D0022916

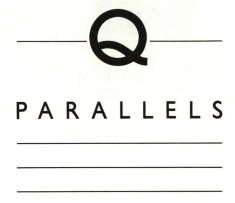

PARALLELS

FOUNDATIONS & FACETS
Editorial Board

Adela Yarbro Collins
University of Notre Dame

John Dominic Crossan
DePaul University

John H. Elliott
University of San Francisco

Robert W. Funk, editor
Polebridge Press

John S. Kloppenborg
University of Windsor

Lane C. McGaughy
Willamette University

Carolyn Osiek
Catholic Theological Union

John L. White
Loyola University of Chicago

PUBLISHED VOLUMES

Robert W. Funk, ed., *New Gospel Parallels. Vol. 1: The Synoptic Gospels*
Robert W. Funk, ed., *New Gospel Parallels. Vol. 2: John and the Other Gospels*
John Dominic Crossan, ed., *Sayings Parallels: A Workbook for the Jesus Tradition*
John S. Kloppenborg, *Q Parallels: Synopsis, Critical Notes, and Concordance*

ATS
REF
226.06
K 698

20.36

Q

PARALLELS

SYNOPSIS

CRITICAL NOTES

& CONCORDANCE

JOHN S. KLOPPENBORG

POLEBRIDGE PRESS

SONOMA, CALIFORNIA

17036

ATS Library
Nyack, NY 10960

Quotations from the Greek New Testament are taken from *Novum Testamentum Graece*, 26th edition, edited by Kurt and Barbara Aland. Copyright © 1898 and 1979 by the Deutsche Bibelstiftung, Stuttgart. Used by permission.

Selections from *The Gospel of the Ebionites, The Gospel of the Hebrews,* and *The Gospel of the Nazarenes* are reprinted from *New Testament Apocrypha: Volume One: Gospels and Related Writings* by Edgar Hennecke; edited by Wilhelm Schneemelcher; English translation edited by R. McL. Wilson. Copyright © 1959 by J. C. B. Mohr (Paul Siebeck), Tübingen; English translation copyright © 1963 by Lutterworth Press, Cambridge. Reprinted and used by permission of The Westminster Press.

Excerpts from *The Apocryphon of James, The Gospel of Mary, The Book of Thomas the Contender, The Gospel of Truth,* and *The Teachings of Silvanus* are taken from *The Nag Hammadi Library,* edited by James M. Robinson. Copyright © 1978 by E. J. Brill. Reprinted by permission of Harper & Row, Publishers, Inc.

Selections from *1 Clement, 2 Clement, Didache,* and *Polycarp to the Philippians* are reprinted by permission of the publishers and The Loeb Classical Library from *The Apostolic Fathers,* translated by Kirsopp Lake, Cambridge, Mass.: Harvard University Press and William Heinemann Ltd., 1919.

Excerpts from *The Dialogue of the Savior* are reprinted from *Nag Hammadi Codex III, 5: The Dialogue of the Savior,* edited with an English translation by Stephen Emmel (Nag Hammadi Studies 26), Copyright © 1984 by E. J. Brill, Leiden. Used by permission.

The Coptic excerpts of the *Teachings of Silvanus* are reprinted from *Les Leçons de Silvanos (NH VII,4),* text established and presented by Yvonne Janssens (Bibliothèque copte de Nag Hammadi, Section «Textes» 13). Copyright © 1983 by Les Presses de l'Université Laval, Quebec. Used by permission.

Selections from the New Testament were translated by the author, John S. Kloppenborg.

The English translation of the *Gospel of Thomas* was provided by Marvin W. Meyer.

Copyright © 1988 Polebridge Press

All rights reserved. No part of this publication may be reproduced, stored in a retrieval system, or transmitted in any form or by any means, electronic, mechanical, photocopying, recording, or otherwise, without prior permission of the copyright owner.

Library of Congress Cataloging-in-Publication Data

Kloppenborg, John S., 1951–
   Q parallels.

   (Foundations & facets. [New Testament])
   Bibliography: p.
   Includes index.
   1. Q hypothesis (Synoptics criticism) 2. Bible.
N.T. Gospels––Harmonies, English. 3. Bible N.T.
Gospels––Concordances, Greek. I. Title II. Series:
Foundations and facets. New Testament.
BS2560.K58 1987   179.'7   87–62921
ISBN 0-944344-00-3
ISBN 0-944344-01-1 (pbk.)

Printed in the United States of America

In gratitude

Gerd Dieter Wilhelm Müller †
and Heinz O. Guenther

Contents

*I*llustrations

Foreword to the Series

Foundations & Facets: New Testament has two major divisions as indicated by the title.

Much of the more creative biblical scholarship on the contemporary scene is devoted to *Facets* of biblical texts: to units of the text smaller than canonical books, or to aspects of the New Testament that ignore the boundaries of books and canon. In one sense, *Facets* refers to any textual unit or group of units that does not coincide with the boundaries of canonical books. In another sense, *Facets* refers to aspects of the biblical materials that are being addressed by newly emerging biblical disciplines: literary criticism and its partner, narratology, and the social sciences in various guises. These two senses of *Facets* produce the second major division of the series with its two subdivisions: Literary Facets and Social Facets.

The creative and innovative impulses in current scholarship are also linked to the creation of new study instruments and tools, based on emerging new methods in biblical criticism or to the reconception of old ones. These instruments are shaping the first division of the series: *Foundations*.

Together, the two divisions of *Foundations & Facets* will form the basis for the next phase of biblical scholarship.

Polebridge Press
Sonoma, California 1987

Robert W. Funk, *editor*

Preface

The origins of this book go back to my days as a graduate student working on a dissertation on the Synoptic Sayings source (Q). Two facts soon became obvious. First, the tools available for the study of the Synoptic gospels in general are not always ideally suited to the examination and reconstruction of Q. The alignment of parallels in the standard synopses of Aland, Huck-Lietzmann, and Huck-Greeven do not always make easily visible the extent of verbal agreements (and disagreements) between Matthew and Luke where Mark is present and even on occasion in non-Markan material. The requirements of economy and readability for a three- or four-gospel synopsis often result in the separation of double tradition pericopae which in Q probably belonged together. Moreover, the division of the texts of Matthew and Luke into short pericopae is made, quite understandably, not on the basis of their likely function in Q but on the basis of their use by Matthew and Luke, or their position *vis à vis* Mark. But for those interested in Q, a sense of the original order and cohesion of the Q document is frequently either lost or obscured. The canon-centered priorities of many of the editors of the standard synopses means that valuable comparative materials, especially from the *Gospel of Thomas*, are either not printed at all, or relegated to the footnotes or appendices.

The blame for such inconveniences cannot, of course, be laid at the doorsteps of the editors of our standard synopses, since their tasks entailed the presentation of three or four gospels in such a manner as to be useful for a very wide range of tasks in gospel criticism. Nevertheless, these features help to explain the second fact, namely, that many scholars who work on Q have been forced to construct their own *Hilfsmittel*.

It was the encouragement of Robert Funk which led me to produce a synopsis specifically for use by those who work with Q-related questions. I am especially grateful to him for including *Q Parallels* in the series "Foundations and Facets." Throughout the development of the synopsis, many have given graciously of their time and learning. James M. Robinson has offered continuous encouragement and support for the project, and his Q Seminar at the Claremont Graduate School offered many helpful suggestions and corrections. To them, and in particular, Sterling Bjorndahl, I am indebted. Dieter Lührmann, Ron Cameron, Wendy

Cotter and Christopher Tuckett have read through the manuscript, providing helpful suggestions in regard to formatting and graphics. I am especially grateful to Frans Neirynck who presented an earlier version of the synopsis to his colleagues in the New Testament Seminar at Leuven and generously communicated extensive suggestions and corrections. Thanks for various kindnesses go also to Harold Attridge, Heinz Guenther, John C. Hurd, Vernon Robbins, Leif Vaage and Caroline Whelan.

Finally, it has been a pleasure to work with Char Matejovsky, Stephanie Funk and Helen Melnis of Polebridge Press. Their care, efficiency and creativity are in evidence throughout.

All translations of biblical texts are my own. The English translations of the Gospel of Thomas are courtesy of Marvin W. Meyer.

The University of Windsor
Windsor, Canada

John S. Kloppenborg

*A*bbreviations, Short Titles and Sigla

1. Quotation of Q Texts

Texts in Q are cited by Lukan versification, prefaced by "Q" (e.g., Q 6:20b = Luke 6:20b // Matt 5:3). This does not necessarily imply that the Lukan wording or order is to be preferred. In instances of Matthean *Sondergut* that may derive from Q, the text is designated as Q/Matt (e.g., Q/Matt 5:41).

2. Abbreviations

Abbreviations used in this volume for journals, series and standard reference works are found in the *Catholic Biblical Quarterly* 46 (1984) 393–408 and the *Journal of Biblical Literature* 95 (1976) 331–46. In addition to these, the following abbreviations are used:

ApJas	*Apocryphon of James*
Clement Alex., *Strom.*	Clement of Alexandria, *Stromata*
1 Clem	*1 Clement*
2 Clem	*2 Clement*
DialSav	*Dialogue of the Savior*
Did	*Didache* or *The Teachings of the Twelve Apostles*
Epiphanius, *Haer.*	Epiphanius, *Haereses* (*Panarion*)
Eusebius, *Hist. eccl.*	Eusebius, *Historia ecclesiastica*
GEbi	*Gospel of the Ebionites*
GEgy	*Gospel of the Egyptians*
GHeb	*Gospel of the Hebrews*
GMary	*Gospel of Mary*
GNaz	*Gospel of the Nazarenes*
GThom	*Gospel of Thomas*
GTruth	*Gospel of Truth*
Jerome, *Comm. in Isaiam*	Jerome, *Commentaria in Isaiam prophetam*
Jerome, *Comm. in Mattheum*	Jerome, *Commentarius in Mattheum*
Jerome, *Dial. contra Pelag.*	Jerome, *Dialogus contra Pelagianos*
Origen, *Hom. in Jer.*	Origen, *Homiliae in Jeremiam*
PEger 2	*Papyrus Egerton 2*
POxy	*Papyrus Oxyrhynchus*
Polycarp, *Phil.*	Polycarp, *Letter to the Philippians*
Ps. Clem. Hom.	*Pseudo–Clementine Homilies*
T. Abr.	*Testament of Abraham*
TeachSilv	*The Teachings of Silvanus*
ThomCont	*Thomas the Contender*

3. Citation of Secondary Sources

Literature is cited in the apparatus by author or author and year. For full bibliographical details, consult the Secondary sources section of the Bibliography. In addition, the following short titles are used:

Migne, *PL* J.-P. Migne, ed., *Patrologiae cursus completus: Series latina.* 221 vols. Paris 1844–64.

NTApoc Edgar Hennecke and Wilhelm Schneemelcher, *New Testament Apocrypha.* trans. R. McL. Wilson. 2 vols. Philadelphia: Westminster Press, 1963–1965.

4. Sigla (see the Introduction for an explanation)

	Unbracketed text: most probably from Q.
( )	*Sondergut* passages which *may* have originated in Q.
⟨ ⟩	Introductory and transitional elements which most probably stood in Q but which have become practically unrecoverable because of the extensive redactional interventions of Matthew and Luke.
[ ]	Not from Q. This siglum marks whole pericopae (e.g., [Q 3:21– 22]) or portions of pericopae which have little or no probability of an origin in Q.
καρπός	Bolded and underscored text is used for all words which display verbatim agreement in inflected form with the parallel Synoptist.
καρπός	Underscoring denotes agreement in dictionary form but not in inflected form.
καρπός	Normal font is used for vocabulary which shows no verbatim agreement with the parallel Synoptist.

5. Textual Notes

The textual notes are based on the apparatus of E. Nestle and Kurt Aland, edd., *Novum Testamentum Graece* (26th ed.; Stuttgart: Deutsche Bibelstiftung, 1979), Kurt Aland, ed., *Synopsis Quattuor Evangeliorum* (10th ed.; Stuttgart: Deutsche Bibelstiftung, 1978; 13. revidierte Aufl., 1985), and Albert Huck, ed., *Synopse der drei ersten Evangelien mit Beigabe der johanneischen Parallelstellen* (13th ed. rev. by Heinrich Greeven; Tübingen: J. C. B. Mohr [Paul Siebeck] 1981).

Witnesses are cited in the customary manner, with papyri first, then uncials and major text types (e.g., Koine), then minuscules, versions and church fathers. The text printed by the major recent editions of the New Testament is given at the end of each variant.

The Papyri

No.	Name	Date	Content
𝔭4	Paris, Bibliothèque nationale, gr. 1120, suppl. 2	III	Luke 1—6*
𝔭19	Oxford Bodleian Library, MS Gr. bibl. d. 6	IV/V	Matt 10:32—11:5
𝔭21	Muhlenberg College, Theol. pap. 3	III	Matt 12:24–33*
𝔭35	Firenze, Biblioteca Laurenziana, PSI 1	IV ?	Matt 25*
𝔭45	Chester Beatty, P. Gr. Vindob. 31974	III	gospels*
𝔭67	P. Barc. 1	early III	Matt 3*, 5*, 27*
𝔭75	P. Bodmer XIV/XV	early III	Luke*, John*
𝔭77	P. Oxy 2683	II	Matt 23*
𝔭82	Strasbourg, Bibliothèque nationale, P. Gr. 2677	IV/V	Luke 7*

Letter Uncials

No.	Name	Date	Content
א	Sinaiticus	IV	NT
A	Alexandrinus	V	NT
B	Vaticanus	IV	gospels, acts, epistles
C	Ephraemi Rescriptus	V	NT
D	Bezae	V/VI	gospel, acts
K	Cyprius	IX	gospels
L	Regius	VIII	gospels*
N	Purpureus Petropolitanus	VI	gospels*
P	Guelferbytanus A	VI	gospels
R	Nitriensis	VI	Luke*
W	Freerianus	IV/V	gospels*
X	Monacensis	IX/X	gospels*
Z	Dublinensis	VI	Matthew*
Γ	Tischendorfianus	X	gospels*
Δ	Sangallensis	IX	gospels*
Θ	Koridethi	IX	gospels*
Ξ	Zacynthius	VI	Luke 1–11*
Π	Petropolitanus	IX	gospels*
Ψ	Athlous Laurae	VIII/IX	gospels, acts, epistles

Number Uncials

No.	Date
063	IX
067	VI
070	VI
0102	VII/VIII
0106	VII
0107	VII
0115	IX/X
0124	VI
0133	IX
0135	IX
0138	VII/VIII
0181	IV/V
0233	VIII
0250	VIII

Families

Siglum	Name	Date
λ	Lake Group	XII–XIV
φ	Ferrar Group	XI–XV

Minuscules

1 2 3 4, etc.	IX–

* indicates fragmentary or defective manuscripts

Versions

co	Coptic versions
sa	Sahidic (Coptic) version
bo	Bohairic (Coptic) version
mae	Middle-Egyptian (Coptic) version
syr^c	Cureton Syriac version
syr^s	Sinaitic Syriac version
syr^p	Peshitta Syriac version
syr^{ph}	Philoxenian Syriac version
syr^h	Harclean Syriac version
syr^{pal}	Palestinian Syriac version
it	Old Latin (Italia)
	Individual Old Latin mss are designated by lower case Roman letters: e.g., a aur b c d ff^1 g^1 h, etc.
vg	Vulgate (Latin)
geo	Georgian version

Church Fathers

Aug	Augustine
Bas	Basil of Caesarea
Cl	Clement of Alexandria
Cyp	Cyprian
Cyr	Cyril of Alexandria
CyrJ	Cyril of Jerusalem
Did	Didymus
Epiph	Epiphanius
Eus	Eusebius
GrNy	Gregory of Nyssa
Ir	Irenaeus
Ju	Justin
Meth	Methodius
Mcion	Marcion
Or	Origen
Tert	Tertullian

Editions of the New Testament

GNT	K. Aland, M. Black, B. M. Metzger and A. Wikgren, edd. *The Greek New Testament.* New York, London, Edinburgh, Amsterdam, Stuttgart: United Bible Societies, 1966.
GNT^2	K. Aland, M. Black, B. M. Metzger and A. Wikgren, edd. *The Greek New Testament.* 2d ed. New York, London, Edinburgh, Amsterdam, Stuttgart: United Bible Societies, 1968.
GNT^3	K. Aland, M. Black, C. M. Martini, B. M. Metzger and A. Wikgren, edd. *The Greek New Testament.* 3d ed. New York, London, Edinburgh, Amsterdam, Stuttgart: United Bible Societies, 1975.
HG	Albert Huck, ed., *Synopse der drei ersten Evangelien mit Beigabe der johanneischen Parallelstellen.* 13th ed. rev. by Heinrich Greeven; Tübingen: J. C. B. Mohr [Paul Siebeck] 1981.
NA^{25}	E. Nestle and Kurt Aland, edd., *Novum Testamentum Graece.* 25th ed.; Stuttgart: Württembergische Bibelanstalt, 1963.
NA^{26}	E. Nestle and Kurt Aland, edd., *Novum Testamentum Graece.* 26th ed.; Stuttgart: Deutsche Bibelstiftung, 1979.

Other Sigla

al	*alii,* other witnesses	vid	*videtur,* as it appears
mg	marginal reading	( )	with minor differences
rell	*reliqui,* the rest	*3 1 2 4*	variation of word order
pc	*pauci,* a few	*	original reading of a ms
pm	*permulti,* many others	c	the corrector of a ms
txt	text	1 2 3	1st, 2d, 3d correctors of a ms

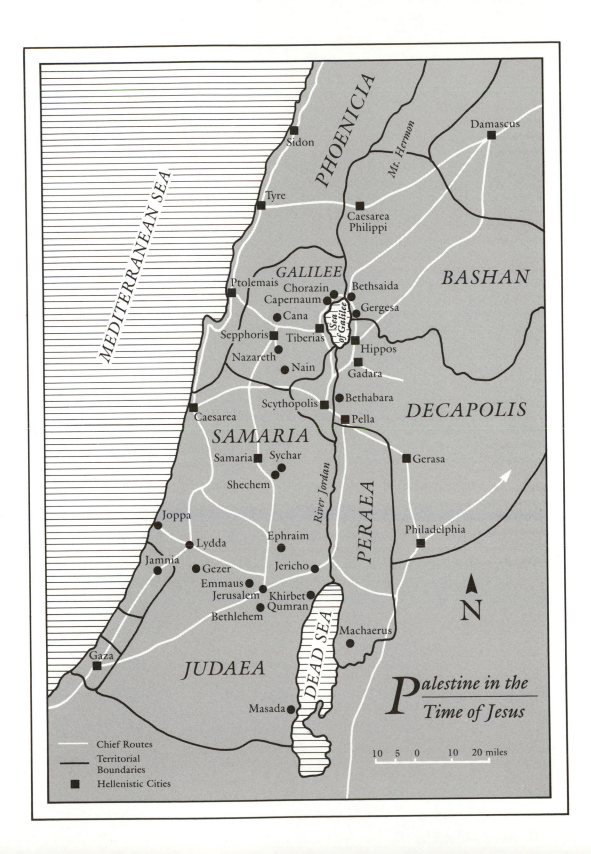

MEDITERRANEAN SEA

PHOENICIA

Damascus

Sidon

Mt. Hermon

Tyre

Caesarea
Philippi

BASHAN

GALILEE

Ptolemais
Chorazin   Bethsaida
Capernaum
Cana   Gergesa
                  Sea
                  of Galilee
Sepphoris   Tiberias
                  Hippos
Nazareth
        Nain   Gadara

                  Bethabara
Scythopolis   DECAPOLIS
Caesarea   Pella

SAMARIA

Samaria   Sychar

Shechem   Gerasa
                  River Jordan

                  PERAEA
Joppa

Lydda   Philadelphia
        Ephraim
Jamnia
    Gezer
                  Jericho
Emmaus
Jerusalem Khirbet
        Qumran
Bethlehem

                  DEAD SEA   Machaerus

Gaza

        JUDAEA   N

                  Palestine in the
                  Time of Jesus

Masada

        Chief Routes
        Territorial
        Boundaries   10 5 0   10   20 miles
        Hellenistic Cities

*I*ntroduction

The last decade has witnessed a burgeoning of the literature on the Synoptic Sayings source (Q). Almost every facet is the subject of discussion, from the viability of the Two Document hypothesis, upon which the very existence of Q is predicated, to a host of literary-critical, tradition-historical, redactional and theological issues. Scholer's bibliography lists over 150 items published between 1981 and June of 1986 (Scholer 1986)!

We are fortunate that previous generations of scholars have already bequeathed important tools for the study of Q. Adolf von Harnack's *Sprüche und Reden Jesu* (1907; ET: *The Sayings of Jesus* [1908]) contained not only a reconstruction of Q in Greek but valuable tables of vocabulary and discussions of Q's syntax, style, constituent forms and original order. Published the following year, G. H. Müller's *Zur Synopse: Untersuchung über die Arbeitsweise des Lk und Mt und ihre Quellen* (1908) contributed importantly to the discussion of the extent and order of Q. In the period since Harnack and Müller, the names of J. C. Hawkins (1911), Walther Haupt (1913), B. H. Streeter (1911, 1924), Wilhelm Bussmann (1929), Burton Easton (1926), Josef Schmid (1930), T. W. Manson (1937) and G. D. Kilpatrick (1946) came to be associated with landmark treatments of the Synoptics to which any serious student of Q is obliged to give due attention.

Recent authors continue to enrich the discipline with significant tools. Robert Morgenthaler's *Statistische Synopse* (1971) provides invaluable statistical tables which register, *inter alia,* the degree of Matthew-Luke agreement in Q sections and the extent of sequential agreement in the reproduction of pericopae. In 1975 Richard Edwards published a concordance to the minimal text of Q, i.e., the vocabulary upon which Matthew and Luke agree. This may now be used in conjuction with the word list of Frans Neirynck and Frans Van Segbroeck, *New Testament Vocabulary* (1984), which registers vocabularic agreements with and against Mark as well as tables of synonyms and substitutes where one synoptist disagrees with another.

Two recent reconstructions of Q exist, one by Wolfgang Schenk (1981) which gives Matthean and Lukan parallels followed by a reconstruction of Q, all in German. Athanasius Polag's *Fragmenta Q: Textheft zur Logienquelle* (1979) provides a reconstruction of Q in Greek (without displaying the Synoptic parallels) along with an apparatus which reports concurring and dissenting opinions on matters of reconstruction and inclusion of various pericopae in Q. The Greek text of Polag has now been translated (without the apparatus) by Ivan Havener and printed as an appendix to *Q: The Sayings of Jesus* (1987).

There are, in addition, a few other tools. Siegfried Schulz produced a set of synoptic texts as a companion volume to his *Q: Die Spruchquelle der Evangelisten* (1972).[1] The arrangement of the texts corresponds to the order of Schulz's treatment of Q in his monograph, an order which follows neither Matthean nor Lukan nor any putative original Q order. Hence the tool has limited utility for most others tasks. Dieter Lührmann has produced and circulated privately a presentation of Synoptic parallels (without a reconstruction) based mainly on the Huck-Lietzmann synopsis, but with a few pericopae taken from Aland.[2] Ulrich Luz in Europe and members of the Society of Biblical Literature Q Seminar in North America have devoted considerable effort to the reconstruction of Q. Partial and preliminary reconstructions with copious apparatus are periodically published in *SBLASP* and elsewhere.[3]

A Synopsis for Q

The present volume does not intend to offer a reconstruction of the Greek text of Q but instead provides a tool to aid in that reconstruction and indeed in any investigation of Q. Even in those instances where the degree of agreement between Matthew and Luke is high and the reconstruction of Q is relatively uncontroversial (e.g., Q 3:7b–9; 7:31–35), no attempt has been made to propose a reconstructed version of Q. A fully documented reconstruction of Q will eventually become available through the efforts of the SBL Q Seminar and the Institute for Antiquity and Christianity.

---

1. Siegfried Schulz, *Griechisch–deutsche Synopse der Q–Überlieferung* (Zurich: Theologischer Verlag, 1972).

2. Dieter Lührmann, *Synopse der Q–Überlierferungen* (1985).

3. James M. Robinson, "The Sermon on the Mount/Plain: Work Sheets for the Reconstruction of Q," *SBLASP* 22 (1983) 451–54; Ronald D. Worden, "The Q Sermon on the Mount/Plain: Variants and Reconstructions," ibid., 455–71; Ulrich Luz, "Sermon on the Mount/Plain: Reconstruction of QMt and QLk," ibid., 473–79; James M. Robinson, "The Preaching of John: Work Sheets for the Reconstruction of Q," *SBLASP* 23 (1984) 305–46; Leif Vaage, "Q 4," ibid., 347–76; Harry Fleddermann, "John and the Coming One (Matt 3:11–12 // Luke 3:16–17)," ibid., 377–84; James M. Robinson, "The Mission and Beelzebul: Pap. Q 10:2–16; 11:14–23," *SBLASP* 24 (1985) 97–99; Ulrich Luz, "Q 10:2–16; 11:14–23," ibid., 101–102; John S. Kloppenborg, "Q 11:14–20: Work Sheets for Reconstruction," ibid., 133–51; Harry Fleddermann, "The Beginning of Q," ibid., 153–59; James M. Robinson, Leif Vaage and Jon Daniels, *Pap. Q* (Claremont: Institute for Antiquity and Christianity, 1985); Harry Fleddermann, "The Householder and the Servant Left in Charge," *SBLASP* 25 (1986) 17–26.

This synopsis is designed to provide a visual indication of the following materials:

1. The *minimal text of Q,* i.e., the verbatim and near-verbatim Matthew–Luke agreements. This is indicated by use of underscored bolded font for agreements in inflected form and underscored normal font for agreements in dictionary form. Agreements of both sorts are marked with an asterisk in the concordance which follows.

ἡ βασιλεία
χορτασθήσεται

2. The *generally accepted extent of Q,* which includes the minimal verbatim agreements and those portions of text which display a general agreement in sense but not exact verbatim agreement. This is printed as unbracketed text. Obviously, this represents a combination of Q elements and redactional interventions. Since the minimal text of Q is not syntactically complete, every reconstruction of Q must identify redactional elements in Matthew and Luke, and then either choose between the two Synoptists or, on occasion, propose conjectural readings which depart from both Matthew and Luke. Some favorite Matthean and Lukan words and phrases are easily recognized, e.g., Matt 5:3, "in spirit" or Luke 6:23, "their fathers." The same goes for parts of verses or even entire verses. Matt 7:12b, "For this is the Law and the Prophets," for example, is considered as Matthean by virtually all except Müller (1908: 8). But in many instances, the choice between Matthew and Luke is not so clear, and decisions regarding the inclusion or exclusion of phrases or verses attested in only one gospel are controverted. Therefore, I have chosen to present the texts as neutrally as possible and therefore to err on the side of inclusiveness. Thus, if any portion of a verse is likely to derive from Q, the entire verse is printed in unbracketed form (apart from obviously redactional introductions or appendices).

The vocabulary of the text printed in unbracketed sections, whether bolded, underscored or not, has been concorded. This means that some Matthean and Lukan words appear in the concordance. Precisely which vocabulary is redactional, however, depends entirely upon how one reconstructs Q.

( )

3. The *probable and possible extent of Q.* This includes selected items of *Sondergut* such as Luke 9:61–62 and 12:49 for which plausible or compelling reasons for inclusion have been cited. And it includes items from the triple tradition (e.g., the baptism story) which various authors have ascribed to Q. Pericopae which are deemed likely to have derived from Q are printed in parentheses and their vocabulary appears in the concordance. Those pericopae for which an origin in Q seems unlikely appear in

[ ]
⟨ ⟩
διώκω ⇨ Matt 5:44 [S9]

square brackets. In a few instances, it is probable that various Q sayings and stories originally had brief introductory or transitional phrases, but that both Matthew and Luke have completely rewritten these phrases so that little or nothing of Q remains. At these points the Matthean and Lukan texts are enclosed in angle brackets. None of the vocabulary of these sections is concorded.

4. The *catchword* connections between Q pericopae are noted at the end of each set of texts.

Following the convention of the SBL Q Seminar, Q texts are designated by their *Lukan* location. Thus, e.g., Q 11:19 is that Q text which is the source of Luke 11:19 // Matt 12:27. This designation, however, does not necessarily imply that Luke's *wording* is that of Q. In the few instances where Matthean *Sondergut* may derive from Q, the Q text is designated as Q/Matt (e.g., Q/Matt 5:41; 7:2a; 10:5–6, 23).

Principles of Selection and Construction

In compiling the synopsis and citing critical opinion, I have not attempted to list pedantically all of those texts which have occasionally been ascribed to Q by one scholar or another. Weiss (1907), for example, attributed not only the double tradition to Q, but a considerable amount of the triple tradition. Müller (1908: 29–30) included several Matthean texts from the sermon on the mount and the woes against the Pharisees that are normally ascribed to Matthean redaction or to other sources (Matt 5:21–26, 27–30, 33–37; 6:1–6, 16–18; 7:6; 21:28–31a; 23:13–22). He also included a few units of Lukan *Sondergut* (Luke 16:14–15 // Matt 5:20; Luke 11:1; 12:37–38; 13:25). More recently, Heinz Schürmann has proposed a Q *Vorlage* for several dozen *Sondergut* texts.[4] Each of these proposals represents a substantial expansion of the extent of Q and, in the case of Weiss, a significant alteration in the character of the source. Since, however, none of these expansions has met with widespread approval and since inclusion of all of the suggested texts would expand the synopsis to rather unmanageable proportions (and correspondingly diminish its usefulness), I have treated only a limited selection of *Sondergut* and triple tradition texts.

This synopsis includes only the following: (1) those texts upon which there is a near unanimous consensus (e.g., Q 3:7b–9; 6:20b–23; 7:18–19, 22, 24–28, 31–35; 12:2–9, 22–31, etc.); (2) those texts over which there has been sustained scholarly debate (e.g., Q 3:21–22; 9:61–62; 14:16–24; 19:12–26, etc.); (3) *Sondergut* texts for which plausible even if not compelling reasons have been advanced by significant numbers of authors for membership in Q (e.g., Q 12:13–20; 15:8–10; 17:20–21; Matt 10:5–6, 23) and (4) pericopae which very probably derived from Q but which have been extensively edited by the synoptic writers (e.g., the incipit, Q 6:20a; 7:1a).

In addition, various Matthean and Lukan texts appear for which there is very little or no likelihood of an origin in Q. Some of these are cited to provide an indication of the *context* in which the evangelists placed Q.

---

4. Frans Neirynck (1982: 38 n. 38) has compiled an extensive list of those verses and pericopae which Schürmann has proposed for membership in Q.

E.g., Matt 9:36 and 10:1 are Matthean reworkings of Mark and Matt 23:1–3, 5, 8–11, 14–22 derive partly from Mark and partly from Matthew's special material. In other instances, redactional *introductions* are cited: e.g., Luke 3:15 and Luke 6:39a, which are Lukan, and Matt 5:38–39a, 42, which are usually taken to be Matthean. Both the contextual materials and the introductions are normally enclosed in square brackets [ ].

The Choice and Alignment of Parallels

The decisions regarding the alignment of parallels are not always easy. Especially in those instances in which the wording and order of Matthew and Luke disagree sharply, uncertainty arises. Matt 7:16–20 // 12:33–35 // Luke 6:43–45 [S13] is especially difficult as it appears that Matthew has not only used portions of this Q pericope twice, but has also amplified the two new settings of the material by creating additional sayings based upon the motifs present in Q 6:43–45 (cf. Matt 7:16a, 17, 20; Matt 12:33) and upon Q sayings taken from John's preaching of judgment (Matt 7:19; Matt 12:34 cf. Q 3:7–9 [S3]). In this synopsis, Luke 6:43 is aligned with Matt 7:18 since both take the form of statements contrary-to-fact while Matt 7:17 and 12:33, which echo phrases of Luke 6:43 // Matt 7:18, are treated as secondary (and redactional) creations. Aland (1978: § 82), Worden (1973: 83) and Schenk (1981: 32) likewise treat Matt 7:18 as parallel to Luke 6:43, as do Huck and Greeven (1981: § 90) who also align Matt 12:33 with these two. By contrast, Neirynck and Van Segbroeck (1984: 267) apparently treat Matt 7:17 and 12:33 as the parallels as well. Moreover, Neirynck and Van Segbroeck appear to treat not only Matt 7:16b and 12:33c as parallel with Luke 6:44 but also Matt 7:16a and 7:20 (1984: 267; cf. Worden 1973: 83–84), which I have considered as secondary redactional creations. The principal effect of these varying alignments is to alter the way in which agreements and disagreements are registered and concorded. Thus there are a few discrepancies between the vocabularic statistics found in the concordance following the synopsis, and the statistics offered by Neirynck and Van Segbroeck.

The commissioning speech (Matt 9:37—10:16 // Luke 10:2–12 [S22]) also presents difficulties in alignment of parallels, which in turn affect the concording of agreements. Presumably, Matthew's conflation of the Q speech with Mark and his rearrangement (and rewriting?) of the entire composition are contributing factors here. In general I prefer the alignment of Huck and Lietzmann (1936: § 139) and Aland (1978: § 177) to that of Huck and Greeven (1981: § 122), although along with Lührmann (1985: 8), I treat Matt 10:11 and Luke 10:8 as parallel. This decision accounts for a few discrepancies between the vocabularic statistics in the concordance and those of Neirynck and Van Segbroeck (1984) who evidently do not consider Matt 10:11 and Luke 10:8 as parallels.

A similar problem exists with Matt 24:23, 26 // Luke 17:23 [S66]. Aland (1978: § 235), followed by Lührmann (1985: 25), considers Matt 24:23 as the parallel for Luke 17:23. However, it seems to me that Matt 24:23 is a Matthean rewriting of Mark 13:21 and that Matt 24:26 is the appropriate parallel to Luke 17:23.[5]

In a few instances, two pericopae in Matthew are treated as parallel to a single Lukan passage. While Matt 12:22–30 [S29] represents the major parallel to Luke 11:14–23, Matt 9:32–34 offers somewhat closer parallels to Luke 11:14–15 than does Matt 12:22–24. It would appear that Matthew has reproduced Q 11:14–15 in an attenuated but relatively accurate form in chap. 9 and in a longer but more periphrastic way in Matt 12. Similarly, Matthew has reproduced the request for a sign (Q 11:16, 29–32 [S32]) once at Matt 12:38–42 and a second time in a shorter form at Matt 16:1–2a, 4. While the latter occurs in parallel sequence with the Markan request for a sign (Mark 8:11–12), Matthew evidently preferred the *wording* of Q to that of Mark.

On the other hand, Matthew fused Q 12:54–56 with the request for a sign with the result that his introduction ὁ δὲ ἀποκριθεὶς εἶπεν αὐτοῖς· ("but answering he said to them," Matt 16:2a) serves not only as a parallel to Luke 11:29a // Matt 12:39 [S32] but also to Luke 12:54a [S47].

In three cases, Luke offers two parallels to a single Matthean verse. Luke 7:20 echoes the wording of Luke 7:19 // Matt 11:3. Since there is a substantial body of opinion that views Matt 11:3 as a Matthean abbreviation of Q, I have noted verbal agreements between both Lukan verses and Matt 11:3 [S16]. Similarly, in Q 10:2–11 [S22] Luke twice reproduces the phrase "the kingdom of God has come near" (10:9b, 11b) while Matthew has it but once (10:7). Since it is a moot point whether Luke replicated Q or Matthew abbreviated it, I have registered both Lukan verses as parallels with Matt 10:7. Finally, in a rare instance of the use of doublets, Luke has evidently used an aphorism from Q twice, once at 14:11 and a second time at 18:14b. Both are treated as parallels to Matt 23:12 [S54].

In several cases, it is questionable whether Matthew offers a parallel to Luke at all. The Matthean and Lukan versions of the parables of the great supper [S55] and the talents [S67] are frequently held to be so disparate as to disqualify them from Q. At least in these cases, however, both the Matthean and Lukan versions of each are represented as parables with comparable narrative lines. A number of verbatim and near-verbatim agreements are found between the two versions of each. It is otherwise with Luke 13:25 [S50]. This verse is printed in parentheses without a

---

5. This is also the decision of Harnack (1908: 105), Huck and Lietzmann (1933: § 184), Huck and Greeven (1981: § 198), Schenk (1981: 120) and Neirynck and Van Segbroeck (1984).

parallel in the Matthean column. Matt 25:10–12 is printed on the right hand page as a secondary parallel (similarly, Aland 1978: § 211). Neirynck and Van Segbroeck (1984) evidently treat the two as parallel and concord vocabularic agreements. The similarities between the two pericopae are clear enough and as the notes suggest, many authors have posited some sort of literary relation between the two. However, it is extremely doubtful that the Matthean parable stood in Q; if anything, Matthew saw Luke 13:25 in Q and created a parable from it and other materials. The portion of the parable which contains verbal parallels to Luke 13:25 now forms the conclusion to the Matthean parable (25:10–12) but it has been integrated so thoroughly into the parable that it can no longer stand alone. In this case, Matt 25:10–12 provides only a rather faint and secondary witness to Q, and is therefore not treated as a primary parallel. Nevertheless, the items of vocabulary in 25:10–12 which are also found in Luke 13:25 are marked and these agreements are flagged in the concordance. Luke 12:35–38 [S43], which displays only minimal verbal agreements with Matt 25:1–10, is not judged to be based on Q and hence is printed in square brackets.

Critical Notes
There are two types of apparatus: (1) a sketch of critical opinion in regard to the inclusion or non-inclusion of various disputed texts and (2) a brief listing of some of the important textual variants of the Matthean and Lukan texts.

The first set of apparatus provides a list of authors who regard the pericope in question as deriving from Q and those who do not. This is usually accompanied by a brief indication of the reasons which are cited for and against inclusion. While I have not attempted to gather from the rather substantial literature on Q all of the authors who have contributed to the discussion of each Q pericope or all of the arguments that have been employed, the apparatus for each pericope has normally taken into account the views of the following authors, spanning some eighty years, who have treated the whole of Q or very significant portions of it: Beare (1962); Bussmann (1929); Crossan (1983); Easton (1926); Edwards (1975, 1976); Fitzmyer (1981–1985); Harnack (1908); Hawkins (1911); Hoffmann (1975); Hunter (1950); Kilpatrick (1946); Kloppenborg (1987); Knox (1957); Lambrecht (1985); Lührmann (1969); Manson (1949); Marshall (1978); Meyer (1967); Müller (1908); Polag (1979); Schenk (1981); Schmithals (1980); Schulz (1972); Streeter (1924); Vassiliadis (1978); Weiss (1907) and Zeller (1984). Hence, the notations "In Q: most authors" and "Not in Q: most authors" includes at least these critics. If any of these represents the contrary position, a notation to that effect will normally appear. In addition, the apparatus notes the contributions of other authors to the discussion of various individual pericopae.

It is often the case that a variety of reasons has been advanced for and against the inclusion of a particular pericope. As will be obvious, not all of the reasons are of equal cogency and some may not be persuasive at all. The arguments pro and con are noted in the apparatus not because the editor necessarily deems all of them equally compelling, but because they have played a part in the history of scholarship. The decision to include a particular pericope in Q (as unbracketed or enclosed in parentheses) indicates that, in the view of the editor, the arguments for inclusion on the whole outweigh those for exclusion. The same applies *mutatis mutandis* for those pericopae which have been enclosed in square brackets ["not in Q"].

It will also become obvious that the rubric "not in Q" encompasses a variety of explanations for the origin of the excluded materials. Among earlier critics (e.g., Manson, Müller, Weiss), appeal to the M and L sources was common, both for *Sondergut* materials, but also at times for those pericopae in which the Matthean and Lukan versions differ substantially (e.g., Q 6:20–23; 11:2–4; 14:16–24; 19:12–26, etc.). Although a few recent scholars are still inclined toward this sort of explanation, it is more usual now to ascribe disagreements between Matthew and Luke and even some *Sondergut* to redaction.

Authors are cited by three methods: (1) by surname alone in the case of the major commentators on Q (Harnack, Hoffmann, Lührmann, Schenk, Schulz, etc.), (2) by surname and "Mt" or "Lk" for commentators on Matthew and Luke who have devoted considerable space to Q (e.g., Easton Lk; Fitzmyer Lk) and (3) by surname and date for all other literature. This corresponds to the way in which the literature is cited in the bibliography. Normally the relevant page references are provided. When no page numbers are given (usually after the notation "Not in Q"), the author in question omits the pericope from his list or table of the contents of Q and hence (presumably) does not consider it to be a part of Q.

Harnack 80

Fitzmyer Lk 452

Hawkins 1911:113

Text and Textual Notes

The Greek text printed is the 26th edition of E. Nestle and K. Aland.[6] Nestle-Aland's use of the square brackets [ ] to designate words about which there is considerable textual insecurity has been preserved. Since this use of bracketing is normally associated with individual words, there should be no confusion with the bracketing of entire verses or clauses which means "not in Q" (see above).

The *textual notes* represent a highly selective number of variant readings. No attempt has been made to duplicate the extensive apparatus of the synopses of Aland or Huck and Greeven. However, all divergences

---

6. E. Nestle and K. Aland, edd., *Novum Testamentum Graece* (26th. ed.; Stuttgart: Deutsche Bibelstiftung, 1979).

NA²⁵
NA²⁶
HG
GNT

between Nestle-Aland²⁶, Nestle-Aland²⁵ and Huck-Greeven are listed (and more rarely, disagreements with the United Bible Society's *Greek New Testament* [1966; 2d ed. 1968]). The sigla NA²⁵, NA²⁶, HG and GNT follow the list of textual witnesses and indicate the variant which has been printed as "text" by these editors. As well, the apparatus provides a selected number of variants that have played a role in the history of attempts to reconstruct Q (e.g., the western reading of Luke 3:22 and Marcion's reading of Luke 11:2). Only orthographic variations (e.g., δανίσητε [NA²⁶], δανείσητε [NA²⁵; HG], at Luke 6:34) are omitted.[7]

omit γαρ (Matt)

Where one variant reading is identical with, or shows strong affinities to, another text (usually the parallel gospel, but occasionally another verse in the same gospel, or Mark, John or the LXX), the source of harmonization is named in parentheses immediately following the variant and before the list of witnesses. For example, Luke 6:33: omit γαρ (Matt): ℵ² A D L W, etc., or Luke 3:22: υιος μου ει συ εγω σημερον γεγεννηκα σε (Ps 2:7): D it; Ju (Cl) Meth, etc.

/
//

Textual notes to the same unit of variation are separated by a single stroke, and units of variation are separated by double strokes. Words in the apparatus are frequently abbreviated but spelled out in full when ambiguities might arise. E.g., βαπτ. at Matt 3:7 refers to βάπτισμα in the text. When a word occurs more than once in a verse and when one of those occurrences is included in a unit of variation, a numerical super-script is used. E.g., Matt 3:16: omit και³ refers to the third καί of the verse.

και³

4 1–3

Transpositions in word order are indicated by italicized Arabic numerals immediately preceding the list of witnesses. E.g., Matt 4:3: ο περι. ειπ. αυτ.: *4 1–3*: C L Koine 0233, etc.

λ φ
Koine

The sigla for textual witnesses are those used in Nestle-Aland²⁶ and Aland's synopsis (using λ and φ respectively for the Lake [family 1] and Ferrar [family 13] groups and "Koine" to designate the so-called "majority text").

Other Parallels

Whenever a Q text quotes or alludes to the Old Testament, the Septuagint text is printed as a parallel. Only when the Masoretic text seems to have exerted influence on Q is the MT quoted.

Parallels from Mark, John, patristic writers, agrapha, apocryphal gospels, etc. are not listed because they necessarily provide independent access to the text of Q, even though Mark, John, the *Gospel of Thomas, P. Oxy.* 1, 654 and 655 and a few other texts arguably attest versions of the

---

7. For a tabulation of divergences between NA²⁵, NA²⁶ and HG (including orthographic variations), see F. Neirynck, "The Synoptic Gospels According to the New Textus Receptus," *ETL* 52 (1976) 364–79; F. Neirynck and F. Van Segbroeck, "Greeven's Text of the Synoptic Gospels," *ETL* 58 (1982) 123–39.

sayings which are as old as those of Q. The parallels are cited as much to reveal post-canonical developments of Synoptic and Q texts and thus to provide a fuller view of the range of forms which a particular saying might take.

In those cases of possible overlap between Mark and Q (e.g., Q 3:2–4; 3:16–17; 4:1–13; 10:2–12; 11:14–23, etc.), the agreements between Matthew // Luke and Mark are indicated by bolding and underscoring.

Order of Presentation

Since it is the *opinio communis* that the Lukan presentation of Q pericopae represents, with minor qualifications, the order of Q, the synopsis has been arranged in Lukan order, except where there are strong grounds for suspecting Lukan dislocations. The most notable instance of a Lukan dislocation is Q 17:33 [S56] which Luke probably transferred to his apocalyptic discourse [S66]. A detailed defense of the general priority of Lukan order is not provided since it is available elsewhere.[8] Disagreements in order *within* a pericope (e.g., Q 6:27–35; 11:39–52; 17:23–37) are discussed in the apparatus, as is the placement of several notoriously difficult pericopae, e.g., Q 13:34–35; 16:16. In a few highly disputed instances (e.g., Q 13:34–35; 16:16; 17:37b), parallels are displayed twice, once at the Matthean location and once at the Lukan location.

Departures from Lukan order

In a few instances, Lukan order is abandoned in favor of Matthean. The sequence of the second and third Lukan temptations (Luke 4:9–12, 5–8) is inverted in accord with the generally held view that Matthew preserves the original order of the Q temptations. Similarly, it is probable that Luke inverted Q 11:42, 39–41 in order to bring Q 11:39–41 into proximity with his redactional introduction to the woes (Luke 11:37–39a). At its Matthean location, Q 16:16 [S18] is given in its Matthean order (16:16b, a) and in its Lukan order (16:16a, b) at the Lukan location [S61]. Q 13:28–29 [S51] is given in the inverse (Matthean) order, since in the view of the editor that corresponds to the order of Q.[9]

8. See recent discussions of the original order of Q in Kloppenborg 1987: 64–80 and Vassiliadis 1982.

9. See Kloppenborg 1987: 224–25.

Contents of the Q Source

Section & Name	Q text	Matthew	Luke
Incipit & The Preaching of John			
1. Incipit	⟨Incipit⟩	[no text]	[no text]
2. The Coming of John the Baptist	[3:2–4]	3:1–6	3:1–4
3. John's Preaching of Repentance	3:7–9, [10–14]	3:7–10	3:7–9, 10–14
4. John's Preaching of the Coming One	3:16b–17	3:11–12	3:15, 16–17
5. The Baptism of Jesus	[3:21–22]	3:13–17	3:21–22
The Temptations of Jesus			
6. The Temptations of Jesus	4:1–13	4:1–11	4:1–13
Jesus' Inaugural Sermon			
7. Introduction	⟨6:20a⟩	5:1–2	6:12, 17, 20a
8. Blessing and Woes	6:20b–23, (24–26)	5:3–12	6:20b–26
9. On Retaliation	6:27–33, (34–35b), 35c; (Q/Matt 5:41)	5:38–47; 7:12	6:27–35
10. On Judging	6:36–37b; (Q/Matt 7:2a); (6:37c–38b), 38c	5:48; 7:1–2	6:36–38
11. Blind Guides, Teachers and Pupils	6:39b–40	15:13–14; 10:24–25	6:39–40
12. On Hypocrisy	6:41–42	7:3–5	6:41–42
13. Good and Evil Men	6:43–45	7:15–20; 12:33–35	6:43–45
14. The Parable of the Builders	6:46–49	7:21–27	6:46–49
John, Jesus and this Generation			
15. The Centurion's Son	7:⟨1a⟩, 1b–2, (3–5), 6–10	8:5–13	7:1–10
16. John's Inquiry	7:18–19, (20), 22–23	11:2–6	7:18–23
17. Jesus' Eulogy of John	7:24–28	11:7–11	7:24–28
18. The Kingdom Suffers Violence	16:16	11:12–15	16:16
19. John and the Tax Collectors	[7:29–30]	21:28–32	7:29–30
20. The Children in the Agora	7:31–35	11:16–19	7:31–35
Discipleship and Mission			
21. Three Followers of Jesus	9:57–60, (61–62)	8:18–22	9:57–62
22. The Mission Speech	10:2–12	9:36–38; 10:1–16	10:1–12
23. Woes on the Galilean Towns	10:13–15 (Q/Matt 11:23b–24)	11:20–24	10:13–15
24. The Authority of Missionaries	10:16, [18–20]	10:40	10:16–20
25. Thanksgiving for Revelation	10:21–22	11:25–27	10:21–22
26. Blessing on the Eye–witnesses	10:23b–24	13:16–17	10:23–24

Section & Name	Q text	Matthew	Luke
On Prayer			
27. The Lord's Prayer	11:2–4	6:7–13	11:1–4
28. Confidence in Prayer	11:[5–8], 9–13	7:7–11	11:5–13
Controversies with this Generation			
29. The Beelzebul Accusation	11:14–18a, 19–20, (21–22), 23	12:22–30; 9:32–34	11:14–23
30. The Return of the Evil Spirit	11:24–26	12:43–45	11:24–26
31. True Blessedness	(11:27–28)	[no parallel]	11:27–28
32. The Sign of Jonah	11:16, 29–32	12:38–42	11:16, 29–32
33. The Lamp and the Eye	11:33–35, (36)	5:14–16; 6:22–23	11:33–36
34. Woes Against the Pharisees	11:39b–44, 46–52; 13:34–35	23:1–39 13:34–35	11:37–54; 13:34–35
On Anxiety			
35. Hidden and Revealed	12:[1], 2–3	10:26–27	12:1–3
36. Appropriate Fear	12:4–7	10:28–31	12:4–7
37. On Confessing Jesus	12:8–9	10:32–33	12:8–9
38. Blasphemy of the Spirit	12:10	12:31–32	12:10
39. The Spirit's Assistance	12:11–12 [Q/Matt 10:23]	10:17–20, 23	12:11–12
40. Foolish Possessions	(12:13–14, 16–21)	[no parallel]	12:13–21
41. Earthly Cares	12:22–31	6:25–34	12:22–32
42. Heavenly Treasure	12:33–34	6:19–21	12:33–34
Sayings on the Coming Judgment			
43. Watchful Servants	[12:35–38]	[no parallel]	12:35–38
44. The Householder and the Thief	12:39–40	24:42–44	12:391–40
45. Faithful and Unfaithful Servants	12:42b–46	24:45–51	12:41–48
46. Fire and Division on Earth	12:(49), 51–53	10:34–36	12:49–53
47. Signs of the Times	12:54–56	16:2–3	12:54–56
48. Agreeing with One's Accuser	12:57–59	5:25–26	12:57–59
Two Parables of Growth			
49. The Mustard and the Leaven	13:18–21	13:31–33	13:18–21
The Two Ways			
50. The Narrow Gate and Closed Door	13:24, (25), 26–27	7:13–14, 22–23	13:22–27
51. Gentiles in the Kingdom	13:28–30	8:11–12; 20:16	13:28–30
52. Lament over Jerusalem	13:34–35	23:37–39	13:31–35
53. Livestock in a Pit	[14:5]	12:11–12	14:1–6
54. Exalting the Humble	14:11/18:14b	23:6–12	14:7–12; 18:14
55. The Great Supper	14:16–24	22:1–10	14:15–24
56. Being My Disciple	14:26–27; 17:33	10:37–39	14:25–27; 17:33
57. Savorless Salt	14:34–35	5:13	14:34–35

C. H. Weisse 1838

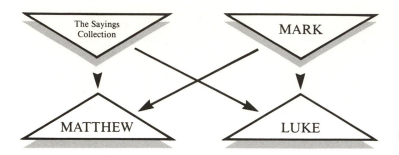

C. H. Weisse, *Die evangelische Geschichte kritisch und philosophisch bearbeitet*. 2 vols. Leipzig, 1838.

H. J. Holtzmann 1863

H. J. Holtzmann, *Die synoptischen Evangelien: Ihr Ursprung und geschichtlicher Charakter*. Leipzig: Wilhelm Engelmann, 1863.

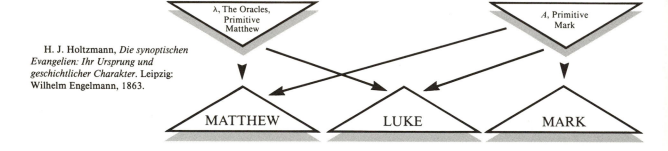

J. Weiss 1890

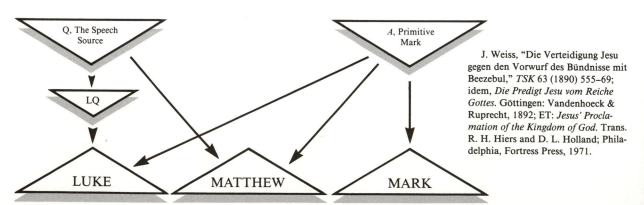

J. Weiss, "Die Verteidigung Jesu gegen den Vorwurf des Bündnisse mit Beezebul," *TSK* 63 (1890) 555–69; idem, *Die Predigt Jesu vom Reiche Gottes*. Göttingen: Vandenhoeck & Ruprecht, 1892; ET: *Jesus' Proclamation of the Kingdom of God*. Trans. R. H. Hiers and D. L. Holland; Philadelphia, Fortress Press, 1971.

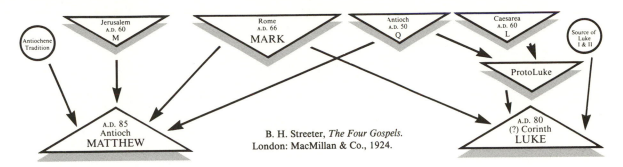

B. H. Streeter 1924

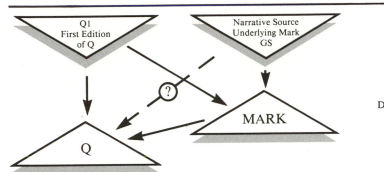

W. Schmithals 1985

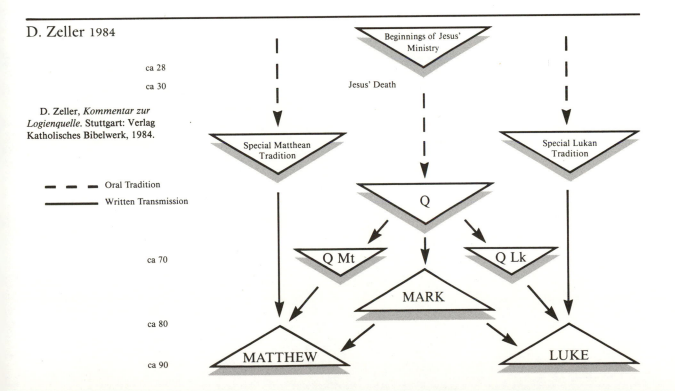

D. Zeller 1984

PARALLELS

Matt

[No text extant]

Luke

[No text extant]

Notes

Although the Synoptic Sayings source presumably had an incipit, the editorial activities of Matthew and Luke have evidently obscured it. Since nothing within the gospels survives to indicate how Q may have begun, we are left only with the analogies afforded by the incipits of other similar sayings collections. There are at least three possibilities.

1. Q may have begun in a way similar to Baruch, *POxy* 654 or the *Gospel of Thomas*, something such as, Οὗτοι οἱ λόγοι οὓς ἐλάλησεν Ἰησοῦς καὶ Ἰωάννης, "These are the sayings which Jesus (and John) spoke."

2. The church father Papias (whose work is quoted in Eusebius, *Hist. eccl.* 3.39.16) refers to the Aramaic *logia* compiled by Matthew. Many have supposed this work to be identical with Q or something very much like it. Hawkins (1911: 119), evidently influenced by the title of Papias' work, "Interpretation of the Oracles [*logia*] of the Lord" (Eusebius, *Hist. eccl.* 3.39.1), suggests the title, Κυριακὰ λόγια, "Oracles of the Lord."

3. Finally, there are several instances in early Christian and Gnostic literature where small clusters of sayings of Jesus are quoted and prefaced with the formula, "remembering the sayings of (the Lord) Jesus."

For example,

Acts 20:35b: μνημονεύειν τε τῶν λόγων τοῦ κυρίου Ἰησοῦ ὅτι αὐτὸς εἶπεν·
"remembering the words of the Lord Jesus, how he said . . ."

1 Clem 13:1–2: μεμνημένοι τῶν λόγων τοῦ κυρίου Ἰησοῦ, οὓς ἐλάλησεν διδάσκων . . . οὕτως γὰρ εἶπεν·
"remembering the words of the Lord Jesus which he spoke when he was teaching . . . For he spoke thus: . . ."

1 Clem 46:7–8: μνήσθητε τῶν λόγων τοῦ κυρίου Ἰησοῦ. εἶπεν γάρ·
"Remember the words of the Lord Jesus; for he said . . ."

ApJas 2:7–15: "Now when the twelve disciples were all sitting together and recalling what the Savior had said to each one of them, whether in secret or openly, and [setting it in order] in books . . ."

If this "remembering" formula contains a technical designation of the sayings of Jesus, the superscription of Q may have been, Λόγοι (τοῦ κυρίου) Ἰησοῦ, "(The) sayings of (the Lord) Jesus." This is an option favored by Polag (28).

Parallels

POxy 654.1–5

Οὗτοι οἱ {οι} λόγοι οἱ [ἀπόκρυφοι οὓς ἐλά]λησεν
᾽Ιη(σοῦ)ς ὁ ζῶν κ[αὶ ἔγραψεν ᾽Ιούδα ὁ] καὶ Θωμᾶ. καὶ
εἶπεν· [ὃς ἂν τὴν ἑρμηνεί]αν τῶν λόγων τούτ[ων εὕρῃ
θανάτου] οὐ μὴ γεύσηται.

POxy 654.1–5

These are the [secret] sayings [which] the living Jesus
[spoke and which Judas, who is] also Thomas, [wrote
down]. And he said, "[Whoever finds the interpretation]
of these sayings will not experience [death]."

GThom Incipit and saying 1

ⲛⲁⲉⲓ ⲛⲉ ⲛ̄ϣⲁϫⲉ ⲉⲑⲏⲡ ⲉⲛⲧⲁ ⲓ̅ⲥ̅ ⲉⲧⲟⲛϩ· ϫⲟⲟⲩ ⲁⲩⲱ
ⲁϥⲥϩⲁⲓ̈ⲥⲟⲩ ⲛ̄ϭⲓ ⲇⲓⲇⲩⲙⲟⲥ ⲓ̈ⲟⲩⲇⲁⲥ ⲑⲱⲙⲁⲥ.
(1) ⲁⲩⲱ ⲡⲉϫⲁϥ ϫⲉ ⲡⲉⲧⲁϩⲉ ⲉⲑⲉⲣⲙⲏⲛⲉⲓⲁ
ⲛ̄ⲛⲉⲉⲓϣⲁϫⲉ ϥⲛⲁϫⲓ †ⲡⲉ ⲁⲛ ⲙ̄ⲡⲙⲟⲩ.

GThom Incipit and saying 1

These are the secret sayings that the living Jesus spoke
and Didymos Judas Thomas recorded. (1) And he said,
"Whoever discovers the interpretation of these sayings
will not taste death."

Mani, *Epistula Fundamenti*

Haec sunt salubria verba ex perenni ac vivo fonte
quae qui audierit et eisdem primum crediderit,
deinde, quae insinuant, custodierit, numquam erit
morti obnoxious, verum aeterna et gloriosa vita
fruetur. Nam profecto beatus est iudicandus, qui
hac divina instructus cognitione fuerit, per quam
liberatus in sempiterna vita permanebit.

Mani, *Epistula Fundamenti*

These are the serviceable words from a lasting and living
source. Whoever listens to them and believes, and then
observes what they teach will never experience death, but
will enjoy an eternal and glorious life. For he is to be
considered perfectly blessed, who is instructed in this
divine wisdom through which he will be remain liberated
in eternal life.

Thom. Cont. 138:1–2

ⲛ̄ϣⲁϫⲉ ⲉⲑⲏⲡ ⲛⲁⲓ̈ ⲉⲛⲧⲁϥϣⲁϫⲉ ⲙ̄ⲙⲟⲟⲩ ⲛ̄ϭⲓ ⲡⲥⲱⲣ
ⲛ̄ⲓ̈ⲟⲩⲇⲁⲥ ⲑⲱⲙⲁⲥ ⲛⲁⲓ̈ ⲉⲛⲧⲁⲓ̈ⲥⲁϩⲟⲩ· ⲁⲛⲟⲕ ϩⲱⲱⲧ
ⲙⲁⲑⲁⲓⲁⲥ.

Thom. Cont. 138:1–2

The secret words that the Savior spoke to Judas Thomas
which I, even I Mathaias, wrote down.

Baruch 1:1

¹Καὶ οὗτοι οἱ λόγοι τοῦ βιβλίου, οὓς ἔγραψεν Βαρουχ
υἱὸς Νηριου υἱοῦ Μαασαιου . . .

Baruch 1:1

¹These are the words of the book which Baruch the son of
Neraiah, son of Mahseiah . . . wrote.

Matt 3:1–6

¹ Ἐν δὲ ταῖς ἡμέραις ἐκείναις

παραγίνεται Ἰωάννης ὁ Βαπτιστὴς κηρύσσων
ἐν τῇ ἐρήμῳ τῆς Ἰουδαίας
(⇨ Matt 3:5)
²[καὶ] λέγων· μετανοεῖτε· ἤγγικεν γὰρ ἡ βασιλεία τῶν
οὐρανῶν. ³οὗτος γάρ ἐστιν
ὁ ῥηθεὶς διὰ Ἡσαΐου τοῦ προφήτου λέγοντος·
φωνὴ βοῶντος ἐν τῇ ἐρήμῳ· ἑτοιμάσατε τὴν
ὁδὸν κυρίου, εὐθείας ποιεῖτε τὰς τρίβους αὐτοῦ.

⁴αὐτὸς δὲ ὁ Ἰωάννης εἶχεν τὸ ἔνδυμα αὐτοῦ ἀπὸ τριχῶν
καμήλου καὶ ζώνην δερματίνην περὶ τὴν ὀσφὺν αὐτοῦ, ἡ
δὲ τροφὴ ἦν αὐτοῦ ἀκρίδες καὶ μέλι ἄγριον. ⁵τότε
ἐξεπορεύετο πρὸς αὐτὸν Ἱεροσόλυμα καὶ πᾶσα
ἡ Ἰουδαία καὶ πᾶσα ἡ περίχωρος τοῦ Ἰορδάνου,
⁶καὶ ἐβαπτίζοντο ἐν τῷ Ἰορδάνῃ ποταμῷ ὑπ' αὐτοῦ
ἐξομολογούμενοι τὰς ἁμαρτίας αὐτῶν.

Luke 3:1–4

¹Ἐν ἔτει δὲ πεντεκαιδεκάτῳ τῆς ἡγεμονίας Τιβερίου
Καίσαρος, ἡγεμονεύοντος Ποντίου Πιλάτου τῆς
Ἰουδαίας, καὶ τετρααρχοῦντος τῆς Γαλιλαίας Ἡρῴδου,
Φιλίππου δὲ τοῦ ἀδελφοῦ αὐτοῦ τετρααρχοῦντος τῆς
Ἰτουραίας καὶ Τραχωνίτιδος χώρας, καὶ Λυσανίου τῆς
Ἀβιληνῆς τετρααρχοῦντος, ²ἐπὶ ἀρχιερέως Ἅννα καὶ
Καϊάφα,
ἐγένετο ῥῆμα θεοῦ ἐπὶ Ἰωάννην τὸν
Ζαχαρίου υἱὸν ἐν τῇ ἐρήμῳ. ³καὶ ἦλθεν εἰς
πᾶσαν [τὴν] περίχωρον τοῦ Ἰορδάνου
κηρύσσων βάπτισμα μετανοίας εἰς ἄφεσιν
ἁμαρτίων, ⁴ὡς γέγραπται ἐν βίβλῳ λόγων
Ἡσαΐου τοῦ προφήτου·
φωνὴ βοῶντος ἐν τῇ ἐρήμῳ· ἑτοιμάσατε τὴν
ὁδὸν κυρίου, εὐθείας ποιεῖτε τὰς τρίβους αὐτοῦ . . .

Matt 3:2: καὶ: C D L W Koine 0233 λ ϕ *pm* lat sy [NA²⁶;
HG] / omit: B ℵ 28 q [NA²⁵].

Luke 3:3: omit τὴν: A B L W 579 *al*; Or [HG].

GEbi 3

ʽΗ δὲ ἀρχὴ τοῦ παρ᾽ αὐτοῖς εὐαγγελίου ἔχει ὅτι ἐγένετο ἐν ταῖς ἡμέραις Ἡρῴδου βασιλέως τῆς Ἰουδαίας ⟨ἐπὶ ἀρχιερέως Καϊάφα⟩, ἦλθεν ⟨τις⟩ Ἰωάννης ⟨ὀνόματι⟩ βαπτίζων βάπτισμα μετανοίας ἐν τῷ Ἰορδάνῃ ποταμῷ, ὃς ἐλέγετο εἶναι ἐκ γένους Ἀαρὼν τοῦ ἱερέως, παῖς Ζαχαρίου καὶ Ἐλισάβετ· καὶ ἐξήρχοντο πρὸς αὐτὸν πάντες.

GEbi 3

And the beginning of their gospel runs: It came to pass in the days of Herod the king of Judaea, ⟨when Caiaphas was high priest⟩, that there came ⟨one⟩, John ⟨by name⟩, and baptized with the baptism of repentance in the river Jordan. It was said of him that he was of the lineage of Aaron the priest, a son of Zacharias and Elisabeth; and all went out to him.

Mark 1:2–6

²Καθὼς γέγραπται ἐν τῷ Ἡσαΐᾳ τῷ προφήτῃ· ἰδοὺ ἀποστέλλω τὸν ἄγγελόν μου πρὸ προσώπου σου, ὃς κατασκευάσει τὴν ὁδόν σου· (⇨ Q 7:27 [S17]) ³**φωνὴ βοῶντος ἐν τῇ ἐρήμῳ· ἑτοιμάσατε τὴν ὁδὸν κυρίου, εὐθείας ποιεῖτε τὰς τρίβους αὐτοῦ.** ⁴ἐγένετο Ἰωάννης [ὁ] Βαπτίζων ἐν τῇ ἐρήμῳ καὶ κηρύσσων βάπτισμα μετανοίας εἰς ἄφεσιν ἁμαρτιῶν. ⁶καὶ ἦν ὁ Ἰωάννης ἐνδεδυμένος τρίχας καμήλου καὶ ζώνην δερματίνην περὶ τὴν ὀσφὺν αὐτοῦ, καὶ ἐσθίων ἀκρίδας καὶ μέλι ἄγριον. ⁵καὶ ἐξεπορεύετο πρὸς αὐτὸν πᾶσα ἡ Ἰουδαία χώρα καὶ οἱ Ἱεροσολυμῖται πάντες καὶ ἐβαπτίζοντο ὑπ᾽ αὐτοῦ ἐν τῷ Ἰορδάνῃ ποταμῷ ἐξομολογούμενοι τὰς ἁμαρτίας αὐτῶν.

Mark 1:2–6

²As it is written in Isaiah the prophet,
"Behold, I send my messenger before your face,
who will prepare your way;
³the voice of one crying in the wilderness:
Prepare the way of the Lord,
make his paths straight—"
⁴John the baptizer appeared in the wilderness, preaching a baptism of repentance for the forgiveness of sins.
⁶And John was clothed in camel's hair, and had a leather girdle around his waist, and was eating locusts and wild honey.
⁵And all the country of Judea and all the people of Jerusalem went out to him; and they were baptized by him in the river Jordan, confessing their sins.

Isaiah 40:3 LXX

³φωνὴ βοῶντος ἐν τῇ ἐρήμῳ· ἑτοιμάσατε τὴν ὁδὸν κυρίου, εὐθείας ποιεῖτε τὰς τρίβους τοῦ θεοῦ ἡμῶν.

Isaiah 40:3 LXX

³the voice of one crying in the wilderness: Prepare the way of the Lord, make the paths of our God straight.

John 1:23

²³ἔφη [Ἰωάννης]· ἐγὼ **φωνὴ βοῶντος ἐν τῇ ἐρήμῳ· εὐθύνατε τὴν ὁδὸν κυρίου,** καθὼς εἶπεν Ἡσαΐας ὁ προφήτης.

John 1:23

²³He [John] said, "I am the voice of one crying in the wilderness, 'Make straight the way of the Lord,' as the prophet Isaiah said."

GEbi 2

καὶ ἐγένετο Ἰωάννης βαπτίζων, καὶ ἐξῆλθον πρὸς αὐτὸν Φαρισαῖοι καὶ ἐβαπτίσθησαν καὶ πᾶσα Ἱεροσόλυμα. καὶ εἶχεν ὁ Ἰωάννης ἔνδυμα ἀπὸ τριχῶν καμήλου καὶ ζώνην δερματίνην περὶ τὴν ὀσφὺν αὐτοῦ. καὶ τὸ βρῶμα αὐτοῦ, φησί, μέλι ἄγριον, οὗ ἡ γεῦσις ἡ τοῦ μάννα, ὡς ἐγκρὶς ἐν ἐλαίῳ.

GEbi 2

It came to pass that John was baptizing; and there went out to him Pharisees and were they were baptized, and all Jerusalem. And John had a garment of camel's hair and a leather girdle about his loins, and his food, as it saith, was wild honey, the taste of which was that of manna, as a cake dipped in oil.

In Q: The principal grounds for tracing this back to Q are (1) the necessity of positing some sort on introduction for Q 3:7–9, (2) the Matthew-Luke agreements against Mark in the omission of the Malachi quotation and in the relative order of the Isaiah quotation and introduction of John, and (3) the 'minor agreement' "the region about the Jordan."

Many conjecture that part of Luke 3:2–4 appeared also in Q. Crossan (1983: 342) suggests that portions of Luke 3:2b, 3a, 4 // Matt 3:1, 3, 5b derived from Q. Easton (Lk 37) argues: "Q began with the mention of John, perhaps with Matthew's historic present" and perhaps with Luke's ῥῆμα ("word") and γίνεσθαι ἐπί ("came upon") which is reminiscent of Jer 1:1. It certainly contained "in the wilderness" but lacked both the quotation of Mal 3:1 and a parallel to Mark 1:5–6.

Harnack (127) includes in his introduction to Q 3:7–9 only "all the region around the Jordan . . ." while Hoffmann (17) regards this as the remains of the original introduction. Jacobson (28–30) includes "In those days, John came preaching in all the region of the Jordan, as it is written in the book of the words of Isaiah the prophet . . . ," the Isa 40:3 (LXX) quotation and perhaps a reference to Herod. Polag (28) includes Luke 3:2b, 3b, 4, 3a as "conjectural." Schürmann (Lk 161) holds that Luke 3:3–4a follows Q (although Markan influence is present too), pointing especially to "region about the Jordan" and Luke's "came."

See also Beare 1962: 38; Marshall Lk 132–37; Schmithals Lk 49; Schneider Lk 84; Streeter 1911b: 186; idem 1924: 205–206, 305; Weiss 1907: 189–90; Wellhausen 1911: 57; Zeller 17 (hesitantly).

Not in Q: The agreements of Matthew and Luke against Mark are slight and can be explained without recourse to a Q *Vorlage*. While one cannot be dogmatic in this case, the large amount of Markan material present in this section as well as the likelihood of Lukan redaction in vv. 1–2 render it unwise to include it in Q.

See Bussmann; Edwards 1975; idem 1976; Fitzmyer Lk 452; Hawkins 1911; Hunter; Kloppenborg 1987: 74; Knox; Manson; Müller 1908: 45; Schenk; Schulz; Wernle 1899: 91.

Matt 3:1–6

[1] Now in those days

John the Baptist came, preaching in the wilderness of Judea

[2] and saying, "Repent, for the reign of heaven is at hand."

[3] For this is he who was spoken of by the prophet Isaiah when he says,

    "The voice of one crying in the wilderness:
    Prepare the way of the Lord,
      make his paths straight."

[4] Now John had a garment of camel's hair, and a leather girdle around his waist; and his food was locusts and wild honey.

[5] Then Jerusalem and all Judea and all the region about the Jordan went out to him,

[6] and they were baptized by him in the river Jordan, confessing their sins.

Luke 3:1–4

[1] Now in the fifteenth year of the reign of Tiberius Caesar, when Pontius Pilate was governor of Judea, and Herod was tetrarch of Galilee, and his brother Philip tetrarch of the region of Ituraea and Trachonitis, and Lysanias tetrarch of Abilene,

[2] during the high-priesthood of Annas and Caiaphas, the word of God came to John the son of Zechariah in the wilderness;

[3] and he went into all the region of the Jordan, preaching a baptism of repentance for the forgiveness of sins,

[4] as it is written in the book of the words of Isaiah the prophet,

    "The voice of one crying in the wilderness:
    Prepare the way of the Lord,
      make his paths straight."

Matt 3:7–10

⁷Ἰδὼν δὲ πολλοὺς τῶν Φαρισαίων καὶ Σαδδουκαίων ἐρχομένους ἐπὶ τὸ βάπτισμα αὐτοῦ εἶπεν αὐτοῖς· γεννήματα ἐχιδνῶν, τίς ὑπέδειξεν ὑμῖν φυγεῖν ἀπὸ τῆς μελλούσης ὀργῆς; ⁸ποιήσατε οὖν καρπὸν ἄξιον τῆς μετανοίας, ⁹καὶ μὴ δόξητε λέγειν ἐν ἑαυτοῖς· πατέρα ἔχομεν τὸν Ἀβραάμ· λέγω γὰρ ὑμῖν ὅτι δύναται ὁ θεὸς ἐκ τῶν λίθων τούτων ἐγεῖραι τέκνα τῷ Ἀβραάμ. ¹⁰ἤδη δὲ   ἡ ἀξίνη πρὸς τὴν ῥίζαν τῶν δένδρων κεῖται· πᾶν οὖν δένδρον μὴ ποιοῦν καρπὸν καλὸν ἐκκόπτεται καὶ εἰς πῦρ βάλλεται.

Luke 3:7–9

⁷Ἔλεγεν οὖν τοῖς ἐκπορευομένοις ὄχλοις βαπτισθῆναι ὑπ' αὐτοῦ· γεννήματα ἐχιδνῶν, τίς ὑπέδειξεν ὑμῖν φυγεῖν ἀπὸ τῆς μελλούσης ὀργῆς; ⁸ποιήσατε οὖν καρποὺς ἀξίους τῆς μετανοίας, καὶ μὴ ἄρξησθε λέγειν ἐν ἑαυτοῖς· πατέρα ἔχομεν τὸν Ἀβραάμ· λέγω γὰρ ὑμῖν ὅτι δύναται ὁ θεὸς ἐκ τῶν λίθων τούτων ἐγεῖραι τέκνα τῷ Ἀβραάμ. ⁹ἤδη δὲ καὶ ἡ ἀξίνη πρὸς τὴν ῥίζαν τῶν δένδρων κεῖται· πᾶν οὖν δένδρον μὴ ποιοῦν καρπὸν καλὸν ἐκκόπτεται καὶ εἰς πῦρ βάλλεται.

Luke 3:10–14

[¹⁰Καὶ ἐπηρώτων αὐτὸν οἱ ὄχλοι λέγοντες· τί οὖν ποιήσωμεν; ¹¹ἀποκριθεὶς δὲ ἔλεγεν αὐτοῖς· ὁ ἔχων δύο χιτῶνας μεταδότω τῷ μὴ ἔχοντι, καὶ ὁ ἔχων βρώματα ὁμοίως ποιείτω. ¹²ἦλθον δὲ καὶ τελῶναι βαπτισθῆναι καὶ εἶπαν πρὸς αὐτόν· διδάσκαλε, τί ποιήσωμεν; ¹³ὁ δὲ εἶπεν πρὸς αὐτούς· μηδὲν πλέον παρὰ τὸ διατεταγμένον ὑμῖν πράσσετε. ¹⁴ἐπηρώτων δὲ αὐτὸν καὶ στρατευόμενοι λέγοντες· τί ποιήσωμεν καὶ ἡμεῖς; καὶ εἶπεν αὐτοῖς· μηδένα διασείσητε μηδὲ συκοφαντήσητε καὶ ἀρκεῖσθε τοῖς ὀψωνίοις ὑμῶν.]

Matt 3:7: βαπτ. αυτου: ℵ¹ C D L W Koine 0233 λ φ latt sy^{s.c.h} bo [NA²⁶; HG] / βαπτ.: ℵ* B 28 sa mae; Or [NA²⁵].

Mark 1:5 ⇨ Q 3:2–4 [S2]

⁵καὶ ἐξεπορεύετο πρὸς αὐτὸν πᾶσα ἡ Ἰουδαία χώρα καὶ οἱ Ἱεροσολυμῖται πάντες καὶ ἐβαπτίζοντο ὑπ᾽ αὐτοῦ ἐν τῷ Ἰορδάνῃ ποταμῷ ἐξομολογούμενοι τὰς ἁμαρτίας αὐτῶν.

Matt 23:33 ⇨ Q 11:39–52 [S34]

³³Ὄφεις, γεννήματα ἐχιδνῶν, πῶς φύγητε ἀπὸ τῆς κρίσεως τῆς γεέννης;

Matt 12:34 ⇨ Q 6:43–45 [S13]

³⁴γεννήματα ἐχιδνῶν, πῶς δύνασθε ἀγαθὰ λαλεῖν πονηροὶ ὄντες;

Matt 7:18–19 ⇨ Q 6:43–45 [S13]

¹⁸οὐ δύναται δένδρον ἀγαθὸν καρποὺς πονηροὺς ποιεῖν οὐδὲ δένδρον σαπρὸν καρποὺς καλοὺς ποιεῖν. ¹⁹πᾶν δένδρον μὴ ποιοῦν καρπὸν καλὸν ἐκκόπτεται καὶ εἰς πῦρ βάλλεται.

ApJas 9:24—10:6

ⲱ̅ ⲛ̅ⲧⲁⲗⲁⲓⲡⲱⲣⲟⲥ ⲱ̅ ⲛ̅ⲕⲁⲕⲟⲇⲁⲓⲙⲱⲛ ⲱ̅ ⲛ̅ϩⲩⲡⲟⲕⲣⲓⲧⲏⲥ ⲛ̅ⲧⲙⲏⲉ· ⲱ̅ ⲛ̅ⲣⲙⲛ̅ⲛⲟⲩϫ ⲛ̅ⲧⲅⲛⲱⲥⲓⲥ ⲱ̅ ⟨ⲙ̅⟩ⲡⲁⲣⲁⲃⲁⲧⲏⲥ ⲙ̅ⲡⲛⲉⲩⲙⲁ ϩⲓⲉ ϣⲁ ϯⲛⲟⲩ ⲁⲛ ⲧⲉⲧⲛ̅ⲣ̅ ϩⲩⲡⲟⲙⲓⲛⲉ ⲁⲥⲱⲧⲙ̅ ⲉϣϣⲉ ⲁⲣⲱⲧⲛ̅ ⲁϣⲉϫⲉ ϫⲓⲛ ⲛ̅ϣⲁⲣⲡ̅ ϩⲓⲉ ϯⲛⲟⲩ ⲁⲛ ⲧⲉⲧⲛ̅ⲣ̅ ϩⲩⲡⲟⲙⲓⲛⲉ ⲁⲛ ⲕⲁⲧⲕⲉ ⲉϣϣⲉ ⲁⲣⲱⲧⲛ̅ ⲁⲣⲁⲓⲥ ϫⲓⲛ ⲛ̅ϣⲁⲣⲡ̅ ϫⲉⲕⲁⲥⲉ ⲉⲥⲛⲁ ϣⲉⲡ ⲧⲏⲛⲉ· ⲁⲣⲁⲥ ⲛ̅ϭⲓ ⲧⲙⲛ̅ⲧⲣ̅ⲣⲟ ⲛⲙⲡⲏⲩⲉ ⲥⲉ ⲙⲙⲁⲛ ϯϫⲟⲩ ⲙⲙⲁⲥ ⲛⲏⲧⲛ̅ ϫⲉ ⲥⲙⲁⲧⲛ̅ ⲁⲧⲣⲉⲟⲩⲡⲉⲧⲟⲩⲁⲁⲃ ⲉⲓ ⲁⲡⲓⲧⲛ̅ ⲁⲩϫⲱϩⲙ̅ ⲁⲩⲱ ⲛ̅ⲧⲉⲟⲩⲣⲙ̅ⲛ̅ⲟⲩⲁⲉⲓⲛ ⲉⲓ ⲁⲡⲓⲧⲛ̅ ⲁⲡⲕⲉⲕⲉⲓ ⲛ̅ϩⲟⲩⲟ ⲁⲣⲱⲧⲛ̅ ⲁⲣ̅ ⲣ̅ⲣⲟ ⲏ ⲁⲧⲙ̅ⲉⲓⲣⲉ.

Mark 1:5 ⇨ Q 3:2–4 [S2]

⁵And there went out to him all the country of Judea, and all the people of Jerusalem; and they were baptized by him in the river Jordan, confessing their sins.

Matt 23:33

³³You serpents, you brood of vipers, how will you flee from the judgment of Gehenna?

Matt 12:34

³⁴You brood of vipers! how can you speak good, if you are evil?

Matt 7:18–19

¹⁸A healthy tree cannot bear bad fruit, nor can a rotten tree bear good fruit. ¹⁹Every tree that does not bear good fruit is cut down and thrown into the fire.

ApJas 9:24—10:6

O you wretches; O you unfortunates; O you pretenders to the truth; O you falsifiers of knowledge; O you sinners against the Spirit: can you still bear to listen when it behooved you to speak from the first? Can you still bear to sleep, when it behooved you to be awake from the first so that the kingdom of heaven might receive you? Verily I say unto you, it is easier for a pure one to fall into defilement, and for a man of light to fall into darkness, than for you to reign or not reign.

Q 3:7–9
In Q: Most authors.

[Luke 3:10–14]
In Q: Marshall Lk 142: The vocabulary in not Lukan, and since Luke's *Sondergut* contained no traditions about John, it is likely that 3:10–14 comes from Q. Plummer Lk 90 (probably in Q); Schürmann Lk 169: Q 7:29–30 (!) also contrasts the unrepentant leaders with toll-collectors. Matthew omitted it so as to reserve ethical instruction for Jesus. Streeter 1924: 291 (with considerable doubt). Sato 1984: 61–62: Q[Lk].

Not in Q: Most authors.

Matt 3:7–10

⁷But when he saw many of the Pharisees and Sadducees coming to his baptism, he said to them, "You brood of vipers! Who warned you to flee from the coming wrath? ⁸Bear fruit worthy of repentance,

⁹and do not presume to say to yourselves, 'We have Abraham as our father'; for I tell you, God is able from these stones to raise up children to Abraham.

¹⁰Even now the axe is laid to the root of the trees; every tree therefore that does not bear good fruit is cut down and thrown into the fire."

Luke 3:7–9

⁷He said therefore to the crowds that were coming out to be baptized by him, "You brood of vipers! Who warned you to flee from the wrath to come?

⁸Bear fruits worthy of repentance, and do not start saying to yourselves, 'We have Abraham as our father'; for I tell you, God is able from these stones to raise up children to Abraham.

⁹Even now the axe is laid to the root of the trees; every tree therefore that does not bear good fruit is cut down and thrown into the fire."

Luke 3:10–14

[¹⁰And the crowds asked him, "What then shall we do?" ¹¹And he answered them, "He who has two tunics, let him share with him who has none; and let the one who has food do likewise." ¹²Tax collectors also came to be baptized, and said to him, "Teacher, what shall we do?" ¹³And he said to them, "Collect no more than you are entitled." ¹⁴Soldiers also asked him, "And we, what shall we do?" And he said to them, "Do not extort or falsely denounce anyone, and be content with your wages."]

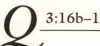

Matt 3:11–12

¹¹ἐγὼ μὲν ὑμᾶς βαπτίζω ἐν ὕδατι εἰς μετάνοιαν,
ὁ δὲ ὀπίσω μου ἐρχόμενος ἰσχυρότερός μού
ἐστιν, οὗ οὐκ εἰμὶ ἱκανὸς τὰ ὑποδήματα
βαστάσαι·
αὐτὸς ὑμᾶς βαπτίσει ἐν πνεύματι ἁγίῳ καὶ πυρί·
¹² οὗ τὸ πτύον ἐν τῇ χειρὶ αὐτοῦ καὶ
διακαθαριεῖ τὴν ἅλωνα αὐτοῦ καὶ συνάξει
τὸν σῖτον αὐτοῦ εἰς τὴν ἀποθήκην,
τὸ δὲ ἄχυρον κατακαύσει πυρὶ ἀσβέστῳ.

Luke 3:15, 16–17

[¹⁵Προσδοκῶντος δὲ τοῦ λαοῦ καὶ διαλογιζομένων
πάντων ἐν ταῖς καρδίαις αὐτῶν περὶ τοῦ Ἰωάννου,
μήποτε αὐτὸς εἴη ὁ χριστός,]
[¹⁶ἀπεκρίνατο λέγων πᾶσιν ὁ Ἰωάννης·]
ἐγὼ μὲν ὕδατι βαπτίζω ὑμᾶς·
ἔρχεται δὲ ὁ ἰσχυρότερός μου,
οὗ οὐκ εἰμὶ ἱκανὸς λῦσαι τὸν ἱμάντα
τῶν ὑποδημάτων αὐτοῦ·
αὐτὸς ὑμᾶς βαπτίσει ἐν πνεύματι ἁγίῳ καὶ πυρί.
¹⁷οὗ τὸ πτύον ἐν τῇ χειρὶ αὐτοῦ
διακαθᾶραι τὴν ἅλωνα αὐτοῦ καὶ συναγαγεῖν
τὸν σῖτον εἰς τὴν ἀποθήκην αὐτοῦ,
τὸ δὲ ἄχυρον κατακαύσει πυρὶ ἀσβέστῳ.

Notes

[Luke 3:15–16a]

In Q: Schürmann (Lk 171) cites five reasons for the inclusion of Luke 3:15–16a in Q: (1) It contains several non-Lukan locutions. (2) If 3:10–14 derives from Q (see S3), some form of transition is required between 3:10–14 and 3:16–17. (3) Luke 3:15–16a serves appropriately to introduce the rejection of an elevated estimation of the Baptist implicit in 3:16. (4) If as is probable, Q 3:7–9 and Q 3:16–17 were originally independent sayings, 3:16–17 would require some form of introduction. (5) Matthew could eliminate Q 3:15–16a because the problem of John's position was not so acute for him. See also Marshall Lk 144 (with hesitations).

Lukan: Jeremias 1980: 109 (except for ἀπεκρίνατο) and most others.

Q 3:16

In Q: Most authors. The strong Matthew-Luke agreements in Matt 3:12 // Luke 3:17 make it highly probable that this derives from Q. Despite the Marcan parallel, the preceding verse (Matt 3:12 // Luke 3:16) was probably also represented in Q. Matthew and Luke agree against Mark in several important respects: (1) in the order of clauses, (2) the use of μέν . . . δέ, (3) the use of a present tense rather than an aorist of "to baptize," (4) the placing of ὑμᾶς before βαπτίσει and (5) the addition of καὶ πυρί.

Not in Q: Bussmann 37 (who also excludes 3:17); Haupt 1913: 97, 98: The agreements of Matthew and Luke against Mark derive from an earlier recension of Mark rather than from Q. See also Hawkins 1911: 113; Lührmann 31.

Matt 3:11–12

Luke 3:15, 16–17

[15 Since the people were in expectation, and everyone was wondering in their hearts concerning John, whether perhaps he were the Christ,]
[16 John answered them all,]

11 "To be sure, I am baptizing you with water for repentance, but the One coming after me is stronger than I, whose sandals I am not worthy to carry; he will baptize you with the Holy Spirit and fire. 12 His winnowing fork is in his hand, and he will clear his threshing floor and gather his wheat into the granary, but the chaff he will burn with unquenchable fire."

"To be sure, I am baptizing you with water; but the One who is stronger than I is coming, the thong of whose sandals I am not worthy to untie; he will baptize you with the Holy Spirit and fire. 17 His winnowing fork is in his hand, to clear his threshing floor, and to gather the wheat into his granary, but the chaff he will burn with unquenchable fire."

Parallels

Mark 1:7–8
7 Καὶ ἐκήρυσσεν λέγων·
ἔρχεται ὁ ἰσχυρότερός
μου ὀπίσω μου, οὗ οὐκ εἰμὶ ἱκανὸς κύψας
λῦσαι τὸν ἱμάντα τῶν ὑποδημάτων αὐτοῦ.
8 ἐγὼ ἐβάπτισα ὑμᾶς ὕδατι,
αὐτὸς δὲ βαπτίσει ὑμᾶς ἐν πνεύματι ἁγίῳ.

Mark 1:7–8
7 And he was preaching, saying, "After me is coming one who is stronger than I, the thong of whose sandals I am not worthy to stoop down and untie. 8 I have baptized you with water; but he will baptize you with the Holy Spirit."

John 1:26–27, 33b
26 ἀπεκρίθη αὐτοῖς ὁ Ἰωάννης λέγων·
ἐγὼ βαπτίζω ἐν ὕδατι·
μέσος ὑμῶν ἔστηκεν ὃν ὑμεῖς οὐκ οἴδατε,
27 ὁ ὀπίσω μου ἐρχόμενος, (⇨ Matt)
οὗ οὐκ εἰμὶ [ἐγὼ] ἄξιος ἵνα
λύσω αὐτοῦ τὸν ἱμάντα τοῦ ὑποδήματος.
33 . . . οὗτός ἐστιν ὁ βαπτίζων ἐν πνεύματι ἁγίῳ.

John 1:26–27, 33b
26 John answered them, "I am baptizing with water; among you stands one whom you do not know, 27 namely, the one coming after me, the thong of whose sandal I am not worthy to untie."
33 . . . this is the one who baptizes with the Holy Spirit.

Acts 13:24–25
24 Προκηρύξαντος Ἰωάννου πρὸ προσώπου τῆς εἰσόδου αὐτοῦ βάπτισμα μετανοίας παντὶ τῷ λαῷ Ἰσραήλ. 25 ὡς δὲ ἐπλήρου Ἰωάννης τὸν δρόμον, ἔλεγεν· τί ἐμὲ ὑπονοεῖτε εἶναι; οὐκ εἰμὶ ἐγώ· ἀλλ᾽ ἰδοὺ ἔρχεται μετ᾽ ἐμὲ οὗ οὐκ εἰμὶ ἄξιος τὸ ὑπόδημα τῶν ποδῶν λῦσαι.

Acts 13:24–25
24 Before his entrance John had preached a baptism of repentance to all the people of Israel. 25 And as John was finishing his course, he said, 'What do you suppose that I am? I am not he. No, but behold, after me one is coming, the sandals of whose feet I am not worthy to untie.'

Mark 1:8: εν πνευματι αγιω (Matt; Luke): ℵ A D K W Koine Δ Θ Π λ φ 28 33 565 700 892 1009 1010 1071 1216 1230 1242 it vg^mss; sy^p sa bo; Or [NA^26; HG] / πνευματι αγιω: B L b t z vg^mss [NA^25].

Matt 3:13–17

¹³Τότε παραγίνεται ὁ ᾽Ιησοῦς ἀπὸ τῆς Γαλιλαίας ἐπὶ τὸν ᾽Ιορδάνην πρὸς τὸν ᾽Ιωάννην τοῦ βαπτισθῆναι ὑπ᾽ αὐτοῦ. ¹⁴ ὁ δὲ ᾽Ιωάννης διεκώλυεν αὐτὸν λέγων· ἐγὼ χρείαν ἔχω ὑπὸ σοῦ βαπτισθῆναι, καὶ σὺ ἔρχῃ πρός με; ¹⁵ ἀποκριθεὶς δὲ ὁ ᾽Ιησοῦς εἶπεν πρὸς αὐτόν· ἄφες ἄρτι, οὕτως γὰρ πρέπον ἐστὶν ἡμῖν πληρῶσαι πᾶσαν δικαιοσύνην. τότε ἀφίησιν αὐτόν.

¹⁶βαπτισθεὶς δὲ ὁ ᾽Ιησοῦς εὐθὺς ἀνέβη ἀπὸ τοῦ ὕδατος· καὶ ἰδοὺ

ἠνεῴχθησαν [αὐτῷ] οἱ οὐρανοί, καὶ εἶδεν [τὸ] πνεῦμα [τοῦ] θεοῦ καταβαῖνον ὡσεὶ περιστερὰν [καὶ] ἐρχόμενον ἐπ᾽ αὐτόν· ¹⁷καὶ ἰδοὺ φωνὴ ἐκ τῶν οὐρανῶν λέγουσα· οὗτός ἐστιν ὁ υἱός μου ὁ ἀγαπητός, ἐν ᾧ εὐδόκησα.

Luke 3:21–22

²¹᾽Εγένετο δὲ ἐν τῷ βαπτισθῆναι ἅπαντα τὸν λαὸν

καὶ ᾽Ιησοῦ βαπτισθέντος καὶ προσευχομένου

ἀνεῳχθῆναι τὸν οὐρανὸν ²²καὶ καταβῆναι τὸ πνεῦμα τὸ ἅγιον σωματικῷ εἴδει ὡς περιστερὰν ἐπ᾽ αὐτόν, καὶ φωνὴν ἐξ οὐρανοῦ γενέσθαι· σὺ εἶ ὁ υἱός μου ὁ ἀγαπητός, ἐν σοὶ εὐδόκησα.

Matt 3:14: omit Ιωαννης: ℵ* B sa; Eus [NA²⁵] / txt: ℵ¹ C D L W 0233 0250 λ φ lat sy mae bo [NA²⁶; HG] // 15: ειπεν αυτω: B φ *pc* [NA²⁵] / txt: 𝔭⁶⁷ ℵ C D L W 0233 λ [NA²⁵; HG] // 16: omit αυτω (Luke): ℵ* B vg sy^s.c sa; Ir CyrJ [NA²⁵] / txt: ℵ¹ C D L W Koine 0233 λ φ lat sy^p.h mae bo [NA²⁶; HG] // omit το, του: ℵ B [NA²⁵] / txt: C D L W Koine 0233 λ φ [NA²⁶; HG] // omit και³: ℵ* B lat [NA²⁵; HG] / txt: ℵ^c C D W L Koine 0233 λ φ f l vg^cl sy [NA²⁶].

Luke 3:22 υιος μου ει συ, εγω σημερον γεγεννηκα σε (Ps 2:7): D it; Ju (Cl) Meth Hil Aug / txt: 𝔭⁴ ℵ B A W Koine Θ λ φ vg sa bo.

Mark 1:9–11

⁹Καὶ ἐγένετο ἐν ἐκείναις ταῖς ἡμέραις ἦλθεν
Ἰησοῦς ἀπὸ Ναζαρὲτ τῆς Γαλιλαίας
καὶ ἐβαπτίσθη εἰς τὸν Ἰορδάνην ὑπὸ
Ἰωάννου. ¹⁰ καὶ εὐθὺς ἀναβαίνων ἐκ τοῦ
ὕδατος εἶδεν σχιζομένους τοὺς οὐρανοὺς καὶ
τὸ πνεῦμα ὡς περιστερὰν καταβαῖνον εἰς
αὐτόν· ¹¹ καὶ φωνὴ ἐγένετο ἐκ τῶν οὐρανῶν·
σὺ εἶ ὁ υἱός μου ὁ ἀγαπητός,
ἐν σοὶ εὐδόκησα.

John 1:32–34

³²Καὶ ἐμαρτύρησεν Ἰωάννης λέγων ὅτι
τεθέαμαι τὸ πνεῦμα καταβαῖνον ὡς
περιστερὰν ἐξ οὐρανοῦ καὶ ἔμεινεν ἐπ' αὐτόν.
³³ κἀγὼ οὐκ ᾔδειν αὐτόν, ἀλλ' ὁ πέμψας με
βαπτίζειν ἐν ὕδατι ἐκεῖνός μοι εἶπεν· ἐφ' ὃν
ἂν ἴδῃς τὸ πνεῦμα καταβαῖνον καὶ μένον ἐπ'
αὐτόν, οὗτός ἐστιν ὁ βαπτίζων ἐν πνεύματι
ἁγίῳ. ³⁴ κἀγὼ ἑώρακα καὶ μεμαρτύρηκα ὅτι
οὗτός ἐστιν ὁ υἱὸς τοῦ θεοῦ.

GHeb 2

Factum est autem cum ascendisset Dominus de
aqua, descendit fons omnis Spiritus sancti, et
requievit super eum, et dixit illi: Fili mi, in omnibus
prophetis exspectabam te, ut venires, et
requiescerem in te. Tu es enim requies mea, tu es
filius meus primogenitus, qui regnas in
sempiternum.

GNaz 2

Ecce mater Domini et fratres eius dicebant ei:
Ioannes Baptista baptizat in remissionem
peccatorum: eamus et baptizemur ab eo. Dixit
autem eis: Quid peccavi, ut vadem et baptizer ab eo?
Nisi forte hoc ipsum quod dixi, ignorantia est.

Ps 2:7 LXX

⁷Κύριος εἶπεν πρός με· Υἱός μου εἶ σύ, ἐγὼ σήμερον
γεγέννηκά σε.

Isa 42:1 LXX

¹Ἰακὼβ ὁ παῖς μου, ἀντιλήμψομαι αὐτοῦ· Ἰσραὴλ ὁ
ἐκλεκτός μου, προσεδέξατο αὐτὸν ἡ ψυχή μου.

Mark 1:9–11

⁹And it happened in those days that Jesus came from
Nazareth of Galilee and was baptized in the Jordan by
John. ¹⁰And just as he rose up from the water, he saw the
heavens tear and the Spirit descending to him like a
dove; ¹¹and a voice came from the heavens, "You are my
beloved son; I am well pleased with you."

John 1:32–34

³²And John bore witness, "I saw the Spirit descending
like a dove from heaven, and it remained on him. ³³I
myself did not know him; but he who sent me to baptize
with water said to me, 'On whomever you see the Spirit
descend and remain, this is he who baptizes with the
Holy Spirit.' ³⁴And I have seen and have borne witness
that this is the Son of God."

GHeb 2

And it came to pass when the Lord came up out of the
water, the whole fount of the Holy Spirit descended upon
him and rested on him and said to him, "My Son, in all
the prophets was I waiting for thee that you should come
and I might rest in you. For you are my rest; you are my
first-begotten Son who reigns forever."

GNaz 2

Behold, the mother of the Lord and his brothers said to
him, "John the Baptist baptized for the remission of sins,
let us go and be baptized by him." But he said to them,
"Wherein have I sinned that I should go and be baptized
by him? Unless what I have said is ignorance (a sin of
ignorance)."

Ps 2:7 LXX

⁷The Lord said to me, "You are my son, today I have
begotten you."

Isa 42:1 LXX

¹Jacob my child, I will assist him; Israel my chosen, my
soul received him favorably.

[Q 3:21–22]

In Q: Crossan 1983: 342 (hesitantly); Grundmann Lk 106–107; Harnack 310–14; Hoffmann 4; Hunter 132; Jacobson 35; Luz 1983: 376; Marshall Lk 152; Polag 30–31 (conjectural); Schmithals Lk 54; Schürmann Lk 197, 218; Streeter 1924: 188; Vassiliadis 1978: 73: Q may have contained a baptismal account which differed widely from that of the canonical gospels [but see below]. Weiss 1907: 191; Zeller 23.

The principal grounds for the inclusion of 3:21–22 derive from (1) some Matthew-Luke agreements against Mark: (a) the use of a participial form of "to baptize", (b) $\dot{\alpha}\nuo\acute{\iota}\gamma\omega$ instead of $\sigma\chi\acute{\iota}\zeta\omega$, (c) the use of $\dot{\epsilon}\pi'\ \alpha\dot{\upsilon}\tau\acute{o}\nu$ in place of $\dot{\epsilon}\iota\varsigma\ \alpha\dot{\upsilon}\tau\acute{o}\nu$, and (d) the placement of $\kappa\alpha\tau\alpha\beta\alpha\acute{\iota}\nu\omega$ before $\dot{\omega}\varsigma(\dot{\epsilon}\iota)$ $\pi\epsilon\rho\iota\sigma\tau\epsilon\rho\acute{\alpha}\nu$ (Schürmann, Jacobson). (2) Some argue that the statements in Q 4:3, 9 presuppose some narrative in which Jesus' divine sonship is manifested (Schmithals, Schürmann, Marshall). (3) Harnack, Polag and Streeter hold that the Western reading of Luke 3:22 reflected a Q version of the voice from heaven.

Not in Q: Bussmann; Easton Lk xiii, xviii, 43; Edwards 1975; idem 1976; Fitzmyer Lk 479; Hawkins 1909: 109; idem, 1911; Kloppenborg 1987: 84–85; Knox 1957: 4; Lührmann; Manson; Müller 1908: 45; Schulz; Schenk; Vassiliadis 1978: 69 [but see above]; Wernle 1899: 91.

The extent of Matthew-Luke agreements is too slight to posit a Q *Vorlage* and all of the "minor agreements" are easily explained as redactional modifications of Mark (Fitzmyer, Kloppenborg). The title "Son of God" in Q 4 does not require an explanatory narrative any more than does the title "Son of Man," which is by far the more common title for Q (Kloppenborg). Finally, the Western reading of Luke 3:22 is not directly relevant to a reconstruction of Q (Vassiliadis).

Matt 3:13–17

13 Then Jesus came from Galilee to the Jordan to John, to be baptized by him. 14 But John tried to prevent him, saying, "I need to be baptized by you, and do you come to me?" 15 But Jesus answered him, "Let it be so now; for thus it is proper for us to fulfil all righteousness." Then he consented. 16 When Jesus was baptized, he went up immediately from the water, and behold, the heavens were opened and he saw the Spirit of God descending as if a dove, and alighting upon him; 17 and behold, a voice from the heavens, saying, "This is my beloved son, with whom I am well pleased."

Luke 3:21–22

21 Now when all the people were baptized,

and when Jesus also had been baptized and was praying, the heaven was opened, 22 and the Holy Spirit descended upon him in bodily form, like a dove, and a voice came from heaven, "You are my beloved son; I am well pleased with you."

Matt 4:1–11

¹Τότε ὁ Ἰησοῦς ἀνήχθη εἰς τὴν ἔρημον ὑπὸ τοῦ **πνεύματος**

πειρασθῆναι ὑπὸ τοῦ διαβόλου. ² καὶ νηστεύσας ἡμέρας τεσσεράκοντα καὶ νύκτας τεσσεράκοντα, ὕστερον ἐπείνασεν. ³καὶ προσελθὼν ὁ πειράζων εἶπεν αὐτῷ· εἰ υἱὸς εἶ τοῦ θεοῦ, εἰπὲ ἵνα οἱ λίθοι οὗτοι ἄρτοι γένωνται. ⁴ὁ δὲ ἀποκριθεὶς εἶπεν· γέγραπται· οὐκ ἐπ' ἄρτῳ μόνῳ ζήσεται ὁ ἄνθρωπος, ἀλλ' ἐπὶ παντὶ ῥήματι ἐκπορευομένῳ διὰ στόματος θεοῦ. ⁵Τότε παραλαμβάνει αὐτὸν ὁ διάβολος εἰς τὴν ἁγίαν πόλιν καὶ ἔστησεν αὐτὸν ἐπὶ τὸ πτερύγιον τοῦ ἱεροῦ ⁶καὶ λέγει αὐτῷ· εἰ υἱὸς εἶ τοῦ θεοῦ, βάλε σεαυτὸν κάτω· γέγραπται γὰρ ὅτι τοῖς ἀγγέλοις αὐτοῦ ἐντελεῖται περὶ σοῦ   καὶ ἐπὶ χειρῶν ἀροῦσίν σε, μήποτε προσκόψῃς πρὸς λίθον τὸν πόδα σου. ⁷ἔφη αὐτῷ ὁ Ἰησοῦς· πάλιν γέγραπται· οὐκ ἐκπειράσεις κύριον τὸν θεόν σου. ⁸Πάλιν παραλαμβάνει αὐτὸν ὁ διάβολος εἰς ὄρος ὑψηλὸν λίαν καὶ δείκνυσιν αὐτῷ πάσας τὰς βασιλείας τοῦ κόσμου καὶ τὴν δόξαν αὐτῶν. ⁹ καὶ εἶπεν αὐτῷ· ταῦτά σοι πάντα δώσω,

ἐὰν πεσὼν προσκυνήσῃς μοι. ¹⁰τότε λέγει αὐτῷ ὁ Ἰησοῦς· ὕπαγε, σατανᾶ· γέγραπται γάρ· κύριον τὸν θεόν σου προσκυνήσεις καὶ αὐτῷ μόνῳ λατρεύσεις. ¹¹Τότε ἀφίησιν αὐτὸν ὁ διάβολος καὶ ἰδοὺ ἄγγελοι προσῆλθον καὶ διηκόνουν αὐτῷ.

Luke 4:1–13

¹Ἰησοῦς δὲ πλήρης πνεύματος ἁγίου ὑπέστρεψεν ἀπὸ τοῦ Ἰορδάνου, καὶ ἤγετο ἐν τῷ πνεύματι ἐν τῇ ἐρήμῳ ²ἡμέρας τεσσεράκοντα πειραζόμενος ὑπὸ τοῦ διαβόλου. Καὶ οὐκ ἔφαγεν οὐδὲν ἐν ταῖς ἡμέραις ἐκείναις καὶ συντελεσθεισῶν αὐτῶν ἐπείνασεν. ³εἶπεν δὲ αὐτῷ ὁ διάβολος· εἰ υἱὸς εἶ τοῦ θεοῦ, εἰπὲ τῷ λίθῳ τούτῳ ἵνα γένηται ἄρτος. ⁴καὶ ἀπεκρίθη πρὸς αὐτὸν ὁ Ἰησοῦς· γέγραπται ὅτι οὐκ ἐπ' ἄρτῳ μόνῳ ζήσεται ὁ ἄνθρωπος.

⁹Ἤγαγεν δὲ αὐτὸν εἰς Ἰερουσαλὴμ

καὶ ἔστησεν ἐπὶ τὸ πτερύγιον τοῦ ἱεροῦ καὶ εἶπεν αὐτῷ· εἰ υἱὸς εἶ τοῦ θεοῦ, βάλε σεαυτὸν ἐντεῦθεν κάτω· ¹⁰γέγραπται γὰρ ὅτι τοῖς ἀγγέλοις αὐτοῦ ἐντελεῖται περὶ σοῦ τοῦ διαφυλάξαι σε ¹¹καὶ ὅτι ἐπὶ χειρῶν ἀροῦσίν σε, μήποτε προσκόψῃς πρὸς λίθον τὸν πόδα σου. ¹²καὶ ἀποκριθεὶς εἶπεν αὐτῷ ὁ Ἰησοῦς ὅτι εἴρηται· οὐκ ἐκπειράσεις κύριον τὸν θεόν σου. ⁵Καὶ ἀναγαγὼν αὐτὸν ἔδειξεν

αὐτῷ πάσας τὰς βασιλείας τῆς οἰκουμένης ἐν στιγμῇ χρόνου ⁶καὶ εἶπεν αὐτῷ ὁ διάβολος· σοὶ δώσω τὴν ἐξουσίαν ταύτην ἅπασαν καὶ τὴν δόξαν αὐτῶν, ὅτι ἐμοὶ παραδέδοται καὶ ᾧ ἐὰν θέλω δίδωμι αὐτήν· ⁷σὺ οὖν ἐὰν προσκυνήσῃς ἐνώπιον ἐμοῦ, ἔσται σοῦ πᾶσα. ⁸καὶ ἀποκριθεὶς ὁ Ἰησοῦς εἶπεν αὐτῷ· γέγραπται· κύριον τὸν θεόν σου προσκυνήσεις καὶ αὐτῷ μόνῳ λατρεύσεις. ¹³Καὶ συντελέσας πάντα πειρασμὸν ὁ διάβολος ἀπέστη ἀπ' αὐτοῦ ἄχρι καιροῦ.

Matt 4:2: τεσσεράκοντα νυκτας: ℵ D 892 [NA²⁵; HG] / txt: B C L W Koine 0233 φ syʰ [NA²⁶] // 3: ο πειρ. ειπ. αυτ.: *4 1-3*: C L Koine 0233 f (k) syʰ [NA²⁵; HG] / *4 1-4*: (D it) sys.c sa / txt: ℵ B W λ 33 700 aur ff¹ l vg syᵖ mae bo [NA²⁶].

Luke 4:8: κυριον τ. θ. σ. προς.: *5 1 2 3 4*: A Θ Koine 0102 a r¹ [NA²⁵; HG] / txt: ℵ B D L W Ξ Ψ λ φ 33 892 1241 1424 lat syᵖ.ʰ [NA²⁶].

18

Mark 1:12–13

¹²Καὶ εὐθὺς τὸ **πνεῦμα** αὐτὸν ἐκβάλλει εἰς τὴν ἔρημον. ¹³καὶ ἦν ἐν τῇ ἐρήμῳ **τεσσεράκοντα ἡμέρας πειραζόμενος ὑπὸ τοῦ** σατανᾶ, καὶ ἦν μετὰ τῶν θηρίων . . . (continued below)

Mark 1:12–13

¹²And the Spirit immediately drove him out into the wilderness. ¹³And he was in the wilderness forty days, tempted by Satan; and he was with the wild animals . . .

GHeb 3

Ἐὰν δὲ προσιῆταί τις τὸ καθ᾽ Ἑβραίους εὐαγγέλιον, ἔνθα αὐτὸς ὁ σωτήρ φησιν· Ἄρτι ἔλαβέ με ἡ μήτηρ μου, τὸ ἅγιον πνεῦμα, ἐν μιᾷ τῶν τριχῶν μου καὶ ἀπήνεγκέ με εἰς τὸ ὄρος τὸ μέγα Θαβώρ.

GHeb 3

And if any accept the Gospel of the Hebrews—here the Saviour says, "Even so did my mother, the Holy Spirit, take me by one of my hairs and carry me away on to the great mountain Tabor."

Deut 8:3b LXX

³. . . οὐκ ἐπ᾽ ἄρτῳ μόνῳ ζήσεται ὁ ἄνθρωπος, ἀλλ᾽ ἐπὶ παντὶ ῥήματι τῷ ἐκπορευομένῳ διὰ στόματος θεοῦ ζήσεται ὁ ἄνθρωπος.

Deut 8:3b LXX

³. . . No one can live by bread alone; but they shall live by every word that comes forth from the mouth of God.

Ps 90:11–12 LXX

¹¹ὅτι τοῖς ἀγγέλοις αὐτοῦ ἐντελεῖται περὶ σοῦ τοῦ διαφυλάξαι σε ἐν πάσαις ταῖς ὁδοῖς σου· ¹²ἐπὶ χειρῶν ἀροῦσίν σε, μήποτε προσκόψῃς πρὸς λίθον τὸν πόδα σου.

Ps 90:11–12 LXX

¹¹For to his angels he will give orders concerning you to guard you in all your ways; ¹²they will lift you on their hands list you strike your foot against a stone.

Deut 6:16 LXX

¹⁶οὐκ ἐκπειράσεις κύριον τὸν θεόν σου.

Deut 6:16 LXX

¹⁶You shall not test the Lord your (MT: your [pl.]) God.

Deut 6:13/10:20 LXX

¹³κύριον τὸν θεόν σου φοβηθήσῃ καὶ αὐτῷ λατρεύσεις.

Deut 6:13/10:20 LXX

¹³You shall fear the Lord your God and him shall you serve.

Deut 5:9 LXX

⁹οὐ προσκυνήσεις αὐτοῖς οὐδὲ μὴ λατρεύσῃς αὐτοῖς, ὅτι ἐγώ εἰμι κύριος ὁ θεός σου.

Deut 5:9 LXX

⁹You shall not worship them nor shall you serve them, for I am the Lord your God.

Mark 1:13b

¹³. . . καὶ οἱ ἄγγελοι διηκόνουν αὐτῷ.

Mark 1:13b

¹³. . . and the angels were serving him.

Q 4:1–13

In Q: Most authors. The extent of Matthew-Luke agreement is strongly suggestive of a Q *Vorlage* and Q elsewhere uses the LXX. Testing and ordeal narratives are found in other wisdom collections (Kloppenborg 1987: 322–24).

Not in Q: Argyle 1952–53: 382: The use of the LXX is inconsistent with an Aramaic *Vorlage*. Lührmann 56: The account falls outside the scope of the contents of Q.

Q 4:9–12, 5–8

The majority opinion is that *Matthean order* best reflects Q and that Luke has inverted the order of the second and third temptations. A variety of explanations are given: (1) Matthew's order, which juxtaposes the two similarly structured desert and temple incidents, is more original than Luke who is conditioned by a topographical schema (Weiss; Dibelius). (2) Matthew's order is more logical, moving to a climax in the offer of sovereignty (Dibelius; Schulz). (3) The Lukan rearrangement makes the sequence the reverse of the first three petitions of the Lukan Lord's Prayer (Rengstorf Lk 63). (4) Luke reversed the order in the interests of his topographical schema (Dibelius; Schulz; Fitzmyer). (5) Luke transposed the two to eliminate an awkward change in scene (Marshall), or (6) to put the last two Deuteronomy quotations in canonical order (Marshall).

See Dibelius 1935: 275; Easton Lk 48–49; Fitzmyer Lk 507; Harnack 44; Marshall Lk 166; Polag 30–32; Schenk 21; Schulz 177; Weiss 1907: 102; Vassiliadis 1982: 383; Zeller 21.

A few hold in favor of *Lukan order*: Bussmann (38–40) thinks that under the influence of Mark 1:13b, Matthew transposed the two temptations in order to contrast Jesus' refusal to worship with the angels serving Jesus. Manson 42–43: Matthew's order is superior to Luke's and therefore a Lukan transposition would be unlikely. Schmid 210–11: A Lukan transposition is not consistent with his editorial procedures observed elsewhere. See also Grundmann Mt 100; Schürmann Lk 218.

Undecided: Plummer Lk 110.

Matt 4:1–11

[1] Then Jesus was led up into the wilderness by the Spirit to be tempted by the devil. [2] And since he had fasted forty days and forty nights, afterward he was hungry. [3] And the tempter came and said to him, "If you are the Son of God, tell these stones to become loaves of bread." [4] But he answered, "It is written,

'No one can live by bread alone,
   but by every word that proceeds from the mouth
      of God.'"

[5] Then the devil took him to the holy city, and set him on the pinnacle of the temple, [6] and said to him, "If you are the Son of God, throw yourself down; for it is written,

'He will give his angels charge of you,'

and

'On their hands they will bear you up,
   lest you strike your foot against a stone.'"

[7] Jesus said to him, "Again it is written, 'You shall not tempt the Lord your God.'"

[8] Again, the devil took him to a very high mountain, and showed him all the kingdoms of the world and the glory of them; [9] and he said to him, "All these I will give you, if you will fall down and worship me."

[10] Then Jesus said to him, "Depart, Satan! for it is written,

'You shall worship the Lord your God
   and him alone shall you serve.'"

[11] Then the devil left him, and behold, angels came and were serving him.

Luke 4:1–13

[1] Jesus, full of the Holy Spirit, returned from the Jordan, and was led by the Spirit [2] for forty days in the wilderness, tempted by the devil. And he ate nothing in those days; and when they were completed, he was hungry. [3] The devil said to him, "If you are the Son of God, tell this stone to become a loaf of bread." [4] And Jesus answered him, "It is written, 'No one can live by bread alone.'"

[9] And he led him to Jerusalem, and set him on the pinnacle of the temple, and said to him, "If you are the Son of God, throw yourself down from here; [10] for it is written,

'He will give his angels charge of you, to guard
      you,'

[11] and

'On their hands they will bear you up,
   lest you strike your foot against a stone.'"

[12] And Jesus answered him, "It is said, 'You shall not tempt the Lord your God.'"

[5] And the devil took him up, and showed him all the kingdoms of the earth in a moment of time, [6] and said to him, "To you I will give all this authority and their glory; for it has been delivered to me, and I give it to whom I wish. [7] If you, therefore, will worship me, it shall all be yours." [8] And Jesus answered him, "It is written,

'You shall worship the Lord your God,
   and him alone shall you serve.'"

[13] And having completed every temptation, the devil departed from him until an opportune time.

Matt 5:1–2

¹Ἰδὼν δὲ τοὺς ὄχλους ἀνέβη εἰς τὸ ὄρος, καὶ καθίσαντος αὐτοῦ προσῆλθαν αὐτῷ οἱ μαθηταὶ αὐτοῦ·

²καὶ ἀνοίξας τὸ στόμα αὐτοῦ ἐδίδασκεν αὐτοὺς λέγων·

Luke 6:12, 17, 20a

¹²Ἐγένετο δὲ ἐν ταῖς ἡμέραις ταύταις ἐξελθεῖν αὐτὸν εἰς τὸ ὄρος προσεύξασθαι, καὶ ἦν διανυκτερεύων ἐν τῇ προσευχῇ τοῦ θεοῦ.

[Luke 6:13–16 = The Choosing of the Twelve]

¹⁷καὶ καταβὰς μετ' αὐτῶν ἔστη ἐπὶ τόπου πεδινοῦ, καὶ ὄχλος πολὺς μαθητῶν αὐτοῦ, καὶ πλῆθος πολὺ τοῦ λαοῦ . . .
²⁰ᵃ καὶ αὐτὸς ἐπάρας τοὺς ὀφθαλμοὺς αὐτοῦ εἰς τοὺς μαθητὰς αὐτοῦ ἔλεγεν·

Notes

⟨Q 6:20a⟩

Some form of transitional phrase is required between Q 4:13 and 6:20b. However, the redactional activities of Matthew and Luke have apparently obscured Q at this point and thus any reconstruction is extremely speculative.

Bussmann (55) observes that some form of introduction is suggested by the basic agreements of Matthew and Luke in directing the speech to the disciples. He argues that Luke's "lifting his eyes" is more likely to reflect Q than is Matthew's "opening his mouth." Easton (Lk 81) argues that the introduction resembled Mark 3:7 and speculates that it may have included the selection of the Twelve. Fitzmyer Lk 632: "Mention of [the disciples] was undoubtedly included in the introduction to the sermon in Q." Harnack (128)

reconstructs: . . . ὄχλοι . . . ἐδίδαξεν τοὺς μαθητὰς λέγων, ". . . crowds . . . he was teaching the disciples saying." Hunter (132), Kilpatrick (1946: 15) and Schenk (24) suggest an introduction resembling Luke 6:20. Polag (32), who designates Q 6:20a as "certainly or very probably in Q," follows Matt 5:1–2 in his reconstruction: (καὶ ὁ Ἰησοῦς) ἀνέβη εἰς τὸ ὄρος. καὶ ἰδὼν τοὺς ὄχλους καὶ τοὺς μαθητὰς αὐτοῦ ἔλεγεν· Weiss (1907: 256) argues that Luke had another version of the sermon from L and that Matthew's version (including his introduction) represents Q. Zeller (26) argues that the sermon was originally directed at disciples but both Matthew and Luke have broadened the audience with a reference to "the crowds."

See further Hawkins 1909: 108 (hesitantly); Marshall Lk 241; Müller 1908: 46; Schmithals Lk 78; Schürmann Lk 323.

Matt 5:1–2

[1] When he saw the crowds, he went up the mountain, and when he sat down his disciples came to him.

[2] And he opened his mouth and taught them, saying:

Luke 6:12, 17, 20a

[12] In these days he went out to the mountain to pray; and he spent all night in prayer to God.

[17] And when he came down with them, he stood on a level place with a great crowd of his disciples and a great multitude of people . . .

[20] And he raised his eyes to his disciples, and said:

Parallels

Mark 3:13, 7

[13] καὶ ἀναβαίνει εἰς τὸ ὄρος, καὶ προσκαλεῖται οὓς ἤθελεν αὐτός, καὶ ἀπῆλθον πρὸς αὐτόν.

[Mark 3:14–19 = The Choosing of the Twelve]

[7] Καὶ ὁ ᾽Ιησοῦς μετὰ τῶν μαθητῶν αὐτοῦ ἀνεχώρησεν πρὸς τὴν θάλασσαν, καὶ πολὺ πλῆθος ἀπὸ τῆς Γαλιλαίας [ἠκολούθησεν] . . .

Mark 3:13, 7

[13] And he went up the mountain, and called those whom he desired; and they came to him.

[7] And Jesus withdrew with his disciples to the sea, and a great multitude from Galilee followed . . .

Mark 3:7: ηκολουθησαν (Matt 4:25): ℵ C K* 0133 0135 1241 1424 l r² syʰ sa boᵖᵗ / omit (Luke): D W 28 124 788 v l r¹ sys boᵖᵗ / txt: A B L 565 579 700 892 λ vg [NA²⁶; HG].

Matt 5:3, 6, 4–5, 7–12

³μακάριοι οἱ πτωχοὶ τῷ πνεύματι
ὅτι αὐτῶν ἐστιν ἡ βασιλεία τῶν οὐρανῶν.
⁶μακάριοι οἱ πεινῶντες καὶ
διψῶντες τὴν δικαιοσύνην,
ὅτι αὐτοὶ χορτασθήσονται.
⁴μακάριοι οἱ πενθοῦντες,
ὅτι αὐτοὶ παρακληθήσονται.

[⁵μακάριοι οἱ πραεῖς ὅτι αὐτοὶ κληρονομήσουσιν τὴν
γῆν. ⁷μακάριοι οἱ ἐλεήμονες, ὅτι αὐτοὶ ἐλεηθήσονται.
⁸μακάριοι οἱ καθαροὶ τῇ καρδίᾳ, ὅτι αὐτοὶ τὸν θεὸν
ὄψονται. ⁹μακάριοι οἱ εἰρηνοποιοί, ὅτι αὐτοὶ υἱοὶ θεοῦ
κληθήσονται. ¹⁰μακάριοι οἱ δεδιωγμένοι ἕνεκεν
δικαιοσύνης, ὅτι αὐτῶν ἐστιν ἡ βασιλεία τῶν οὐρανῶν].
¹¹μακάριοί ἐστε ὅταν

ὀνειδίσωσιν ὑμᾶς καὶ διώξωσιν καὶ εἴπωσιν
πᾶν πονηρὸν καθ᾽ ὑμῶν [ψευδόμενοι]
ἕνεκεν ἐμοῦ.
¹²χαίρετε καὶ ἀγαλλιᾶσθε, ὅτι
ὁ μισθὸς ὑμῶν πολὺς ἐν τοῖς οὐρανοῖς·
οὕτως γὰρ ἐδίωξαν τοὺς προφήτας τοὺς πρὸ ὑμῶν.

Luke 6:20b–23

²⁰ᵝ μακάριοι οἱ πτωχοί,
ὅτι ὑμετέρα ἐστὶν ἡ βασιλεία τοῦ θεοῦ.
²¹μακάριοι οἱ πεινῶντες νῦν,

ὅτι   χορτασθήσεσθε.
μακάριοι οἱ κλαίοντες νῦν,
ὅτι γελάσετε.

²²μακάριοί ἐστε ὅταν μισήσωσιν ὑμᾶς οἱ
ἄνθρωποι, καὶ ὅταν ἀφορίσωσιν ὑμᾶς καὶ
ὀνειδίσωσιν καὶ ἐκβάλωσιν τὸ ὄνομα ὑμῶν
ὡς πονηρὸν
ἕνεκα τοῦ υἱοῦ τοῦ ἀνθρώπου·
²³χάρητε ἐν ἐκείνῃ τῇ ἡμέρᾳ καὶ σκιρτήσατε,
ἰδοὺ γὰρ ὁ μισθὸς ὑμῶν πολὺς ἐν τῷ οὐρανῷ·
κατὰ τὰ αὐτὰ γὰρ ἐποίουν τοῖς προφήταις
οἱ πατέρες αὐτῶν.

Luke 6:24–26

(²⁴Πλὴν οὐαὶ ὑμῖν τοῖς πλουσίοις, ὅτι ἀπέχετε τὴν
παράκλησιν ὑμῶν. ²⁵οὐαὶ ὑμῖν, οἱ ἐμπεπλησμένοι νῦν,
ὅτι πεινάσετε. οὐαί, οἱ γελῶντες νῦν, ὅτι πενθήσετε καὶ
κλαύσετε. ²⁶οὐαὶ ὅταν ὑμᾶς καλῶς εἴπωσιν πάντες οἱ
ἄνθρωποι· κατὰ τὰ αὐτὰ γὰρ ἐποίουν τοῖς
ψευδοπροφήταις οἱ πατέρες αὐτῶν).

διώκω ⇨ Matt 5:44 [S9]

μισέω ⇨ Luke 6:27 [S9]

Matt 5:4-5: *5-4:* D Δ 28 33 543 544 565 700 *pc* vg syᶜ
boᵖᵗ; Cl / txt: ℵ B K W Koine Θ λ φ b f q sʸˢ·ᵖ sa boᵖᵗ // 11:
omit ψευδομενοι: D it sʸˢ; Tert [HG] / txt: *rell* [NA²⁵·²⁶].

Luke 6:26: καλως υμας ειπωσιν: (D) Q R W Koine Θ 0135
λ φ [NA²⁵; HG] / καλως ειπωσιν υμας: ℵ A L Ψ 33 892 *al* it
/ txt: 𝔭⁷⁵ B e q vg [NA²⁶].

GThom 54

ⲡⲉϫⲉ ⲓ̅ⲥ̅ ϫⲉ ϩⲛ̅ⲙⲁⲕⲁⲣⲓⲟⲥ ⲛⲉ ⲛϩⲏⲕⲉ ϫⲉ ⲧⲱⲧⲛ̅ ⲧⲉ ⲧⲙⲛ̅ⲧⲉⲣⲟ ⲛⲙ̅ⲡⲏⲩⲉ.

GThom 69b

ϩⲙ̅ⲙⲁⲕⲁⲣⲓⲟⲥ ⲛⲉⲧϩⲕⲁⲉⲓⲧ ϣⲓⲛⲁ ⲉⲩⲛⲁⲧⲥⲓⲟ ⲛ̅ⲑⲏ ⲙ̅ⲡⲉⲧⲟⲩⲱϣ.

Isaiah 61:1–2 LXX

¹ Πνεῦμα κυρίου ἐπ᾽ ἐμέ, οὗ εἵνεκεν ἔχρισέν με· εὐαγγελίσασθαι πτωχοῖς ἀπέσταλκέν με, ἰάσασθαι τοὺς συντετριμμένους τῇ καρδίᾳ, κηρύξαι αἰχμαλώτοις ἄφεσιν καὶ τυφλοῖς ἀνάβλεψιν, ² καλέσαι ἐνιαυτὸν κυρίου δεκτὸν καὶ ἡμέραν ἀνταποδόσεως, παρακαλέσαι πάντας τοὺς πενθοῦντας.

1 Pet 3:14

¹⁴ εἰ καὶ πάσχοιτε διὰ δικαιοσύνην, μακάριοι.

1 Pet 4:13–14

¹³ ἀλλὰ καθὸ κοινωνεῖτε τοῖς τοῦ Χριστοῦ παθήμασιν χαίρετε, ἵνα καὶ ἐν τῇ ἀποκαλύψει τῆς δόξης αὐτοῦ χαρῆτε ἀγαλλιώμενοι. ¹⁴ εἰ ὀνειδίζεσθε ἐν ὀνόματι Χριστοῦ, μακάριοι, ὅτι τὸ τῆς δόξης καὶ τὸ τοῦ θεοῦ πνεῦμα ἐφ᾽ ὑμᾶς ἀναπαύεται.

Polycarp, *Phil.* **2:3**

³ μακάριοι οἱ πτωχοὶ καὶ οἱ διωκόμενοι ἕνεκεν δικαιοσύνης, ὅτι αὐτῶν ἐστιν ἡ βασιλεία τοῦ θεοῦ.

Clement Alex., *Strom.* **4.6.41.2**

μακάριοι, φησίν, οἱ δεδιωγμένοι ἕνεκεν δικαιοσύνης, ὅτι αὐτοὶ υἱοὶ θεοῦ κληθήσονται, ἢ ὥς τινες τῶν μετατιθέντων τὰ εὐαγγέλια· μακάριοι, φησίν, οἱ δεδιωγμένοι ὑπὲρ τῆς δικαιοσύνης, ὅτι αὐτοὶ ἔσονται τέλειοι καὶ μακάριοι οἱ δεδιωγμένοι ἕνεκα ἐμοῦ, ὅτι ἕξουσι τόπον ὅπου οὐ διωχθήσονται.

GThom 68

ⲡⲉϫⲉ ⲓ̅ⲥ̅ ϫⲉ ⲛ̅ⲧⲱⲧⲛ̅ ϩⲙ̅ⲙⲁⲕⲁⲣⲓⲟⲥ ϩⲟⲧⲁ(ⲛ) ⲉⲩϣⲁⲛⲙⲉⲥⲧⲉ ⲑⲏⲩⲧⲛ̅ ⲛ̅ⲥⲉⲣⲇⲓⲱⲕⲉ ⲙ̅ⲙⲱⲧⲛ̅ ⲁⲩⲱ ⲥⲉⲛⲁϩⲉ ⲁⲛ ⲉⲧⲟⲡⲟⲥ ϩⲙ̅ ⲡⲙⲁ ⲉⲛⲧⲁⲩⲇⲓⲱⲕⲉ ⲙ̅ⲙⲱⲧⲛ̅ ϩⲣⲁⲓ̈ ⲛ̅ϩⲏⲧϥ.

GThom 69a

ⲡⲉϫⲉ ⲓ̅ⲥ̅ ϩⲙ̅ⲙⲁⲕⲁⲣⲓⲟⲥ ⲛⲉ ⲛⲁⲉⲓ ⲛ̅ⲧⲁⲩⲇⲓⲱⲕⲉ ⲙ̅ⲙⲟⲟⲩ ϩⲣⲁⲓ̈ ϩⲙ̅ ⲡⲟⲩϩⲏⲧ ⲛⲉⲧⲙ̅ⲙⲁⲩ ⲛⲉⲛⲧⲁϩⲥⲟⲩⲱⲛ ⲡⲉⲓⲱⲧ ϩⲛ̅ ⲟⲩⲙⲉ.

GThom 54

Jesus said, "Blessed are the poor, for yours is the kingdom of heaven."

GThom 69b

Blessed are the hungry, that the stomach of the one in want may be filled.

Isaiah 61:1–2 LXX

¹ The Spirit of the Lord is upon me, because he has anointed me. He has sent me to preach good news to the poor, to heal those whose hearts are broken, to proclaim release to captives and sight to the blind, ² to proclaim the acceptable year of the Lord and the day of recompense, to comfort all those that mourn.

1 Pet 3:14

¹⁴ But even if you do suffer for righteousness' sake, you are blessed.

1 Pet 4:13–14

¹³ But rejoice in so far as you share Christ's sufferings, that you may also rejoice and be glad at the revelation of his glory. ¹⁴ If you are reproached for the name of Christ, you are blessed, because the spirit of glory and of God rests upon you.

Polycarp, *Phil.* **2:3**

³ Blessed are the poor, and they who are persecuted for righteousness' sake, for theirs is the Kingdom of God.

Clement Alex., *Strom.* **4.6.41.2**

"Blessed are those who are persecuted on account of righteousness, for they will be called the children of God," or, as those who transpose the gospels say, "Blessed are those who are persecuted because of righteousness, for they will be perfect" and "Blessed are those who are persecuted on my account, for they will have a place where they will not be persecuted."

GThom 68

Jesus said, "Blessed are you when you are hated and persecuted, and no place will be found, wherever you have been persecuted."

GThom 69a

Jesus said, "Blessed are those who have been persecuted in their hearts: they are the ones who have truly come to know the Father."

Q 6:20b–21

In Q: Most authors. Easton (Lk 83), however, holds that Luke 6:20b–23 is from L. Hawkins (1911: 116) ascribes these verse to Q but only "with considerable probability." Weiss (1907: 256–57) argues that Luke 6:20–38, 46–49 derives from L but holds that Matthew used Q.

The order is the first three Q beatitudes is in dispute. The originality of the Lukan order is supported by Crossan 1983: 342; Hunter 132; Lambrecht 1985: 48; Polag 32; Schenk 24; Schulz 76; Schürmann Lk 330 n. 30; Worden 547; Zeller 27. According to Schürmann, Matthew reversed the second and third beatitudes in order to enhance the parallels between Matt 5:3–4 and Isa 61:1–2. Schulz argues that while Luke offered his beatitudes without interpolations, Matthew expanded and schematized his list, dividing the beatitudes into those concerning human needs (5:3, 4) and those concerning Christian virtues (5:5–10). On the other hand, Dupont (1969: 271–72, 298) holds that Luke redactionally associated poverty with hunger just as he associated riches with satiety in 6:24–25a and thus concludes that the Matthean order is original. The same conclusion is drawn by Harnack 50, 128 and Michaelis 1968: 157.

[Matt 5:5, 7–10]

Apart from Michaelis (1968: 148–61), who holds that Q began with four beatitudes displaying π-alliteration and that Luke omitted Q/Matt 5:5, the consensus is that the additional beatitudes, including 5:5, did not belong to Q. A few earlier critics excluded 5:5 even from Matthew on textual grounds, arguing that the textual disruption with respect to the order of verses 4–5 (see the textual notes) indicates a later addition. See Bultmann 1963: 110; Harnack 48 n. 1; Klostermann Mt 37; Wellhausen Mt 14–15.

There is near universal agreement that Matt 5:10 is due to Matthew himself. This verse, created from 5:3 and 5:11–12, serves as a transition between the two main groups of Matthean beatitudes, 5:3–10 and 5:11–12. See Bultmann 1963: 110; Dupont 1969: 223–27; Guelich 1976b: 431; Lambrecht 1985: 61–62; Luz Mt 200; Sato 1984: 55; Strecker 1971b: 260; Tuckett 1983: 201–202; Walter 1968: 247.

For the remainder, opinion is divided. The additional beatitudes may be due entirely to Matthean redaction. Thus Dupont 1969: 256–64; Frankemölle 1971: 54–58; Kilpatrick 1946: 16–17; Lambrecht 1985: 60–62; Tuckett 1983: 202; Walter 1968: 247–49. Alternatively, they may derive from Matthean special source material (Manson 47), or more likely, from a pre-Matthean expansion of Q,

Q^{Mt}, a position favored by Guelich 1976b: 423–24; Luz Mt 200; idem, 1983: 474; Sato 1984: 55; Strecker 1971b: 259–264. Guelich (1976b: 423) argues that vv. 5–7 are closely related to sayings occurring later in the Q sermon (Q 6:36, 45) but which Matthew either relocated outside the chaps. 5–7 (Q 6:45 = Matt 12:35) or reworded (Q 6:26). Hence these verses are neither editorial nor from M but represent an expansion of Q. Strecker argues that none of the vocabulary is distinctively Matthean.

(Q 6:24–26)

In Q. The striking parallelism between the beatitudes and the Lukan woes exludes the possibility that the woes ever circulated independently of the blessings. Bussmann 44; Crossan 1983: 169–70 ("very tentatively"). Frankemölle (1971: 64) argues (1) that Matthew omitted the woes because they did not fit his redactional purposes in the Sermon on the Mount, (2) Matthew betrays knowledge of vocabulary in the woes (see Schürmann) and (3) that Matthew compensated for the omission by including a woe-sermon in Matt 23. Hawkins 1911: 134: Matthew omitted the verses as inappropriate for catechetical purposes. Hunter 133; Kilpatrick 1946: 15 (hesitantly); Knox 1957: 12; Manson 49 (hesitantly); Marshall Lk 247; Polag 84 (uncertain); Schmithals Lk 81; Schürmann Lk 339: $\pi\epsilon\nu\theta\epsilon\omega$ and $\pi\alpha\rho\alpha\kappa\alpha\lambda\epsilon\omega$ in Matthew's beatitudes are reminiscences of the woes. Matthew was more interested in positive demands on disciples and hence omitted woes. Streeter 1924: 252: Matthew omitted the woes, regarding riches and poverty as ethically neutral. Tuckett 1983: 199.

A smaller group of critics ascribe the woes to Q^{Lk}: Grundmann Lk 144; Lührmann 105; Luz 1983: 475. Müller (1908: 19, 46) seems to think that the woes are pre-Lukan and while not original in Q, were community constructions which eventually influenced Q. Steck (1967: 21–22) argues that Matthew had no reason to omit the woes, but neither are they Lukan. Also Walter 1968: 249–50; Zeller 26.

Not in Q: Easton Lk 83 ascribes the the whole of Luke 6:20–26 to L. On the other hand, Dupont (1969: 299–342) holds that there is no positive indication that Matthew omitted the woes and no indication that the woes functioned in a context different than the present Lukan context. Dupont, Fitzmyer (Lk 627, 636–37) and Lambrecht (1985: 51–52) all adduce Lukan vocabulary and ascribe the verses to redaction. Several authors do not mention the woes at all: Edwards 1976; Harnack; Hoffmann; Meyer; Schenk; Schulz; Vassiliadis. Edwards (1975: 98–99) lists Luke 6:20–26 but concords no vocabulary (including $\pi\epsilon\nu\theta\epsilon\omega$) from 6:24–26.

Matt 5:3, 6, 4–5, 7–12

³ Blessed are the poor in spirit, for theirs is the reign of heaven.

⁶ Blessed are those who hunger and thirst for righteousness, for they shall be filled.

⁴ Blessed are those who mourn, for they shall be comforted.

[⁵ Blessed are the meek, for they shall inherit the earth. ⁷ Blessed are the merciful, for mercy will be shown them. ⁸ Blessed are the pure in heart, for they shall see God. ⁹ Blessed are the peacemakers, for they shall be called sons of God. ¹⁰ Blessed are those who are persecuted for righteousness' sake, for theirs is the reign of heaven.]

¹¹ Blessed are you when they reproach you and persecute you and say every evil against you falsely on my account.

¹² Rejoice and be glad, for your reward is great in heaven, for so they persecuted the prophets who came before you.

Luke 6:20–23

²⁰ . . . Blessed are you poor, for yours is the reign of God.

²¹ Blessed are you that hunger now, for you shall be filled.

Blessed are you that weep now, for you shall laugh.

²² Blessed are you when people hate you, and when they exclude you and reproach you, and cast out your name as evil, on account of the Son of man! ²³ Rejoice in that day, and leap for joy, for behold, your reward is great in heaven; for so their fathers did to the prophets.

Luke 6:24–26

(²⁴ But woe to you rich, for you have received your consolation. ²⁵ Woe to you who are full now, for you shall go hungry. Woe to you who laugh now, for you shall mourn and weep. ²⁶ Woe to you, when all people speak well of you, for so their fathers did to the false prophets.)

Matt 5:43–44, 38–42; 7:12; 5:46–47, 45

[⁴³Ἠκούσατε ὅτι ἐρρέθη· ἀγαπήσεις τὸν πλησίον σου καὶ μισήσεις τὸν ἐχθρόν σου.]
⁴⁴ἐγὼ δὲ λέγω ὑμῖν·   ἀγαπᾶτε
τοὺς ἐχθροὺς ὑμῶν καὶ

προσεύχεσθε ὑπὲρ τῶν διωκόντων ὑμᾶς.
[³⁸Ἠκούσατε ὅτι ἐρρέθη· ὀφθαλμὸν ἀντὶ ὀφθαλμοῦ καὶ ὀδόντα ἀντὶ ὀδόντος. ³⁹ἐγὼ δὲ λέγω ὑμῖν μὴ ἀντιστῆναι τῷ πονηρῷ· ἀλλ’]
ὅστις σε ῥαπίζει εἰς τὴν δεξιὰν σιαγόνα
[σου], στρέψον αὐτῷ καὶ τὴν ἄλλην· ⁴⁰καὶ
τῷ θέλοντί σοι κριθῆναι καὶ τὸν χιτῶνά σου
λαβεῖν, ἄφες αὐτῷ καὶ τὸ ἱμάτιον·
(⁴¹καὶ ὅστις σε ἀγγαρεύσει μίλιον ἕν, ὕπαγε μετ’ αὐτοῦ
δύο).
⁴²τῷ αἰτοῦντί σε δός, καὶ τὸν θέλοντα ἀπὸ σοῦ
δανίσασθαι μὴ ἀποστραφῇς.

¹²Πάντα οὖν ὅσα ἐὰν θέλητε ἵνα ποιῶσιν
ὑμῖν οἱ ἄνθρωποι, οὕτως καὶ ὑμεῖς ποιεῖτε αὐτοῖς·
οὗτος γάρ ἐστιν ὁ νόμος καὶ οἱ προφῆται.

⁴⁶ἐὰν γὰρ ἀγαπήσητε τοὺς ἀγαπῶντας ὑμᾶς,
τίνα μισθὸν ἔχετε; οὐχὶ καὶ οἱ τελῶναι τὸ
αὐτὸ ποιοῦσιν;
⁴⁷καὶ   ἐὰν ἀσπάσησθε τοὺς ἀδελφοὺς ὑμῶν
μόνον, τί περισσὸν ποιεῖτε; οὐχὶ
καὶ οἱ ἐθνικοὶ τὸ αὐτὸ ποιοῦσιν;

⇨ Matt 5:42

⇨ Matt 5:44a

⁴⁵ὅπως γένησθε υἱοὶ τοῦ πατρὸς ὑμῶν τοῦ ἐν οὐρανοῖς,
ὅτι τὸν ἥλιον αὐτοῦ ἀνατέλλει ἐπὶ
πονηροὺς καὶ ἀγαθοὺς καὶ βρέχει ἐπὶ δικαίους καὶ
ἀδίκους.

Luke 6:27–35

²⁷Ἀλλὰ ὑμῖν λέγω τοῖς ἀκούουσιν· ἀγαπᾶτε
τοὺς ἐχθροὺς ὑμῶν, καλῶς ποιεῖτε τοῖς μισοῦσιν ὑμᾶς,
²⁸εὐλογεῖτε τοὺς καταρωμένους ὑμᾶς,
προσεύχεσθε περὶ τῶν ἐπηρεαζόντων ὑμᾶς.

²⁹τῷ τύπτοντί σε ἐπὶ τὴν   σιαγόνα
πάρεχε   καὶ τὴν ἄλλην, καὶ ἀπὸ τοῦ
αἴροντός σου τὸ ἱμάτιον καὶ τὸν χιτῶνα μὴ κωλύσῃς.

³⁰παντὶ αἰτοῦντί σε δίδου, καὶ ἀπὸ τοῦ
αἴροντος τὰ σὰ μὴ ἀπαίτει.

³¹ Καὶ καθὼς θέλετε ἵνα ποιῶσιν
ὑμῖν οἱ ἄνθρωποι, ποιεῖτε αὐτοῖς ὁμοίως.

³²καὶ   εἰ ἀγαπᾶτε τοὺς ἀγαπῶντας ὑμᾶς,
ποία ὑμῖν χάρις ἐστίν; καὶ γὰρ οἱ ἁμαρτωλοὶ τοὺς
ἀγαπῶντας αὐτοὺς ἀγαπῶσιν;
³³καὶ [γὰρ] ἐὰν ἀγαθοποιῆτε τοὺς
ἀγαθοποιοῦντας ὑμᾶς, ποία ὑμῖν χάρις ἐστίν;
καὶ οἱ ἁμαρτωλοὶ τὸ αὐτὸ ποιοῦσιν.

(³⁴καὶ ἐὰν δανίσητε παρ’ ὧν ἐλπίζετε λαβεῖν, ποία ὑμῖν
χάρις [ἐστίν]; καὶ ἁμαρτωλοὶ ἁμαρτωλοῖς δανίζουσιν ἵνα
ἀπολάβωσιν τὰ ἴσα).
(³⁵πλὴν ἀγαπᾶτε τοὺς ἐχθροὺς ὑμῶν καὶ ἀγαθοποιεῖτε
καὶ δανίζετε μηδὲν ἀπελπίζοντες· καὶ ἔσται ὁ μισθὸς
ὑμῶν πολύς,)
καὶ ἔσεσθε υἱοὶ ὑψίστου,

    ὅτι αὐτὸς χρηστός ἐστιν ἐπὶ τοὺς
ἀχαρίστους καὶ πονηρούς.

Matt 5:39: ραπισει: D L Koine Θ λ φ ; Eus [HG] / τω
ραπιζοντι σε: Epiph / txt: ℵ B W 33 700 1424 [NA²⁵·²⁶] //
δεξ. σιαγ. σου: 1 3 2: K L Δ Θ φ 28 565 700 1424 syᵖ·ʰ?
[HG] / 1 2: ℵ W λ 33 892 1010 1241 a f (h); Ad Cyr Epiph
Or / 2 3: D k sysˢ·ᶜ / txt: B D syᵖ·ʰ?; Eus [NA²⁵·²⁶] // 47: το
αυτο· ℵ B D Z λ φ [NA²⁵·²⁶] / ουτως· K L W Δ Θ Koine 565
1010 h syᶜ·ʰ bo [HG].

Luke 6:33: omit γαρ (Matt): ℵ² A D L W Koine Θ Ξ Ψ
0135 φ latt sy co [HG] / txt: 𝔭⁷⁵ ℵ* B 700 [NA²⁵·²⁶].

Did 1:3–5

³Τούτων δὲ τῶν λόγων ἡ διδαχή ἐστιν αὕτη· εὐλογεῖτε τοὺς καταρωμένους ὑμῖν καὶ προσεύχεσθε ὑπὲρ τῶν ἐχθρῶν ὑμῶν, νηστεύετε δὲ ὑπὲρ τῶν διωκόντων ὑμᾶς· ποία γὰρ χάρις, ἐὰν ἀγαπᾶτε τοὺς ἀγαπῶντας ὑμᾶς; οὐχὶ καὶ τὰ ἔθνη τὸ αὐτὸ ποιοῦσιν; ὑμεῖς δὲ ἀγαπᾶτε τοὺς μισοῦντας ὑμᾶς, καὶ οὐχ ἕξετε ἐχθρόν. ⁴ἀπέχου τῶν σαρκικῶν καὶ σωματικῶν ἐπιθυμιῶν· ἐάν τίς σοι δῷ ῥάπισμα εἰς τὴν δεξιὰν σιαγόνα, στρέψον αὐτῷ καὶ τὴν ἄλλην, καὶ ἔσῃ τέλειος. ἐὰν ἀγγαρεύσῃ σέ τις μίλιον ἕν, ὕπαγε μετ᾽ αὐτοῦ δύο. ἐὰν ἄρῃ τις τὸ ἱμάτιόν σου, δὸς αὐτῷ καὶ τὸν χιτῶνα· ἐὰν λάβῃ τις ἀπὸ σοῦ τὸ σόν, μὴ ἀπαίτει· οὐδὲ γὰρ δύνασαι. ⁵παντὶ τῷ αἰτοῦντί σε δίδου καὶ μὴ ἀπαίτει· πᾶσι γὰρ θέλει δίδοσθαι ὁ πατὴρ ἐκ τῶν ἰδίων χαρισμάτων.

Rom 12:14

¹⁴εὐλογεῖτε τοὺς διώκοντας [ὑμᾶς], εὐλογεῖτε καὶ μὴ καταρᾶσθε.

POxy 1224 fr 2 recto col. i

κ]αὶ π[ρ]οσεύχεσθε ὑπὲρ [τῶν ἐχθ]ρῶν ὑμῶν· ὁ γὰρ μὴ ὢν [κατὰ ὑμ]ῶν ὑπὲρ ὑμῶν ἐστιν. [ὁ σήμερον ὢ]ν μακρὰν αὔριον [ἐγγὺς ὑμῶν γ]ενήσεται, καὶ ἐν [. . .]

GThom 95

[ⲡⲉⲭⲁϥ ⲛϭⲓ ⲓ̅ⲥ̅] ⲉϣⲱⲡⲉ ⲟⲩⲛ̄ⲧⲏⲧⲛ̄ ϩⲟⲙⲧ ⲙ̄ⲡⲣ̄ϯ ⲉⲧⲙⲏⲥⲉ ⲁⲗⲗⲁ ϯ [. . .] ⲙⲡⲉ[ⲧⲉ] ⲧⲛⲁϫⲓⲧⲟⲩ ⲁⲛ ⲛ̄ⲧⲟⲟⲧϥ.

Did 1:2

² . . . πάντα δὲ ὅσα ἐὰν θελήσῃς μὴ γίνεσθαί σοι, καὶ σὺ ἄλλῳ μὴ ποίει.

Acts 15:29 (Western text)

²⁹ . . . καὶ ὅσα μὴ θέλετε ἑαυτοῖς γίνεσθαι, ἑτέρῳ μὴ ποιεῖν . . .

2 Clem 13:4

⁴Ὅταν γὰρ ἀκούσωσιν παρ᾽ ἡμῶν, ὅτι λέγει ὁ θεός· Οὐ χάρις ὑμῖν, εἰ ἀγαπᾶτε τοὺς ἀγαπῶντας ὑμᾶς, ἀλλὰ χάρις ὑμῖν, εἰ ἀγαπᾶτε τοὺς ἐχθροὺς καὶ τοὺς μισοῦντας ὑμᾶς· ταῦτα ὅταν ἀκούσωσιν, θαυμάζουσιν τὴν ὑπερβολὴν τῆς ἀγαθότητος.

1 Pet 3:9 ⇨ Q 6:27–29

⁹μὴ ἀποδιδόντες κακὸν ἀντὶ κακοῦ ἢ λοιδορίαν ἀντὶ λοιδορίας, τοὐναντίον δὲ εὐλογοῦντες ὅτι εἰς τοῦτο ἐκλήθητε ἵνα εὐλογίαν κληρονομήσητε.

Polycarp, *Phil.* 12:3 ⇨ Q 6:28

³Pro omnibus sanctis orate. Orate etiam pro regibus et potestatibus et principibus atque pro persequentibus et odientibus vos et pro inimicis crucis, ut fructus vester manifestus sit in omnibus, ut sitis in illo perfecti.

Tobit 4:15 LXX ⇨ Q 6:31

¹⁵καὶ ὃ μισεῖς, μηδενὶ ποιήσῃς.

POxy 654.36–37 ⇨ Q 6:31

λέγει Ἰη(σοῦ)ς· [μὴ ψεύδεσθε καὶ ὅ τι μισ]εῖται μὴ ποιεῖ[τε·

GThom 6b ⇨ Q 6:31

ⲡⲉⲭⲉ ⲓ̅ⲥ̅ ϫⲉ ⲙ̄ⲡⲣ̄ϫⲉ ϭⲟⲗ ⲁⲩⲱ ⲡⲉⲧⲉⲧⲛ̄ⲙⲟⲥⲧⲉ ⲙ̄ⲙⲟϥ ⲙ̄ⲡⲣ̄ⲁⲁϥ.

Did 1:3–5

³Now, the teaching of these words is this: Bless those that curse you, and and pray for your enemies, and fast for those that persecute you. For what credit is it to you if you love those that love you? Do not even the Gentiles do the same? But, for your part, love those that hate you and you will have no enemy. ⁴Abstain from carnal and bodily lusts. If any one smites you on the right cheek, turn to him the other cheek also and you will be perfect. If any one compels you to go with him one mile, go with him two. If anyone takes your coat, give him your shirt also. If anyone takes from you what is yours, refuse it not, even if you are able. ⁵Give to everyone that asks and do not refuse, for the Father's will is that we give to all from the gifts we have received.

Rom 12:14

¹⁴Bless those who persecute you; bless and do not curse them.

POxy 1224 fr 2 recto col. i

And] pray for your [enemies]. For he who is not [against you] is for you. [He who today is] far off will be [near you] tomorrow, and [. . .]

GThom 95

[Jesus said], "If you have money, do not lend it at interest. Rather, give [it] to someone from whom you will not get it back."

Did 1:2

² . . . whatsoever you would not have done to yourself, do not do to another.

Acts 15:29 (Western text)

²⁹And whatsoever you do not wish done to you yourselves, do not do to others.

2 Clem 13:4

⁴For when they [the Gentiles] hear from use that God says: "It is no credit to you, if you love them that love you, but it is a credit to you if you love your enemies and those that hate you"; — when they hear this they wonder at this extraordinary goodness . . .

1 Pet 3:9

⁹Do not return evil for evil or insult for insult; but on the contrary bless, for to this you have been called, and that you may obtain a blessing.

Polycarp, *Phil.* 12:3

³Pray for all the saints. Pray also for the emperors and for the potentates, and princes, and for those who persecute you and hate you and for the enemies of the Cross that your fruit may be manifest among all men, that you may be perfected in him.

Tobit 4:15 LXX

¹⁵And that which you hate, do to no one.

POxy 654.36–37

Jesus said, "[Do not tell lies, and] do not do what you [hate]."

GThom 6b

Jesus said, "Do not lie, and do not do what you hate, . . ."

Q 6:27–33, 35c

In Q: Most authors. Percy (1953: 149–50) conjectures that Matt 5:38–39a and 5:43 stood in Q, but it is much more likely that these verses are Matthean. Thus Broer 1975: 50–63; Bultmann 1963: 148; Guelich 1976a: 449–50; Grundmann Mt 169–70, 175; Lambrecht 1985: 104; Luz Mt 291; Schenk 26–27; Schulz 121; Suggs 1975 and most others. While Müller (1908: 29, 46) also includes Matt 5:21–24, 27–29, 30, 33–37, most exclude these verses. Easton (Lk 89) holds that Luke 6:27–35 derives from L.

A more serious matter of dispute is the original order of sayings. In favor of *Lukan order*: Catchpole 1986: 303; Crossan 1983: 342; Grundmann Lk 146; Guelich 1976a: 449–50; Hunter 133; Jacobson 56; Kloppenborg 1987: 173; Lührmann 1972: 413–14; Manson 50, 54; Müller 1908: 29 (but Q 6:31 originally occurred in its Matthean position, i.e., afer Q 11:11–13 // Matt 7:9–11); Polag 34 (but 6:31 is placed after 6:38); Schürmann Lk 345; Streeter 1924: 248; Worden 547–48. The usual defense of Lukan order is based on the argument that it is less likely that Luke would have broken up Q 6:27–28, 32–33, 35c by inserting Q 6:29–31 than that Matthew would have rearranged and rationalized the materials when he created the series of antitheses in Matt 5:21–48. To this Catchpole adds the observation that Luke does not deliberately use the "sandwich technique" (i.e., positioning 6:29–31 inside the main body of sayings).

Others favor *Matthean order*: Bultmann 1963: 96: Luke created a unitary composition by a redactional introduction (v. 27a) and by inserting vv. 29–30 and 31. Dupont 1969: 191–92; Harnack 58–63, 129 (but 6:31 is placed after 6:36); Hoffmann 1984: 64–71; Lambrecht 1985: 104–105; Schmid 228–29; Schulz 120–21: Luke employed the sayings on love of enemy as a frame for the other sayings. Zeller 26. Schenk (26–29) dissents from both views and suggests as the original order 6:27–28, 35, 29–30, 31, 32–33.

(Q/Matt 5:41)

In Q: Crossan 1985: 15; Harnack 182–83 (possibly); Hoffmann 1984: 61; Luz Mt 291 (?): It is possible that Luke omitted the verse because he lived in a senatorial province or in Rome where no troops were stationed. Marshall Lk 260; Piper 1979: 58; Polag 34 (probably); Schweizer Mt 67, 79 (?): Outside Palestine the example of military requisition would not be useful; therefore Luke omitted it. A few others suggest that this was present in Q^{Mt}: Luz Mt 291 (?); Luz 1983: 475; Schweizer Mt 67 (?): The verse may have been added to Q at a time of tension with Rome. Strecker 1978: 64 (perhaps).

Not in Q: Bussmann 45; Lührmann 1972: 418: There is no reason for Luke to have omitted the verse. See also Kilpatrick 1946: 20; Manson 160; Schenk 27; Schmithals Lk 85; Schulz 123; Strecker 1978: 64 (perhaps); Worden 206; Zeller 1977: 55.

(Q 6:34–35b)

In Q: Bussmann 45 (hesitantly); Catchpole (1986: 303) regards 6:35a as the summarizing restatement typical of form of both Q 12:22–31 and 6:27–35. He is hesitant in regard to 6:34 (305 n 36). Guelich 1976a: 449–50; Hunter 133; Luz 1983: 476 (Q^{Lk}); Manson 54–55; Marshall Lk 263: Matthew omitted v. 34 because of its difficulty. Schürmann (Lk 354) suggests that δανείζω in v. 34 is a reminiscence of original form of Q 6:30 = Matt 5:42. Matthew omitted Q 6:34–35 altogether, preserving only a reminiscence in 5:42.

Not in Q: Bultmann 1963: 96: Luke wished to utilize δανείζω which he had passed over in 6:30. Lührmann 1972: 420: Luke 6:34 + 35aβγ–35b is a Lukan creation recalling Q 6:30 = Matt 5:42; however 35aα· ἀγαπᾶτε τοὺς ἐχθροὺς ὑμῶν is from Q as the parallel of Matt 5:44–45 // Luke 6:35aα, 36 shows. See also Fitzmyer Lk 640; Hoffmann 1984: 54–56; Müller 1908: 19; Polag 35 (only 35a ἀγαπᾶτε τοὺς ἐχθροὺς ὑμῶν is from Q); Schulz 131; Strecker 1978: 67; Weiss 1907: 260. Edwards (1975: 100–101) concords vocabulary from 6:35a–c but not from 6:34.

Matt 5:43–44, 38–42

[43 You have heard that it was said, 'You shall love your countryman and hate your enemy.']

44 But I tell you, Love your enemies and pray for those who persecute you.

[38 You have heard that it was said, 'An eye for an eye and a tooth for a tooth.' 39 But I tell you, do not oppose one who is evil. But]

if any one strikes you on the right cheek, turn to him the other also; 40 and if any one wants to sue you and take your tunic, let him have your cloak as well;

(41 and if any one presses you into service for one mile, go with him two miles.)

42 Give to one who begs from you, and do not refuse one who wants to borrow from you.

Matt 7:12

12 So whatever you wish that people would do to you, do so also to them; for this is the law and the prophets.

Matt 5:46–47, 45

46 For if you love those who love you, what reward have you? Do not even the tax collectors do the same? 47 And if you greet your brothers alone, what are you doing that is out of the ordinary? Do not even the Gentiles do the same?

45 Thus you will become sons of your Father who is in heaven; for he makes his sun rise on the evil and on the good, and sends rain on the just and on the unjust.

Luke 6:27–35

27 But I tell you who listen, Love your enemies, do good to those who hate you, 28 bless those who curse you, pray for those who mistreat you.

29 When someone strikes you on the cheek, offer the other also; and when someone takes away your cloak do not withhold even your tunic.

30 Give to every one who begs from you; and if someone takes away your belongings do not ask them back again.

31 And as you wish that people would do to you, do so to them.

32 If you love those who love you, what credit is that to you? For even sinners love those who love them. 33 For if you also do good to those who do good to you, what credit is that to you? For even sinners do the same.

(34 And if you lend to those from whom you expect repayment, what credit is that to you? Even sinners lend to sinners, to receive as much again. 35 Instead, love your enemies, and do good, and lend, expecting nothing back; and your reward will be great,) and you will be sons of the Most High; for he is kind to the ungrateful and the evil.

Matt 5:48; 7:1–2

⁴⁸ἔσεσθε οὖν ὑμεῖς τέλειοι ὡς ὁ **πατὴρ ὑμῶν**
ὁ οὐράνιος τέλειός **ἐστιν**.
¹ Μὴ **κρίνετε**, ἵνα <u>μὴ **κριθῆτε**·</u>
(²ἐν ᾧ γὰρ κρίματι κρίνετε κριθήσεσθε),

καὶ ἐν <u>ᾧ **μέτρῳ μετρεῖτε**</u> <u>μετρηθήσεται</u> **ὑμῖν**.

Luke 6:36–38

³⁶Γίνεσθε οἰκτίρμονες καθὼς [καὶ] ὁ **πατὴρ**
ὑμῶν   οἰκτρίμων **ἐστίν**.
³⁷Καὶ μὴ **κρίνετε**, καὶ οὐ <u>μὴ **κριθῆτε**·</u>

καὶ μὴ καταδικάζετε, καὶ οὐ μὴ καταδικασθῆτε.
(ἀπολύετε, καὶ ἀπολυθήσεσθε·
³⁸δίδοτε, καὶ δοθήσεται ὑμῖν· μέτρον καλὸν πεπιεσμένον
σεσαλευμένον ὑπερεκχυννόμενον δώσουσιν εἰς τὸν
κόλπον ὑμῶν)·
ᾧ γὰρ <u>**μέτρῳ μετρεῖτε**</u> <u>ἀντιμετρηθήσεται</u> **ὑμῖν**.

Luke 6:36: omit καὶ (Matt): 𝔓⁷⁵ᵛⁱᵈ ℵ B L W Ξ Ψ λ *pc* c d
syᶜ; Mcion Cl [NA²⁵] / txt: A D Koine Θ φ *pm* lat syᵖ·ʰ;
Cyp Bas Cyr [NA²⁶; HG].

Rom 2:1

¹Διὸ ἀναπολόγητος εἶ, ὦ ἄνθρωπε πᾶς ὁ κρίνων· ἐν ᾧ γὰρ κρίνεις τὸν ἕτερον, σεαυτὸν κατακρίνεις, τὰ γὰρ αὐτὰ πράσσεις ὁ κρίνων.

Rom 2:1

¹Therefore you are without excuse, O friend, you who are judging; for in judging another you condemn yourself, because you, the judge, are doing the very same things.

Matt 12:37

³⁷ἐκ γὰρ τῶν λόγων σου δικαιωθήσῃ, καὶ ἐκ τῶν λόγων σου καταδικασθήσῃ.

Matt 12:37

³⁷for by your words you will be justified, and by your words you will be condemned.

1 Clem 13:1–2

¹ . . . μάλιστα μεμνημένοι τῶν λόγων τοῦ κυρίου Ἰησοῦ, οὓς ἐλάλησεν διδάσκων ἐπιείκειαν καὶ μακροθυμίαν. ²οὕτως γὰρ εἶπεν· Ἐλεᾶτε, ἵνα ἐλεηθῆτε· ἀφίετε, ἵνα ἀφεθῇ ὑμῖν· ὡς ποιεῖτε, οὕτω ποιηθήσεται ὑμῖν· ὡς δίδοτε, οὕτως δοθήσεται ὑμῖν· ὡς κρίνετε, οὕτως κριθήσεσθε· ὡς χρηστεύεσθε, οὕτως χρηστευθήσεται ὑμῖν· ᾧ μέτρῳ μετρεῖτε, ἐν αὐτῷ μετρηθήσεται ὑμῖν.

1 Clem 13:1–2

¹ . . . especially remembering the words of the Lord Jesus which he spoke when he was teaching gentleness and longsuffering. ²For he spoke thus: "Be merciful, that you may obtain mercy. Forgive, that you may be forgiven. As you do, so shall it be done to you. As you give, so shall it be given to you. As you judge, so shall you be judged. As you are kind, so shall kindness be shown you. With what measure you measure, it shall be measured to you."

Mark 4:24–25

²⁴Καὶ ἔλεγεν αὐτοῖς· βλέπετε τί ἀκούετε. ἐν ᾧ μέτρῳ μετρεῖτε μετρηθήσεται ὑμῖν καὶ προστεθήσεται ὑμῖν. ²⁵ὃς γὰρ ἔχει, δοθήσεται αὐτῷ· καὶ ὃς οὐκ ἔχει, καὶ ὃ ἔχει ἀρθήσεται ἀπ' αὐτοῦ.

Mark 4:24–25

²⁴And he said to them, "Take care what you hear; by the standard with which you measure, it will be measured to you, and still more will be given you. ²⁵For the one who has will be given more; and from the one who has not, even what he has will be taken away."

Polycarp, *Phil.* 2:3

³μεμημονεύοντες δὲ ὧν εἶπεν ὁ κύριος διδάσκων· Μὴ κρίνετε, ἵνα μὴ κριθῆτε· ἀφίετε, καὶ ἀφεθήσεται ὑμῖν· ἐλεᾶτε, ἵνα ἐλεηθῆτε· ᾧ μέτρῳ μετρεῖτε, ἀντιμετρηθήσεται ὑμῖν.

Polycarp, *Phil.* 2:3

³ . . . but remembering what the Lord taught when he said, "Judge not that you be not judged, forgive and it shall be forgiven you, be merciful that you may obtain mercy, with what measure you measure, it shall be measured to you again."

Lev 19:2 LXX ▷ Q 6:36

²Λάλησον τῇ συναγωγῇ τῶν υἱῶν Ἰσραὴλ καὶ ἐρεῖς πρὸς αὐτούς· ἅγιοι ἔσεσθε, ὅτι ἐγὼ ἅγιος, κύριος ὁ θεὸς ὑμῶν.

Lev 19:2 LXX ▷ Q 6:36

²Speak to the assembly of the children of Israel and say to them: "Be holy because I, the Lord your God, am holy."

Deut 18:13 LXX ▷ Matt 5:48

¹³τέλειος ἔσῃ ἐναντίον κυρίου τοῦ θεοῦ σου.

Deut 18:13 LXX ▷ Matt 5:48

¹³Be perfect before the Lord your God.

James 4:11–12 ▷ Q 6:37–38

¹¹Μὴ καταλαλεῖτε ἀλλήλων, ἀδελφοί· ὁ καταλαλῶν ἀδελφοῦ ἢ κρίνων τὸν ἀδελφὸν αὐτοῦ καταλαλεῖ νόμου καὶ κρίνει νόμον· εἰ δὲ νόμον κρίνεις, οὐκ εἶ ποιητὴς νόμου ἀλλὰ κριτής. ¹²εἷς ἐστιν ὁ νομοθέτης καὶ κριτὴς ὁ δυνάμενος σῶσαι καὶ ἀπολέσαι· σὺ δὲ τίς εἶ, ὁ κρίνων τὸν πλησίον;

James 4:11–12 ▷ Q 6:37–38

¹¹Do not slander one another, brothers. Whoever slanders a brother or judges his brother, slanders the law and judges the law. But if you judge the law, you do not observe the law but judge it. ¹²There is only one lawgiver and judge who is able to save and to destroy. But who are you that you judge your neighbor?

Did 6:2 ▷ Matt 5:48

²εἰ μὲν γὰρ δύνασαι βαστάσαι ὅλον τὸν ζυγὸν τοῦ κυρίου, τέλειος ἔσῃ· εἰ δ' οὐ δύνασαι, ὃ δύνῃ, τοῦτο ποίει.

Did 6:2 ▷ Matt 5:48

²For it you can bear the whole yoke of the Lord, you will be perfect, but if you cannot, do what you can.

Q 6:36–37a, 38c

In Q: Most authors. Easton (Lk 89) attributes this to L.

(Q/Matt 7:2a)

In Q: Harnack 9; Schulz 146, 147 n. 46: Q 6:38c cannot follow directly on 6:37a but requires Q/Matt 7:2a as a connective which shifts attention from judgment itself to the standard of judgment. Weiss 1907: 261; Worden 323–25 (probably). Klostermann (Mt 65), Luz (1983: 477), and Sato 1984: 59 ascribe the verse to Q^{Mt}.

Not in Q: Crossan 1983: 180; Schenk 30; Schürmann Lk 362 (but 7:2a is based on Q/Luke 6:37bc); Zeller 1977: 13.

Q 6:37b

In Q: Catchpole 1986: 310; Crossan 1983: 180–81; Hunter 133; Manson 55–56; Schürmann Lk 362: Matt 7:2a abbreviates and presupposes the double judgment mentioned in Q/Luke 6:37b.c. Moreover, Matt 12:37 is a reminiscence of Q/Luke 6:37b. See also Manson 55; Polag 34; Worden 323–25 (probably). Harnack (9–10, hesitantly) and Luz (1983: 477) consider the possibility of Q^{Lk}.

Not in Q: Müller 1908: 19; Schenk 30; Schulz 146: Luke's double prohibition is probably secondary to Matthew's simple prohibition. Weiss 1907: 261 (from L).

(Q 6:37c–38b)

In Q: Catchpole 1986: 310: V. 38b presupposes "the Palestinian custom of using the fold of a garment as a container for wheat" which Luke would hardly have added himself (similarly Schürmann). Crossan 1983: 180–81; Hunter 130; Manson 55: Luke's form is poetic and therefore original. Marshall Lk 258; Polag 34. Schürmann Lk 363: Matthew simplified the unit by omitting Q/Luke 6:38ab in order to focus only on the idea of judging. Harnack (9–10, hesitantly), Luz (1983: 477) and Sato 1984: 62 consider the possibility of Q^{Lk}.

Not in Q: Bultmann 1963: 86–87; Dupont 1969: 51: The shift of focus between 6:37ab and 37c–38b indicates secondary expansion. Whereas 6:37a, 38c express the "rigorous equivalence" of judgment given and judgment received, 6:38ab appeals to generosity "and promises in return not just equal measure but rather superabundance." Fitzmyer Lk 627, 641; Müller 1908: 4, 19, 47 (6:38a and c derive from Q but 38b is from L). Schenk 30; Schmid 246; Schmithals Lk 86; Schulz 146: Luke 6:38b disrupts the formal structure of 37–38 and is secondarily attached ad vocem μέτρον. Weiss 1907: 261 (from L). Edwards (1975: 102–104) concords no vocabulary from Matt 7:2 // Luke 6:37b–38 (including Matt 7:2b // Luke 6:38c).

Matt 5:48; 7:1–2

[48] Be perfect, therefore, as your heavenly Father is perfect.

[1] "Do not judge, lest you be judged. ([2] For with the judgment you pronounce you will be judged,)

and by the standard with which you measure, it will be measured to you."

Luke 6:36–38

[36] Be merciful, even as your Father is merciful.

[37] And judge not, and you will not be judged; condemn not, and you will not be condemned; (forgive, and you will be forgiven; [38] give, and it will be given to you; they will put into your lap a full measure, pressed down, shaken together, overflowing.)

For by the standard with which you measure, it will be measured back to you.

Matt 15:13–14

[¹³ὁ δὲ ἀποκριθεὶς εἶπεν· πᾶσα φυτεία ἣν οὐκ ἐφύτευσεν ὁ πατήρ μου ὁ οὐράνιος ἐκριζωθήσεται].

¹⁴ἄφετε αὐτούς· τυφλοί εἰσιν ὁδηγοὶ [τυφλῶν]· **τυφλὸς** δὲ **τυφλὸν** ἐὰν ὁδηγῇ, **ἀμφότεροι εἰς βόθυνον** πεσοῦνται.

Matt 10:24–25

²⁴<u>Οὐκ ἔστιν μαθητὴς ὑπὲρ τὸν διδάσκαλον</u> οὐδὲ δοῦλος ὑπὲρ τὸν κύριον αὐτοῦ. ²⁵ἀρκετὸν τῷ μαθητῇ ἵνα γένηται **ὡς ὁ διδάσκαλος αὐτοῦ** καὶ ὁ δοῦλος ὡς ὁ κύριος αὐτοῦ. [εἰ τὸν οἰκοδεσπότην Βεελζεβοὺλ ἐπεκάλεσαν, πόσῳ μᾶλλον τοὺς οἰκιακοὺς αὐτοῦ].

Luke 6:39–40

[³⁹Εἶπεν δὲ καὶ παραβολὴν αὐτοῖς·] μήτι δύναται **τυφλὸς τυφλὸν** ὁδηγεῖν; οὐχὶ **ἀμφότεροι εἰς βόθυνον** ἐμπεσοῦνται;

⁴⁰<u>οὐκ ἔστιν μαθητὴς ὑπὲρ τὸν διδάσκαλον</u>· κατηρτισμένος δὲ πᾶς ἔσται

ὡς ὁ διδάσκαλος αὐτοῦ.

Matt 15:14: τυφ. εις. οδηγ. τυφ.: *3 2 1 4*: C W Koine 0106 q / *3 2 4*: K *pc* sys.c / *3 2 1*: ℵ*.²; Epiph / *1–3*: B D 0237 / txt: ℵ¹ L Z λ φ 33 700 892 1241 1424 *al* lat syp.h [NA²⁶; HG] // πεσουνται εις βοθυνον: L Z 0237 λ [HG] / πεσουνται εις τον βοθυννον: Θ φ *pc* / εμπεσουνται εις βοθρον: D λ *pc*; Did / εις βοθυννον εμπεσ. (Luke): W Φ Koine lat sy mae / txt: *rell*; lat sy; Bas Cyp [NA²⁵.²⁶].

GThom 40

ⲡⲉⲭⲉ ⲓⲥ ⲟⲩⲃⲉ ⲛⲉⲗⲟⲟⲗⲉ ⲁⲩⲧⲟⲃⲥ ⲙ̄ⲡⲥⲁ ⲛ̄ⲃⲟⲗ
ⲙ̄ⲡⲉⲓⲱⲧ ⲁⲩⲱ ⲉⲥⲧⲁⲭⲣⲏⲩ ⲁⲛ ⲥⲉⲛⲁⲡⲟⲣⲕ̄ⲥ̄ ϩⲁ
ⲧⲉⲥⲛⲟⲩⲛⲉ ⲛ̄ⲥⲧⲁⲕⲟ.

GThom 34

ⲡⲉⲭⲉ ⲓⲥ ϫⲉ ⲟⲩⲃⲗ̄ⲗⲉ ⲉϥϣⲁⲛⲥⲱⲕ ϩⲏⲧϥ̄ ⲛ̄ⲛⲟⲩⲃⲗ̄ⲗⲉ
ϣⲁⲩϩⲉ ⲙ̄ⲡⲉⲥⲛⲁⲩ ⲉⲡⲉⲥⲏⲧ· ⲉⲩϩⲓⲉⲓⲧ·

John 13:16

[16]ἀμὴν ἀμὴν λέγω ὑμῖν, οὐκ ἔστιν δοῦλος μείζων τοῦ
κυρίου αὐτοῦ οὐδὲ ἀπόστολος μείζων τοῦ πέμψαντος
αὐτόν.

John 15:20a

[20]μνημονεύετε τοῦ λόγου οὗ ἐγὼ εἶπον ὑμῖν· οὐκ ἔστιν
δοῦλος μείζων τοῦ κυρίου αὐτοῦ. εἰ ἐμὲ ἐδίωξαν, καὶ ὑμᾶς
διώξουσιν . . .

DialSav 53

ⲡⲉⲭⲁⲥ ⲛ̄ϭⲓⲙⲁⲣⲓϩⲁⲙ ϫⲉϩⲓⲛⲁⲓ̈ ⲉⲧⲕⲁⲕⲓⲁ ⲙ̄ⲡⲉϩⲟⲟⲩ
ⲡⲉϩⲟⲟⲩ ⲁⲩⲱ ⲡⲉⲣⲅⲁⲧⲏⲥ ⲙ̄ⲡϣⲁ ⲛ̄ⲧⲉϥⲧⲣⲟⲫⲏ· ⲁⲩⲱ
ⲡⲙⲁⲑⲏⲧⲏⲥ ⲛ̄ϥⲉⲓⲛⲉ ⲙ̄ⲡⲉϥⲥⲁϩ· ⲡⲉⲉⲓϣⲁϫⲉ ⲁⲥϫⲟⲟϥ
ϩⲱⲥ ⲥϩⲓⲙⲉ ⲉⲁⲥⲉⲓⲙⲉ ⲉⲡⲧⲏⲣϥ̄.

GThom 40

Jesus said, "A grapevine has been planted apart from the
Father. Since it is not strong, it will be pulled up by its
root and will perish."

GThom 34

Jesus said, "If one blind person leads another blind
person, both of them will fall into a hole."

John 13:16

[16]Amen, amen, I say to you, a servant is not greater than
his master; nor is he who is sent greater than he who sent
him.

John 15:20

[20]Remember the word that I said to you, 'A servant is not
greater than his master.' If they persecuted me, they will
persecute you . . .

DialSav 53

Mary said, "Thus with respect to 'the wickedness of each
day,' and 'the laborer is worthy of his food,' and 'the
disciple resembles his teacher.'" She uttered this as a
woman who had understood completely.

[Q/Matt 15:13]

In Q: Hawkins 1911: 134: Luke omitted this anti-Pharisaic polemic.

Not in Q: Most authors.

[Luke 6:39a]

In Q: Bussmann 48 n. 1: The introduction was omitted by Matthew when he relocated 6:39. Knox 1957: 10: Q/Luke 6:39a survives from a period when the sermon was a collection of sayings introduced by "and he said." Marshall Lk 268: Lukan, but "may be based on a source." Schürmann Lk 367: Despite some Lukan vocabulary Luke elsewhere prefers πρός to the dative with verbs of speaking.

Not in Q: Most authors. The use of δὲ καί is typically Lukan (see Jeremias 1980: 78) and the phrase εἶπεν or λέγει παραβολήν is also redactional at 5:36; 20:9, 19; 21:29 and appears in non-Markan material at 4:23; 6:39; 12:16; 13:6; 14:7; 15:3; 18:1, 9; 19:11.

Q 6:39bc–40

In Q: Crossan 1983: 342; Easton Lk 91–92; Edwards 1975: 102–104; Fitzmyer Lk 641; Harnack 81, 179 ("more or less probable"); Hawkins 1911: 116–117 (with considerable probability); Hunter 133; Jacobson 50. Kilpatrick (1946: 26) suggests that Matthew has conflated Q 6:40 with a version in another source. Kloppenborg 1987: 180–81; Lührmann 54; Manson 57: The Matthean versions of the sayings (10:24–25 and 15:14) are from M. Müller 1908: 47, 49; Polag 36; Schenk 31; Schulz 472–74; Steinhauser 1981: 184–93; Weiss 1907: 93, 95 n. 2; Worden 342.

Not in Q: Luz Mt 376 (not in Matthew's copy of Q); Vassiliadis 1978: 66, 68: "Short apophthegms or sayings of a proverbial character, especially those found in a different context in Matthew and Luke should be excluded [from Q] as possibly due to the oral tradition." Zeller 16 (uncertain).

The original location of Q 6:39 and 6:40 is controverted and a decision depends mainly upon whether one supposes that Matthew reorganized sayings which did not originally fit together smoothly, or that Luke created the awkwardness by his insertion. Many argue or assume that the Lukan placement of both sayings is original: Crossan 1983: 342; Hunter 133; Jacobson 50; Kloppenborg 1987: 181; Müller 1908: 29; Polag 36; Schenk 30–31; Schürmann Lk 369–70; Steinhauser 1981: 184; Taylor 1972: 105; Zeller 1977: 114. Catchpole (1986: 297, 313–14) agrees that the placement of 6:39bc is original in Luke, arguing that the redactional nature of 6:39a in no way implies that the saying itself has been relocated. However, the poor connection of Q 6:40 with the present Lukan context suggests that its position is not original. Against this, however, it may be argued that since Q 6:40 does fit so poorly with Q 6:39 and Q 6:41–42, it must already have been attached to 6:39 prior to its association with 6:41–41 (Kloppenborg; Schürmann).

Easton (Lk 91) argues that Matthew's anti-Pharisaic setting of Q 6:39 is more original and that Q 6:40 is artificially placed here by Luke. Fitzmyer (Lk 641), Lambrecht (1985: 213) and Schmithals (Lk 87) likewise argue that Luke has artificially relocated both sayings. Lührmann (54) and Schmid (247) conclude that the redactional nature of Luke 6:39a suggests that Luke has inserted Q 6:39b–40 into a previously existing unit. Schmid (247, 271, 301) suggests that the original position of Q 6:40 is in the commissioning speech (Matt 10).

[Matt 10:25b]

Matthean: Schmid 271; Steinhauser 1981: 186 and most authors.

Matt 15:13–14

[13 He answered, "Every plant which my heavenly Father did not plant will be uprooted.]

14 Let them alone; guides of the blind are themselves blind. And if a blind man leads a blind man, both will fall into a pit."

Matt 10:24–25

24 "A disciple is not above the teacher, nor a servant above his master; 25 it is enough for the disciple to be like his teacher, and the servant like his master.
[If they called the master of the house Beelzebul, how much more will they say it of those of his household."]

Luke 6:39–40

[39 He also told them a parable:]
"Surely a blind man cannot lead a blind man? Will they not both fall into a pit?

40 A disciple is not above his teacher, but every one when he is fully trained will be like his teacher."

Matt 7:3–5

³τί δὲ βλέπεις τὸ κάρφος τὸ ἐν τῷ ὀφθαλμῷ
τοῦ ἀδελφοῦ σου, τὴν δὲ ἐν τῷ σῷ
ὀφθαλμῷ δοκὸν οὐ κατανοεῖς;
⁴ ἢ πῶς ἐρεῖς　　　　τῷ ἀδελφῷ σου·
　　ἄφες ἐκβάλω τὸ κάρφος ἐκ τοῦ
ὀφθαλμοῦ σου, καὶ ἰδοὺ ἡ δοκὸς ἐν τῷ ὀφθαλμῷ σου;
⁵ὑποκριτά, ἔκβαλε πρῶτον ἐκ
τοῦ ὀφθαλμοῦ σοῦ τὴν δοκόν, καὶ τότε
διαβλέψεις ἐκβαλεῖν τὸ κάρφος ἐκ τοῦ ὀφθαλμοῦ τοῦ
ἀδελφοῦ σου.

Luke 6:41–42

⁴¹τί δὲ βλέπεις τὸ κάρφος τὸ ἐν τῷ ὀφθαλμῷ
τοῦ ἀδελφοῦ σου, τὴν δὲ δοκὸν τὴν ἐν τῷ ἰδίῳ
ὀφθαλμῷ οὐ κατανοεῖς;
⁴²πῶς δύνασαι λέγειν τῷ ἀδελφῷ σου·
ἀδελφέ, ἄφες ἐκβάλω τὸ κάρφος τὸ ἐν τῷ
ὀφθαλμῷ σου, αὐτὸς τὴν ἐν τῷ ὀφθαλμῷ σου δοκὸν
οὐ βλέπων; ὑποκριτά, ἔκβαλε πρῶτον
τὴν δοκὸν ἐκ τοῦ ὀφθαλμοῦ σου, καὶ τότε
διαβλέψεις τὸ κάρφος τὸ ἐν τῷ ὀφθαλμῷ τοῦ
ἀδελφοῦ σου ἐκβαλεῖν.

Matt 7:4: απο του οφθ.: W Koine Δ Θ λ φ 565 700 1010
[HG] // 5: την δοκον εκ τ. οφθ. σου (Luke): L W Koine Θ
0233 λ φ latt [HG] / txt: ℵ B Cᵛⁱᵈ [NA²⁵·²⁶].

Notes

Q 6:41–42
In Q: Most authors.

Matt 7:3–5

³ Why do you see the speck that is in your brother's eye, but do not notice the beam that is in your own eye? ⁴ Or how can you say to your brother, 'Let me remove the speck from your eye,' when behold there is the beam in your own eye? ⁵ Hypocrite, first remove the beam from your own eye, and then you will see clearly to remove the speck from your brother's eye.

Luke 6:41–42

⁴¹ Why do you see the speck that is in your brother's eye, but do not notice the beam that is in your own eye? ⁴² How can you say to your brother, 'Brother, let me remove the speck that is in your eye,' when you yourself do not see the beam that is in your own eye? You hypocrite, first remove the beam from your own eye, and then you will see clearly to remove the speck that is in your brother's eye.

Parallels

POxy 1. 1–4

[. . .   . . .] καὶ τότε διαβλέψεις ἐκβαλεῖν τὸ κάρφος τὸ ἐν τῷ ὀφθαλμῷ τοῦ ἀδελφοῦ σου.

GThom 26

ⲡⲉϫⲉ ⲓ̅ⲥ̅ ϫⲉ ⲡϫⲏ ⲉⲧϩⲙ̅ ⲡⲃⲁⲗ ⲙ̅ⲡⲉⲕⲥⲟⲛ ⲕⲛⲁⲩ ⲉⲣⲟϥ ⲡⲥⲟⲉⲓ ⲇⲉ ⲉⲧϩⲙ̅ ⲡⲉⲕⲃⲁⲗ ⲕⲛⲁⲩ ⲁⲛ ⲉⲣⲟϥ ϩⲟⲧⲁⲛ ⲉⲕϣⲁⲛⲛⲟⲩϫⲉ ⲙ̅ⲡⲥⲟⲉⲓ ⲉⲃⲟⲗ ϩⲙ̅ ⲡⲉⲕⲃⲁⲗ ⲧⲟⲧⲉ ⲕⲛⲁⲛⲁⲩ ⲉⲃⲟⲗ ⲉⲛⲟⲩϫⲉ ⲙ̅ⲡϫⲏ ⲉⲃⲟⲗ ϩⲙ̅ ⲡⲃⲁⲗ ⲙ̅ⲡⲉⲕⲥⲟⲛ.

POxy 1. 1–4

[. . .] and then you (sg.) will see clearly to cast the mote from your (sg.) brother's eye.

GThom 26

Jesus said, "You see the speck that is in your brother's eye, but you do not see the beam that is in your own eye. When you take the beam out of your own eye, then you will see well enough to take the speck out of your brother's eye."

Matt 7:15–20

[¹⁵Προσέχετε ἀπὸ τῶν ψευδοπροφητῶν, οἵτινες ἔρχονται πρὸς ὑμᾶς ἐν ἐνδύμασιν προβάτων, ἔσωθεν δέ εἰσιν λύκοι ἅρπαγες].
[¹⁶ἀπὸ τῶν καρπῶν αὐτῶν ἐπιγνώσεσθε αὐτούς].
μήτι συλλέγουσιν ἀπὸ ἀκανθῶν σταφυλὰς ἢ ἀπὸ τριβόλων σῦκα;
[¹⁷οὕτως πᾶν δένδρον ἀγαθὸν καρποὺς καλοὺς ποιεῖ, τὸ δὲ σαπρὸν δένδρον καρποὺς πονηροὺς ποιεῖ].
¹⁸οὐ δύναται δένδρον ἀγαθὸν καρποὺς πονηροὺς ποιεῖν οὐδὲ δένδρον σαπρὸν καρποὺς καλοὺς ποιεῖν.
[¹⁹πᾶν δένδρον μὴ ποιοῦν καρπὸν καλὸν ἐκκόπτεται καὶ εἰς πῦρ βάλλεται].
[²⁰ἄρα γε ἀπὸ τῶν καρπῶν αὐτῶν ἐπιγνώσεσθε αὐτούς].

Matt 12:33–35

[³³Ἢ ποιήσατε τὸ δένδρον καλὸν καὶ τὸν καρπὸν αὐτοῦ καλόν, ἢ ποιήσατε τὸ δένδρον σαπρὸν καὶ τὸν καρπὸν αὐτοῦ σαπρόν·]
ἐκ γὰρ τοῦ καρποῦ τὸ δένδρον γινώσεται.
(7:16) μήτι συλλέγουσιν ἀπὸ ἀκανθῶν σταφυλὰς ἢ ἀπὸ τριβόλων σῦκα;
[³⁴γεννήματα ἐχιδνῶν, πῶς δύνασθε ἀγαθὰ λαλεῖν πονηροὶ ὄντες;]
ἐκ γὰρ τοῦ περισσεύματος τῆς καρδίας τὸ στόμα λαλεῖ.
³⁵ὁ ἀγαθὸς ἄνθρωπος ἐκ τοῦ ἀγαθοῦ θησαυροῦ ἐκβάλλει ἀγαθά, καὶ ὁ πονηρὸς ἄνθρωπος ἐκ τοῦ πονηροῦ θησαυροῦ ἐκβάλλει πονηρά.
⇨ Matt 12:34b

Luke 6:43–45

⇨ Luke 6:44a

⁴⁴. . . οὐ γὰρ ἐξ ἀκανθῶν συλλέγουσιν σῦκα οὐδὲ ἐκ βάτου σταφυλὴν τρυγῶσιν.
⇨ Luke 6:43

⁴³Οὐ γὰρ ἐστιν δένδρον καλὸν ποιοῦν καρπὸν σαπρόν, οὐδὲ πάλιν δένδρον σαπρὸν ποιοῦν καρπὸν καλόν.
⇨ Q 3:9 [S3]

⇨ Luke 6:43

⁴⁴ἕκαστον γὰρ δένδρον ἐκ τοῦ ἰδίου καρποῦ γινώσκεται·
οὐ γὰρ ἐξ ἀκανθῶν συλλέγουσιν σῦκα οὐδὲ ἐκ βάτου σταφυλὴν τρυγῶσιν.
⇨ Q 3:7b [S3]

⇨ Luke 6:45c

⁴⁵ὁ ἀγαθὸς ἄνθρωπος ἐκ τοῦ ἀγαθοῦ θησαυροῦ τῆς καρδίας προφέρει τὸ ἀγαθόν, καὶ ὁ πονηρὸς ἐκ τοῦ πονηροῦ προφέρει τὸ πονηρόν· ἐκ γὰρ περισσεύματος καρδίας λαλεῖ τὸ στόμα αὐτοῦ.

Matt 7:18: ποιειν . . . ποιειν: ℵᶜ C K L W X Δ Θ Π 0250 λ φ 33 565 700 892 1010 1071 1079 1195 1216 1230 (1242ᵛⁱᵈ) 1242 1253 1365 1546 1646 2174 it vg syᶜ·ᵖ·ʰ sa bo goth arm geo [NA²⁶; HG] / ενεγκειν . . . ποιειν: B syᵖᵃˡ? / ενεγκειν . . . ενεγκειν: Tert Or [NA²⁵] / ποιειν . . . ενεγκειν· ℵ* syᵖᵃˡ?; Tert Or.

Luke 6:45: καρδιας + αυτου: C A (D) L W Θ λ φ *pl* latt syˢ·ᵖ sa bo [HG] / txt: 𝔭⁷⁵ ℵ B; Cl [NA²⁵·²⁶].

Did 11:8

8οὐ πᾶς δὲ ὁ λαλῶν ἐν πνεύματι προφήτης ἐστίν, ἀλλ᾽ ἐὰν ἔχῃ τοὺς τρόπους κυρίου. ἀπὸ οὖν τῶν τρόπων γνωθήσεται ὁ ψευδοπροφήτης καὶ ὁ προφήτης.

Did 11:8

8But not everyone who speaks in a spirit is a prophet, except that he have the behaviour of the Lord. From his behaviour, then, the false prophet and the true prophet shall be known.

James 3:12

12μὴ δύναται, ἀδελφοί μου, συκῆ ἐλαίας ποιῆσαι ἢ ἄμπελος σῦκα; οὔτε ἁλυκὸν γλυκὺ ποιῆσαι ὕδωρ.

James 3:12

12Can a fig tree, my brothers, yield olives, or a grapevine figs? Nor can salt water yield fresh.

GThom 43

πεχαγ ναϥ ⲛϭι ⲛεϥμαθητης ϫε· ⲛⲧⲁⲕ ⲛⲓⲙ ⲉⲕϫⲱ ⲛⲛⲁϊ ⲛⲁⲛ ⟨ⲡⲉϫⲉ ⲓⲥ ⲛⲁⲩ ϫⲉ⟩ ⲍⲛ ⲛⲉⲧϫⲱ ⲙⲙⲟⲟⲩ ⲛⲏⲧⲛ ⲛⲧⲉⲧⲛⲉⲓⲙⲉ ⲁⲛ ϫⲉ ⲁⲛⲟⲕ ⲛⲓⲙ ⲁⲗⲗⲁ ⲛⲧⲱⲧⲛ ⲁⲧⲉⲧⲛϣⲱⲡⲉ ⲛⲑⲉ ⲛⲛⲓϊⲟⲩⲇⲁⲓⲟⲥ ϫⲉ ⲥⲉⲙⲉ ⲙⲡϣⲏⲛ ⲥⲉⲙⲟⲥⲧⲉ ⲙⲡⲉϥⲕⲁⲣⲡⲟⲥ ⲁⲩⲱ ⲥⲉⲙⲉ ⲙⲡⲕⲁⲣⲡⲟⲥ ⲥⲉⲙⲟⲥⲧⲉ ⲙⲡϣⲏⲛ.

GThom 43

His disciples said to him, "Who are you to say these things to us?" ⟨Jesus said to them,⟩ "You do not know who I am from what I say to you. Rather, you have become like the Jews, for they love the tree but hate its fruit, or they love the fruit but hate the tree."

GThom 45

ⲡⲉϫⲉ ⲓⲥ ⲙⲁⲩϫⲉⲗⲉ ⲉⲗⲟⲟⲗⲉ ⲉⲃⲟⲗ ⲍⲛ ϣⲟⲛⲧⲉ ⲟⲩⲧⲉ ⲙⲁⲩⲕⲱⲧϥ ⲕⲛⲧⲉ ⲉⲃⲟⲗ ⲍⲛ ⲥⲣϭⲁⲙⲟⲩⲗ ⲙⲁⲩϯ ⲕⲁⲣⲡⲟⲥ ⲅⲁⲣ ⲟⲩⲁⲅⲁⲑⲟⲥ ⲣⲣⲱⲙⲉ ϣⲁϥⲉⲓⲛⲉ ⲛⲟⲩⲁⲅⲁⲑⲟⲛ ⲉⲃⲟⲗ ⲍⲙ ⲡⲉϥⲉⲍⲟ ⲟⲩⲕⲁ[ⲕⲟⲥ] ⲣⲣⲱⲙⲉ ϣⲁϥⲉⲓⲛⲉ ⲛⲍⲛⲡⲟⲛⲏⲣⲟⲛ ⲉⲃⲟⲗ ⲍⲙ ⲡⲉϥⲉⲍⲟ ⲉⲑⲟⲟⲩ ⲉⲧⲍⲛ ⲡⲉϥⲍⲏⲧ ⲁⲩⲱ ⲛϥϫⲱ ⲛⲍⲛⲡⲟⲛⲏⲣⲟⲛ ⲉⲃⲟⲗ ⲅⲁⲣ ⲍⲙ ⲡϩⲟⲩⲟ ⲙⲫⲏⲧ ϣⲁϥⲉⲓⲛⲉ ⲉⲃⲟⲗ ⲛⲍⲛⲡⲟⲛⲏⲣⲟⲛ.

GThom 45

Jesus said, "Grapes are not harvested from thorn trees, nor are figs gathered from thistles, for they yield no fruit. A good person brings forth good from the storehouse, while a bad person brings forth evil things from the corrupt storehouse in the heart, and says evil things. For from the abundance of the heart this person brings forth evil things."

Prov 12:14 LXX

14ἀπὸ καρπῶν στόματος ψυχὴ ἀνδρὸς πλησθήσεται ἀγαθῶν, ἀνταπόδομα δὲ χειλέων αὐτοῦ δοθήσεται αὐτῷ.

Prov 12:14 LXX

14From the fruit of his mouth will the soul of a man be filled with good, and the reward of his lips will be given him.

Q 6:43–45

In Q: Most authors, though Harnack (68–69) makes no mention of Q 6:45. Here it appears that Matthew has split up material in Q, using the first part (Q 6:43) in conjunction with his warning against false prophets (Matt 7:15–20) and a second part as a concluding warning to the Beelzebul accusation (12:22–37). He has also repeated and reformulated Q 3:7, 9, using them in 7:19 and again in 12:34. Matthew betrays knowledge of the original connection of Q 6:43 with Q 6:44 in his use of the phrase "by their fruits you shall know them" which he uses twice in Matt 7 (7:16, 20; cf. Q 6:44). He presumably delayed Q 6:44–45 because it has to do with *evil speech* and this cohered well with the emphases in the Beelzebul accusation in which Matthew uses Q and Markan sayings on blasphemy (⇨ S38) and which concludes with a warning about idle words (12:36–37). Easton (Lk 92), Lührmann (54) and Weiss (1907: 96), however, think that these sayings were already a doublet in Q.

While a few take Matt 7:15 to derive from Q (Dupont 1969: 126–27; Moffatt 1918: 197; Weiss 1907: 93; Wellhausen 1911: 57), most think the saying comes from M or from Matthean redaction: Barth 1963: 73 n. 2: πρόβατον is a favorite Matthean word. Beare 1962: 68: The connection of v. 15 with the following is editorial, though v. 15 may be an originally independent saying. Luz Mt: 401: The vocabulary is thoroughly Matthean, e.g., προσέχω ἀπό, ὅστις, ἔνδυμα, πρόβατον. See also Bultmann 1963: 124, 127; Grundmann Mt 229; Kilpatrick 1946: 24, 35; Manson 175–76; Minear 1970: 80; Müller 1908: 47; Polag; Schulz 317; Schweizer, 1974: 126; Strecker 1985: 166.

Matt 7:16a and 7:20 are best regarded as Matthean editorializing, but based on Q 6:44a. Luz (Mt 401) observes that the *inclusio* formed by 7:16a and 7:20 is typical of Matthean style and the plural of "fruit" is Matthean in both vv. 16a and 20. See also Barth 1963: 74; Bultmann 1963: 91; Grundmann Mt 229; Knox 1957: 16; Lambrecht 1985: 192; Minear 1970: 81; Müller 1908: 47; Schulz 316; Schürmann Lk 375; Schweizer 1974: 127–28.

Matt 7:17 is the source of some debate. Harnack (69) conjectures that Luke may have omitted the verse as superfluous. Strecker 1985: 169: Although the negative formulation in v. 18 seems to presuppose v. 16 rather than v. 17, Matthew may nevertheless have found v. 17 at this point. Strecker adduces the similar formulation of Matt 12:33 as support. More, however, are inclined to see Matthean editing: Barth 1963: 74: V. 17 is "a pedantic positive new construction to offset the negative statement in 7:18." Lambrecht 1985: 192; Schmid 249: V. 17 is a transitional phrase which presupposes the negative formulation of the saying in v.18 (Q 6:43); Schulz 318; Schürmann Lk 375; Steinhauser 1981: 314.

In respect to Matt 12:33ab, while the vocabulary is plainly influenced by Q 6:43, and while the use of "fruit" in the singular agrees with Luke 6:43 against Matt 7:18 (and 7:16a, 17, 20), Matt 12:33 is a redactional reformulation used to introduce 12:34–35. See Bultmann 1963: 52; Harnack 69, 130; Grundmann Mt 331; Polag 36–37; Schenk 32; Schulz 316; Schürmann Lk 375–76; Steinhauser 1981: 314–15.

Matt 7:15–20

[¹⁵ Beware of false prophets, who come to you in sheep's clothing but inside are rapacious wolves.]

[¹⁶ From their fruits you will know them.]

Are grapes gathered from thorns, or figs from thistles?

[¹⁷ So, every healthy tree bears good fruit, but the rotten tree bears bad fruit.]

¹⁸ A healthy tree cannot bear bad fruit, nor can a rotten tree bear good fruit.

> [¹⁹ Every tree that does not bear good fruit is cut down and thrown into the fire.]

[²⁰ Therefore from their fruits you will know them.]

Luke 6:43–45

⁴⁴ for each tree is known by its own fruit. For figs are not gathered from thorns, nor are grapes picked from a bramble bush.

⁴³ For no healthy tree bears bad fruit, nor again does an unhealthy tree bear good fruit;

Matt 12:33–35

[³³ Either suppose that the tree is good, and its fruit good; or suppose that the tree is bad, and its fruit bad;]

for by its fruit the tree is known.

> [³⁴ You brood of vipers! how can you speak good, if you are evil?]

For from what overflows the heart the mouth speaks.

³⁵ The good man out of his good treasure brings forth good, and the evil man out of his evil treasure brings forth evil.

⁴⁴ for each tree is known by its own fruit. For figs are not gathered from thorns, nor are grapes picked from a bramble bush.

⁴⁵ The good man out of the good treasure of his heart produces good, and the evil man out of his evil treasure produces evil; for from what overflows the heart his mouth speaks.

Matt 7:21–27

²¹Οὐ πᾶς ὁ λέγων μοι· κύριε κύριε, εἰσελεύσεται εἰς τὴν βασιλείαν τῶν οὐρανῶν, ἀλλ᾽ ὁ ποιῶν τὸ θέλημα τοῦ πατρός μου τοῦ ἐν τοῖς οὐρανοῖς.

²²πολλοὶ ἐροῦσίν μοι ἐν ἐκείνῃ τῇ ἡμέρᾳ· κύριε κύριε, οὐ τῷ σῷ ὀνόματι ἐπροφητεύσαμεν, καὶ τῷ σῷ ὀνόματι δαιμόνια ἐξεβάλομεν, καὶ τῷ σῷ ὀνόματι δυνάμεις πολλὰς ἐποιήσαμεν; ²³ καὶ τότε ὁμολογήσω αὐτοῖς ὅτι οὐδέποτε ἔγνων ὑμᾶς· ἀποχωρεῖτε ἀπ᾽ ἐμοῦ οἱ ἐργαζόμενοι τὴν ἀνομίαν.

²⁴Πᾶς οὖν ὅστις ἀκούει μου τοὺς λόγους τούτους καὶ ποιεῖ αὐτούς, ὁμοιωθήσεται ἀνδρὶ φρονίμῳ, ὅστις ᾠκοδόμησεν αὐτοῦ τὴν οἰκίαν ἐπὶ τὴν πέτραν· ²⁵ καὶ κατέβη ἡ βροχὴ καὶ ἦλθον οἱ ποταμοὶ καὶ ἔπνευσαν οἱ ἄνεμοι καὶ προσέπεσαν τῇ οἰκίᾳ ἐκείνῃ, καὶ οὐκ ἔπεσεν, τεθεμελίωτο γὰρ ἐπὶ τὴν πέτραν. ²⁶καὶ πᾶς ὁ ἀκούων μου τοὺς λόγους τούτους καὶ μὴ ποιῶν αὐτοὺς ὁμοιωθήσεται ἀνδρὶ μωρῷ, ὅστις ᾠκοδόμησεν αὐτοῦ τὴν οἰκίαν ἐπὶ τὴν ἄμμον· ²⁷ καὶ κατέβη ἡ βροχὴ καὶ ἦλθον οἱ ποταμοὶ καὶ ἔπνευσαν οἱ ἄνεμοι καὶ προσέκοψαν τῇ οἰκίᾳ ἐκείνῃ, καὶ ἔπεσεν, καὶ ἦν ἡ πτῶσις αὐτῆς μεγάλη.

κύριε ➪ Matt 8:8 [S15]
λόγος ➪ Matt 8:8 [S15]
ποιέω ➪ Matt 8:9 [S15]
ἄνεμος ➪ Matt 11:7 [S17]

Luke 6:46, 47–49

⁴⁶Τί δέ με καλεῖτε· κύριε κύριε καὶ οὐ ποιεῖτε ἃ λέγω;

➪ Q 13:26–27 [S50]

⁴⁷Πᾶς ὁ ἐρχόμενος πρός με καὶ ἀκούων μου τῶν λόγων καὶ ποιῶν αὐτούς, ὑποδείξω ὑμῖν τίνι ἐστὶν ὅμοιος· ⁴⁸ ὅμοιός ἐστιν ἀνθρώπῳ οἰκοδομοῦντι οἰκίαν ὃς ἔσκαψεν καὶ ἐβάθυνεν καὶ ἔθηκεν θεμέλιον ἐπὶ τὴν πέτραν· πλημμύρης δὲ γενομένης προσέρηξεν ὁ ποταμὸς τῇ οἰκίᾳ ἐκείνῃ, καὶ οὐκ ἴσχυσεν σαλεῦσαι αὐτὴν διὰ τὸ καλῶς οἰκοδομῆσθαι αὐτήν. ⁴⁹ὁ δὲ ἀκούσας καὶ μὴ ποιήσας ὅμοιός ἐστιν ἀνθρώπῳ οἰκοδομήσαντι οἰκίαν ἐπὶ τὴν γῆν χωρὶς θεμελίου, ᾗ προσέρηξεν ὁ ποταμός, καὶ εὐθὺς συνέπεσεν καὶ ἐγένετο τὸ ῥῆγμα τῆς οἰκίας ἐκείνης μέγα.

κύριε ➪ Luke 7:6 [S15]
λόγος ➪ Luke 7:7 [S15]
ποιέω ➪ Luke 7:8 [S15]
σαλεύω ➪ Luke 7:24 [S17]

Notes

Q 6:46

In Q: Most authors. Harnack 71: "The common source perhaps lies far in the background of time, and we may not with absolute certainty claim the verse for Q."

Matt 7:22–23 (= Q 13:26–27)

While most assume that the Matthean placement is secondary, Strecker (1985: 172, hesitantly) proposes that if 2 Clem 4:5 shows no influence of the text of Matthew, it reflects a pre–Matthean juxtaposition of Matt 7:21 and 7:22–23.

Q 6:47–49

In Q: Most authors.

Matt 7:21–27

21 Not every one who says to me, 'Lord, Lord,' will enter the kingdom of heaven, but the one who does the will of my Father who is in heaven. 22 On that day many will say to me, 'Lord, Lord, did we not prophesy in your name, and exorcise demons in your name, and perform many miracles in your name?' 23 And then will I declare to them, 'I never knew you; depart from me, you who act against the law.'

24 Therefore every one who hears these words of mine and practices them will be like a wise man who built his house upon the rock; 25 and the rain fell, and the torrents came, and the winds blew and beat upon that house, and it did not fall, for it had been founded on the rock. 26 And every one who hears these words of mine and does not practice them will be like a foolish man who built his house upon the sand; 27 and the rain fell, and the torrents came, and the wind blew and beat against that house, and it fell; and its fall was great.

Luke 6:46–49

46 Why do you call me 'Lord, Lord,' and not do what I tell you?

47 Every one who comes to me and hears my words and practices them, I will show you what he is like: 48 he is like a person building a house, who dug down deep, and laid the foundation upon the rock; and when a flood came, the torrent broke against that house, and could not shake it, since it was well built. 49 But he who hears and does not practice them is like a person who built a house on the ground without a foundation. The torrent broke against it, and immediately it collapsed, and the ruin of that house was great.

Parallels

PEger 2 fr. 2 recto

[Παραγε]νόμενοι πρὸς αὐτὸν ἐξ[ετασ]τικῶς ἐπείραζον αὐτὸν λ[έγοντες] διδάσκαλε ᾿Ιη(σοῦ) οἴδαμεν ὅτι [ἀπὸ θ(εο)ῦ] ἐλήλυθας ἃ γὰρ ποιεῖς μα[ρτυρεῖ] ὑπὲρ το[ὺ]ς προφ(ήτ)ας πάντας. [εἰπὲ οὖν] ἡμεῖν· ἐξὸν βα(σι)λεῦσ[ιν ἀποδοῦ]ναι τὰ ἀν[ή]κοντα τῃ ἀρχῃ ἀπ[οδῶμεν αὐ]τοῖς ἢ μ[ή]; ὁ δὲ ᾿Ιη(σοῦς) εἰδὼς [τὴν διάνοιαν [αὐτ]ῶν ἐμβρειμ[ησάμενος] εἶπεν α[ὐτοῖς]· τί με καλεῖτ[ε τῷ στό]ματι ὑμ[ῶν δι]δάσκαλον· μ[ὴ ἀκού]οντες ὃ [λ]έγω· καλῶς ῾Η[σ(αΐ)ας περὶ ὑ]μῶν ἐπ[ρο]φ(ήτευ)σεν εἰπών· ὁ [λαὸς οὗ]τος τοῖς [χεί]λεσιν αὐτ[ῶν τιμῶσιν] με ἡ [δὲ καρδί]α αὐτῶ[ν πόρρω ἀπέ]χει ἀπ᾿ ἐ[μοῦ μ]άτη[ν με σέβονται ἐντάλ]ματα . . .

PEger 2 fr. 2 recto

. . . coming to him began to tempt him with a question, saying, "Master Jesus, we know that you are come from God, for the things which you do testify above all the prophets. Tell us therefore: Is it lawful [? to render] unto kings that which pertains to their rule? [Shall we render unto them], or not?" But Jesus, knowing their thought, being moved with indignation, said to them, "Why do you call me with your mouth teacher when you do not hear what I say? Well did Isaiah prophesy of you, saying, 'This people honours me with their lips, but their heart is far from me. In vain do they worship me, [teaching as their doctrines the] precepts [of men] . . .'"

2 Clem 4:1–2, 4–5

1 Μὴ μόνον οὖν αὐτὸν καλῶμεν κύριον· οὐ γὰρ τοῦτο σώσει ἡμᾶς. 2 λέγει γάρ· οὐ πᾶς ὁ λέγων μοι· Κύριε, κύριε, σωθήσεται, ἀλλ᾽ ὁ ποιῶν τὴν δικαιοσύνην.

4 καὶ οὐ δεῖ ἡμᾶς φοβεῖσθαι τοὺς ἀνθρώπους μᾶλλον, ἀλλὰ τὸν θεόν. 5 διὰ τοῦτο, ταῦτα ὑμῶν πρασσόντων, εἶπεν ὁ κύριος· ἐὰν ἦτε μετ᾽ ἐμοῦ συνηγμένοι ἐν τῷ κόλπῳ μου καὶ μὴ ποιῆτε τὰς ἐντολάς μου, ἀποβαλῶ ὑμᾶς καὶ ἐρῶ ὑμῖν· ὑπάγετε ἀπ᾽ ἐμοῦ, οὐκ οἶδα ὑμᾶς, πόθεν ἐστέ, ἐργάται ἀνομίας.

2 Clem 4:1–2, 4–5

1 Let us, then, not merely call him Lord, for this will not save us. 2 For he says, "Not everyone that says to me Lord, Lord, shall be saved, but he that does righteousness."

4 And we must not fear men rather than God. 5 For this reason, if you do these things, the Lord said, "If you are gathered together with me in my bosom, and do not my commandments, I will cast you out, and will say to you, 'Depart from me, I know not whence you are, you workers of iniquity.'"

Matt 7:28–29; 8:5–13

⟨²⁸Καὶ ἐγένετο ὅτε ἐτέλεσεν ὁ ᾽Ιησοῦς τοὺς λόγους τούτους, ἐξεπλήσσοντο οἱ ὄχλοι ἐπὶ τῇ διδαχῇ αὐτοῦ·⟩

[²⁹ἦν γὰρ διδάσκων αὐτοὺς ὡς ἐξουσίαν ἔχων καὶ οὐχ ὡς οἱ γραμματεῖς αὐτῶν.]

⁵Εἰσελθόντος δὲ αὐτοῦ **εἰς Καφαρναοὺμ** προσῆλθεν αὐτῷ **ἑκατόνταρχος** παρακαλῶν **αὐτὸν** ⁶καὶ λέγων· κύριε, ὁ παῖς μου βέβληται ἐν τῇ οἰκίᾳ παραλυτικός, δεινῶς βασανιζόμενος.

⁷καὶ λέγει αὐτῷ· ἐγὼ **ἐλθὼν** θεραπεύσω αὐτόν.

⁸καὶ ἀποκριθεὶς ὁ **ἑκατόνταρχος** ἔφη·
κύριε   **οὐκ   εἰμὶ ἱκανὸς ἵνα
μου ὑπὸ τὴν στέγην εἰσέλθῃς**

ἀλλὰ **μόνον εἰπὲ λόγῳ, καὶ ἰαθήσεται ὁ παῖς μου.**
⁹**καὶ γὰρ ἐγὼ ἄνθρωπός εἰμι ὑπὸ ἐξουσίαν,**
                    **ἔχων ὑπ᾽ ἐμαυτὸν στρατιώτας,
καὶ λέγω τούτῳ· πορεύθητι, καὶ πορεύεται,
καὶ ἄλλῳ· ἔρχου, καὶ ἔρχεται, καὶ τῷ δούλῳ
μου· ποίησον τοῦτο, καὶ ποιεῖ.**
¹⁰**ἀκούσας δὲ   ὁ ᾽Ιησοῦς ἐθαύμασεν
καὶ εἶπεν** τοῖς ἀκολουθοῦσιν·
ἀμὴν λέγω ὑμῖν, παρ᾽ οὐδενὶ **τοσαύτην πίστιν
ἐν τῷ ᾽Ισραὴλ εὗρον.**

¹¹λέγω δὲ ὑμῖν ὅτι πολλοὶ ἀπὸ ἀνατολῶν καὶ δυσμῶν ἥξουσιν καὶ ἀνακλιθήσονται μετὰ ᾽Αβραὰμ καὶ ᾽Ισαὰκ καὶ ᾽Ιακὼβ ἐν τῇ βασιλείᾳ τῶν οὐρανῶν, ¹² οἱ δὲ υἱοὶ τῆς βασιλείας ἐκβληθήσονται εἰς τὸ σκότος τὸ ἐξώτερον· ἐκεῖ ἔσται ὁ κλαυθμὸς καὶ ὁ βρυγμὸς τῶν ὀδόντων. ¹³καὶ εἶπεν ὁ ᾽Ιησοῦς τῷ ἑκατοντάρχῃ· ὕπαγε, ὡς ἐπίστευσας γενηθήτω σοι. καὶ ἰάθη ὁ παῖς [αὐτοῦ] ἐν τῇ ὥρᾳ ἐκείνῃ.

Luke 7:1–10

⟨¹᾽Επειδὴ ἐπλήρωσεν πάντα τὰ ῥήματα αὐτοῦ εἰς τὰς ἀκοὰς τοῦ λαοῦ⟩,

εἰσῆλθεν **εἰς Καφαρναούμ.**
²῾**Εκατοντάρχου** δέ τινος δοῦλος κακῶς ἔχων ἤμελλεν τελευτᾶν, ὃς ἦν αὐτῷ ἔντιμος.

³ἀκούσας δὲ περὶ τοῦ ᾽Ιησοῦ ἀπέστειλεν πρὸς αὐτὸν πρεσβυτέρους τῶν ᾽Ιουδαίων ἐρωτῶν αὐτὸν ὅπως **ἐλθὼν** διασώσῃ τὸν δοῦλον αὐτοῦ.
⁴οἱ δὲ παραγενόμενοι πρὸς τὸν ᾽Ιησοῦν παρεκάλουν **αὐτὸν** σπουδαίως λέγοντες ὅτι ἄξιός ἐστιν ᾧ παρέξῃ τοῦτο.
⁵ἀγαπᾷ γὰρ τὸ ἔθνος ἡμῶν καὶ τὴν συναγωγὴν αὐτὸς ᾠκοδόμησεν ἡμῖν.
⁶ὁ δὲ ᾽Ιησοῦς ἐπορεύετο σὺν αὐτοῖς. ἤδη δὲ αὐτοῦ οὐ μακρὰν ἀπέχοντος ἀπὸ τῆς οἰκίας ἔπεμψεν φίλους ὁ **ἑκατοντάρχης** λέγων αὐτῷ·
κύριε, μὴ σκύλλου, **οὐ** γὰρ **ἱκανός εἰμι ἵνα
ὑπὸ τὴν στέγην** μου **εἰσέλθῃς·** ⁷διὸ οὐδὲ ἐμαυτὸν ἠξίωσα πρὸς σὲ ἐλθεῖν·
ἀλλὰ   **εἰπὲ λόγῳ, καὶ ἰαθήτω ὁ παῖς μου.**
⁸**καὶ γὰρ ἐγὼ ἄνθρωπός εἰμι ὑπὸ ἐξουσίαν**
τασσόμενος, **ἔχων ὑπ᾽ ἐμαυτὸν στρατιώτας,
καὶ λέγω τούτῳ· πορεύθητι, καὶ πορεύεται,
καὶ ἄλλῳ· ἔρχου, καὶ ἔρχεται, καὶ τῷ δούλῳ
μου· ποίησον τοῦτο, καὶ ποιεῖ.**
⁹**ἀκούσας δὲ** ταῦτα ὁ ᾽Ιησοῦς **ἐθαύμασεν**
αὐτὸν καὶ στραφεὶς τῷ ἀκολουθοῦντι αὐτῷ ὄχλῳ **εἶπεν·**
λέγω ὑμῖν, οὐδὲ **ἐν τῷ ᾽Ισραὴλ τοσαύτην
πίστιν εὗρον.**

⇨ Q 13:28–29 [S50]

¹⁰**Καὶ** ὑποστρέψαντες εἰς τὸν οἶκον οἱ πεμφθέντες εὗρον τὸν δοῦλον ὑγιαίνοντα.

Mark 1:21–22
²¹Καὶ εἰσπορεύονται εἰς Καφαρναούμ· καὶ εὐθὺς τοῖς σάββασιν εἰσελθὼν εἰς τὴν συναγωγὴν ἐδίδασκεν. ²²καὶ ἐξεπλήσσοντο ἐπὶ τῇ διδαχῇ αὐτοῦ· ἦν γὰρ διδάσκων αὐτοὺς ὡς ἐξουσίαν ἔχων καὶ οὐκ ὡς οἱ γραμματεῖς.

John 4:46–54
⁴⁶Ἦλθεν οὖν πάλιν εἰς τὴν Κανὰ τῆς Γαλιλαίας, ὅπου ἐποίησεν τὸ ὕδωρ οἶνον.
καὶ ἦν τις βασιλικὸς οὗ ὁ υἱὸς ἠσθένει ἐν Καφαρναούμ. ⁴⁷οὗτος ἀκούσας ὅτι Ἰησοῦς ἥκει ἐκ τὴν Ἰουδαίας εἰς τὴν Γαλιλαίαν ἀπῆλθεν πρὸς αὐτὸν καὶ ἠρώτα ἵνα καταβῇ καὶ ἰάσηται αὐτοῦ τὸν υἱόν, ἤμελλεν γὰρ ἀποθνῄσκειν.
⁴⁸εἶπεν οὖν ὁ Ἰησοῦς πρὸς αὐτόν, ἐὰν μὴ σημεῖα καὶ τέρατα ἴδητε, οὐ μὴ πιστεύσητε.
⁴⁹λέγει πρὸς αὐτὸν ὁ βασιλικός, **Κύριε**, κατάβηθι πρὶν ἀποθανεῖν τὸ παιδίον **μου**. ⁵⁰λέγει αὐτῷ ὁ Ἰησοῦς, πορεύου· ὁ υἱός σου ζῇ. ἐπίστευσεν ὁ ἄνθρωπος τῷ λόγῳ ὃν εἶπεν αὐτῷ ὁ Ἰησοῦς καὶ ἐπορεύετο.
⁵¹ἤδη δὲ αὐτοῦ καταβαίνοντος οἱ δοῦλοι αὐτοῦ ὑπήντησαν αὐτῷ λέγοντες ὅτι ὁ παῖς αὐτοῦ ζῇ. ⁵² ἐπύθετο οὖν τὴν ὥραν παρ' αὐτῶν ἐν ᾗ κομψότερον ἔσχεν· εἶπαν οὖν αὐτῷ ὅτι ἐχθὲς ὥραν ἑβδόμην ἀφῆκεν αὐτὸν ὁ πυρετός. ⁵³ἔγνω οὖν ὁ πατὴρ ὅτι [ἐν] ἐκείνῃ τῇ ὥρᾳ ἐν ᾗ εἶπεν αὐτῷ ὁ Ἰησοῦς, ὁ υἱός σου ζῇ, καὶ ἐπίστευσεν αὐτὸς καὶ ἡ οἰκία αὐτοῦ ὅλη. ⁵⁴Τοῦτο [δὲ] πάλιν δεύτερον σημεῖον ἐποίησεν ὁ Ἰησοῦς ἐλθὼν ἐκ τῆς Ἰουδαίας εἰς τὴν Γαλιλαίαν.

Mark 1:21–22
²¹ And they came to Capernaum; and immediately on the sabbath he entered the synagogue and taught. ²² And they were astonished at his teaching, for he was teaching them as one who had authority, and not like the scribes.

John 4:46–54
⁴⁶ Then he came again to Cana in Galilee, where he had made the water wine. And at Capernaum there was a certain royal official whose son was ill. ⁴⁷ When he heard that Jesus had come from Judea to Galilee, he went and begged him to come down and heal his son, for he was about to die.

⁴⁸ Jesus therefore said to him, "Unless you people see signs and wonders you will not believe." ⁴⁹ The royal official said to him, "Sir, come down before my child dies." ⁵⁰ Jesus said to him, "Go; your son will live." The man trusted the word that Jesus spoke to him and went his way. ⁵¹ As he was going down, his servants met him and told him that his son was going to live. ⁵² So he inquired of them the hour when he started to improve, and they said to him, "Yesterday at the seventh hour the fever left him." ⁵³ The father knew that was the hour when Jesus had said to him, "Your son will live"; and he and all his household believed. ⁵⁴ This was now the second sign that Jesus performed on returning to Galilee from Judaea.

Matt 8:7: omit καί: B 700 it sy^s.c.p sa mae bo^mss [NA²⁵] / txt: ℵ C L W Koine Θ 0233 0250 λ φ lat sy^h bo; Cyr [NA²⁶; HG] // 8: αποκριθεις δε ο εκατ.: ℵ* B 33 pc sa [NA²⁵] / txt: ℵ¹ C L W Koine Θ 0233 λ φ lat bo [NA²⁶; HG] // 13: omit αυτου: ℵ B 0250 λ 33 pc latt bo mae [NA²⁵; HG] / txt: C L W Koine Θ φ sy sa? [NA²⁶].

Luke 7:10: δουλον: 𝔭⁷⁵ ℵ B L W λ 700 892* 1241 it sy^s sa bo [NA²⁵.²⁶] / ασθενουντα: D d / ασθενουντα δουλον: A C K X Θ φ 28 33 565 1010 1071 1079 1195 1216 1230 1242 f vg sy^p.h [HG].

⟨Q 7:1a⟩

In Q: Bussmann 56; Easton Lk 94; Harnack 74; Polag 37; Schenk 37; Schmithals Lk 90; Strecker 1985: 179–80; Streeter 1924: 262; Wegner 1985: 102–26 and most critics. The lack of significant agreement between Matthew and Luke, coupled with the presence of Matthean and Lukan elements and Markan influence suggests that both evangelists have thoroughly reworked Q at this point.

Q 7:1–2, 6–10

In Q: Most authors. Manson (63–65) and Schweizer (Mt 137) assign only the dialogue portions (vv. 6b–9) and the terms 'child' and 'centurion from Capharnaum' to Q and suggests that Matthew and Luke independently created the narrative setting. Dibelius (1935: 244–45) and Hawkins (1911: 110, 114, 119) suggest that the story takes for granted that the cure occurred and concludes with Jesus' word to the centurion (Q 7:9).

⟨Q 7:3–5⟩

Substantial disagreement exists in regard to the status of Luke 7:3–5. Several critics includes these verses in Q: Grundmann Mt 249; Hawkins 1909: 158–60, 195; Hunter 124; Marshall Lk 278 (hesitantly); Schmid 253–54; Schürmann Lk 396. The usual grounds for the inclusion of vv. 3–5 in Q are (1) that Matthew's tendency to abbreviate his source materials allows for the possibility that he has done so here, and (2) that the Lukan scenario involving Jewish intermediaries is historically more plausible than Matthew's scene.

Others see the verses as a Lukan addition: Busse 1979: 147–50, 158–59: Vv. 3–5 is Lukan in vocabulary. Luke wishes to project "the moral–religious qualities of those who already believe" into the story. Creed Lk 100: Luke's presentation is artificial and vv. 6b–8 are phrased as if the centurion himself is speaking directly. Fitzmyer Lk 649: Matthew's omission of the double delegation is more difficult to explain than a Lukan addition. Harnack 76; Meyer 1970: 410–11; Polag 39; Schmithals Lk 91–92; Schulz 237–38: The vocabulary of vv. 3–5 is Lukan. Schweizer Lk 86: Luke created vv. 3–5 from oral tradition or assimilated it to Acts 10:2, 5, 22. Wernle 86; Wilson 1973: 12 n. 1: Luke focuses on the faith of the centurion, enhances the parallel with Cornelius (Acts 10), and treats 7:1–10 as a prophetic reception of the Gentiles.

Easton (Lk xviii, 96–97), Müller (1908: 11, 20, 47) and Wegner (1985: 239–54) think that Luke followed a longer L version which had already incorporated Q, while Sato (1984: 62) posits Q^{Lk}.

Matt 8:11–12 (= Q 13:28–29 [S51])

The majority view is that Matthew has relocated this saying to its present location. Contrary opinions are expressed by: Ernst Lk 238: Luke omitted the threatening saying because he was interested in overcoming the opposition between Jew and Gentile. Manson 63, 65 (hesitantly); Wernle 1899: 65, 89: Luke considered such a harsh saying premature in chap. 7.

Matt 7:28–29

⟨²⁸And it happened that when Jesus finished these sayings, the crowds were astonished at his teaching,⟩ [²⁹for he was teaching them as one who had authority, and not like their scribes.]

Matt 8:5–13

⁵When he entered Capernaum, a centurion came forward to him, appealing to him ⁶and saying, "Lord, my serving boy is lying paralyzed at home, suffering dreadfully." ⁷And he said to him, "I will come and heal him."

⁸And the centurion answered him, "Lord, I am not worthy to have you come under my roof; but only speak a word, and my serving boy will be healed. ⁹For I myself am a man under authority, with soldiers under me; and I say to one, 'Go,' and he goes, and to another, 'Come,' and he comes, and to my slave, 'Do this,' and he does it."

¹⁰When Jesus heard him, he marveled, and said to those who followed him, "Amen, I tell you, I have not found such trust in anyone in Israel. ¹¹Now I tell you, many will come from east and west and sit at table with Abraham, Isaac, and Jacob in the kingdom of heaven, ¹²but the sons of the kingdom will be thrown into the outer darkness; out there will be weeping and gnashing of teeth." ¹³And to the centurion Jesus said, "Depart. As you have trusted, may it be done to you." And his serving boy was healed in that hour.

Luke 7:1–10

⟨¹After he had completed all his speech in the hearing of the people⟩

he entered Capernaum. ²Now a centurion had a certain slave who was dear to him, who was sick and at the point of death. ³When he heard about Jesus, he sent to him elders of the Jews, asking him to come and heal his slave. ⁴And when they came to Jesus, they appealed to him earnestly, saying, "He is worthy to have you do this for him, ⁵for he loves our nation, and he himself built the synagogue for us." ⁶So Jesus went with them.
When he was not far from the house, the centurion sent friends, saying to him, "Lord, do not trouble yourself, for I am not worthy to have you come under my roof; ⁷that is why I did not consider myself fit to come to you. But speak a word, and let my serving boy be healed. ⁸For I myself am a man set under authority, with soldiers under me: and I say to one, 'Go,' and he goes; and to another, 'Come,' and he comes; and to my slave, 'Do this,' and he does it."
⁹When Jesus heard this he marveled at him, and turning to the crowd that followed him, he said "I tell you, I have not found such trust in Israel."

¹⁰And when the delegation returned to the house, they found the slave well.

Matt 11:2–6

²Ὁ δὲ ᾽Ιωάννης ἀκούσας ἐν τῷ δεσμωτηρίῳ
τὰ ἔργα τοῦ Χριστοῦ πέμψας διὰ
τῶν μαθητῶν αὐτοῦ ³εἶπεν αὐτῷ·

σὺ εἶ ὁ ἐρχόμενος ἢ ἕτερον προσδοκῶμεν;

⁴καὶ ἀποκριθεὶς ὁ ᾽Ιησοῦς εἶπεν αὐτοῖς·
πορευθέντες ἀπαγγείλατε ᾽Ιωάννῃ ἃ ἀκούετε
καὶ βλέπετε· ⁵τυφλοὶ ἀναβλέπουσιν καὶ
χωλοὶ περιπατοῦσιν, λεπροὶ καθαρίζονται καὶ
κωφοὶ ἀκούουσιν, καὶ νεκροὶ ἐγείρονται καὶ
πτωχοὶ εὐαγγελίζονται· ⁶καὶ μακάριός ἐστιν
ὃς ἐὰν μὴ σκανδαλισθῇ ἐν ἐμοί.

ἔργα ⇨ Matt 11:19 [S20]
᾽Ιωάννης ⇨ Matt 11:7, 11 [S17]

Luke 7:18–23

¹⁸Καὶ ἀπήγγειλαν ᾽Ιωάννῃ οἱ μαθηταὶ αὐτοῦ
περὶ πάντων τούτων. καὶ προσκαλεσάμενος
δύο τινὰς τῶν μαθητῶν αὐτοῦ ὁ ᾽Ιωάννης
¹⁹ἔπεμψεν πρὸς τὸν κύριον λέγων·
σὺ εἶ ὁ ἐρχόμενος ἢ ἄλλον προσδοκῶμεν;
(²⁰παραγενόμενοι δὲ πρὸς αὐτὸν οἱ ἄνδρες
εἶπαν· ᾽Ιωάννης ὁ Βαπτιστὴς ἀπέστειλεν ἡμᾶς
πρὸς σὲ λέγων· σὺ εἶ ὁ ἐρχόμενος ἢ ἄλλον
προσδοκῶμεν;)
[²¹ἐν ἐκείνῃ τῇ ὥρᾳ ἐθεράπευσεν πολλοὺς ἀπὸ νόσων
καὶ μαστίγων καὶ πνευμάτων πονηρῶν καὶ τυφλοῖς
πολλοῖς ἐχαρίσατο βλέπειν.]
²²καὶ ἀποκριθεὶς   εἶπεν αὐτοῖς·
πορευθέντες ἀπαγγείλατε ᾽Ιωάννῃ ἃ εἴδετε
καὶ ἠκούσατε· τυφλοὶ ἀναβλέπουσιν,
χωλοὶ περιπατοῦσιν, λεπροὶ καθαρίζονται καὶ
κωφοὶ ἀκούουσιν,   νεκροὶ ἐγείρονται,
πτωχοὶ εὐαγγελίζονται· ²³καὶ μακάριός
ἐστιν ὃς ἐὰν μὴ σκανδαλισθῇ ἐν ἐμοί.

᾽Ιωάννης ⇨ Luke 7:24, 28 [S17]

Luke 7:22: ηκουσατε οτι: A D R Koine *al* lat syʰ [HG] /
txt: 𝔓⁷⁵ ℵ B C L W Θ λ φ 700 892 1241 1424 saᵐˢ bo
[NA²⁵·²⁶].

Notes

Q 7:18–19, 22–23

In Q: Most authors. Weiss (1907: 240–41) assigns the
entire Lukan version to L and the Matthean to Q.

(Q 7:20)

While there is a relatively strong consensus that Luke
7:21 is redactional, opinion is divided in regard to 7:20,
with a number of critics ascribing it to Q: Easton Lk 101;
Lührmann 26; Manson 66; Marshall Lk 290; Schmid 283;
Schürmann Lk 410; Vassiliadis 1978: 72. The usual
support for this assertion derives from Matthew's
tendency to abbreviate his source material, especially
narrative portions. Schürmann adds that the repetition of
v. 20 is un-Lukan.

On the other hand, many treat both 7:20 and 7:21 as

Lukan: Bultmann 1963: 23; Dibelius 1911: 33; Fitzmyer
Lk 663; Harnack 132; Hawkins 1911: 114; Hoffmann
193: The repetition of John's charge may be Lukan. Both
verses contain Lukan vocabulary. Jacobson 71; Müller
1908: 13; Polag 40–41; Schenk 40; Schmithals Lk 94;
Schönle 1982: 38–39: Since Matt 11:2b contains no
Matthean vocabulary, while Luke 7:18–20 reflects Lukan
vocabulary and style, it is reasonable to assume that Luke
has expanded Q/Matt 11:2b. Schulz 191–92: Luke's
version is a novelistic expansion containing typically
Lukan vocabulary. Streeter 1924: 273; Vögtle 1971b: 220:
Luke underlines that the two disciples are eye-witnesses
by placing them at the scene of the healings performed in
v. 21. The focus on seeing and hearing is clearly a Lukan
interest. Wink 1968: 24.

Matt 11:2–6

²Now when John heard in prison about the works of the Christ, he sent word by his disciples ³and said to him, "Are you the one who is to come, or should we expect someone else?"

⁴And Jesus answered them, "Go and tell John what you hear and see: ⁵the blind recover their sight and the lame walk, lepers are cleansed and the deaf hear, and the dead are raised, and the poor are given good news. ⁶And whoever is not offended by me is blessed."

Luke 7:18–23

¹⁸And the disciples of John told him of all these things. ¹⁹And John, summoning two of his disciples, sent them to the Lord, saying, "Are you the one who is to come, or should we expect another?"
(²⁰When the men had come to him, they said, "John the Baptist sent us to you, saying, 'Are you the one who is to come, or should we expect another?'")
[²¹In that hour he cured many of diseases and afflictions and evil spirits, and to many who were blind he granted sight.]
²²And he answered them, "Go and tell John what you have seen and heard: the blind recover their sight, the lame walk, lepers are cleansed, and the deaf hear, the dead are raised up, the poor are given good news. ²³And whoever is not offended by me is blessed."

Parallels

Isa 26:19 LXX

¹⁹ἀναστήσονται οἱ νεκροί, καὶ ἐγερθήσονται οἱ ἐν τοῖς μνημείοις, καὶ εὐφρανθήσονται οἱ ἐν τῇ γῇ· ἡ γὰρ δρόσος ἡ παρὰ σοῦ ἴαμα αὐτοῖς ἐστιν, ἡ δὲ γῆ τῶν ἀσεβῶν πεσεῖται.

Isa 26:19 LXX

¹⁹The dead shall rise and those in the tombs shall be raised and those on the earth shall rejoice. For your course is healing for them, but the land of the impious will fall.

Isa 29:18–19 LXX

¹⁸καὶ ἀκούσονται ἐν τῇ ἡμέρᾳ ἐκείνῃ κωφοὶ λόγους βιβλίου, καὶ οἱ ἐν τῷ σκότει καὶ οἱ ἐν τῇ ὁμίχλῃ ὀφθαλμοὶ τυφλῶν βλέψονται· ¹⁹καὶ ἀγαλλιάσονται πτωχοὶ διὰ κύριον ἐν εὐφροσύνῃ, καὶ οἱ ἀπηλπισμένοι τῶν ἀνθρώπων ἐμπλησθήσονται εὐφροσύνης.

Isa 29:18–19 LXX

¹⁸And in that day the deaf shall hear the words of a book and those who are in darkness and the misted eyes of the blind will see. ¹⁹And the poor will rejoice in the Lord and those who despair will be filled with joy.

Isa 35:5–6 LXX

⁵τότε ἀνοιχθήσονται ὀφθαλμοὶ τυφλῶν, καὶ ὦτα κωφῶν ἀκούσονται. ⁶τότε ἁλεῖται ὡς ἔλαφος ὁ χωλός, καὶ τρανὴ ἔσται γλῶσσα μογιλάλων, ὅτι ἐρράγη ἐν τῇ ἐρήμῳ ὕδωρ καὶ φάραγξ ἐν γῇ διψώσῃ.

Isa 35:5–6 LXX

⁵Then the eyes of the blind will be opened and the ears of the deaf will hear. ⁶Then the lame man shall leap like a deer and the tongue of the dumb will be clear. For water broke forth in the desert and a gully in the thirsty land.

Isa 42:6–7 LXX

⁶ἐγὼ κύριος ὁ θεὸς ἐκάλεσά σε ἐν δικαιοσύνῃ καὶ κρατήσω τῆς χειρός σου καὶ ἐνισχύσω σε καὶ ἔδωκά σε εἰς διαθήκην γένους, εἰς φῶς ἐθνῶν ⁷ἀνοῖξαι ὀφθαλμοὺς τυφλῶν, ἐξαγαγεῖν ἐκ δεσμῶν δεδεμένους καὶ ἐξ οἴκου φυλακῆς καθημένους ἐν σκότει.

Isa 42:6–7 LXX

⁶I the Lord God called you in righteousness and I will hold your hand and strengthen you. I gave you as a covenant for the people, as a light to the nations, ⁷to open the eyes of the blind, to bring out prisoners from the dungeons and from the prison those who sit in darkness.

Isa 61:1 LXX

¹Πνεῦμα κυρίου ἐπ᾽ ἐμέ, οὗ εἵνεκεν ἔχρισέν με· εὐαγγελίσασθαι πτωχοῖς ἀπέσταλκέν με, ἰάσασθαι τοὺς συντετριμμένους τῇ καρδίᾳ, κηρύξαι αἰχμαλώτοις ἄφεσιν καὶ τυφλοῖς ἀνάβλεψιν.

Isa 61:1 LXX

¹The spirit of the Lord is upon me, because he has anointed me. He has sent me to preach good news to the poor, to heal those whose hearts are broken, to proclaim release to captives and sight to the blind.

Matt 11:7–11

⁷Τούτων δὲ πορευομένων ἤρξατο ὁ Ἰησοῦς
λέγειν τοῖς ὄχλοις περὶ Ἰωάννου·
τί ἐξήλθατε εἰς τὴν ἔρημον θεάσασθαι;
κάλαμον ὑπὸ ἀνέμου σαλευόμενον; ⁸ἀλλὰ τί
ἐξήλθατε ἰδεῖν; ἄνθρωπον ἐν μαλακοῖς
ἠμφιεσμένον; ἰδοὺ οἱ τὰ μαλακὰ
φοροῦντες   ἐν τοῖς οἴκοις τῶν
βασιλέων εἰσίν. ⁹ἀλλὰ τί ἐξήλθατε ἰδεῖν;
προφήτην; ναί, λέγω ὑμῖν, καὶ περισσότερον προφήτου.
¹⁰οὗτός ἐστιν περὶ οὗ γέγραπται· ἰδοὺ ἐγὼ
ἀποστέλλω τὸν ἄγγελόν μου πρὸ προσώπου σου,
ὃς κατασκευάσει τὴν ὁδόν σου ἔμπροσθέν σου.
¹¹ἀμὴν λέγω ὑμῖν· οὐκ ἐγήγερται ἐν γεννητοῖς
γυναικῶν μείζων Ἰωάννου τοῦ Βαπτιστοῦ·
ὁ δὲ μικρότερος ἐν τῇ βασιλείᾳ
τῶν οὐρανῶν μείζων αὐτοῦ ἐστιν.

προφήτης ⇨ Matt 11:13 [S18]
Ἰωάννης ⇨ Matt 11:12–13, 18 [S18, 20]
βαπτιστής ⇨ Matt 11:12 [S18]; Luke 7:33 [S20]
βασιλεία ⇨ Matt 11:12 [S18]

Matt 11:8: omit ειϲιν: ℵ* B [NA²⁵] / txt: ℵ² C D L W Z
Koine Θ λ φ *pl* [NA²⁶; HG] // 9: εξηλθατε ιδειν προφητην
(Luke): ℵ¹ B* C D L Koine Θ λ φ latt sy sa [NA²⁶] /
εξηλθατε προφητην ιδειν: ℵ* B¹ W Z 892 *pc* bo; Or [NA²⁵;
HG].

Luke 7:24–28

²⁴Ἀπελθόντων δὲ τῶν ἀγγέλων Ἰωάννου
ἤρξατο λέγειν πρὸς τοὺς ὄχλους περὶ Ἰωάννου·
τί ἐξήλθατε εἰς τὴν ἔρημον θεάσασθαι;
κάλαμον ὑπὸ ἀνέμου σαλευόμενον; ²⁵ἀλλὰ τί
ἐξήλθατε ἰδεῖν; ἄνθρωπον ἐν μαλακοῖς
ἱματίοις ἠμφιεσμένον; ἰδοὺ οἱ ἐν ἱματισμῷ
ἐνδόξῳ καὶ τρυφῇ ὑπάρχοντες ἐν τοῖς
βασιλείοις εἰσίν. ²⁶ἀλλὰ τί ἐξήλθατε ἰδεῖν;
προφήτην; ναί, λέγω ὑμῖν, καὶ περισσότερον προφήτου.
²⁷οὗτός ἐστιν περὶ οὗ γέγραπται· ἰδοὺ
ἀποστέλλω τὸν ἄγγελόν μου πρὸ προσώπου σου,
ὃς κατασκευάσει τὴν ὁδόν σου ἔμπροσθέν σου.
²⁸   λέγω ὑμῖν· μείζων ἐν γεννητοῖς
γυναικῶν Ἰωάννου οὐδείς ἐστιν·
              ὁ δὲ μικρότερος ἐν τῇ βασιλείᾳ
τοῦ θεοῦ μείζων αὐτοῦ ἐστιν.

προφήτης ⇨ Luke 16:16 [S18]
Ἰωάννης ⇨ Luke 16:16; 7:29, 33 [S18, 19, 20]
βασιλεία ⇨ Luke 16:16 [S18]

Luke 7:26: εξελθατε: 𝔓⁷⁵ ℵ B D L Ξ φ 565 1241 1424
[NA²⁵·²⁶] / εξεληλυθατε: A W Koine Θ Ψ; Or [HG] // 28:
προφητης Ιωαννου: A Koine Θ φ (892) (1241) f q r¹ z vg
sy^{p.h} bo^{pt} [HG] / Ιωαννου: 𝔓⁷⁵ ℵ B L W Ξ λ *pc* sa^{mss} bo^{pt};
Or [NA²⁵·²⁶].

Notes

Q 7:24–28
In Q: Most authors.

Matt 11:7-11

7 When they had gone on their way, Jesus began to speak to the crowds concerning John: "What did you go out to the wilderness to see? A reed shaken by the wind? 8 But what did you go out to see? Someone luxuriously dressed? Behold, those who wear luxurious garments are in the houses of kings. 9 But what did you go out to see? A prophet? Yes, I tell you, and more than a prophet. 10 This is the one about whom it is written,

'Behold I send my messenger before your face,
who will prepare your way before you.'

11 Amen, I tell you, among those born of women there has not arisen one greater than John the Baptist; yet the least in the kingdom of heaven is greater than he."

Luke 7:24-28

24 When the messengers of John had departed, he began to speak to the crowds concerning John: "What did you go out into the wilderness to see? A reed shaken by the wind? 25 But what did you go out to see? A man clothed in luxurious clothing? Behold, those who are gorgeously appareled and live in luxury are in royal palaces. 26 But what did you go out to see? A prophet? Yes, I tell you, and more than a prophet. 27 This is the one about whom it is written,

'Behold, I send my messenger before your face,
who will prepare your way before you.'

28 I tell you, among those born of women none is greater than John; yet the least in the kingdom of God is greater than he."

Parallels

GThom 78

ⲡⲉϫⲉ ⲓ̅ⲥ̅ ϫⲉ ⲉⲧⲃⲉ ⲟⲩ ⲁⲧⲉⲧⲛ̅ⲉⲓ ⲉⲃⲟⲗ ⲉⲧⲥⲱϣⲉ ⲉⲛⲁⲩ ⲉⲩⲕⲁϣ ⲉϥⲕⲓⲙ ⲉ[ⲃⲟⲗ] ϩⲓⲧⲙ̅ ⲡⲧⲏⲩ ⲁⲩⲱ ⲉⲛⲁⲩ ⲉⲩⲣ[ⲱⲙⲉ ⲉϩ]ⲛ̅ϣⲧⲏⲛ ⲉⲩϭⲏⲛ ϩⲓⲱⲱϥ· [. . .]ⲣ̅ⲣⲱⲟⲩ ⲙⲛ̅ ⲛⲉⲧⲙ̅ⲙⲉⲅⲓⲥⲧⲁⲛⲟⲥ ⲛⲁⲉⲓ ⲉⲛ[ϣⲧⲏ]ⲛ [ⲉⲧ]ϭⲏⲛ ϩⲓⲱⲟⲩ ⲁⲩⲱ ⲥⲉ[ⲛⲁ]ϣ ⲥⲟⲩⲛ ⲧⲙⲉ ⲁⲛ.

GThom 78

Jesus said, "Why have you come out to the countryside? To see a reed shaken by the wind? And to see a person dressed in rich clothing, [like your] rulers and your powerful ones? They are dressed in rich [clothing], but they cannot understand truth."

Mal 3:1 LXX

1 ἰδοὺ ἐγὼ ἐξαποστέλλω τὸν ἄγγελόν μου, καὶ ἐπιβλέψεται ὁδὸν πρὸ προσώπου μου.

Mal 3:1 LXX

1 Behold, I send my messenger, and he will look upon the road before my face.

Mal 3:1 MT

הִנְנִי שֹׁלֵחַ מַלְאָכִי וּפִנָּה־דֶרֶךְ לְפָנָי

Mal 3:1 MT

1 Behold, I send my messenger to prepare the way before me.

Exod 23:20 LXX

20 Καὶ ἰδοὺ ἐγὼ ἀποστέλλω τὸν ἄγγελόν μου πρὸ προσώπου σου, ἵνα φυλάξῃ σε ἐν τῇ ὁδῷ.

Exod 23:20 LXX

20 And behold, I send my messenger before your face, to guard you on the way.

Exod 23:20 MT

הִנֵּה אָנֹכִי שֹׁלֵחַ מַלְאָךְ לְפָנֶיךָ לִשְׁמָרְךָ בַּדָּרֶךְ

Exod 23:20 MT

20 Behold, I send an angel [messenger] before you, to guard you on the way.

Mark 1:2

2 Καθὼς γέγραπται ἐν τῷ Ἠσαΐᾳ τῷ προφήτῃ· ἰδοὺ ἀποστέλλω τὸν ἄγγελόν μου πρὸ προσώπου σου, ὃς κατασκευάσει τὴν ὁδόν σου·

Mark 1:2

2 As it is written in Isaiah the prophet,
"Behold, I send my messenger before your face,
who will prepare your way."

GThom 46

ⲡⲉϫⲉ ⲓ̅ⲥ̅ ϫⲉ ϫⲓⲛ ⲁⲇⲁⲙ ϣⲁ ⲓ̈ⲱϩⲁ(ⲛ)ⲛⲏⲥ ⲡⲃⲁⲡⲧⲓⲥⲧⲏⲥ ϩⲛ̅ ⲛ̅ϫⲡⲟ ⲛ̅ⲛ̅ϩⲓⲟⲙⲉ ⲙⲛ̅ ⲡⲉⲧϫⲟⲥⲉ ⲁⲓ̈ⲱϩⲁⲛⲛⲏⲥ ⲡⲃⲁⲡⲧⲓⲥⲧⲏⲥ ϣⲓⲛⲁ ϫⲉ ⲛⲟⲩⲱϭⲡ ⲛ̅ϭⲓ ⲛⲉϥⲃⲁⲗ ⲁⲉⲓϫⲟⲟⲥ ⲇⲉ ϫⲉ ⲡⲉⲧⲛⲁϣⲱⲡⲉ ϩⲛ̅ ⲧⲏⲩⲧⲛ̅ ⲉϥⲟ ⲛ̅ⲕⲟⲩⲉⲓ ϥⲛⲁⲥⲟⲩⲱⲛ ⲧⲙⲛ̅ⲧⲉⲣⲟ ⲁⲩⲱ ϥⲛⲁϫⲓⲥⲉ ⲁⲓ̈ⲱϩⲁⲛⲛⲏⲥ.

GThom 46

Jesus said, "From Adam to John the Baptist, among those born of women, no one is so much greater than John the Baptist that the person's eyes should not be averted (lit.: be broken). But I have said that whoever among you becomes a child will know the kingdom, and will become greater than John."

Matt 11:12–15 ⇨ S61

¹²Ἀπὸ δὲ τῶν ἡμερῶν Ἰωάννου τοῦ
Βαπτιστοῦ ἕως ἄρτι **ἡ βασιλεία τῶν οὐρανῶν**
βιάζεται καὶ βιασταὶ **ἁρπάζουσιν αὐτήν.**
¹³**πάντες** γὰρ **οἱ προφῆται καὶ ὁ νόμος** ἕως Ἰωάννου
ἐπροφήτευσαν·

[¹⁴καὶ εἰ θέλετε δέξασθαι, αὐτός ἐστιν Ἡλίας ὁ
μέλλων ἔρχεσθαι. ¹⁵ὁ ἔχων ὦτα ἀκουέτω].

Ἰωάννης ⇨ Matt 11:18 [S20]
βαπτιστής ⇨ Luke 7:33 [S20]

Luke 16:16 ⇨ S61

¹⁶ᵇἀπὸ τότε

ἡ βασιλεία τοῦ θεοῦ εὐαγγελίζεται
καὶ πᾶς **εἰς αὐτὴν βιάζεται.**
¹⁶ᵃ   ῾Ο **νόμος καὶ οἱ προφῆται** μέχρι Ἰωάννου·

Ἰωάννης ⇨ Luke 7:29, 34 [S19, S20]

Notes

Q 16:16

The majority of authors holds that these verses derive
from Q. The main point of disagreement has to do with
the relative placement of the passage. A number argue
that the Matthean placement is original (i.e., following Q
7:28): Edwards 1982: 264; Harnack 16; Bultmann 1963:
164; Fitzmyer Lk 662 (but see p. 1114!); Jacobson 82–84;
Lührmann 27–28; Müller 1908: 29; Polag 74; Schenk 44;
Schönle 1982: 33; Weiss 1907: 65.

Lührmann observes that while the Lukan setting
betrays obvious Lukan interests, Matthew's own
theological interest is found not in 11:12–13 but in
11:14–15. Hence, he argues, there is no reason to think
that Matthew moved the text. Schönle observes that the
fact that both Matthew and Luke place an additional
saying about the Baptist after Q 7:28 suggests that either
Luke 16:16 // Matt 11:12–13 or Luke 7:29–30 // Matt
21:32 stood here in Q. Since Luke 7:29–30 fits very poorly
with the context of Q 7, it is preferable to assume that Q
16:16 occurred at this point.

Others support Lukan order as original: Bussmann 62;
Chilton 1979: 206–9; Crossan 1983: 345; Dupont 1969:
113–16; Hunter 144; Knox 1957: 99; Manson 68;

Schlosser 1980: 509–10; Schmid 284–85; Schürmann
1968: 130–31; Streeter 1911: 156–57; Trilling 1959: 275–
76; Wilson 1973: 64; Zeller 43.

Since Johannes Weiss (1900: 192) it has been argued
that it is highly unlikely that Luke would have moved Q
16:16 to its current awkward Lukan location had he seen
it in Q in the context of a series of Baptist-related
materials. Luke's context is the "connexio difficilior."
Dupont argues that although the grouping of the three
sayings in Luke is highly artificial, Luke cannot be
credited with this collection since he shows no interest in
questions of the Law. Schürmann argues, further, that
Matt 5:17–20 betrays knowledge of the original Q order
of the sayings (Q 16:16–18). Matthew's τὸν νόμον ἢ τοὺς
προφήτας (5:17) is a reminiscence of Q 16:16; he employs
Q 16:17 at Matt 5:18; and εἰσέλθητε εἰς τὴν βασιλείαν in
5:20 echoes εἰς αὐτὴν βιάζεται in Q 16:16.

Several take the view that both settings are secondary,
or that the original setting is unrecoverable: Easton Lk
103, 249; Hoffmann 51; Kloppenborg 1987: 113–14;
Kümmel 1957: 121–22; Marshall Lk 627; Schmithals Lk
168; Schulz 261; Wink 1968: 20.

Matt 11:12–15

12 From the days of John the Baptist until now the reign of heaven has suffered violence, and the violent have seized it. 13 For all the prophets and the law prophesied until John;

[14 and if you are willing to accept it, he is Elijah who is to come. 15 Let whoever has ears listen.]

Luke 16:16

16b From then the good news of the reign of God is proclaimed, and everybody is trying to enter by force. 16a The law and the prophets were until John.

Parallels

Mark 9:13 ⇨ Matt 11:14–15

13 ἀλλὰ λέγω ὑμῖν ὅτι καὶ Ἠλίας ἐλήλυθεν, καὶ ἐποίησαν αὐτῷ ὅσα ἤθελον, καθὼς γέγραπται ἐπ᾽ αὐτόν.

Matt 17:12–13 ⇨ Matt 11:14–15

12 λέγω δὲ ὑμῖν ὅτι Ἠλίας ἤδη ἦλθεν, καὶ οὐκ ἐπέγνωσαν αὐτόν, ἀλλὰ ἐποίησαν ἐν αὐτῷ ὅσα ἠθέλησαν· οὕτως καὶ ὁ υἱὸς τοῦ ἀνθρώπου μέλλει πάσχειν ὑπ᾽ αὐτῶν. 13 τότε συνῆκαν οἱ μαθηταὶ ὅτι περὶ Ἰωάννου τοῦ βαπτιστοῦ εἶπεν αὐτοῖς.

Mark 9:13

13 But I tell you that Elijah has indeed come, and they did to him whatever they pleased, as it is written of him.

Matt 17:12–13

12 But I tell you that Elijah has already come, and they did not recognize him, but did to him whatever they pleased. So also the Son of man is about to suffer at their hands. 13 Then the disciples understood that he was speaking to them of John the Baptist.

Matt 21:28–32

²⁸Τί δὲ ὑμῖν δοκεῖ; ἄνθρωπος εἶχεν τέκνα δύο. καὶ προσελθὼν τῷ πρώτῳ εἶπεν· τέκνον, ὕπαγε σήμερον ἐργάζου ἐν τῷ ἀμπελῶνι. ²⁹ὁ δὲ ἀποκριθεὶς εἶπεν· οὐ θέλω, ὕστερον δὲ μεταμεληθεὶς ἀπῆλθεν. ³⁰ προσελθὼν δὲ τῷ ἑτέρῳ εἶπεν ὡσαύτως. ὁ δὲ ἀποκριθεὶς εἶπεν· ἐγώ, κύριε, καὶ οὐκ ἀπῆλθεν. ³¹ τίς ἐκ τῶν δύο ἐποίησεν τὸ θέλημα τοῦ πατρός; λέγουσιν· ὁ πρῶτος. λέγει αὐτοῖς ὁ Ἰησοῦς·
ἀμὴν λέγω ὑμῖν ὅτι **οἱ τελῶναι καὶ** αἱ πόρναι προάγουσιν ὑμᾶς εἰς τὴν βασιλείαν τοῦ θεοῦ. ³² ἦλθεν γὰρ Ἰωάννης πρὸς ὑμᾶς ἐν ὁδῷ δικαιοσύνης, καὶ οὐκ ἐπιστεύσατε αὐτῷ, οἱ δὲ τελῶναι καὶ αἱ πόρναι ἐπίστευσαν αὐτῷ· ὑμεῖς δὲ ἰδόντες οὐδὲ μετεμελήθητε ὕστερον τοῦ πιστεῦσαι αὐτῷ.

ἦλθεν γὰρ Ἰωάννης ⇨ Matt 11:18 [S20]
τελῶναι ⇨ Matt 11:19 [S20]

Luke 7:29–30

²⁹Καὶ πᾶς ὁ λαὸς ἀκούσας **καὶ οἱ τελῶναι** ἐδικαίωσαν τὸν θεὸν βαπτισθέντες τὸ βάπτισμα Ἰωάννου· ³⁰οἱ δὲ Φαρισαῖοι καὶ οἱ νομικοὶ τὴν βουλὴν τοῦ θεοῦ ἠθέτησαν εἰς ἑαυτοὺς μὴ βαπτισθέντες ὑπ᾽ αὐτοῦ.

δικαιόω ⇨ Luke 7:35 [S20]
τελῶναι ⇨ Luke 7:34 [S20]

Notes

[Matt 21:28–31a]

Hawkins (1911: 134) and Müller (1908: 10, 48) hold that Matthew preserves Q and that Luke omitted the anti-Pharisaic polemic (Hawkins) or that Luke abbreviated Q/Matt 21:28–32 and created 7:29–30 on the basis of the motifs found there (Müller). Most authors do no consider Matt 21:28–31a to derive from Q.

[Luke 7:29–30]

In Q: Bussmann (60) argues that 7:29–30 coheres well with Q 7:31–35 and suggests that Matthew deleted it when he interpolated Q 16:16. Easton Lk 103: "It is unlikely that Luke would have inserted such an unimportant section" in the middle of a continuous discourse. Edwards (1975: 114–18) lists Luke 7:24–35 as Q but concords no vocabulary from Luke 7:29–30 // Matt 21:31–32. See also idem, 1976: xi, 97 (?); Grundmann Łk 162; Haupt 1913: 53, 258; Hawkins 1911: 118, 126 (with slight probability); Hunter 135; Lührmann 28: Luke 7:29–30 may derive from Q, but Luke is responsible for its present location. Marshall Lk 297 (hesitantly); Schenk 46: Both Matthew and Luke share the same basic contrast of two different reactions to John. Schmithals Lk 97; Schneider Lk 172; Schönle 1982: 32–33 (the Lukan setting is secondary); Schürmann Lk 422 (the Lukan setting is original); Trilling 1959: 275–76 (perhaps); Strecker 1971a: 153 n. 1; Weiss 1907: 65.

Not in Q: Beare 1962: 88; Crossan 1983; Fitzmyer Lk 77, 671; Harnack 118–19: It is not clear that the two pericopae derive from a common source. Both versions reflect the stylistic characteristics of their respective editors, and both exhibit literary dependence on their contexts. Hoffmann 194–95: Although Luke 7:29–30 recalls Matt 21:31–32, it is formulated by Luke himself, and betrays Lukan vocabulary and interests. Manson 70; Polag; Schulz; Zeller 16. Sato (1984: 62–63) posits Q^Lk.

Matt 21:28–32

28 "What do you think? A man had two sons; and going to the first he said, 'Child, go and work in the vineyard today.' 29 But he answered, 'I will not'; but afterward he changed his mind and went. 30 Going to the second he said the same; and he answered, 'I go, sir,' but did not go. 31 Which of the two did the will of his father?" They said, "The first." Jesus said to them, "Amen, I tell you, the tax collectors and the prostitutes are entering the kingdom of God before you. 32 For John came to you on the road of righteousness, and you did not believe him, but the tax collectors and the prostitutes believed him; and even when you saw that, you did not afterward change your mind and believe him."

Luke 7:29–30

29 And when they heard this all the people and the tax collectors vindicated God, having been baptized with the baptism of John; 30 but the Pharisees and the lawyers rejected the purpose of God for themselves, not having been baptized by him.

Matt 11:16–19

¹⁶τίνι δὲ ὁμοιώσω   τὴν
γενεὰν ταύτην; ὁμοία ἐστὶν παιδίοις
καθημένοις ἐν ταῖς ἀγοραῖς ἃ προσφωνοῦντα
τοῖς ἑτέροις ¹⁷λέγουσιν·
ηὐλήσαμεν ὑμῖν καὶ οὐκ ὠρχήσασθε,
ἐθρηνήσαμεν καὶ οὐκ ἐκόψασθε.
¹⁸ἦλθεν γὰρ Ἰωάννης   μήτε
ἐσθίων   μήτε πίνων,   καὶ λέγουσιν·
δαιμόνιον ἔχει. ¹⁹ἦλθεν ὁ υἱὸς τοῦ ἀνθρώπου
ἐσθίων καὶ πίνων, καὶ λέγουσιν· ἰδοὺ
ἄνθρωπος φάγος καὶ οἰνοπότης, τελωνῶν
φίλος καὶ ἁμαρτωλῶν. καὶ ἐδικαιώθη ἡ σοφία
ἀπὸ τῶν ἔργων αὐτῆς.

ὁ υἱὸς τοῦ ἀνθρώπου ⇨ Matt 8:20 [S21]

Luke 7:31–35

³¹τίνι οὖν ὁμοιώσω τοὺς ἀνθρώπους τῆς
γενεᾶς ταύτης καὶ τίνι εἰσὶν ὅμοιοι; ³²ὅμοιοί
εἰσιν παιδίοις τοῖς ἐν ἀγορᾷ καθημένοις καὶ
προσφωνοῦσιν ἀλλήλοις ἃ λέγει·
ηὐλήσαμεν ὑμῖν καὶ οὐκ ὠρχήσασθε,
ἐθρηνήσαμεν καὶ οὐκ ἐκλαύσατε.
³³ἐλήλυθεν γὰρ Ἰωάννης ὁ βαπτιστὴς μὴ
ἐσθίων ἄρτον μήτε πίνων οἶνον, καὶ λέγετε·
δαιμόνιον ἔχει. ³⁴ἐλήλυθεν ὁ υἱὸς τοῦ
ἀνθρώπου ἐσθίων καὶ πίνων, καὶ λέγετε· ἰδοὺ
ἄνθρωπος φάγος καὶ οἰνοπότης, φίλος
τελωνῶν καὶ ἁμαρτωλῶν. ³⁵καὶ ἐδικαιώθη ἡ σοφία
ἀπὸ πάντων τῶν τέκνων αὐτῆς.

ὁ υἱὸς τοῦ ἀνθρώπου ⇨ Luke 9:58 [S21]

Luke 7:32: α λεγει: ℵ* B λ 700* [NA²⁵·²⁶] / και λεγουσιν
(Matt): A Θ Ψ Koine vg syʰ / λεγοντες: D L φ it sa bo
[HG] / λεγοντα: ℵ² W Ξ *pc* // 33: εσθιων αρτον . . . πινων
οινον: 𝔭⁸² ℵ B L W Ξ 1241 f r² z vg syᵖ [NA²⁵·²⁶] / αρτον
εσθιων . . . οινον πινων: A Θ Ψ Koine r¹ syʰ [HG] / omit
αρτον, οινον (Matt): λ φ 700 *pc* it syˢ·ᶜ // 35: παντων των
τεκνων αυτης: (ℵ*) B W φ 579 892 syˢ·ᵖ [NA²⁵·²⁶] / των
τεκνων αυτης παντων: A Koine Ξ [HG] / των τεκνων
αυτης: D L Θ Ψ λ 28 700 1241 *al*; Ir.

Notes

Q 7:31–35
In Q: Most authors.

Matt 11:16–19

¹⁶ Now to what shall I compare this generation? It is like children seated in the agoras and addressing their playmates,

¹⁷ 'We piped to you, and you did not dance;
we sang a dirge, and you did not mourn.'

¹⁸ For John came neither eating nor drinking, and they say, 'He has a demon.' ¹⁹ The Son of man came eating and drinking, and they say, 'Behold, a glutton and a drunk, a friend of tax collectors and sinners!' Yet wisdom is vindicated by her works.

Luke 7:31–35

³¹ To what then shall I compare the people of this generation, and what are they like? ³² They are like children seated in the agora and addressing one another,

'We piped to you, and you did not dance;
we sang a dirge, and you did not weep.'

³³ For John the Baptist has come neither eating bread nor drinking wine; and you say, 'He has a demon.' ³⁴ The Son of man has come eating and drinking; and you say, 'Behold, a glutton and a drunk, a friend of tax collectors and sinners!' ³⁵ Yet wisdom is vindicated by all her children.

Parallels

Sir 4:11

¹¹ ἡ σοφία υἱοὺς αὐτῆς ἀνύψωσεν καὶ ἐπιλαμβάνεται τῶν ζητούντων αὐτήν.

Origen, *Hom. in Jer.* 14.5

Καὶ ἐν τῷ εὐαγγελίῳ ἀναγέγραπται· καὶ ἀποστέλλει ἡ σοφία τὰ τέκνα αὐτῆς.

Sir 4:11

¹¹ Wisdom exalts her sons and gives help to those who seek her.

Origen, *Hom. in Jer.* 14.5

And it is written in the gospel, "And Wisdom sends forth her children."

Matt 8:18–22

[¹⁸᾽Ιδὼν δὲ ὁ ᾽Ιησοῦς ὄχλον περὶ αὐτὸν ἐκέλευσεν ἀπελθεῖν εἰς τὸ πέραν].
¹⁹καὶ προσελθὼν εἷς γραμματεὺς εἶπεν αὐτῷ· διδάσκαλε, ἀκολουθήσω σοι ὅπου ἐὰν ἀπέρχῃ.
²⁰καὶ λέγει αὐτῷ ὁ ᾽Ιησοῦς· αἱ ἀλώπεκες φωλεοὺς ἔχουσιν καὶ τὰ πετεινὰ τοῦ οὐρανοῦ κατασκηνώσεις, ὁ δὲ υἱὸς τοῦ ἀνθρώπου οὐκ ἔχει ποῦ τὴν κεφαλὴν κλίνῃ.
²¹ἕτερος δὲ τῶν μαθητῶν [αὐτοῦ] εἶπεν αὐτῷ· κύριε, ἐπίτρεψόν μοι πρῶτον ἀπελθεῖν καὶ θάψαι τὸν πατέρα μου. ²²ὁ δὲ ᾽Ιησοῦς λέγει αὐτῷ· ἀκολούθει μοι καὶ ἄφες τοὺς νεκροὺς θάψαι τοὺς ἑαυτῶν νεκρούς.

Luke 9:57–62

⁵⁷Καὶ πορευομένων αὐτῶν ἐν τῇ ὁδῷ εἶπέν τις πρὸς αὐτόν· ἀκολουθήσω σοι ὅπου ἐὰν ἀπέρχῃ.
⁵⁸καὶ εἶπεν αὐτῷ ὁ ᾽Ιησοῦς· αἱ ἀλώπεκες φωλεοὺς ἔχουσιν καὶ τὰ πετεινὰ τοῦ οὐρανοῦ κατασκηνώσεις, ὁ δὲ υἱὸς τοῦ ἀνθρώπου οὐκ ἔχει ποῦ τὴν κεφαλὴν κλίνῃ.
⁵⁹Εἶπεν δὲ πρὸς ἕτερον· ἀκολούθει μοι. ὁ δὲ εἶπεν· [κύριε], ἐπίτρεψόν μοι ἀπελθόντι πρῶτον θάψαι τὸν πατέρα μου. ⁶⁰εἶπεν δὲ αὐτῷ· ἄφες τοὺς νεκροὺς θάψαι τοὺς ἑαυτῶν νεκρούς, σὺ δὲ ἀπελθὼν διάγγελε τὴν βασιλείαν τοῦ θεοῦ.
(⁶¹Εἶπεν δὲ καὶ ἕτερος· ἀκολουθήσω σοι, κύριε· πρῶτον δὲ ἐπίτρεψόν μοι ἀποτάξασθαι τοῖς εἰς τὸν οἶκόν μου. ⁶²εἶπεν δὲ [πρὸς αὐτὸν] ὁ ᾽Ιησοῦς· οὐδεὶς ἐπιβαλὼν τὴν χεῖρα ἐπ᾽ ἄροτρον καὶ βλέπων εἰς τὰ ὀπίσω εὔθετός ἐστιν τῇ βασιλείᾳ τοῦ θεοῦ).

βασιλεία τοῦ θεοῦ ⇨ Luke 10:9, 11 [S22]

Matt 8:18: πολλους οχλους: ℵ² C L Koine Θ 0233 φ lat sy [HG] / πολυν οχλον: (W) 1424 *al* sa^{mss} mae / οχλους: ℵ* λ *pc* bo / txt: B sa^{mss} [NA²⁵·²⁶] // 21: μαθητων αυτου: C L W Koine Θ 0250 λ φ lat sy mae bo [NA²⁶] / μαθητων: ℵ B 33 *pc* it sa [NA²⁵; HG].

Luke 9:59: omit κυριε: B* D V *pc* g² sy^s; Or [NA²⁵; HG] / txt (v. 61): 𝔭⁴⁵·⁷⁵ ℵ B² C L W Koine Θ Ξ Ψ λ φ lat sy^{c.p.h} co [NA²⁶] / 62: χειρα αυτου: 𝔭⁴⁵ ℵ A C L W Koine Θ φ *al* [HG] / χειρα: 𝔭⁷⁵ B 0181 λ *pc* a b l q; Cyp Tert Or [NA²⁵·²⁶].

Mark 4:35

³⁵Καὶ λέγει αὐτοῖς ἐν ἐκείνῃ τῇ ἡμέρᾳ ὀψίας γενομένης· διέλθωμεν εἰς τὸ πέραν.

GThom 86

ⲡⲉϫⲉ ⲓ̅ⲥ̅ ϫⲉ [ⲛⲃⲁϣⲟⲣ ⲟⲩⲛ̅ⲧⲁ]ⲩ ⲛ[ⲉⲩⲃⲏⲃ] ⲁⲩⲱ ⲛ̅ϩⲁⲗⲁⲧⲉ ⲟⲩⲛ̅ⲧⲁⲩ ⲙⲙⲁⲩ ⲙ̅[ⲡⲉ]ⲩⲙⲁϩ ⲡϣⲏⲣⲉ ⲇⲉ ⲙ̅ⲡⲣⲱⲙⲉ ⲙⲛ̅ⲧⲁϥ ⲛⲛ[ⲟⲩ]ⲙⲁ ⲉⲣⲓⲕⲉ ⲛ̅ⲧⲉϥⲁⲡⲉ ⲛϥⲙ̅ⲧⲟⲛ ⲙ̅ [ⲙⲟ]ϥ.

1 Kgs 19:19–21 (3 Kgdms LXX)

¹⁹Καὶ ἀπῆλθεν [Ηλιου] ἐκεῖθεν καὶ εὑρίσκει τὸν Ελισαιε υἱὸν Σαφατ, καὶ αὐτὸς ἠροτρία ἐν βουσίν — δώδεκα ζεύγη βοῶν ἐνώπιον αὐτοῦ, καὶ αὐτὸς ἐν τοῖς δώδεκα —, καὶ ἐπῆλθεν ἐπ' αὐτὸν καὶ ἐπέρριψε τὴν μηλωτὴν αὐτοῦ ἐπ' αὐτόν. ²⁰καὶ κατέλιπεν Ελισαιε τὰς βόας καὶ κατέδραμεν ὀπίσω Ηλιου καὶ εἶπεν· καταφιλήσω τὸν πατέρα μου καὶ ἀκολουθήσω ὀπίσω σου· καὶ εἶπεν Ηλιου· ἀνάστρεφε, ὅτι πεποίηκά σοι. ²¹ καὶ ἀνέστρεψεν ἐξόπισθεν αὐτοῦ καὶ ἔλαβεν τὰ ζεύγη τῶν βοῶν καὶ ἔθυσεν καὶ ἥψησεν αὐτὰ ἐν τοῖς σκεύεσι τῶν βοῶν καὶ ἔδωκεν τῷ λαῷ, καὶ ἔφαγον· καὶ ἀνέστη καὶ ἐπορεύθη ὀπίσω Ηλιου καὶ ἐλειτούργει αὐτῷ.

Mark 4:35

³⁵On that day, when evening had come, he said to them, "Let us go across to the other shore."

GThom 86

Jesus said, "[Foxes have their dens] and birds have their nests, but the son of man has no place to lay his head and rest."

1 Kgs 19:19–21 (3 Kgdms LXX)

¹⁹So he [Elijah] departed from there and found Elisha the son of Shaphat, who was ploughing, — with twelve yoke of oxen before him, and he was with the twelve. And he went to him and threw his sheepskin on him. ²⁰And Elisha left the oxen and ran after Elijah, and said, "I shall kiss my father and follow after you." And Elijah said, "Turn back. What have I done to you?" ²¹And he turned back and took the yoke of oxen and slaughtered and boiled them with the oxen's gear and gave it to the people and they ate. And he arose and went after Elijah and ministered to him.

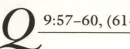

Q 9:57–60
In Q: Most authors.

(Q 9:61–62)
In Q: Crossan 1983: 243, 343; Edwards 1976: xi, 100 (?); Hahn 1969: 80, 119 (from Q[Lk]); Hawkins 1911: 134; Hengel 1981: 4 n. 5; Hunter 136; Kloppenborg 1987: 189–90; Knox 1957: 46; Marshall Lk 408; Polag 43; Schürmann 1975: 132; idem, 1968: 121; Streeter 1911b: 192; Vassiliadis 1978: 67, 70; Wernle 1899: 99.

Of all the Lukan *Sondergut*, this has the strongest probability of deriving from Q since it is found in a Q context, the saying coheres with the preceding sayings formally, and it evinces the same theology of discipleship typical of other Q sayings. Vassiliadis' criteria for the inclusion of *Sondergut* (1978: 67) appear to fit 9:61–62 well. "In the special material of Luke or Matthew which is ... without parallel ..., only those passages which fulfil some of the following conditions seem *likely* to stem from Q: (a) they have to do with components of either a text [already] assigned to Q [by other considerations] ...; (b) they accord with the theological ideas of the Q-Document ...; (c) they accord with the country–life language of Q; (d) they do not show any sign of editorial activity; (e) there are good reasons for the other Synoptist to have

omitted them; (f) they fall into the Q–blocks of the so-called Great Insertion of Luke (ix 51—xviii 14)."

Several reasons for Matthew's omission have been offered: Matthew eliminated the saying because it was liable to be misconstrued by Jewish Christians (Hawkins) or because it added nothing to Matt 8:21–22 (Hengel; Schürmann; Streeter). Knox suggests that Matthew's copy of Q may have been "defective." However, Matthew betrays knowledge of Q/Luke 9:61: ἕτερος δὲ ... εἶπεν (v. 21) is a reminiscence of Q 9:61, and κύριε in Matt 8:21 (diff Luke 9:59 *var. lect.*) echoes Q's κύριε (9:61). Moreover, Marshall observes that since 9:61–62 is so closely parallel to 9:59–60, there is no reason for Luke to have added the saying.

Not in Q: Bussmann 63; Dibelius 1935: 160 n. 1; Fitzmyer Lk 833: It is either Lukan or from L. Harnack 10–11; Hoffmann 251 (from L); Jacobson 131; Lührmann 58 n. 5 (Lukan); Manson 72; Müller 1908: 7; Schenk 48; Schmithals Lk 120: Since it is not clear why Matthew would have omitted the saying, it may not have been in Q. Schulz 435 n. 239; Weiss 1907: 239; Zeller 45, 49. Sato (1984: 16, 63) posits Q[Lk].

Undecided: Easton Lk 156; Schmid 257. Streeter 1924: 289–90: "I now feel less confidence" in the arguments used in Streeter 1911b (see above).

Matt 8:18–22

[18 Now when Jesus saw a crowd around him, he gave orders to go over to the other shore.]
19 And a scribe came up and said to him, "Teacher, I will follow you wherever you go." 20 And Jesus said to him, "Foxes have holes, and birds of the sky have nests; but the Son of man has nowhere to lay his head." 21 Another of his disciples said to him, "Lord, let me first go and bury my father." 22 But Jesus said to him, "Follow me, and leave the dead to bury their own dead."

Luke 9:57–62

57 And as they were going along the road, someone said to him, "I will follow you wherever you go." 58 And Jesus said to him, "Foxes have holes, and birds of the sky have nests; but the Son of man has nowhere to lay his head." 59 To another he said, "Follow me." But he said, "Lord, let me first go and bury my father." 60 But he said to him, "Leave the dead to bury their own dead; but as for you, go and proclaim the reign of God."
(61 Yet another said, "I will follow you, Lord; but first let me say farewell to those at my home." 62 Jesus said to him, "No one who puts his hand to the plow and looks back is fit for the reign of God.")

Matt 9:36—38

[³⁶ Ἰδὼν δὲ τοὺς ὄχλους ἐσπλαγχνίσθη περὶ αὐτῶν, ὅτι ἦσαν ἐσκυλμένοι καὶ ἐρριμμένοι ὡσεὶ πρόβατα μὴ ἔχοντα ποιμένα].

³⁷τότε λέγει τοῖς μαθηταῖς αὐτοῦ·
ὁ μὲν θερισμὸς πολύς, οἱ δὲ ἐργάται ὀλίγοι·
³⁸δεήθητε οὖν τοῦ κυρίου τοῦ θερισμοῦ ὅπως ἐκβάλῃ ἐργάτας εἰς τὸν θερισμὸν αὐτοῦ.

Matt 10:1, 5–6, 16, 9–10a, 11–13, 10b–11, 7–8, 14, 7, 15

[¹Καὶ προσκαλεσάμενος τοὺς δώδεκα μαθητὰς αὐτοῦ ἔδωκεν αὐτοῖς ἐξουσίαν πνευμάτων ἀκαθάρτων ὥστε ἐκβάλλειν αὐτὰ καὶ θεραπεύειν πᾶσαν νόσον καὶ πᾶσαν μαλακίαν. . .].
[⁵Τούτους τοὺς δώδεκα ἀπέστειλεν ὁ Ἰησοῦς παραγγείλας αὐτοῖς λέγων· εἰς ὁδὸν ἐθνῶν μὴ ἀπέλθητε, καὶ εἰς πόλιν Σαμαριτῶν μὴ εἰσέλθητε· ⁶πορεύεσθε δὲ μᾶλλον πρὸς τὰ πρόβατα τὰ ἀπολωλότα οἴκου Ἰσραήλ].
¹⁶   ἰδοὺ ἐγὼ ἀποστέλλω ὑμᾶς ὡς πρόβατα ἐν μέσῳ λύκων·
[γίνεσθε οὖν φρόνιμοι ὡς οἱ ὄφεις καὶ ἀκέραιοι ὡς αἱ περιστεραί].

Luke 10:1–12

[¹Μετὰ δὲ ταῦτα ἀνέδειξεν ὁ κύριος ἑτέρους ἑβδομήκοντα [δύο], καὶ ἀπέστειλεν αὐτοὺς ἀνὰ δύο [δύο] πρὸ προσώπου αὐτοῦ εἰς πᾶσαν πόλιν καὶ τόπον οὗ ἤμελλεν αὐτὸς ἔρχεσθαι].
²ἔλεγεν δὲ πρὸς αὐτούς·
ὁ μὲν θερισμὸς πολύς, οἱ δὲ ἐργάται ὀλίγοι·
δεήθητε οὖν τοῦ κυρίου τοῦ θερισμοῦ ὅπως ἐργάτας ἐκβάλῃ εἰς τὸν θερισμὸν αὐτοῦ.

³ὑπάγετε· ἰδοὺ ἀποστέλλω ὑμᾶς ὡς ἄρνας ἐν μέσῳ λύκων·

Luke 10:1: και ετερους: ℵ A C D W Koine Θ Ψ λ φ lat syᶜ·ʰ; Mcion [HG] / txt: 𝔭⁷⁵ B L 0181 892 1424 *pc* r¹ syˢ·ᵖ [NA²⁵·²⁶] // ανα δυο δυο: B K Θ φ 565 *al* syʰ; Eus [NA²⁶] / ανα δυο: ℵ A C D L W Koine Θ Ψ 0181 λ [NA²⁵; HG].

     Continued on p. 68

Mark 6:34 ⇨ Matt 9:36

³⁴Καὶ ἐξελθὼν εἶδεν πολὺν ὄχλον καὶ ἐσπλαγχίσθη ἐπ' αὐτούς, ὅτι ἦσαν ὡς πρόβατα μὴ ἔχοντα ποιμένα, καὶ ἤρξατο διδάσκειν αὐτοὺς πολλά.

Mark 6:6b–7 ⇨ Luke 10:1

⁶. . .Καὶ περιῆγεν τὰς κώμας κύκλῳ διδάσκων. ⁷καὶ προσκαλεῖται τοὺς δώδεκα, καὶ ἤρξατο αὐτοὺς ἀποστέλλειν δύο δύο, καὶ ἐδίδου αὐτοῖς ἐξουσίαν τῶν πνευμάτων τῶν ἀκαθάρτων·

GThom 73

ⲡⲉϫⲉ ⲓ̅ⲥ̅ ϫⲉ ⲡⲱⲥ ⲙⲉⲛ ⲛⲁϣⲱϥ ⲛⲉⲣⲅⲁⲧⲏⲥ ⲇⲉ ⲥⲟⲃⲕ ⲥⲟⲡ̅ ⲇⲉ ⲙ̅ⲡϫⲟⲉⲓⲥ ϣⲓⲛⲁ ⲉϥⲛⲁⲛⲉϫ ⲉⲣⲅⲁⲧⲏⲥ ⲉⲃⲟⲗ ⲉⲡⲱϩ̅ⲥ̅.

Mark 3:13–15 ⇨ Matt 10:1

¹³Καὶ ἀναβαίνει εἰς τὸ ὄρος καὶ προσκαλεῖται οὓς ἤθελεν αὐτός, καὶ ἀπῆλθον πρὸς αὐτόν. ¹⁴καὶ ἐποίησεν δώδεκα [οὓς καὶ ἀποστόλους ὠνόμασεν] ἵνα ὦσιν μετ' αὐτοῦ καὶ ἵνα ἀποστέλλῃ αὐτοὺς κηρύσσειν ¹⁵καὶ ἔχειν ἐξουσίαν ἐκβάλλειν τὰ δαιμόνια.

2 Clem 5:2

²λέγει γὰρ ὁ κύριος· ἔσεσθε ὡς ἀρνία ἐν μέσῳ λύκων.

GEgy (?) frag. 3 apud Ps-Titum.

. . .ipso exortante domino: Audite me, inquid, quos elegi agnos et nolite timere lupos.

GThom 39b

ⲛ̅ⲧⲱⲧⲛ̅ ⲇⲉ ϣⲱⲡⲉ ⲙ̅ⲫⲣⲟⲛⲓⲙⲟⲥ ⲛ̅ⲑⲉ ⲛ̅ⲛ̅ϩⲟϥ ⲁⲩⲱ ⲛ̅ⲁⲕⲉⲣⲁⲓⲟⲥ ⲛ̅ⲑⲉ ⲛ̅ⲛ̅ϭⲣⲟⲙⲡⲉ.

POxy 655 ii 19–23

[ὑμεῖς] δὲ γεί[νεσθε φρόνι]μοι ὡ[ς ὄφεις καὶ ἀ]κέραι[οι ὡς περιστε]ρα[ί].

Mark 6:34

³⁴And as he went ashore he saw a great crowd, and he had compassion on them, because they were like sheep without a shepherd; and he began to teach them many things.

Mark 6:6b–7

⁶. . . And he made the rounds of the villages teaching. ⁷And he summoned the twelve, and began to send them out two by two, and gave them authority over the unclean spirits.

GThom 73

Jesus said, "The harvest is large but the workers are few, so beg the lord to send out workers to the harvest."

Mark 3:13–15

¹³And he went up the mountain, and summoned those whom he desired; and they came to him. ¹⁴And he appointed twelve, whom he also named apostles, to be with him, and to be sent out to preach ¹⁵and have authority to exorcise demons:

2 Clem 5:2

²For the Lord says, "You shall be as lambs in the midst of wolves."

GEgy (?)

The Lord himself said, "Hear me, you whom I have chosen as lambs, and fear not the wolves."

GThom 39b

. . . As for you, be as clever as snakes and as innocent as doves.

POxy 655 ii 19–23

[You], however, [be as wise as serpents and as] innocent [as doves].

⁹Μὴ κτήσησθε χρυσὸν μηδὲ ἄργυρον μηδὲ χαλκὸν εἰς τὰς ζώνας ὑμῶν,
¹⁰ᵃ **μὴ πήραν** εἰς ὁδὸν μηδὲ δύο χιτῶνας μηδὲ **ὑποδήματα** μηδὲ ῥάβδον·

¹¹ **εἰς ἣν** δ' **ἂν πόλιν ἢ κώμην εἰσέλθητε,** ἐξετάσατε τίς ἐν αὐτῇ ἄξιός ἐστιν· κἀκεῖ μείνατε ἕως ἂν ἐξέλθητε.
¹² εἰσερχόμενοι δὲ εἰς τὴν **οἰκίαν** ἀσπάσασθε αὐτήν·

¹³ καὶ ἐὰν μὲν **ᾖ** ἡ οἰκία ἀξία, ἐλθάτω ἡ εἰρήνη ὑμῶν ἐπ' αὐτήν, ἐὰν δὲ μὴ **ᾖ** ἀξία, ἡ εἰρήνη ὑμῶν πρὸς ὑμᾶς ἐπιστραφήτω.
⇨ Matt 10:11 // Luke 10:8

¹⁰ᵇ ἄξιος γὰρ ὁ ἐργάτης τῆς τροφῆς αὐτοῦ.

¹¹ **εἰς ἣν** δ' **ἂν πόλιν ἢ κώμην εἰσέλθητε,** ἐξετάσατε τίς ἐν αὐτῇ ἄξιός ἐστιν· κἀκεῖ μείνατε ἕως ἂν ἐξέλθητε.

⁴ **μὴ βαστάζετε βαλλάντιον,**

μὴ πήραν,
μὴ **ὑποδήματα,**
καὶ μηδένα κατὰ τὴν ὁδὸν ἀσπάσησθε.
⇨ Luke 10:8

⁵ **εἰς ἣν** δ' **ἂν εἰσέλθητε οἰκίαν,** πρῶτον λέγετε· εἰρήνη τῷ οἴκῳ τούτῳ.
⁶ καὶ ἐὰν ἐκεῖ **ᾖ** υἱὸς εἰρήνης, ἐπαναπαήσεται ἐπ' αὐτὸν ἡ εἰρήνη ὑμῶν· εἰ δὲ μή γε, ἐφ' ὑμᾶς ἀνακάμψει.

⁷ ἐν αὐτῇ δὲ τῇ οἰκίᾳ μένετε, ἐσθίοντες καὶ πίνοντες τὰ παρ' αὐτῶν· ἄξιος γὰρ ὁ ἐργάτης τοῦ μισθοῦ αὐτοῦ. μὴ μεταβαίνετε ἐξ οἰκίας εἰς οἰκίαν. ⁸ καὶ **εἰς ἣν ἂν πόλιν** εἰσέρχεσθε καὶ δέχωνται ὑμᾶς, ἐσθίετε τὰ παρατιθέμενα ὑμῖν,

Continued on p. 70

Luke 10:6: εκει η: 𝔓⁷⁵ B 0181 *pc* it; Or [NA²⁵·²⁶] / η εκει: ℵ A C D L R W Koine Θ Ψ λ φ [HG].

Mark 6:8–13 ⇨ Q 10:4–11

⁸καὶ παρήγγειλεν αὐτοῖς ἵνα μηδὲν αἴρωσιν εἰς ὁδὸν εἰ μὴ ῥάβδον μόνον, μὴ ἄρτον, **μὴ πήραν**, μὴ εἰς τὴν ζώνην χαλκόν, ⁹ἀλλὰ ὑποδεδεμένους σανδάλια καὶ μὴ ἐνδύσησθε δύο χιτῶνας. ¹⁰καὶ ἔλεγεν αὐτοῖς· ὅπου ἐὰν εἰσέλθητε εἰς **οἰκίαν**, ἐκεῖ μένετε ἕως ἂν ἐξέλθητε ἐκεῖθεν. ¹¹καὶ ὃς ἂν τόπος μὴ δέξηται ὑμᾶς μηδὲ ἀκούσωσιν ὑμῶν, ἐκπορευόμενοι ἐκεῖθεν ἐκτινάξατε τὸν χοῦν τὸν ὑποκάτω τῶν ποδῶν ὑμῶν εἰς μαρτύριον αὐτοῖς. ¹²καὶ ἐξελθόντες ἐκήρυξαν ἵνα μετανοῶσιν, ¹³καὶ δαιμόνια πολλὰ ἐξέβαλλον, καὶ ἤλειφον ἐλαίῳ πολλοὺς ἀρρώστους καὶ ἐθεράπευον.

Luke 9:2–6 ⇨ Q 10:4–11

²καὶ ἀπέστειλεν αὐτοὺς κηρύσσειν τὴν βασιλείαν τοῦ θεοῦ καὶ ἰᾶσθαι [τοὺς ἀσθενεῖς]. ³καὶ εἶπεν πρὸς αὐτούς, μηδὲν αἴρετε εἰς τὴν ὁδόν, μήτε ῥάβδον μήτε **πήραν** μήτε ἄρτον μήτε ἀργύριον, μήτε [ἀνὰ] δύο χιτῶνας ἔχειν. ⁴καὶ εἰς ἣν ἂν **οἰκίαν** εἰσέλθητε, ἐκεῖ μένετε καὶ ἐκεῖθεν ἐξέρχεσθε. ⁵καὶ ὅσοι ἂν μὴ δέξωνται ὑμᾶς, ἐξερχόμενοι ἀπὸ τῆς πόλεως ἐκείνης τὸν κονιορτὸν ἀπὸ τῶν ποδῶν ὑμῶν ἀποτινάσσετε εἰς μαρτύριον ἐπ᾽ αὐτούς. ⁶ἐξερχόμενοι δὲ διήρχοντο κατὰ τὰς κώμας εὐαγγελιζόμενοι καὶ θεραπεύοντες πανταχοῦ.

DialSav 53 ⇨ Q 10:7b

ⲡⲉⲭⲁⲥ ⲛ̅ϭⲓ ⲙⲁⲣⲓϩⲁⲙ ϫⲉ ϩⲓⲛⲁⲓ̈ ⲉⲧⲕⲁⲕⲓⲁ ⲙ̅ⲡⲉϩⲟⲟⲩ ⲡⲉϩⲟⲟⲩ ⲁⲩⲱ ⲡⲉⲣⲅⲁⲧⲏⲥ ⲙ̅ⲡϣⲁ ⲛ̅ⲧⲉϥⲧⲣⲟⲫⲏ· ⲁⲩⲱ ⲡⲙⲁⲑⲏⲧⲏⲥ ⲛ̅ϥⲉⲓⲛⲉ ⲙ̅ⲡⲉϥⲥⲁϩ· ⲡⲉⲓ̈ϣⲁϫⲉ ⲁⲥϫⲟⲟϥ ϩⲱⲥ ⲥϩⲓⲙⲉ ⲉⲁⲥⲉⲓⲙⲉ ⲉⲡⲧⲏⲣϥ̅.

1 Tim 5:18 ⇨ Q 10:7b

¹⁸λέγει γὰρ ἡ γραφή· βοῦν ἀλοῶντα οὐ φιμώσεις, καί· ἄξιος ὁ ἐργάτης τοῦ μισθοῦ αὐτοῦ.

Did 13:1–2 ⇨ Q 10:7b

¹Πᾶς δὲ προφήτης ἀληθινὸς θέλων καθῆσθαι πρὸς ὑμᾶς ἄξιός ἐστι τῆς τροφῆς αὐτοῦ. ²ὡσαύτως διδάσκαλος ἀληθινός ἐστιν ἄξιος καὶ αὐτὸς ὥσπερ ὁ ἐργάτης τῆς τροφῆς αὐτοῦ.

Mark 6:8–13

⁸He instructed them to take nothing for their journey except a staff; no bread, no knapsack, no copper coins in their belts. ⁹"But wear sandals and do not put on two tunics." ¹⁰And he said to them, "Whatever house you enter, remain there until you leave the place. ¹¹And if any place does not welcome you and listen to you, when you leave, shake off the dust that is on your feet for a testimony against them." ¹²And they went out and preached repentance. ¹³And they exorcised many demons, and anointed with oil many that were sick and healed them.

Luke 9:2–6

²And he sent them to proclaim the reign of God and to heal the sick. ³And he said to them, "Take nothing for your journey, no staff, nor knapsack, nor bread, nor silver; and do not have two tunics. ⁴And whatever house you enter, remain there, and from there depart. ⁵And wherever they do not welcome you, when you leave that city shake off the dust from your feet as a testimony against them." ⁶And they departed and went through the villages, evangelizing and healing everywhere.

DialSav 53

Mary said, "Thus with respect to 'the wickedness of each day,' and 'the laborer is worthy of his food,' and 'the disciple resembles his teacher.'" She uttered this as a woman who had understood completely.

1 Tim 5:18

¹⁸for the scripture says, "You shall not muzzle an ox when it is treading out the grain," and "The laborer deserves his wages."

Did 13:1–2

¹But every true prophet who wishes to settle among you is worthy of his food. ²Likewise a true teacher is himself worthy, like the workman, of his food.

⁷πορευόμενοι δὲ κηρύσσετε λέγοντες ὅτι
ἤγγικεν ἡ βασιλεία <u>τῶν οὐρανῶν</u>.
⁸ἀσθενοῦντας **θεραπεύετε**, νεκροὺς ἐγείρετε, λεπροὺς
καθαρίζετε, δαιμόνια ἐκβάλλετε· δωρεὰν ἐλάβετε,
δωρεὰν δότε.
¹⁴καὶ ὃς **ἂν μὴ** δέξηται **ὑμᾶς** μηδὲ ἀκούσῃ
τοὺς λόγους ὑμῶν, ἐξερχόμενοι ἔξω τῆς οἰκίας
ἢ **τῆς πόλεως** ἐκείνης ἐκτινάξατε **τὸν κονιορτὸν**
τῶν ποδῶν ὑμῶν.

⁷πορευόμενοι δὲ κηρύσσετε λέγοντες ὅτι
ἤγγικεν ἡ βασιλεία <u>τῶν οὐρανῶν</u>.
¹⁵**ἀμὴν λέγω ὑμῖν**, ἀνεκτότερον ἔσται γῇ Σοδόμων
καὶ Γομόρρων **ἐν ἡμέρα** κρίσεως **ἢ τῇ**
πόλει ἐκείνῃ.

⁹καὶ **θεραπεύετε** τοὺς ἐν αὐτῇ ἀσθενεῖς, καὶ
λέγετε αὐτοῖς· **ἤγγικεν** ἐφ᾽ ὑμᾶς **ἡ βασιλεία** τοῦ θεοῦ.

¹⁰εἰς ἣν δ᾽ **ἂν** πόλιν εἰσέλθητε καὶ **μὴ**
δέχωνται **ὑμᾶς**, ἐξελθόντες εἰς τὰς πλατείας
αὐτῆς εἴπατε· ¹¹ καὶ **τὸν κονιορτὸν** τὸν
κολληθέντα ὑμῖν ἐκ **τῆς πόλεως** ὑμῶν εἰς
τοὺς πόδας ἀπομασσόμεθα ὑμῖν·
πλὴν τοῦτο γινώσκετε ὅτι
ἤγγικεν ἡ βασιλεία τοῦ θεοῦ.
¹² **λέγω ὑμῖν** ὅτι Σοδόμοις
ἐν τῇ ἡμέρᾳ ἐκείνῃ ἀνεκτότερον ἔσται ἢ τῇ
πόλει ἐκείνῃ.

ἀποστέλλω ⇨ Matt 10:40 [S24]
δέχομαι ⇨ Matt 10:40 [S24]
ἀκούω ⇨ Luke 10:16 [S24]
Σόδομα ⇨ Matt 11:23, 24 [S23]
ἡμέρα κρίσεως ⇨ Matt 11:22, 24 [S23]

ἀποστέλλω ⇨ Luke 10:16 [S24]
δέχομαι ⇨ Matt 10:40 [S24]
Σόδομα ⇨ Matt 11:23, 24 [S23]
ἀνεκτότερος ⇨ Luke 10:24 [S23]

Matt 10:14: omit εξω: *rell* [HG] / απο (Luke 9:5): 1579 /
εκ: L *pc* / txt: ℵ B C D W Θ 33 579 892 lat [NA²⁵·²⁶].

GThom 14b ⇨ Q 10:8–9

ⲁⲩⲱ ⲉⲧⲉⲧⲛ̅ϣⲁⲛⲃⲱⲕ ⲉϩⲟⲩⲛ ⲉⲕⲁϩ ⲛⲓⲙ ⲁⲩⲱ ⲛ̅ⲧⲉⲧⲛ̅
ⲙⲟⲟϣⲉ ϩⲛ̅ ⲛ̅ⲭⲱⲣⲁ ⲉⲩϣⲁⲣ̅ⲡⲁⲣⲁⲇⲉⲭⲉ ⲙ̅ⲙⲱⲧⲛ̅
ⲡⲉⲧⲟⲩⲛⲁⲕⲁⲁϥ ϩⲁⲣⲱⲧⲛ̅ ⲟⲩⲟⲙϥ̅ ⲛⲉⲧϣⲱⲛⲉ
ⲛ̅ϩⲏⲧⲟⲩ ⲉⲣⲓⲑⲉⲣⲁⲡⲉⲩⲉ ⲙ̅ⲙⲟⲟⲩ ⲡⲉⲧⲛⲁⲃⲱⲕ ⲅⲁⲣ
ⲉϩⲟⲩⲛ ϩⲛ̅ ⲧⲉⲧⲛ̅ⲧⲁⲡⲣⲟ ϥⲛⲁϫⲱϩⲙ̅ ⲑⲏⲩⲧⲛ̅ ⲁⲛ ⲁⲗⲗⲁ
ⲡⲉⲧⲛ̅ⲛⲏⲩ ⲉⲃⲟⲗ ϩⲛ̅ ⲧⲉⲧⲛ̅ⲧⲁⲡⲣⲟ ⲛ̅ⲧⲟϥ ⲡⲉⲧⲛⲁϫⲁϩⲙ̅
ⲑⲏⲩⲧⲛ̅.

GThom 14b

. . . When you go into any country and walk from place to place, when the people receive you, eat what they serve you and heal the sick among them. For what goes into your mouth will not defile you; rather, it is what comes out of your mouth that will defile you.

Q 10:2–10

Luke has *two* commissioning speeches, the first (9:3–6) taken largely from Mark 6:8–13 but influenced slightly by Q, especially in the prohibition of a staff (Matt 10:10 // Luke 9:3; cf. Mark 6:8) and in the instructions regarding rejection (Luke 9:5 // 10:10–11 // Matt 10:14; cf. Mark 6:11). His second speech (Luke 10:2–16) derives, presumably, from Q. Matthew, by contrast, has conflated Mark 6:8–13 with Q and special material to produce a single speech, which he concludes with Markan material relocated from Mark 13:9–13 and a small cluster of Q sayings (Matt 10:26–39) which are found scattered throughout Luke. In both Matthew and Luke, Q 10:16 (Matt 10:40) retains its function as the aphorism concluding the mission speech.

Although the reconstruction of the speech is controverted, it seems reasonable to ascribe to Q at least those verses on which Matthew and Luke agree and where Mark has no counterpart (10:2, 3, 6, 7b, 8a, 9, 12) and those verses where Matthew and Luke offer a version differing slightly from Mark (10:4, 5, 7a, 10–11). See Polag 44–46; Schulz 404–7. Hawkins (1909: 109) includes all these except Luke 10:10–11 par. Harnack expresses reservations on 10:3 and 10:7b since both are short (pp. 12–13); he omits mention of 10:7a and 10:10–11 (because of the Markan parallels?) and he hesitates to reconstruct 10:4 but states that 10:5–6 was preceded by "some words which can still be supplied with some degree of certainty" from 10:4 (p. 134). He also prints Luke 9:2 rather than 10:9 as the parallel for Matt 10:7, but allows that it is "questionable whether the verse belonged to Q" (p. 80).

Concerning the order of the Q speech, Luke is probably nearer the order of Q. Matthew clearly has rearranged Mark and Q in order to produce Matt 9:35—10:42. Schulz adds that Luke's tendency is to treat the speech in a historicizing fashion and hence not to revise it for application to missionary activities of his own day. Q 10:9 (Matt 10:7–8) has been re-positioned to serve as the continuation of Matt 10:5–6 (*Sondergut*). He has employed Q 10:3 as a transition to his Markan section (Matt 10:17–25 // Mark 13:9–13). Matthew then inserted the command concerning cities and villages (Matt 10:11 // Luke 10:7–8) prior to those concerning houses (Matt 10:12–13 // Luke 10:5–6).

The originality of Lukan order is supported by: Bultmann 1963: 325; Bussmann 63; Hahn 1963: 42–43; Hoffmann 287–88; Jacobson 128–30; idem, 1982b: 420; Kloppenborg 1987: 77–78; Polag 44–46; Schenk 50–56; Schmid 262; Schulz 404; Schürmann 1968: 270. Beare (1970: 7 ?) and Harnack (175, 261–62) appear to favor Matthean order.

[Luke 10:1]

In Q: Polag 44–45; Schürmann 1968: 144–46; Vassiliadis 1978: 69.

Not in Q: Bultmann 1963: 334; Bussmann 63; Crossan 1983: 343; Easton Lk 159; Fitzmyer Lk 842; Harnack 12; Haupt 1913: 27. Hoffmann 248–49: Luke 10:1 betrays Lukan vocabulary and appears to have been influenced by Mark 6:7, 11. Hunter; Laufen 1980: 203–4. Manson 74: Since 10:1 relates to the material in 10:17–20, which derives from L, 10:1 must also come from L. Müller 1908: 7, 50. Schulz 404: The vocabulary of 10:1 is strongly Lukan and 10:1b presupposes the plan of the entire Lukan travel narrative. Weiss 1907: 124, 208.

[Q/Matt 10:5b–6]

In Q: Haupt 1913: 14, 27; Hawkins 1911: 134; Müller 1908: 30, 51; Polag 44 (probably); Sato 1984: 16, 29–30 (possibly in Q); Schelkle 1983: 87–88; Schmid 262, 268; Schürmann 1968: 137–48; Schweizer Mt 152; Weiss 1907: 130.

It is usually argued that Luke would have omitted such particularistic or obscure material (Haupt; Hawkins). Schürmann asserts that since Matthew did not omit any of the verses from Q 10:1–16 (apart from 10:7c) and since he used no other sources besides what was available to him from Mark and Q for the composition of Matt 10, it is likely that 10:5b–6 is also from Q. Luke omitted the saying as no longer relevant. Since Q/Matt 10:5–6 plainly concerns mission, it must have occurred in Q 10, probably between Q 10:7 and 10:8, attached to the latter by the catchword εἰσέρχομαι.

Not in Q: Beare 1970: 8–9; Hahn 1963: 54; Harnack; Hoffmann 258–61, 293; Kilpatrick 1946: 27. Laufen 1980: 233–43: The saying contradicts the theology of Q (its positive assessment of Gentiles) and its actual missionary practice. Lührmann 60 n. 4; Schenk 50; Schulz 416 n. 92. Streeter 1924: 255–56: Q displays too positive a view of Gentiles to have included such a particularistic saying. Zeller 46.

[Matt 10:16b]

In Q: Carlston 1982: 111 (very hesitantly). Knox 1957: 51: Luke omitted the "unedifying command to be as prudent as serpents." Vassiliadis 1978: 70.

Not in Q: Harnack 13; Hoffmann 263; Laufen 1980: 206. Schmid 261: There is no reason for Luke to have omitted the saying. Schulz 405; Steinhauser 1981: 281–82 and most authors.

Matt 9:36–38

[36 When he saw the crowds, he had compassion for them, because they were weary and lying down, like sheep without a shepherd.]

37 Then he said to his disciples, "The harvest is large, but the workers are few; 38 beg therefore the master of the harvest to send out workers into his harvest."

Matt 10:1, 5–6, 16, 9–10a, 11–13, 10b–11, 7–8, 14, 7, 15

[1 And he summoned his twelve disciples and gave them authority over unclean spirits, to expel them, and to heal every disease and every infirmity . . .]
[5 These twelve Jesus sent out, instructing them, "Do not go to the Gentiles, and enter no city of the Samaritans, 6 but go instead to the lost sheep of the house of Israel.]
16 Behold, I am sending you as sheep among wolves;
   [therefore be as clever as snakes and as innocent as doves."]
9 Take no gold, nor silver, nor copper in your belts, 10 no knapsack for your journey, nor two tunics, nor sandals, nor a staff; . . .
11 Into whatever city or village you enter, determine who in it is worthy, and stay with that person until you depart.
12 As you enter the house, salute it. 13 And if the house is worthy, let your peace come upon it; but if it is not worthy, let your peace return to you.

10b for the worker deserves his food. 11 Into whatever city or village you enter, determine who in it is worthy, and stay with that person until you depart.
7 Preach as you go, saying, 'The reign of heaven is at hand.' 8 Heal the sick, raise the dead, cleanse lepers, exorcise demons. You received without payment, give without charge.
14 And whoever does not welcome you or listen to your words, shake off the dust from your feet as you leave that house or city.
7 Preach as you go, saying, 'The reign of heaven is at hand.'
15 Amen, I tell you, it shall be more tolerable on the day of judgment for the land of Sodom and Gomorrah than for that city.

Luke 10:1–12

[1 After this the Lord appointed an additional seventy [two] others, and sent them on ahead of him, two by two, into every city and place where he himself was about to come.]
2 And he said to them, "The harvest is large, but the workers are few; beg therefore the master of the harvest to send out workers into his harvest.

3 Go; behold, I am sending you out as lambs among wolves.

4 Carry no purse, no knapsack, no sandals; and greet no one on the road.

5 Into whatever house you enter, first say, 'Peace be to this house!' 6 And if a child of peace is there, your peace shall rest upon him; but if not, it shall return to you.

7 And stay in the same house, eating and drinking whatever they have, for the worker deserves his wages. Do not go from house to house. 8 And if you enter a city and they welcome you, eat what is set before you;
9 and heal the sick in it and say to them, 'The reign of God has come near to you.'

10 But if you enter a city and they do not welcome you, go into its streets and say, 11 'Even the dust of your city that clings to our feet, we wipe off against you; but know this, that the reign of God has come near.'

12 I tell you, it shall be more tolerable on that day for Sodom than for that city."

Matt 11:20–24

[²⁰Τότε ἤρξατο ὀνειδίζειν τὰς πόλεις ἐν αἷς ἐγένοντο αἱ πλεῖσται δυνάμεις αὐτοῦ, ὅτι οὐ μετενόησαν·]
²¹οὐαί σοι, Χοραζίν· οὐαί σοι, Βηθσαϊδά· ὅτι εἰ ἐν Τύρῳ καὶ Σιδῶνι ἐγένοντο   αἱ δυνάμεις αἱ γενόμεναι ἐν ὑμῖν, πάλαι ἂν ἐν σάκκῳ καὶ σποδῷ   μετενόησαν.
²²πλὴν λέγω ὑμῖν, Τύρῳ καὶ Σιδῶνι ἀνεκτότερον ἔσται ἐν ἡμέρᾳ κρίσεως ἢ ὑμῖν.
²³καὶ σύ, Καφαρναούμ, μὴ ἕως οὐρανοῦ ὑψωθήσῃ; ἕως   ᾅδου καταβήσῃ·
(ὅτι εἰ ἐν Σοδόμοις ἐγενήθησαν αἱ δυνάμεις αἱ γενόμεναι ἐν σοί, ἔμεινεν ἂν μέχρι τῆς σήμερον. ²⁴ πλὴν λέγω ὑμῖν ὅτι γῇ Σοδόμων ἀνεκτότερον ἔσται ἐν ἡμέρᾳ κρίσεως ἢ σοί.)

Luke 10:13–15

¹³Οὐαί σοι, Χοραζίν· οὐαί σοι, Βηθσαϊδά· ὅτι εἰ ἐν Τύρῳ καὶ Σιδῶνι ἐγενήθησαν αἱ δυνάμεις αἱ γενόμεναι ἐν ὑμῖν, πάλαι ἂν ἐν σάκκῳ καὶ σποδῷ καθήμενοι μετενόησαν.
¹⁴πλὴν   Τύρῳ καὶ Σιδῶνι ἀνεκτότερον ἔσται ἐν τῇ κρίσει ἢ ὑμῖν.
¹⁵καὶ σύ, Καφαρναούμ, μὴ ἕως οὐρανοῦ ὑψωθήσῃ; ἕως τοῦ ᾅδου καταβήσῃ.

Luke 10:15: ουρανου (Matt): 𝔭⁴⁵·⁷⁵ ℵ B* D *pc* [NA²⁵·²⁶] / του ουρανου: A B² C R W Koine Θ Ψ λ φ 700 lat syᵖ·ʰ [HG] // του αδου: 𝔭⁷⁵ B L 0115 1010 *pc* [NA²⁵·²⁶] / αδου (Matt): 𝔭⁴⁵ ℵ A C D R W Koine Θ Ψ λ φ; Cyr [HG] // καταβιβασθησῃ: 𝔭⁴⁵ ℵ A C L R W Koine Θ Ψ λ φ lat syᵖ·ʰ co [HG] / txt: 𝔭⁷⁵ B D *pc* 569 syˢ·ᶜ [NA²⁵·²⁶].

Matt 11:23: καταβιβασθησῃ: ℵ C L Koine Θ λ φ syᵖ·ʰ mae bo [HG] / txt (Isa 14:15): B D W 372 it syˢ·ᶜ sa; Ir [NA²⁵·²⁶].

Notes

[Matt 11:20]

In Q: Manson 77; Marshall Lk 424.
Not in Q: Edwards 1982: 269; Schmid 286; Schönle 1982: 134 and most authors.

(Q/Matt 11:23b–24)

In Q: Bultmann 1963: 112. Edwards 1982: 270: Vv. 21–24 form a carefully balanced saying employing the second person plural in the first saying (vv. 21–22) and the second singular in the second (vv. 23–24). The use of λέγω ὑμῖν in v. 24 is purely formulaic and does not interfere with the consistent second person singular address in v. 23 (καὶ σύ . . . ἐν σοί) and v. 24 (ἢ σοί). Fitzmyer Lk 851: The longer Matthean form "undoubtedly reflects the original Q version"; Luke omitted Q/Matt 11:24 because it duplicated Q 10:12.

Manson 77: Matthew preserves the "strophic parallelism" which is characteristic of Jesus' teaching. Müller 1908: 10: Luke omitted the verse as repetitious.
Not in Q: Harnack 135; Hoffmann 284–85; Lührmann 62; Schenk 56; Schmid 287; Schönle 1982: 46–47. Schulz 361: V. 23b is formulated from Q 10:13b, and v. 24 is based upon Q 10:12. Weiss 1907: 69 n. 1: "A mechanical imitation of 11:21." Zeller 46. The usual grounds for excluding these verses as redactional are: (1) Matthew's λέγω ὑμῖν in v. 24 is inconsistent with the second person singular address of v. 23a and (2) there is no reason for Luke to have destroyed the parallelism had he found it in Q.
Undecided: Grundmann Mt 314; Marshall Lk 426; Strecker 1971: 102 n. 2.

Matt 11:20–24

[²⁰ Then he began to reproach the cities where most of his miracles had been done, because they did not repent.]

²¹ "Woe to you, Chorazin! woe to you, Bethsaida! for if the miracles done in you had been done in Tyre and Sidon, they would have repented long ago with sackcloth and ashes. ²² But I tell you, it shall be more tolerable on the day of judgment for Tyre and Sidon than for you. ²³ And you, Capernaum, will you be exalted to heaven? You shall be brought down to Hades.

(For if the miracles done in you had been done in Sodom, it would be standing today. ²⁴ But I tell you that it shall be more tolerable on the day of judgment for the land of Sodom than for you.")

Luke 10:13–15

¹³ "Woe to you, Chorazin! woe to you, Bethsaida! for if the miracles done in you had been done in Tyre and Sidon, they would have repented long ago, sitting in sackcloth and ashes. ¹⁴ But it shall be more tolerable in the judgment for Tyre and Sidon than for you. ¹⁵ And you, Capernaum, will you be exalted to heaven? You shall be brought down to Hades."

Parallels

Isa 14:13–15 LXX

¹³σὺ δὲ εἶπας ἐν τῇ διανοίᾳ σου· εἰς τὸν οὐρανὸν ἀναβήσομαι, ἐπάνω τῶν ἄστρων τοῦ οὐρανοῦ θήσω τὸν θρόνον μου, καθιῶ ἐν ὄρει ὑψηλῷ ἐπὶ τὰ ὄρη τὰ ὑψηλὰ τὰ πρὸς βορρᾶν, ¹⁴ἀναβήσομαι ἐπάνω τῶν νεφελῶν, ἔσομαι ὅμοιος τῷ ὑψίστῳ. ¹⁵νῦν δὲ εἰς ἅδου καταβήσῃ καὶ εἰς τὰ θεμέλια τῆς γῆς.

Isa 14:13–15 LXX

¹³But you said in your mind, "I will ascend into heaven and set my thone above the stars of heaven; I will sit on the highest mountain in the highest mountains of the north; ¹⁴I will ascend above the clouds; I will be like the Most High." ¹⁵But now you are brought down to Hades and to the foundations of the earth.

Matt 10:40

⁴⁰ὁ δεχόμενος ὑμᾶς ἐμὲ δέχεται, καὶ ὁ ἐμὲ δεχόμενος δέχεται τὸν ἀποστείλαντά με.

Luke 10:16

¹⁶Ὁ ἀκούων ὑμῶν ἐμοῦ ἀκούει, καὶ ὁ ἀθετῶν ὑμᾶς ἐμὲ ἀθετεῖ· ὁ δὲ ἐμὲ ἀθετῶν ἀθετεῖ τὸν ἀποστείλαντά με.

ἀκούω ⇨ Luke 10:24 [S26]

Luke 10:17–20

[¹⁷Ὑπέστρεψαν δὲ οἱ ἑβδομήκοντα [δύο] μετὰ χαρᾶς λέγοντες, Κύριε, καὶ τὰ δαιμόνια ὑποτάσσεται ἡμῖν ἐν τῷ ὀνόματί σου].
[¹⁸εἶπεν δὲ αὐτοῖς, ἐθεώρουν τὸν Σατανᾶν ὡς ἀστραπὴν ἐκ τοῦ οὐρανοῦ πεσόντα. ¹⁹ἰδοὺ δέδωκα ὑμῖν τὴν ἐξουσίαν τοῦ πατεῖν ἐπάνω ὄφεων καὶ σκορπίων, καὶ ἐπὶ πᾶσαν τὴν δύναμιν τοῦ ἐχθροῦ, καὶ οὐδὲν ὑμᾶς οὐ μὴ ἀδικήσῃ. ²⁰πλὴν ἐν τούτῳ μὴ χαίρετε ὅτι τὰ πνεύματα ὑμῖν ὑποτάσσεται, χαίρετε δὲ ὅτι τὰ ὀνόματα ὑμῶν ἐγγέγραπται ἐν τοῖς οὐρανοῖς].

Luke 10:19: αδικησει: ℵ A D L W Γ Θ 1 28 1241 *al*; Did [NA²⁵; HG] / txt: 𝔓⁴⁵·⁷⁵ B C Ψ 0115 Koine φ; Or Cyp [NA²⁶].

Notes

Q 10:16

In Q: Most authors. Harnack (90) hesitates to include Q 10:16 because of the "marked differences" between Matthew and Luke, while Kilpatrick (1946: 26–27) remarks that Matt 10:40 does not differ sufficiently from Mark 9:37 to justify the view that Matthew used another source. Müller (1908: 4) suggests that the Lukan version is from L.

[Luke 10:18–20]

In Q: Easton Lk xxi, 163; Marshall Lk 427; Schmithals Lk 124 (v. 18 only); Schürmann 1968: 146 n. 37; Streeter 1911b: 192 (but see 1924: 289–90!); Vassiliadis 1978: 71 (vv. 19–20 only); Weiss 1907: 69. Several arguments are employed in support of the inclusions of these verses: (1)

Schürmann argues that Matt 7:22–23 contains "reminiscences" of this Q text: κύριε, ἐν τῷ ὀνόματι σου, δαιμόνια, δύναμιν. Moreover, Matt 7:21–23 has been influenced by Q 10:21, the original context for Q 10:17–20. (2) Matthew's omission is explicable. In the course of the conflation of the mission speeches in Mark and Q, Matthew omitted an account of the disciples' departure and return, and hence the occasion for this saying (Easton; Streeter; Weiss). (3) Matthew may have found difficult the suggestion that Satan fell from heaven, since for Matthew, Satan's demise was still to come (Streeter).

Not in Q: Bussmann 65; Fitzmyer Lk 859; Harnack; Hoffmann 248–54; Jacobson; Lührmann; Manson 258–59; Müller 1908: 7, 13, 51; Schenk; Zeller and most other authors. Sato (1984: 63–64) ascribes vv. 18–19 to Q^Lk.

Matt 10:40

⁴⁰ Whoever welcomes you welcomes me, and whoever welcomes me welcomes him who sent me.

Luke 10:16

¹⁶ Whoever hears you hears me, and he who rejects you rejects me, and whoever rejects me rejects him who sent me.

Luke 10:17–20

[¹⁷ The seventy [two] returned with joy, saying, "Lord, even the demons are subject to us through your name!"] [¹⁸ And he said to them, "I saw Satan fall like lightning from heaven. ¹⁹ Behold, I have given you authority to walk upon snakes and scorpions, and over all the power of the enemy; and nothing shall injure you. ²⁰ Still, do not rejoice in the fact that the spirits are subject to you; but rejoice that your names are written in heaven."]

Parallels

Mark 9:37

³⁷ ὃς ἂν ἓν τῶν τοιούτων παιδίων δέξηται ἐπὶ τῷ ὀνόματί μου, ἐμὲ δέχεται· καὶ ὃς ἂν ἐμὲ δέχηται, οὐκ ἐμὲ δέχεται ἀλλὰ τὸν ἀποστείλαντά με.

Mark 9:37

³⁷ Whoever welcomes one such child in my name welcomes me; and whoever welcomes me, welcomes not me but him who sent me.

John 13:20

²⁰ Ἀμὴν ἀμὴν λέγω ὑμῖν, ὁ λαμβάνων ἄν τινα πέμψω ἐμὲ λαμβάνει, ὁ δὲ ἐμὲ λαμβάνων λαμβάνει τὸν πέμψαντά με.

John 13:20

²⁰ Amen, amen, I tell you, whoever receives any one whom I send receives me; and the one who receives me receives him who sent me.

John 12:44–45

⁴⁴ Ἰησοῦς δὲ ἔκραξεν καὶ εἶπεν· ὁ πιστεύων εἰς ἐμὲ οὐ πιστεύει εἰς ἐμὲ ἀλλὰ εἰς τὸν πέμψαντά με, ⁴⁵ καὶ ὁ θεωρῶν ἐμὲ θεωρεῖ τὸν πέμψαντά με.

John 12:44–45

⁴⁴ Then Jesus cried out and said, "The one who believes in me, believes not in me but in him who sent me." ⁴⁵ And the one who sees me sees him who sent me.

Matt 11:25–27

²⁵Ἐν ἐκείνῳ τῷ καιρῷ ἀποκριθεὶς ὁ Ἰησοῦς εἶπεν·

ἐξομολογοῦμαί σοι, πάτερ, κύριε τοῦ οὐρανοῦ καὶ τῆς γῆς, ὅτι ἔκρυψας ταῦτα ἀπὸ σοφῶν καὶ συνετῶν καὶ ἀπεκάλυψας αὐτὰ νηπίοις· ²⁶ναί, ὁ πατήρ, ὅτι οὕτως εὐδοκία ἐγένετο ἔμπροσθέν σου.

²⁷Πάντα μοι παρεδόθη ὑπὸ τοῦ πατρός μου, καὶ οὐδεὶς ἐπιγινώσκει τὸν υἱὸν   εἰ μὴ ὁ πατήρ, οὐδὲ τὸν πατέρα τις ἐπιγινώσκει εἰ μὴ ὁ υἱὸς καὶ ᾧ ἐὰν βούληται ὁ υἱὸς ἀποκαλύψαι.

Luke 10:21–22

²¹Ἐν αὐτῇ τῇ ὥρᾳ ἠγαλλιάσατο [ἐν] τῷ πνεύματι τῷ ἁγίῳ καὶ εἶπεν·

ἐξομολογοῦμαί σοι, πάτερ, κύριε τοῦ οὐρανοῦ καὶ τῆς γῆς, ὅτι ἀπέκρυψας ταῦτα ἀπὸ σοφῶν καὶ συνετῶν καὶ ἀπεκάλυψας αὐτὰ νηπίοις· ναί, ὁ πατήρ, ὅτι οὕτως εὐδοκία ἐγένετο ἔμπροσθέν σου.

²²Πάντα μοι παρεδόθη ὑπὸ τοῦ πατρός μου, καὶ οὐδεὶς γινώσκει τίς ἐστιν ὁ υἱὸς εἰ μὴ ὁ πατήρ, καὶ τίς ἐστιν ὁ πατήρ   εἰ μὴ ὁ υἱὸς καὶ ᾧ ἐὰν βούληται ὁ υἱὸς ἀποκαλύψαι.

πατήρ ⇨ Luke 11:2 [S27]

Luke 10:21: τω πνευματι τω αγιω: 𝔭⁷⁵ B C K Θ λ 1424 *al* vg [NA²⁵; HG] / εν τω πνευματι τω αγιω: ℵ D L Ξ 33 1241 *al* it [NA²⁶] / τω πνευματι: A W Koine Ψ f / εν τω πνευματι: 𝔭⁴⁵ 0115 892 *pc* q // εγενετο ευδοκια: 𝔭⁴⁵ ℵ A C³ D W Koine Θ 0115 φ [HG] / txt: 𝔭⁷⁵ B C* L Ξ Ψ 0124 1 33 892 *pc* it [NA²⁵·²⁶].

Notes

Q 10:21–22
In Q: Most authors.

Matt 11:25–27

²⁵ At that time Jesus said, "I praise you, Father, Lord of heaven and earth, that you have hidden these things from sages and the learned and revealed them to babes. ²⁶ Yes, Father, for such was your gracious will. ²⁷ All things have been handed over to me by my Father; and no one knows the Son except the Father, and no one knows the Father except the Son and any one to whom the Son wishes to reveal him."

Luke 10:21–22

²¹ In that very hour he rejoiced in the Holy Spirit and said, "I praise you, Father, Lord of heaven and earth, that you have hidden these things from sages and the learned and revealed them to babes. Yes, Father, for such was your gracious will. ²² All things have been handed over to me by my Father; and no one knows who the Son is except the Father, or who the Father is except the Son and any one to whom the Son wishes to reveal him."

Parallels

John 3:35–36

³⁵ ὁ πατὴρ ἀγαπᾷ τὸν υἱὸν καὶ πάντα δέδωκεν ἐν τῇ χειρὶ αὐτοῦ. ³⁶ ὁ πιστεύων εἰς τὸν υἱὸν ἔχει ζωὴν αἰώνιον· ὁ δὲ ἀπειθῶν τῷ υἱῷ οὐκ ὄψεται ζωήν, ἀλλ᾽ ἡ ὀργὴ τοῦ θεοῦ μένει ἐπ᾽ αὐτόν.

John 17:1b–2

¹ . . . πάτερ, ἐλήλυθεν ἡ ὥρα· δόξασόν σου τὸν υἱόν, ἵνα ὁ υἱὸς δοξάσῃ σε, ² καθὼς ἔδωκας αὐτῷ ἐξουσίαν πάσης σαρκός, ἵνα πᾶν ὃ δέδωκας αὐτῷ δώσῃ αὐτοῖς ζωὴν αἰώνιον.

John 10:15

¹⁵ καθὼς γινώσκει με ὁ πατὴρ κἀγὼ γινώσκω τὸν πατέρα, καὶ τὴν ψυχήν μου τίθημι ὑπὲρ τῶν προβάτων.

POxy 654.21–27

[λέγει ᾽Ιη(σοῦ)ς· οὐκ ἀποκνήσει ἄνθ[ρωπος παλαιὸς ἡμε]ρῶν ἐπερωτῆσε πα[ιδίον ἑπτὰ ἡμε]ρῶν περὶ τοῦ τόπου τῆ[ς ζωῆς, καὶ ζή]σετε· ὅτι πολλοὶ ἔσονται π[ρῶτοι ἔσχατοι καὶ] οἱ ἔσχατοι πρῶτοι, καὶ [εἰς ἓν καταντήσου]σιν.

John 3:35–36

³⁵ The Father loves the Son, and has given all things into his hand. ³⁶ Whoever believes in the Son has eternal life; whoever does not obey the Son shall not see life, but the wrath of God remains upon him.

John 17:1b–2

¹ . . . "Father, the hour has come; glorify your Son that the Son may glorify you, ² since you gave him authority over all flesh, to give eternal life to all whom you gave him."

John 10:15

¹⁵ As the Father knows me, I know the Father; and I lay down my life for the sheep.

POxy 654.21–27

[Jesus said], "The [man old in days] will not hesitate to ask [a small child seven days old] about the place [of life, and] he will [live]. For many who are [first] will become [last, and] the last will be first, and [they will become one and the same]."

GThom 4

ⲡⲉϫⲉ ⲓ̅ⲥ̅ ϥⲛⲁϫⲛⲁⲩ ⲁⲛ ⲛ̄ϭⲓ ⲡⲣⲱⲙⲉ ⲛ̄ϩⲗ̄ⲗⲟ ϩⲛ̄ ⲛⲉϥϩⲟⲟⲩ ⲉϫⲛⲉ ⲟⲩⲕⲟⲩⲉⲓ ⲛ̄ϣⲏⲣⲉ ϣⲏⲙ ⲉϥϩⲛ̄ ⲥⲁϣϥ̄ ⲛ̄ϩⲟⲟⲩ ⲉⲧⲃⲉ ⲡⲧⲟⲡⲟⲥ ⲙ̄ⲡⲱⲛϩ ⲁⲩⲱ ϥⲛⲁⲱⲛϩ ϫⲉ ⲟⲩⲛ̄ ϩⲁϩ ⲛ̄ϣⲟⲣⲡ ⲛⲁⲣ̄ ϩⲁⲉ ⲁⲩⲱ ⲛ̄ⲥⲉϣⲱⲡⲉ ⲟⲩⲁ ⲟⲩⲱⲧ.

GTruth 19:18–34

ⲙ̄ⲛⲁ ⲛ̄ϫⲓ ⲥⲃⲱ ⲁϥⲓ ⲁⲧⲙⲏⲧⲉ ⲁϥϫⲉ ⲡⲓϣⲉϫⲉ· ⲉϥⲟⲉⲓ ⲛ̄ⲟⲩⲥⲁϩ· ⲁⲅⲉⲓ ϣⲁⲣⲁⲉⲓ ⲛ̄ϭⲓ ⲛ̄ⲥⲟⲫⲟⲥ ⲛ̄ϩⲣⲁⲓ̈ ϩⲙ̄ ⲡⲟⲩϩⲏⲧ· ⲟⲩⲁⲉⲉⲧⲟⲩ ⲉⲩⲡⲓⲣⲁⲍⲉ ⲙ̄ⲙⲁϥ ⲛ̄ⲧⲁϥ ⲇⲉ ⲛⲉϥϫⲡⲓⲟ ⲙ̄ⲙⲁⲩ ϫⲉ ⲛⲉϩⲛ̄ⲡⲉⲧϣⲟⲩⲉⲓⲧ ⲛⲉ· ⲁⲩⲙⲉⲥⲧⲱϥ ϫⲉ ⲛⲉϩⲛ̄ⲣⲙ̄ⲛ̄ϩⲏⲧ ⲉⲛ ⲛⲉ ⲙⲁⲙⲏⲉ. ⲙⲛ̄ⲛ̄ⲥⲁ ⲛⲉⲉⲓ ⲧⲏⲣⲟⲩ ⲁⲩⲉⲓ ϣⲁⲣⲁⲓ̈ ⲛ̄ϭⲓ ⲛ̄ⲕⲉⲕⲟⲩⲓ̈ ϣⲏⲙ· ⲛⲉⲉⲓ ⲉⲧⲉ ⲡⲱⲟⲩ ⲡⲉ· ⲡⲥⲁⲩⲛⲉ ⲙ̄ⲡⲓⲱⲧ· ⲉⲁⲩⲧⲱⲕ ⲛⲉⲁⲩϫⲓ ⲥⲃⲱ ⲁⲛⲓⲙⲟⲩⲛⲅ̄ ⲛ̄ϩⲟ ⲛ̄ⲧⲉ ⲡⲓⲱⲧ· ⲁⲩⲥⲁⲩⲛⲉ ⲁⲩⲥⲟⲩⲱⲛⲟⲩ ⲁⲩϫⲓ ⲉⲁⲩ ⲁⲩϯ ⲉⲁⲩ ⲁϥⲟⲩⲱⲛϩ ⲁⲃⲁⲗ.

GThom 4

Jesus said, "The person old in days will not hesitate to ask a little child seven days old about the place of life, and that person will live. For many of the first will be last, and will become a single one."

GTruth 19:18–34

He went into the midst of the schools (and) he spoke the word as a teacher. There came the wise men—in their own estimation—putting him to the test. But he confounded them because they were foolish. They hated him because they were not really wise.
After all these, there came the little children also, those to whom the knowledge of the Father belongs. Having been strengthened, they learned about the impressions of the Father. They knew, they were known; they were glorified, they glorified.

Matt 13:16–17

[16]ὑμῶν δὲ **μακάριοι οἱ ὀφθαλμοὶ** ὅτι βλέπουσιν,
καὶ τὰ ὦτα ὑμῶν ὅτι ἀκούουσιν.
[17]ἀμὴν γὰρ **λέγω ὑμῖν ὅτι πολλοὶ προφῆται καὶ**
δίκαιοι ἐπεθύμησαν ἰδεῖν ἃ   **βλέπετε καὶ**
οὐκ εἶδαν, καὶ ἀκοῦσαι ἃ ἀκούετε καὶ οὐκ
ἤκουσαν.

Luke 10:23–24

[[23]Καὶ στραφεὶς πρὸς τοὺς μαθητὰς κατ᾽ ἰδίαν εἶπεν·]
            μακάριοι οἱ ὀφθαλμοὶ οἱ βλέποντες
ἃ βλέπετε,
[24]**λέγω γὰρ ὑμῖν ὅτι πολλοὶ προφῆται καὶ**
βασιλεῖς ἠθέλησαν ἰδεῖν ἃ ὑμεῖς **βλέπετε καὶ**
οὐκ εἶδαν, καὶ ἀκοῦσαι ἃ ἀκούετε καὶ οὐκ
ἤκουσαν.

Notes

[Luke 10:23a]

In Q: Hunter 137; Manson 80; Polag 89 (uncertain);
Schmithals Lk 126; Schürmann 1968: 236.

Not in Q: Bultmann 1963: 335; Bussmann 66;
Grundmann Lk 220; Harnack 135; Hoffmann 105;
Kloppenborg 1978: 134; Müller 1908: 51; Schenk 59.
Marshall (Lk 438) and Schulz (419) hold that although v.
23a is Lukan, Q 10:23b–24 originally had an introduction
in Q.

Q 10:23b–24

In Q: Most authors.

Matt 13:16–17

[16] But your eyes are blessed, because they see, and your ears, because they hear. [17] Amen, I tell you, many prophets and righteous ones longed to see what you are seeing, and did not see it, and to hear what you are hearing, and did not hear it.

Luke 10:23–24

[[23] And turning to the disciples he said privately,] "Blessed are the eyes which see what you see! [24] For I tell you that many prophets and kings desired to see what you are seeing, and did not see it, and to hear what you are hearing, and did not hear it."

Parallels

GThom 38

ⲡⲉϫⲉ ⲓ̅ⲥ̅ ϫⲉ ϩⲁϩ ⲛ̅ⲥⲟⲡ ⲁⲧⲉⲧⲛ̅ⲣ̅ⲉⲡⲓⲑⲩⲙⲉⲓ ⲉⲥⲱⲧⲙ̅
ⲁⲛⲉⲉⲓϣⲁϫⲉ ⲛⲁⲉⲓ ⲉϯϫⲱ ⲙ̅ⲙⲟⲟⲩ ⲛⲏⲧⲛ̅ ⲁⲩⲱ
ⲙⲛ̅ⲧⲏⲧⲛ̅ ⲕⲉⲟⲩⲁ ⲉⲥⲟⲧⲙⲟⲩ ⲛ̅ⲧⲟⲟⲧϥ ⲟⲩⲛ̅ ϩⲛ̅ϩⲟⲟⲩ
ⲛⲁϣⲱⲡⲉ ⲛ̅ⲧⲉⲧⲛ̅ϣⲓⲛⲉ ⲛ̅ⲥⲱⲉⲓ ⲧⲉⲧⲛⲁϩⲉ ⲁⲛ ⲉⲣⲟⲉⲓ.

GThom 38

Jesus said, "Often you have desired to hear these sayings that I am speaking to you, and you have no one else from whom to hear them. There will be days when you will seek me but will not find me."

Matt 6:7–13

[⁷Προσευχόμενοι δὲ μὴ βατταλογήσητε ὥσπερ οἱ ἐθνηκοί, δοκοῦσιν γὰρ ὅτι ἐν τῇ πολυλογίᾳ αὐτῶν εἰσακουσθήσονται. ⁸μὴ οὖν ὁμοιωθῆτε αὐτοῖς· οἶδεν γὰρ ὁ πατὴρ ὑμῶν ὧν χρείαν ἔχετε πρὸ τοῦ ὑμᾶς αἰτῆσαι αὐτόν].

⁹Οὕτως οὖν προσεύχεσθε ὑμεῖς·
Πάτερ ἡμῶν ὁ ἐν τοῖς οὐρανοῖς·
ἁγιασθήτω τὸ ὄνομά σου·
¹⁰ἐλθέτω ἡ βασιλεία σου· γενηθήτω τὸ θέλημά σου, ὡς ἐν οὐρανῷ καὶ ἐπὶ γῆς·
¹¹τὸν ἄρτον ἡμῶν τὸν ἐπιούσιον δὸς ἡμῖν σήμερον·
¹²καὶ ἄφες ἡμῖν τὰ ὀφειλήματα ἡμῶν,
ὡς καὶ ἡμεῖς ἀφήκαμεν τοῖς ὀφειλέταις ἡμῶν·
¹³ καὶ μὴ εἰσενέγκῃς ἡμᾶς εἰς πειρασμόν, ἀλλὰ ῥῦσαι ἡμᾶς ἀπὸ τοῦ πονηροῦ.

Luke 11:1–4

[¹Καὶ ἐγένετο ἐν τῷ εἶναι αὐτὸν ἐν τόπῳ τινὶ προσευχόμενον, ὡς ἐπαύσατο, εἶπέν τις τῶν μαθητῶν αὐτοῦ πρὸς αὐτόν· κύριε, δίδαξον ἡμᾶς προσεύχεσθαι, καθὼς καὶ Ἰωάννης ἐδίδαξεν τοὺς μαθητὰς αὐτοῦ].
²εἶπεν δὲ αὐτοῖς· ὅταν προσεύχησθε λέγετε·

Πάτερ
ἁγιασθήτω τὸ ὄνομά σου·
ἐλθέτω ἡ βασιλεία σου·

³τὸν ἄρτον ἡμῶν τὸν ἐπιούσιον δίδου ἡμῖν τὸ καθ᾽ ἡμέραν·
⁴καὶ ἄφες ἡμῖν τὰς ἁμαρτίας ἡμῶν,
καὶ γὰρ αὐτοὶ ἀφίομεν παντὶ ὀφείλοντι ἡμῖν·
καὶ μὴ εἰσενέγκῃς ἡμᾶς εἰς πειρασμόν.

ἄρτος ⇨ Luke 11:5; Matt 7:9 [S28]
πατήρ ⇨ Luke 11:13 [S28]
δίδωμι ⇨ Luke 11:8, 9, 13 [S28]

Luke 11:2: instead of αγιασθητω . . . σου: ελθετω το αγιον πνευμα σου εφ ημας και καθαρισατω ημας: Mcion // εφ ημας ελθετω σου η βασιλεια (Luke 10:9; 11:20): D / omit ελθετω . . . σου: geo / ελθετω το πνευμα σου το αγιον εφ ημιν και καθαρισατω ημιν: (162) 700; GrNy Max / txt: B *rell* [NA²⁵·²⁶; HG].

Did 8:2

²μηδὲ προσεύχεσθε ὡς οἱ ὑποκριταί, ἀλλ᾽ ὡς ἐκέλευσεν ὁ κύριος ἐν τῷ εὐαγγελίῳ αὐτοῦ, οὕτω προσεύχεσθε· Πάτερ ἡμῶν ὁ ἐν τῷ οὐρανῷ, ἁγιασθήτω τὸ ὄνομά σου, ἐλθέτω ἡ βασιλεία σου, γενηθήτω τὸ θέλημά σου ὡς ἐν οὐρανῷ καὶ ἐπὶ γῆς· τὸν ἄρτον ἡμῶν τὸν ἐπιούσιον δὸς ἡμῖν σήμερον, καὶ ἄφες ἡμῖν τὴν ὀφειλὴν ἡμῶν, ὡς καὶ ἡμεῖς ἀφίεμεν τοῖς ὀφειλέταις ἡμῶν, καὶ μὴ εἰσενέγκῃς ἡμᾶς εἰς πειρασμόν, ἀλλὰ ῥῦσαι ἡμᾶς ἀπὸ τοῦ πονηροῦ· ὅτι σοῦ ἐστιν ἡ δύναμις καὶ ἡ δόξα εἰς τοὺς αἰῶνας.

ApJas 4:22–31

ⲁϩⲓⲟⲩⲱϣⲃ̅ ⲇⲉ ⲡⲁⲭⲏⲓ̈ ⲛⲉϥ ⲭⲉ ⲡⲭⲁⲉⲓⲥ ⲟⲩⲛ̄ ⳓⲁⲙ ⲙ̄ⲙⲁⲛ ⲁⲡⲓⲑⲉ ⲛⲉⲕ ⲱⲡⲉ ϩⲛⲉⲕ ⲁϩⲛ̄ⲕⲱⲉ ⲅⲁⲣ ⲛ̄ⲥⲱⲛ ⲛⲛⲉⲛⲉⲓⲁϯ ⲛ̄ϩⲁⲟⲩⲧ· ⲙⲛ̄ ⲛⲉⲛⲙⲉⲉⲩ ⲙⲛ̄ ⲛⲉⲛϯⲙⲉ ⲁϩⲛⲟⲩⲁϩⲛ̄ ⲛ̄ⲥⲱⲕ ϯ ⲑⲉ ⳓ[ⲉ] ⲛⲉⲛ ⲁⲧⲙ̄ⲧⲣⲟⲩⲡⲓⲣⲁⲍⲉ ⲙ̄ⲙⲁⲛ ⲁⲃⲁⲗ ϩⲓ̈ⲧⲟⲟⲧϥ̄ ⲙ̄ⲡⲇⲓⲁⲃⲟⲗⲟⲥ ⲉⲑⲁⲩ.

GNaz 5

In euaggelio, quod appellatur secundum Hebraeos, "pro supersubstantiali pane" "mahar" reperi, quod dicitur "crastinum," ut sit sensus: "panem nostrum crastinum, id est futurum, da nobis hodie."

Did 8:2

²And do not pray as the hypocrites, but as the Lord commanded in his gospel, pray thus: "Our Father, who art in Heaven, hallowed by thy Name, thy Kingdom come, thy will be done, as in Heaven so also upon earth; give us today our daily bread, and forgive us our debt as we forgive our debtors, and lead us not into trial, but deliver us from the Evil One, for thine is the power and the glory for ever."

ApJas 4:22–31

But I answered and said to him, "Lord, we can obey you if you wish, for we have forsaken our fathers and our mothers and our villages and followed you. Grant us not to be tempted by the devil, the evil one."

GNaz 5

In the so-called Gospel according to the Hebrews instead of "essential to existence" I found "*mahar*," which means "of tomorrow," so that the sense is: Our bread of tomorrow—that is, of the future—give us this day.

[Luke 10:1]

In Q: Bussmann 67 (hesitantly). Easton Lk 176: Luke would not have introduced a reference to John on his own. Marshall Lk 456 (?): Despite Lukan vocabulary, the mention of John adds nothing to Luke's scene but is an interest of both Q and L. Polag 88 (uncertain).

Not in Q: Creed Lk 156: "A characteristically Lucan construction." Dibelius 1911: 43; Fitzmyer Lk 897–98; Jeremias 1980: 194; Schmithals Lk 131; Schulz 84 n. 185: The doubling of the introduction (11:1; 11:2a) and the presence of Lukan vocabulary in 11:1 suggests that it is editorial. Wernle 1899: 68.

Q 11:2–4

In Q: Bussmann 51, 66–68; Creed Lk 155 (probably); Crossan 1983: 97, 343; Easton Lk 176; Edwards 1975: 130–31; idem, 1976: xii, 38, 107; Fitzmyer Lk 78, 897; Hawkins 1911: 113; Hoffmann 4; Kilpatrick 1946: 20; Kloppenborg 1987: 202–5; Lambrecht 1985: 133. Marshall Lk 455: Luke has drawn from Q while Matthew substituted an alternate version. Müller 1908: 51; Polag 48; Schenk 61–62; Schmid 232; Schulz 84–86; Vassiliadis 1978: 70 (with hesitation); Zeller 56–57 and many others.

Harnack (63–66, 114, 179, 208) hesitantly assigns the prayer to Q. He contends that the original text of Luke 11:2 contained only a petition for the spirit (see textual notes). Accordingly, the disagreements between Matthew and Luke in wording, and the serious divergence in relative placement make it only "more or less probable" that the prayer belonged to Q.

Not in Q: The differences in wording and order between Matthew and Luke as well as the possibility of an independent liturgical transmission of the prayer have inclined some critics to exclude the prayer from Q. Hunter 64; Manson 167, 265. Streeter 1924: 277: Regardless of whether the reading of ms 700 or Codex Vaticanus is accepted for Luke 11:2 (see Harnack [above] and the textual notes), the differences between Matthew and Luke are too great for the prayer to derive from Q. Matthew's prayer occurs in an M block, and Luke's in a section of L.

Matt 6:7–13

[⁷"When praying do not babble as the Gentiles do; for they think that by their wordiness they will obtain a hearing. ⁸Do not be like them, for your Father knows what you need before you ask him.]

⁹Pray then like this:
   Our Father in heaven,
   May your name be holy.
¹⁰May your reign come,
   Your will be done,
      On earth as it is in heaven.
¹¹Give us today our daily bread;
¹²And forgive us our debts,
      As we also have forgiven our debtors;
¹³And do not lead us to the test,
      But deliver us from the evil one."

Luke 11:1–4

   [¹And it happenened that he was in a certain place praying, and when he finished, one of his disciples said to him, "Lord teach us to pray, as John also taught his disciples."]
²He said to them, "When you pray, say:
   "Father,
may your name be holy.
May your reign come.

³Give us each day our daily bread;
⁴and forgive us our sins,
for we ourselves forgive every one who is indebted to us;
and do not lead us to the test."

Matt 7:7–11

Luke 11:5–8, 9–13

[⁵Καὶ εἶπεν πρὸς αὐτούς· τίς ἐξ ὑμῶν ἕξει φίλον καὶ
πορεύσεται πρὸς αὐτὸν μεσονυκτίου καὶ εἴπῃ αὐτῷ·
φίλε, χρῆσόν μοι τρεῖς ἄρτους, ⁶ἐπειδὴ φίλος μου
παρεγένετο ἐξ ὁδοῦ πρός με καὶ οὐκ ἔχω ὃ παραθήσω
αὐτῷ· ⁷κἀκεῖνος ἔσωθεν ἀποκριθεὶς εἴπῃ· μή μοι κόπους
πάρεχε· ἤδη ἡ θύρα κέκλεισται καὶ τὰ παιδία μου μετ’
ἐμοῦ εἰς τὴν κοίτην εἰσίν· οὐ δύναμαι ἀναστὰς δοῦναί
σοι. ⁸λέγω ὑμῖν, εἰ καὶ οὐ δώσει αὐτῷ ἀναστὰς διὰ τὸ
εἶναι φίλον αὐτοῦ, διά γε τὴν ἀναίδειαν αὐτοῦ ἐγερθεὶς
δώσει αὐτῷ ὅσων χρῄζει].

⁷<u>Αἰτεῖτε καὶ δοθήσεται</u>
<u>ὑμῖν, ζητεῖτε καὶ εὑρήσετε, κρούετε καὶ</u>
<u>ἀνοιγήσεται ὑμῖν·</u> ⁸<u>πᾶς γὰρ ὁ αἰτῶν</u>
<u>λαμβάνει καὶ ὁ ζητῶν εὑρίσκει καὶ τῷ</u>
<u>κρούοντι ἀνοιγήσεται.</u> ⁹ἢ <u>τίς ἐστιν ἐξ ὑμῶν</u>
ἄνθρωπος, ὃν <u>αἰτήσει ὁ υἱὸς</u> αὐτοῦ <u>ἄρτον,</u>
μὴ <u>λίθον ἐπιδώσει αὐτῷ;</u> ¹⁰ἢ καὶ <u>ἰχθύν αἰτήσει,</u>
μὴ <u>ὄφιν ἐπιδώσει αὐτῷ;</u>
¹¹<u>εἰ οὖν ὑμεῖς πονηροὶ</u> ὄντες   <u>οἴδατε</u>
<u>δόματα ἀγαθὰ διδόναι τοῖς τέκνοις ὑμῶν,</u>
<u>πόσῳ μᾶλλον ὁ πατὴρ</u> ὑμῶν ὁ ἐν τοῖς
οὐρανοῖς <u>δώσει ἀγαθὰ</u>   <u>τοῖς αἰτοῦσιν αὐτόν.</u>

⁹<u>Κἀγὼ ὑμῖν λέγω·</u> <u>αἰτεῖτε καὶ δοθήσεται</u>
<u>ὑμῖν, ζητεῖτε καὶ εὑρήσετε, κρούετε καὶ</u>
<u>ἀνοιγήσεται ὑμῖν·</u> ¹⁰<u>πᾶς γὰρ ὁ αἰτῶν</u>
<u>λαμβάνει καὶ ὁ ζητῶν εὑρίσκει καὶ τῷ</u>
<u>κρούοντι ἀνοιγ[ήσ]εται.</u> ¹¹ <u>τίνα</u> δὲ <u>ἐξ ὑμῶν</u>
τὸν πατέρα <u>αἰτήσει ὁ υἱὸς</u> <u>ἰχθὺν</u> καὶ ἀντὶ
ἰχθύος <u>ὄφιν αὐτῷ ἐπιδώσει;</u> ¹²ἢ καὶ <u>αἰτήσει</u>
ᾠόν, <u>ἐπιδώσει αὐτῷ</u> σκορπίον;
¹³<u>εἰ οὖν ὑμεῖς πονηροὶ</u> ὑπάρχοντες <u>οἴδατε</u>
<u>δόματα ἀγαθὰ διδόναι τοῖς τέκνοις ὑμῶν,</u>
<u>πόσῳ μᾶλλον ὁ πατὴρ</u>   [ὁ] ἐξ
οὐρανοῦ <u>δώσει</u> πνεῦμα ἅγιον <u>τοῖς αἰτοῦσιν αὐτόν.</u>

Luke 11:10: ανοιγεται: 𝔓⁷⁵ B D sy bo [GNT] /
ανοιχθησεται: A K W Γ Δ 565 1010 1424 *pc* / txt (Matt):
𝔓⁴⁵ ℵ B C L R Θ Ψ λ φ 28 33 700 892 1241 *pm* [NA²⁵·²⁶;
HG] // 11: μη αντι ιχθυος: ℵ A C D L R W Koine Θ λ φ latt
[NA²⁵; HG] / μη και αντι ιχθυος: Γ 1012 / txt: 𝔓⁴⁵·⁷⁵ B sa
[NA²⁶] // 12: μη επιδωσει: ℵ A (C) D R W Koine Θ Ψ λ φ
latt saᵐˢˢ bo; Mcion [HG] / txt: 𝔓⁴⁵·⁷⁵ B L 892 *pc* saᵐˢˢ
[NA²⁵·²⁶].

GThom 92

ⲡⲉⲭⲉ ⲓ̅ⲥ̅ ⲭⲉ ϣⲓⲛⲉ ⲁⲩⲱ ⲧⲉⲧⲛⲁϭⲓⲛⲉ ⲁⲗⲗⲁ ⲛⲉⲧⲁⲧⲉⲧⲛ̅ϫⲛⲟⲩⲉⲓ ⲉⲣⲟⲟⲩ ⲛ̅ⲛⲓⲍⲟⲟⲩ ⲉⲙⲡⲓⲭⲟⲟⲩ ⲛⲏⲧⲛ̅ ⲙ̅ⲫⲟⲟⲩ ⲉⲧⲙ̅ⲙⲁⲩ ⲧⲉⲛⲟⲩ ⲉⲍⲛⲁⲓ̈ ⲉⲭⲟⲟⲩ ⲁⲩⲱ ⲧⲉⲧⲛ̅ϣⲓⲛⲉ ⲁⲛ ⲛ̅ⲥⲱⲟⲩ.

GThom 94

[ⲡⲉⲭⲉ] ⲓ̅ⲥ̅ ⲡⲉⲧϣⲓⲛⲉ ϥⲛⲁϭⲓⲛⲉ [ⲁⲩⲱ ⲡⲉⲧⲧⲱϩⲙ ⲉ]ϩⲟⲩⲛ ⲥⲉⲛⲁⲟⲩⲱⲛ ⲛⲁϥ.

John 14:13–14

¹³καὶ ὅ τι ἂν αἰτήσητε ἐν τῷ ὀνόματί μου τοῦτο ποιήσω, ἵνα δοξασθῇ ὁ πατὴρ ἐν τῷ υἱῷ. ¹⁴ ἐάν τι αἰτήσητέ με ἐν τῷ ὀνόματί μου ἐγὼ ποιήσω.

John 15:7

⁷ἐὰν μείνητε ἐν ἐμοὶ καὶ τὰ ῥήματά μου ἐν ὑμῖν μείνῃ, ὃ ἐὰν θέλητε αἰτήσασθε, καὶ γενήσεται ὑμῖν.

John 16:23–24

²³Καὶ ἐν ἐκείνῃ τῇ ἡμέρᾳ ἐμὲ οὐκ ἐρωτήσετε οὐδέν. ἀμὴν ἀμὴν λέγω ὑμῖν, ἄν τι αἰτήσητε τὸν πατέρα ἐν τῷ ὀνόματί μου δώσει ὑμῖν. ²⁴ἕως ἄρτι οὐκ ᾐτήσατε οὐδὲν ἐν τῷ ὀνόματί μου· αἰτεῖτε καὶ λήμψεσθε, ἵνα ἡ χαρὰ ὑμῶν ᾖ πεπληρωμένη.

POxy 654.5–9

[λέγει ᾽Ιη(σοῦ)ς]· μὴ παυσάσθω ὁ ζη[τῶν τοῦ ζητεῖν ἕως ἂν] εὕρῃ, καὶ ὅταν εὕρῃ [θαμβηθήσεται, καὶ θαμ]βηθεὶς βασιλεύσῃ, κα[ὶ βασιλεύσας ἐπαναπα]ήσεται.

GThom 2

ⲡⲉⲭⲉ ⲓ̅ⲥ̅ ⲙⲛ̅ⲧⲣⲉϥⲗⲟ ⲛ̅ϭⲓ ⲡⲉⲧϣⲓⲛⲉ ⲉϥϣⲓⲛⲉ ϣⲁⲛⲧⲉϥϭⲓⲛⲉ ⲁⲩⲱ ϩⲟⲧⲁⲛ ⲉϥϣⲁⲛϭⲓⲛⲉ ϥⲛⲁϣⲧⲣ̅ⲧⲣ̅ ⲁⲩⲱ ⲉϥϣⲁⲛϣⲧⲟⲣ̅ⲧⲣ̅ ϥⲛⲁⲣ̅ (blank) ϣⲡⲏⲣⲉ ⲁⲩⲱ ϥⲛⲁⲣ̅ ⲣ̅ⲣⲟ ⲉϫⲙ̅ ⲡⲧⲏⲣϥ.

GHeb 4a, 4b

⁴ᵃἧ, κἂν τῷ καθ᾽ ῾Εβραίους εὐαγγελίῳ, ὁ θαυμάσας βασιλεύσει, γέγραπται, καὶ ὁ βασιλεύσας ἀναπαήσεται.

⁴ᵇ῎Ισον γὰρ τούτοις ἐκεῖνα δύναται· οὐ παύσεται ὁ ζητῶν, ἕως ἂν εὕρῃ, εὑρὼν δὲ θαμβηθήσεται· θαμβηθεὶς δὲ βασιλεύσει, βασιλεύσας δὲ ἐπαναπαήσεται.

GThom 92

Jesus said, "Seek and you will find. In the past I did not tell you the things about which you asked me then. Now I am willing to tell them, but you are not seeking them."

GThom 94

Jesus [said], "One who seeks will find, and to [one who knocks] it will be opened."

John 14:13–14

¹³Whatever you ask in my name, I will do it, that the Father may be glorified in the Son; ¹⁴if you ask anything in my name, I will do it.

John 15:7

⁷If you abide in me, and my discourses abide in you, ask whatever you wish, and it shall be done for you.

John 16:23–24

²³And in that day you will ask nothing of me. Amen, amen, I tell you, if you ask anything of the Father in my name, he will give it to you. ²⁴Hitherto you have asked nothing in my name; ask, and you will receive, that your joy may be full.

POxy 654.5–9

[Jesus said], "Let him who seeks continue [seeking until] he finds. When he finds, [he will be amazed. And] when he becomes [amazed], he will rule. And [once he has ruled], he will [attain rest]."

GThom 2

Jesus said, "Let one who seeks not stop seeking until one finds. When one finds, one will be disturbed. When one is disturbed, one will marvel, and will reign over all."

GHeb 4a, 4b

⁴ᵃAs also it stands in the Gospel of the Hebrews: "He that marvels shall reign, and he that has reigned shall rest." ⁴ᵇTo those words this is equivalent: "He that seeks will not rest until he finds; and he that has found shall marvel; and he that has marvelled shall reign; and he that has reigned shall rest."

[Luke 11:5–8]

In Q: Catchpole (1983a: 418–19) offers three arguments: (1) V. 9 provides a "concluding inference" for 11:5–8 which by itself lacks an application. (2) The transition between vv. 5–8 and vv. 9–13 is smooth and the "three metaphors — asking, seeking, and knocking — in [vv. 9–13] are envisaged by [vv. 5–8]." (3) Both vv. 5–8 and vv. 9–13 make the same point concerning God's provision. As elsewhere in Q (12:24–28; 9:57–60; 7:33–34; 11:31–32), two parallel illustrations are employed. Easton Lk xxi, 177: The connection with Q 11:9–13 is excellent and τίς ἐξ ὑμῶν (v. 5) is frequent in Q. Since he transferred Q 11:9–13 to the Sermon on the Mount, Matthew could not use the parable. Knox 1957: 30: Matthew omitted it because it added nothing to the teaching which follows. Marshall Lk 463 (possible, but lacks proof); Polag 84 (uncertain). Schmid 241–42: Q 11:9–13 is the application of the parable (11:5–8). The mention of "knocking" in vv. 9–10 presupposes the preceeding story. Schürmann 1968: 119, 213, 222: The phrase καὶ εἶπεν πρός (11:5) is un–Lukan. Matthew's knowledge of Q 11:5–8 is suggested by his use of ὧν χρείαν ἔχετε in his introduction to the Lord's prayer (Matt 6:8 [S27]), which is an echo of ὅσων χρῄζει (Luke 11:8); Weiss 1907: 72.

Not in Q: Most authors. Sato (1984: 64) ascribes vv. 5–8 to Q^Lk.

Q 11:9–13

In Q: Most authors.

Matt 7:7–11

Luke 11:5–13

[⁵And he said to them, "Which of you who has a friend will go to him at midnight and say to him, 'Friend, lend me three loaves; ⁶for a friend of mine has come from a journey, and I have nothing to set before him'; ⁷and he will answer from within, 'Do not bother me; the door is now shut, and my children are with me in bed; I cannot get up and give you anything'? ⁸I tell you, though he will not get up and give him anything because he is his friend, yet because of his persistence he will rise and give him whatever he needs.]

⁷Ask, and it will be given you; seek, and you will find; knock, and it will be opened to you. ⁸For every one who asks receives, and whoever seeks finds, and whoever knocks is admitted. ⁹Or who among you, if his son asks him for bread, will give him a stone? ¹⁰Or if he asks for a fish, will give him a snake? ¹¹If you then, being selfish, know how to give good gifts to your children, how much more will your Father who is in heaven give good things to those who ask him!

⁹And I tell you, Ask, and it will be given you; seek, and you will find; knock, and it will be opened to you. ¹⁰For every one who asks receives, and whoever seeks finds, and whoever knocks is admitted. ¹¹What father among you, if his son asks for a fish, will instead of a fish give him a snake; ¹²or if he asks for an egg, will give him a scorpion? ¹³If you then, being selfish, know how to give good gifts to your children, how much more will the heavenly Father give the Holy Spirit to those who ask him!"

Matt 12:22–30

²²Τότε προσηνέχθη αὐτῷ δαιμονιζόμενος
τυφλὸς καὶ κωφός, καὶ ἐθεράπευσεν αὐτόν,
ὥστε τὸν κωφὸν λαλεῖν καὶ βλέπειν.
²³καὶ ἐξίσταντο πάντες οἱ ὄχλοι καὶ ἔλεγον· μήτι οὗτός
ἐστιν ὁ υἱὸς Δαυίδ;
²⁴οἱ δὲ Φαρισαῖοι ἀκούσαντες εἶπον·
οὗτος οὐκ ἐκβάλλει τὰ δαιμόνια εἰ μὴ
ἐν τῷ Βεελζεβοὺλ ἄρχοντι τῶν δαιμονίων.

Matt 12:38 ⇨ Q 11:29–32 [S32]

²⁵   εἰδὼς δὲ   τὰς ἐνθυμήσεις αὐτῶν
εἶπεν αὐτοῖς·
πᾶσα βασιλεία   μερισθεῖσα καθ᾽
ἑαυτῆς ἐρημοῦται καὶ πᾶσα πόλις ἢ οἰκία μερισθεῖσα
καθ᾽ ἑαυτῆς οὐ σταθήσεται.
²⁶καὶ εἰ   ὁ σατανᾶς τὸν σατανᾶν ἐκβάλλει,
ἐφ᾽ ἑαυτὸν   ἐμερίσθη· πῶς οὖν σταθήσεται
ἡ βασιλεία αὐτοῦ;

²⁷καὶ εἰ ἐγὼ ἐν Βεελζεβοὺλ ἐκβάλλω τὰ
δαιμόνια, οἱ υἱοὶ ὑμῶν ἐν τίνι ἐκβάλλουσιν;
διὰ τοῦτο αὐτοὶ κριταὶ ἔσονται ὑμῶν.
²⁸εἰ δὲ ἐν πνεύματι θεοῦ ἐγὼ ἐκβάλλω τὰ
δαιμόνια, ἄρα ἔφθασεν ἐφ᾽ ὑμᾶς ἡ βασιλεία
τοῦ θεοῦ.
(²⁹ἢ πῶς δύναταί τις εἰσελθεῖν εἰς τὴν οἰκίαν
τοῦ ἰσχυροῦ καὶ τὰ σκεύη αὐτοῦ ἁρπάσαι,
ἐὰν μὴ πρῶτον δήσῃ τὸν ἰσχυρόν;

καὶ τότε τὴν οἰκίαν αὐτοῦ διαρπάσει).
³⁰ὁ μὴ ὢν μετ᾽ ἐμοῦ κατ᾽ ἐμοῦ ἐστιν, καὶ
ὁ μὴ συνάγων μετ᾽ ἐμοῦ σκορπίζει.

Luke 11:14–23

¹⁴Καὶ ἦν ἐκβάλλων δαιμόνιον [καὶ αὐτὸ ἦν]
κωφόν· ἐγένετο δὲ τοῦ δαιμονίου ἐξελθόντος
ἐλάλησεν ὁ κωφός
καὶ ἐθαύμασαν οἱ ὄχλοι,

¹⁵τινὲς δὲ ἐξ αὐτῶν εἶπον·

ἐν   Βεελζεβοὺλ τῷ ἄρχοντι τῶν δαιμονίων
ἐκβάλλει τὰ δαιμόνια·
¹⁶ἕτεροι δὲ πειράζοντες σημεῖον ἐξ οὐρανοῦ ἐζήτουν παρ᾽
αὐτοῦ.
¹⁷αὐτὸς δὲ εἰδὼς αὐτῶν τὰ διανοήματα
εἶπεν αὐτοῖς·
πᾶσα βασιλεία ἐφ᾽ ἑαυτὴν διαμερισθεῖσα
ἐρημοῦται καὶ οἶκος ἐπὶ οἶκον πίπτει.

¹⁸   εἰ δὲ καὶ ὁ σατανᾶς
ἐφ᾽ ἑαυτὸν διεμερίσθη, πῶς   σταθήσεται ἡ
βασιλεία αὐτοῦ;
   [ὅτι λέγετε ἐν Βεελζεβοὺλ ἐκβάλλειν με τὰ δαιμόνια.]
¹⁹εἰ δὲ ἐγὼ ἐν Βεελζεβοὺλ ἐκβάλλω τὰ
δαιμόνια, οἱ υἱοὶ ὑμῶν ἐν τίνι ἐκβάλλουσιν;
διὰ τοῦτο αὐτοὶ ὑμῶν κριταὶ ἔσονται.
²⁰εἰ δὲ ἐν δακτύλῳ θεοῦ [ἐγὼ] ἐκβάλλω τὰ
δαιμόνια, ἄρα ἔφθασεν ἐφ᾽ ὑμᾶς ἡ βασιλεία
τοῦ θεοῦ.
(²¹ὅταν ὁ ἰσχυρὸς καθωπλισμένος φυλάσσῃ τὴν ἑαυτοῦ
αὐλήν, ἐν εἰρήνῃ ἐστὶν τὰ ὑπάρχοντα αὐτοῦ.
²²ἐπὰν δὲ ἰσχυρότερος αὐτοῦ ἐπελθὼν νικήσῃ αὐτόν,
τὴν πανοπλίαν αὐτοῦ αἴρει ἐφ᾽ ᾗ ἐπεποίθει,
καὶ τὰ σκῦλα αὐτοῦ διαδίδωσιν).
²³ὁ μὴ ὢν μετ᾽ ἐμοῦ κατ᾽ ἐμοῦ ἐστιν, καὶ
ὁ μὴ συνάγων μετ᾽ ἐμοῦ σκορπίζει.

Matt 12:24, 27: Βεελζεβουλ: ℵ B [NA²⁵] / Beelzebub: c (ff²)
vg sy^{s.c.p} / txt: 𝔭²¹ C D (L) W Koine Θ λ φ it sy^h (co); Or
[NA²⁶; HG: Βεελ Ζεβουλ].

Luke 11:14: και αυτο ην: A^c C W X Koine Δ Θ Π Ψ φ pm
latt sy^{p.h} geo [NA²⁵·²⁶; HG] / omit: 𝔭⁴⁵ 𝔭⁷⁵ ℵ A* B L λ 33
892 1241 sy^{c.s} sa bo arm eth // 15, 18, 19: Βεελζεβουλ: ℵ B
[NA²⁵] / Beelzebub: aur c vg sy^{s.c.p} / txt: 𝔭⁴⁵·⁷⁵ A C D (L)
R W Koine Θ Ψ λ φ sy^h sa bo; Or [NA²⁶; HG: Βεελ
Ζεβουλ] // 19: αυτοι υμων κριται εσονται: 𝔭⁷⁵ B D 579 700
pc c [NA²⁵·²⁶] / αυτοι κριται εσονται υμων (Matt): ℵ it vg /

αυτοι εσονται υμων κριται: 𝔭⁴⁵ 477 1194 1604 / αυτοι
κριται υμων εσονται: A C K L W Θ Ψ λ φ 33 892 1241 pm
[HG] / κριται υμων εσονται αυτοι: R Γ Δ 28 565 1010
1424 pm // 20: ει δε εγω εν δακτυλω θεου (v. 19): N D pc c
sa bo; Mcion Bas / ει δε εγω εν δακτυλω θεου εγω: 𝔭⁷⁵ ℵ¹ B C L
R φ 33 579 892 1071 al ff² l q r¹ sy [NA²⁵·²⁶] / ει δε εν
δακτυλω θεου: 𝔭⁴⁵ ℵ* A W Koine Θ Ψ λ φ lat sy sa bo // 23:
σκορπιζει με: ℵ*·² C² L Θ Ψ 33 892 pc sy bo eth [HG] / txt:
𝔭⁴⁵ 𝔭⁷⁵ ℵ¹ A B C* D R W Koine λ φ lat sy sa bo^{mss}
[NA²⁵·²⁶].

Matt 9:32–34

³²Αὐτῶν δὲ ἐξερχομένων ἰδοὺ προσήνεγκαν αὐτῷ ἄνθρωπον **κωφὸν** δαιμονιζόμενον. ³³καὶ ἐκβληθέντος **τοῦ δαιμονίου ἐλάλησεν ὁ κωφός.** καὶ ἐθαύμασαν οἱ ὄχλοι λέγοντες· οὐδέποτε ἐφάνη οὕτως ἐν τῷ Ἰσραήλ. ³⁴οἱ δὲ Φαρισαῖοι ἔλεγον·

ἐν   τῷ ἄρχοντι τῶν δαιμονίων
ἐκβάλλει τὰ δαιμόνια.

Matt 9:32–34

³²As they were going away, behold, they brought to him a mute who was demon-possessed. ³³And when the demon had been exorcised, the mute spoke; and the crowds marveled, saying, "Never was anything like this seen in Israel." ³⁴But the Pharisees were saying, "He exorcises demons by the prince of demons."

Mark 3:22–26

²²Καὶ οἱ γραμματεῖς οἱ ἀπὸ Ἱεροσολύμων καταβάντες ἔλεγον ὅτι **Βεελζεβοὺλ** ἔχει καὶ ὅτι
ἐν   τῷ ἄρχοντι τῶν δαιμονίων
ἐκβάλλει τὰ δαιμόνια.
²³καὶ προσκαλεσάμενος αὐτοὺς ἐν παραβολαῖς ἔλεγεν αὐτοῖς·
πῶς δύναται σατανᾶς σατανᾶν ἐκβάλλειν;
²⁴καὶ ἐὰν **βασιλεία** ἐφ' ἑαυτὴν μερισθῇ, οὐ δύναται σταθῆναι ἡ βασιλεία ἐκείνη· ²⁵καὶ ἐὰν οἰκία ἐφ' ἑαυτὴν μερισθῇ, οὐ δυνήσεται ἡ οἰκία ἐκείνη σταθῆναι.
²⁶καὶ εἰ ὁ **σατανᾶς** ἀνέστη ἐφ' ἑαυτὸν καὶ ἐμερίσθη, οὐ δύναται στῆναι ἀλλὰ τέλος ἔχει.

Mark 3:22–26

²²And the scribes who came down from Jerusalem said, "He is possessed by Beelzebul," and "by the prince of demons he exorcises the demons." ²³And summoning them, he said to them in parables, "How can Satan exorcise Satan? ²⁴If a kingdom is divided against itself, that kingdom cannot last. ²⁵And if a household is divided against itself, that household will not be able to survive. ²⁶And if Satan has risen up against himself and is divided, he cannot endure, but is finished."

Mark 3:27

²⁷ἀλλ' οὐ δύναται οὐδεὶς εἰς τὴν οἰκίαν τοῦ **ἰσχυροῦ** εἰσελθὼν τὰ σκεύη αὐτοῦ διαρπάσαι, ἐὰν μὴ πρῶτον τὸν ἰσχυρὸν δήσῃ, καὶ τότε τὴν οἰκίαν αὐτοῦ διαρπάσει.

Mark 3:27

²⁷But no one can enter a strong man's house and plunder his goods, unless he first binds the strong man; then indeed he may plunder his house.

GThom 35

ⲡⲉϫⲉ ⲓ̅ⲥ̅ ⲙⲛ̅ ϭⲟⲙ ⲛ̅ⲧⲉⲟⲩⲁ ⲃⲱⲕ ⲉϩⲟⲩⲛ ⲉⲡⲏⲉⲓ ⲙ̅ⲡϫⲱⲱⲣⲉ ⲛ̅ϥϫⲓⲧϥ̅ ⲛ̅ϫⲛⲁϩ ⲉⲓⲙⲏⲧⲓ ⲛ̅ϥⲙⲟⲩⲣ ⲛ̅ⲛⲉϥϭⲓϫ ⲧⲟⲧⲉ ϥⲛⲁⲡⲱⲱⲛⲉ ⲉⲃⲟⲗ ⲙ̅ⲡⲉϥⲏⲉⲓ.

GThom 35

Jesus said, "One cannot enter the house of the strong and take it by force without tying the person's hands. Then one will loot the person's house."

Mark 9:40

⁴⁰ὃς γὰρ οὐκ ἔστιν καθ' ἡμῶν, ὑπὲρ ἡμῶν ἐστιν.

Mark 9:40

⁴⁰For whoever is not against us is for us.

POxy 1224 fr 2 recto col. i ⇨ S9

ὁ γὰρ μὴ ὢν [κατ' ὑμ]ῶν ὑπὲρ ὑμῶν ἐστιν. [ὁ σήμερον ὢ]ν μακρὰν αὔριον [ἐγγὺς ὑμῶν γ]ενήσεται.

POxy 1224 fr 2 recto col. i ⇨ S9

For whoever is not against you is for you. [Whoever today is] far-off tomorrow will [be near you].

Q 11:14-15, 17-20, 23

In Q: Most authors. A few verses are disputed. Harnack (21, 133) excludes vv. 15 and 18, and reconstructs Q (largely following Matthew) with Matt 12:22b, 23a, 25b, 27-28. Hawkins (1909: 109) includes only Luke 11:14, 19-20, presumably because of the Markan overlap of vv. 15, 17-18. The agreements between Matt 12:22-23; 9:32-33 and Luke 11:14 against Mark in relating an exorcism of a dumb demoniac, with mention of his speaking and the astonishment of the crowd, indicate that 11:14 is indeed from Q. The agreements between Matthew and Luke against Mark in 11:15 and 17 and the necessity of stating the accusation to which Q 11:19-20 responds likewise justify their ascription to Q.

[Luke 11:18b]

In Q: Easton Lk 183: The verse is too difficult to be Lukan. Marshall Lk 474.

Not in Q: This appears to be a Lukan insertion, influenced by Mark 3:30: ὅτι ἔλεγον· πνεῦμα ἀκάθαρτον ἔχει. Thus Bultmann 1963: 90, 327; Creed Lk 160; Fitzmyer Lk 918; Laufen 1980: 129; Lührmann 33; Meyer 71 n 1; Müller 1908: 13; Polag 51; Schenk 66; Schmithals Lk 133; Schulz 205.

(Q 11:21-22)

In Q: Bultmann 1963: 13-14; Creed Lk 161; Easton 1913: 63; idem, Lk 183; Edwards 1976: xii, 110 (but idem, 1975: 134-36 concords no vocabulary from vv. 21-22); Fitzmyer Lk 918, 922 (probably); Hunter 137; Laufen 1980: 30; Käsemann 1964: 245; Kloppenborg 1987: 125; Manson 84; Marshall Lk 476-77; Müller 1908: 4, 48; Polag 52; Schmid 292; Schmithals Lk 134 (perhaps); Schweizer Lk 128; Mt 184-85; Steinhauser 1981: 143; Vassiliadis 1978: 70; Weiss 1907: 117; Zeller 59. The main argument for the inclusion of the parable in Q is that the agreement of Matthew and Luke in independently placing the parable of the strong man between Q 11:20 and 11:23 cannot be coincidental, but indicates that the parable also stood in Q at this point. Matthew preferred Mark to Q at this point.

Not in Q: Crossan 1983: 189; Jacobson 158; Legasse 1962: 5-9; Lührmann 33; Meyer 71; Schenk 136; Schulz 203: The Matthew-Luke agreements are too slight to posit Q; Matthew depends on Mark, and Luke rewrites Mark.

Matt 12:22–30

²²Then a blind and dumb man who was demon-possessed was brought to him, and he healed him, so that the dumb man spoke and saw. ²³And all the crowds were amazed, he said, "Can this be the Son of David?"
²⁴But when the Pharisees heard it they said, "It is only by Beelzebul, the prince of demons, that this man exorcises demons."

²⁵Knowing their thoughts, he said to them, "Every kingdom divided against itself is laid waste, and a city or household divided against itself will not survive.
²⁶And if Satan exorcises Satan, he is divided against himself; how then will his kingdom endure?

²⁷And if I exorcise demons by Beelzebul, by whom do your sons exorcise? Therefore they shall be your judges.
²⁸But if it is by the Spirit of God that I exorcise demons, then the reign of God has come upon you.
(²⁹Or how can one enter a strong man's house and plunder his property, unless he first binds the strong man? And then he may plunder his house.)

³⁰Whoever is not with me is against me, and whoever does not gather with me scatters."

Luke 11:14–23

¹⁴And he was exorcising a demon that was dumb; when the demon had gone out, the mute spoke, and the crowds marveled.

¹⁵But some of them said, "He exorcises demons by Beelzebul, the prince of demons."

¹⁶Now others, to test him, sought from him a sign from heaven.
¹⁷But he, knowing their thoughts, said to them, "Every kingdom divided against itself is laid waste, and house that is against house collapses.
¹⁸And if Satan also is divided against himself, how will his kingdom endure?
[For you say that I exorcise demons by Beelzebul.]
¹⁹And if I exorcise demons by Beelzebul, by whom do your sons exorcise? Therefore they shall be your judges.
²⁰But if it is by the finger of God that I exorcise demons, then the reign of God has come upon you.
(²¹When a strong man, fully armed, guards his own courtyard, his goods are safe; ²²but when one stronger than he overpowers him and conquers him, he takes away his armor in which he trusted, and divides his spoil.)
²³Whoever is not with me is against me, and whoever does not gather with me scatters."

Matt 12:43–45

⁴³Ὅταν δὲ τὸ ἀκάθαρτον πνεῦμα ἐξέλθῃ ἀπὸ τοῦ ἀνθρώπου, διέρχεται δι᾽ ἀνύδρων τόπων ζητοῦν ἀνάπαυσιν καὶ οὐχ εὑρίσκει. ⁴⁴ τότε λέγει· εἰς τὸν οἶκόν μου ἐπιστρέψω ὅθεν ἐξῆλθον· καὶ ἐλθὸν εὑρίσκει σχολάζοντα σεσαρωμένον καὶ κεκοσμημένον.
⁴⁵τότε πορεύεται καὶ παραλαμβάνει μεθ᾽ ἑαυτοῦ ἑπτὰ ἕτερα πνεύματα πονηρότερα ἑαυτοῦ καὶ εἰσελθόντα κατοικεῖ ἐκεῖ· καὶ γίνεται τὰ ἔσχατα τοῦ ἀνθρώπου ἐκείνου χείρονα τῶν πρώτων.
[οὕτως ἔσται καὶ τῇ γενεᾷ ταύτῃ τῇ πονηρᾷ].

Luke 11:24–26

²⁴Ὅταν   τὸ ἀκάθαρτον πνεῦμα ἐξέλθῃ ἀπὸ τοῦ ἀνθρώπου, διέρχεται δι᾽ ἀνύδρων τόπων ζητοῦν ἀνάπαυσιν καὶ μὴ εὑρίσκον [τότε] λέγει· ὑποστρέψω εἰς τὸν οἶκόν μου ὅθεν ἐξῆλθον· ²⁵καὶ ἐλθὸν εὑρίσκει σεσαρωμένον καὶ κεκοσμημένον.
²⁶τότε πορεύεται καὶ παραλαμβάνει
          ἕτερα πνεύματα πονηρότερα ἑαυτοῦ ἑπτὰ καὶ εἰσελθόντα κατοικεῖ ἐκεῖ· καὶ γίνεται τὰ ἔσχατα τοῦ ἀνθρώπου ἐκείνου χείρονα τῶν πρώτων.

Matt 12:44: σχολ. και: א C* 565 1424 it sy [NA²⁵] / txt: B C² Koine D L W Z Θ λ φ *pm* lat; Cyr [NA²⁶; HG] .

Luke 11:24: τοτε: 𝔭⁷⁵ א² Bᶜ L X Θ Ξ 0124 33 892 1241 *pc* it syʰ sa bo [NA²⁶] / omit: 𝔭⁴⁵ א* A C D W Koine λ φ lat sy [NA²⁵; HG] .

Notes

Q 11:24–26

Most authors place this in Q. The only point of dispute is its relative placement. Some put it after Q 11:23, i.e., in Lukan order: Bussmann 69; Creed Lk 161; Harnack 136, 266; Hoffmann 37, 299; Hunter 138; Kloppenborg 1987: 73; Lührmann 34; Manson 87; Marshall Lk 479 (hesitantly); Müller 1908: 30; Polag 52; Schenk 68; Schmid 294; Schmithals Lk 135; Schulz 476 n. 562; Strecker 1971: 103; Streeter 1911a: 153; Taylor 1972: 115; Vassiliadis 1982: 384; Zeller 59. The usual supposition is that Matthew transferred the saying to the end of the controversy section, where it could serve as a summary. Vassiliadis argues that Q used a "cyclical concentric" structure (a . . . b . . . x . . . b' . . . a') with the climax occurring in the middle. Hence 11:24–26, which serves as the climax, was originally placed between 11:14–23 and 11:29–32, but Matthew later moved the conclusion to the end.

Others argue that Matthew has preserved the original position, i.e., after Q 11:29–32: Crossan 1983: 344. Easton Lk 185: In Q, as in Matthew, this section served to summarize the controversy section. Jacobson 157, 160. Wernle 1899: 70: Since Q 11:24–26 has to do with impenitence, not blasphemy, Matthew's placement is more original.
Undecided: Fitzmyer Lk 924.

[Matt 12:45c]

In Q: Bultmann 164; Jacobson 158.
Not in Q: Creed Lk 161; Hoffmann 299; Manson 87; Müller 1908: 52; Polag 53; Schenk 69; Schmid 295; Schulz 477; Strecker 1971: 103.
Undecided: Fitzmyer Lk 924.

Matt 12:43–45

[43] Now when the unclean spirit has gone out of a person, he goes through arid places seeking a resting place, and he finds none. [44] Then he says, 'I will return to my house whence I came.' And when he comes he finds it unoccupied, swept, and put in order. [45] Then he goes and brings with him seven other spirits more evil than himself, and they enter and dwell there; and the last state of that person becomes worse than the first.

[So shall it be also with this evil generation.]

Luke 11:24–26

[24] When the unclean spirit has gone out of a person, he goes through arid places seeking a resting place; and having found none, then he says, 'I will return to my house whence I came.' [25] And when he comes he finds it swept and put in order. [26] Then he goes and brings seven other spirits more evil than himself, and they enter and dwell there; and the last state of that person becomes worse than the first.

Luke 11:27–28

(²⁷Ἐγένετο δὲ ἐν τῷ λέγειν αὐτὸν ταῦτα ἐπάρασά τις φωνὴν γυνὴ ἐκ τοῦ ὄχλου εἶπεν αὐτῷ· μακαρία ἡ κοιλία ἡ βαστάσασά σε καὶ μαστοὶ οὓς ἐθήλασας. ²⁸αὐτὸς δὲ εἶπεν· μενοῦν μακάριοι οἱ ἀκούοντες τὸν λόγον τοῦ θεοῦ καὶ φυλάσσοντες).

Notes

(Q 11:27–28)

In Q: Crossan 1983: 344; Hawkins 1911: 134: Matthew omitted this as unsuitable. Hunter 138 (but possibly from L). Jacobson 158: Although Mark has a story about Jesus' relatives (3:31–35) at the end of his Beelzebul accusation (3:24–27), Matthew and Luke concur in placing the saying concerning hearing and doing immediately after the return of the evil spirit (Matt 12:43–45 // Luke 11:24–26 ⇨ [S30]). This suggests that the saying occurred in Q and that while Matthew followed Mark, he was influenced by the Q setting of Q 11:27–28. Manson 85, 88: While the introduction is Lukan, the substance of the story is from Q. Schmid 295: If Matthew inverted the order of Q 11:24–26 and 11:29–32 (⇨ [S30]) then his omission of Q 11:27–28 is understandable, since he would have replaced it with a version of Mark 3:31–35. Schürmann 1968: 231; Streeter 1924: 278–79; Vassiliadis 1978: 70.

Not in Q: Bussmann; Easton Lk 184; Edwards 1975; idem 1976. Fitzmyer Lk 926–27: There is not the slightest hint that Matthew knew the story. Harnack; Hoffmann; Marshall Lk 481; Müller 1908: 7, 52; Polag; Schenk; Schmithals Lk 135; Schulz; Weiss 1907: 206; Zeller.

Luke 11:27–28

(²⁷As he was saying these things, a woman from the crowd raised her voice and said to him, "Blessed is the womb that bore you, and the breasts that you sucked!" ²⁸But he said, "Blessed rather are those who listen to the word of God and keep it!")

Parallels

GThom 79

πεχε ογς2ιμ[ε] ναϥ 2Μ πμηϣε χε νεειατ[c
ν]θ2η Ντα2ϥι 2αροκ αγω Νκι[β]ε
 εντα2cα2νογϣκ. πεχαϥ να[c] χε νεειατογ
Ννεντα2cωτΜ απλογος Μπειωτ αγαρε2 εροϥ
2Ν ογμε ογΝ 2Ν2οογ γαρ ναϣωπε Ντετνχοος
χε νεειατⲥ Νθ2η ταει ετε μπcω αγω Νκιβε
ναει εμπογϯ ερωτε.

Mark 3:31–35

³¹Καὶ ἔρχεται ἡ μήτηρ αὐτοῦ καὶ οἱ ἀδελφοὶ αὐτοῦ καὶ ἔξω στήκοντες ἀπέστειλαν πρὸς αὐτὸν καλοῦντες αὐτόν. ³²καὶ ἐκάθητο περὶ αὐτὸν ὄχλος, καὶ λέγουσιν αὐτῷ· ἰδοὺ ἡ μήτηρ σου καὶ οἱ ἀδελφοί σου [καὶ αἱ ἀδελφαί σου] ἔξω ζητοῦσίν σε. ³³ καὶ ἀποκριθεὶς αὐτοῖς λέγει· τίς ἐστιν ἡ μήτηρ μου καὶ οἱ ἀδελφοί [μου]; ³⁴καὶ περιβλεψάμενος τοὺς περὶ αὐτὸν κύκλῳ καθημένους λέγει· ἴδε ἡ μήτηρ μου καὶ οἱ ἀδελφοί μου. ³⁵ὃς [γὰρ] ἂν ποιήσῃ τὸ θέλημα τοῦ θεοῦ, οὗτος ἀδελφός μου καὶ ἀδελφὴ καὶ μήτηρ ἐστίν.

Matt 12:46–50

⁴⁶῎Ετι αὐτοῦ λαλοῦντος τοῖς ὄχλοις ἰδοὺ ἡ μήτηρ καὶ οἱ ἀδελφοὶ αὐτοῦ εἱστήκεισαν ἔξω ζητοῦντες αὐτῷ λαλῆσαι. ⁴⁷[εἶπεν δέ τις αὐτῷ· ἰδοὺ ἡ μήτηρ σου καὶ οἱ ἀδελφοί σου ἔξω ἑστήκασιν ζητοῦντές σοι λαλῆσαι]. ⁴⁸ὁ δὲ ἀποκριθεὶς εἶπεν τῷ λέγοντι αὐτῷ· τίς ἐστιν ἡ μήτηρ μου καὶ τίνες εἰσιν οἱ ἀδελφοί μου; ⁴⁹καὶ ἐκτείνας τὴν χεῖρα αὐτοῦ ἐπὶ τοὺς μαθητὰς αὐτοῦ εἶπεν· ἰδοὺ ἡ μήτηρ μου καὶ οἱ ἀδελφοί μου. ⁵⁰ὅστις γὰρ ἂν ποιήσῃ τὸ θέλημα τοῦ πατρός μου τοῦ ἐν οὐρανοῖς, αὐτός μου ἀδελφὸς καὶ ἀδελφὴ καὶ μήτηρ ἐστίν.

Luke 23:28–29

²⁸στραφεὶς δὲ πρὸς αὐτὰς [ὁ] ᾽Ιησοῦς εἶπεν· θυγατέρες ᾽Ιερουσαλήμ, μὴ κλαίετε ἐπ᾽ ἐμέ· πλὴν ἐφ᾽ ἑαυτὰς κλαίετε καὶ ἐπὶ τὰ τέκνα ὑμῶν, ²⁹ὅτι ἰδοὺ ἔρχονται αἱ ἡμέραι ἐν αἷς ἐροῦσιν· μακάριαι αἱ στεῖραι καὶ αἱ κοιλίαι αἳ οὐκ ἐγέννησαν καὶ μαστοὶ οἳ οὐκ ἔθρεψαν.

GThom 79

A woman in the crowd said to him, "Blessed are the womb that bore you and the breasts that fed you." He said to her, "Blessed are those who have heard the word of the Father and have truly kept it. For the days will come when you will say, 'Blessed are the womb that has not conceived and the breasts that have not produced milk.'"

Mark 3:31–35

³¹And his mother and his brothers came; and standing outside they sent to him and called him. ³²And a crowd was sitting about him; and they said to him, "Behold, your mother and your brothers [and your sisters] are outside, asking for you." ³³And he replied, "Who are my mother and my brothers?" ³⁴And looking around at those seated about him in a circle, he said, "Here are my mother and my brothers! ³⁵[For] whoever does the will of God is my brother, and sister, and mother."

Matt 12:46–50

⁴⁶While he was still speaking to the crowds, behold, his mother and his brothers stood outside, asking to speak to him. ⁴⁷[Someone said to him, "Behold, your mother and your brothers are standing outside, asking to speak to you."] ⁴⁸But he replied to the man who told him, "Who is my mother, and who are my brothers?" ⁴⁹And stretching out his hand toward his disciples, he said, "Behold my mother and my brothers! ⁵⁰For whoever does the will of my Father in heaven is my brother, and sister, and mother."

Luke 23:28–29

²⁸But turning to them Jesus said, "Daughters of Jerusalem, do not weep for me. Weep instead for yourselves and for your children, ²⁹for behold, the days are coming when they will say, 'Blessed are the barren, and the wombs that never bore, and the breasts that never gave suck!'"

Matt 12:38–42

³⁸Τότε ἀπεκρίθησαν αὐτῷ τινες τῶν γραμματέων καὶ Φαρισαίων λέγοντες· διδάσκαλε, θέλομεν ἀπὸ σοῦ σημεῖον ἰδεῖν.

³⁹ὁ δὲ ἀποκριθεὶς εἶπεν αὐτοῖς·

γενεὰ πονηρὰ καὶ μοιχαλὶς σημεῖον ἐπιζητεῖ, καὶ σημεῖον οὐ δοθήσεται αὐτῇ εἰ μὴ τὸ σημεῖον Ἰωνᾶ τοῦ προφήτου.

⁴⁰ὥσπερ γὰρ ἦν Ἰωνᾶς ἐν τῇ κοιλίᾳ τοῦ κήτους τρεῖς ἡμέρας καὶ τρεῖς νύκτας, οὕτως ἔσται ὁ υἱὸς τοῦ ἀνθρώπου ἐν τῇ καρδίᾳ τῆς γῆς τρεῖς ἡμέρας καὶ τρεῖς νύκτας.

⁴²βασίλισσα νότου ἐγερθήσεται ἐν τῇ κρίσει μετὰ τῆς γενεᾶς ταύτης καὶ κατακρινεῖ αὐτήν, ὅτι ἦλθεν ἐκ τῶ περάτων τῆς γῆς ἀκοῦσαι τὴν σοφίαν Σολομῶνος, καὶ ἰδοὺ πλεῖον Σολομῶνος ὧδε.

⁴¹ἄνδρες Νινευῖται ἀναστήσονται ἐν τῇ κρίσει μετὰ τῆς γενεᾶς ταύτης καὶ κατακρινοῦσιν αὐτήν, ὅτι μετενόησαν εἰς τὸ κήρυγμα Ἰωνᾶ, καὶ ἰδοὺ πλεῖον Ἰωνᾶ ὧδε.

Luke 11:16, 29–32

¹⁶ἕτεροι δὲ **πειράζοντες σημεῖον ἐξ οὐρανοῦ** ἐζητοῦν παρ᾽ αὐτοῦ.

⇨ 11:14–23 [S29]

²⁹τῶν δὲ ὄχλων ἐπαθροιζομένων ἤρξατο λέγειν· ἡ γενεὰ αὕτη γενεὰ πονηρά ἐστιν· σημεῖον ζητεῖ, καὶ σημεῖον οὐ δοθήσεται αὐτῇ εἰ μὴ τὸ σημεῖον Ἰωνᾶ.

³⁰καθὼς γὰρ ἐγένετο Ἰωνᾶς τοῖς Νινευίταις σημεῖον, οὕτως ἔσται καὶ ὁ υἱὸς τοῦ ἀνθρώπου τῇ γενεᾷ ταύτῃ.

³¹βασίλισσα νότου ἐγερθήσεται ἐν τῇ κρίσει μετὰ τῶν ἀνδρῶν τῆς γενεᾶς ταύτης καὶ κατακρινεῖ αὐτούς, ὅτι ἦλθεν ἐκ τῶν περάτων τῆς γῆς ἀκοῦσαι τὴν σοφίαν Σολομῶνος, καὶ ἰδοὺ πλεῖον Σολομῶνος ὧδε.

³²ἄνδρες Νινευῖται ἀναστήσονται ἐν τῇ κρίσει μετὰ τῆς γενεᾶς ταύτης καὶ κατακρινοῦσιν αὐτήν, ὅτι μετενόησαν εἰς τὸ κήρυγμα Ἰωνᾶ, καὶ ἰδοὺ πλεῖον Ἰωνᾶ ὧδε.

Luke 11:30: ο Ιωνας: B *pc* [NA²⁵] / Ιωνας: 𝔭⁷⁵ ℵ A C D W Koine Θ Ξ Ψ 0124 λ φ *pl* [NA²⁶; HG] // omit v. 32: D.

Matt 16:1–2a, 4

¹Καὶ προσελθόντες οἱ Φαρισαῖοι καὶ Σαδδουκαῖοι **πειράζοντες** ἐπηρώτησαν αὐτὸν **σημεῖον** ἐκ τοῦ <u>οὐρανοῦ</u> ἐπιδεῖξαι αὐτοῖς. ²ὁ δὲ ἀποκριθεὶς εἶπεν αὐτοῖς . . .

   ⇨ Q 12:54–56 [S47]

⁴**γενεὰ** πονηρὰ καὶ μοιχαλὶς **σημεῖον** ἐπιζητεῖ, καὶ σημεῖον οὐ δοθήσεται αὐτῇ εἰ μὴ τὸ σημεῖον Ἰωνᾶ.

Matt 16:1–2a, 4

¹ And the Pharisees and Sadducees came, and to test him they asked him to show them a sign from heaven. ² He answered them, . . .

⁴ An evil and adulterous generation seeks for a sign, and no sign shall be given to it except the sign of Jonah."

Mark 8:11–12

¹¹Καὶ ἐξῆλθον οἱ Φαρισαῖοι καὶ ἤρξαντο συζητεῖν αὐτῷ, ζητοῦντες παρ' αὐτοῦ **σημεῖον** ἀπὸ τοῦ οὐρανοῦ, **πειράζοντες** αὐτόν. ¹²καὶ ἀναστενάξας τῷ πνεύματι αὐτοῦ λέγει· τί ἡ **γενεὰ** αὕτη ζητεῖ **σημεῖον**; ἀμὴν λέγω ὑμῖν, εἰ δοθήσεται τῇ γενεᾷ ταύτῃ **σημεῖον**.

Mark 8:11–12

¹¹ And the Pharisees came and began to argue with him, seeking from him a sign from heaven, to test him. ¹² And sighing deeply in his spirit, he said, "Why does this generation seek a sign? Amen, I tell you, no sign shall be given to this generation."

John 6:30

³⁰Εἶπον οὖν αὐτῷ· τί οὖν ποιεῖς σὺ **σημεῖον**, ἵνα ἴδωμεν καὶ πιστεύσωμέν σοι; τί ἐργάζῃ;

John 6:30

³⁰ So they said to him, "Then what sign do you do, that we may see, and believe you? What will you perform?"

Jonah 2:1 LXX ⇨ Matt 12:40

¹Καὶ προσέταξεν κύριος κήτει μεγάλῳ καταπιεῖν τὸν Ἰωνᾶν· καὶ ἦν Ἰωνᾶς ἐν τῇ κοιλίᾳ τοῦ κήτους τρεῖς ἡμέρας καὶ τρεῖς νύκτας.

Jonah 2:1 LXX

¹ And the Lord commanded a large sea monster to swallow Jonah. And Jonah was three days and three nights in the belly of the sea monster.

17036

ATS Library 99
Nyack, NY 10960

Q 11:16, 29–32

Matthew has used the sign of Jonah tradition twice, once at its Q location (following the Beelzebul accusation and in conjunction with the return of the evil spirit) and once at its Markan location, i.e., following the feeding of the four thousand (Mark 8:1–10 // Matt 15:32–39) and prior to the warning against the leaven of the Pharisees (Mark 8:14–21 // Matt 16:5–12). While in the second version of the request for a sign the location is due to Mark, Matthew has assimilated the wording to that of Q by avoiding several peculiar features of Mark 8:12 (ἀναστενάζω, the oath formula εἰ δοθήσεται, and the solemn introduction), and by adding the exception clause (16:4c = 12:39c). For a full discussion see Edwards 1971 and Vögtle 1971a.

Q 11:31–32

The only dispute here concerns order. Most favor Lukan order: Bultmann 1963: 112; Crossan 1983: 344; Easton Lk 188; Hunter 138; Manson 91; Marshall Lk 486; Meyer 8 n. 1; Polag 52–54; Schenk 71; Schmid 297; Schulz 252; Vassiliadis 1982: 384; Vögtle 1971a; Zeller

62. Bultmann argues that the historical order (Solomon followed by Jonah) is the natural and original order, and that Matthew transposed the sayings in order to bring v. 32 into closer association with Q 11:30 which also speaks of Jonah and the Ninevites. Vögtle holds that the Lukan order is the more difficult and therefore the more original.

A few favor Matthean order: Bussmann 69: Luke inverted the two in order to achieve chronological order (Solomon followed by Jonah). Harnack 23: The reversal of the order of v. 31 and v. 32 is either due to "an ancient scribal error" or Luke 11:32 is an interpolation into the text of Luke (see textual notes). Lührmann 37–38: For stylistic reasons Luke placed v. 32 last. Plummer Lk 307: Luke inverts the order for the sake of chronology or because the case of the Ninevites was the stronger of the two. Rengstorf Lk 151 (as Bussmann).

Undecided: Fitzmyer Lk 931–32: While Matthew may have brought v. 41 into closer proximity to v. 40, alternatively, the Matthean order may reflect the topical grouping of Q and Luke may have altered the sequence in order to invest Jonah's preaching with sapiential overtones.

Matt 12:38–42

³⁸Then some of the scribes and Pharisees said to him, "Teacher, we wish to see a sign from you."

³⁹But he answered them, "An evil and adulterous generation seeks for a sign; and no sign shall be given to it except the sign of Jonah the prophet. ⁴⁰For as Jonah was three days and three nights in the belly of the sea monster, so will the Son of man be three days and three nights in the heart of the earth. ⁴²The queen of the South will arise at the judgment with this generation and condemn it; for she came from the ends of the earth to hear the wisdom of Solomon, and behold, something greater than Solomon is here.

⁴¹The Ninevite men will arise at the judgment with this generation and condemn it; for they repented at the preaching of Jonah, and behold, something greater than Jonah is here."

Luke 11:16

¹⁶Now others, to test him, were seeking from him a sign from heaven.

Luke 11:29–32

²⁹When the crowds were increasing, he began to say, "This generation is an evil generation; it seeks a sign, and no sign shall be given to it except the sign of Jonah. ³⁰For as Jonah became a sign to the Ninevites, so will the Son of man be to this generation.

³¹The queen of the South will arise at the judgment with the men of this generation and condemn them; for she came from the ends of the earth to hear the wisdom of Solomon, and behold, something greater than Solomon is here. ³²The Ninevite men will arise at the judgment with this generation and condemn it; for they repented at the preaching of Jonah, and behold, something greater than Jonah is here."

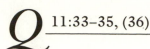

Matt 5:14–16

[¹⁴ᶜ Ὑμεῖς ἐστε τὸ φῶς τοῦ κόσμου. οὐ δύναται πόλις κρυβῆναι ἐπάνω ὄρους κειμένη·]
¹⁵οὐδὲ καίουσιν λύχνον καὶ τιθέασιν αὐτὸν ὑπὸ τὸν μόδιον ἀλλ’ ἐπὶ τὴν λυχνίαν, καὶ λάμπει πᾶσιν τοῖς ἐν τῇ οἰκίᾳ.

[¹⁶οὕτως λαμψάτω τὸ φῶς ὑμῶν ἔμπροσθεν τῶν ἀνθρώπων, ὅπως ἴδωσιν ὑμῶν τὰ καλὰ ἔργα καὶ δοξάσωσιν τὸν πατέρα ὑμῶν τὸν ἐν τοῖς οὐρανοῖς].

Matt 6:22–23

²²Ὁ λύχνος τοῦ σώματός ἐστιν ὁ ὀφθαλμός. ἐὰν οὖν ᾖ ὁ ὀφθαλμός σου ἁπλοῦς, ὅλον τὸ σῶμά σου φωτεινὸν ἔσται· ²³ἐὰν δὲ ὁ ὀφθαλμός σου πονηρὸς ᾖ, ὅλον τὸ σῶμά σου σκοτεινὸν ἔσται. εἰ οὖν τὸ φῶς τὸ ἐν σοὶ σκότος ἐστίν, τὸ σκότος πόσον.

Luke 11:33

³³Οὐδεὶς λύχνον ἅψας εἰς κρύπτην τίθησιν [οὐδὲ ὑπὸ τὸν μόδιον] ἀλλ’ ἐπὶ τὴν λυχνίαν, ἵνα οἱ εἰσπορευόμενοι τὸ φῶς βλέπωσιν.

Luke 11:34–36

³⁴Ὁ λύχνος τοῦ σώματός ἐστιν ὁ ὀφθαλμός σου. ὅταν ὁ ὀφθαλμός σου ἁπλοῦς ᾖ, καὶ ὅλον τὸ σῶμά σου φωτεινὸν ἐστιν. ἐπὰν δὲ πονηρὸς ᾖ, καὶ τὸ σῶμά σου σκοτεινόν. ³⁵σκόπει οὖν μὴ τό φῶς τὸ ἐν σοὶ σκότος ἐστίν. (³⁶εἰ οὖν τὸ σῶμά σου ὅλον φωτεινόν, μὴ ἔχον μέρος τι σκοτεινόν, ἔσται φωτεινὸν ὅλον ὡς ὅταν ὁ λύχνος τῇ ἀστραπῇ φωτίζῃ σε).

κρύπτη ⇨ Luke 12:2 (κρυπτόν) [S35]
φῶς ⇨ Luke 12:3 [S35]
οἱ εἰσπορευόμενοι ⇨ Luke 11:52 [S34]
σῶμα ⇨ Luke 12:4 [S36]
σκότος ⇨ Luke 12:3 (σκοτία) [S35]

Luke 11:33: ουδε υπο τον μοδιον: ℵ A B C D W Koine Θ Ψ φ *pm* latt [NA²⁵·²⁶; HG] / omit: 𝔓⁴⁵·⁷⁵ L Ξ 0124 (λ) 700* *al* syˢ sa // φεγγος: 𝔓⁴⁵ A K L W Koine Γ Δ Ψ 28 565 700 1010 *pm* [NA²⁵; HG] / φως (Luke 8:16): 𝔓⁷⁵ ℵ B C D Θ 0124 (λ) φ 33 892 1241 1424 *al* [NA²⁶].

Mark 4:21

²¹Καὶ ἔλεγεν αὐτοῖς· μήτι ἔρχεται ὁ λύχνος ἵνα ὑπὸ τὸν μόδιον τεθῇ ἢ ὑπὸ τὴν κλίνην; οὐχ ἵνα ἐπὶ τὴν λυχνίαν τεθῇ;

Luke 8:16

¹⁶Οὐδεὶς δὲ λύχνον ἄψας καλύπτει αὐτὸν σκεύει ἢ ὑποκάτω κλίνης τίθησιν, ἀλλ᾽ ἐπὶ λυχνίας τίθησιν, ἵνα οἱ εἰσπορευόμενοι βλέπωσιν τὸ φῶς.

GThom 33 ⇨ S35

ⲡⲉϫⲉ ⲓ̅ⲥ̅ ⲡⲉⲧⲕⲛⲁⲥⲱⲧⲙ̅ ⲉⲣⲟϥ ϩⲙ̅ ⲡⲉⲕⲙⲁⲁϫⲉ ϩⲙ̅ ⲡⲕⲉⲙⲁⲁϫⲉ ⲧⲁϣⲉⲟⲉⲓϣ ⲙ̅ⲙⲟϥ ϩⲓϫⲛ̅ ⲛⲉⲧⲛ̅ϫⲉⲛⲉⲡⲱⲣ ⲙⲁⲣⲉⲗⲁⲁⲩ ⲅⲁⲣ ϫⲉⲣⲉ ϩⲏⲃ̅ⲥ̅ ⲛ̅ϥⲕⲁⲁϥ· ϩⲁ ⲙⲁⲁϫⲉ ⲟⲩⲇⲉ ⲙⲁϥⲕⲁⲁϥ ϩⲙ̅ ⲙⲁ ⲉϥϩⲏⲡ· ⲁⲗⲗⲁ ⲉϣⲁⲣⲉϥⲕⲁⲁϥ ϩⲓϫⲛ̅ ⲧⲗⲩⲭⲛⲓⲁ ϫⲉⲕⲁⲁⲥ ⲟⲩⲟⲛ ⲛⲓⲙ ⲉⲧⲃⲏⲕ ⲉϩⲟⲩⲛ ⲁⲩⲱ ⲉⲧⲛ̅ⲛⲏⲩ ⲉⲃⲟⲗ ⲉⲩⲛⲁⲛⲁⲩ ⲁⲡⲉϥⲟⲩⲟⲉⲓⲛ.

GThom 24

ⲡⲉϫⲉ ⲛⲉϥⲙⲁⲑⲏⲧⲏⲥ ϫⲉ ⲙⲁⲧⲥⲉⲃⲟⲛ ⲉⲡⲧⲟⲡⲟⲥ ⲉⲧⲕⲙ̅ⲙⲁⲩ ⲉⲡⲉⲓ ⲧⲁⲛⲁⲅⲕⲏ ⲉⲣⲟⲛ ⲧⲉ ⲉⲧⲣⲛ̅ϣⲓⲛⲉ ⲛ̅ⲥⲱϥ. ⲡⲉϫⲁϥ ⲛⲁⲩ ϫⲉ ⲡⲉⲧⲉⲩⲛ̅ ⲙⲁⲁϫⲉ ⲙ̅ⲙⲟϥ ⲙⲁⲣⲉϥⲥⲱⲧⲙ̅ ⲟⲩⲛ̅ ⲟⲩⲟⲉⲓⲛ ϣⲟⲟⲡ ⲙ̅ⲫⲟⲩⲛ ⲛ̅ⲛⲟⲩⲣⲙ̅ⲟⲩⲟⲉⲓⲛ ⲁⲩⲱ ϥⲣ̅ ⲟⲩⲟⲉⲓⲛ ⲉⲡⲕⲟⲥⲙⲟⲥ ⲧⲏⲣϥ ⲉϥⲧⲙ̅ⲣ̅ ⲟⲩⲟⲉⲓⲛ ⲟⲩⲕⲁⲕⲉ ⲡⲉ.

DialSav 8

ⲡⲉ[ϫⲁϥ ⲛ̅ϭ]ⲓⲡⲥⲱⲧⲏⲣ ϫⲉⲡϩⲏⲃ̅ⲥ̅ [ⲙ̅ⲡⲥ]ⲱⲙⲁ ⲡⲉ ⲡⲛⲟⲩⲥ ⲉϥ ⲟⲥⲟⲛ [ⲛⲉⲧⲛ̅ϩⲏ]ⲧⲕ ⲥⲟⲩⲧⲱⲛ ⲉⲧⲉⲧⲁⲓ̈ ⲧⲉ [. . .].ⲥ ⲛⲉⲧⲛ̅ⲥⲱⲙⲁ ϩⲉⲛⲟⲩ[ⲟⲉⲓⲛ] ⲛⲉ· ⲉϥ ⲟⲥⲟⲛ ⲡⲉⲧⲛ̅ϩⲏⲧ [ⲟⲩⲕⲁ]ⲕⲉ ⲡⲉ· ⲡⲉⲧⲛ̅ⲟⲩⲟⲉⲓⲛ ⲉⲧⲉⲧⲛ̅ϭⲱϣⲧ ⲉⲃⲟⲗ ϩⲏ[ⲧϥ̅. . .]

Mark 4:21

²¹ And he said to them, "Is a lamp brought in to be put under a grain basket, or under a bed? Is it not to be placed on a lampstand?"

Luke 8:16

¹⁶ No one having lit a lamp covers it with a vessel, or puts it under a bed, but puts it on a lampstand, that those who enter may see the light.

GThom 33

Jesus said, "What you will hear in your ear (text adds: in the other ear) proclaim from your rooftops. For no one lights a lamp and puts it under a basket, nor does one put it in a hidden place. Rather, one puts it on a stand so that all who come and go will see its light."

GThom 24

His disciples said, "Show us the place where you are, for we must seek it."
He said to them, "Whoever has ears ought to listen. There is light within a person of light, and it (or: he) shines on the whole world. If it (or: he) does not shine, it (or: he) is dark."

DialSav 8

The Savior [said], "The lamp [of the body] is the mind. As long as [the things inside] you are set in order, that is [. . .] . . . your bodies are [luminous]. As long as your hearts are [dark], the luminosity you anticipate [. . .]"

Q 11:33

In Q: Most authors.

Not in Q: Neither Hawkins (1911) nor Vassiliadis (1978: 72) lists 11:33 although Hawkins includes 11:34–35 (p. 113). Edwards (1975; 1976) does not list 11:33.

Q 11:34–35 (36)

In Q: Most authors. The status of v. 36 is unclear. Some authors (Harnack, Müller 1908: 7; Schulz 469; Schenk 73; Zeller 36–37) exclude it because of the lack of strong agreement with Matthew. However, there is a slight agreement and it is as difficult to explain why Luke would have added such an obscure if not tautologous phrase as it is to explain its meaning in Q.

Not in Q: Vassiliadis 1978: 66, 68: Short sayings of a proverbial character, especially if placed differently by Matthew and Luke, should be excluded as possibly due to oral tradition. Sato (1984: 64) ascribes v. 36 to Q^{Lk}.

Q 11:33, 34–36

The placement of the two sayings is somewhat uncertain. Many authors assume that these two sayings belonged together and most place them between Q 11:14–32 and Q 11:39–52. Thus Crossan 1983: 344; Easton Lk 188; Jacobson 193; Kloppenborg 1987: 79; Manson 92; Polag 54; Schenk 73; Schürmann 1975: 134–45; Taylor 1972: 101; Wanke 1980: 221. Müller (1908: 30) agrees that the Lukan order is original, but places Q 14:34–35 (//Matt 5:13) prior to 11:33. Harnack (180), who supports the Matthean order of Q as original, argues that they belonged together in the Sermon on the Mount. Marshall (Lk 487) agrees that 11:33 and 11:34–36 were linked, but is uncertain whether they followed 11:29–32 in Q, while Schulz (475 n. 558) and Hoffmann (5) appear to think that both settings are redactional. Zeller (72–73; 1977: 191 n. 233 and 1982: 398) suggests that 11:33–36 was originally attached to Q 12:2–7 by the catchwords φῶς (11:33; 12:3), σκοτία, σκότος, σκοτεινός (Q 11:35; 12:3) and σῶμα (Q 11:34–36; 12:4). He adds that Luke's εἰς κρύπτην (11:33) may recall κρυπτόν (Q 12:2).

Matt 5:14–16

[¹⁴ You are the light of the world. A city set on a hill cannot be hid.]
¹⁵ Nor do they light a lamp and put it under a grain basket, but on a lampstand, and it gives light to all in the house.

[¹⁶ Let your light so shine before people, that they may see your good works and glorify your Father who is in heaven.]

Matt 6:22–23

²² The eye is the lamp of the body. So, if your eye is generous, your whole body will be full of light; ²³ but if your eye is evil, your whole body will be full of darkness. If then the light in you is darkness, how great is the darkness!

Luke 11:33

³³ No one having lit a lamp puts it in a cellar or under a grain basket, but on a lampstand, that those who enter may see the light.

Luke 11:34–36

³⁴ Your eye is the lamp of your body; when your eye is generous, your whole body is also full of light; but when it is evil, your body is also full of darkness. ³⁵ Therefore watch lest the light in you be darkness. (³⁶ If then your whole body is full of light, having no part dark, it will be completely full of light, as when a lamp with its rays illuminates you.)

Matt 23:1–36

[¹Τότε ὁ Ἰησοῦς ἐλάλησεν τοῖς ὄχλοις καὶ τοῖς
μαθηταῖς αὐτοῦ ²λέγων· ἐπὶ τῆς Μωϋσέως καθέδρας
ἐκάθισαν οἱ γραμματεῖς καὶ οἱ Φαρισαῖοι. ³ πάντα οὖν
ὅσα ἐὰν εἴπωσιν ὑμῖν ποιήσατε καὶ τηρεῖτε, κατὰ δὲ
τὰ ἔργα αὐτῶν μὴ ποιεῖτε· λέγουσιν γὰρ καὶ οὐ
ποιοῦσιν].
⁴δεσμεύουσιν δὲ **φορτία** βαρέα [καὶ
δυσβάστακτα] καὶ ἐπιτιθέασιν ἐπὶ τοὺς
<u>ὤμους τῶν ἀνθρώπων</u>, **αὐτοὶ** δὲ τῷ δακτύλῳ αὐτῶν <u>οὐ</u>
θέλουσιν κινῆσαι αὐτά.
    [⁵πάντα δὲ τὰ ἔργα αὐτῶν ποιοῦσιν πρὸς τὸ θεαθῆναι
    τοῖς ἀνθρώποις· πλατύνουσιν γὰρ τὰ φυλακτήρια
    αὐτῶν καὶ μεγαλύνουσιν τὰ κράσπεδα],
⁶φιλοῦσιν δὲ τὴν πρωτοκλισίαν ἐν τοῖς
δείπνοις καὶ τὰς πρωτοκαθεδρίας **ἐν ταῖς**
συναγωγαῖς ⁷**καὶ τοὺς ἀσπασμοὺς ἐν ταῖς**
ἀγοραῖς καὶ καλεῖσθαι ὑπὸ τῶν ἀνθρώπων ῥαββί.
    [⁸ὑμεῖς δὲ μὴ κληθῆτε ῥαββί· εἷς γάρ ἐστιν ὑμῶν ὁ
    διδάσκαλος, πάντες δὲ ὑμεῖς ἀφελφοί ἐστε. ⁹ καὶ
    πατέρα μὴ καλέσητε ὑμῶν ἐπὶ τῆς γῆς, εἷς γάρ ἐστιν
    ὑμῶν ὁ πατὴρ ὁ οὐράνιος. ¹⁰μηδὲ κληθῆτε καθηγηταί,
    ὅτι καθηγητὴς ὑμῶν ἐστιν εἷς ὁ Χριστός. ¹¹ὁ μείζων
    ὑμῶν ἔσται ὑμῶν διάκονος].
¹²Ὅστις δὲ ὑψώσει ἑαυτὸν ταπεινωθήσεται καὶ ὅστις
ταπεινώσει ἑαυτὸν ὑψωθήσεται.
¹³**Οὐαὶ** δὲ **ὑμῖν**, γραμματεῖς καὶ Φαρισαῖοι
ὑποκριταί, **ὅτι** κλείετε τὴν βασιλείαν τῶν
οὐρανῶν ἔμπροσθεν τῶν ἀνθρώπων· ὑμεῖς γὰρ
<u>**οὐκ εἰσέρχεσθε**</u> οὐδὲ **τοὺς εἰσερχομένους**
ἀφίετε εἰσελθεῖν.
    [¹⁵Οὐαὶ ὑμῖν, γραμματεῖς καὶ Φαρισαῖοι ὑποκριταί, ὅτι
    περιάγετε τὴν θάλασσαν καὶ τὴν ξηρὰν ποιῆσαι ἕνα
    προσήλυτον, καὶ ὅταν γένηται ποιεῖτε αὐτὸν υἱὸν
    γεέννης διπλότερον ὑμῶν].
    [¹⁶Οὐαὶ ὑμῖν, ὁδηγοὶ τυφλοὶ οἱ λέγοντες· ὃς ἂν ὀμόσῃ
    ἐν τῷ ναῷ, οὐδέν ἐστιν· ὃς δ᾽ ἂν ὀμόσῃ ἐν τῷ χρυσῷ
    τοῦ ναοῦ, ὀφείλει. ¹⁷μωροὶ καὶ τυφλοί, τίς γὰρ μείζων
    ἐστίν, ὁ χρυσὸς ἢ ὁ ναὸς ὁ ἁγιάσας τὸν χρυσόν; ¹⁸καὶ
    ὃς ἂν ὀμόσῃ ἐν τῷ θυσιαστηρίῳ, οὐδέν ἐστιν· ὃς δ᾽ ἂν
    ὀμόσῃ ἐν τῷ δώρῳ τῷ ἐπάνω αὐτοῦ, ὀφείλει.
    ¹⁹τυφλοί, τί γὰρ μεῖζον, τὸ δῶρον ἢ τὸ θυσιαστήριον
    τὸ ἁγιάζον τὸ δῶρον; ²⁰ὁ οὖν ὀμόσας ἐν τῷ
    θυσιαστηρίῳ ὀμνύει ἐν αὐτῷ καὶ ἐν πᾶσι τοῖς ἐπάνω
    αὐτοῦ· ²¹καὶ ὁ ὀμόσας ἐν τῷ ναῷ ὀμνύει ἐν αὐτῷ καὶ ἐν
    τῷ κατοικοῦντι αὐτόν, ²²καὶ ὁ ὀμόσας ἐν τῷ οὐρανῷ
    ὀμνύει ἐν τῷ θρόνῳ τοῦ θεοῦ καὶ ἐν τῷ καθημένῳ
    ἐπάνω αὐτοῦ].

Luke 11:37–52

⁴⁶ὁ δὲ εἶπεν· καὶ ὑμῖν τοῖς νομικοῖς οὐαί,
ὅτι φορτίζετε τοὺς ἀνθρώπους **φορτία**
δυσβάστακτα,

            καὶ **αὐτοὶ** ἑνὶ τῶν δακτύλων
ὑμῶν <u>οὐ</u> προσψαύετε τοῖς φορτίοις.

⁴³οὐαὶ ὑμῖν τοῖς Φαρισαίοις, ὅτι ἀγαπᾶτε
            τὴν πρωτοκαθεδρίαν **ἐν ταῖς**
συναγωγαῖς καὶ τοὺς ἀσπασμοὺς ἐν ταῖς
ἀγοραῖς.

⇨ Q 14:11/18:14 [S54]

⁵²οὐαὶ ὑμῖν τοῖς νομικοῖς
ὅτι ἤρατε τὴν κλεῖδα τῆς γνώσεως· αὐτοὶ

<u>**οὐκ εἰσήλθατε**</u> καὶ **τοὺς εἰσερχομένους** ἐκωλύσατε.

    [³⁷Ἐν δὲ τῷ λαλῆσαι ἐρωτᾷ αὐτὸν Φαρισαῖος ὅπως
    ἀριστήσῃ παρ᾽ αὐτῷ· εἰσελθὼν δὲ ἀνέπεσεν. ³⁸ ὁ δὲ
    Φαρισαῖος ἰδὼν ἐθαύμασεν ὅτι οὐ πρῶτον ἐβαπτίσθη
    πρὸ τοῦ ἀρίστου. ³⁹εἶπεν δὲ ὁ κύριος πρὸς αὐτόν·]

Continued on p. 108

Mark 12:37b–40 ⇨ Matt 23:6//Luke 11:43

³⁷Καὶ [ὁ] πολὺς οχλος ἤκουεν αὐτοῦ ἡδέως. ³⁸καὶ ἐν τῇ διδαχῇ αὐτοῦ ἔλεγεν· βλέπετε ἀπὸ τῶν γραμματέων τῶν θελόντων ἐν στολαῖς περιπατεῖν **καὶ ἀσπασμοὺς ἐν ταῖς ἀγοραῖς** ³⁹ καὶ πρωτοκαθεδρίας **ἐν ταῖς συναγωγαῖς** καὶ πρωτοκλισίας ἐν τοῖς δείπνοις, ⁴⁰οἱ κατεσθίοντες τὰς οἰκίας τῶν χηρῶν καὶ προφάσει μακρὰ προσευχόμενοι, οὗτοι λήμψονται περισσότερον κρίμα.

Mark 7:1–2, 5–6a ⇨ Luke 11:37–38

¹Καὶ συνάγονται πρὸς αὐτὸν οἱ Φαρισαῖοι καί τινες τῶν γραμματέων ἐλθόντες ἀπὸ Ἱεροσολύμων. ²καὶ ἰδόντες τινὰς τῶν μαθητῶν αὐτοῦ ὅτι κοιναῖς χερσίν, τοῦτ' ἔστιν ἀνίπτοις, ἐσθίουσιν τοὺς ἄρτους . . . ⁵ καὶ ἐπερωτῶσιν αὐτὸν οἱ Φαρισαῖοι καὶ οἱ γραμματεῖς· διὰ τί οὐ περιπατοῦσιν οἱ μαθηταί σου κατὰ τὴν παράδοσιν τῶν πρεσβυτέρων, ἀλλὰ κοιναῖς χερσὶν ἐσθίουσιν τὸν ἄρτον; ⁶ὁ δὲ εἶπεν αὐτοῖς· . . .

Luke 7:36 ⇨ Luke 11:37–38

³⁶Ἠρώτα δέ τις αὐτὸν τῶν Φαρισαίων ἵνα φάγῃ μετ' αὐτοῦ· καὶ εἰσελθὼν εἰς τὸν οἶκον τοῦ Φαρισαίου κατεκλίθη.

Mark 12:37b–40

³⁷. . . And the great crowd heard him gladly.
³⁸And in his teaching he said, "Beware of the scribes, who like to walk around in long robes, and to have salutations in the market places ³⁹and the front seats in the synagogues and the places of honor at feasts, ⁴⁰who devour widows' houses and for a pretense make long prayers. They will receive the greater condemnation."

Mark 7:1–2, 5–6a

¹And the Pharisees and some of the scribes, who had come from Jerusalem, gathered together to him. ²And when they saw that some of his disciples ate with hands defiled, that is, unwashed . . . ⁵And the Pharisees and the scribes asked him, "Why do your disciples not live according to the tradition of the elders, but eat their food with defiled hands?" ⁶And he said to them, . . .

Luke 7:36

³⁶One of the Pharisees asked him to dine with him, and when he entered the Pharisee's house, he took his place at table.

²³   Οὐαὶ ὑμῖν, γραμματεῖς καὶ Φαρισαῖοι
ὑποκριταί, ὅτι ἀποδεκατοῦτε τὸ ἡδύοσμον
καὶ τὸ ἄνηθον καὶ τὸ κύμινον καὶ ἀφήκατε
τὰ βαρύτερα τοῦ νόμου,
τὴν κρίσιν καὶ τὸ ἔλεος καὶ τὴν πίστιν·
ταῦτα [δὲ] ἔδει ποιῆσαι κἀκεῖνα μὴ ἀφιέναι.
    [²⁴ὁδηγοὶ τυφλοί, οἱ διϋλίζοντες τὸν κώνωπα, τὴν δὲ
κάμηλον καταπίνοντες].
²⁵Οὐαὶ ὑμῖν, γραμματεῖς καὶ **Φαρισαῖοι**
ὑποκριταί, ὅτι **καθαρίζετε τὸ ἔξωθεν τοῦ**
ποτηρίου καὶ τῆς παροψίδος, **ἔσωθεν δὲ**
γέμουσιν ἐξ ἁρπαγῆς καὶ ἀκρασίας.
²⁶Φαρισαῖε τυφλέ, καθάρισον πρῶτον τὸ ἐντὸς τοῦ
ποτηρίου, ἵνα γένηται καὶ τὸ
ἐκτὸς αὐτοῦ καθαρόν.
⁶φιλοῦσιν δὲ τὴν πρωτοκλισίαν ἐν τοῖς
δείπνοις καὶ τὰς πρωτοκαθεδρίας **ἐν ταῖς**
συναγωγαῖς ⁷**καὶ τοὺς ἀσπασμοὺς ἐν ταῖς**
ἀγοραῖς καὶ καλεῖσθαι ὑπὸ τῶν ἀνθρώπων ῥαββί.
²⁷Οὐαὶ ὑμῖν, γραμματεῖς καὶ Φαρισαῖοι ὑποκριταί,
ὅτι παρομοιάζετε τάφοις κεκονιαμένοις, οἵτινες ἔξωθεν
μὲν φαίνονται ὡραῖοι, ἔσωθεν δὲ γέμουσιν ὀστέων
νεκρῶν καὶ πάσης ἀκαθαρσίας. ²⁸ οὕτως καὶ ὑμεῖς ἔξωθεν
μὲν φαίνεσθε τοῖς ἀνθρώποις δίκαιοι, ἔσωθεν δέ ἐστε
μεστοὶ ὑποκρίσεως καὶ ἀνομίας.

⁴δεσμεύουσιν δὲ **φορτία** βαρέα [καὶ
δυσβάστακτα] καὶ ἐπιτιθέασιν ἐπὶ τοὺς
ὤμους τῶν ἀνθρώπων, **αὐτοὶ** δὲ τῷ δακτύλῳ
αὐτῶν **οὐ** θέλουσιν κινῆσαι αὐτά.
²⁹Οὐαὶ ὑμῖν, γραμματεῖς καὶ Φαρισαῖοι
ὑποκριταί, **ὅτι οἰκοδομεῖτε** τοὺς τάφους **τῶν**
προφητῶν καὶ κοσμεῖτε **τὰ μνημεῖα** τῶν
δικαίων, ³⁰καὶ λέγετε· εἰ ἤμεθα ἐν ταῖς
ἡμέραις τῶν πατέρων ἡμῶν, οὐκ ἂν ἤμεθα αὐτῶν
κοινωνοὶ ἐν τῷ αἵματι τῶν προφητῶν.
³¹ὥστε μαρτυρεῖτε ἑαυτοῖς ὅτι υἱοί **ἐστε**
τῶν φονευσάντων τοὺς προφήτας.
³²καὶ **ὑμεῖς** πληρώσατε τὸ μέτρον τῶν πατέρων ὑμῶν.
    [³³ὄφεις, γεννήματα ἐχιδνῶν, πῶς φύγητε ἀπὸ τῆς
κρίσεως τῆς γεέννης;]

⁴²ἀλλὰ **οὐαὶ ὑμῖν** τοῖς Φαρισαίοις,
        ὅτι ἀποδεκατοῦτε τὸ ἡδύοσμον
καὶ τὸ πήγανον καὶ **πᾶν** λάχανον **καὶ**
παρέρχεσθε
τὴν κρίσιν καὶ τὴν ἀγάπην τοῦ θεοῦ·
ταῦτα δὲ ἔδει ποιῆσαι κἀκεῖνα μὴ παρεῖναι.

³⁹. . . νῦν ὑμεῖς οἱ **Φαρισαῖοι**
        τὸ ἔξωθεν τοῦ ποτηρίου
καὶ τοῦ πίνακος **καθαρίζετε**, τὸ δὲ **ἔσωθεν**
ὑμῶν γέμει **ἁρπαγῆς καὶ** πονηρίας.
⁴⁰ἄφρονες, οὐχ ὁ ποιήσας τὸ ἔξωθεν καὶ τὸ
ἔσωθεν ἐποίησεν; ⁴¹ πλὴν τὰ ἐνόντα δότε
ἐλεημοσύνην, καὶ ἰδοὺ πάντα καθαρὰ ὑμῖν ἐστιν.
⁴³οὐαὶ ὑμῖν τοῖς Φαρισαίοις, ὅτι ἀγαπᾶτε
        τὴν πρωτοκαθεδρίαν ἐν ταῖς
συναγωγαῖς καὶ τοὺς ἀσπασμοὺς ἐν ταῖς
ἀγοραῖς.
⁴⁴**οὐαὶ ὑμῖν**,
        ὅτι ἐστὲ ὡς τὰ μνημεῖα τὰ ἄδηλα, καὶ οἱ
ἄνθρωποι [οἱ] περιπατοῦντες ἐπάνω οὐκ οἴδασιν.

[⁴⁵Ἀποκριθεὶς δέ τις τῶν νομικῶν λέγει αὐτῷ·
    διδάσκαλε, ταῦτα λέγων καὶ ἡμᾶς ὑβρίζεις].
⁴⁶ὁ δὲ εἶπεν· καὶ ὑμῖν τοῖς νομικοῖς οὐαί,
ὅτι φορτίζετε τοὺς ἀνθρώπους **φορτία**
δυσβάστακτα,
        καὶ **αὐτοὶ** ἑνὶ τῶν δακτύλων
ὑμῶν **οὐ** προσψαύετε τοῖς φορτίοις.
⁴⁷**Οὐαὶ ὑμῖν**,
        ὅτι οἰκοδομεῖτε τὰ μνημεῖα τῶν
προφητῶν,

οἱ δὲ πατέρες ὑμῶν ἀπέκτειναν αὐτούς.

⁴⁸ἄρα μάρτυρές **ἐστε** καὶ συνευδοκεῖτε τοῖς
ἔργοις τῶν πατέρων ὑμῶν, ὅτι αὐτοὶ μὲν
ἀπέκτειναν αὐτούς, **ὑμεῖς** δὲ οἰκοδομεῖτε.
⇨ Q 3:7 [S3]

Mic 6:8 LXX

⁸εἰ ἀνηγγέλη σοι, ἄνθρωπε, τί καλόν; ἢ τί κύριος ἐκζητεῖ παρὰ σοῦ ἀλλ' ἢ τοῦ ποιεῖν κρίμα καὶ ἀγαπᾶν ἔλεον καὶ ἕτοιμον εἶναι τοῦ πορεύεσθαι μετὰ κυρίου θεοῦ σου;

GThom 89

ΠΕΧΕ ΙC ΧΕ ΕΤΒΕ ΟΥ ΤΕΤΝΕΙѠΕ ΜΠCΑ ΝΒΟΛ ΜΠΠΟΤΗΡΙΟΝ ΤΕΤΝ̄Ρ̄ΝΟΕΙ ΑΝ ΧΕ ΠΕΝΤΑϨΤΑΜΙΟ ΜΠCΑ Ν̄ϨΟΥΝ Ν̄ΤΟϤ ΟΝ ΠΕΝΤΑϤΤΑΜΙΟ ΜΠCΑ ΝΒΟΛ.

POxy 840.2

ὁ σωτὴρ πρὸς αὐτὸν ἀπο[κρι]θεὶς εἶπεν· Οὐαὶ τυφλοὶ μὴ ὁρῶντ[ε]ς· σὺ ἐλούσω τούτοις τοῖς χεομένοις ὔ[δ]ασίν, ἐν οἷς κύνες καὶ χοῖροι βέβλην[ται] νυκτὸς καὶ ἡμέρας, καὶ νιψάμε[ν]ος τὸ ἐκτὸς δέρμα ἐσμήξω, ὅπερ [κα]ὶ αἱ πόρναι καὶ α[ἱ] αὐλητρίδες μυρί[ζ]ου[σαι κ]αὶ λούουσιν καὶ σμήχουσι [καὶ κ]αλλωπίζουσι πρὸς ἐπιθυμί[αν τ]ῶν ἀνθρώπων, ἔνδοθεν δὲ ἐκεῖ[ναι πεπλ]ήρω⟨ν⟩ται σκορπίων καὶ [πάσης ἀδι]κίας. ἐγὼ δὲ καὶ οἱ [μαθηταί μου,] οὓς λέγεις μὴ βεβα[μμένους, βεβά]μμεθα ἐν ὕδασι ζω[ῆς αἰωνίου τοῖς κα]τελθοῦσιν ἀπὸ [τοῦ θεοῦ ἐκ τοῦ οὐρανοῦ. ἀλ]λὰ οὐαὶ [τ]οῖς [. . .

Mic 6:8 LXX

⁸Has he told you, O man, what is good? Or what does the Lord seek from you except that you do justice and love mercy and be prepared to walk with your Lord God?

GThom 89

Jesus said, "Why do you wash the outside of the cup? Do you not understand that the one who made the inside is also the one who made the outside?"

POxy 840.2

Then said the Savior to him [a Pharisaic chief priest], "Woe unto you blind that see not! You have bathed yourself in water that is poured out, in which dogs and swine lie night and day and you have washed yourself and have chafed your outer skin, which prostitutes also and flute–girls anoint, bathe, chafe and rouge, in order to arouse desire in men, but within they are full of scorpions and of [bad]ness [of every kind]. But I and [my disciples], of whom you say that we have not im[mersed] ourselves, [have been im]mersed in the liv[ing . . .] water which comes down from [. . . B]ut woe unto them that . . ."

³⁴διὰ τοῦτο ἰδοὺ ἐγὼ   ἀποστέλλω
πρὸς ὑμᾶς **προφήτας καὶ σοφοὺς καὶ**
γραμματεῖς· ἐξ αὐτῶν ἀποκτενεῖτε καὶ
σταυρώσετε καὶ ἐξ αὐτῶν μαστιγώσετε ἐν
ταῖς συναγωγαῖς ὑμῶν **καὶ** διώξετε ἀπὸ
πόλεως εἰς πόλιν· ³⁵ὅπως ἔλθῃ ἐφ᾽ ὑμᾶς πᾶν
αἷμα δίκαιον **ἐκχυννόμενον** ἐπὶ τῆς γῆς
ἀπὸ τοῦ **αἵματος** Ἄβελ τοῦ δικαίου **ἕως τοῦ**
αἵματος Ζαχαρίου υἱοῦ Βαραχίου, ὃν
ἐφονεύσατε μεταξὺ τοῦ ναοῦ **καὶ τοῦ**
θυσιαστηρίου. ³⁶ ἀμὴν λέγω ὑμῖν, ἥξει ταῦτα
πάντα ἐπὶ τὴν γενεὰν ταύτην.
¹³Οὐαὶ δὲ ὑμῖν, γραμματεῖς καὶ Φαρισαῖοι
ὑποκριταί, ὅτι κλείετε τὴν βασιλείαν τῶν
οὐρανῶν ἔμπροσθεν τῶν ἀνθρώπων· ὑμεῖς γὰρ
οὐκ εἰσέρχεσθε οὐδὲ **τοὺς εἰσερχομένους** ἀφίετε
εἰσελθεῖν.

⁴⁹διὰ τοῦτο καὶ ἡ σοφία τοῦ θεοῦ εἶπεν·
ἀποστελῶ εἰς αὐτοὺς **προφήτας καὶ**
ἀποστόλους, καὶ **ἐξ αὐτῶν** ἀποκτενοῦσιν

καὶ διώξουσιν,
        ⁵⁰ἵνα ἐκζητηθῇ τὸ **αἷμα** πάντων
τῶν προφητῶν τὸ **ἐκκεχυμένον** ἀπὸ
καταβολῆς κόσμου ἀπὸ τῆς γενεᾶς ταύτης,
⁵¹ἀπὸ **αἵματος** Ἄβελ   **ἕως** αἵματος
Ζαχαρίου   τοῦ ἀπολομένου **μεταξὺ τοῦ**
θυσιαστηρίου καὶ τοῦ οἴκου· ναὶ λέγω ὑμῖν,
ἐκζητηθήσεται ἀπὸ τῆς γενεᾶς ταύτης.
⁵²οὐαί ὑμῖν τοῖς νομικοῖς
ὅτι ἤρατε τὴν κλεῖδα τῆς γνώσεως·

αὐτοὶ οὐκ εἰσήλθατε καὶ **τοὺς εἰσερχομένους** ἐκωλύσατε.
[⁵³Κἀκεῖθεν ἐξελθόντος αὐτοῦ ἤρξαντο οἱ γραμματεῖς
καὶ οἱ Φαρισαῖοι δεινῶς ἐνέχειν καὶ ἀποστοματίζειν
αὐτὸν περὶ πλειόνων, ⁵⁴ἐνεδρεύοντες αὐτὸν θηρεῦσαί
τι ἐκ τοῦ στόματος αὐτοῦ].

⇨ Q 13:34–35 [S52]
³⁷Ἰερουσαλὴμ Ἰερουσαλήμ, ἡ ἀποκτείνουσα
τοὺς προφήτας καὶ λιθοβολοῦσα τοὺς
ἀπεσταλμένους πρὸς αὐτήν, ποσάκις ἠθέλησα
ἐπισυναγαγεῖν τὰ τέκνα σου, ὃν τρόπον ὄρνις
ἐπισυνάγει τὰ νοσσία αὐτῆς ὑπὸ τὰς
πτέρυγας, καὶ οὐκ ἠθελήσατε. ³⁸ἰδοὺ ἀφίεται
ὑμῖν ὁ οἶκος ὑμῶν ἔρημος. ³⁹λέγω γὰρ ὑμῖν, οὐ
μή με ἴδητε ἀπ᾽ ἄρτι ἕως ἂν εἴπητε·
εὐλογημένος ὁ ἐρχόμενος ἐν ὀνόματι κυρίου.

Luke 13:34–35
³⁴Ἰερουσαλὴμ Ἰερουσαλήμ, ἡ ἀποκτείνουσα
τοὺς προφήτας καὶ λιθοβολοῦσα τοὺς
ἀπεσταλμένους πρὸς αὐτήν, ποσάκις ἠθέλησα
ἐπισυνάξαι τὰ τέκνα σου ὃν τρόπον ὄρνις
        τὴν ἑαυτῆς νοσσιὰν ὑπὸ τὰς
πτέρυγας, καὶ οὐκ ἠθελήσατε. ³⁵ἰδοὺ ἀφίεται
ὑμῖν ὁ οἶκος ὑμῶν.   λέγω [δὲ] ὑμῖν, οὐ
μὴ ἴδητέ με   ἕως [ἥξει ὅτε] εἴπητε·
εὐλογημένος ὁ ἐρχόμενος ἐν ὀνόματι κυρίου.

Matt 23:4: βαρεα και δυσβαστακτα: B D W Δ Θ 0107
0138 φ Koine lat syʰ sa (mae) [NA²⁶] / βαρεα: L λ 892
1589 *pc* it syˢ·ᶜ·ᵖ bo; Ir Or [NA²⁵; HG] / δυσβαστακτα
(Matt): 544 700 1010 1293 *pc* / μεγαλα βαρεα: א // τω δε
δακτυλω: W Koine Θ 0107 0138 λ φ lat syʰ [HG] / αυτοι
δε τω δακτυλω: א B D L 33 892 1010 1293 *pc* sy⁽ˢ⁾·ᵖ bo; Ir
Or [NA²⁵·²⁶] / αυτοι δε ενι των δακτυλων (Luke): 1093 syᶜ
sa // 6: ραββι ραββι: D W 0107 φ 69 565 700 syˢ·ᶜ·ʰ [HG] /
txt: א B L Δ Θ 0138 λ 892 1241 *al* lat syᵖ sa bo [NA²⁵·²⁶] //
23: ταυτα εδει: א D Γ 0133 λ φ 28 700 1241 1424 *pm* lat
saᵐˢ mae bo; Or [HG] / ταυτα δε εδει: B C K L W Δ 0138
33 565 892 1010 *pm* a d h sy saᵐˢˢ; Or [NA²⁶] // 36:

παντα ταυτα: B K W Koine Δ Γ 0138 λ 33 700 892 *pm*; Ir
[HG] / txt: א C D L Φ φ 28 565 1010 1241 1424 *pm*; Or
Eus [NA²⁵·²⁶] // 38: ο οικος υμων (Luke): B L ff² syˢ sa boᵖᵗ;
Or [NA²⁵] / ο οικος υμων ερημος: 𝔭⁷⁷ א C D W Koine Θ
0138 λ φ lat syᵖ·ʰ mae boᵖᵗ; Eus [NA²⁶; HG].

Luke 11:42: ταυτα εδει: א* A W λ a ff² syˢ bo [HG] // txt:
𝔭⁴⁵·⁷⁵ א¹ B C K L X Θ 0108 0124 φ 33 579 892 c z vg
syᶜ·ᵖ·ʰ sa [NA²⁵·²⁶] // omit ταυτα δε εδει ποιησαι κακεινα μη
παρειναι: D // 49: εκδιωξουσιν: A D W Koine Ψ φ [HG] /
διωξουσιν (Matt): 𝔭⁷⁵ א B C L Θ 1 33 1241 1424 *pc*
[NA²⁵·²⁶].

Origen, *Hom. in Jer.* 14.5

Καὶ ἐν τῷ εὐαγγελίῳ ἀναγέγραπται· καὶ ἀποστέλλει ἡ σοφία τέκνα αὐτῆς.

Origen, *Hom. in Jer.* 14.5

And it is written in the gospel, "And Wisdom sends forth her children."

POxy 655 ii 11–23

[λέγει Ἰ(ησοῦ)ς· οἱ Φαρισαῖοι καὶ οἱ γραμματεῖς] ἔλ[αβον τὰς κλεῖδας] τῆς [γνώσεως. αὐτοὶ ἔ]κρυψ[αν αὐτάς. οὔτε] εἰσῆλ[θον, οὔτε τοὺς] εἰσερ[χομένους ἀφῆ]καν [εἰσελθεῖν. ὑμεῖς] δὲ γεί[νεσθε φρόνι]μοι ὡ[ς ὄφεις καὶ ἀ]κέραι[οι ὡς περιστε]ρα[ί].

POxy 655 ii 11–23

[Jesus said, "The Pharisees and the scribes have taken the keys] of [knowledge (gnosis) and] hidden [them. They themselves have not] entered, [nor have they allowed to enter those who were about to] come in. [You], however, [be as wise as serpents and as] innocent [as doves]."

GThom 39

ⲡⲉϫⲉ ⲓ̅ⲥ̅ ϫⲉ ⲙⲫⲁⲣⲓⲥⲁⲓⲟⲥ ⲙⲛ̅ ⲛ̅ⲅⲣⲁⲙⲙⲁⲧⲉⲩⲥ ⲁⲩϫⲓ ⲛ̅ϣⲁϣⲧ ⲛ̅ⲧⲅⲛⲱⲥⲓⲥ ⲁⲩϩⲟⲡⲟⲩ ⲟⲩⲧⲉ ⲙ̅ⲡⲟⲩⲃⲱⲕ ⲉϩⲟⲩⲛ ⲁⲩⲱ ⲛⲉⲧⲟⲩⲱϣ ⲉⲃⲱⲕ ⲉϩⲟⲩⲛ ⲙⲡⲟⲩⲕⲁⲁⲩ ⲛ̅ⲧⲱⲧⲛ̅ ⲇⲉ ϣⲱⲡⲉ ⲙ̅ⲫⲣⲟⲛⲓⲙⲟⲥ ⲛ̅ⲑⲉ ⲛ̅ⲛ̅ϩⲟϥ ⲁⲩⲱ ⲛ̅ⲁⲕⲉⲣⲁⲓⲟⲥ ⲛ̅ⲑⲉ ⲛ̅ⲛ̅ϭⲣⲟⲙⲡⲉ.

GThom 39

Jesus said, "The Pharisees and the scribes have taken the keys to knowledge and have hidden them. They have not entered, nor have they allowed those who want to enter to do so. As for you, be as clever as snakes and as innocent as doves."

GThom 102

ⲡⲉϫⲉ ⲓ̅ⲥ̅ [ϫⲉ ⲟ]ⲩⲟⲉⲓ ⲛⲁⲩ ⲙ̅ⲫⲁⲣⲓⲥⲁⲓⲟⲥ ϫⲉ ⲉⲩⲉⲓⲛⲉ [ⲛ]ⲟⲩⲟⲩϩⲟⲣ· ⲉϥⲛ̅ⲕⲟⲧⲕ ϩⲓϫⲛ̅ ⲡⲟⲩⲟⲛⲉϥ· ⲛ̅[ϩⲉⲛ]ⲉϩⲟⲟⲩ ϫⲉ ⲟⲩⲧⲉ ϥⲟⲩⲱⲙ ⲁⲛ ⲟⲩⲧⲉ ϥⲕ[ⲱ ⲁ]ⲛ ⲛ̅ⲛⲉϩⲟⲟⲩ ⲉⲟⲩⲱⲙ.

GThom 102

Jesus said, "Woe to the Pharisees, for they are like a dog sleeping in the food trough of cows: the dog neither eats nor lets the cows eat."

Although there is considerable disagreement between Matthew and Luke in the setting and order of the woes, recent scholarship has tended to assume that a Q text underlies Matt 23 and Luke 11:39–52 (see Haenchen 1951). Bultmann (1963: 113–14), Bussmann (73–74), Streeter (1924: 253–54) and Wernle (1899: 91) included at least 11:39, 41–44, 46–52 in Q. Harnack (95–105) and Hawkins (1911: 111, 113, 115) excluded 11:43 as possibly due to Markan influence, while Manson (96) argued that Luke 11:37–41 and 11:53–54 formed a single story deriving from L, and that the parallel between Luke 11:39–41 and Matt 23:25–26 was an instance of overlap between L and M. He assigned only Luke 11:42–44, 46–52 and par. to Q. Schmid (323) argues that Luke may have omitted Matt 23:2–3 because of its Jewish-Christian tone, and Matt 23:5, 15, 16–21 because these held little interest for his audience. Müller (1908: 10) goes even further, asserting that Matt 23:15–22 and 23:33 comes from Q and that Luke omitted the former because of his Gentile audience and the latter because it formed a doublet with Q 3:7. Weiss (1907: 262–67) thought that Luke took his woes from L and that Matthew followed Q. Sato (1984: 59) ascribes Matt 23:15–19, 24 to Q^Mt.

A few have urged that Luke 11:37–39a derives from Q: Hunter 139; Marshall Lk 491; Polag 88–89 (uncertain); Streeter 1924: 279. Schürmann (1968: 115, 220, 224–25) argues that πρῶτον in 11:38 is a reminiscence of Matt 23:26 diff Luke 11:40 (p. 115) and that κύριος is used frequently by the Q–redactor in transitional phrases (Q 7:19; 10:1; 11:39; 12:42; 17:5) (p. 225) (see, however, Schürmann 1982: 174!). Most, however, argue that the verses are Lukan, modelled on Mark 7:1–2 and Luke 7:36. Verse 39a (εἶπεν δὲ ... πρὸς αὐτόν) is a Lukan introduction (see Jeremias 1980: 33) and the absolute κύριος is Lukan (Fitzmyer Lk 202–3).

A difficult question is that of the original order of the woes. Garland (1979: 17, 93–94), Kloppenborg (1987: 139–40), Schürmann (1975: 174) and Zeller (65–66) assume that Luke inverted the order of the first two woes to bring 11:39b–41 into proximity with his redactional introduction (11:37–39a) and that in the remainder, Luke

represents the order of Q. Jacobson (183–86) concurs that Luke displaced 11:39–41, but then argues that Q 11:44 and 11:47–48 were originally linked by the catchwords τάφος (Matt) or μνημεῖον (Luke). Luke broke this connection by his insertion of v. 45 and his placement of Q 11:46 programatically at the beginning of the woes against the lawyers. Nevertheless, Luke preserved the original programmatic function of 11:46. Q 11:43 "obviously stood near the beginning" and 11:52, a dangling saying, cannot be placed with certainty. Thus the original Q order is: 11:46, 42, 39–41, 44, 47–48, 49–51.

Schenk (75–82) restores the Q order as 11:39, 42–44, 46, 52, 47–48, 49–51; 13:34–35, while Schmid (323) and Schulz (94 n. 5) assume that the Lukan order is original throughout.

Q 11:42d
In Q: Bultmann 1963: 131; Hoffmann 59; Polag 54; Schulz 101; Zeller 67 and most others.
Not in Q: Easton (Lk 194), Harnack (101), Klostermann (Mt 186), Wellhausen (Lk 61) and Manson (98) argue on the basis of the absence of this phrase in Codex Bezae and Marcion (see textual notes) that it did not belong to the original text of Luke (or Q), but was interpolated into Luke from Matt 23:23.

[Luke 11:45]
In Q: Bussmann 74: Matthew omitted 11:45 when he rearranged the woes. Hunter 139; Marshall Lk 499 (hesitantly); Polag 88–89 (uncertain); Schmid 324–25; Schürmann 1968: 218 (but see idem, 1982: 174).
Not in Q: Most authors.

[Luke 11:53–54]
In Q: Haupt 1913: 67, 258; Knox 1957: 67–68; Marshall Lk 491 (perhaps).
Not in Q: Most authors.

Q 13:34–35 ⇨ S52

Matt 23:1–26

[¹ Then Jesus spoke to the crowds and to his disciples, ² "The scribes and the Pharisees sit on Moses' seat; ³ so practice and observe everything they tell you. But do not do what they do; for they preach, but do not practice.]
⁴ They bind heavy loads, hard to bear, and lay them on people's shoulders; but they themselves will not move them with their finger.

[⁵ They do all their deeds to be seen in public; for they widen their phylacteries and wear long tassels.]
⁶ They love the place of honor at feasts and the front seats in the synagogues, ⁷ and salutations in the market places, and being called rabbi by people.

[⁸ But you are not to be called rabbi, for you have one teacher, and you are all brothers. ⁹ And call no one your father on earth, for you have one Father, the heavenly One. ¹⁰ Do not be called teachers, for you have one teacher, the Christ. ¹¹ He who is greatest among you shall be your servant.]
¹² Whoever exalts himself will be humbled, and whoever humbles himself will be exalted.

¹³ "Woe to you, scribes and Pharisees, hypocrites! because you lock the kingdom of heaven away from people; for you neither enter yourselves, nor allow those who are trying to enter to go in.

[¹⁴ ¹⁵ Woe to you, scribes and Pharisees, hypocrites! for you travel sea and land to make a single proselyte, and when that happens, you make him twice as much a son of Gehenna as yourselves.] [¹⁶ "Woe to you, blind guides, who say, 'If any one swears by the temple, it is nothing; but if any one swears by the gold of the temple, he is obligated.' ¹⁷ Blind fools! For which is greater, the gold or the temple that sanctified the gold? ¹⁸ And (you say), 'If any one swears by the altar, it is nothing; but if any one swears by the gift that is on the altar, he is obligated.'
¹⁹ You blind men! For which is greater, the gift or the altar that sanctifies the gift? ²⁰ So whoever swears by the altar, is swearing by it and by everything on it; ²¹ and whoever swears by the temple, is swearing by it and by him who dwells in it; ²² and whoever swears by heaven, is swearing by the throne of God and by him who sits upon it.]
²³ "Woe to you, scribes and Pharisees, hypocrites! for you tithe mint and dill and cummin, and leave aside the weightier matters of the law, justice and mercy and faithfulness; these you ought to have done, without leaving aside the others. [²⁴ Blind guides! You strain out the gnat and swallow the camel!]

²⁵ "Woe to you, scribes and Pharisees, hypocrites! for you cleanse the outside of the cup and of the dish, but inside they are full of extortion and rapacity. ²⁶ You blind Pharisee! first cleanse the inside of the cup, that its outside also may be clean."

Luke 11:46

⁴⁶ He said, "Woe to you lawyers also! for you load people with burdens hard to bear, and you yourselves do not touch the burdens with one of your fingers."

Luke 11:43

⁴³ "Woe to you Pharisees! for you love the front seat in the synagogues and salutations in the market places."

Luke 11:52

⁵² "Woe to you lawyers! for you have taken away the key of knowledge; you yourselves did not enter, and you prevented those who were trying to enter."

Luke 11:37–39a

[³⁷ While he was speaking, a Pharisee asked him to dine with him; so he went in and sat at table. ³⁸ Seeing this, the Pharisee was surprised that he did not first wash before dinner. ³⁹ But the Lord said to him, . . .]

Luke 11:42

⁴² "But woe to you Pharisees! for you tithe mint and rue and every herb, and neglect the justice and love of God; these you ought to have done, without neglecting the others."

Luke 11:39b–41

³⁹ . . . "Now you Pharisees cleanse the outside of the cup and of the plate, but inside you are full of extortion and evil. ⁴⁰ You fools! Did not he who made the outside make the inside also? ⁴¹ But give as alms what is inside; and behold, everything is clean for you." *Continued on p. 115*

The incipit and first
seven sayings of the
Gospel of Thomas,
preserved on papyrus
Oxyrhynchus 654,
third century C.E.

Photograph reproduced with
permission from The British
Library, London, England.

Matt 23:6

⁶ They love the place of honor at feasts and the front seats in the synagogues,

Matt 23:27–28

²⁷ "Woe to you, scribes and Pharisees, hypocrites! for you are like whitewashed tombs, which outwardly appear beautiful, but within they are full of dead men's bones and all uncleanness. ²⁸ So you also outwardly appear righteous to men, but within you are full of hypocrisy and iniquity.

Matt 23:4

⁴ They bind heavy loads, hard to bear, and lay them on people's shoulders; but they themselves will not move them with their finger.

Matt 23:29–36

²⁹ "Woe to you, scribes and Pharisees, hypocrites! for you build the tombs of the prophets and beautify the graves of the righteous, ³⁰ and say, 'If we had lived in the days of our fathers, we would not have collaborated with them in shedding the blood of the prophets.' ³¹ Thus you witness against yourselves, that you are sons of those who murdered the prophets. ³² Fill up, then, the measure of your fathers. [³³ You serpents, you brood of vipers, how will you flee from the judgment of Gehenna?] ³⁴ Therefore behold, I am sending you prophets and sages and scribes, some of whom you will kill and crucify, and some you will scourge in your synagogues and persecute from city to city, ³⁵ that upon you may come all the righteous blood shed on earth, from the blood of innocent Abel to the blood of Zechariah the son of Barachiah, whom you murdered between the sanctuary and the altar. ³⁶ Amen, I tell you, all this will come upon this generation.

Matt 23:13

¹³ "Woe to you, scribes and Pharisees, hypocrites! because you lock the kingdom of heaven away from people; for you neither enter yourselves, nor allow those who are trying to enter to go in.

Matt 23:37–39

³⁷ O Jerusalem, Jerusalem, you kill the prophets and stone those who are sent to you! How often would I have gathered your children together as a hen gathers her brood under her wings, and you refused! ³⁸ Behold, your house is forsaken and desolate. ³⁹ For I tell you, you will not see me again, until you say, 'Blessed is he who comes in the name of the Lord.'

Luke 11:43–54

⁴³ "Woe to you Pharisees! for you love the front seat in the synagogues and salutations in the market places."

⁴⁴ "Woe to you! for you are like unmarked graves, and people who walk over them do not know it."

[⁴⁵ One of the lawyers answered him, "Teacher, in saying this you insult us also."]
⁴⁶ He said, "Woe to you lawyers also! for you load people with burdens hard to bear, and you yourselves do not touch the burdens with one of your fingers.

⁴⁷ Woe to you! for you build the graves of the prophets but it was your fathers who killed them. ⁴⁸ So you are witnesses and consent to the deeds of your fathers; for they killed them, and you build.

⁴⁹ Therefore also the Wisdom of God said, 'I will send them prophets and apostles, some of whom they will kill and persecute,' ⁵⁰ that the blood of all the prophets, shed from the foundation of the world, may be required of this generation, ⁵¹ from the blood of Abel to the blood of Zechariah, who perished between the altar and the sanctuary. Yes, I tell you, it shall be required of this generation.

⁵² Woe to you lawyers! for you have taken away the key of knowledge; you yourselves did not enter, and you prevented those who were trying to enter."
[⁵³ When he went away from there, the scribes and the Pharisees began to be very hostile and to interrogate him on many subjects, ⁵⁴ waiting to catch him in something he might say.]

Luke 13:34–35

³⁴ O Jerusalem, Jerusalem, you kill the prophets and stone those who are sent to you! How often would I have gathered your children together as a hen gathers her brood under her wings, and you refused! ³⁵ Behold, your house is forsaken. Now I tell you, you will not see me until the time comes when you say, 'Blessed is he who comes in the name of the Lord!'

Matt 10:26–27

Luke 12:1, 2–3

[¹ Ἐν οἷς ἐπισυναχθεισῶν τῶν μυριάδων τοῦ ὄχλου, ὥστε καταπατεῖν ἀλλήλους, ἤρξατο λέγειν πρὸς τοὺς μαθητὰς αὐτοῦ πρῶτον· προσέχετε ἑαυτοῖς ἀπὸ τῆς ζύμης, ἥτις ἐστὶν ὑπόκρισις, τῶν Φαρισαίων].

²⁶Μὴ οὖν φοβηθῆτε αὐτούς· οὐδὲν γάρ ἐστιν κεκαλυμμένον ὃ οὐκ ἀποκαλυφθήσεται καὶ κρυπτὸν ὃ οὐ γνωσθήσεται.

² Οὐδὲν δὲ συγκεκαλυμμένον ἐστὶν ὃ οὐκ ἀποκαλυφθήσεται καὶ κρυπτὸν ὃ οὐ γνωσθήσεται.

²⁷ὃ λέγω ὑμῖν ἐν τῇ σκοτίᾳ εἴπατε ἐν τῷ φωτί,   καὶ ὃ εἰς τὸ οὖς ἀκούετε κηρύξατε ἐπὶ τῶν δωμάτων.

³ἀνθ' ὧν ὅσα ἐν τῇ σκοτίᾳ εἴπατε ἐν τῷ φωτὶ ἀκουσθήσεται, καὶ ὃ πρὸς τὸ οὖς ἐλαλήσατε ἐν τοῖς ταμείοις κηρυχθήσεται ἐπὶ τῶν δωμάτων.

Mark 8:14–15 ⇨ Luke 12:1

¹⁴Καὶ ἐπελάθοντο λαβεῖν ἄρτους καὶ εἰ μὴ ἕνα ἄρτον οὐκ εἶχον μεθ' ἑαυτῶν ἐν τῷ πλοίῳ. ¹⁵ καὶ διεστέλλετο αὐτοῖς λέγων· ὁρᾶτε, βλέπετε ἀπὸ τῆς ζύμης τῶν Φαρισαίων καὶ τῆς ζύμης Ἡρῴδου.

Matt 16:5–6 ⇨ Luke 12:1

⁵Καὶ ἐλθόντες οἱ μαθηταὶ εἰς τὸ πέραν ἐπελάθαντο ἄρτους λαβεῖν. ⁶ὁ δὲ Ἰησοῦς εἶπεν αὐτοῖς· ὁρᾶτε καὶ προσέχετε ἀπὸ τῆς ζύμης τῶν Φαρισαίων καὶ Σαδδουκαίων.

Mark 4:22 ⇨ Q 12:2

²²οὐ γάρ ἐστιν κρυπτὸν ἐὰν μὴ ἵνα φανερωθῇ, οὐδὲ ἐγένετο ἀπόκρυφον, ἀλλ' ἵνα ἔλθῃ εἰς φανερόν.

Luke 8:17 ⇨ Q 12:2

¹⁷οὐ γάρ ἐστιν κρυπτὸν ὃ οὐ φανερὸν γενήσεται, οὐδὲ ἀπόκρυφον ὃ οὐ μὴ γνωσθῇ καὶ εἰς φανερὸν ἔλθῃ.

POxy 654.27–31 ⇨ Q 12:2

λέγει Ἰη(σοῦ)ς· γ[νῶθι τὸ ὂν ἔμπροσ]θεν τῆς ὄψεώς σου, καὶ [τὸ κεκαλυμμένον] ἀπό σου ἀποκαλυφ⟨θ⟩ήσετ[αί σοι· οὐ γάρ ἐσ]τιν κρυπτὸν ὃ οὐ φανε[ρὸν γενήσεται], καὶ θεθαμμένον ὃ ο[ὐκ ἐγερθήσεται].

GThom 5 ⇨ Q 12:2

ⲡⲉϫⲉ ⲓ̅ⲥ̅ ⲥⲟⲩⲱⲛ ⲡⲉⲧⲙ̅ⲡⲙ̅ⲧⲟ ⲙ̅ⲡⲉⲕϩⲟ ⲉⲃⲟⲗ ⲁⲩⲱ ⲡⲉⲑⲏⲡ ⲉⲣⲟⲕ ϥⲛⲁϭⲱⲗⲡ ⲉⲃⲟⲗ ⲛⲁⲕ· ⲙ̅ⲛ ⲗⲁⲁⲩ ⲅⲁⲣ ⲉϥϩⲏⲡ ⲉϥⲛⲁⲟⲩⲱⲛϩ ⲉⲃⲟⲗ ⲁⲛ.

POxy 654.36–40 ⇨ Q 12:2

λέγει Ἰη(σοῦ)ς· [μὴ ψεύδεσθε καὶ ὅτι μισ]εῖται, μὴ ποιεῖτ[ε· ὅτι πάντα ἐνώπιον τ]ῆς ἀληθ[ε]ίας ἀν[αφαίνεται. οὐδὲν γάρ ἐστι]ν ἀ[π]οκεκρ[υμμένον ὃ οὐ φανερὸν ἔσται].

GThom 6b ⇨ Q 12:2

ⲡⲉϫⲉ ⲓ̅ⲥ̅ ϫⲉ ⲙ̅ⲡⲣ̅ϫⲉ ϭⲟⲗ ⲁⲩⲱ ⲡⲉⲧⲉⲧⲙ̅ⲙⲟⲥⲧⲉ ⲙ̅ⲙⲟϥ ⲙ̅ⲡⲣ̅ⲁⲁϥ ϫⲉ ⲥⲉⲃⲟⲗⲡ ⲧⲏⲣⲟⲩ ⲉⲃⲟⲗ ⲙ̅ⲡⲉⲙⲧⲟ ⲉⲃⲟⲗ ⲛ̅ⲧⲡⲉ ⲙ̅ⲛ ⲗⲁⲁⲩ ⲅⲁⲣ ⲉϥϩⲏⲡ ⲉϥⲛⲁⲟⲩⲱⲛϩ ⲉⲃⲟⲗ ⲁⲛ ⲁⲩⲱ ⲙ̅ⲛ ⲗⲁⲁⲩ ⲉϥϩⲟⲃⲥ̅ ⲉⲩⲛⲁϭⲱ ⲟⲩⲉϣⲛ̅ ϭⲟⲗⲡϥ.

POxy 1.41–42 ⇨ Q 12:3

λέγει Ἰη(σοῦ)ς· ⟨ὃ⟩ ἀκούεις [ε]ἰς τὸ ἓν ὠτίον σου, το[ῦτο κήρυξον ...].

GThom 33 ⇨ Q 12:3 (⇨ S33)

ⲡⲉϫⲉ ⲓ̅ⲥ̅ ⲡⲉⲧⲕⲛⲁⲥⲱⲧⲙ̅ ⲉⲣⲟϥ ϩⲙ̅ ⲡⲉⲕⲙⲁⲁϫⲉ ϩⲙ̅ ⲡⲕⲉⲙⲁⲁϫⲉ ⲧⲁϣⲉⲟⲉⲓϣ ⲙ̅ⲙⲟϥ ϩⲓϫⲛ̅ ⲛⲉⲧⲛϫⲉⲛⲉⲡⲱⲣ ⲙⲁⲣⲉⲗⲁⲁⲩ ⲅⲁⲣ ϫⲉⲣⲉ ϩⲏ̅ⲃ̅ⲥ̅ ⲛ̅ϥⲕⲁⲁϥ ϩⲁ ⲙⲁⲁϫⲉ ⲟⲩⲇⲉ ⲙⲁϥⲕⲁⲁϥ ϩⲙ̅ ⲙⲁ ⲉϥϩⲏⲡ ⲁⲗⲗⲁ ⲉϣⲁⲣⲉϥⲕⲁⲁϥ ϩⲓϫⲛ̅ ⲧⲗⲩⲭⲛⲓⲁ ϫⲉⲕⲁⲁⲥ ⲟⲩⲟⲛ ⲛⲓⲙ ⲉⲧⲃⲏⲕ ⲉϩⲟⲩⲛ ⲁⲩⲱ ⲉⲧⲛ̅ⲛⲏⲩ ⲉⲃⲟⲗ ⲉⲩⲛⲁⲛⲁⲩ ⲁⲡⲉϥⲟⲩⲟⲉⲓⲛ.

Mark 8:14–15

¹⁴And they had forgotten to bring bread; and they had only one loaf with them in the boat. ¹⁵And he instructed them, saying, "Take heed, beware of the leaven of the Pharisees and the leaven of Herod."

Matt 16:5–6

⁵And when the disciples reached the other side, they had forgotten to bring any bread. ⁶Jesus said to them, "Take heed and beware of the leaven of the Pharisees and Sadducees."

Mark 4:22

²²For there is nothing hid, except to be made manifest; nor is anything secret, except to come to light.

Luke 8:17

¹⁷For nothing is hid that shall not be made manifest, nor anything secret that shall not be known and come to light.

POxy 654.27–31

Jesus said, "[Recognize what is in] your (sg.) sight, and [that which is hidden] from you (sg.) will become plain [to you (sg.). For there is nothing] hidden which [will] not [become] manifest, nor buried that [will not be raised]."

GThom 5

Jesus said, "Know what is before your face, and what is hidden from you will be disclosed to you. For there is nothing hidden that will not be revealed."

POxy 654.36–40

Jesus said, "[Do not tell lies, and] do not do what you [hate, for all things are plain in the sight] of truth. [For nothing] hidden [will not become manifest]."

GThom 6b

Jesus said, "Do not lie, and do not do what you hate, because all things are disclosed before heaven. For there is nothing hidden that will not be revealed, and there is nothing covered that will remain without being disclosed."

POxy 1.41–42

Jesus said, "That which you (sg.) hear in one of your (sg.) ears, [preach . . .]"

GThom 33

Jesus said, "What you will hear in your ear (text adds: in the other ear) proclaim from your rooftops. For no one lights a lamp and puts it under a basket, nor does one put it in a hidden place. Rather, one puts it on a stand so that all who come and go will see its light."

[Luke 12:1]

In Q: Bussmann 76–77: Luke 12:1 is found between two blocks of Q, and fits well with these. Knox 1957: 68; Marshall Lk 510; Polag 86–87 (uncertain); Schneider Lk 277. Schürmann 1968: 123–24: Matthew's designation of the Pharisees as "hypocrites" in his woes against the Pharisees (▷ S34) is a reminiscence of ὑπόκρισις in Q/Luke 12:1b. Additionally, Matthew's προσέχετε in 16:6 (diff Mark 8:15) may be a reminiscence of Q, although Luke himself displays a tendency to add προσέχετε (17:3; 20:46; 21:34). Streeter 1924: 279: Matthew omitted the saying here because he had it already in another (Markan) context.

Not in Q: Most authors.

Q 12:2–3

In Q: Most authors.

Matt 10:26–27

²⁶ So do not fear them; for nothing is covered that will not be revealed, or hidden that will not be known. ²⁷ What I tell you in the dark, speak in the light; and what you hear whispered, proclaim upon the housetops.

Luke 12:1–3

[¹ Meantime, a crowd of thousands had gathered together so that they were stepping upon one another. He began to say to his disciples first, "Beware of the leaven of the Pharisees, which is hypocrisy.] ² Nothing is covered up that will not be revealed, or hidden that will not be known. ³ Therefore whatever you have said in the dark shall be heard in the light, and what you have whispered in secret rooms shall be proclaimed upon the housetops."

Matt 10:28–31

²⁸καὶ <u>μὴ</u> <u>φοβεῖσθε</u> <u>ἀπὸ</u> <u>τῶν</u> <u>ἀποκτεννόντων</u> <u>τὸ σῶμα</u>,
τὴν δὲ ψυχὴν <u>μὴ</u> δυναμένων ἀποκτεῖναι·

<u>φοβεῖσθε</u> δὲ μᾶλλον <u>τὸν</u> δυνάμενον καὶ ψυχὴν
καὶ σῶμα ἀπολέσαι ἐν <u>γεέννῃ</u>.

²⁹<u>οὐχὶ</u> δύο   <u>στρουθία</u> ἀσσαρίου πωλεῖται;
<u>καὶ</u> <u>ἓν</u> <u>ἐξ</u> <u>αὐτῶν</u> <u>οὐ</u> πεσεῖται ἐπὶ τὴν
<u>γῆν</u> ἄνευ <u>τοῦ</u> <u>πατρὸς ὑμῶν.</u> ³⁰<u>ὑμῶν</u> <u>δὲ</u> <u>καὶ</u>
<u>αἱ</u> <u>τρίχες</u> <u>τῆς</u> <u>κεφαλῆς</u> <u>πᾶσαι</u> <u>ἠριθμημέναι</u>
<u>εἰσίν.</u> ³¹ <u>μὴ</u> οὖν <u>φοβεῖσθε·</u> <u>πολλῶν</u> <u>στρουθίων</u>
<u>διαφέρετε</u> <u>ὑμεῖς.</u>

σῶμα ⇨ Matt 6:25 [S41]
ψυχή ⇨ Matt 6:25 [S41]

Luke 12:4–7

⁴Λέγω δὲ ὑμῖν τοῖς φίλοις μου,
<u>μὴ</u> <u>φοβηθῆτε</u> <u>ἀπὸ</u> <u>τῶν</u> <u>ἀποκτεινόντων</u> <u>τὸ σῶμα</u>
καὶ μετὰ ταῦτα <u>μὴ</u> ἐχόντων περισσότερόν
τι ποιῆσαι. ⁵ὑποδείξω δὲ ὑμῖν τίνα φοβηθῆτε·
<u>φοβηθῆτε</u> <u>τὸν</u> μετὰ τὸ ἀποκτεῖναι ἔχοντα
ἐξουσίαν ἐμβαλεῖν εἰς τὴν <u>γέενναν.</u> ναὶ λέγω ὑμῖν,
τοῦτον φοβηθῆτε.
⁶<u>οὐχὶ</u> πέντε <u>στρουθία</u> πωλοῦνται ἀσσαρίων δύο;
<u>καὶ</u> <u>ἓν</u> <u>ἐξ</u> <u>αὐτῶν</u> <u>οὐκ</u> ἔστιν
ἐπιλελησμένον ἐνώπιον <u>τοῦ</u> θεοῦ. ⁷ἀλλὰ <u>καὶ</u>
<u>αἱ</u> <u>τρίχες</u> <u>τῆς</u> <u>κεφαλῆς</u> <u>ὑμῶν</u> <u>πᾶσαι</u> <u>ἠρίθμηνται.</u>
       <u>μὴ</u>   <u>φοβεῖσθε·</u> <u>πολλῶν</u> <u>στρουθίων</u>
<u>διαφέρετε.</u>

ἐξουσία ⇨ Luke 12:11 [S39]
σῶμα ⇨ Luke 12:23 [S41]

Notes

Q 12:4–7
In Q: Most authors.

Matt 10:28–31

²⁸ And do not fear those who kill the body but are not powerful enough to kill the soul; fear instead him who can destroy both soul and body in Gehenna. ²⁹ Are not two sparrows sold for an *assarion*? And not one of them will fall to the ground without your Father's consent. ³⁰ But even the hairs of your head are all numbered. ³¹ Fear not, therefore; you are worth more than many sparrows.

Luke 12:4–7

⁴ I tell you, my friends, do not fear those who kill the body, and afterwards are able to do no more. ⁵ But I will warn you whom to fear: fear him who, after he has killed, has power to cast into Gehenna; yes, I tell you, fear him! ⁶ Are not five sparrows sold for two *assaria*? And not one of them is forgotten before God. ⁷ But, even the hairs of your head are all numbered. Fear not; you are worth more than many sparrows.

Parallels

2 Clem 5:1–4 ⇨ Q 10:3 [S22]

¹ Ὅθεν, ἀδελφοί, καταλείψαντες τὴν παροικίαν τοῦ κόσμου τούτου ποιήσωμεν τὸ θέλημα τοῦ καλέσαντος ἡμᾶς, καὶ μὴ φοβηθῶμεν ἐξελθεῖν ἐκ τοῦ κόσμου τούτου. ² λέγει γὰρ ὁ κύριος· ἔσεσθε ὡς ἀρνία ἐν μέσῳ λύκων. ³ ἀποκριθεὶς δὲ ὁ Πέτρος αὐτῷ λέγει· ἐὰν οὖν διασπαράξωσιν οἱ λύκοι τὰ ἀρνία; ⁴ εἶπεν ὁ Ἰησοῦς τῷ Πέτρῳ· μὴ φοβείσθωσαν τὰ ἀρνία τοὺς λύκους μετὰ τὸ ἀποθανεῖν αὐτά· καὶ ὑμεῖς μὴ φοβεῖσθε τοὺς ἀποκτέννοντας ὑμᾶς καὶ μηδὲν ὑμῖν δυναμένους ποιεῖν, ἀλλὰ φοβεῖσθε τὸν μετὰ τὸ ἀποθανεῖν ὑμᾶς ἔχοντα ἐξουσίαν ψυχῆς καὶ σώματος τοῦ βαλεῖν εἰς γέενναν πυρός.

2 Clem 5:1–4

¹ Wherefore, brothers, let us forsake our sojourning in this world, and do the will of him who called us, and let us not fear to go forth from this world, ² for the Lord said, "You shall be as lambs in the midst of wolves." ³ Peter answered and said to him, "If then the wolves tear the lambs?" ⁴ Jesus said to him, "Let the lambs have no fear of the wolves after their death; and do not have fear of those that slay you, and can do nothing more to you, but fear him who after your death has power over soul and body, to cast them into the flames of hell."

Luke 21:18

¹⁸ καὶ θρὶξ ἐκ τῆς κεφαλῆς ὑμῶν οὐ μὴ ἀπόληται.

Luke 21:18

¹⁸ But not a hair of your head will perish.

Acts 27:34

³⁴ Διὸ παρακαλῶ ὑμᾶς μεταλαβεῖν τροφῆς· τοῦτο γὰρ πρὸς τῆς ὑμετέρας σωτηρίας ὑπάρχει· οὐδενὸς γὰρ ὑμῶν θρὶξ ἀπὸ τῆς κεφαλῆς ἀπολεῖται.

Acts 27:34

³⁴ Therefore I urge you to take some food; it will give you strength, since not a hair is to perish from the head of any of you.

Matt 10:32–33

³²Πᾶς οὖν ὅστις ὁμολογήσει <u>ἐν ἐμοὶ</u>
<u>ἔμπροσθεν τῶν ἀνθρώπων</u>,
<u>ὁμολογήσω κἀγὼ ἐν αὐτῷ ἔμπροσθεν</u> τοῦ
πατρός μου τοῦ ἐν [τοῖς] οὐρανοῖς·
³³ὅστις δ' ἂν ἀρνήσεταί με ἔμπροσθεν <u>τῶν</u>
<u>ἀνθρώπων</u>, ἀρνήσομαι κἀγὼ αὐτὸν ἔμπροσθεν
τοῦ πατρός μου τοῦ ἐν [τοῖς] οὐρανοῖς.

Luke 12:8–9

⁸Λέγω δὲ ὑμῖν, **πᾶς ὃς ἂν** ὁμολογήσῃ <u>ἐν ἐμοὶ</u>
<u>ἔμπροσθεν τῶν ἀνθρώπων</u>, καὶ ὁ υἱὸς τοῦ
ἀνθρώπου <u>ὁμολογήσει ἐν αὐτῷ ἔμπροσθεν</u>
τῶν ἀγγέλων τοῦ θεοῦ·
⁹ὁ δὲ ἀρνησάμενός με ἐνώπιον <u>τῶν</u>
<u>ἀνθρώπων</u>, ἀπαρνηθήσεται ἐνώπιον τῶν ἀγγέλων τοῦ
θεοῦ.

πᾶς ὅς ⇨ Luke 12:10 [S38]
ὁ υἱὸς τοῦ ἀνθρώπου ⇨ Luke 12:10 [S38]

Matt 10:32: εν ουρανοις: 𝔭¹⁹ ℵ D L W Koine Θ λ; Cl Or
[GNT; HG] / εν τοις ουρανοις: B C K X φ 565 892 *al*; Or
Eus [NA²⁵·²⁶] // 33: αυτον καγω: C L Koine φ [HG] / txt
(v. 32): 𝔭¹⁹ ℵ B D W Δ Θ λ 33 892 *al* [NA²⁵·²⁶] // εν
ουρανοις: 𝔭¹⁹ ℵ C D L W Koine Θ λ; Or [GNT; HG] / εν
τοις ουρανοις: B X φ 892 1424 *al*; Or [NA²⁵·²⁶].

Notes

Q 12:8–9
In Q: Most authors.

Matt 10:32–33

³²So every one who acknowledges me in public, I also will acknowledge before my Father who is in heaven; ³³but whoever denies me in public, I also will deny before my Father who is in heaven.

Luke 12:8–9

⁸I tell you, every one who acknowledges me in public, the Son of man also will acknowledge before the angels of God; ⁹but he who denies me in public will be denied before the angels of God.

Parallels

Mark 8:38

³⁸ὃς γὰρ ἐὰν ἐπαισχυνθῇ με καὶ τοὺς ἐμοὺς λόγους ἐν τῇ γενεᾷ ταύτῃ τῇ μοιχαλίδι καὶ ἁμαρτωλῷ, καὶ ὁ υἱὸς τοῦ ἀνθρώπου ἐπαισυνθήσεται αὐτόν, ὅταν ἔλθῃ ἐν τῇ δόξῃ τοῦ πατρὸς αὐτοῦ μετὰ τῶν ἀγγέλων τῶν ἁγίων.

Mark 8:38

³⁸For whoever is ashamed of me and of my words in this adulterous and sinful generation, of him will the Son of man also be ashamed, when he comes in the glory of his Father with the holy angels.

Luke 9:26

²⁶ὃς γὰρ ἂν ἐπαισχυνθῇ με καὶ τοὺς ἐμοὺς λόγους, τοῦτον ὁ υἱὸς τοῦ ἀνθρώπου ἐπαισυνθήσεται, ὅταν ἔλθῃ ἐν τῇ δόξῃ αὐτοῦ καὶ τοῦ πατρὸς καὶ τῶν ἁγίων ἀγγέλων.

Luke 9:26

²⁶For whoever is ashamed of me and of my words, of him will the Son of man be ashamed when he comes in his glory and the glory of the Father and of the holy angels.

2 Clem 3:2

²λέγει δὲ καὶ αὐτός· τὸν ὁμολογήσαντά με ἐνώπιον τῶν ἀνθρώπων, ὁμολογήσω αὐτὸν ἐνώπιον τοῦ πατρός μου.

2 Clem 3:2

²And he [the Lord] himself also says, "Whosoever confessed me before men, I will confess him before my Father."

2 Tim 2:11–13

¹¹πιστὸς ὁ λόγος· εἰ γὰρ συναπεθάνομεν, καὶ συζήσομεν· ¹²εἰ ὑπομένομεν, καὶ συμβασιλεύσομεν· εἰ ἀρνησόμεθα, κἀκεῖνος ἀρνήσεται ἡμᾶς· ¹³εἰ ἀπιστοῦμεν, ἐκεῖνος πιστὸς μένει, ἀρνήσασθαι γὰρ ἑαυτὸν οὐ δύναται.

2 Tim 2:11–13

¹¹The saying is sure: If we have died with him, we shall also live with him; ¹²if we endure, we shall also reign with him; if we deny him, he also will deny us; ¹³if we are faithless, he remains faithful— for he cannot deny himself.

Rev 3:5

⁵ὁ νικῶν οὕτως περιβαλεῖται ἐν ἱματίοις λευκοῖς καὶ οὐ μὴ ἐξαλείψω τὸ ὄνομα αὐτοῦ ἐκ τῆς βίβλου τῆς ζωῆς καὶ ὁμολογήσω τὸ ὄνομα αὐτοῦ ἐνώπιον τοῦ πατρός μου καὶ ἐνώπιον τῶν ἀγγέλων αὐτοῦ.

Rev 3:5

⁵He who conquers shall be clad thus in white garments, and I will not blot his name out of the book of life; I will confess his name before my Father and before his angels.

Matt 12:31–32

[³¹Διὰ τοῦτο λέγω ὑμῖν, πᾶσα ἁμαρτία καὶ
βλασφημία ἀφεθήσεται τοῖς ἀνθρώποις, ἡ δὲ τοῦ
πνεύματος βλασφημία οὐκ ἀφεθήσεται].
³²καὶ <u>ὃς</u> <u>ἐὰν</u> <u>εἴπῃ</u> <u>λόγον</u> <u>κατὰ</u> <u>τοῦ</u> <u>υἱοῦ</u> **τοῦ**
ἀνθρώπου, <u>ἀφεθήσεται</u> <u>αὐτῷ·</u> ὃς δ᾽ ἂν εἴπῃ
κατὰ τοῦ πνεύματος τοῦ ἁγίου, <u>οὐκ</u>
<u>ἀφεθήσεται</u> αὐτῷ οὔτε ἐν τούτῳ τῷ αἰῶνι οὔτε ἐν τῷ
μέλλοντι.

Luke 12:10

¹⁰<u>Καὶ</u> <u>πᾶς</u> <u>ὃς</u> <u>ἐρεῖ</u> <u>λόγον</u> <u>εἰς</u> <u>τὸν</u> <u>υἱὸν</u> **τοῦ**
ἀνθρώπου, <u>ἀφεθήσεται</u> <u>αὐτῷ·</u> τῷ δὲ <u>εἰς</u> <u>τὸ</u>
ἅγιον πνεῦμα βλασφημήσαντι <u>οὐκ</u>
<u>ἀφεθήσεται.</u>

τὸ ἅγιον πνεῦμα ⇨ Luke 12:12 [S39]

Notes

Q 12:10

In Q: Most authors. Matthew's version of the saying is
generally acknowledged to be a conflation of Mark 3:28–
29 and Q, with Matt 12:31 derived exclusively from
Mark. Luke is less influenced by Mark although his
βλασφημήσαντι may be due to Mark.

Matt 12:31–32
[³¹ Therefore I tell you, every sin and blasphemy will be forgiven people, but the blasphemy against the Spirit will not be forgiven.]
³² And whoever says a word against the Son of man will be forgiven, but whoever speaks against the Holy Spirit will not be forgiven, either in this age or in the coming one.

Luke 12:10

¹⁰ And every one who says a word against the Son of man will be forgiven; but the one who blasphemes against the Holy Spirit will not be forgiven.

Parallels

Mark 3:28–30
²⁸ Ἀμὴν λέγω ὑμῖν ὅτι πάντα ἀφεθήσεται τοῖς υἱοῖς τῶν ἀνθρώπων τὰ ἁμαρτήματα καὶ αἱ βλασφημίαι ὅσα ἐὰν βλασφημήσωσιν· ²⁹ ὃς δ' ἂν βλασφημήσῃ εἰς τὸ πνεῦμα τὸ ἅγιον οὐκ ἔχει ἄφεσιν εἰς τὸν αἰῶνα, ἀλλὰ ἔνοχός ἐστιν αἰωνίου ἁμαρτήματος. ³⁰ ὅτι ἔλεγον· πνεῦμα ἀκάθαρτον ἔχει.

GThom 44
ⲡⲉϫⲉ ⲓ̅ⲥ̅ ϫⲉ ⲡⲉⲧⲁϫⲉ ⲟⲩⲁ ⲁⲡⲉⲓⲱⲧ ⲥⲉⲛⲁⲕⲱ ⲉⲃⲟⲗ ⲛⲁϥ ⲁⲩⲱ ⲡⲉⲧⲁϫⲉ ⲟⲩⲁ ⲉⲡϣⲏⲣⲉ ⲥⲉⲛⲁⲕⲱ ⲉⲃⲟⲗ ⲛⲁϥ ⲡⲉⲧⲁϫⲉ ⲟⲩⲁ ⲇⲉ ⲁⲡⲡ̅ⲛ̅ⲁ̅ ⲉⲧⲟⲩⲁⲁⲃ ⲥⲉⲛⲁⲕⲱ ⲁⲛ ⲉⲃⲟⲗ ⲛⲁϥ ⲟⲩⲧⲉ ϩ̅ⲙ ⲡⲕⲁϩ ⲟⲩⲧⲉ ϩ̅ⲛ ⲧⲡⲉ.

Did 11:7
⁷ Καὶ πάντα προφήτην λαλοῦντα ἐν πνεύματι οὐ πειράσετε οὐδὲ διακρινεῖτε· πᾶσα γὰρ ἁμαρτία ἀφεθήσεται, αὕτη δὲ ἡ ἁμαρτία οὐκ ἀφεθήσεται.

2 Clem 13:2
² Λέγει γὰρ ὁ κύριος· διὰ παντὸς τὸ ὄνομά μου βλασφημεῖται ἐν πᾶσιν τοῖς ἔθνεσιν, καὶ πάλιν· οὐαὶ δι' ὃν βλασφημεῖται τὸ ὄνομά μου.

Mark 3:28–30
²⁸ "Amen, I tell you, all sins will be forgiven the sons of men, and whatever blasphemies they utter; ²⁹ but whoever blasphemes the Holy Spirit never has forgiveness, but is guilty of an eternal sin"— ³⁰ for they were saying, "He has an unclean spirit."

GThom 44
Jesus said, "Whoever blasphemes against the Father will be forgiven, and whoever blasphemes against the son will be forgiven. But whoever blasphemes against the holy spirit will not be forgiven, either on earth or in heaven."

Did 11:7
⁷ Do not test or examine any prophet who is speaking in the a spirit, for every sin shall be forgiven, but this sin shall not be forgiven.

2 Clem 13:2
² For the Lord says, "Every way is my name blasphemed among all the heathen," and again, "Woe unto him on whose account my name is blasphemed."

Matt 10:17–20

[¹⁷Προσέχετε δὲ ἀπὸ τῶν ἀνθρώπων· παραδώσουσιν
γὰρ ὑμᾶς εἰς συνέδρια καὶ ἐν ταῖς συναγωγαῖς αὐτῶν
μαστιγώσουσιν ὑμᾶς· ¹⁸καὶ ἐπὶ ἡγεμόνας δὲ καὶ
βασιλεῖς ἀχθήσεσθε ἕνεκεν ἐμοῦ εἰς μαρτύριον αὐτοῖς
καὶ τοῖς ἔθνεσιν].
¹⁹ὅταν δὲ παραδῶσιν ὑμᾶς,

μὴ μεριμνήσητε πῶς ἢ τί λαλήσατε·
δοθήσεται γὰρ ὑμῖν ἐν ἐκείνῃ τῇ ὥρᾳ τί λαλήσητε·

[²⁰οὐ γὰρ ὑμεῖς ἐστε οἱ λαλοῦντες, ἀλλὰ τὸ πνεῦμα
τοῦ πατρὸς ὑμῶν τὸ λαλοῦν ἐν ὑμῖν].

Matt 10:23

[²³ὅταν δὲ διώκωσιν ὑμᾶς ἐν τῇ πόλει ταύτῃ, φεύγετε εἰς
τὴν ἑτέραν· ἀμὴν γὰρ λέγω ὑμῖν, οὐ μὴ τελέσητε τὰς
πόλεις τοῦ Ἰσραὴλ ἕως ἂν ἔλθῃ ὁ υἱὸς τοῦ ἀνθρώπου].

Matt 10:23: εως αν: C D L W Koine Θ λ φ [NA²⁶; HG] /
εως: א* B X 248 [NA²⁵] / εως ου: א² pc.

Luke 12:11–12

¹¹ὅταν δὲ εἰσφέρωσιν ὑμᾶς ἐπὶ τὰς
συναγωγὰς καὶ τὰς ἀρχὰς καὶ τὰς ἐξουσίας,
μὴ μεριμνήσητε πῶς ἢ τί ἀπολογήσησθε ἢ τί εἴπητε·
¹²τὸ γὰρ ἅγιον πνεῦμα διδάξει ὑμᾶς ἐν αὐτῇ τῇ ὥρᾳ ἃ δεῖ
εἰπεῖν.

μὴ μεριμνήσητε ⇨ Luke 12:22 [S41]

Notes

Q 12:11–12

In Q: Most authors.

Not in Q: Harnack and Hawkins (1911) omit all
discussion of Q 12:11–12. Müller (1908: 52) argues that
Luke 12:11–12 // Matt 10:19 is from Mark.

[Matt 10:23]

In Q: Coppens 1981: 182; Crossan 1983: 344; Easton
Lk 199; Haupt 1913: 22–23; Hawkins 1911: 134; Polag 60
(conjectural); Sato 1984: 16, 30 (possibly in Q);
Schnackenburg 1963: 204; Schürmann 1968: 151–52;
Tödt 1963: 47–48.

The principal grounds for including Matt 10:23 in Q
are: (1) It is difficult to explain the verse as a redactional
creation by Matthew (Easton). (2) "Ὅταν δὲ διώκωσιν in
Matt 10:23 seems as if it formed the immediate
continuation for ὅταν παραδῶσιν in v. 19 . . ." (Haupt;
Schürmann). (3) Q/Matt 10:23 is attached to its context
by the phonetic accord between ὅταν δὲ εἰσφέρωσιν ὑμᾶς
ἐπὶ τὰς . . . , μὴ μεριμνήσητε (Q 12:11) and ὅταν δὲ διώκωσιν
ὑμᾶς ἐν τῇ . . . , οὐ μὴ τελέσητε (Matt 10:23) and by the
catchword "Son of Man" (in Q 12:8–9, 10) (Schürmann).
(4) Matt 10:23 derives from early Palestinian tradition
and is similar to other Q sayings both materially and in its
history of tradition (Tödt). (5) Luke's omission is
explicable on the basis that it was "distasteful to his
readers" (Hawkins; cf. Easton; Haupt).

Not in Q: Most authors.

Matt 10:17–20

[17 Beware of those people; for they will deliver you up to courts, and flog you in their synagogues, 18 and you will be dragged before governors and kings for my sake, as a witness to them and the Gentiles.]
19 When they deliver you up, do not be anxious how or what you will say; for what you are to say will be given to you in that hour;

[20 for it is not you who speak, but the Spirit of your Father speaking through you.]

Matt 10:23

[23 When they persecute you in one city, flee to the next; Amen I tell you, you will not finish going through the cities of Israel before the Son of man comes.]

Luke 12:11–12

11 When they bring you before the synagogues and the rulers and the authorities, do not be anxious how or what you are to answer or what you are to say; 12 for the Holy Spirit will teach you in that very hour what you ought to say.

Parallels

Mark 13:9–11

9 Βλέπετε δὲ ὑμεῖς ἑαυτούς· παραδώσουσιν ὑμᾶς εἰς συνέδρια καὶ εἰς συναγωγὰς δαρήσεσθε καὶ ἐπὶ ἡγεμόνων καὶ βασιλέων σταθήσεσθε ἕνεκεν ἐμοῦ εἰς μαρτύριον αὐτοῖς. 10 καὶ εἰς πάντα τὰ ἔθνη πρῶτον δεῖ κηρυχθῆναι τὸ εὐαγγέλιον.
11 καὶ **ὅταν** ἄγωσιν ὑμᾶς παραδιδόντες, **μὴ** προμεριμνᾶτε τί λαλήσατε, ἀλλ᾽ ὃ ἐὰν δοθῇ ὑμῖν **ἐν ἐκείνῃ τῇ ὥρᾳ** τοῦτο λαλεῖτε· οὐ γάρ ἐστε ὑμεῖς οἱ λαλοῦντες ἀλλὰ τὸ πνεῦμα τὸ ἅγιον.

Luke 21:14–15

14 θέτε οὖν ἐν ταῖς καρδίαις ὑμῶν μὴ προμελετᾶν ἀπολογηθῆναι· 15 ἐγὼ γὰρ δώσω ὑμῖν στόμα καὶ σοφίαν ᾗ οὐ δυνήσονται ἀντιστῆναι ἢ ἀντειπεῖν ἅπαντες οἱ ἀντικείμενοι ὑμῖν.

Mark 13:9–11

9 But take heed for yourselves; for they will deliver you up to courts; and you will be beaten in synagogues; and you will stand before governors and kings for my sake, for a witness to them. 10 And the gospel must first be preached to all nations.
11 And when they bring you to trial and deliver you up, do not be anxious beforehand what you are to say; but say whatever is given you in that hour, for it is not you who speak, but the Holy Spirit.

Luke 21:14–15

14 Settle it therefore in your minds, not to practice an apologia; 15 for I will give you a mouth and wisdom, which none of your adversaries will be able to withstand or contradict.

Luke 12:13–15, 16–21

(¹³Εἶπεν δέ τις ἐκ τοῦ ὄχλου αὐτῷ· διδάσκαλε, εἰπὲ τῷ ἀδελφῷ μου
μερίσασθαι μετ᾽ ἐμοῦ τὴν κληρονομίαν.
¹⁴ὁ δὲ εἶπεν αὐτῷ· ἄνθρωπε, τίς με κατέστησεν κριτὴν ἢ μεριστὴν ἐφ᾽ ὑμᾶς;)
[¹⁵εἶπεν δὲ πρὸς αὐτούς· ὁρᾶτε καὶ φυλάσσεσθε ἀπὸ πάσης πλεονεξίας, ὅτι
οὐκ ἐν τῷ περισσεύειν τινὶ ἡ ζωὴ αὐτοῦ ἐστιν ἐκ τῶν ὑπαρχόντων αὐτῷ].
(¹⁶Εἶπεν δὲ παραβολὴν πρὸς αὐτοὺς λέγων· ἀνθρώπου τινὸς πλουσίου
εὐφόρησεν ἡ χώρα. ¹⁷καὶ διελογίζετο ἐν ἑαυτῷ λέγων· τί ποιήσω, ὅτι οὐκ ἔχω
ποῦ συνάξω τοὺς καρπούς μου; ¹⁸καὶ εἶπεν· τοῦτο ποιήσω, καθελῶ μου τὰς
ἀποθήκας καὶ μείζονας οἰκοδομήσω καὶ συνάξω ἐκεῖ πάντα τὸν σῖτον καὶ τὰ
ἀγαθά μου ¹⁹καὶ ἐρῶ τῇ ψυχῇ μου· ψυχή, ἔχεις πολλὰ ἀγαθὰ κείμενα εἰς ἔτη
πολλά· ἀναπαύου, φάγε, πίε, εὐφραίνου. ²⁰εἶπεν δὲ αὐτῷ ὁ θεός· ἄφρων,
ταύτῃ τῇ νυκτὶ τὴν ψυχήν σου ἀπαιτοῦσιν ἀπὸ σοῦ· ἃ δὲ ἡτοίμασας, τίνι
ἔσται; ²¹οὕτως ὁ θησαυρίζων ἑαυτῷ καὶ μὴ εἰς θεὸν πλουτῶν).

Luke 12:18: παντα τα γενηματα μου: ℵ* D b ff²
i l q r¹ (sysᵉ) [HG] / τους καρπους: a c d e /
παντα τα γενηματα και τα αγαθα μου: A Q W
Koine Θ Ψ *pm* sypʰ vg / παντα τον σιτον και τα
αγαθα μου: 𝔭⁴⁵·⁷⁵ ℵ² B L X 070 λ φ (33) 579
892 1241 *pc* sa bo [NA²⁵·²⁶] // 21: αυτω: ℵ* B
[NA²⁵] / εν αυτω: (L) W Γ *al* / εαυτω: 𝔭⁷⁵ ℵ² A
Q Θ Ψ 070 λ φ [NA²⁶; HG].

ἀποθήκη ⇨ Luke 12:24 [S41]
ψυχή ⇨ Luke 12:22 [S41]
φάγε ⇨ Luke 12:22, 29 [S41]
πίε ⇨ Matt 6:25; Luke 12:29 [S41]
θησαυρίζω ⇨ Matt 6:19, 20 [S42]

Notes

(Q 12:13–14, 16–21)

In Q: Dupont 1969 (but see idem 1973: 115–17);
Easton Lk xxi, 201 ("undoubtedly from Q"); Haupt 1913:
69, 193–94 (12:13–14 only); Kloppenborg 1987: 215;
Marshall Lk 522 (hesitantly); Soiron 1916: 30;
Schürmann 1968: 119–20, 232, Steinhauser 1981: 228–
29; Weiss 1901: 441; idem 1907: 78, 81–82.

While the vocabulary and syntax of v. 15 is Lukan,
several scholars propose that Luke 12:13–14, 16–21
derived from Q. The principal grounds for inclusion are:
(1) Luke 12:13–14 and 12:16–21 occur in a
predominantly Q section of Luke and are closely
connected with the following Q section (Easton;
Kloppenborg). (2) The two sections are characterized by
the same key words: "barn," "soul," "eat" and "drink"
(Schürmann; Steinhauser; Weiss). Moreover, πιῆτε in
Matt 6:25 (mss! diff Luke) provides an original catchword
connection with Luke 12:19 (πίε) (Schürmann).
Schürmann takes θησαυρίζω in Matt 6:19, 20 to be a
reminiscence of the word in Q 12:21. (3) Διὰ τοῦτο (Q
12:22) more logically follows on 12:13–21 than it does on
12:11–12 (Schürmann; Steinhauser). (3) The chriic style
of 12:13–14 is strikingly similar to other chriae in Q (e.g.,
Q 9:57–58, 59–60) (Kloppenborg) and (4) the criticism of

riches coheres with Q 12:33–34 and Q 16:13
(Kloppenborg). (5) Matthew may have omitted the story
when he transferred Q 12:22–31 to the Sermon on the
Mount (Easton; Steinhauser) because its apophthegmatic
(12:13–14) and narrative forms (12:16–21) did not fit well
within the Sermon on the Mount or because Jesus'
rejection of the role of judge no longer cohered with later
church praxis (Schürmann).

Not in Q: Most authors, including Crossan 1983;
Edwards; Harnack; Hoffmann; Hunter; Jacobson;
Lührmann; Meyer; Schenk; Schulz and Zeller, do not
discuss Luke 12:13–14, 16–21 at all. Dupont (1973: 116–
17) argues that θησαυρίζω is probably original in Q 12:33–
34 and therefore not a reminiscence of Luke 12:21 (*pace*
Schürmann). Fitzmyer (Lk 968) dismisses as farfetched
the suggestion that Matthew would have omitted the
verses or that Matt 6:19–20, 25 contains reminiscences of
Q. Lambrecht (1982: 302) holds that the Lukan character
of vv. 15 and 21 indicates that Luke is responsible to the
position of the parable. Fitzmyer (Lk 968, 971),
Grundmann (Lk 256), Manson (270), Müller (1908: 7, 52)
and Schmithals (Lk 144) assign both units to L. Sato
(1984: 65) ascribes vv. 16–21 to QᴸᵏLk.

Luke 12:13–21

(¹³Someone from the crowd said to him, "Teacher, tell my brother to divide the inheritance with me." ¹⁴But he said to him, "Friend, who set me up as a judge or divider over you?")

[¹⁵Then he said to them, "Take heed, and guard against all greed; for a man's life does not consist in the abundance of his possessions."]

(¹⁶He told them a parable, saying, "The land of a rich man brought forth plentifully; ¹⁷and he thought to himself, 'What shall I do, for I have nowhere to store my crops?' ¹⁸And he said, 'I will do this: I will pull down my granaries, and build larger ones; and there I will store all my grain and my goods. ¹⁹And I will say to myself, Soul, you have many goods laid up for many years; rest, eat, drink, be merry.' ²⁰But God said to him, 'Fool! This night your soul is required of you; and the things you have prepared, whose will they be?' ²¹So is whoever lays up treasure for himself, and is not rich in the sight of God.")

Parallels

GThom 72

[ⲡⲉⲝ]ⲉ ⲟ[ⲩⲣⲱⲙⲉ] ⲛⲁϥ ϫⲉ ϫⲟⲟⲥ ⲛⲛⲁⲥⲛⲏⲩ ϣⲓⲛⲁ ⲉⲩⲛ[ⲁ]ⲡⲱϣⲉ ⲛ̄ⲛ̄ϩⲛⲁⲁⲩ ⲙ̄ⲡⲁⲉⲓⲱⲧ ⲛⲙ̄ⲙⲁⲉⲓ ⲡⲉϫⲁϥ ⲛⲁϥ ϫⲉ ⲱ ⲡⲣⲱⲙⲉ ⲛⲓⲙ ⲡⲉ ⲛ̄ⲧⲁϩⲁⲁⲧ ⲛ̄ⲣⲉϥⲡⲱϣⲉ ⲁϥⲕⲟⲧϥ̄ ⲁⲛⲉϥⲙⲁⲑⲏⲧⲏⲥ ⲡⲉϫⲁϥ ⲛⲁⲩ ϫⲉ ⲙⲏ ⲉⲉⲓϣⲟⲟⲡ ⲛ̄ⲣⲉϥⲡⲱϣⲉ.

GThom 63

ⲡⲉϫⲉ ⲓ̅ⲥ̅ ϫⲉ ⲛⲉⲩⲛ̄ ⲟⲩⲣⲱⲙⲉ ⲙ̄ⲡⲗⲟⲩⲥⲓⲟⲥ ⲉⲩⲛ̄ⲧⲁϥ ⲙ̄ⲙⲁⲩ ⲛ̄ϩⲁϩ ⲛ̄ⲭⲣⲏⲙⲁ ⲡⲉϫⲁϥ ϫⲉ ϯⲛⲁⲣ̄ⲭⲣⲱ ⲛ̄ⲛⲁⲭⲣⲏⲙⲁ ϫⲉⲕⲁⲁⲥ ⲉⲉⲓⲛⲁϫⲟ ⲛ̄ⲧⲁⲱⲥϩ ⲛ̄ⲧⲁⲧⲱϭⲉ ⲛ̄ⲧⲁⲙⲟⲩϩ ⲛ̄ⲛⲁⲉϩⲱⲣ ⲛ̄ⲕⲁⲣⲡⲟⲥ ϣⲓⲛⲁ ϫⲉ ⲛⲓⲣ̄ ϭⲣⲱϩ ⲗ̄ⲗⲁⲁⲩ ⲛⲁⲉⲓ ⲛⲉ ⲛⲉϥⲙⲉⲉⲩⲉ ⲉⲣⲟⲟⲩ ϩⲙ̄ ⲡⲉϥϩⲏⲧ ⲁⲩⲱ ϩⲛ̄ ⲧⲟⲩϣⲏ ⲉⲧⲙ̄ⲙⲁⲩ ⲁϥⲙⲟⲩ ⲡⲉⲧⲉⲩⲙ̄ ⲙⲁϫⲉ ⲙ̄ⲙⲟϥ· ⲙⲁⲣⲉϥⲥⲱⲧⲙ̄.

GThom 72

[A person said] to him, "Tell my relatives (lit.: brothers) to divide my father's property with me." He said to the person, "Sir, who made me a divider?" He turned to his disciples and said to them, "I am not a divider, am I?"

GThom 63

Jesus said, "There was a rich person who had a great deal of money. He said, 'I shall invest my money so that I may sow, reap, plant, and fill my storehouses with produce, that I may lack nothing.' These were his plans, but that very night he died. Whoever has ears ought to listen."

Matt 6:25–34

²⁵Διὰ τοῦτο λέγω ὑμῖν· μὴ μεριμνᾶτε τῇ
ψυχῇ ὑμῶν τί φάγητε [ἢ τί πίητε], μηδὲ τῷ
σώματι ὑμῶν τί ἐνδύσησθε. οὐχὶ ἡ ψυχὴ
πλεῖόν ἐστιν τῆς τροφῆς καὶ τὸ σῶμα τοῦ ἐνδύματος;
²⁶ἐμβλέψατε εἰς τὰ πετεινὰ τοῦ οὐρανοῦ
ὅτι οὐ σπείρουσιν οὐδὲ θερίζουσιν οὐδὲ
συνάγουσιν εἰς ἀποθήκας, καὶ ὁ πατὴρ ὑμῶν
ὁ οὐράνιος τρέφει αὐτά· οὐχ ὑμεῖς μᾶλλον διαφέρετε
αὐτῶν;
²⁷τίς δὲ ἐξ ὑμῶν μεριμνῶν δύναται
προσθεῖναι ἐπὶ τὴν ἡλικίαν αὐτοῦ πῆχυν ἕνα;
²⁸καὶ περὶ ἐνδύματος τί μεριμνᾶτε;
καταμάθετε τὰ κρίνα τοῦ ἀγροῦ πῶς
αὐξάνουσιν· οὐ κοπιῶσιν οὐδὲ νήθουσιν·
²⁹λέγω δὲ ὑμῖν ὅτι οὐδὲ Σολομὼν ἐν πάσῃ
τῇ δόξῃ αὐτοῦ περιεβάλετο ὡς ἓν τούτων.
³⁰εἰ δὲ τὸν χόρτον τοῦ ἀγροῦ σήμερον ὄντα
καὶ αὔριον εἰς κλίβανον βαλλόμενον ὁ θεὸς
οὕτως ἀμφιέννυσιν, οὐ πολλῷ μᾶλλον ὑμᾶς,
ὀλιγόπιστοι; ³¹μὴ οὖν μεριμνήσητε λέγοντες·
τί φάγωμεν; ἤ· τί πίωμεν; ἤ· τί περιβαλώμεθα;
³²πάντα γὰρ ταῦτα τὰ ἔθνη ἐπιζητοῦσιν,
οἶδεν γὰρ ὁ πατὴρ ὑμῶν ὁ οὐράνιος ὅτι χρῄζετε
τούτων ἁπάντων.
³³ζητεῖτε δὲ πρῶτον τὴν βασιλείαν [τοῦ θεοῦ] καὶ τὴν
δικαιοσύνην αὐτοῦ, καὶ ταῦτα πάντα
προστεθήσεται ὑμῖν.
[³⁴μὴ οὖν μεριμνήσητε εἰς τὴν αὔριον, ἡ γὰρ αὔριον
μεριμνήσει ἑαυτῆς· ἀρκετὸν τῇ ἡμέρᾳ ἡ κακία αὐτῆς].

Luke 12:22–32

²²Εἶπεν δὲ πρὸς τοὺς μαθητὰς [αὐτοῦ]·
διὰ τοῦτο λέγω ὑμῖν· μὴ μεριμνᾶτε τῇ
ψυχῇ τί φάγητε, μηδὲ τῷ
σώματι τί ἐνδύσησθε. ²³ἡ γὰρ ψυχὴ
πλεῖόν ἐστιν τῆς τροφῆς καὶ τὸ σῶμα τοῦ ἐνδύματος;
²⁴κατανοήσατε τοὺς κόρακας
ὅτι οὐ σπείρουσιν οὐδὲ θερίζουσιν, οἷς οὐκ
ἔστιν ταμεῖον οὐδὲ ἀποθήκη, καὶ ὁ θεὸς
τρέφει αὐτούς· πόσῳ μᾶλλον ὑμεῖς
διαφέρετε τῶν πετεινῶν;
²⁵τίς δὲ ἐξ ὑμῶν μεριμνῶν δύναται ἐπὶ τὴν
ἡλικίαν αὐτοῦ προσθεῖναι πῆχυν;
²⁶εἰ οὖν οὐδὲ ἐλάχιστον δύνασθε, τί περὶ
τῶν λοιπῶν μεριμνᾶτε; ²⁷κατανοήσατε τὰ κρίνα
πῶς αὐξάνει· οὐ κοπιᾷ οὐδὲ νήθει·
λέγω δὲ ὑμῖν οὐδὲ Σολομὼν ἐν πάσῃ τῇ
δόξῃ αὐτοῦ περιεβάλετο ὡς ἓν τούτων.
²⁸εἰ δὲ ἐν ἀγρῷ τὸν χόρτον ὄντα σήμερον
καὶ αὔριον εἰς κλίβανον βαλλόμενον ὁ θεὸς
οὕτως ἀμφιέζει, πόσῳ μᾶλλον ὑμᾶς,
ὀλιγόπιστοι; ²⁹καὶ ὑμεῖς μὴ ζητεῖτε τί φάγητε καὶ
τί πίητε, καὶ μὴ μετεωρίζεσθε· ³⁰ταῦτα γὰρ
πάντα τὰ ἔθνη τοῦ κόσμου ἐπιζητοῦσιν,
ὑμῶν δὲ ὁ πατὴρ οἶδεν ὅτι χρῄζετε
τούτων.
³¹πλὴν ζητεῖτε τὴν βασιλείαν αὐτοῦ,
καὶ ταῦτα
προστεθήσεται ὑμῖν.
[³²Μὴ φοβοῦ, τὸ μικρὸν ποίμνιον, ὅτι εὐδόκησεν ὁ
πατὴρ ὑμῶν δοῦναι ὑμῖν τὴν βασιλείαν].

Matt 6:25: η τι πιητε: B W φ 33 *al* c f g¹ h q z sa^mss mae bo
[NA²⁵·²⁶] / και τι πιητε (Luke 12:29): L Θ 0233 syp.h / omit:
א λ 892 *pc* a b ff² l vg sy^c sa^mss; Cl [HG] // 33: βασιλεια του
θεου: L W Koine Θ 0233 λ φ lat sy mae bo [NA²⁶; HG] /
βασιλεια: א B k g² l sa bo; Eus Tert [NA²⁵] / βασιλεια των
ουρανων (Matt 5:3): 301; Cl.

Luke 12:22 σωματι υμων (Matt): B 070 φ 28 33 1241 *al* a
syp [NA²⁵] / txt: 𝔓⁴⁵·⁷⁵ א A D L Q W Koine Θ Ψ λ lat
sy^s.c.h; Cl [NA²⁶; HG] // 24: ουτε σπειρουσιν ουτε
θεριζουσιν: א D L Q 579 892 *pc* e [NA²⁵; HG] / txt (Matt):
𝔓⁴⁵·⁷⁵ A B W Koine Θ Ψ (070) λ φ lat sa; Cl [NA²⁶] // 25:
προσθειναι επι τ. ηλικιαν αυτου (Matt): 𝔓⁴⁵ א A D L Q W
Θ Ψ λ φ [HG] / txt: 𝔓⁷⁵ B 579 *pc* [NA²⁵·²⁶] // 27: ουτε
νηθει ουτε υφαινει: D d sy^s.c; Cl [NA²⁵] / ου κοπια ουδε
νηθει: 𝔓⁴⁵·⁷⁵ א B A W Koine Θ 070 λ φ lat syp sa bo [NA²⁶;
HG].

POxy 655 i 1–17

[λέγει Ἰ(ησοῦ)ς· μὴ μεριμνᾶτε ἀ]πὸ πρωὶ ἔ[ως ὀψὲ
μήτ]ε ἀφ᾽ ἑσπ[έρας ἕως π]ρωὶ μήτε [τῇ τροφῇ ὑ]μῶν τί
φά[γητε, μήτε] τῇ στ[ολῇ ὑμῶν] τί ἐνδύ[ση]σθε.
[πολ]λῷ κρεί[σσον]ές ἐ[στε] τῶν [κρί]νων, ἅτι[να ο]ὐ
ξα[ί]νει οὐδὲ ν[ήθ]ει. μ[ηδ]ὲν ἔχοντ[ες ἔ]νδ[υ]μα, τί
ἐν[δύεσθε] καὶ ὑμεῖς; τίς ἂν προσθ⟨εί⟩η ἐπὶ τὴν ἡλικίαν
ὑμῶν; αὐτὸ[ς δ]ώσει ὑμεῖν τὸ ἔνδυμα ὑμῶν.

POxy 655 i 1–17

[Jesus said, "Do not be concerned] from morning [until
evening and] from evening [until] morning, neither
[about] your [food] and what [you will] eat, [nor] about
[your clothing] and what you [will] wear.
[You are far] better than the [lilies] which [neither] card
nor [spin]. As for you, when you have no garment, what
[will you put on]? Who might add to your stature? He it is
who will give you your cloak."

GThom 36

ⲡⲉϫⲉ ⲓ̅ⲥ̅ ⲙ̅ⲛ̅ϥⲓ ⲣⲟⲟⲩϣ ϫⲓ(ⲛ) ϩⲧⲟⲟⲩⲉ ϣⲁ ⲣⲟⲩϩⲉ
ⲁⲩⲱ ϫⲓⲛ ϩⲓⲣⲟⲩϩⲉ ϣⲁ ϩⲧⲟⲟⲩⲉ ϫⲉ ⲟⲩ ⲡⲉ
ⲉⲧⲛⲁⲧⲁⲁϥ ϩⲓⲱⲧ ⲧⲏⲩⲧⲛ̅.

GThom 36

Jesus said, "Do not worry, from morning to evening and
from evening to morning, about what you will wear."

Origen, *De oratione* 2.2; 14.1

Αἰτεῖτε τὰ μεγάλα, καὶ τὰ μικρὰ ὑμῖν προστεθήσεται·
καὶ αἰτεῖτε τὰ ἐπουράνια, καὶ τὰ ἐπίγεια ὑμῖν
προστεθήσεται.

Origen, *De oratione* 2.2; 14.1

Ask for great things and the small things will be added to
you; and ask for heavenly things, and the earthly will be
added to you.

Clement Alex., *Strom.* 1.24.158.2

Αἰτεῖσθε γάρ, φησί, τὰ μεγάλα, καὶ τὰ μικρὰ ὑμῖν
προστεθήσεται.

Clement Alex., *Strom.* 1.24.158.2

"For," it is said, "seek what is great and the little things
shall be added to you."

Q 12:22–31
In Q: Most authors.

[Matt 6:34]
In Q: Harnack 183 (possibly); Luz Mt: 364: V. 34 derives from Q^{Mt}; Sato 1984: 57: Q^{Mt}.

Not in Q: Dupont 1969: 121; Easton Lk 204; Grundmann Mt 214; Hawkins 1911: 110; Hoffmann; Knox 1957: 29; Lambrecht 1985: 168; Müller 1908: 52; Polag 63; Schenk; Schulz. Strecker 1985: 141, 145: V. 34 is an addition, but may be pre–Matthean. Weiss 1907: 83; Zeller 1977: 93.

[Luke 12:32]
In Q: Bussmann 83; Chilton 1979: 236–37 (Q^{Lk}); Crossan 1983: 344; Hunter 141; Manson 114; Polag 62 (probably). Schmid 237: Matthew may have omitted Luke 12:32 because it did not fit well with the themes of the Sermon on the Mount. Schürmann 1982: 136, 159–60: Matt 21:43 betrays knowledge of a Q version of Luke 12:32. Sato 1984: 65: v 34 is from Q^{Lk}. Strecker 1985: 141: Perhaps this belonged already to Q^{Lk}. Vassiliadis 1978: 68, 68 n. 114: The absence of a parallel to Luke 12:32 is due to Matthew's omission. Weiss 1907: 83.

Not in Q: Easton Lk 204; Fitzmyer Lk 976; Grundmann Lk 259; Harnack 4–8; Hawkins 1911: 110; Hoffmann; Müller 1908: 7, 53; Schenk; Schlosser 1980; Schmithals Lk 146; Schweizer Lk 138; Schulz; Zeller. The abrupt shift from the second person plural address in Q 12:22–31 to the second person singular and the differing perspectives on the kingdom as an object of human striving (Q 12:31) and a gift of God (12:32) are regularly cited as evidence of the secondary nature of v. 32.

Matt 6:25–34

²⁵ "Therefore I tell you, do not be anxious about yourself, what you shall eat or what you shall drink, nor about your body, what you shall wear. Is not the soul more than food, and the body more than clothing? ²⁶ Look at the birds of the sky: they neither sow nor reap nor gather into granaries, and yet your heavenly Father feeds them. Are you not worth more than they? ²⁷ Which of you by being anxious can add one cubit to his span of life? ²⁸ And concerning clothing, why are you anxious? Consider the lilies of the field, how they grow; they neither toil nor spin; ²⁹ but I tell you, even Solomon in all his glory was not arrayed like one of these. ³⁰ But if God so clothes the grass of the field, which is growing today and tomorrow is thrown into the oven, will he not much more clothe you, O weak in faith? ³¹ Therefore do not be anxious, saying, 'What shall we eat?' or 'What shall we drink?' or 'What shall we wear?' ³² For all these things the Gentiles seek; but your heavenly Father knows that you need them all. ³³ But seek first God's reign over you and his righteousness, and all these things will be added to you.

[³⁴ "Therefore do not be anxious about tomorrow, for tomorrow will be anxious for itself. Today's trouble is quite sufficient."]

Luke 12:22–32

²² And he said to his disciples, "Therefore I tell you, do not be anxious about yourself, what you shall eat, nor about your body, what you shall wear. ²³ For the soul is more than food, and the body more than clothing. ²⁴ Consider the ravens: they neither sow nor reap, they have neither storehouse nor granary, and yet God feeds them. Are you not worth much more than the birds! ²⁵ Which of you by being anxious can add a cubit to his span of life? ²⁶ If then you are not able to do such a small thing, why are you anxious about the rest? ²⁷ Consider the lilies, how they grow; they neither toil nor spin; but I tell you, even Solomon in all his glory was not arrayed like one of these. ²⁸ But if God so clothes the grass which is growing in the field today and tomorrow is thrown into the oven, how much more will he clothe you, O weak in faith! ²⁹ And do not seek what you are to eat and what you are to drink, nor be worried. ³⁰ For all the nations of the world seek these things; but your Father knows that you need them. ³¹ Instead, seek his reign over you, and these things will be added to you.

[³² "Fear not, little flock, for your Father takes pleasure in giving you the kingdom."]

Matt 6:19–21

¹⁹Μὴ θησαυρίζετε ὑμῖν θησαυροὺς ἐπὶ τῆς γῆς, ὅπου σὴς
καὶ βρῶσις ἀφανίζει καὶ ὅπου κλέπται διορύσσουσιν καὶ
κλέπτουσιν·
²⁰θησαυρίζετε δὲ ὑμῖν θησαυροὺς <u>ἐν οὐρανῷ</u>,
<u>ὅπου</u> οὔτε <u>σὴς</u> οὔτε βρῶσις ἀφανίζει καὶ
<u>ὅπου κλέπται</u> οὐ διορύσσουσιν οὐδὲ κλέπτουσιν·
²¹<u>ὅπου γάρ ἐστιν ὁ θησαυρός</u> σου,
<u>ἐκεῖ ἔσται καὶ ἡ καρδία</u> σου.

κλέπτης ⇨ Matt 24:43 [S44]
διορύσσω ⇨ Matt 24:43 [S44]

Luke 12:33–34

³³Πωλήσατε τὰ ὑπάρχοντα ὑμῶν καὶ δότε ἐλεημοσύνην·
ποιήσατε ἑαυτοῖς βαλλάντια μὴ παλαιούμενα,

θησαυρὸν ἀνέκλειπτον <u>ἐν τοῖς οὐρανοῖς</u>,
<u>ὅπου κλέπτης</u> οὐκ ἐγγίζει οὐδὲ <u>σὴς</u> διαφθείρει·

³⁴<u>ὅπου γάρ ἐστιν ὁ θησαυρὸς</u> ὑμῶν,
<u>ἐκεῖ καὶ ἡ καρδία</u> ὑμῶν <u>ἔσται</u>.

κλέπτης ⇨ Luke 12:39 [S44]

Notes

Q 12:33–34

In Q: Most authors. Bussmann (82) and Manson (114)
argue that Luke took 12:33–34 from Q while Matthew
derived his version from M and that both versions ended
with a proverb (Matt 6:21 = Luke 12:34). Grundmann
(Lk 262) and Weiss (1907: 230) argue the reverse: the
Lukan version derives from L, and the Matthean from Q.

Not in Q: Easton Lk xxiii, 204. Vassiliadis (1978: 68)
includes Luke 12:33 // Matt 6:19–20 in Q but argues that
Luke 12:34 par., since it is a proverbial saying and is
placed differently by Matthew and Luke, should be
excluded from Q.

Matt 6:19–21

[19] Do not lay up for yourselves treasures on earth, where moth and rust corrode and where thieves dig through and steal, [20] but lay up for yourselves treasures in heaven, where neither moth nor rust corrodes and where thieves do not dig through and steal.

[21] For where your treasure is, there will your heart be also.

Luke 12:33–34

[33] Sell your possessions, and give alms; provide yourselves with purses that do not wear out, with an unfailing treasure in the heavens, where no thief approaches and no moth destroys.

[34] For where your treasure is, there will your heart be also.

Parallels

GThom 76

ⲡⲉϫⲉ ⲓ̅ⲥ̅ ϫⲉ ⲧⲙⲛ̅ⲧⲉⲣⲟ ⲙ̅ⲡⲉⲓⲱⲧ ⲉⲥⲧⲛ̅ⲧⲱⲛ ⲁⲩⲣⲱⲙⲉ ⲛ̅ⲉϣⲱⲧ ⲉⲩⲛ̅ⲧⲁϥ ⲙ̅ⲙⲁⲩ ⲛ̅ⲟⲩⲫⲟⲣⲧⲓⲟⲛ ⲉⲁϩⲉ ⲁⲩⲙⲁⲣⲅⲁⲣⲓⲧⲏⲥ ⲡⲉϣⲱⲧ ⲉⲧⲙ̅ⲙⲁⲩ ⲟⲩⲥⲁⲃⲉ ⲡⲉ ⲁϥϯ ⲡⲉϥⲟⲣⲧⲓⲟⲛ ⲉⲃⲟⲗ ⲁϥⲧⲟⲟⲩ ⲛⲁϥ ⲙ̅ⲡⲓⲙⲁⲣⲅⲁⲣⲓⲧⲏⲥ ⲟⲩⲱⲧ. ⲛ̅ⲧⲱⲧⲛ̅ ϩⲱⲧ ⲧⲏⲩⲧⲛ̅ ϣⲓⲛⲉ ⲛ̅ⲥⲁ ⲡⲉϥⲉϩⲟ ⲉⲙⲁϥⲱϫⲛ̅ ⲉϥⲙⲏⲛ ⲉⲃⲟⲗ ⲡⲙⲁ ⲉⲙⲁⲣⲉⲭⲟⲟⲗⲉⲥ ⲧϩⲛⲟ ⲉϩⲟⲩⲛ ⲉⲙⲁⲩ ⲉⲟⲩⲱⲙ ⲟⲩⲇⲉ ⲙⲁⲣⲉϥϥⲛ̅ⲧ ⲧⲁⲕⲟ.

TeachSilv 88:15–22

ⲁⲣⲓⲡⲟⲗⲓⲧⲉⲩⲉ ϩⲙ̅ ⲡⲉⲭ̅ⲥ̅· ⲁⲩⲱ ⲕⲛⲁϫⲡⲟ ⲛⲁⲕ ⲛ̅ⲛⲟⲩⲁϩⲟ ϩⲛ̅ ⲧⲡⲉ· ⲙ̅ⲡⲣ̅ϣⲱⲡⲉ ⲙ̅ⲙⲟⲛⲑⲩⲗⲟⲥ ⲛ̅ϩⲁϩ ⲛ̅ϩⲱⲃ ⲉⲙⲛ̅ ϩⲏⲩ ⲙ̅ϩⲏⲧⲟⲩ· ⲁⲩⲱ ⲙ̅ⲡⲣ̅ϣⲱⲡⲉ ⲙ̅ⲣⲉϥϫⲓⲙⲟⲉⲓⲧ ϩⲏⲧⲥ̅ ⲛ̅ⲧⲉⲕⲙⲛ̅ⲧⲁⲧⲥⲟⲟⲩⲛ ⲉⲧⲟ ⲛ̅ⲃ̅ⲗ̅ⲗ̅ⲏ.

GMary 10:1–16

ⲡⲉϫⲉ ⲡⲉⲧⲣⲟⲥ ⲙⲙⲁⲣⲓϩⲁⲙ ϫⲉ ⲧⲥⲱⲛⲉ ⲧⲛ̅ⲥⲟⲟⲩⲛ ϫⲉ ⲛⲉⲣⲉⲡⲥ̅ⲱ̅ⲣ̅ ⲟⲩⲁϣⲉ ⲛ̅ϩⲟⲩⲟ ⲡⲁⲣⲁ ⲡⲕⲉⲥⲉⲉⲡⲉ ⲛ̅ⲥ̅ϩⲓⲙⲉ ϫⲱ ⲛⲁⲛ ⲛ̅ⲛ̅ϣⲁϫⲉ ⲡ̅ⲙ̅ⲡ̅ⲥ̅ⲱ̅ⲣ̅ ⲉⲧⲉⲉⲓⲣⲉ ⲙⲡⲉⲩⲙⲉⲉⲩⲉ ⲛⲁⲓ̈ ⲉⲧⲉⲥⲟⲟⲩⲛ ⲙ̅ⲙⲟⲟⲩ ⲛ̅ⲛⲁⲛⲟⲛ ⲁⲛ ⲟⲩⲇⲉ ⲙⲡⲛ̅ⲥⲟⲧⲙⲟⲩ ⲁⲥⲟⲩⲱϣⲃ̅ ⲛ̅ϭⲓ ⲙⲁⲣⲓϩⲁⲙ ⲡⲉϫⲁⲥ ϫⲉ ⲡⲉⲑⲏⲡ ⲉⲣⲱⲧⲛ̅ ϯⲛⲁⲧⲁⲙⲁ ⲧⲏⲩⲧⲛ̅ ⲉⲣⲟϥ ⲁⲩⲱ ⲁⲥⲁⲣⲭⲉⲭⲉⲓ ⲛ̅ϫⲱ ⲛⲁⲩ ⲛ̅ⲛⲉⲓ̈ϣⲁϫⲉ ϫⲉ ⲁ{ⲓ̈}ⲛⲟⲕ ⲡⲉϫⲁⲥ ⲁⲓⲛⲁⲩ ⲉⲡⲭ̅ⲥ̅ ϩⲛ̅ ⲟⲩϩⲟⲣⲟⲙⲁ ⲁⲩⲱ ⲁⲉⲓϫⲟⲟⲥ ⲛⲁϥ ϫⲉ ⲡⲭ̅ⲥ̅ ⲁⲓ̈ⲛⲁⲩ ⲉⲣⲟⲕ ⲙⲡⲟⲟⲩ ϩⲛ̅ ⲟⲩϩⲟⲣⲟⲙⲁ ⲁϥⲟⲩⲱϣⲃ̅ ⲡⲉϫⲁϥ ⲛⲁⲓ̈ ϫⲉ ⲛⲁⲓ̈ⲁⲧⲉ ϫⲉ ⲛ̅ⲧⲉⲕⲓⲙ ⲁⲛ ⲉⲣⲉⲛⲁⲩ ⲉⲣⲟⲉⲓ ⲡⲙⲁ ⲅⲁⲣ ⲉⲧⲉⲣⲉⲡⲛⲟⲩⲥ ⲙ̅ⲙⲁⲩ ⲉϥⲙⲙⲁⲩ ⲛ̅ϭⲓ ⲡⲉϩⲟ.

GThom 76

Jesus said, "The kingdom of the Father is like a merchant who had a supply of merchandise, and then found a pearl. That merchant was prudent: he sold the merchandise and bought the single pearl for himself. So also with you: seek the treasure that is unfailing, that is abiding, where no moth comes to consume and no worm destroys."

TeachSilv 88·15–22

Live in Christ, and you will acquire a treasure in heaven. Do not become a sausage (made) of many things which are useless, and do not become a guide on behalf of your blind ignorance.

GMary 10:1–16

Peter said to Mary, "Sister, we know that the Savior loved you more than the rest of women. Tell us the words of the Savior which you remember—which you know (but) we do not, nor have we heard them." Mary answered and said, "What is hidden from you I will proclaim to you." And she began to speak to them these words: "I," she said, "I saw the Lord in a vision and I said to him, 'Lord, I saw you today in a vision.' He answered and said to me, 'Blessed are you, that you did not waver at the sight of me. For where the mind is, there is the treasure.'"

Luke 12:35–38 ⇨ Matt 25:1–13 (p. 137)

[³⁵ Ἔστωσαν ὑμῶν αἱ ὀσφύες περιεζωσμέναι καὶ οἱ λύχνοι καιόμενοι· ³⁶καὶ ὑμεῖς ὅμοιοι ἀνθρώποις προσδεχομένοις τὸν κύριον ἑαυτῶν πότε ἀναλύσῃ ἐκ τῶν γάμων, ἵνα ἐλθόντος καὶ κρούσαντος εὐθέως ἀνοίξωσιν αὐτῷ. ³⁷μακάριοι οἱ δοῦλοι ἐκεῖνοι, οὓς ἐλθὼν ὁ κύριος εὑρήσει γρηγοροῦντας· ἀμὴν λέγω ὑμῖν ὅτι περιζώσεται καὶ ἀνακλινεῖ αὐτοὺς καὶ παρελθὼν διακονήσει αὐτοῖς. ³⁸κἂν ἐν τῇ δευτέρᾳ κἂν ἐν τῇ τρίτῃ φυλακῇ ἔλθῃ καὶ εὕρῃ οὕτως, μακάριοί εἰσιν ἐκεῖνοι].

φυλακή ⇨ Matt 24:43 [S44]
ἐκεῖνοι ⇨ Matt 24:43 [S44]

Notes

[Luke 12:35–38]

In Q: Beare 1962: 169; Bultmann 1963: 118; Bussmann 83 (hesitantly); Creed Lk 176; Crossan 1983: 58, 344 (possibly); Edwards 1976: xii; Haupt 1913: 73–74, 221; Hoffmann 44; Hunter 141; Lührmann 69, 71 (very hesitantly); Manson 115–16; Marshall Lk 533 (hesitantly); März 1985: 486; Müller 7 (hesitantly); Polag 62; idem 1977: 4, 81 (certainly or very probably in Q); Schmithals Lk 147 (who thinks that Mark 13:33–37 betrays knowledge of Q); Schneider Lk 288; Schürmann 1968: 124, 213, 233; Streeter 1924: 279; Vassiliadis 1978: 70; Wellhausen 1911: 58; Wernle 1899: 91 (uncertain); Zeller 1977:191 (uncertain).

The main reasons for attributing Luke 12:35–38 to Q are: (1) Matt 25:1–13 has a few features in common with Luke 12:35–38 which might suggest that both are working from a common source, or that Matthew omitted Q 12:35–38 because he had a similar story in Matt 25:1–13. (2) Schürmann argues that the fact that Matthew places an abbreviated version of Mark 13:33–37 (Matt 24:42) in a Q context (before Matt 24:43–44) suggests that he has seen Q/Luke 12:35–38, esp. v. 37. Moreover, φυλακή in Matt 24:43 (diff Luke 12:39) betrays knowledge of Q/Luke 12:38 and ἐκεῖνο of Matt 24:43 (diff Luke 12:39) is influenced by Q/Luke 12:38.

Not in Q: Easton Lk 206; Fitzmyer Lk 984; Grundmann Lk 264; Harnack; Hawkins 1911; Schenk; Schulz; Weiss 1907: 240; Zeller. The agreement between Matt 25:1–13 and Luke 12:35–38 in the use of the theme of watchfulness is so minor, and the disagreement in the basic plot so major, that this cannot safely be ascribed to Q. Sato 1984: 65–66: Vv. 35–38 derive from Q^{Lk}.

Luke 12:35–38

[³⁵ Let your belts be fastened and your lamps burning,
³⁶ and be like people who are expecting their master to
come home from the marriage feast, so that when he
comes and knocks they may open the door immediately
to him. ³⁷ Blessed are those servants whom the master
finds awake when he comes; Amen, I tell you, he will put
on an apron and have them recline, and he will come and
serve them. ³⁸ Even if he comes in the second watch, or in
the third, and finds them so, blessed are those servants!]

Parallels

Matt 25:1–13 ⇨ S50

¹Τότε ὁμοιωθήσεται ἡ βασιλεία τῶν οὐρανῶν δέκα
παρθένοις, αἵτινες λαβοῦσαι τὰς λαμπάδας ἑαυτῶν
ἐξῆλθον εἰς ὑπάντησιν τοῦ νυμφίου. ²πέντε δὲ ἐξ αὐτῶν
ἦσαν μωραὶ καὶ πέντε φρόνιμοι. ³αἱ γὰρ μωραὶ λαβοῦσαι
τὰς λαμπάδας αὐτῶν οὐκ ἔλαβον μεθ' ἑαυτῶν ἔλαιον. ⁴αἱ
δὲ φρόνιμοι ἔλαβον ἔλαιον ἐν τοῖς ἀγγείοις μετὰ τῶν
λαμπάδων ἑαυτῶν. ⁵χρονίζοντος δὲ τοῦ νυμφίου
ἐνύσταξαν πᾶσαι καὶ ἐκάθευδον. ⁶μέσης δὲ νυκτὸς
κραυγὴ γέγονεν· ἰδοὺ ὁ νυμφίος, ἐξέρχεσθε εἰς
ἀπάντησιν [αὐτοῦ]. ⁷τότε ἠγέρθησαν πᾶσαι αἱ παρθένοι
ἐκεῖναι καὶ ἐκόσμησαν τὰς λαμπάδας ἑαυτῶν. ⁸αἱ δὲ
μωραὶ ταῖς φρονίμοις εἶπαν· δότε ἡμῖν ἐκ τοῦ ἐλαίου
ὑμῶν, ὅτι αἱ λαμπάδες ἡμῶν σβέννυνται. ⁹ἀπεκρίθησαν
δὲ αἱ φρόνιμοι λέγουσαι· μήποτε οὐ μὴ ἀρκέσῃ ἡμῖν καὶ
ὑμῖν· πορεύεσθε μᾶλλον πρὸς τοὺς πωλοῦντας καὶ
ἀγοράσατε ἑαυταῖς. ¹⁰ἀπερχομένων δὲ αὐτῶν ἀγοράσαι
ἦλθεν ὁ νυμφίος, καὶ αἱ ἕτοιμοι εἰσῆλθον μετ' αὐτοῦ
εἰς τοὺς γάμους καὶ ἐκλείσθη ἡ θύρα. ¹¹ὕστερον δὲ
ἔρχονται καὶ αἱ λοιπαὶ παρθένοι λέγουσαι· κύριε, κύριε,
ἄνοιξον ἡμῖν. ¹²ὁ δὲ ἀποκριθεὶς εἶπεν· ἀμὴν λέγω ὑμῖν,
οὐκ οἶδα ὑμᾶς. ¹³Γρηγορεῖτε οὖν, ὅτι οὐκ οἴδατε τὴν
ἡμέραν οὐδὲ τὴν ὥραν.

Matt 24:42–44 ⇨ S44

⁴²Γρηγορεῖτε οὖν, ὅτι οὐκ οἴδατε ποίᾳ ἡμέρᾳ ὁ κύριος
ὑμῶν ἔρχεται. ⁴³Ἐκεῖνο δὲ γινώσκετε ὅτι εἰ ᾔδει ὁ
οἰκοδεσπότης ποίᾳ φυλακῇ ὁ κλέπτης ἔρχεται,
ἐγρηγόρησεν ἂν καὶ οὐκ ἂν εἴασεν διορυχθῆναι τὴν
οἰκίαν αὐτοῦ. ⁴⁴διὰ τοῦτο καὶ ὑμεῖς γίνεσθε ἕτοιμοι, ὅτι ᾗ
οὐ δοκεῖτε ὥρᾳ ὁ υἱὸς τοῦ ἀνθρώπου ἔρχεται.

Did 16:1

¹Γρηγορεῖτε ὑπὲρ τῆς ζωῆς ὑμῶν· οἱ λύχνοι ὑμῶν μὴ
σβεσθήτωσαν, καὶ αἱ ὀσφύες ὑμῶν μὴ ἐκλυέσθωσαν,
ἀλλὰ γίνεσθε ἕτοιμοι. οὐ γὰρ οἴδατε τὴν ὥραν, ἐν ᾗ ὁ
κύριος ἡμῶν ἔρχεται.

Matt 25:1–13

¹Then the reign of heaven shall be compared to ten
maidens who took their lamps and went to receive the
bridegroom. ²Five of them were foolish, and five were
wise. ³For when the foolish took their lamps, they took
no oil with them; ⁴but the wise took oil in flasks along
with their lamps. ⁵Since the bridegroom was delayed,
they all slumbered and slept. ⁶But at midnight there was
a cry, 'Behold, the bridegroom! Come out to receive
him.' ⁷Then all those maidens rose and got their lamps
ready. ⁸But the foolish said to the wise, 'Give us some of
your oil, for our lamps are going out.' ⁹But the wise
replied, 'Perhaps there will not be enough for us and for
you; go instead to the merchants and buy for yourselves.'
¹⁰And while they went to buy, the bridegroom came, and
those who were ready went in with him to the marriage
feast; and the door was locked. ¹¹Afterward the other
maidens came also, saying, 'Lord, lord, open for us.'
¹²But he replied, 'Amen, I tell you, I do not know you.'
¹³Watch therefore, for you know neither the day nor the
hour.

Matt 24:42–44

⁴²Watch therefore, for you do not know on what day your
Lord is coming. ⁴³But know this, that if the house owner
had known in what part of the night the thief was coming,
he would have watched and would not have let his house
be dug into. ⁴⁴Therefore you also must be ready; for the
Son of man is coming at an hour you do not expect.

Did 16:1

¹Watch over your life: let your lamps be not quenched
and your loins be not ungirded, but be ready, for ye know
not the hour in which our Lord cometh.

Matt 24:42, 43–44

[⁴²Γρηγορεῖτε οὖν, ὅτι οὐκ οἴδατε ποίᾳ ἡμέρᾳ ὁ κύριος ὑμῶν ἔρχεται].
⁴³Ἐκεῖνο δὲ <u>γινώσκετε ὅτι εἰ ᾔδει ὁ</u>
<u>οἰκοδεσπότης ποίᾳ</u> φυλακῇ <u>ὁ κλέπτης ἔρχεται,</u>
ἐγρηγόρησεν ἂν καὶ <u>οὐκ ἂν</u> εἴασεν <u>διορυχθῆναι</u>
<u>τὴν οἰκίαν αὐτοῦ.</u> ⁴⁴ διὰ τοῦτο <u>καὶ ὑμεῖς</u>
<u>γίνεσθε ἕτοιμοι, ὅτι ᾗ</u> οὐ <u>δοκεῖτε ὥρᾳ ὁ υἱὸς τοῦ</u>
<u>ἀνθρώπου ἔρχεται.</u>

Luke 12:39–40

³⁹Τοῦτο δὲ <u>γινώσκετε ὅτι εἰ ᾔδει ὁ</u>
<u>οἰκοδεσπότης ποίᾳ</u> ὥρᾳ <u>ὁ κλέπτης ἔρχεται,</u>
                    <u>οὐκ ἂν</u> ἀφῆκεν <u>διορυχθῆναι</u>
<u>τὸν οἶκον αὐτοῦ.</u> ⁴⁰   <u>καὶ ὑμεῖς</u>
<u>γίνεσθε ἕτοιμοι, ὅτι ᾗ</u> ὥρᾳ οὐ <u>δοκεῖτε ὁ υἱὸς τοῦ</u>
<u>ἀνθρώπου ἔρχεται.</u>

ᾗ ὥρᾳ οὐ δοκεῖτε ⇨ Luke 12:46 [S45]

Matt 24:43: διορυγηναι: B W Koine Θ λ φ; Or [HG] /
διορυχθηναι (Luke): ℵ D L 067 33 892 *pc* [NA²⁵·²⁶].

Notes

Q 12:39–40
In Q: Most authors.

Matt 24:42–44

[⁴²Watch therefore, for you do not know on what day your Lord is coming.] ⁴³But know this, that if the houseowner had known in what part of the night the thief was coming, he would have watched and would not have let his house be dug into. ⁴⁴Therefore you also must be ready; for the Son of man is coming at an hour you do not expect.

Luke 12:39–40

³⁹But know this, that if the houseowner had known at what hour the thief was coming, he would not have left his house to be dug into. ⁴⁰You also must be ready; for the Son of man is coming at an hour you do not expect.

Parallels

Mark 13:35 ⇨ Matt 24:42

³⁵γρηγορεῖτε οὖν· οὐκ οἴδατε γὰρ πότε ὁ κύριος τῆς οἰκίας ἔρχεται, ἢ ὀψὲ ἢ μεσονύκτιον ἢ ἀλεκτοροφωνίας ἢ πρωΐ.

GThom 21

ⲡⲉⲭⲉ ⲙⲁⲣⲓϩⲁⲙ ⲛ̄ⲓ̅ⲥ̅ ⲭⲉ ⲉⲛⲉⲕⲙⲁⲑⲏⲧⲏⲥ ⲉⲓⲛⲉ ⲛ̄ⲛⲓⲙ. ⲡⲉⲭⲁϥ ⲭⲉ ⲉⲩⲉⲓⲛⲉ ⲛ̄ϩ̄ⲛϣⲏⲣⲉ ϣⲏⲙ ⲉⲩ[ϭ]ⲉⲗⲓⲧ ⲁⲩⲥⲱϣⲉ ⲉⲧⲱⲟⲩ ⲁⲛ ⲧⲉ. ϩⲟⲧⲁⲛ ⲉⲩϣⲁⲉⲓ ⲛ̄ϭⲓ ⲛ̄ⲭⲟⲉⲓⲥ ⲛ̄ⲧⲥⲱϣⲉ ⲥⲉⲛⲁⲭⲟⲟⲥ ⲭⲉ ⲕⲉ ⲧⲛ̄ⲥⲱϣⲉ ⲉⲃⲟⲗ ⲛⲁⲛ ⲛ̄ⲧⲟⲟⲩ ⲥⲉⲕⲁⲕ ⲁϩⲏⲩ ⲙ̄ⲡⲟⲩⲙⲧⲟ ⲉⲃⲟⲗ ⲉⲧⲣⲟⲩⲕⲁⲁⲥ ⲉⲃⲟⲗ ⲛⲁⲩ ⲛ̄ⲥⲉϯ ⲧⲟⲩⲥⲱϣⲉ ⲛⲁⲩ. ⲇⲓⲁ ⲧⲟⲩⲧⲟ ϯⲭⲱ ⲙ̄ⲙⲟⲥ ⲭⲉ ⲉϥϣⲁⲉⲓⲙⲉ ⲛ̄ϭⲓ ⲡⲭⲉⲉ[.] ⲛ̄ⲛⲉⲓ ⲭⲉ ϥⲛⲏⲩ ⲛ̄ϭⲓ ⲡⲣⲉϥⲭⲓⲟⲩⲉ ϥⲛⲁⲣⲟⲉⲓⲥ ⲉⲙⲡⲁⲧⲉϥⲉⲓ ⲛ̄ϥⲧⲙ̄ⲕⲁⲁϥ ⲉϣⲟϫⲧ ⲉϩⲟⲩⲛ ⲉⲡⲉϥⲏⲉⲓ ⲛ̄ⲧⲉ ⲧⲉϥⲙⲛ̄ⲧⲉⲣⲟ ⲉⲧⲣⲉϥϥⲓ ⲛ̄ⲛⲉϥⲥⲕⲉⲩⲟⲥ. ⲛ̄ⲧⲱⲧⲛ̄ ⲇⲉ ⲣⲟⲉⲓⲥ ϩⲁⲧⲉϩⲏ ⲙ̄ⲡⲕⲟⲥⲙⲟⲥ ⲙⲟⲩⲣ ⲙ̄ⲙⲱⲧⲛ ⲉϫⲛ̄ ⲛⲉⲧⲛ̄ϯⲡⲉ ϩⲛ̄ ⲟⲩⲛⲟϭ ⲛ̄ⲇⲩⲛⲁⲙⲓⲥ ϣⲓⲛⲁ ϫⲉ ⲛⲉⲛⲗⲏⲥⲧⲏⲥ ϩⲉ ⲉϩⲓⲏ ⲉⲉⲓ ϣⲁⲣⲱⲧⲛ̄ ⲉⲡⲉⲓ ⲧⲉⲭⲣⲉⲓⲁ ⲉⲧⲉⲧⲛ̄ϭⲱϣⲧ ⲉⲃⲟⲗ ϩⲏⲧⲥ̄ ⲥⲉⲛⲁϩⲉ ⲉⲣⲟⲥ . . .

GThom 103

ⲡⲉⲭⲉ ⲓ̅ⲥ̅ ϫⲉ ⲟⲩⲙ[ⲁⲕⲁ]ⲣⲓⲟⲥ ⲡⲉ ⲡⲣⲱⲙⲉ ⲡⲁⲉⲓ ⲉⲧⲥⲟⲟⲩ(ⲛ) ϫⲉ ϩ[ⲛ ⲁϣ] ⲙ̄ⲙⲉⲣⲟⲥ ⲉⲛⲗⲏⲥⲧⲏⲥ ⲛⲏⲩ ⲉϩⲟⲩ(ⲛ) ϣⲓⲛ[ⲁ ⲉϥⲛ]ⲁⲧⲱⲟⲩⲛ ⲛ̄ϥⲥⲱⲟⲩϩ ⲛ̄ⲧⲉϥⲙⲛ̄ⲧ.[..] ⲁⲩⲱ ⲛ̄ϥⲙⲟⲩⲣ ⲙ̄ⲙⲟϥ ⲉϫⲛ̄ ⲧⲉϥϯⲡⲉ [ϩⲁ] ⲧⲉϩⲏ ⲉⲙⲡⲁⲧⲟⲩⲉⲓ ⲉϩⲟⲩⲛ.

1 Thess 5:1–2

¹Περὶ δὲ τῶν χρόνων καὶ τῶν καιρῶν, ἀδελφοί, οὐ χρείαν ἔχετε ὑμῖν γράφεσθαι, ²αὐτοὶ γὰρ ἀκριβῶς οἴδατε ὅτι ἡμέρα κυρίου ὡς κλέπτης ἐν νυκτὶ οὕτως ἔρχεται.

2 Pet 3:10

¹⁰Ἥξει δὲ ἡμέρα κυρίου ὡς κλέπτης, ἐν ᾗ οἱ οὐρανοὶ ῥοιζηδὸν παρελεύσονται, στοιχεῖα δὲ καυσούμενα λυθήσεται, καὶ γῆ καὶ τὰ ἐν αὐτῇ ἔργα εὑρεθήσεται.

Rev 16:15

¹⁵Ἰδοὺ ἔρχομαι ὡς κλέπτης. μακάριος ὁ γρηγορῶν καὶ τηρῶν τὰ ἱμάτια αὐτοῦ, ἵνα μὴ γυμνὸς περιπατῇ καὶ βλέπωσιν τὴν ἀσχημοσύνην αὐτοῦ.

Mark 13:35

Therefore watch, for you do not know when the master of the house will come, whether in the evening, or at midnight, or at cockcrow, or in the morning.

GThom 21

Mary said to Jesus, "Whom are your disciples like?" He said, "They are like little children living in a field that is not theirs. When the owners of the field come, they will say, 'Give our field back to us.' They (the children) take off their clothes in their presence in order to give the field back and return it to them. For this reason I say: if the owner of a house knows that a thief is coming, the owner will be on guard before the thief arrives, and will not let the thief break into the house of his domain and steal his possessions. As for you, then, be on guard against the world. Gird yourselves with great strength, lest the robbers find a way to get to you, for the trouble you expect will come . . ."

GThom 103

Jesus said, "Blessed is the person who knows where the robbers are going to enter, so that he may arise, bring together his [domain], and gird himself before they enter."

1 Thess 5:1–2

¹But concerning the times and the seasons, brothers, you have no need to have anything written to you. ²For you yourselves know full well that the day of the Lord will come like a thief in the night.

2 Pet 3:10

¹⁰But the day of the Lord will come like a thief, and then the heavens will pass away with a roar, and the elements will be dissolved by fire, and the earth and the works that are upon it will be exposed.

Rev 16:15

¹⁵"Behold, I am coming like a thief! Blessed is the one who is awake, keeping his garments that he may not go naked and people see his shame!"

Matt 24:45–51

⁴⁵Τίς ἄρα ἐστὶν ὁ πιστὸς δοῦλος καὶ
φρόνιμος ὃν κατέστησεν ὁ κύριος ἐπὶ τῆς οἰκετείας
αὐτοῦ τοῦ δοῦναι αὐτοῖς τὴν τροφὴν ἐν καιρῷ;
⁴⁶μακάριος ὁ δοῦλος ἐκεῖνος ὃν ἐλθὼν
ὁ κύριος αὐτοῦ εὑρήσει οὕτως ποιοῦντα·
⁴⁷ἀμὴν λέγω ὑμῖν ὅτι ἐπὶ πᾶσιν τοῖς ὑπάρχουσιν
αὐτοῦ καταστήσει αὐτόν. ⁴⁸ἐὰν δὲ εἴπῃ ὁ κακὸς
δοῦλος ἐκεῖνος ἐν τῇ καρδίᾳ αὐτοῦ· χρονίζει μου ὁ κύριος,
⁴⁹ καὶ ἄρξηται τύπτειν τοὺς συνδούλους
αὐτοῦ, ἐσθίῃ δὲ καὶ πίνῃ μετὰ τῶν μεθυόντων,
⁵⁰ἥξει ὁ κύριος τοῦ δούλου ἐκείνου ἐν ἡμέρᾳ ᾗ οὐ
προσδοκᾷ καὶ ἐν ὥρᾳ ᾗ οὐ γινώσκει,
⁵¹καὶ διχοτομήσει αὐτὸν καὶ τὸ μέρος αὐτοῦ μετὰ τῶν
ὑποκριτῶν θήσει· ἐκεῖ ἔσται ὁ κλαυθμὸς καὶ ὁ βρυγμὸς
τῶν ὀδόντων.

Luke 12:41, 42–46, 47–48

[⁴¹Εἶπεν δὲ ὁ Πέτρος· κύριε, πρὸς ἡμᾶς τὴν παραβολὴν
ταύτην λέγεις ἢ καὶ πρὸς πάντας; ⁴²καὶ εἶπεν ὁ κύριος·]
τίς ἄρα ἐστὶν ὁ πιστὸς οἰκονόμος ὁ
φρόνιμος, ὃν καταστήσει ὁ κύριος ἐπὶ τῆς θεραπείας
αὐτοῦ τοῦ διδόναι ἐν καιρῷ [τὸ] σιτομέτριον;
⁴³μακάριος ὁ δοῦλος ἐκεῖνος, ὃν ἐλθὼν
ὁ κύριος αὐτοῦ εὑρήσει ποιοῦντα οὕτως·
⁴⁴ἀληθῶς λέγω ὑμῖν ὅτι ἐπὶ πᾶσιν τοῖς ὑπάρχουσιν
αὐτοῦ καταστήσει αὐτόν. ⁴⁵ἐὰν δὲ εἴπῃ ὁ
δοῦλος ἐκεῖνος ἐν τῇ καρδίᾳ αὐτοῦ· χρονίζει ὁ κύριός μου
ἔρχεσθαι, καὶ ἄρξηται τύπτειν τοὺς παῖδας
καὶ τὰς παιδίσκας, ἐσθίειν τε καὶ πίνειν καὶ μεθύσκεσθαι,
⁴⁶ἥξει ὁ κύριος τοῦ δούλου ἐκείνου ἐν ἡμέρᾳ ᾗ οὐ
προσδοκᾷ καὶ ἐν ὥρᾳ ᾗ οὐ γινώσκει,
καὶ διχοτομήσει αὐτὸν καὶ τὸ μέρος αὐτοῦ μετὰ τῶν
ἀπίστων θήσει·

[⁴⁷Ἐκεῖνος δὲ ὁ δοῦλος ὁ γνοὺς τὸ θέλημα τοῦ κυρίου
αὐτοῦ καὶ μὴ ἑτοιμάσας ἢ ποιήσας πρὸς τὸ θέλημα
αὐτοῦ δαρήσεται πολλάς· ⁴⁸ὁ δὲ μὴ γνούς, ποιήσας δὲ
ἄξια πληγῶν δαρήσεται ὀλίγας. παντὶ δὲ ᾧ ἐδόθη πολύ,
πολὺ ζητηθήσεται παρ' αὐτοῦ, καὶ ᾧ παρέθεντο πολύ,
περισσότερον αἰτήσουσιν αὐτόν].

Matt 24:48: ο κυριος μου ελθειν (Luke): W 0133 Koine (λ)
φ latt sy mae bo^mss / μου ο κυριος ελθειν: C D L Θ 067 1010
1424 *al* [HG] / txt: ℵ B 33 700 892 *pc* sa bo [NA²⁵·²⁶].

Notes

[Luke 12:41–42a]

In Q: Hunter 141; Manson 117 (hesitantly); Polag
1977: 4 (possibly). Marshall Lk 533, 539–40 (citing
Moule): Matthew dropped v. 41 as unintelligible.
Moreover, without an introduction such as v. 41, ἄρα in Q
12:42 is otiose. Schmid 340: Both the question in v. 41
and the answer in vv. 42–46 refer not to 12:39–40 but to
12:35–38. Therefore 12:39–40 must be an interpolation
into an original unit consisting of 12:35–38, 41, 42–46.
Since Matthew used only Q 12:39–40, 42–46, he dropped
the question (v. 41) as no longer useful.

Not in Q: Bultmann 1963: 335; Easton Lk 207: "An
obvious Lukan transition." Fitzmyer Lk 985;
Grundmann Lk 266; Kloppenborg 1987: 151 n. 212;
März 1985: 486; Schmithals Lk 148; Schulz 271 and n.
33; Schweizer Lk 141; Weiser 1971: 216–19; Zeller 81
and most authors.

Q 12:42b–46

In Q: Most authors.

[Luke 12:47–48]

In Q: Beare 1962: 169; Crossan 1983: 60–61, 344–45
(tentatively); Hunter 141; Manson 119; Polag 86
(uncertain); Schmid 341: Matthew omitted vv. 47–48
because of the context into which he placed Q 12:39–40,
42–46. Wernle 1899: 91 (uncertain); Weiss 1907: 240:
Luke 12:48b may be from Q.

Not in Q: Easton Lk 208; Fitzmyer Lk 991;
Grundmann Lk 266; Marshall Lk 533; März 1985: 486;
Müller 1908: 7, 19; Schmithals Lk 148; Schweizer Lk 140;
Weiser 1971: 222–24 and most authors. Sato (1984: 66)
ascribes the verses to Q^Lk.

Matt 24:45–51

⁴⁵Who then is the faithful and wise servant, whom his master has put in charge of his household, to give them their meals on time? ⁴⁶Blessed is that servant whom his master when he comes will find so doing. ⁴⁷Amen, I tell you, he will put him in charge of all his possessions. ⁴⁸But if that wicked servant says to himself, 'My master is delayed,' ⁴⁹and begins to beat his fellow servants, and eats and drinks with the drunkards, ⁵⁰the master of that servant will come on a day when he does not expect him and at an hour he does not know, ⁵¹and will punish him severely, and assign him a place with the hypocrites; and there will be weeping and gnashing of teeth.

Luke 12:41–48

[⁴¹Peter said, "Lord, are you telling this parable for us or for everyone?" ⁴²And the Lord said,] "Who then is the faithful and wise steward, whom his master will put in charge of his household staff, to give them their food allowance on time? ⁴³Blessed is that servant whom his master when he comes will find so doing. ⁴⁴Truly, I tell you, he will put him in charge of all his possessions. ⁴⁵But if that servant says to himself, 'My master is delayed in coming,' and begins to beat the housemen and the maids, and to eat and drink and get drunk, ⁴⁶the master of that servant will come on a day when he does not expect him and at an hour he does not know, and will punish him severly, and assign him a place with the unfaithful.

[⁴⁷But that servant who knew his master's will, but did not make ready or obey his will, shall receive a severe beating. ⁴⁸But he who did not know, and did what deserved a beating, shall receive a light beating. Much is expected from one to whom much has been given; they will require more of somebody who has been entrusted with much."]

Parallels

GNaz 18

Ἐπεὶ δὲ τὸ εἰς ἡμᾶς ἧκον Ἑβραϊκοῖς χαρακτῆρσιν εὐαγγέλιον τὴν ἀπειλὴν οὐ κατὰ τοῦ ἀποκρύψαντος ἐπῆγεν, ἀλλὰ κατὰ τοῦ ἀσώτως ἐζηκότος· τρεῖς γὰρ δούλους περιεῖχε, τὸν μὲν καταφαγόντα τὴν ὕπαρξιν τοῦ δεσπότου μετὰ πορνῶν καὶ αὐλητρίδων, τὸν δὲ πολλαπλασιάσαντα τὴν ἐργασίαν, τὸν δὲ κατακρύψαντα τὸ τάλαντον· εἶτα τὸν μὲν ἀποδεχθῆναι, τὸν δὲ μεμφθῆναι μόνον, τὸν δὲ συγκλεισθῆναι δεσμωτηρίῳ· ἐφίστημι, μήποτε κατὰ τὸν Ματθαῖον μετὰ τὴν συμπλήρωσιν τοῦ λόγου τοῦ κατὰ τοῦ μηδὲν ἐργασαμένου ἡ ἑξῆς ἐπιλεγομένη ἀπειλὴ οὐ περὶ αὐτοῦ, ἀλλὰ περὶ τοῦ προτέρου κατ᾽ ἐπανάληψιν λέλεκται, τοῦ ἐσθίοντος καὶ πίνοντος μετὰ τῶν μεθυόντων.

GNaz 18

But since the Gospel [written] in Hebrew characters which has come into our hands enters the threat not against the man who had hid [the talent], but against him who had lived dissolutely — for he [the master] had three servants: one who squandered his master's substance with harlots and flute-girls, one who multiplied the gain, and one who his the talent; and accordingly one was accepted [with joy], another merely rebuked, and another cast into prison — I wonder whether in Matthew the threat which is uttered after the word against the man who did nothing may refer not to him, but by epanalepsis to the first who had feasted and drunk with the drunken.

Matt 10:34–36

Luke 12:49–53

(⁴⁹Πῦρ ἦλθον βαλεῖν ἐπὶ τὴν γῆν, καὶ τί θέλω εἰ ἤδη ἀνήφθη).

[⁵⁰βάπτισμα δὲ ἔχω βαπτισθῆναι, καὶ πῶς συνέχομαι ἕως ὅτου τελεσθῇ].

³⁴Μὴ νομίσητε **ὅτι** ἦλθον βαλεῖν **εἰρήνην** ἐπὶ τὴν γῆν· οὐκ ἦλθον βαλεῖν εἰρήνην **ἀλλὰ** μάχαιραν.

⁵¹δοκεῖτε **ὅτι εἰρήνην** παρεγενόμην δοῦναι ἐν τῇ γῇ; οὐχί, λέγω ὑμῖν, **ἀλλὰ** ἢ διαμερισμόν.

³⁵ἦλθον **γὰρ** διχάσαι ἄνθρωπον κατὰ τοῦ πατρὸς αὐτοῦ **καὶ** θυγατέρα κατὰ τῆς μητρὸς αὐτῆς **καὶ** νύμφην κατὰ τῆς πενθερᾶς αὐτῆς,
³⁶καὶ ἐχθροὶ τοῦ ἀνθρώπου οἱ οἰκιακοὶ αὐτοῦ.

⁵²ἔσονται **γὰρ** ἀπὸ τοῦ νῦν πέντε ἐν ἑνὶ οἴκῳ διαμεμερισμένοι, τρεῖς ἐπὶ δυσὶν καὶ δύο ἐπὶ τρισίν,
⁵³διαμερισθήσονται πατὴρ ἐπὶ υἱῷ καὶ υἱὸς ἐπὶ πατρί, μητὴρ ἐπὶ τὴν θυγατέρα **καὶ** θυγάτηρ ἐπὶ τὴν μητέρα πενθερὰ ἐπὶ τὴν νύμφην **αὐτῆς, καὶ** νύμφη ἐπὶ τὴν πενθεράν.

Luke 12:53: την θυγατερα: 𝔓⁴⁵·⁷⁵ L Θ λ (070) 700 892 (1241) *pc*; Eus [NA²⁶] / θυγατερα: ℵ B D [NA²⁵; HG] / θυγατρι: A (W) Koine Ψ φ; Mcion.

Notes

(Q 12:49)

In Q: Arens 1976: 64–65; Creed Lk 178; Crossan 1983: 345; Edwards 1976: 127–28; Grundmann Lk 251, 269 (possibly in Q); Hawkins 1911: 134; Hunter 44, 142 (hesitantly); Kloppenborg 1987: 151; Manson 120; Marshall Lk 545 (hesitantly); März 1985: 480–87; Polag 64; Sato 1984: 48; Schmid 276; Schürmann 1968: 213, 234, 280; Schweizer Lk 142 (hesitantly); Vassiliadis 1978: 70; Wernle 1899: 91. The usual grounds for inclusion are: (1) the formal and verbal similarities between Matt 10:34 = Q 12:51 and Luke 12:49 in the formula ἦλθον βαλεῖν ... ἐπὶ τὴν γῆν suggest that v. 49 belonged to Q. (2) Matthew would have omitted the verse because it did not cohere thematically with the content of Matt 10 or because it was unsuited to catechetical purposes (Hawkins). (3) None of the vocabulary of v. 49 is Lukan and the verse is thematically coherent with other parts of Q.

Not in Q: Bussmann 78, 122–23; Easton Lk 209; Fitzmyer Lk 994; Harnack; Haupt 1913: 233; Müller 1908: 8; Schenk; Schmithals Lk 149; Schulz 258: Luke

formed v. 49 on the pattern of Q 12:51 (ἦλθον βαλεῖν). Zeller.

[Luke 12:50]

In Q: Crossan 1983: 345; Edwards 1976: 127–28; Hunter 78, 142 (hesitantly); Manson 120; Polag 64; Sato 1984: 48.

Not in Q: Arens 1976: 65–66; Bussmann 78, 122–23; Fitzmyer Lk 994; Harnack; Haupt 1913: 233; Kloppenborg 1987: 151; März 1985: 482; Müller 1908: 8; Schenk; Schmithals Lk 149; Schulz; Weiss 1907: 255; Zeller. Since v. 50 contains several Lukanisms, it is most likely due to Luke, and based on Mark 10:38.

Q 12:51–53

In Q: Most authors. Fitzmyer (Lk 994), Harnack (86–87) and Schmithals (Lk 149) exclude v. 52.

Not in Q: Easton Lk 210: The source is uncertain, though Matt 10:34–35 may be from Q.

Matt 10:34–36

Luke 12:49–53

(⁴⁹I have come to bring fire upon the earth; and how I wish that it were already kindled!)

[⁵⁰I have a baptism to be baptized with; and how I am in anguish until it is over!]

³⁴Do not think that I have come to bring peace on earth; I have not come to bring peace, but a sword.

⁵¹Do you suppose that I have come to give peace on earth? No, I tell you, but rather division; ⁵²for from now on in one house there will be five divided, three against two and two against three;

³⁵For I have come to set a man against his father, and a daughter against her mother, and a daughter-in-law against her mother-in-law;

⁵³they will be divided, father against son and son against father, mother against daughter and daughter against her mother, mother-in-law against her daughter-in-law and daughter-in-law against her mother-in-law.

³⁶and a man's enemies will be his own kin.

Parallels

Mark 10:38b

³⁸ὁ δὲ Ἰησοῦς εἶπεν αὐτοῖς· οὐκ οἴδατε τί αἰτεῖσθε. δύνασθε πιεῖν τὸ ποτήριον ὃ ἐγὼ πίνω ἢ τὸ βάπτισμα ὃ ἐγὼ βαπτίζομαι βαπτισθῆναι;

Mark 10:38

³⁸But Jesus said to them, "You do not know what you are asking. Are you able to drink the cup that I drink, or to be baptized with the baptism with which I am baptized?"

GThom 10

ⲡⲉϫⲉ ⲓ̅ⲥ̅ ϫⲉ ⲁⲉⲓⲛⲟⲩϫⲉ ⲛ̅ⲟⲩⲕⲱϩⲧ̅ ⲉϫⲛ̅ ⲡⲕⲟⲥⲙⲟⲥ ⲁⲩⲱ ⲉⲓⲥ ϩⲏⲏⲧⲉ ϯⲁⲣⲉϩ ⲉⲣⲟϥ ϣⲁⲛⲧⲉϥϫⲉⲣⲟ.

GThom 10

Jesus said, "I have cast fire upon the world, and behold, I am guarding it until it is ablaze."

GThom 16

ⲡⲉϫⲉ ⲓ̅ⲥ̅ ϫⲉ ⲧⲁⲭⲁ ⲉⲩⲙⲉⲉⲩⲉ ⲛ̅ϭⲓ ⲣ̅ⲣⲱⲙⲉ ϫⲉ ⲛ̅ⲧⲁⲉⲓⲉⲓ ⲉⲛⲟⲩϫⲉ ⲛ̅ⲟⲩⲉⲓⲣⲏⲛⲏ ⲉϫⲙ̅ ⲡⲕⲟⲥⲙⲟⲥ ⲁⲩⲱ ⲥⲉⲥⲟⲟⲩⲛ ⲁⲛ ϫⲉ ⲛ̅ⲧⲁⲉⲓⲉⲓ ⲁⲛⲟⲩϫⲉ ⲛ̅ϩⲛ̅ⲡⲱⲣϫ ⲉϫⲛ̅ ⲡⲕⲁϩ ⲟⲩⲕⲱϩⲧ̅ ⲟⲩⲥⲏϥⲉ ⲟⲩⲡⲟⲗⲉⲙⲟⲥ. ⲟⲩⲛ̅ ϯⲟⲩ ⲅⲁⲣ ⲛⲁϣⲱⲡ[ⲉ] ϩⲛ̅ ⲟⲩⲏⲉⲓ ⲟⲩⲛ̅ ϣⲟⲙⲧ̅ ⲛⲁϣⲱⲡⲉ ⲉϫⲛ̅ ⲥⲛⲁⲩ ⲁⲩⲱ ⲥⲛⲁⲩ ⲉϫⲛ̅ ϣⲟⲙⲧ̅· ⲡⲉⲓⲱⲧ ⲉϫⲙ̅ ⲡϣⲏⲣⲉ ⲁⲩⲱ ⲡϣⲏⲣⲉ ⲉϫⲙ̅ ⲡⲉⲓⲱⲧ ⲁⲩⲱ ⲥⲉⲛⲁⲱϩⲉ ⲉⲣⲁⲧⲟⲩ ⲉⲩⲟ ⲙ̅ⲙⲟⲛⲁⲭⲟⲥ.

GThom 16

Jesus said, "Perhaps people think that I have come to cast peace upon the world. They do not know that I have come to cast conflict upon the earth: fire, sword, war. For there will be five in a house: there will be three against two and two against three, father against son and son against father, and they will stand alone."

Mic 7:6 LXX

⁶διότι υἱὸς ἀτιμάζει πατέρα, θυγάτηρ ἐπαναστήσεται ἐπὶ τὴν μητέρα αὐτῆς, νύμφη ἐπὶ τὴν πενθερὰν αὐτῆς, ἐχθροὶ ἀνδρὸς πάντες οἱ ἄνδρες οἱ ἐν τῷ οἴκῳ αὐτοῦ.

Mic 7:6 LXX

⁶Therefore a son dishonors his father, a daughter will rebel against her mother, a daughter-in-law against her mother-in- law, and all of a man's enemies are the men of his own house.

GThom 82

ⲡⲉϫⲉ ⲓ̅ⲥ̅ ϫⲉ ⲡⲉⲧϩⲏⲛ ⲉⲣⲟⲉⲓ ⲉϥϩⲏⲛ ⲉⲧⲥⲁⲧⲉ ⲁⲩⲱ ⲡⲉⲧⲟⲩⲏⲩ ⲙ̅ⲙⲟⲉⲓ ϥⲟⲩⲏⲩ ⲛ̅ⲧⲙⲛ̅ⲧⲉⲣⲟ.

GThom 82

Jesus said, "Whoever is near me is near the fire, and whoever is far from me is far from the kingdom."

Origen, *Hom. in Jer.* 3.3

Ait autem ibi Salvator: qui iuxta me est, iuxta ignem est; qui longe est a me, longe est a regnos.

Origen, *Hom. in Jer.* 3.3

The savior says there, "He who is near me is near the fire, and he who is far from me is far from the Kingdom."

Matt 16:2–3 ⇨ Q 11:16, 29–32 [S32]

²ʿΟ δὲ ἀποκριθεὶς εἶπεν αὐτοῖς· ὀψίας γενομένης **λέγετε**· εὐδία, πυρράζει γὰρ ὁ οὐρανός· ³**καὶ** πρωΐ· σήμερον χειμών, πυρράζει γὰρ στυγνάζων ὁ οὐρανός.

<u>τὸ</u> μὲν <u>πρόσωπον τοῦ οὐρανοῦ</u> γινώσκετε διακρίνειν, <u>τὰ</u> δὲ <u>σημεῖα τῶν καιρῶν οὐ</u> δύνασθε;

Luke 12:54–56

⁵⁴Ἔλεγεν δὲ καὶ τοῖς ὄχλοις· ὅταν ἴδητε [τὴν] νεφέλην ἀνατέλλουσαν ἐπὶ δυσμῶν, εὐθέως **λέγετε** ὅτι ὄμβρος ἔρχεται, καὶ γίνεται οὕτως· ⁵⁵**καὶ** ὅταν νότον πνέοντα, λέγετε ὅτι καύσων ἔσται, καὶ <u>γίνεται</u>. ⁵⁶ὑποκριταί, τὸ <u>πρόσωπον</u> τῆς γῆς καὶ <u>τοῦ οὐρανοῦ</u> οἴδατε δοκιμάζειν, <u>τὸν καιρὸν</u> δὲ τοῦτον πῶς <u>οὐκ</u> οἴδατε δοκιμάζειν.

Matt 16:2-3: omit οψιας γενομενης . . . ου δυνασθε (Matt 12:39): ℵ B V X Y Γ φ 157 1216 *al* sy^s.c sa mae bo^pt; Or Jerome / txt: C D K L W Koine Δ Θ Π λ 33 565 700 892 1010 1230 1241 1242 it vg sy^p.h bo^pt; Eus [NA²⁵·²⁶; HG].

Luke 12:54: την νεφελην: 𝔓⁴⁵ D W Koine Θ 070 [NA²⁶] / νεφελην: 𝔓⁷⁵ ℵ A B L N Δ Ψ λ φ 33 700 892 1241 *al* sa bo [NA²⁵; HG] // 56: πως ου δοκιμαζετε: 𝔓⁴⁵ A W Koine Ψ λ φ lat sy^p.h [NA²⁵; HG] / ου δοκιμαζετε: D it sy^c / πως ουκ οιδατε δοκιμαζετε: 070 / πως ουκ οιδατε δοκιμαζειν: 𝔓⁷⁵ ℵ B L Θ 33 892 1241 *pc* sy^hmg (co) [NA²⁶].

Notes

Q 12:54–56

In Q: Bussmann 53, 80; Carlston 1982: 111–12; Crossan 1983: 244–50; Edwards 1975: 164; idem, 1976: 128; Haupt 1913: 70–71; Hunter 142; Knox 1957: 21; Manson 16, 121; März 1985: 486–87; idem 1986; Meyer 1967: 63; Polag 66 (vv. 54–55 are "conjectural"; v. 56 is in Q). Schürmann 1968: 116: The use of διακρίνειν in Matt 16:3 (diff Luke) is a reminiscence of κρίνετε in the next saying, Q 12:57, and provides the basis for a catchword association of the two sayings. Schmithals Lk 150; Schneider Lk 293–94 (probably from Q); Steinhauser 1981: 252 (apparently); Taylor 1972: 117 (probably from Q); Vassiliadis 1978: 70; Weiss 1901: 500; idem, 1907: 91.

Not in Q: Easton Lk 211: The source is uncertain. Fitzmyer Lk 999: The passage may be pre–Lukan, but scarcely from Q. Harnack; Hawkins 1911: 110; Hoffmann; Klein 1964: 374; Müller 1908: 8, 53; Schenk; Schulz; Wernle 1899: 92; Zeller 16 (uncertain). The usual grounds for suspicion (when it is expressed) is the text–critical uncertainty of Matt 16:2–3, and the relative lack of verbal agreement between Matthew and Luke. Sato (1984: 17, 67) ascribes Luke 12:54–56 to Q^Lk.

Matt 16:2–3

[2] But he answered them, "When it is evening you say, 'Good weather, for the sky is red,' [3] and in the morning, 'Today will be stormy, for the sky is red and dark.'

You know how to judge the appearance of the sky, but cannot judge the signs of the times?"

Luke 12:54–56

[54] He also said to the crowds, "When you see a cloud rising in the west, you say immediately, 'Rain is coming'; and so it happens. [55] And when there is a south wind blowing, you say, 'It will be hot'; and it happens. [56] Hypocrites! You know how to interpret the appearance of the earth and sky; but why do you not know how to interpret the present time?"

Parallels

GThom 91

ⲡⲉⲭⲁⲩ ⲛⲁϥ ⲭⲉ ⲭⲟⲟⲥ ⲉⲣⲟⲛ ⲭⲉ ⲛ̄ⲧⲕ ⲛⲓⲙ ϣⲓⲛⲁ
ⲉⲛⲁⲣ̄ⲡⲓⲥⲧⲉⲩⲉ ⲉⲣⲟⲕ ⲡⲉⲭⲁϥ ⲛⲁⲩ ⲭⲉ ⲧⲉⲧⲛ̄ⲣ̄ⲡⲓⲣⲁⲍⲉ
ⲙ̄ⲡϩⲟ ⲛ̄ⲧⲡⲉ ⲙⲛ̄ ⲡⲕⲁϩ ⲁⲩⲱ ⲡⲉⲧⲛ̄ⲡⲉⲧⲛⲙ̄ⲧⲟ ⲉⲃⲟⲗ
ⲙ̄ⲡⲉⲧⲛ̄ⲥⲟⲩⲱⲛϥ ⲁⲩⲱ ⲡⲉⲉⲓⲕⲁⲓⲣⲟⲥ ⲧⲉⲧⲛ̄ⲥⲟⲟⲩⲛ ⲁⲛ
ⲛ̄ⲣ̄ⲡⲓⲣⲁⲍⲉ ⲙ̄ⲙⲟϥ.

GThom 91

They said to him, "Tell us who you are so we may believe in you."
He said to them, "You examine the face of heaven and earth, but you have not come to know the one who is in your presence, and you do not know how to examine this moment."

Matt 5:25–26

²⁵ἴσθι εὐνοῶν τῷ <u>ἀντιδίκῳ</u> <u>σου</u> ταχύ, ἕως
ὅτου <u>εἶ</u> <u>μετ'</u> αὐτοῦ <u>ἐν τῇ ὁδῷ</u>,

<u>μήποτέ</u>

<u>σε</u> <u>παραδῷ</u> ὁ ἀντίδικος <u>τῷ κριτῇ</u> <u>καὶ ὁ κριτὴς</u>
   <u>τῷ</u> ὑπηρέτῃ, <u>καὶ</u>
<u>εἰς</u> <u>φυλακὴν</u> <u>βληθήσῃ·</u>
²⁶ἀμὴν <u>λέγω σοι, οὐ μὴ ἐξέλθῃς ἐκεῖθεν, ἕως</u>
ἂν <u>ἀποδῷς</u> τὸν <u>ἔσχατον</u> κοδράντην.

Luke 12:57–59

⁵⁷Τί δὲ καὶ ἀφ' ἑαυτῶν οὐ κρίνετε τὸ δίκαιον;
⁵⁸ὡς γὰρ ὑπάγεις <u>μετὰ</u> <u>τοῦ ἀντιδίκου</u>
<u>σου</u> ἐπ' ἄρχοντα, <u>ἐν τῇ ὁδῷ</u> δὸς
ἐργασίαν ἀπηλλάχθαι ἀπ' αὐτοῦ, <u>μήποτε</u>
κατασύρῃ <u>σε</u> πρὸς τὸν κριτήν, <u>καὶ ὁ κριτής</u>
<u>σε</u> <u>παραδώσει</u> τῷ πράκτορι, <u>καὶ</u> ὁ πράκτωρ
<u>σε</u> βαλεῖ <u>εἰς φυλακήν.</u>
⁵⁹   <u>λέγω σοι, οὐ μὴ ἐξέλθῃς ἐκεῖθεν, ἕως</u>
καὶ τὸ <u>ἔσχατον</u> λεπτὸν <u>ἀποδῷς.</u>

Notes

Q 12:57–59
In Q: Most authors. Harnack (57) and Schenk (98) omit
v. 57.

Matt 5:25–26

25 Come to terms quickly with a plaintiff against you while you are going with him on the way, lest the plaintiff hand you over to the judge, and the judge to the guard, and you be thrown into prison. 26 Amen, I tell you, you will not leave there till you have paid the last *quadran*.

Luke 12:57–59

57 And why do you not judge for yourselves what is right? 58 As you go with a plaintiff against you before the magistrate, make an effort to settle with him on the way, lest he drag you to the judge, and the judge hand you over to the bailiff, and the bailiff throw you in prison. 59 I tell you, you will not leave there till you have paid the very last copper.

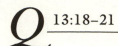

Matt 13:31–32, 33

³¹ Ἄλλην παραβολὴν παρέθηκεν αὐτοῖς λέγων·
<u>ὁμοία ἐστὶν ἡ βασιλεία</u> τῶν οὐρανῶν

      κόκκῳ
σινάπεως, ὃν λάβων ἄνθρωπος ἔσπειρεν ἐν τῷ
ἀγρῷ αὐτοῦ· ³² ὃ μικρότερον μέν ἐστιν
πάντων τῶν σπερμάτων, ὅταν δὲ <u>αὐξηθῇ</u>,
μεῖζον τῶν λαχάνων ἐστὶν καὶ γίνεται
<u>δένδρον</u> ὥστε ἐλθεῖν <u>τὰ πετεινὰ τοῦ οὐρανοῦ</u> καὶ
<u>κατασκηνοῦν</u> <u>ἐν τοῖς κλάδοις αὐτοῦ</u>.

Luke 13:18–19, 20–21

¹⁸ Ἔλεγεν οὖν·
<u>τίνι ὁμοία ἐστὶν ἡ βασιλεία</u> τοῦ θεοῦ καὶ
τίνι ὁμοιώσω αὐτήν; ¹⁹ <u>ὁμοία ἐστὶν</u> **κόκκῳ**
σινάπεως, ὃν λάβων ἄνθρωπος ἔβαλεν εἰς
κῆπον ἑαυτοῦ,

      καὶ ηὔξησεν
     καὶ <u>ἐγένετο εἰς</u>
<u>δένδρον</u>, καὶ <u>τὰ πετεινὰ τοῦ οὐρανοῦ</u>
<u>κατασκήνωσεν</u> <u>ἐν τοῖς κλάδοις αὐτοῦ</u>.

³³ Ἄλλην παραβολὴν ἐλάλησεν αὐτοῖς·
     <u>ὁμοία ἐστὶν ἡ βασιλεία</u> τῶν
οὐρανῶν **ζύμῃ, ἣν λαβοῦσα γυνὴ** <u>ἐνέκρυψεν</u>
εἰς ἀλεύρου σάτα τρία ἕως οὗ ἐζυμώθη ὅλον.

²⁰ Καὶ πάλιν εἶπεν·
τίνι ὁμοιώσω τὴν βασιλείαν τοῦ θεοῦ;
²¹ <u>ὁμοία ἐστὶν</u> **ζύμῃ, ἣν λαβοῦσα γυνὴ** [ἐν]έκρυψεν
εἰς ἀλεύρου σάτα τρία ἕως οὗ ἐζυμώθη ὅλον.

Luke 13:21: εκρυψεν: 𝔭⁴⁵ B K L N Π 047 λ 892 1010
1071 1424 *al* [NA²⁵; HG] / ενεκρυψεν (Matt): 𝔭⁷⁵ ℵ A D
W Koine Θ 070 φ 1 [NA²⁶; GNT].

Mark 4:30–32

³⁰Καὶ ἔλεγεν· πῶς ὁμοιώσωμεν τὴν βασιλείαν τοῦ θεοῦ ἢ ἐν τίνι αὐτὴν παραβολῇ θῶμεν; ³¹ὡς *κόκκῳ σινάπεως*, ὃς ὅταν σπαρῇ ἐπὶ τῆς γῆς, μικρότερον ὂν πάντων τῶν σπερμάτων τῶν ἐπὶ τῆς γῆς, ³²καὶ ὅταν σπαρῇ, ἀναβαίνει καὶ γίνεται μεῖζον πάντων τῶν λαχάνων καὶ ποιεῖ κλάδους μεγάλους, ὥστε δύνασθαι ὑπὸ τὴν σκιὰν αὐτοῦ *τὰ πετεινὰ τοῦ οὐρανοῦ κατασκηνοῦν*.

Mark 4:30–32

³⁰And he said, "With what can we compare the reign of God, or what parable shall we use for it? ³¹It is like a grain of mustard seed, which, when sown upon the ground, is the smallest of all the seeds on earth; ³²yet when it is sown it grows up and becomes the greatest of all shrubs, and produces large branches, so that the birds of the sky can make nests in its shade."

GThom 20

ⲡⲉϫⲉ ⲙⲙⲁⲑⲏⲧⲏⲥ ⲛ̄ⲓⲥ̄ ϫⲉ ϫⲟⲟⲥ ⲉⲣⲟⲛ ϫⲉ ⲧⲙⲛ̄ⲧⲉⲣⲟ ⲛ̄ⲙⲡⲏⲩⲉ ⲉⲥⲧⲛ̄ⲧⲱⲛ ⲉⲛⲓⲙ ⲡⲉϫⲁϥ ⲛⲁⲩ ϫⲉ ⲉⲥⲧⲛ̄ⲧⲱⲛ ⲁⲩⲃ̄ⲃⲓⲗⲉ ⲛ̄ϣⲗ̄ⲧⲁⲙ ⲥⲟⲃⲕ̄ ⲡⲁⲣⲁ ⲛ̄ϭⲣⲟϭ ⲧⲏⲣⲟⲩ ϩⲟⲧⲁⲛ ⲇⲉ ⲉⲥϣⲁ(ⲛ)ϩⲉ ⲉϫⲙ̄ ⲡⲕⲁϩ ⲉⲧⲟⲩⲣ̄ ϩⲱⲃ ⲉⲣⲟϥ ϣⲁϥⲧⲉⲩⲟ ⲉⲃⲟⲗ ⲛ̄ⲛⲟⲩⲛⲟϭ ⲛ̄ⲧⲁⲣ ⲛϥ̄ϣⲱⲡⲉ ⲛ̄ⲥⲕⲉⲡⲏ ⲛ̄ϩⲁⲗⲁⲧⲉ ⲛ̄ⲧⲡⲉ.

GThom 20

The disciples said to Jesus, "Tell us what the kingdom of heaven is like."
He said to them, "It is like a mustard seed, the tiniest of all seeds. But when it falls on prepared soil, it produces a large plant and becomes a shelter for birds of heaven."

GThom 96

[ⲡⲉϫⲉ] ⲓⲥ̄ ϫⲉ ⲧⲙⲛⲧⲉⲣⲟ ⲙ̄ⲡⲉⲓⲱⲧ ⲉⲥⲧⲛ̄ⲧⲱ[ⲛ ⲉⲟⲩ]ⲥϩⲓⲙⲉ ⲁⲥϫⲓ ⲛ̄ⲟⲩⲕⲟⲅⲉⲓ ⲛ̄ⲥⲁⲉⲓⲣ[ⲉ] ⲁⲥϩⲟ]ⲡϥ̄ ϩⲛ̄ ⲟⲩϣⲱⲧⲉ ⲁⲥⲁⲁϥ ⲛ̄ϩⲛ̄ⲛⲟ[ϭ] ⲛ̄ⲟⲉⲓⲕ ⲡⲉⲧⲉⲩⲙ̄ ⲙⲁⲁϫⲉ ⲙ̄ⲙⲟϥ ⲙⲁ[ⲣⲉϥ]ⲥⲱⲧⲙ̄.

GThom 96

Jesus [said], "The kingdom of the Father is like [a] woman who took a little yeast, [hid] it in dough, and made large loaves of bread. Whoever has ears ought to listen."

Dan 4:20–21 LXX

²⁰τὸ δένδρον τὸ ἐν τῇ γῇ πεφυτευμένον, οὗ ἡ ὅρασις μεγάλη, σὺ εἶ, βασιλεῦ. ²¹καὶ πάντα τὰ πετεινὰ τοῦ οὐρανοῦ τὰ νοσσεύοντα ἐν αὐτῷ· ἡ ἰσχὺς τῆς γῆς καὶ τῶν ἐθνῶν καὶ τῶν γλωσσῶν πασῶν ἕως τῶν περάτων τῆς γῆς καὶ πᾶσαι αἱ χῶραι σοι δουλεύουσι.

Dan 4:20–21 LXX

²⁰The tree that is planted in the earth, whose appearance is large — it is you, King. ²¹And all the birds of the sky built their nests in it. The power of the earth and of the nations and of all tongues, to the ends of the earth, and all the lands will serve you.

Dan 4:20–21 Theod

²⁰τὸ δένδρον, ὃ εἶδες, τὸ μεγαλυνθὲν καὶ τὸ ἰσχυκός, οὗ τὸ ὕψος ἔφθασεν εἰς τὸν οὐρανὸν καὶ τὸ κύτος αὐτοῦ εἰς πᾶσαν τὴν γῆν ²¹καὶ τὰ φύλλα αὐτοῦ εὐθαλῆ καὶ ὁ καρπὸς αὐτοῦ πολὺς καὶ τροφὴ πᾶσιν ἐν αὐτῷ, ὑποκάτω αὐτοῦ κατῴκουν τὰ θηρία τὰ ἄγρια καὶ ἐν τοῖς κλάδοις αὐτοῦ κατεσκήνουν τὰ ὄρνεα τοῦ οὐρανοῦ.

Dan 4:20–21 Theod

²⁰The tree that you see which grew great and strong so that its top reached heaven and its trunk (as visible) to all the earth ²¹and its leaves were fair and its fruit abundant and food for all who lived in it. Under it lived the beasts of the field and in its branches dwelt the birds of the sky.

Ps 103:10–12 LXX

¹⁰ὁ ἐξαποστέλλων πηγὰς ἐν φάραγξιν, ἀνὰ μέσον τῶν ὀρέων διελεύσονται ὕδατα· ¹¹ποτιοῦσιν πάντα τὰ θηρία τοῦ ἀγροῦ, προσδέξονται ὄναγροι εἰς δίψαν αὐτῶν· ¹²ἐπ' αὐτὰ τὰ πετεινὰ τοῦ οὐρανοῦ κατασκηνώσει, ἐκ μέσου τῶν πετρῶν δώσουσιν φωνήν.

Ps 103:10–12 LXX

¹⁰He who sends forth springs in the ravines, (whose) waters flow between the hills. ¹¹They give drink to all the beasts of the field, and wild asses wait to drink of them. ¹²Beside them the birds of the sky dwell, and sing from amid the rocks.

Q 13:18–19, 20–21
In Q: Most authors.

Matt 13:31–33

[31] Another parable he proposed to them, saying, "The reign of heaven is like a grain of mustard seed which a man took and sowed in his field; [32] it is the smallest of all seeds, but when it has grown it is the greatest of shrubs and becomes a tree, so that the birds of the sky come and make nests in its branches."

[33] He told them another parable. "The reign of heaven is like leaven which a woman took and hid in three measures of flour, till it leavened the whole mass."

Luke 13:18–21

[18] He said therefore, "What is the reign of God like? And to what shall I compare it? [19] It is like a grain of mustard seed which a man took and put into his garden; and it grew and became a tree, and the birds of the sky made nests in its branches."

[20] And again he said, "To what shall I compare the reign of God? [21] It is like leaven which a woman took and hid in three measures of flour, till it leavened the whole mass."

Matt 7:13–14

¹³ εἰσέλθατε **διὰ τῆς στενῆς** πύλης·
ὅτι πλατεῖα ἡ πύλη καὶ εὐρύχωρος ἡ ὁδὸς ἡ ἀπάγουσα
εἰς τὴν ἀπώλειαν καὶ **πολλοί**
εἰσιν οἱ εἰσερχόμενοι δι᾽ αὐτῆς·
¹⁴τί στενὴ ἡ πύλη καὶ τεθλιμμένη ἡ ὁδὸς ἡ ἀπάγουσα εἰς
τὴν ζωὴν καὶ ὀλίγοι εἰσὶν οἱ εὑρίσκοντες αὐτήν·

⇨ Matt 25:10–12 (p. 153)

Matt 7:22–23 ⇨ Q 6:46–49 [S14]
²²Πολλοὶ ἐροῦσίν μοι ἐν ἐκείνῃ τῇ ἡμέρᾳ·
κύριε κύριε, οὐ τῷ σῷ ὀνόματι
ἐπροφητεύσαμεν, **καὶ** τῷ σῷ ὀνόματι δαιμόνια
ἐξεβάλομεν, **καὶ** τῷ σῷ ὀνόματι δυνάμεις
πολλὰς ἐποιήσαμεν; ²³**καὶ** τότε ὁμολογήσω
αὐτοῖς ὅτι οὐδέποτε ἔγνων **ὑμᾶς·**
ἀποχωρεῖτε **ἀπ᾽ ἐμοῦ** οἱ ἐργαζόμενοι τὴν ἀνομίαν.

Luke 13:22–27
[²²Καὶ διεπορεύετο κατὰ πόλεις καὶ κώμας διδάσκων
καὶ πορείαν ποιούμενος εἰς Ἱεροσόλυμα].
[²³εἶπεν δέ τις αὐτῷ· κύριε, εἰ ὀλίγοι οἱ σῳζόμενοι; ὁ δὲ
εἶπεν πρὸς αὐτούς·]
²⁴ἀγωνίζεσθε εἰσελθεῖν **διὰ τῆς στενῆς** θύρας,
ὅτι

        πολλοί, λέγω ὑμῖν, ζητήσουσιν
εἰσελθεῖν
καὶ οὐκ ἰσχύσουσιν.

(²⁵ἀφ᾽ οὗ ἂν ἐγερθῇ ὁ οἰκοδεσπότης **καὶ** ἀποκλείσῃ τὴν
θύραν, καὶ ἄρξησθε ἔξω ἑστάναι καὶ κρούειν τὴν θύραν
λέγοντες· κύριε, ἄνοιξον ἡμῖν, καὶ ἀποκριθεὶς ἐρεῖ ὑμῖν·
οὐκ οἶδα ὑμᾶς πόθεν ἐστέ).
²⁶τότε ἄρξεσθε λέγειν·

        ἐφάγομεν ἐνώπιόν σου
καὶ ἐπίομεν **καὶ** ἐν ταῖς πλατείαις ἡμῶν
ἐδίδαξας·

        ²⁷**καὶ** ἐρεῖ λέγων ὑμῖν·
οὐκ οἶδα [ὑμᾶς] πόθεν ἐστέ·
ἀπόστητε **ἀπ᾽ ἐμοῦ** πάντες ἐργάται ἀδικίας·

Matt 7:14: τι: א² (B²) C L W Koine Θ λ φ 892 1006 1342
1506 lat sy [NA²⁶; HG] / οτι (Luke): א² 700ᶜ *pc* saᵐˢˢ mae
bo [NA²⁵] / οτι δε: B* saᵐˢˢ / και: 205 209.

Luke 13:27: λεγω υμιν: 𝔓⁷⁵* A D L R W Koine Θ Ψ 070
λ φ syˢ·⁽ᶜ⁾·ʰ boᵐˢ [HG] / txt: 𝔓⁷⁵ᶜ B 892 1424 *pc* [NA²⁵·²⁶] //
ουκ οιδα ποθεν εστε: 𝔓⁷⁵ B L R 070 1241 *pc* it [NA²⁵; HG]
/ ουδεποτε ειδον υμας (Matt): D (e) / txt: א W Koine Θ Ψ λ
φ lat sy [NA²⁶].

T. Abraham (A) 11

Καὶ εἶδεν ᾿Αβραὰμ δύο ὁδούς· ἡ μία ὁδὸς στενὴ καὶ
τεθλιμμένη καὶ ἡ ἐτέρα πλατεῖα καὶ εὐρύχωρος ⟨καὶ εἶδεν
δύο πύλας· μία πύλη πλατεῖα⟩, κατὰ τῆς πλατείας ὁδοῦ,
καὶ μία πύλη στενὴ κατὰ τῆς στενῆς ὁδοῦ· ἔξωθεν δὲ τῶν
πυλῶν τῶν ἐκεῖσε τῶν δύο, ἰδὸν ἄνδρα καθήμενον ἐπὶ
θρόνου κεχρυσωμένου . . . εἶπεν δὲ ὁ ἀσώματος· οὗτός
ἐστιν ὁ πρωτόπλαστος ᾿Αδὰμ . . . καὶ ὅτε ἴδῃ ψυχὰς
πολλὰς εἰσερχομένας διὰ τῆς στενῆς πύλας, τότε
ἀνίσταται καὶ κάθηται ἐπὶ τοῦ θρόνου αὐτοῦ χαίρων καὶ
ἀγαλλόμενος ἐν εὐφροσύνῃ, ὅτι αὕτη ἡ πύλη ἡ στενὴ
τῶν δικαίων ἐστί⟨ν⟩, ἡ ἀπάγουσα εἰς τὴν ζωήν, καὶ οἱ
εἰσερχόμενοι δι᾿ αὐτῆς εἰς τὸν παράδεισον ἔρχονται . . .
καὶ ὅταν ἴδῃ ψυχὰς πολλὰς εἰσερχομένας διὰ τῆς
πλατείας πύλης, τότε ἀνασπᾷ τὰς τρίχας τῆς κεφαλῆς
αὐτοῦ καὶ ῥίπτει ἑαυτὸν χαμαὶ κλαίων καὶ ὀδυρόμενος
πικρῶς· διότι ἡ πύλη ἡ πλατεῖα τῶν ἁμαρτωλῶν ἐστιν, ἡ
ἀπάγουσα εἰς τὴν ἀπώλειαν καὶ εἰς τὴν κόλασιν τὴν
αἰώνιον.

T. Abraham (A) 11

And Abraham saw two ways: the one way was narrow
and tortuous and the other was wide and spacious; ⟨and
he saw there two gates, one gate wide⟩ on the wide way
and one gate narrow on the narrow way. Outside of the
two gates there, they saw a man sitting on a golden throne
. . . The incorporeal one said, "This is Adam, the first
created one . . . When he sees many souls being led
through the narrow gate, then he rises up and sits upon
his throne rejoicing and being happy in gladness, for this
narrow gate is that of the righteous which leads to life and
those who enter through it go to paradise . . . But
whenever he sees many souls being led through the wide
gate, then he pulls out the hair of his head and throws
himself upon the earth weeping and mourning bitterly,
for the wide gate is that of the wicked, which leads to
destruction and to eternal punishment."

Matt 25:10–12 ⇨ Luke 13:25

¹⁰ἀπερχομένων δὲ αὐτῶν ἀγοράσαι ἦλθεν ὁ νυμφίος, καὶ
αἱ ἕτοιμαι εἰσῆλθον μετ᾿ αὐτοῦ εἰς τοὺς γάμους καὶ
ἐκλείσθη ἡ θύρα. ¹¹ὕστερον δὲ ἔρχονται καὶ αἱ λοιπαὶ
παρθένοι λέγουσαι· κύριε, κύριε, ἄνοιξον ἡμῖν. ¹²ὁ δὲ
ἀποκριθεὶς εἶπεν· ἀμὴν λέγω ὑμῖν, οὐκ οἶδα ὑμᾶς.

Matt 25:10–12

¹⁰ And while they went to buy, the bridegroom came, and
those who were ready went in with him to the marriage
feast; and the door was locked. ¹¹ Afterward the other
maidens came also, saying, 'Lord, lord, open for us.'
¹² But he replied, 'Amen, I say to you, I do not know you.'

Ps 6:9 LXX

⁹ἀπόστητε ἀπ᾿ ἐμοῦ, πάντες οἱ ἐργαζόμενοι τὴν
ἀνομίαν, ὅτι εἰσήκουσεν κύριος τῆς φωνῆς τοῦ κλαυθμοῦ
μου.

Ps 6:9 LXX

⁹Depart from me, all who work lawlessness, for the Lord
has heard to the sound of my weeping.

GNaz 6

Τὸ ᾿Ιουδαϊκὸν ἐνταῦθα οὕτως ἔχει· ἐὰν ἦτε ἐν τῷ κόλπῳ
μου καὶ τὸ θέλημα τοῦ πατρός μου τοῦ ἐν οὐρανοῖς μὴ
ποιῆτε, ἐκ τοῦ κόλπου μου ἀπορρίψω ὑμᾶς.

GNaz 6

The Jewish Gospel reads here as follows: If ye be in my
bosom and do not the will of my Father in heaven, I will
cast you out of my bosom.

2 Clem 4:5

⁵διὰ τοῦτο, ταῦτα ὑμῶν πρασσόντων, εἶπεν ὁ κύριος· ἐὰν
ἦτε μετ᾿ ἐμοῦ συνηγμένοι ἐν τῷ κόλπῳ μου καὶ μὴ
ποιῆτε τὰς ἐντολάς μου, ἀποβαλῶ ὑμᾶς καὶ ἐρῶ ὑμῖν·
ὑπάγετε ἀπ᾿ ἐμοῦ, οὐκ οἶδα ὑμᾶς, πόθεν ἐστέ, ἐργάται
ἀνομίας.

2 Clem 4:5

⁵For this reason, if you do these things, the Lord said, "If
ye be gathered together with me in my bosom, and do not
my commandments, I will cast you out, and will say to
you, Depart from me, I know not whence ye are, ye
workers of iniquity."

[Q 13:23]

In Q: Crossan 1983: 244–45. Dupont 1969: 100: The question of the number of those who will be saved is not an exclusively Lukan interest. Hawkins 1909: 195 (who includes also v. 22); idem, 1911: 116. Hunter 143; Manson 125: V. 23 has formal parallels elsewhere in Q, e.g., Q 9:57–62. Mussner 1967: 113; Polag 90 (uncertain). Schmid 244: One cannot argue that Luke has created the introduction out of the saying. Vassiliadis 1978: 70.

Not in Q: Bultmann 359–60; Bussmann 77; Creed Lk 185; Dibelius 1935: 162. Easton Lk 220: Luke created the question from the conclusion of v. 24. Fitzmyer Lk 1021; Harnack. Hoffmann 1967: 193 n. 16: The use of a question to introduce paraenesis is Lukan. Kilpatrick 1946: 22; Kloppenborg 1987: 222; Klostermann Lk 146; idem, Mt 68; Müller 1908: 14, 53; Schenk 102; Schmithals Lk 155; Schulz 310: The vocabulary is thoroughly Lukan. Steinhauser 1981: 148–49; Weiss 1907: 94 n. 1.

Q 13:24

In Q: Most authors. Easton (Lk 220) suggests that in Q the saying probably followed Q 12:59. Kilpatrick (1946: 22), Manson (125) and Streeter (1924: 283) ascribe Luke's version to Q and Matthew's to M.

(Q 13:25)

In Q: Bussmann 77; Crossan 1983: 345; Dupont 1969: 95: Easton Lk 220; Fitzmyer Lk 1021–22 (hesitantly); Hunter 143; Kilpatrick 1946: 32; Knox 1957: 80; Lührmann 69, 105; Manson 124; Marshall Lk 563; Müller 1908: 8 (hesitantly); Neirynck and Van Segbroeck 1984; Polag 68; Schenk 103; Schmithals Lk 154; Soiron 1916: 103; Streeter 1924: 279; Vassiliadis 1978: 70; Weiss 1907: 97 n. 1.

The principal reasons for including 13:25 in Q are: (1) Luke would not have shortened Matt 25:1–13 and must have had access to a short form of the parable (Dupont; Easton). (2) The original catchword connection between v. 24 and v. 25 is still visible in θύρα, a word which cannot easily be ascribed to Luke (Dupont; Soiron). (3) Matthew omitted the saying because he had a more impressive form in his parable of the maidens (Kilpatrick) or simply in the course of his use of the two adjoining sayings in the Sermon on the Mount (Marshall). Weiss, however, thinks that Luke knew the parable of the ten maidens from Q but omitted it, interpolating parts of it to create an introduction for Q 13:26.

Not in Q: Bultmann 1963: 130; Harnack; Hoffmann 1967: 198–99; Kloppenborg 1987: 223 n. 217; Klostermann Lk 146; Mussner 1967: 117; Schulz 424.

The main grounds for suspecting this verse as redactional are the clumsiness of the verse and its abrupt shift in *Bildlogik* (Bultmann; Kloppenborg), the meal setting (see also 12:37; 14:15; 22:30), which is a favorite Lukanism (Hoffmann; Kloppenborg; Mussner) and the presence of some Lukan vocabulary (Hoffmann; Mussner; Schulz).

Q 13:26–27

In Q: Most authors.

Not in Q: Harnack 71: Matt 7:22–23 and Luke 13:26–27 are independent of each other, though ultimately they derive from a common source. [However, on p. 183 he entertains the possibility that Matt 7:22–23 was from Q]. Manson (125) ascribes the Matthean parallel to M and the Lukan version to Q.

Matt 7:13–14

[13] Enter through the narrow gate; for the gate is wide and the way is easy, that leads to destruction, and those who enter through it are many. [14] But how narrow is the gate and how hard the way that leads to life, and those who find it are few.

Matt 7:22–23

[22] On that day many will say to me, 'Lord, Lord, did we not prophesy in your name, and exorcise demons in your name, and perform many miracles in your name?' [23] And then will I declare to them, 'I never knew you; depart from me, you who act against the law.'

Luke 13:22–27

[[22] He went on his way through cities and villages, teaching, and making his way to Jerusalem.]
[[23] And some one said to him, "Lord, will those who are saved be few?" And he said to them,]
[24] "Strive to enter through the narrow door; for many, I tell you, will seek to enter and will not be able.

([25] When once the house owner has stood up and locked the door, you will begin to stand outside and to knock at the door, saying, 'Lord, open for us.' He will answer you, 'I do not know where you come from.')

[26] Then you will start saying, 'We ate and drank with you, and you taught in our streets.' [27] And he will say to you, 'I do not know where you come from; away from me, all you workers of injustice!'"

Matt 8:11–12 ⇨ **Q 7:1–10 [S15]**

¹¹λέγω δὲ ὑμῖν ὅτι πολλοὶ ἀπὸ ἀνατολῶν
καὶ δυσμῶν ἥξουσιν
καὶ ἀνακλιθήσονται μετὰ ᾿Αβραὰμ καὶ ᾿Ισαὰκ
καὶ ᾿Ιακὼβ ἐν τῇ βασιλείᾳ τῶν οὐρανῶν,
¹²οἱ δὲ υἱοὶ τῆς βασιλείας ἐκβληθήσονται
εἰς τὸ σκότος τὸ ἐξώτερον· ἐκεῖ ἔσται ὁ
κλαυθμὸς καὶ ὁ βρυγμὸς τῶν ὀδόντων.

Matt 20:16

¹⁶Οὕτως ἔσονται οἱ ἔσχατοι πρῶτοι καὶ οἱ
πρῶτοι ἔσχατοι.

Luke 13:29, 28, 30

²⁹   καὶ ἥξουσιν ἀπὸ ἀνατολῶν
καὶ δυσμῶν καὶ ἀπὸ βορρᾶ καὶ νότου
καὶ ἀνακλιθήσονται
         ἐν τῇ βασιλείᾳ τοῦ θεοῦ.
²⁸ἐκεῖ ἔσται ὁ κλαυθμὸς καὶ ὁ βρυγμὸς τῶν
ὀδόντων ὅταν ὄψησθε ᾿Αβραὰμ καὶ ᾿Ισαὰκ καὶ
᾿Ιακὼβ καὶ πάντας τοὺς προφήτας ἐν τῇ
βασιλείᾳ τοῦ θεοῦ, ὑμᾶς δὲ ἐκβαλλομένους ἔξω.

³⁰καὶ ἰδοὺ εἰσὶν ἔσχατοι οἳ ἔσονται πρῶτοι, καὶ
εἰσὶν πρῶτοι οἳ ἔσονται ἔσχατοι.

Notes

Q 13:28–29

In Q: Most authors. The main difficulty has to do with
the order of the two parts of the saying. While Schenk
(104), Schlosser (1980: 609–11), Schmid (255), Strecker
(1971: 100) and Trilling (1964: 88) take the Lukan order
(28, 29) to be original, v. 28a cannot have functioned as
the introduction to an originally independent saying.
More probably, Luke inverted the order of the two parts
of the saying and used v. 28a as a bridge connecting v. 27
("depart from me") and vv. 28b–29. Thus Dupont 1967:
156; Hahn 1965: 34 n. 1; Harnack 78; Hoffmann 1967:
207; Kloppenborg 1987: 225; Meyer 16; idem, 1970:
411–12; Polag 68; Schulz 323; Zeller 87; idem, 1971–72:
223.

Not in Q: Vassiliadis (1978: 68) excludes 13:28a (Matt
8:12b) on the basis that it is a proverbial saying possibly
due to the oral tradition.

Q 13:30

In Q: Bussmann 6 (possibly); Crossan 1983: 42–47;
Easton Lk 220; Edwards 1975: 168–69 (but E. concords
no vocabulary from Luke 13:30 // Matt 19:30); idem,
1976: xii; Hunter 143; Kloppenborg 1987: 226. Knox
1957: 80–81: Matthew omitted the saying when he
moved Q 13:28–29 to its new setting in the miracle
account. Marshall Lk 564 (probably in Q); Müller 1908:
4, 54; Polag 68; Schenk 104. Schmithals Lk 154: Mark
10:31 is dependent upon an early recension of Q. Streeter
1924: 279.

Not in Q: Fitzmyer Lk 1022; Harnack; Hoffmann;
Schulz; Vassiliadis 1978: 68: Luke 13:30 is a proverbial
saying whose presence here is possibly due to oral
tradition. Weiss 1907: 98; Zeller.

Matt 8:11–12
¹¹ Now I tell you, many will come from east and west and
sit at table with Abraham, Isaac, and Jacob in the
kingdom of heaven, ¹²but the sons of the kingdom will be
thrown into the outer darkness; out there will be weeping
and gnashing of teeth.

Matt 20:16
¹⁶ So the last will be first, and the first last.

Luke 13:28–30
²⁹ And people will come from east and west, and from
north and south, and sit at table in the kingdom of God.
²⁸ There will be weeping and gnashing of teeth, when you
see Abraham and Isaac and Jacob and all the prophets in
the kingdom of God but you yourselves thrust out.

³⁰ And behold, the last will be first, and the first will be
last.

Parallels

Ps 106:3 LXX
³ ἐκ τῶν χωρῶν συνήγαγεν αὐτοὺς ἀπὸ ἀνατολῶν καὶ
δυσμῶν καὶ βορρᾷ καὶ θαλάσσης.

Mark 10:31
³¹πολλοὶ δὲ ἔσονται πρῶτοι ἔσχατοι καὶ [οἱ] ἔσχατοι
πρῶτοι.

Matt 19:30
³⁰Πολλοὶ δὲ ἔσονται πρῶτοι ἔσχατοι καὶ ἔσχατοι
πρῶτοι.

POxy 654.21–27
[λέγει ᾿Ιη(σοῦ)ς]· οὐκ ἀποκνήσει ἄνθ[ρωπος παλαιὸς
ἡμε]ρῶν ἐπερωτῆσε πα[ιδίον ἑπτὰ ἡμε]ρῶν περὶ τοῦ
τόπου τῆ[ς ζωῆς, καὶ ζή]σετ⟨αι⟩· ὅτι πολλοὶ ἔσονται
π[ρῶτοι ἔσχατοι καὶ] οἱ ἔσχατοι πρῶτοι, καὶ [εἰς ἓν
καταντήσου]σιν.

GThom 4
ⲡⲉϫⲉ ⲓ̅ⲥ̅ ϥⲛⲁϫⲛⲁⲩ ⲁⲛ ⲛ̅ϭⲓ ⲡⲣⲱⲙⲉ ⲛ̅ϩⲗ̅ⲗⲟ ϩⲛ̅
ⲛⲉϥϩⲟⲟⲩ ⲉⲭⲛⲉ ⲟⲩⲕⲟⲩⲉⲓ ⲛ̅ϣⲏⲣⲉ ϣⲏⲙ ⲉϥϩⲛ̅ ⲥⲁϣϥ̅
ⲛ̅ϩⲟⲟⲩ ⲉⲧⲃⲉ ⲡⲧⲟⲡⲟⲥ ⲙ̅ⲡⲱⲛϩ ⲁⲩⲱ ϥⲛⲁⲱⲛϩ ϫⲉ
ⲟⲩⲛ̅ ϩⲁϩ ⲛ̅ϣⲟⲣⲡ ⲛⲁⲣ̅ ϩⲁⲉ ⲁⲩⲱ ⲛ̅ⲥⲉϣⲱⲡⲉ ⲟⲩⲁ
ⲟⲩⲱⲧ.

Ps 106:3 LXX
³From the lands he gathered them, from east and west
and the north and the sea.

Mark 10:31
³¹ But many that are first will be last, and the last first.

Matt 19:30
³⁰ But many that are first will be last, and the last first.

POxy 654.21–27
[Jesus said], "The [man old in days] will not hesitate to
ask [a small child seven days old] about the place [of life,
and] he will [live]. For many who are [first] will become
[last, and] the last will be first, and [they will become one
and the same]."

GThom 4
Jesus said, "The person old in days will not hesitate to
ask a little child seven days old about the place of life,
and that person will live. For many of the first will be last,
and will become a single one."

Matt 23:37–39 ⇨ Q 11:39–44, 46–52 [S34]

Luke 13:31–33, 34–35

[³¹ Ἐν αὐτῇ τῇ ὥρᾳ προσῆλθάν τινες Φαρισαῖοι
λέγοντες αὐτῷ· ἔξελθε καὶ πορεύου ἐντεῦθεν, ὅτι
Ἡρῴδης θέλει σε ἀποκτεῖναι· ³²καὶ εἶπεν αὐτοῖς·
πορευθέντες εἴπατε τῇ ἀλώπεκι ταύτῃ· ἰδοὺ ἐκβάλλω
δαιμόνια καὶ ἰάσεις ἀποτελῶ σήμερον καὶ αὔριον καὶ
τῇ τρίτῃ τελειοῦμαι. ³³πλὴν δεῖ με σήμερον καὶ αὔριον
καὶ τῇ ἐχομένῃ πορεύεσθαι, ὅτι οὐκ ἐνδέχεται
προφήτην ἀπολέσθαι ἔξω Ἰερουσαλήμ].

³⁷Ἰερουσαλὴμ Ἰερουσαλήμ, ἡ ἀποκτείνουσα
τοὺς προφήτας καὶ λιθοβολοῦσα τοὺς
ἀποσταλμένους πρὸς αὐτήν, ποσάκις ἠθέλησα
ἐπισυναγαγεῖν τὰ τέκνα σου, ὃν τρόπον ὄρνις
ἐπισυνάγει τὰ νοσσία αὐτῆς ὑπὸ τὰς
πτέρυγας, καὶ οὐκ ἠθελήσατε. ³⁸ἰδοὺ ἀφίεται
ὑμῖν ὁ οἶκος ὑμῶν ἔρημος. ³⁹λέγω γὰρ ὑμῖν, οὐ
μή με ἴδητε ἀπ᾽ ἄρτι ἕως ἂν εἴπητε·
εὐλογημένος ὁ ἐρχόμενος ἐν ὀνόματι κυρίου.

³⁴Ἰερουσαλὴμ Ἰερουσαλήμ, ἡ ἀποκτείνουσα
τοὺς προφήτας καὶ λιθοβολοῦσα τοὺς
ἀποσταλμένους πρὸς αὐτήν, ποσάκις ἠθέλησα
ἐπισυνάξαι τὰ τέκνα σου ὃν τρόπον ὄρνις
τὴν ἑαυτῆς νοσσιὰν ὑπὸ τὰς
πτέρυγας, καὶ οὐκ ἠθελήσατε. ³⁵ἰδοὺ ἀφίεται
ὑμῖν ὁ οἶκος ὑμῶν. λέγω [δὲ] ὑμῖν, οὐ
μὴ ἴδητέ με ἕως [ἥξει ὅτε] εἴπητε·
εὐλογημένος ὁ ἐρχόμενος ἐν ὀνόματι κυρίου.

Matt 23:38: ο οικος υμων (Luke): B L ff² syˢ sa boᵖᵗ; Or
[NA²⁵] / ο οικος υμων ερημος: 𝔓⁷⁷ ℵ C D W Koine Θ 0138
λ φ lat syᵖ·ʰ mae boᵖᵗ; Eus [NA²⁶; HG].

Notes

Q 13:34–35

In Q: Most authors. The principal debate concerns the
placement of this pericope. In favor of the Matthean
location (after Q 11:49–51): Bultmann 1963: 114–15;
Easton Lk 224; Fitzmyer Lk 1034; Grundmann Lk 287;
Harnack 168–69; Lührmann 45, 48; Marshall Lk 502,
573; März 1985: 486; Meyer 25–26; Müller 1908: 29;
Schenk 81; Schmithals Lk 155; Schneider Lk 309. The
grounds for advocating Matthean priority are: (1) Since Q
13:34–35 seems to have been spoken by Sophia, it is
probably a part of the Sophia oracle in Q 11:49–51
(Bultmann; Harnack). (2) The character and content of Q
13:34–35 fit more naturally with 11:49–51 than in the
Lukan context (Easton; Lührmann). (3) There is an
implicit connection between λιθοβολέω in 13:34 and the
mention of the death of Zechariah in 11:50 (cf. 2 Chr
24:21) (Marshall).

Others favor the Lukan location (after Q 13:30):
Bussman 73 (?); Crossan 1983: 345; Hunter 143; Sato
1984: 48; Taylor 1972: 112, 117.

Several, however, suspect that both locations are
secondary: Hoffmann 172; Jacobson 210–11; Knox 1957:
82. Polag 66; idem, 1977: 13: Q 13:34–35 followed Q
12:54–59. Schmid 332–33; Schulz 347; Steck 1967: 40–
48. The grounds for suspecting the Matthean setting are:
(1) Matthew's setting of the saying is superior and
therefore probably secondary (Hoffmann; Knox) and due
to the systematizing tendencies of Matthew (Bussmann;
Schmid; Soiron). (2) It is unlikely that Luke would move
the saying had he found it in its Matthean location
(Kümmel 1957: 80; Schmid). (3) Q 11:49–51 and 13:34–
35 do not form a continuous Sophia saying, but reflect
two different temporal vantage points for the implied
speakers (Haenchen 1951: 56–57; Steck).

The reasons for suspecting the Lukan setting are: (1) By
removing Q 13:34–35 from its Lukan location, the
banquet theme in Q 13:28–29 and Q 14:16–24 is not
interrupted (Meyer). (2) Luke appears to have attached
the oracle to a new context (Luke 13:31–33) *ad vocem*
"Jerusalem" (Bultmann; Schmid; Steck).

Matt 23:37–39

Luke 13:31–35

[³¹ At that very hour some Pharisees came, and said to him, "Get away from here, for Herod wants to kill you." ³² And he said to them, "Go and tell that fox, 'Behold, I exorcise demons and perform cures today and tomorrow, and the third day I finish.
³³ Nevertheless I must proceed today and tomorrow and the day following; for it cannot be that a prophet should perish away from Jerusalem.']

³⁷O Jerusalem, Jerusalem, you kill the prophets and stone those who are sent to you! How often would I have gathered your children together as a hen gathers her brood under her wings, and you refused! ³⁸Behold, your house is forsaken and desolate. ³⁹For I tell you, you will not see me again, until you say, 'Blessed is he who comes in the name of the Lord.'

³⁴O Jerusalem, Jerusalem, you kill the prophets and stone those who are sent to you! How often would I have gathered your children together as a hen gathers her own brood under her wings, and you refused! ³⁵Behold, your house is forsaken. Now I tell you, you will not see me until the time comes when you say, 'Blessed is he who comes in the name of the Lord!'"

Parallels

2 Esdr 1:28–34 (5 Ezra 1:28–34)
²⁸Haec dicit dominus omnipotens: nonne ego vos rogavi ut pater filios et ut mater filias et nutrix parvulos suos, ²⁹Ut essetis mihi in populum, et ego vobis in deum, et vos mihi in filios, et ego vobis in patrem? ³⁰Ita vos collegi ut gallina pullos suos sub alas suas. Modo autem quid faciam vobis? proiciam vos a facie mea. ³¹Oblationes mihi cum obtuleris, avertam faciem meam a vobis; dies enim festos vestros et neomenias et circumcisiones carnis repudiavi. ³²Ego misi pueros meos prophetas ad vos, quos acceptos interfecistis et laniastis corpora illorum: quorum sanguinem exquiram, dicit dominus. ³³Haec dicit dominus omnipotens: domus vestra deserta est, proiciam vos sicut ventus stipulam. ³⁴Et filii procreationem non facient, quoniam mandatum meum vobiscum neglexerunt et quod malum est coram me fecerunt.

2 Esdr 1:28–34 (5 Ezra 1:28–34)
²⁸Thus says the Lord Almighty: Have I not entreated you as a father entreats his sons or a mother her daughters or a nurse her children, ²⁹that you should be my people and I should be your God, and that you should be my sons and I should be your father? ³⁰I gathered you as a hen gathers her brood under her wings. But now, what shall I do? I will cast you out of my presence. ³¹When you offer oblations to me, I will turn my face from you; for I have rejected your feast days, and new moons, and circumcisions of the flesh. ³²I sent to you my servants the prophets, but you have taken and slain them and torn their bodies in pieces; their blood I will require of you, says the Lord.
³³Thus says the Lord Almighty: Your house is desolate; I will drive you out as the wind drives straw; ³⁴and your sons will have no children, because with you they have neglected the commandment and have done what is evil in my sight.

Ps 117:26 LXX
²⁶εὐλογημένος ὁ ἐρχόμενος ἐν ὀνόματι κυρίου· εὐλογήκαμεν ὑμᾶς ἐξ οἴκου κυρίου.

Ps 117:26 LXX
²⁶Blessed is the one who comes in the name of the Lord. We have blessed you (pl.) from the house of the Lord.

Matt 12:11–12

Luke 14:1–6

[¹Καὶ ἐγένετο ἐν τῷ ἐλθεῖν αὐτὸν εἰς οἶκόν τινος τῶν ἀρχόντων [τῶν] Φαρισαίων σαββάτῳ φαγεῖν ἄρτον καὶ αὐτοὶ ἦσαν παρατηρούμενοι αὐτόν. ² καὶ ἰδοὺ ἄνθρωπός τις ἦν ὑδρωπικὸς ἔμπροσθεν αὐτοῦ. ³καὶ ἀποκριθεὶς ὁ Ἰησοῦς εἶπεν πρὸς τοὺς νομικοὺς καὶ Φαρισαίους λέγων· ἔξεστιν τῷ σαββάτῳ θεραπεῦσαι ἢ οὔ; ⁴οἱ δὲ ἡσύχασαν. καὶ ἐπιλαβόμενος ἰάσατο αὐτὸν καὶ ἀπέλυσεν].

[¹¹ὁ δὲ **εἶπεν** αὐτοῖς·
τίς ἔσται ἐξ <u>ὑμῶν</u> ἄνθρωπος ὃς ἕξει πρόβατον ἕν, καὶ ἐὰν <u>ἐμπέσῃ</u> τοῦτο τοῖς σάββασιν <u>εἰς</u> βόθυνον, οὐχὶ κρατήσει <u>αὐτὸ καὶ ἐγερεῖ</u>; ¹² πόσῳ οὖν διαφέρει ἄνθρωπος προβάτου;]

[⁵καὶ πρὸς αὐτοὺς **εἶπεν**·
τίνος <u>ὑμῶν</u> υἱὸς ἢ <u>βοῦς εἰς</u> φρέαρ πεσεῖται, καὶ οὐκ εὐθέως ἀνασπάσει <u>αὐτὸν</u> ἐν ἡμέρᾳ τοῦ σαββάτου;]

[⁶καὶ οὐκ ἴσχυσαν ἀνταποκριθῆναι πρὸς ταῦτα].

Notes

[Luke 14:5]

In Q: Bussmann 100–1, 123: Both Matthew and Luke took the saying from Q and attached it to an appropriate narrative context. Haupt 1913: 59: Luke 14:1–5 is from Q! Hawkins 1911: 118 (with slight probability); Kilpatrick 1946: 27 (hesitantly); Marshall Lk 578: Luke 14:1–5 may be from Q. Polag 72 (conjectural): Polag places the saying prior to Q 15:3–7, presumably because of a possible catchword association (based on πρόβατον) of the two units, or perhaps to suggest that the saying is illustrated by the parable. Schenk 105; Schneider Lk 312; Schürmann 1968: 213: Luke 14:1–6 is from Q; Matthew combined it with Mark 3:1–6.

Not in Q: Crossan 1983; Easton Lk 225; Edwards 1976; Fitzmyer Lk 1039; Harnack; Hoffmann; Hunter 177

(from L); Manson 277; Müller 1908: 54; Schmithals Lk 157; Schulz; Vassiliadis 1978: 68: Proverbial sayings are possibly due to the influence of the oral tradition. Weiss 1907: 206; Zeller 16.

Matt 12:11 is a redactional addition to a Markan story. Luke 14:5, however, is integral to Luke 14:1–6 and cannot be separated from the story without destroying the story completely. Either 14:1–6 belonged to Q, for which there is no proof whatsoever, or 14:5 alone belonged to Q and Luke created the story from the saying. The latter possibility is unlikely since 14:5 by itself has no obvious point unless it is connected with another saying. Polag suggests 15:3–7 as a context, but this is rather conjectural and besides, 15:3–7 is already complete in itself.

Matt 12:11–12

[11 He said to them, "Who among you, if he has one sheep and it falls into a pit on the sabbath, will not lay hold of it and lift it out? 12 Then how much more valuable is a man than a sheep?"]

Luke 14:1–6

[1 And when he went on the Sabbath to dine at the house of a certain ruler who belonged to the Pharisees, they were watching him. 2 And behold, there was a man before him who had dropsy. 3 And Jesus spoke to the lawyers and Pharisees, saying, "Is it lawful to heal on the sabbath, or not?" 4 But they were silent. And taking hold of him he healed him, and let him go.]

[5 And he said to them, "Which of you, having a son or an ox that has fallen into a well, will not immediately pull him out on a sabbath day?"]

[6 And they could not reply to this.]

Matt 23:6–11, 12 ⇨ Q 11:39–44, 46–52 [S34]

[⁶φιλοῦσιν δὲ *τὴν πρωτοκλισίαν* ἐν τοῖς δείπνοις καὶ τὰς πρωτοκαθεδρίας ἐν ταῖς συναγωγαῖς ⁷ καὶ τοὺς ἀσπασμοὺς ἐν ταῖς ἀγοραῖς καὶ καλεῖσθαι ὑπὸ τῶν ἀνθρώπων ῥαββί. ⁸ὑμεῖς δὲ μὴ κληθῆτε ῥαββί· εἷς γάρ ἐστιν ὑμῶν ὁ διδάσκαλος, πάντες δὲ ὑμεῖς ἀφελφοί ἐστε. ⁹καὶ πατέρα μὴ καλέσητε ὑμῶν ἐπὶ τῆς γῆς, εἷς γάρ ἐστιν ὑμῶν ὁ πατὴρ ὁ οὐράνιος. ¹⁰μηδὲ κληθῆτε καθηγηταί, ὅτι καθηγητὴς ὑμῶν ἐστιν εἷς ὁ Χριστός. ¹¹ὁ μείζων ὑμῶν ἔσται ὑμῶν διάκονος].

¹²Ὅστις δὲ <u>ὑψώσει ἑαυτὸν ταπεινωθήσεται</u> καὶ ὅστις <u>ταπεινώσει ἑαυτὸν ὑψωθήσεται</u>.

Luke 14:7–10, 11

[⁷Ἔλεγεν δὲ πρὸς τοὺς κεκλημένους παραβολήν, ἐπέχων πῶς τὰς πρωτοκλισίας ἐξελέγοντο, λέγων πρὸς αὐτούς· ⁸ὅταν κληθῇς ὑπό τινος εἰς γάμους, μὴ κατακλιθῇς εἰς *τὴν πρωτοκλισίαν*, μήποτε ἐντιμότερός σου ᾖ κεκλημένος ὑπ᾽ αὐτοῦ, ⁹καὶ ἐλθὼν ὁ σὲ καὶ αὐτὸν καλέσας ἐρεῖ σοι· δὸς τούτῳ τόπον, καὶ τότε ἄρξῃ μετὰ αἰσχύνης τὸν ἔσχατον τόπον κατέχειν. ¹⁰ἀλλ᾽ ὅταν κληθῇς, πορευθεὶς ἀνάπεσε εἰς τὸν ἔσχατον τόπον, ἵνα ὅταν ἔλθῃ ὁ κεκληκώς σε ἐρεῖ σοι· φίλε, προσανάβηθι ἀνώτερον· τότε ἔσται σοι δόξα ἐνώπιον πάντων τῶν συνανακειμένων σοι].

¹¹ὅτι πᾶς ὁ <u>ὑψῶν ἑαυτὸν ταπεινωθήσεται</u>, καὶ ὁ <u>ταπεινῶν ἑαυτὸν ὑψωθήσεται</u>.

Luke 18:14

[¹⁴λέγω ὑμῖν, κατέβη οὗτος δεδικαιωμένος εἰς τὸν οἶκον αὐτοῦ παρ᾽ ἐκεῖνον·] ὅτι πᾶς ὁ <u>ὑψῶν ἑαυτὸν ταπεινωθήσεται</u>, ὁ δὲ <u>ταπεινῶν ἑαυτὸν ὑψωθήσεται</u>.

Notes

Q 14:11/18:14b

In Q: Easton Lk 227, 269; Fitzmyer Lk 1044: Harnack 29; Haupt 1913: 45; Hawkins 1911: 117 (with considerable probability); Hunter 143. Müller (1908: 9, 54) includes 18:14b in Q but assigns 14:11 to L and places Q 18:14b in the woes against the Pharisees. Polag 86 (uncertain); idem, 1977: 5 (possibly); Schenk 106; Schmithals Lk 158; Schulz 451; Streeter 1924: 285 (hesitantly). Weiss (1907: 268 n. 1) argues that Matt 23:12 derives from Q and Luke 14:11 from L.

Not in Q: Crossan 1983; Edwards 1976; Hoffmann; Manson 279, 312. Vassiliadis 1978: 68: Proverbial sayings are possibly due to the influence of the oral tradition. Zeller 16.

Matt 23:6–12

[⁶They love the place of honor at feasts and the front seats in the synagogues, ⁷and salutations in the market places, and being called rabbi by people. ⁸But you are not to be called rabbi, for you have one teacher, and you are all brothers. ⁹And call no one your father on earth, for you have one Father, the heavenly One. ¹⁰Do not be called teachers for you have one teacher, the Christ. ¹¹He who is greatest among you shall be your servant.]

¹²Whoever exalts himself will be humbled, and whoever humbles himself will be exalted.

Luke 14:7–11

[⁷Now he told a parable to those who were invited, when he noticed how they chose the places of honor, saying to them, ⁸"When you are invited by any one to a marriage feast, do not sit down in a place of honor, lest a more respected person than you be invited by him; ⁹and the one who invited you both will come and say to you, 'Give place to this man,' and then you will proceed in your shame to take the worst seat. ¹⁰But when you are invited, go and sit in the worst seat, so that when your host comes he may say to you, 'Friend, go up higher'; then you will have honor in the presence of all your fellow guests.]
¹¹For every one who exalts himself will be humbled, and he who humbles himself will be exalted."

Luke 18:14

[¹⁴"I tell you, this man went down to his house justified rather than the other;]
for every one who exalts himself will be humbled, but he who humbles himself will be exalted."

Parallels

TeachSilv 104:21–24

ⲉⲕϣⲁⲛ ⲑ̄ⲃ̄ⲃⲓⲟⲕ ⲉⲩⲛⲁϫⲉⲥⲧⲕ̄ ⲛ̄ϩ̄ⲟⲩⲟ· ⲁⲩⲱ
ⲉⲕϣⲁⲛϫⲁⲥⲧⲕ̄ ⲥⲉⲛⲁⲑ̄ⲃ̄ⲃⲓⲟⲕ ⲉⲙⲁⲧⲉ.

TeachSilv 104:21–24

If you humble yourself, you will be greatly exalted. And if you exalt yourself, you will be exceedingly humbled.

163

Matt 22:1–10

^{1}Καὶ ἀποκριθεὶς ὁ Ἰησοῦς πάλιν **εἶπεν** ἐν παραβολαῖς αὐτοῖς λέγων·
^{2}ὡμοιώθη ἡ βασιλεία τῶν οὐρανῶν ἀνθρώπῳ βασιλεῖ, ὅστις ἐποίησεν γάμους τῷ υἱῷ αὐτοῦ.
^{3}καὶ **ἀπέστειλεν** τοὺς δούλους **αὐτοῦ** καλέσαι τοὺς κεκλημένους εἰς τοὺς γάμους, καὶ οὐκ ἤθελον ἐλθεῖν.
^{4}πάλιν ἀπέστειλεν ἄλλους δούλους λέγων· εἴπατε **τοῖς κεκλημένοις**· ἰδοὺ τὸ ἄριστόν μου ἡτοίμακα, οἱ ταῦροί μου καὶ τὰ σιτιστὰ τεθυμένα καὶ πάντα **ἕτοιμα**· δεῦτε εἰς τοὺς γάμους.
^{5}οἱ δὲ ἀμελήσαντες ἀπῆλθον, ὃς μὲν εἰς τὸν ἴδιον **ἀγρόν**, ὃς δὲ ἐπὶ τὴν ἐμπορίαν αὐτοῦ· ^{6}οἱ δὲ λοιποὶ κρατήσαντες τοὺς δούλους αὐτοῦ ὕβρισαν καὶ ἀπέκτειναν.

^{7}ὁ δὲ βασιλεὺς ὠργίσθη, καὶ πέμψας τὰ στρατεύματα αὐτοῦ ἀπώλεσεν τοὺς φονεῖς ἐκείνους καὶ τὴν πόλιν αὐτῶν ἐνέπρησεν. ^{8}**τότε** λέγει τοῖς δούλοις **αὐτοῦ**· ὁ μὲν γάμος ἕτοιμός ἐστιν, οἱ δὲ κεκλημένοι οὐκ ἦσαν ἄξιοι· ^{9}πορεύεσθε οὖν ἐπὶ τὰς διεξόδους τῶν ὁδῶν **καὶ** ὅσους ἐὰν εὕρητε καλέσατε εἰς τοὺς γάμους.

^{10}καὶ ἐξελθόντες οἱ δοῦλοι ἐκεῖνοι **εἰς τὰς ὁδοὺς** συνήγαγον πάντας οὓς εὗρον, πονηρούς τε καὶ ἀγαθούς· καὶ ἐπλήσθη ὁ γάμος ἀνακειμένων.

Luke 14:15, 16–24

[^{15}Ἀκούσας δέ τις τῶν συνανακειμένων ταῦτα εἶπεν αὐτῷ· μακάριος ὅστις φάγεται ἄρτον ἐν τῇ βασιλείᾳ τοῦ θεοῦ].
^{16}ὁ δὲ **εἶπεν** **αὐτῷ**·

ἄνθρωπός τις ἐποίει δεῖπνον μέγα,

καὶ ἐκάλεσεν πολλοὺς ^{17}**καὶ ἀπέστειλεν** τὸν δοῦλον **αὐτοῦ** τῇ ὥρᾳ τοῦ δείπνου

εἰπεῖν **τοῖς κεκλημένοις**· ἔρχεσθε, ὅτι ἤδη **ἕτοιμά** ἐστιν.

^{18}καὶ ἤρξαντο ἀπὸ μιᾶς πάντες παραιτεῖσθαι. ὁ πρῶτος εἶπεν αὐτῷ· **ἀγρὸν** ἠγόρασα καὶ ἔχω ἀνάγκην ἐξελθὼν ἰδεῖν αὐτόν· ἐρωτῶ σε, ἔχε με παρῃτημένον. ^{19}καὶ ἕτερος εἶπεν· ζεύγη βοῶν ἠγόρασα πέντε καὶ πορεύομαι δοκιμάσαι αὐτά· ἐρωτῶ σε, ἔχε με παρῃτημένον. ^{20}καὶ ἕτερος εἶπεν· γυναῖκα ἔγημα καὶ διὰ τοῦτο οὐ δύναμαι ἐλθεῖν. ^{21}καὶ παραγενόμενος ὁ δοῦλος ἀπήγγειλεν τῷ κυρίῳ αὐτοῦ ταῦτα.
τότε ὀργισθεὶς ὁ οἰκοδεσπότης

εἶπεν τῷ δούλῳ **αὐτοῦ**·
ἔξελθε ταχέως εἰς τὰς πλατείας καὶ ῥύμας τῆς πόλεως **καὶ** τοὺς πτωχοὺς καὶ ἀναπείρους καὶ τυφλοὺς καὶ χωλοὺς εἰσάγαγε ὧδε. ^{22}καὶ εἶπεν ὁ δοῦλος· κύριε, γέγονεν ὃ ἐπέταξας, καὶ ἔτι τόπος ἐστίν. ^{23}καὶ εἶπεν ὁ κύριος πρὸς τὸν δοῦλον· ἔξελθε **εἰς τὰς ὁδοὺς** καὶ φραγμοὺς καὶ ἀνάγκασον εἰσελθεῖν, ἵνα γεμισθῇ μου ὁ οἶκος·
^{24}λέγω γὰρ ὑμῖν ὅτι οὐδεὶς τῶν ἀνδρῶν ἐκείνων τῶν κεκλημένων γεύσεταί μου τοῦ δείπνου.

Matt 22:10: γυμφων ανακειμενων: ℵ B* L 0138 892 1010 *pc* [NA^{25}; HG] / γαμος ανακειμενων: B^1 D W Koine Θ 085 0161 λ φ [NA^{26}].

GThom 64

πεχε ιс χε ογρωμε νεγṄтαϥ ϩṄϣμμο αγω
Ṅтареϥсовте μπλιπνον αϥχοογ μπεϥϩμϩ̄ᾱλ
ϣινα εϥνατωϩμ ṄṄϣμμοει· αϥвωκ μπϣορπ
πεχαϥ ναϥ χε παχοεις τωϩμ μμοκ· πεχαϥ χε
ογṄтаει ϩṄϩομτ αϩενεμπορος сеṄνηγ ϣαροει
εрогϩε †ναвωκ Ṅтаоγεϩсаϩνε ναγ
†р̄παραιτει μπλιπνον. αϥвωκ ϣα κεογα πεχαϥ
ναϥ χε απαχοεις тωϩμ μμοκ. πεχαϥ ναϥ χε
αειτοογ ογηει αγω сер̄αιτει μμοει Ṅογϩημερα
†νаср̄ϥε α(ν). αϥει ϣα κεογα πεχαϥ ναϥ χε
παχοεις тωϩμ μμοκ. πεχαϥ ναϥ χε παϣвηр
νар̄ ϣελεετ αγω ανοκ ετνар̄ λιπνον †ναϣ ι αν
†р̄παραιτει μπλιπνον· αϥвωκ ϣα κεογα πεχαϥ
ναϥ χε παχοεις тωϩμ μμοκ. πεχαϥ ναϥ χε
αειτοογ Ṅογκωμη εειвηκ αχι Ṅϣωμ †ναϣ ι αν
†р̄παραιτει. αϥει Ṅϭι πϩμϩ̄ᾱλ αϥχοос
απεϥχοεις χε νεντακταϩμογ απλιπνον
αγπαραιτει. πεχε πχοεις μπεϥϩμϩ̄ᾱλ χε вωκ
επса νвоλ ανϩιοογε νετκναϩε ερоογ ενιογ
χεκαας εγνар̄λιπνει Ṅреϥтоογ μṄ νεϣο[те
εγναвω]κ αν εϩογν εντοπος μπαιωτ.

GThom 64

Jesus said, "A person was receiving guests. When he had
prepared the dinner, he sent a servant to invite the
guests. The servant went to the first and said to that one,
'My lord invites you.' The guest said, 'Some merchants
owe me money, and they are coming to me tonight. I
must go and give instructions to them. Please excuse me
from dinner.' The servant went to another and said to
that one, 'My lord invites you.' The guest said to the
servant, 'I have bought a house, and I have been called
away for a day. I shall have no time.' The servant went to
another and said to that one, 'My lord invites you.' The
guest said to the servant, 'My friend is to be married, and
I am to arrange the dinner. I shall not be able to come.
Please excuse me from dinner.' The servant went to
another and said to that one, 'My lord invites you.' The
guest said to the servant, 'I have bought an estate, and I
am going to collect the rent. I shall not be able to come.
Please excuse me.' The servant returned and said to the
lord, 'Those whom you invited to dinner have asked to
be excused.' The lord said to his servant, 'Go out on the
streets, and bring back whomever you find to have
dinner.' Buyers and merchants [will] not enter the places
of my Father."

Q 14:16–24

In Q: Bussmann 84–85; Crossan 1983: 345; Edwards 1975: 172–73; idem, 1976: 8, 134; Fitzmyer Lk 78, 1052; Hahn 1970: 52 n. 5 (the parable is either from divergent forms of Q or from *Sondergut*); Hoffmann 5, 41; Kilpatrick 1946: 30; Kloppenborg 1987: 228; Lührmann 87; Manson 129–30; Marshall Lk 584 (with hesitations); Meyer 18; Polag 70; idem 1977: 5 (probably in Q); Schenk 108; Schmithals Lk 159–60; Schulz 391–98; Weiss 1907: 268–69: The Lukan version is from L and the Matthean from Q. Wernle 1899: 91; Zeller 87.

Not in Q: Easton Lk 230 (uncertain); Grundmann Lk 296; Harnack 119–22: Either the parable did not belong to Q at all, or Matthew knew a different version of Q. Hawkins 1911: 127; Müller 1908: 54; Streeter 243–44; Weiser 1971: 59–60 (with hesitations); Vassiliadis 1978: 69. The usual ground for rejecting the parable from Q is the minimal verbal agreements between Matthew and Luke. Those who argue for its inclusion point out, however, that there are some verbal agreements and a basic agreement in plot, and account for the differences by appeal to the tendency of Luke and especially Matthew to edit parables.

Matt 22:1–10

¹ And again Jesus spoke to them in parables, saying, ² "The reign of heaven may be compared to a king who gave a marriage feast for his son, ³ and sent his servants to summon those who were invited to the marriage feast; but they refused to come. ⁴ Again he sent other servants, saying, 'Tell those who are invited, Behold, I have prepared my dinner, my oxen and my fat calves are killed, and everything is ready; come to the marriage feast.' ⁵ But they made light of it and went off, one to his farm, another to his business, ⁶ while the rest seized his servants, abused them, and killed them. ⁷ The king was angry, and he sent his soldiers and destroyed those murderers and burned their city. ⁸ Then he said to his servants, 'The wedding is ready, but those invited were not worthy. ⁹ Go therefore to the byroads, and invite to the marriage feast anyone you find.' ¹⁰ And when those servants went out into the roads, they gathered all whom they found, both bad and good; so the wedding hall was filled with banqueters."

Luke 14:15–24

[¹⁵ When one of the fellow guests heard this, he said to him, "Blessed is the one who shall eat bread in the kingdom of God!"]
¹⁶ But he said to him, "A certain person gave a great banquet, and invited many; ¹⁷ and at the time for the banquet he sent his servant to say to those who had been invited, 'Come; for all is now ready.' ¹⁸ But they all alike began to make excuses. The first said to him, 'I have bought a field, and I must go out and inspect it; I ask you, have me excused.' ¹⁹ And another said, 'I have bought five yoke of oxen, and I go to examine them; I ask you, have me excused.' ²⁰ And another said, 'I have married a wife, and therefore I cannot come.' ²¹ And the servant came and reported this to his master. Then the householder was angry and said to his servant, 'Go out quickly to the streets and alleys of the city, and bring in the poor and maimed and blind and lame.' ²² And the servant said, 'Sir, what you commanded has been done, and still there is room.' ²³ And the master said to the servant, 'Go out to the roads and hedges, and force people to come in, that my house may be filled. ²⁴ For I tell you, none of those men who were invited shall taste my banquet.'"

Matt 10:37–39

³⁷Ὁ φιλῶν **πατέρα** ἢ **μητέρα** ὑπὲρ ἐμὲ

οὐκ ἔστιν μου ἄξιος, καὶ ὁ φιλῶν υἱὸν ἢ θυγατέρα ὑπὲρ
ἐμὲ οὐκ ἔστιν μου ἄξιος.
³⁸καὶ ὃς οὐ λαμβάνει **τὸν σταυρὸν** αὐτοῦ
καὶ ἀκολουθεῖ ὀπίσω μου, οὐκ ἔστιν μου ἄξιος.

³⁹   ὁ εὑρὼν **τὴν ψυχὴν αὐτοῦ**
            ἀπολέσει αὐτήν, καὶ ὁ ἀπολέσας
τὴν ψυχὴν αὐτοῦ ἕνεκεν ἐμοῦ εὑρήσει **αὐτήν**.

ἀπόλλυμι ⇨ Luke 15:4 [S58]
εὑρίσκω ⇨ Luke 15:4, 5 [S58]

Luke 14:25, 26–27
[²⁵Συνεπορεύοντο δὲ αὐτῷ ὄχλοι πολλοί, καὶ
στραφεὶς εἶπεν πρὸς αὐτούς·]
²⁶εἴ τις ἔρχεται πρός με καὶ οὐ μισεῖ τὸν **πατέρα** ἑαυτοῦ
καὶ τὴν **μητέρα** καὶ τὴν γυναῖκα καὶ τὰ τέκνα καὶ τοὺς
ἀδελφοὺς καὶ τὰς ἀδελφὰς ἔτι τε καὶ τὴν **ψυχὴν** ἑαυτοῦ,
οὐ δύναταί εἶναί μου μαθητής.

²⁷ὅστις οὐ βαστάζει **τὸν σταυρὸν** ἑαυτοῦ καὶ
ἔρχεται ὀπίσω μου, οὐ δύναταί εἶναί μου μαθητής.

Luke 17:33 ⇨ Q 17:23–37 [S66]
³³ὃς ἐὰν ζητήσῃ **τὴν ψυχὴν αὐτοῦ**
περιποιήσασθαι, **ἀπολέσει αὐτήν**, ὃς δ᾽ ἂν ἀπολέσῃ,
ζωογονήσει **αὐτήν**.

Luke 14:26: πατερα αυτου: 𝔭⁴⁵ ℵ D W Koine Θ λ φ
[NA²⁵; HG] / πατερα (Matt): 579 e; Cl Or / πατερα εαυτου:
𝔭⁷⁵ B L R Ψ *pc* [NA²⁶] // ετι δε: 𝔭⁴⁵ ℵ D W Koine Θ Ψ λ
φ lat syʰ [HG] / ετι: 𝔭⁷⁵ it / ετι τε: B L R Δ 33 892 *pc*
[NA²⁵·²⁶] // εαυτου ψυχην: 𝔭⁴⁵ A D L R W Koine Θ λ φ
[HG] / ψυχην εαυτου (9:24; 17:33; Matt 10:39): 𝔭⁷⁵ ℵ B
(1241) *pc* [NA²⁵·²⁶].

Luke 17:33: και ος² (ε)αν: A (D) R W Koine Θ 063 λ sa
[NA²⁵; HG] / ος δ᾽ αν (Mark 8:35): 𝔭⁷⁵ ℵ B L Ψ 579 892
pc bo [NA²⁶] / και ος δ᾽ αν: φ // απολεσει²: A L N R Γ Δ
063 1010 *al* [NA²⁵] / απολεση: B D W Koine Θ Ψ λ φ
[NA²⁶; HG].

GThom 55

ⲡⲉϫⲉ ⲓ̅ⲥ̅ ϫⲉ ⲡⲉⲧⲁⲙⲉⲥⲧⲉ ⲡⲉϥⲉⲓⲱⲧ ⲁⲛ ⲙ̄ⲛ ⲧⲉϥⲙⲁⲁⲩ
ϥⲛⲁϣ ⲣ̄ ⲙⲁⲑⲏⲧⲏⲥ ⲁⲛ ⲛⲁⲉⲓ ⲁⲩⲱ ⲛ̄ϥⲙⲉⲥⲧⲉ ⲛⲉϥⲥⲛⲏⲩ ⲙ̄ⲛ
ⲛⲉϥⲥⲱⲛⲉ ⲛ̄ϥϥⲉⲓ ⲙ̄ⲡⲉϥⲥ(ⲧⲁⲩⲣ)ⲟⲥ ⲛ̄ⲧⲁϩⲉ ϥⲛⲁϣⲱⲡⲉ ⲁⲛ
ⲉϥⲟ ⲛ̄ⲁⲝⲓⲟⲥ ⲛⲁⲉⲓ.

GThom 101

⟨ⲡⲉϫⲉ ⲓ̅ⲥ̅ ϫⲉ⟩ ⲡⲉⲧⲁⲙⲉⲥⲧⲉ ⲡⲉϥⲉⲓ[ⲱⲧ ⲁ]ⲛ ⲙ̄ⲛ ⲧⲉϥⲙⲁⲁⲩ
ⲛ̄ⲧⲁϩⲉ ϥⲛⲁϣ ⲣ̄ ⲙ[ⲁⲑⲏⲧⲏ]ⲥ ⲛⲁⲉⲓ ⲁ(ⲛ) ⲁⲩⲱ ⲡⲉⲧⲁⲙ̄ⲣⲣⲉ
ⲡⲉ[ϥⲉⲓⲱⲧ ⲁⲛ ⲙ]ⲛ̄ ⲧⲉϥⲙⲁⲁⲩ ⲛ̄ⲧⲁϩⲉ ϥⲛⲁϣ ⲣ̄ ⲙ̄ⲁⲑⲏⲧⲏⲥ
ⲛⲁ]ⲉⲓ ⲁⲛ ⲧⲁⲙⲁⲁⲩ ⲅⲁⲣ ⲛ̄ⲧⲁ[. . .ⲉⲃ]ⲟⲗ [ⲧⲁⲙⲁⲁⲩ] ⲇⲉ ⲙ̄ⲙⲉ
ⲁⲥϯ ⲛⲁⲉⲓ ⲙ̄ⲡⲱⲛϩ.

Mark 8:34–35

³⁴Καὶ προσκαλεσάμενος τὸν ὄχλον σὺν τοῖς μαθηταῖς αὐτοῦ
εἶπεν αὐτοῖς· εἴ τις θέλει **ὀπίσω μου** ἀκολουθεῖν, ἀπαρνησάσθω
ἑαυτὸν καὶ ἀράτω **τὸν σταυρὸν** αὐτοῦ καὶ ἀκολουθείτω μοι. ³⁵ὃς
γὰρ ἐὰν θέλῃ **τὴν ψυχὴν αὐτοῦ** σῶσαι, **ἀπολέσει αὐτήν·** ὃς δ᾽
ἂν ἀπολέσει τὴν ψυχὴν αὐτοῦ ἕνεκεν ἐμοῦ καὶ τοῦ εὐαγγελίου,
σώσει **αὐτήν.**

Luke 9:23–24

²³Ἔλεγεν δὲ πρὸς πάντας· εἴ τι θέλει **ὀπίσω μου** ἔρχεσθαι,
ἀρνησάσθω ἑαυτὸν καὶ ἀράτω **τὸν σταυρὸν** αὐτοῦ καθ᾽ ἡμέραν
καὶ ἀκολουθείτω μοι. ²⁴ὃς γὰρ ἂν θέλῃ **τὴν ψυχὴν αὐτοῦ** σῶσαι
ἀπολέσει αὐτήν· ὃς δ᾽ ἂν ἀπολέσῃ τὴν ψυχὴν αὐτοῦ ἕνεκεν
ἐμοῦ οὗτος σώσει **αὐτήν.**

Matt 16:24–25

²⁴Τότε ὁ Ἰησοῦς εἶπεν τοῖς μαθηταῖς αὐτοῦ· εἴ τις θέλει
ὀπίσω μου ἐλθεῖν, ἀπαρνησάσθω ἑαυτὸν καὶ ἀράτω
τὸν σταυρὸν αὐτοῦ καὶ ἀκολουθείτω μοι. ²⁵ὃς γὰρ ἐὰν θέλῃ **τὴν**
τὴν ψυχὴν αὐτοῦ σῶσαι, **ἀπολέσει αὐτήν·** ὃς δ᾽ ἂν ἀπολέσῃ
τὴν ψυχὴν αὐτοῦ ἕνεκεν ἐμοῦ εὑρήσει **αὐτήν.**

John 12:25

²⁵ὁ φιλῶν **τὴν ψυχὴν αὐτοῦ** ἀπολλύει **αὐτήν,** καὶ ὁ μισῶν τὴν
ψυχὴν αὐτοῦ ἐν τῷ κόσμῳ τούτῳ εἰς ζωὴν αἰώνιον φυλάξει
αὐτήν.

Mark 10:29–30 ⇨ Q 14:26

²⁹ἔφη ὁ Ἰησοῦς· ἀμὴν λέγω ὑμῖν, οὐδείς ἐστιν ὃς ἀφῆκεν οἰκίαν
ἢ ἀδελφοὺς ἢ ἀδελφὰς ἢ μητέρα ἢ πατέρα ἢ τέκνα ἢ ἀγροὺς
ἕνεκεν ἐμοῦ καὶ ἕνεκεν τοῦ εὐαγγελίου, ³⁰ἐὰν μὴ λάβῃ
ἑκατονταπλασίονα νῦν ἐν τῷ καιρῷ τούτῳ οἰκίας καὶ ἀδελφοὺς
καὶ ἀδελφὰς καὶ μητέρας καὶ τέκνα καὶ ἀγροὺς μετὰ διωγμῶν,
καὶ ἐν τῷ αἰῶνι τῷ ἐρχομένῳ ζωὴν αἰώνιον.

GThom 55

Jesus said, "Whoever does not hate father and mother cannot
be a disciple to me, and whoever does not hate brothers and
sisters, and bear the cross as I do, will not be worthy of me."

GThom 101

⟨Jesus said,⟩ "Whoever does not hate [father] and mother as I
do cannot be my [disciple], and whoever does [not] love [father
and] mother as I do cannot be my [disciple]. For my mother
[. . .], but my true [mother] gave me life."

Mark 8:34–35

³⁴And summoning the crowd with his disciples he said to them,
"If any one would follow after me, let him deny himself and take
up his cross and follow me. ³⁵For whoever wants to preserve his
life will lose it; but whoever loses his life for my sake and the
gospel's will preserve it."

Luke 9:23–24

²³He said to all, "If any one would come after me, let him deny
himself and take up his cross daily and follow me. ²⁴For
whoever wants to preserve his life will lose it; and whoever loses
his life for my sake, he will preserve it."

Matt 16:24–25

²⁴Then Jesus told his disciples, "If any man would come after
me, let him deny himself and take up his cross and follow me.
²⁵For whoever wants to preserve his life will lose it, and
whoever loses his life for my sake will find it."

John 12:25

²⁵Whoever loves his life loses it, and whoever hates his life in
this world will keep it for eternal life.

Mark 10:29–30 ⇨ Q 14:26

²⁹Jesus said, "Amen, I tell you, there is no one who has left
house or brothers or sisters or mother or father or children or
lands, for my sake and for the gospel, ³⁰who will not receive a
hundredfold now in this time, houses and brothers and sisters
and mothers and children and lands, with persecutions, and in
the age to come eternal life."

Q 14:26–27

In Q: Most authors. Easton (Lk 233) ascribes only v. 27 to Q; v. 26 is from L.

Q 17:33

In Q: Most authors. Even though Luke 17:33 has been assimilated to Mark 8:35, Luke's general tendency to avoid doublets (see Schürmann 1968: 272–78) and the fact that Matthew and Luke concur in using Q 17:33 in a Q context (thus Marshall Lk 666) suggest that here we have an instance of Mark–Q overlap.

The original placement of Q 17:33 is controverted. Some argue that the Lukan placement is secondary and that Matthew preserves the original setting (i.e., after Q 14:26–27): Fitzmyer Lk 1165 (?); Haupt 1913: 16; Kloppenborg 1987: 158–59; Lambrecht 1982: 294–95; Laufen 1980: 319–20; Lührmann 74–75; Marshall Lk 664; Müller 1908: 30; Schenk 110–11; Schulz 278; Schürmann Lk 544; Wanke 1980: 224–25. If Q 17:33 were originally juxtaposed with Q 17:30, the saying would make nonsense out of the correlative (17:28–30). Only the Lukan redactional insertion of Luke 17:31–32 permits the use of Q 17:33 in the context of Luke 17. Schürmann observes that τὴν ψυχὴν ἑαυτοῦ (Luke 14:26 diff Matt 10:38) is influenced by the original proximity of Q 14:26–27 and 17:33.

Others hold that the Lukan location is original: Bussmann 93; Hunter 145; Manson 145; Polag 78. Schnackenburg 1971: 224: Q 17:33 was attached to 17:29 by the catchword ἀπολέσει. Still others argue that the original setting is no longer recoverable: Crossan 1983: 92, 178; Hoffmann 5.

Not in Q: Grundmann Lk 344. Meyer 52 n. 1: Luke 17:33 is due to the influence of the oral tradition. Neirynck 1982: 49–51; Schmid 335 n. 2; idem, Lk 277. Zmijewski 1972: 479–82: Luke 17:33 is a Lukan editing of Mark 8:35 or a repetition of Luke 9:24. If περιποιήσασθαι and ζῳογονήσει are Lukan, the remainder of the saying may be derived exclusively from Mark.

Matt 10:37–39

37 Whoever loves father or mother more than me is not worthy of me; and whoever loves son or daughter more than me is not worthy of me;

38 and whoever does not take his cross and follow me is not worthy of me.

39 Whoever finds his life will lose it, and he who loses his life for my sake will find it.

Luke 14:25–27

[25 Now great crowds accompanied him; and turning he said to them,]

26 "If any one comes to me and does not hate his own father and mother and wife and children and brothers and sisters, and indeed even his own life, he cannot be my disciple.

27 Whoever does not bear his own cross and come after me, cannot be my disciple."

Luke 17:33

33 Whoever seeks to gain his life will lose it, but whoever loses his life will keep it.

Matt 5:13

¹³ὑμεῖς ἐστε τὸ <u>ἅλας</u> τῆς γῆς· ἐὰν δὲ
    τὸ <u>ἅλας μωρανθῇ, ἐν τίνι</u> ἁλισθήσεται; εἰς οὐδὲν
ἰσχύει ἔτι εἰ μὴ <u>βληθὲν ἔξω</u> καταπατεῖσθαι ὑπὸ τῶν
ἀνθρώπων.

Luke 14:34–35

³⁴καλὸν οὖν τὸ <u>ἅλας·</u>   ἐὰν δὲ καὶ
τὸ <u>ἅλας μωρανθῇ, ἐν τίνι</u> ἀρτυθήσεται; ³⁵οὔτε εἰς γῆν
οὔτε εἰς κοπρίαν εὔθετόν ἐστιν, <u>ἔξω βάλλουσιν</u> αὐτό. ὁ
ἔχων ὦτα ἀκούειν ἀκουέτω.

Notes

Q 14:34–35

In Q: Most authors. Hoffmann omits mention of the
saying. Müller (1908: 30) argues that the original position
of Q 14:34–35 was between Q 11:16, 29–32 and Q 11:33,
i.e., in the context Matthew has given it (Matt 5:13, 14–
16).

Matt 5:13

[13] You are the salt of the earth; but if salt becomes insipid, with what could it be salted? It is no longer good for anything except to be thrown out and trodden under foot by people.

Luke 14:34–35

[34] Salt is good; but if salt becomes insipid, with what could it be seasoned? [35] It is fit neither for the soil nor for the dunghill; they throw it away. Let whoever has ears listen.

Parallels

Mark 9:49–50

[49]Πᾶς γὰρ πυρὶ ἁλισθήσεται. [50]καλὸν τὸ ἅλας· ἐὰν δὲ τὸ ἅλας ἄναλον γένηται, ἐν τίνι αὐτὸ ἀρτύσετε; ἔχετε ἐν ἑαυτοῖς ἅλα καὶ εἰρηνεύετε ἐν ἀλλήλοις.

Mark 9:49–50

[49] For every one will be salted with fire. [50] Salt is good; but if the salt has lost its saltness, how will you season it? Have salt in yourselves, and be at peace with one another.

Matt 18:10, 12–14

[¹⁰ᶜ Ὁρᾶτε μὴ καταφρονήσητε ἑνὸς τῶν μικρῶν
τούτων· λέγω γὰρ ὑμῖν ὅτι οἱ ἄγγελοι αὐτῶν ἐν
οὐρανοῖς διὰ παντὸς βλέπουσι τὸ πρόσωπον τοῦ
πατρός μου τοῦ ἐν οὐρανοῖς·]

¹²τί ὑμῖν δοκεῖ;
ἐὰν γένηταί τινι ἀνθρώπῳ **ἑκατὸν πρόβατα καὶ** πλανηθῇ
ἓν ἐξ αὐτῶν, οὐχὶ ἀφήσει **τὰ ἐνενήκοντα ἐννέα**
ἐπὶ τὰ ὄρη **καὶ** πορευθεὶς ζητεῖ τὸ πλανώμενον;
¹³**καὶ** ἐὰν γένηται εὑρεῖν **αὐτό**,

ἀμὴν **λέγω ὑμῖν ὅτι** χαίρει ἐπ' αὐτῷ μᾶλλον
ἢ ἐπὶ τοῖς **ἐνενήκοντα ἐννέα** τοῖς μὴ πεπλανημένοις.

[¹⁴οὕτως οὐκ ἔστιν θέλημα ἔμπροσθεν τοῦ πατρὸς
ὑμῶν τοῦ ἐν οὐρανοῖς ἵνα ἀπόληται ἓν τῶν μικρῶν
τούτων].

Luke 15:1–2, 3–7

[¹⁹Ἦσαν δὲ αὐτῷ ἐγγίζοντες πάντες οἱ τελῶναι καὶ οἱ
ἁμαρτωλοὶ ἀκούειν αὐτοῦ. ²καὶ διεγόγγυζον οἵ τε
Φαρισαῖοι καὶ οἱ γραμματεῖς λέγοντες ὅτι οὗτος
ἁμαρτωλοὺς προσδέχεται καὶ συνεσθίει αὐτοῖς·]
[³εἶπεν δὲ πρὸς αὐτοὺς τὴν παραβολὴν ταύτην λέγων·]
⁴τίς
ἄνθρωπος ἐξ ὑμῶν ἔχων **ἑκατὸν πρόβατα καὶ** ἀπολέσας
ἐξ αὐτῶν ἓν οὐ καταλείπει **τὰ ἐνενήκοντα ἐννέα** ἐν τῇ
ἐρήμῳ **καὶ** πορεύεται ἐπὶ τὸ ἀπολωλὸς ἕως εὕρῃ **αὐτό**;
⁵**καὶ εὑρὼν** ἐπιτίθησιν ἐπὶ τοὺς ὤμους αὐτοῦ χαίρων ⁶**καὶ**
ἐλθὼν εἰς τὸν οἶκον συγκαλεῖ τοὺς φίλους καὶ τοὺς
γείτονας λέγων αὐτοῖς· συγχάρητέ μοι, ὅτι εὗρον τὸ
πρόβατόν μου τὸ ἀπολωλός.
⁷   **λέγω ὑμῖν ὅτι** οὕτως χαρὰ ἐν τῷ οὐρανῷ ἔσται
ἐπὶ ἑνὶ ἁμαρτωλῷ μετανοοῦντι
ἢ ἐπὶ ἐνενήκοντα ἐννέα δικαίοις οἵτινες οὐ χρείαν
ἔχουσιν μετανοίας.

ἀπόλλομι ⇨ Luke 15:8 [S59]
καὶ εὑρὼν . . . συγκαλεῖ ⇨ Luke 15:9 [S59]
συγχάρητέ μοι . . . ἀπολωλός ⇨ Luke 15:9 [S59]
οὕτως . . . μετανοοῦντι ⇨ Luke 15:10 [S59]

Notes

[Luke 15:3] ⇨ S11 on Luke 6:39a.

Q 15:4–7

In Q: Bussmann 86–87; Creed Lk 196; Crossan 1983:
345; Easton Lk 235; Edwards 1975: 175; idem, 1976: xiii;
Fitzmyer Lk 79, 1073; Grundmann Lk 306; Harnack 91–
93; Hoffmann 5; Kilpatrick 1946: 28–29; Lührmann 90,
114, 116; Müller 1908: 8, 54; Polag 72; Schenk 112–14;
Schmid 305; Schmithals Lk 164; Schneider Lk 324–25;
Schulz 387–89; Weiss 1907: 246–48; Zeller 70. Streeter
(185, 244–46, 265) holds that the differences between the

two versions preclude derivation from a single source. He
suggests that Q overlaps with M, and that Matthew has
used M. [Presumably Luke uses Q, though for a different
view of Streeter, see Taylor 1972: 109].

Not in Q: Beare (1962: 178), Hunter (178) and Manson
(283) argue that the parallels between Matt 18:12–14 and
Luke 15:4–7 are due to an overlap between M and L.
Marshall Lk 602: The discrepancies between Matthew
and Luke make derivation from a common source
unlikely. Taylor 1972: 109–10.

Matt 18:10, 12–14

[¹⁰See that you do not despise one of these little ones; for I tell you that their angels in heaven constantly behold the face of my Father who is in heaven.]

¹²What do you think? If a man has a hundred sheep, and one of them has wandered away, will he not leave the ninety-nine on the hills and go in search of the one that wandered away? ¹³And if he should find it, amen, I tell you, he rejoices over it more than over the ninety-nine that never went astray.

[¹⁴So it is not the will of my Father who is in heaven that one of these little ones should perish.]

Luke 15:1–7

[¹Now the tax collectors and sinners were all drawing near to listen to him. ²And the Pharisees and the scribes were grumbling, saying, "This man welcomes sinners and eats with them."]

[³So he told them this parable:]

⁴"Which one of you, having a hundred sheep, if he has lost one of them, does not leave the ninety-nine in the wilderness, and go after the one which is lost, until he finds it? ⁵And when he has found it, he puts it on his shoulders, rejoicing, ⁶and when he comes home, he invites his friends and his neighbors, saying to them, 'Rejoice with me, for I have found my sheep which was lost.' ⁷Likewise, I tell you, there will be more joy in heaven over one sinner repenting than over ninety-nine righteous persons who need no repentance."

Parallels

GThom 107

ⲡⲉϫⲉ ⲓ̅ⲥ̅ ϫⲉ ⲧⲙⲛ̅ⲧⲉⲣⲟ ⲉⲥⲧⲛ̅ⲧⲱ(ⲛ) ⲉⲩⲣⲱⲙⲉ ⲛ̅ϣⲱⲥ ⲉⲩⲛ̅ⲧⲁϥ ⲙ̅ⲙⲁⲩ ⲛ̅ϣⲉ ⲛ̅ⲉⲥⲟⲟⲩ ⲁⲟⲩⲁ ⲛ̅ϩⲏⲧⲟⲩ ⲥⲱⲣⲙ ⲉⲡⲛⲟϭ ⲡⲉ ⲁϥⲕⲱ ⲙ̅ⲡⲥⲧⲉⲯⲓⲧ ⲁϥϣⲓⲛⲉ ⲛ̅ⲥⲁ ⲡⲓⲟⲩⲁ· ϣⲁⲛⲧⲉϥϩⲉ ⲉⲣⲟϥ· ⲛ̅ⲧⲁⲣⲉϥϩⲓⲥⲉ ⲡⲉϫⲁϥ ⲙ̅ⲡⲉⲥⲟⲟⲩ ϫⲉ ϯⲟⲩⲟϣⲕ ⲡⲁⲣⲁ ⲡⲥⲧⲉⲯⲓⲧ.

GThom 107

Jesus said, "The kingdom is like a shepherd who had a hundred sheep. One of them, the largest, wandered away. The shepherd left the ninety-nine and sought the one until he found it. After he had toiled, he said to the sheep, 'I love you more than the ninety-nine.'"

GTruth 31:35—32:4

ⲉⲛⲧⲁϥ ⲡⲉ ⲡϣⲱⲥ ⲉⲛⲧⲁϩⲕⲱⲉ ⲛ̅ⲥⲱϥ ⲙ̅ⲡⲓⲡⲥⲧⲉⲯⲓⲥ ⲛ̅ⲉⲥⲁⲩ ⲉⲧⲉⲙ̅ⲡⲟⲩⲥⲱⲣⲙ̅. ⲁϥⲉⲓ ⲁϥϣⲓⲛⲉ ⲛ̅ⲥⲁ ⲡⲉⲉⲓ ⲛ̅ⲧⲁϥⲥⲱⲣⲙ̅. ⲁϥⲣⲉϣⲉ ⲛ̅ⲧⲁⲣⲉϥϭⲓⲛⲉ ⲙ̅ⲙⲁϥ.

GTruth 31:35—32:4

He [the Son] is the shepherd who left behind the ninety-nine sheep which were not lost. He went searching for the one which was lost. He rejoiced when he found it.

Luke 15:8–10

(⁸Ἢ τίς γυνὴ δραχμὰς ἔχουσα δέκα ἐὰν ἀπολέσῃ
δραχμὴν μίαν, οὐχὶ ἅπτει λύχνον καὶ σαροῖ τὴν οἰκίαν
καὶ ζητεῖ ἐπιμελῶς ἕως οὗ εὕρῃ; ⁹καὶ εὑροῦσα συγκαλεῖ
τὰς φίλας καὶ γείτονας λέγουσα· συγχάρητέ μοι, ὅτι
εὗρον τὴν δραχμὴν ἣν ἀπώλεσα. ¹⁰οὕτως, λέγω ὑμῖν,
γίνεται χαρὰ ἐνώπιον τῶν ἀγγέλων τοῦ θεοῦ ἐπὶ ἑνὶ
ἁμαρτωλῷ μετανοοῦντι.)

Notes

(Q 15:8–10)

In Q: Creed Lk 196; Crossan 1983: 345; Easton Lk 236;
Grundmann Lk 306 (with hesitation); Knox 92; Polag 72
(probably in Q); Schmid 305–306; Schneider Lk 324–25;
Schürmann 1968: 123, 224, 280 n. 15; Weiss 1907: 248–
49; Wernle 1899: 88.

The grounds for the inclusion of 15:8–10 are: (1) The
strong verbal and formal parallels between the parable of
the lost sheep and the parable of the lost coin indicate
either that the two originally belonged together, or that
the latter was formed (by Luke?) on the pattern of the lost
sheep. Bultmann (1963: 171) holds that if 15:4–7, 8–10
had been originally a double parable, there would have
been only one application appearing at the end. The
repetition of the application (vv. 7, 10) suggests that vv.
8–10 have been secondarily formulated on the pattern of
15:4–7 (▷ S58). Bultmann's argument, however, does not
preclude a secondary expansion in or prior to Q, which
clearly already contains several other double sayings (Q
9:57–60; 10:13–15; 11:11–12; 11:31–32; 13:18–21.

(2) Luke's redactional introduction (v. 3: ταύτην
παραβολήν) is at variance with the fact that three parables
follow. In the case of the third (15:11–32), Luke's
introduction, εἶπεν δέ, signals a new beginning. The first
two, however, are linked only by ἤ. This may suggest that
Luke found the two already joined and treated them as a
unit. (3) Schürmann opines that Matthew's οἱ ἄγγελοι . . .
τὸ πρόσωπον τοῦ πατρός (18:10 ▷ S58) betrays knowledge
of Q/Luke 15:10: ἐνώπιον τῶν ἀγγέλων τοῦ θεοῦ. This
suggests that Matthew has read 15:8–10 in Q.
(4) Matthew did not use this parable since it would
"overload" his section (Easton) or because it had nothing
to do with his theme of being led astray (Schmid).

Not in Q: Beare 1962: 178; Edwards 1976; Fitzmyer Lk
1073: Luke either formulated the parable himself, or,
more likely, found it in L. Harnack; Hoffmann; Hunter
179 (from L); Manson 282–83; Marshall Lk 602–603;
Müller 8, 54; Schenk; Schmithals Lk 164; Schulz; Streeter
291; Zeller.

Luke 15:8–10

([8] Or what woman, having ten drachmae, if she loses one drachma, does not light a lamp and sweep the house and seek diligently until she finds it? [9] And when she has found it, she invites her friends and neighbors, saying, 'Rejoice with me, for I have found the drachma which I had lost.' [10] Likewise, I tell you, there is joy before the angels of God over one sinner repenting.)

Matt 6:24

²⁴Οὐδεὶς   δύναται δυσὶ κυρίοις δουλεύειν·
ἢ γὰρ τὸν ἕνα μισήσει καὶ τὸν ἕτερον ἀγαπήσει,
ἢ ἑνὸς ἀνθέξεται καὶ τοῦ ἑτέρου καταφρονήσει.
οὐ δύνασθε θεῷ δουλεύειν καὶ μαμωνᾷ.

Luke 16:13

¹³Οὐδεὶς οἰκέτης δύναται δυσὶ κυρίοις δουλεύειν·
ἢ γὰρ τὸν ἕνα μισήσει καὶ τὸν ἕτερον ἀγαπήσει,
ἢ ἑνὸς ἀνθέξεται καὶ τοῦ ἑτέρου καταφρονήσει.
οὐ δύνασθε θεῷ δουλεύειν καὶ μαμωνᾷ.

Notes

Q 16:13

In Q: Most authors. Müller (1908: 30) places the saying
between Q 12:10 and Q 12:22–31, arguing that Matthew's
association of the saying with the sayings on anxiety (Q
12:22–31 // Matt 6:25–33) is original.

Not in Q: Vassiliadis 1978: 68: Short proverbial sayings
may be due to the influence of the oral tradition.

Matt 6:24

24 No one can serve two masters; for either he will hate the one and love the other, or he will be loyal to one and despise the other. You cannot serve God and mammon.

Luke 16:13

13 No servant can serve two masters; for either he will hate the one and love the other, or he will be loyal to the one and despise the other. You cannot serve God and mammon.

Parallels

GThom 47a

πεχε ι̅c̅ χε μ̅ν̅ 6ομ ν̅τεογρωμε τελο α2το cναγ ν̅qχωλκ μ̅πιτε cν̅τε αγω μ̅ν̅ 6ομ ν̅τεογ2μ5̅α̅λ̅ ϣμ̅ϣ̅ε χοειc cναγ η qναρ̅τιμα μ̅πογα αγω πκεογα qναρ̅2γβριζε μ̅μοq.

GThom 47a

Jesus said, "A person cannot mount two horses or bend two bows. And a servant cannot serve two lords; that servant will honor one and offend the other."

2 Clem 6:1

1 Λέγει δὲ ὁ κύριος· οὐδεὶς οἰκέτης δύναται δυσὶ κυρίοις δουλεύειν. ἐὰν ἡμεῖς θέλωμεν καὶ θεῷ δουλεύειν καὶ μαμωνᾷ, ἀσύμφορον ἡμῖν ἐστίν.

2 Clem 6:1

1 And the Lord says, "No servant can serve two masters. If we desire to serve both God and Mammon it is unprofitable to us."

Matt 11:12–13 ⇨ S18

¹³πάντες γὰρ <u>οἱ προφῆται καὶ ὁ νόμος</u> ἕως <u>Ἰωάννου</u>
ἐπροφήτευσαν·
¹²Ἀπὸ δὲ τῶν ἡμερῶν Ἰωάννου τοῦ
Βαπτιστοῦ ἕως ἄρτι <u>ἡ βασιλεία</u> τῶν οὐρανῶν
<u>βιάζεται</u> καὶ βιασταὶ ἀρπάζουσιν <u>αὐτήν</u>.

Matt 5:18

¹⁸Ἀμὴν γὰρ λέγω ὑμῖν· <u>ἕως ἂν παρέλθῃ ὁ οὐρανὸς
καὶ ἡ γῆ</u>, ἰῶτα ἓν ἢ <u>μία κεραία</u> οὐ μὴ <u>παρέλθῃ</u> ἀπὸ
<u>τοῦ νόμου</u>, ἕως ἂν πάντα γένηται.

Matt 5:32

³²Ἐγὼ δὲ λέγω ὑμῖν ὅτι <u>πᾶς ὁ ἀπολύων</u>
<u>τὴν γυναῖκα αὐτοῦ</u> παρεκτὸς λόγου πορνείας
ποιεῖ αὐτὴν μοιχευθῆναι,
καὶ ὃς ἐὰν <u>ἀπολελυμένην</u> γαμήσῃ, μοιχᾶται.

Luke 16:16

¹⁶   <u>Ὁ νόμος καὶ οἱ προφῆται</u> μέχρι
<u>Ἰωάννου</u>·
<u>ἀπὸ τότε</u>
          <u>ἡ βασιλεία</u> τοῦ θεοῦ εὐαγγελίζεται
καὶ πᾶς εἰς <u>αὐτὴν βιάζεται</u>.

Luke 16:17:

¹⁷   εὐκοπώτερον δέ ἐστιν <u>τὸν οὐρανὸν
καὶ τὴν γῆν παρελθεῖν</u> ἢ <u>τοῦ νόμου</u> <u>μίαν κεραίαν</u> πεσεῖν.

Luke 16:18

¹⁸   <u>πᾶς ὁ ἀπολύων</u>
<u>τὴν γυναῖκα αὐτοῦ</u>   καὶ γαμῶν
ἑτέραν μοιχεύει,
καὶ ὁ <u>ἀπολελυμένην</u> ἀπὸ ἀνδρὸς <u>γαμῶν</u> μοιχεύει.

Notes

Q 16:16

In Q: Most authors. For a discussion of its placement ⇨
S18.

Q 16:17–18

In Q: Most authors. Edwards (1976) does not list Q
16:18 and although he lists it in idem, 1975 (177), no
vocabulary is concorded. Müller (1908: 29), influenced by
Matthew's positioning of the saying, places it between Q
6:20–23 and Q 6:27–30.

Matt 11:12–13

¹³For all the prophets and the law prophesied until John. ¹²From the days of John the Baptist until now the reign of heaven has suffered violence, and the violent have seized it.

Matt 5:18

¹⁸For amen, I tell you, till heaven and earth pass away, not an iota, not a serif, will pass from the law until all is accomplished.

Matt 5:32

³²But I tell you that every one who divorces his wife, except on the ground of unchastity, forces her to commit adultery; and whoever marries a divorcée commits adultery.

Luke 16:16

¹⁶The law and the prophets were until John; from then the good news of the reign of God is proclaimed, and everybody is trying to enter by force.

Luke 16:17

¹⁷But it is easier for heaven and earth to pass away, than for one serif of the law to be dropped.

Luke 16:18

¹⁸Every one who divorces his wife and marries another commits adultery, and he who marries a woman divorced from her husband commits adultery.

Parallels

GThom 11 ⇨ Q 16:17

ⲡⲉⲝⲉ ⲓ̅ⲥ̅ ϫⲉ ⲧⲉⲉⲓⲡⲉ ⲛⲁⲣ̄ⲡⲁⲣⲁⲅⲉ ⲁⲩⲱ ⲧⲉⲧⲛ̄ⲧⲡⲉ ⲙ̄ⲙⲟⲥ ⲛⲁⲣ̄ⲡⲁⲣⲁⲅⲉ ⲁⲩⲱ ⲛⲉⲧⲙⲟⲟⲩⲧ ⲥⲉⲟⲛϩ ⲁⲛ ⲁⲩⲱ ⲛⲉⲧⲟⲛϩ ⲥⲉⲛⲁⲙⲟⲩ ⲁⲛ ⲛ̄ϩⲟⲟⲩ ⲛⲉⲧⲉⲧⲛ̄ⲟⲩⲱⲙ ⲙ̄ⲡⲉⲧⲙⲟⲟⲩⲧ ⲛⲉⲧⲉⲧⲛ̄ⲉⲓⲣⲉ ⲙ̄ⲙⲟϥ ⲙ̄ⲡⲉⲧⲟⲛϩ ϩⲟⲧⲁⲛ ⲉⲧⲉⲧⲛ̄ϣⲁⲛϣⲱⲡⲉ ϩⲙ̄ ⲡⲟⲩⲟⲉⲓⲛ ⲟⲩ ⲡⲉⲧⲉⲧⲛⲁⲁϥ ϩⲙ̄ ⲫⲟⲟⲩ ⲉⲧⲉⲧⲛ̄ⲟ ⲛ̄ⲟⲩⲁ ⲁⲧⲉⲧⲛ̄ⲉⲓⲣⲉ ⲙ̄ⲡⲥⲛⲁⲩ ϩⲟⲧⲁⲛ ⲇⲉ ⲉⲧⲉⲧⲛ̄ϣⲁϣⲱⲡⲉ ⲛ̄ⲥⲛⲁⲩ ⲟⲩ ⲡⲉ ⲉⲧⲉⲧⲛ̄ⲛⲁⲁϥ.

Mark 10:11–12 ⇨ Q 16:18

¹¹καὶ λέγει αὐτοῖς· ὃς ἂν ἀπολύσῃ τὴν γυναῖκα αὐτοῦ καὶ γαμήσῃ ἄλλην μοιχᾶται ἐπ' αὐτήν·
¹²καὶ ἐὰν αὐτὴ ἀπολύσασα τὸν ἄνδρα αὐτῆς γαμήσῃ ἄλλον, μοιχᾶται.

Matt 19:9 ⇨ Q 16:18

⁹λέγω δὲ ὑμῖν ὅτι ὃς ἂν ἀπολύσῃ τὴν γυναῖκα αὐτοῦ μὴ ἐπὶ πορνείᾳ καὶ γαμήσῃ ἄλλην μοιχᾶται.

GThom 11

Jesus said, "This heaven will pass away, and the one above it will pass away. The dead are not alive, and the living will not die. During the days when you ate what is dead, you made it alive. When you are in the light, what will you do? On the day when you were one, you became two. But when you become two, what will you do?"

Mark 10:11–12

¹¹And he said to them, "Whoever divorces his wife and marries another, commits adultery against her; ¹²and if she, having divorced her husband, marries another, she commits adultery."

Matt 19:9

⁹But I tell you: whoever divorces his wife, except for unchastity, and marries another, commits adultery.

Matt 18:7, 6

⁷οὐαὶ τῷ κόσμῳ ἀπὸ τῶν σκανδάλων·
ἀνάγκη γὰρ **ἐλθεῖν τὰ σκάνδαλα, πλὴν οὐαὶ**
τῷ ἀνθρώπῳ **δι' οὗ** τὸ σκάνδαλον **ἔρχεται.**
⁶**ὃς δ' ἂν σκανδαλίσῃ ἕνα τῶν μικρῶν τούτων**
τῶν πιστευόντων εἰς ἐμέ,
συμφέρει **αὐτῷ** ἵνα κρεμασθῇ μύλος ὀνικὸς **περὶ τὸν**
τράχηλον αὐτοῦ καὶ καταποντισθῇ ἐν τῷ πελάγει
τῆς θαλάσσης.

Luke 17:1–2

[¹Εἶπεν δὲ πρὸς τοὺς μαθητὰς αὐτοῦ·]

ἀνένδεκτόν ἐστιν τοῦ **τὰ σκάνδαλα μὴ ἐλθεῖν, πλὴν οὐαὶ**
δι' οὗ ἔρχεται.

²λυσιτελεῖ **αὐτῷ** εἰ λίθος μυλικὸς περίκειται
περὶ τὸν τράχηλον αὐτοῦ καὶ ἔρριπται εἰς
τὴν θάλασσαν
ἢ ἵνα **σκανδαλίσῃ τῶν μικρῶν τούτων ἕνα.**

Matt 18:6: εις τον τραχηλον: W Koine Γ Δ Θ λ φ *al* sa bo [HG] / επι τον τραχηλον: D U 565 1424 *pc* / περι τον τραχηλον (Mark; Luke): ℵ A B L N R Z 33 579 892 1241 *al* [NA²⁵·²⁶].

Luke 17:1: οuαι δε: A (W) Koine Θ 063 vg syᵖ·ʰ [NA²⁵; HG] / πλην οuαι: 𝔭⁷⁵ ℵ B D L Ψ λ φ 33 892 1241 *pc* it sysᵐᵍ sa bo [NA²⁶] // 2: ενα των μικρων τουτων (Matt; Mark): ℵ² A D W Koine Θ 063 λ φ [HG] / των μικρων τουτων ενα: ℵ* B L Ψ 892 *pc* [NA²⁵·²⁶].

Notes

Q 17:1b

In Q: Most authors, including those mentioned for Q 17:2 ("in Q"). Harnack 190 ("probably" in Q).

Not in Q: Schulz; Vassiliadis 1978: 70 (insufficient verbal agreement).

Q 17:2

In Q: Bussmann 87; Creed Lk 214; Easton Lk 256. Fitzmyer Lk 1137; Hunter 145; Knox 1957: 101; Manson 138; Marshall Lk 640–41; Polag 74; Schmid 305; Schmithals Lk 172; Schneider Lk 345; Streeter 1924: 281; Taylor 1972: 110; Weiss 1907: 145; Wernle 1899: 91.

While Luke seems to have been influenced by Mark 9:42, which he omitted earlier, he appears to depend on Q which had the verses in the reverse order of Mark (= Matthew).

Not in Q: Crossan 1983: 148–49, 345; Edwards 1976: 71, 138–39: Both Matthew and Luke combine Mark with Q. Harnack; Hawkins 1911; Hoffmann; Müller 1908: 54; Neirynck 1982: 52: Luke 17:1–2 is a combination of Q (17:1) and Mark 9:42 (17:2). Schenk; Schulz; Vassiliadis 1978: 70: There is insufficient verbal agreement to posit Q. Zeller.

Matt 18:7, 6

⁷Woe to the world from scandals. For it is necessary that scandals come, but woe to the person by whom the scandal comes!
⁶But whoever leads astray one of these little ones who believe in me, it would be better for him to have a millstone fastened round his neck and to be drowned in the depth of the sea.

Luke 17:1–2
[¹ And he said to his disciples,]
"Scandals are sure to come; but woe to him by whom they come!

²It would be better for him if a millstone were hung round his neck and he were cast into the sea, than that he should lead astray one of these little ones."

Parallels

Mark 9:42
⁴²Καὶ ὃς ἂν σκανδαλίσῃ ἕνα τῶν μικρῶν τούτων τῶν πιστευόντων [εἰς ἐμέ], καλόν ἐστιν αὐτῷ μᾶλλον εἰ περίκειται μύλος ὀνικὸς περὶ τὸν τράχηλον αὐτοῦ καὶ βέβληται εἰς τὴν θάλασσαν.

Mark 9:42
⁴²And whoever leads astray one of these little ones who believe in me, it would be better for him if a millstone were hung round his neck and he were thrown into the sea.

1 Clem 46:7b–8
⁷. . . μνήσθητε τῶν λόγων τοῦ κυρίου Ἰησοῦ· ⁸Εἶπεν γάρ· οὐαὶ τῷ ἀνθρώπῳ ἐκείνῳ· καλὸν ἦν αὐτῷ εἰ οὐκ ἐγεννήθη, ἢ ἕνα τῶν ἐκλεκτῶν μου σκανδαλίσαι· κρεῖττον ἦν αὐτῷ περιτεθῆναι μύλον καὶ καταποντισθῆναι εἰς τὴν θάλασσαν, ἢ ἕνα τῶν ἐκλεκτῶν μου διαστρέψαι.

1 Clem 46:7b–8
⁷. . . Remember the words of the Lord Jesus; ⁸for he said, "Woe unto that man: it were good for him if he had not been born, than that he should offend one of my elect; it were better for him that a millstone be hung on him, and he be cast into the sea, than that he should turn aside one of my elect."

Ps. Clem. Hom. 12.29.1
ὁ τῆς ἀληθείας προφήτης ἔφη· τὰ ἀγαθὰ ἐλθεῖν δεῖ, μακάριος δέ φησιν δι' οὗ ἔρχεται· ὁμοίως καὶ τὰ κακὰ ἀνάγκη ἐλθεῖν, οὐαὶ δὲ δι' οὗ ἔρχεται.

Ps. Clem. Hom. 12.29.1
The prophet of the truth said, "Good things must come, and blessed, (he said), is the one through whom they come. Similarly, evil things must come, but woe to to the one through whom they come."

Matt 18:15–17, 21–22

¹⁵ἐὰν δὲ <u>ἁμαρτήσῃ</u> [εἰς σὲ] <u>ὁ ἀδελφός σου</u>
ὕπαγε ἔλεγξον αὐτὸν μεταξὺ σοῦ καὶ αὐτοῦ μόνου.
ἐάν σου ἀκούσῃ ἐκέρδησας τὸν ἀδελφόν σου·

[¹⁶ἐὰν δὲ μὴ ἀκούσῃ παράλαβε μετὰ σοῦ ἔτι ἕνα ἢ δύο,
ἵνα ἐπὶ στόματος δύο μαρτύρων ἢ τριῶν σταθῇ πᾶν
ῥῆμα· ¹⁷ἐὰν δὲ παρακούσῃ αὐτῶν, εἰπὲ τῇ ἐκκλησίᾳ·
ἐὰν δὲ καὶ τῆς ἐκκλησίας παρακούσῃ, ἔστω σοι ὥσπερ
ὁ ἐθνικὸς καὶ ὁ τελώνης].

[²¹Τότε προσελθὼν ὁ Πέτρος εἶπεν αὐτῷ·]
κύριε, ποσάκις ἁμαρτήσει <u>εἰς ἐμὲ</u> ὁ ἀδελφός μου καὶ
<u>ἀφήσω</u> <u>αὐτῷ</u>; <u>ἕως</u> <u>ἑπτάκις</u>; ²²λέγει αὐτῷ ὁ Ἰησοῦς· οὐ
λέγω σοι ἕως <u>ἑπτάκις</u> ἀλλὰ ἕως ἑβδομηκοντάκις ἑπτά.

Luke 17:3–4

[³προσέχετε ἑαυτοῖς·]
ἐὰν   <u>ἁμάρτῃ</u>   <u>ὁ ἀδελφός σου</u> ἐπιτίμησον
<u>αὐτῷ</u>,
καὶ <u>ἐὰν</u> μετανοήσῃ ἄφες αὐτῷ.

⁴καὶ ἐὰν <u>ἑπτάκις</u> τῆς ἡμέρας <u>ἁμαρτήσῃ</u> <u>εἰς σὲ</u> καὶ <u>ἑπτάκις</u>
ἐπιστρέψῃ πρὸς σὲ λέγων· μετανοῶ, <u>ἀφήσεις</u> <u>αὐτῷ</u>.

Matt 18:15: ειϲ ϲε: D L W Koine Θ 078 λ latt sy mae bo^pt
[NA²⁶; HG] / omit (Luke): ℵ B 1 544 sa bo^pt; Or [NA²⁵] //
16: μετα σεαυτου: ℵ K L N Θ λ φ 28 33 892 1010 *pm* [HG]
/ μετα σου: B D W Koine *al* [NA²⁵·²⁶] // 17: ειπε: [NA²⁶;
HG] / ειπον: [NA²⁵].

Notes

Q 17:3b–4
In Q: Bussmann 88; Crossan 1983: 345. Catchpole
1983b: 80: Portions of Matt 18:16–17 also derive from Q.
Easton Lk 257; Edwards 1976: 139; Fitzmyer Lk 79,
1139; Grundmann Lk 331; Harnack 95–96; Hawkins
1911: 115; Hoffmann 5, 41; Hunter 145; Kilpatrick 1946:
29, 38; Lührmann 111–14; Manson 139; Marshall Lk
640–41; Müller 1908: 54–55; Polag 76; Schenk 117;
Schmid 308–309; Schmithals Lk 172; Schulz 320–22;
Streeter 1924: 281–82; Taylor 1972: 110; Wernle 1899:
91; Zeller 1977: 61. Manson, Marshall, Streeter and
Taylor hold that Luke preserves Q while Matthew
reproduces M.
Not in Q: Vassiliadis 1978: 72; Weiss 1907: 252–53.

Matt 18:15–17, 21–22

¹⁵ "If your brother sins against you, go and point out his fault, between you and him alone. If he listens to you, you have gained your brother.

[¹⁶ But if he does not listen, take one or two others along with you, that every case may be established by the evidence of two or three witnesses. ¹⁷ If he ignores them, tell it to the church; and if he ignores the church, let him be to you as a Gentile and a tax collector."]

[²¹ Then Peter came up and said to him,] "Lord, how often shall my brother sin against me, and I forgive him? Seven times?" ²² Jesus said to him, "I tell you, not seven times, but seventy times seven."

Luke 17:3–4

[³ Take heed to yourselves;] if your brother sins, rebuke him, and if he repents, forgive him;

⁴ and if he sins against you seven times a day, and turns to you seven times, and says, 'I repent,' you must forgive him.

Parallels

GNaz 15

"Si peccaverit," inquit, "frater tuus in verbo, et sais tibi fecerit, septies in die suscipe eum." Dixit illi Simon discipulus eius: "Septies in die?" respondit dominus, et dixit ei: "Etiam ego dico tibi, usque setuagies septies. Etenim in prophetis quoque postquam uncti sunt Spiritu sancto, inventus est sermo peccati."

GNaz 15

He [Jesus] said, "If thy brother has sinned with a word and has made thee reparation, receive him seven times in a day." Simon his disciple said to him, "Seven times a day?" He answered and said to him, "Yea, I say to thee, until seventy times seven times. For in the prophets also after they were anointed with the Holy Spirit, the word of sin [sinful discourse?] was found."

Did 15:3

³ Ἐλέγχετε δὲ ἀλλήλους μὴ ἐν ὀργῇ, ἀλλ᾽ ἐν εἰρήνῃ ὡς ἔχετε ἐν τῷ εὐαγγελίῳ· καὶ παντὶ ἀστοχοῦντι κατὰ τοῦ ἑτέρου μηδεὶς λαλείτω μηδὲ παρ᾽ ὑμῶν ἀκουέτω, ἕως οὗ μετανοήσῃ.

Did 15:3

³ And reprove one another not in wrath but in peace as you find in the Gospel, and let none speak with any who has done a wrong to his neighbour, nor let him hear a word from you until he repents.

Matt 17:19–20

[¹⁹Τότε προσελθόντες οἱ μαθηταὶ τῷ ᾽Ιησοῦ κατ᾽
ἰδίαν εἶπον· διὰ τί ἡμεῖς οὐκ ἠδυνήθημεν ἐκβαλεῖν
αὐτό; ²⁰ὁ δὲ λέγει αὐτοῖς· διὰ τὴν ὀλιγοπιστίαν ὑμῶν·]

ἀμὴν γὰρ λέγω ὑμῖν, ἐὰν ἔχητε **πίστιν ὡς κόκκον
σινάπεως**, ἐρεῖτε τῷ ὄρει τούτῳ· μετάβα ἔνθεν ἐκεῖ, **καὶ**
μεταβήσεται· καὶ οὐδὲν ἀδυνατήσει **ὑμῖν.**

Luke 17:5–6

[⁵καὶ εἶπαν οἱ ἀπόστολοι τῷ κυρίῳ· πρόσθες ἡμῖν
πίστιν].

[⁶εἶπεν δὲ ὁ κύριος·]
            εἰ ἔχετε **πίστιν ὡς κόκκον
σινάπεως**, ἐλέγετε ἂν τῇ συκαμίνῳ [ταύτῃ]· ἐκριζώθητι
καὶ φυτεύθητι ἐν τῇ θαλάσσῃ· καὶ ὑπήκουσεν ἂν **ὑμῖν.**

Luke 17:6: συκαμινω ταυτη (Matt): A B W Koine Θ 063
0135 λ φ *pl* [NA²⁵·²⁶] / συκαμινω: 𝔭⁷⁵ ℵ D L X *pc* syᶜ bo
[HG].

Notes

Q 17:6b

In Q: Bussmann 89–90: V. 5 is also from Q. Crossan
1983: 345; Easton Lk 258 (possibly); Edwards 1976: 139–
40; Fitzmyer Lk 79, 1141; Harnack 91; Hawkins 1911:
117 (with considerable probability); Hoffmann 5, 41;
Hunter 145. Manson 141: Matt 17:20 is from M and Luke
17:6 comes from Q. Manson also includes v. 5 in Q.
Marshall Lk 643–45; Müller 1908: 55. Polag (76, 90) also
includes v. 6a as "uncertain." Schenk 118; Schmithals Lk
173; Schulz 465–68; Taylor 1972: 114; Wernle 1899: 91.
Not in Q: Vassiliadis 1978: 72; Weiss 1907: 252–53.

Matt 17:19–20

[¹⁹Then the disciples came to Jesus privately and said, "Why could we not exorcise it?" ²⁰He said to them, "Because of your weak faith.]

For amen I tell you, if you have faith as a grain of mustard seed, you will say to this mountain, 'Move from here to there,' and it will move; and nothing will be impossible to you."

Luke 17:5–6

[⁵And the apostles said to the Lord, "Increase our faith!"]

[⁶And the Lord said,]
"If you have faith as a grain of mustard seed, you could say to this sycamine tree, 'Be uprooted, and be planted in the sea,' and it would obey you."

Parallels

Mark 9:28–29 ⇨ Matt 17:19

²⁸Καὶ εἰσελθόντος αὐτοῦ εἰς οἶκον οἱ μαθηταὶ αὐτοῦ κατ᾽ ἰδίαν ἐπηρώτων αὐτόν· ὅτι ἡμεῖς οὐκ ἠδυνήθημεν ἐκβαλεῖν αὐτό; ²⁹καὶ εἶπεν αὐτοῖς· τοῦτο τὸ γένος ἐν οὐδενὶ δύναται ἐξελθεῖν εἰ μὴ ἐν προσευχῇ.

Mark 9:28–29

²⁸And when he had entered the house, his disciples asked him privately, "Why could we not exorcise it?" ²⁹And he said to them, "This kind cannot be driven out by anything but prayer."

Mark 11:22–23

²²Καὶ ἀποκριθεὶς ὁ Ἰησοῦς λέγει αὐτοῖς· ἔχετε **πίστιν** θεοῦ. ²³ἀμὴν λέγω ὑμῖν ὅτι ὃς ἂν εἴπῃ τῷ ὄρει τούτῳ· ἄρθητι **καὶ** βλήθητι εἰς τὴν θάλασσαν, καὶ μὴ διακριθῇ ἐν τῇ καρδίᾳ αὐτοῦ ἀλλὰ πιστεύῃ ὅτι ὃ λαλεῖ γίνεται, ἔσται αὐτῷ.

Mark 11:22–23

²²And Jesus answered them, "Have faith in God. ²³Amen, I tell you, whoever says to this mountain, 'Be taken up and cast into the sea,' and does not doubt in his heart, but believes that what he says will happen, it will be done for him."

Matt 21:21

²¹ἀποκριθεὶς δὲ ὁ Ἰησοῦς εἶπεν αὐτοῖς· ἀμὴν λέγω ὑμῖν, ἐὰν ἔχητε **πίστιν** καὶ μὴ διακριθῆτε, οὐ μόνον τὸ τῆς συκῆς ποιήσετε, ἀλλὰ κἂν τῷ ὄρει τούτῳ εἴπητε· ἄρθητι **καὶ** βλήθητι εἰς τὴν θάλασσαν, γενήσεται.

Matt 21:21

²¹And Jesus answered them, "Amen, I tell you, if you have faith and do not doubt, you will not only do what has been done to the fig tree, but even if you say to this mountain, 'Be taken up and cast into the sea,' it will happen."

GThom 48

ⲡⲉϫⲉ ⲓ̅ⲥ̅ ϫⲉ ⲉⲣϣⲁⲥⲛⲁⲩ ⲣ̅ ⲉⲓⲣⲏⲛⲏ ⲙⲛ̅ ⲛⲟⲩⲉⲣⲏⲩ ϩⲙ̅ ⲡⲉⲓⲏⲉⲓ ⲟⲩⲱⲧ ⲥⲉⲛⲁϫⲟⲟⲥ ⲙ̅ⲡⲧⲁⲩ ϫⲉ ⲡⲱⲱⲛⲉ ⲉⲃⲟⲗ ⲁⲩⲱ ϥⲛⲁⲡⲱⲱⲛⲉ.

GThom 48

Jesus said, "If two make peace with each other in a single house, they will say to the mountain, 'Move from here!' and it will move."

Luke 17:20–21

²⁰ Ἐπερωτηθεὶς δὲ ὑπὸ τῶν Φαρισαίων πότε ἔρχεται ἡ βασιλεία τοῦ θεοῦ ἀπεκρίθη αὐτοῖς καὶ εἶπεν· οὐκ ἔρχεται ἡ βασιλεία τοῦ θεοῦ μετὰ παρατηρήσεως, ²¹ οὐδὲ ἐροῦσιν· ἰδοὺ ὧδε ἤ· ἐκεῖ, ἰδοὺ γὰρ ἡ βασιλεία τοῦ θεοῦ ἐντὸς ὑμῶν ἐστιν.

Notes

[Luke 17:20b–21]

In Q: Easton (Lk 262) conjectures that 17:20–21 stood as a preface to 17:23–37 though originally it was an independent saying. Schnackenburg 1971: 221–24; Schürmann 1968: 237 (but see idem, 1982: 124); Streeter 1924: 290.

Schnackenburg offers several grounds for attributing this to Q: (1) Both units use the formula, "They will say to you, 'Behold here,' or 'there'" (vv. 21a, 23a). (2) While 17:20–21 is conceivable as an independent saying, the similarity between 17:20–21 and 17:23–37 makes it possible that the two units belonged together and that Matthew omitted the first for various reasons. (3) The juxtaposition of a kingdom saying with a Son of Man saying poses no problem, since Q uses both kinds of sayings. (4) The separation of vv. 20b–21 (directed at the Pharisees) from vv. 23–37 (directed at the disciples) results from Lukan redaction and thus does not necessarily bespeak an original separation of the units. Schürmann and Streeter suggest that the visible coming of the eschaton was so crucial for Matthew that he omitted this saying as misleading.

Not in Q: Bussmann 91; Edwards 1976; Fitzmyer Lk 1158; Harnack; Hoffmann; Hunter 73, 182; Kloppenborg 1987: 154–55; Manson 303; Marshall Lk 653–54; Meyer 51; Müller 1908: 55; Polag; Schenk; Schulz; Schürmann 1982: 124; Vassiliadis 1978; Zeller; Zmijewski 1972: 379–97.

Luke 17:20–21

²⁰ Being asked by the Pharisees when the reign of God was coming, he answered them, "The reign of God does not come by empirical observation; ²¹ nor can it be said, 'Lo, here it is!' or 'There!' for behold, the reign of God is in the midst of you."

Parallels

POxy 654.9–21

λέγει Ἰ[η(σοῦ)ς· ἐὰν] οἱ ἔλκοντες ⟨ὑ⟩μᾶς [εἴπωσιν ὑμῖν· ἰδοὺ] ἡ βασιλεία ἐν οὐρα[νῷ, ὑμᾶς φθήσεται] τὰ πετεινὰ τοῦ οὐρ[ανοῦ· ἐὰν δ᾽ εἴπωσιν ὅ]τι ὑπὸ τὴν γῆν ἐστ[ιν, εἰσελεύσονται] οἱ ἰχθύες τῆς θαλά[σσης προφθάσαν]τες ὑμᾶς· καὶ ἡ βασ[ιλεία τοῦ θεοῦ] ἐντὸς ὑμῶν [ἐσ]τι [κἀκτός· ὃς ἂν ἑαυτὸν] γνῷ, ταύτην εὑρή[σει, καὶ ὅτε ὑμεῖς] ἑαυτοὺς γνώσεσθα[ι, εἴσεσθε ὅτι υἱοί] ἐστε ὑμεῖς τοῦ πατρὸς τοῦ ζ[ῶντος· εἰ δὲ μὴ] γνώσ⟨εσ⟩θε ἑαυτοὺς, ἐν [τῇ πτωχείᾳ ἐστὲ] καὶ ὑμεῖς ἐστε ἡ πτω[χεία].

POxy 654.9–21

Jesus said, "[If] those who lead you [say to you, 'See], the kingdom is in the sky,' then the birds of the sky [will precede you. If they say that] it is under the earth, then the fish of the sea [will enter it, preceding] you. And, the [kingdom of God] is inside of you, [and it is outside of you. Whoever] knows [himself] will discover this. [And when you] come to know yourselves, [you will realize that] you are [sons of the [living] father. [But if you] will [not] know yourselves, [you dwell] in [poverty] and it is you who are that poverty."

GThom 3

ⲡⲉϫⲉ ⲓ̅ⲥ̅ ϫⲉ ⲉⲅϣⲁϫⲟⲟⲥ ⲛⲏⲧⲛ̅ ⲛ̅ϭⲓ ⲛⲉⲧⲥⲱⲕ ϩⲏⲧ ⲧⲏⲩⲧⲛ̅ ϫⲉ ⲉⲓⲥ ϩⲏⲏⲧⲉ ⲉⲧⲙⲛ̅ⲧⲉⲣⲟ ϩⲛ̅ ⲧⲡⲉ ⲉⲉⲓⲉ ⲛ̅ϩⲁⲗⲏⲧ ⲛⲁⲣ̅ ϣⲟⲣⲡ ⲉⲣⲱⲧⲛ̅ ⲛ̅ⲧⲉ ⲧⲡⲉ ⲉⲅϣⲁⲛϫⲟⲟⲥ ⲛⲏⲧⲛ̅ ϫⲉ ⲥϩⲛ̅ ⲑⲁⲗⲁⲥⲥⲁ ⲉⲉⲓⲉ ⲛ̅ⲧⲃⲧ ⲛⲁⲣ̅ ϣⲟⲣⲡ ⲉⲣⲱⲧⲛ̅ ⲁⲗⲗⲁ ⲧⲙⲛ̅ⲧⲉⲣⲟ ⲥⲙ̅ⲡⲉⲧⲛ̅ϩⲟⲩⲛ ⲁⲩⲱ ⲥⲙ̅ⲡⲉⲧⲛ̅ⲃⲁⲗ ϩⲟⲧⲁⲛ ⲉⲧⲉⲧⲛ̅ϣⲁⲛⲥⲟⲩⲱⲛ ⲧⲏⲩⲧⲛ̅ ⲧⲟⲧⲉ ⲥⲉⲛⲁⲥⲟⲩⲱ(ⲛ) ⲧⲏⲛⲉ ⲁⲩⲱ ⲧⲉⲧⲛⲁⲉⲓⲙⲉ ϫⲉ ⲛ̅ⲧⲱⲧⲛ̅ ⲡⲉ ⲛ̅ϣⲏⲣⲉ ⲙ̅ⲡⲉⲓⲱⲧ ⲉⲧⲟⲛϩ ⲉϣⲱⲡⲉ ⲇⲉ ⲧⲉⲧⲛⲁⲥⲟⲩⲱⲛ ⲧⲏⲩⲧⲛ̅ ⲁⲛ ⲉⲉⲓⲉ ⲧⲉⲧⲛ̅ϣⲟⲟⲡ ϩⲛ̅ ⲟⲩⲙⲛ̅ⲧϩⲏⲕⲉ ⲁⲩⲱ ⲛ̅ⲧⲱⲧⲛ̅ ⲡⲉ ⲧⲙⲛ̅ⲧϩⲏⲕⲉ.

GThom 3

Jesus said, "If your leaders say to you, 'Behold, the kingdom is in heaven,' then the birds of heaven will precede you. If they say to you, 'It is in the sea,' then the fish will precede you. Rather, the kingdom is inside you and it is outside you. When you know yourselves, then you will be known, and will understand that you are children of the living Father. But if you do not know yourselves, then you dwell in poverty, and you are the poverty."

GThom 113

ⲡⲉϫⲁⲩ ⲛⲁϥ ⲛ̅ϭⲓ ⲛⲉϥⲙⲁⲑⲏⲧⲏⲥ ϫⲉ ⲧⲙⲛ̅ⲧⲉⲣⲟ ⲉⲥⲛⲏⲩ ⲛ̅ⲁϣ ⲛ̅ϩⲟⲟⲩ ⟨ⲡⲉϫⲉ ⲓ̅ⲥ̅ ϫⲉ⟩ ⲉⲥⲛⲏⲩ ⲁⲛ ϩⲛ̅ ⲟⲩϭⲱϣⲧ ⲉⲃⲟⲗ· ⲉⲩⲛⲁϫⲟⲟⲥ ⲁⲛ ϫⲉ ⲉⲓⲥ ϩⲏⲏⲧⲉ ⲙ̅ⲡⲓⲥⲁ ⲏ ⲉⲓⲥ ϩⲏⲏⲧⲉ ⲧⲏ ⲁⲗⲗⲁ ⲧⲙⲛ̅ⲧⲉⲣⲟ ⲙ̅ⲡⲉⲓⲱⲧ ⲉⲥⲡⲟⲣϣ ⲉⲃⲟⲗ ϩⲓϫⲙ̅ ⲡⲕⲁϩ ⲁⲩⲱ ⲣ̅ⲣⲱⲙⲉ ⲛⲁⲩ ⲁⲛ ⲉⲣⲟⲥ.

GThom 113

His disciples said to him, "When will the kingdom come?" ⟨Jesus said,⟩ "It will not come by looking for it, nor will it do to say, 'Behold, over here!' or 'Behold, over there!' Rather, the kingdom of the Father is spread out on the earth, but people do not see it."

Matt 24:23–28, 37–42

[²³Τότε ἐάν τις ὑμῖν εἴπῃ· ἰδοὺ ὧδε ὁ χριστός, ἤ· ὧδε, μὴ πιστεύσητε. ²⁴ἐγερθήσονται γὰρ ψευδόχριστοι καὶ ψευδοπροφῆται καὶ δώσουσιν σημεῖα μεγάλα καὶ τέρατα ὥστε πλανῆσαι, εἰ δυνατόν, καὶ τοὺς ἐκλετούς. ²⁵ἰδοὺ προείρηκα ὑμῖν].
²⁶ἐὰν οὖν εἴπωσιν ὑμῖν· ἰδοὺ ἐν τῇ ἐρήμῳ ἐστίν, μὴ ἐξέλθητε· ἰδοὺ ἐν τοῖς ταμείοις, μὴ πιστεύσητε·
²⁷ ὥσπερ γὰρ ἡ ἀστραπὴ ἐξέρχεται ἀπὸ ἀνατολῶν καὶ φαίνεται ἕως δυσμῶν, οὕτως ἔσται ἡ παρουσία τοῦ υἱοῦ τοῦ ἀνθρώπου·

²⁸ὅπου ἐὰν ᾖ τὸ πτῶμα, ἐκεῖ συναχθήσονται οἱ ἀετοί.
³⁷ὥσπερ γὰρ αἱ ἡμέραι τοῦ Νῶε, οὕτως ἔσται ἡ παρουσία τοῦ υἱοῦ τοῦ ἀνθρώπου·
³⁸ὡς γὰρ ἦσαν ἐν ταῖς ἡμέραις [ἐκείναις] ταῖς πρὸ τοῦ κατακλυσμοῦ τρώγοντες καὶ πίνοντες, γαμοῦντες καὶ γαμίζοντες, ἄχρι ἧς ἡμέρας εἰσῆλθεν Νῶε εἰς τὴν κιβωτόν, ³⁹ καὶ οὐκ ἔγνωσαν ἕως ἦλθεν ὁ κατακλυσμὸς καὶ ἦρεν ἅπαντας,

οὕτως ἔσται [καὶ] ἡ παρουσία τοῦ υἱοῦ τοῦ ἀνθρώπου·

Continued on p. 192

Luke 17:22–37

[²²Εἶπεν δὲ πρὸς τοὺς μαθητάς· ἐλεύσονται ἡμέραι ὅτε ἐπιθυμήσετε μίαν τῶν ἡμερῶν τοῦ υἱοῦ τοῦ ἀνθρώπου ἰδεῖν καὶ οὐκ ὄψεσθε].

²³καὶ ἐροῦσιν ὑμῖν· ἰδοὺ ἐκεῖ, [ἤ] ἰδοὺ ὧδε· μὴ ἀπέλθητε μηδὲ διώξητε.
²⁴ὥσπερ γὰρ ἡ ἀστραπὴ ἀστράπτουσα ἐκ τῆς ὑπὸ τὸν οὐρανὸν εἰς τὴν ὑπ᾽ οὐρανὸν λάμπει, οὕτως ἔσται ὁ υἱὸς τοῦ ἀνθρώπου [ἐν τῇ ἡμέρᾳ αὐτοῦ].
[²⁵πρῶτον δὲ δεῖ αὐτὸν πολλὰ παθεῖν καὶ ἀποδοκιμασθῆναι ἀπὸ τῆς γενεᾶς ταύτης].
[³⁷ καὶ ἀποκριθέντες λέγουσιν αὐτῷ· ποῦ κύριε; ὁ δὲ εἶπεν αὐτοῖς·]
ὅπου τὸ σῶμα, ἐκεῖ καὶ οἱ ἀετοὶ ἐπισυναχθήσονται.
²⁶καὶ καθὼς ἐγένετο ἐν ταῖς ἡμέραις Νῶε, οὕτως ἔσται καὶ ἐν ταῖς ἡμέραις τοῦ υἱοῦ τοῦ ἀνθρώπου.

²⁷   ἤσθιον, ἔπινον, ἐγάμουν, ἐγαμίζοντο, ἄχρι ἧς ἡμέρας εἰσῆλθεν Νῶε εἰς τὴν κιβωτόν, καὶ ἦλθεν ὁ κατακλυσμὸς καὶ ἀπώλεσεν πάντας.
(²⁸ὁμοίως καθὼς ἐγένετο ἐν ταῖς ἡμέραις Λώτ· ἤσθιον, ἔπινον, ἠγόραζον, ἐπώλουν, ἐφύτευον, ᾠκοδόμουν· ²⁹ᾗ δὲ ἡμέρᾳ ἐξῆλθεν Λὼτ ἀπὸ Σοδόμων, ἔβρεξεν πῦρ καὶ θεῖον ἀπ᾽ οὐρανοῦ καὶ ἀπώλεσεν πάντας).
³⁰κατὰ τὰ αὐτὰ ἔσται ᾗ ἡμέρᾳ ὁ υἱὸς τοῦ ἀνθρώπου ἀποκαλύπτεται.

Matt 24:38: ημεραις του Νωε: 1424 / ημεραις: ℵ L W Koine Θ 067 0133 λ φ lat mae bo [HG] / ημεραις εκειναις: B D *pc* it sa [NA²⁵·²⁶] // γαμισκοντες: B *pc* / εκγαμισκοντες: W 1424 *pc* / εκγαμιζοντες: L Koine Θ 067 0133 λ [HG] / εγγαμιζοντες: Σ 047 φ 892 1241 *al* / γαμιζοντες: ℵ D 33 *pc* [NA²⁵·²⁶].

Luke 17:23 εκει ιδου ωδε: ℵ L *pc* (sys·c) [NA²⁵; HG] / ωδε, ιδου εκει: D K W 063 28 33 *al* lat (syᵖ) / ωδε η ιδου εκει: A R Koine Θ Ψ 0272 φ it vgᵐˢˢ syʰ / ωδε, μη διωξητε· η ιδου εκει ο Χριστος: λ / εκει η ιδου ωδε: 𝔭⁷⁵ B [NA²⁶] // 24: εν τη ημερα αυτου: ℵ A L R W Koine Θ Ψ λ φ lat sy bo [NA²⁵·²⁶; HG] / omit: 𝔭⁷⁵ B D 220 it sa.

Mark 13:21–23 ⇨ Matt 24:23–25

²¹Καὶ τότε ἐάν τις ὑμῖν εἴπῃ· ἴδε ὧδε ὁ χριστός, ἴδε ἐκεῖ, μὴ πιστεύετε· ²²ἐγερθήσονται γὰρ ψευδόχριστοι καὶ ψευδοπροφῆται καὶ δώσουσιν σημεῖα καὶ τέρατα πρὸς τὸ ἀποπλανᾶν, εἰ δυνατόν, τοὺς ἐκλετούς. ²³ὑμεῖς δὲ βλέπετε· προείρηκα ὑμῖν πάντα.

Mark 13:21–23

²¹ And then if any one says to you, 'Look, here is the Christ!' or 'Look, there he is!' do not believe it. ²² False Christs and false prophets will arise and produce signs and wonders, to lead astray, if possible, the elect. ²³ But you take heed; I have told you all things beforehand.

GThom 113

ⲡⲉⲭⲁⲩ ⲛⲁϥ ⲛ̄ϭⲓ ⲛⲉϥⲙⲁⲑⲏⲧⲏⲥ ϫⲉ ⲧⲙⲛ̄ⲧⲉⲣⲟ ⲉⲥⲛ̄ⲛⲏⲩ ⲛ̄ⲁϣ ⲛ̄ϩⲟⲟⲩ ⟨ⲡⲉϫⲉ ⲓ̅ⲥ̅ ϫⲉ⟩ ⲉⲥⲛ̄ⲛⲏⲩ ⲁⲛ ϩⲛ̄ ⲟⲩϭⲱϣⲧ ⲉⲃⲟⲗ· ⲉⲩⲛⲁϫⲟⲟⲥ ⲁⲛ ϫⲉ ⲉⲓⲥ ϩⲏⲏⲧⲉ ⲙ̄ⲡⲓⲥⲁ ⲏ ⲉⲓⲥ ϩⲏⲏⲧⲉ ⲧⲏ. ⲁⲗⲗⲁ ⲧⲙⲛ̄ⲧⲉⲣⲟ ⲙ̄ⲡⲉⲓⲱⲧ ⲉⲥⲡⲟⲣϣ ⲉⲃⲟⲗ ϩⲓϫⲙ̄ ⲡⲕⲁϩ ⲁⲩⲱ ⲣ̄ⲣⲱⲙⲉ ⲛⲁⲩ ⲁⲛ ⲉⲣⲟⲥ.

GThom 113

His disciples said to him, "When will the kingdom come?" ⟨Jesus said,⟩ "It will not come by looking for it, nor will it do to say, 'Behold, over here!' or 'Behold, over there!' Rather, the kingdom of the Father is spread out on the earth, but people do not see it."

GMary 8:15–22

ⲁⲣⲉϩ ⲙ̄ⲡⲣ̄ⲧⲣⲉⲗⲁⲁⲩ ⲣ̄ⲡⲗⲁⲛⲁ ⲙⲙⲱⲧⲛ̄ ⲉϥϫⲱ ⲙⲙⲟⲥ ϫⲉ ⲉⲓⲥ ϩⲏⲡⲉ ⲙ̄ⲡⲉⲓⲥⲁ ⲏ ⲉⲓⲥ ϩⲏⲡⲉ ⲙ̄ⲡⲉⲉⲓⲙⲁ. ⲡϣⲏⲣⲉ ⲅⲁⲣ ⲙ̄ⲡⲣⲱⲙⲉ ⲉϥϣⲟⲟⲡ ⲙ̄ⲡⲉⲧⲛ̄ϩⲟⲩⲛ ⲟⲩⲉϩⲧⲏⲩⲧⲛ̄ ⲛ̄ⲥⲱϥ ⲛⲉⲧϣⲓⲛⲉ ⲛ̄ⲥⲱϥ ⲥⲉⲛⲁϭⲛ̄ⲧϥ̄ ⲃⲱⲕ ϭⲉ ⲛ̄ⲧⲉⲧⲛ̄ⲧⲁϣⲉⲟⲉⲓ[ϣ] ⲙ̄ⲡⲉⲩⲁⲅⲅⲉⲗⲓⲟⲛ ⲛ̄ⲧⲙⲛ̄ⲧⲉⲣⲟ.

GMary 8:15–22

Beware that no one lead you astray, saying, 'Lo here!' or 'Lo there!' For the Son of Man is within you. Follow after him. Those who seek him will find him. Go then and preach the gospel of the kingdom.

Gen 7:6–7, 10–13 LXX

⁶Νωε δὲ ἦν ἐτῶν ἑξακοσίων, καὶ ὁ κατακλυσμὸς ἐγένετο ὕδατος ἐπὶ τῆς γῆς. ⁷εἰσῆλθεν δὲ Νωε . . . εἰς τὴν κιβωτὸν διὰ τὸ ὕδωρ τοῦ κατακλυσμοῦ. . . ¹⁰ καὶ ἐγένετο μετὰ τὰς ἑπτὰ ἡμέρας καὶ τὸ ὕδωρ τοῦ κατακλυσμοῦ ἐγένετο ἐπὶ τῆς γῆς. ¹¹ἐν τῷ ἑξακοσιοστῷ ἔτει ἐν τῇ ζωῇ τοῦ Νωε, τοῦ δευτέρου μηνός, ἑβδόμῃ καὶ εἰκάδι τοῦ μηνός, τῇ ἡμέρᾳ ταύτῃ ἐρράγησαν πᾶσαι αἱ πηγαὶ τῆς ἀβύσσου, καὶ οἱ καταρράκται τοῦ οὐρανοῦ ἠνεῴχθησαν, ¹²καὶ ἐγένετο ὁ ὑετὸς ἐπὶ τῆς γῆς τεσσαράκοντα ἡμέρας καὶ τερραράκοντα νύκτας. ¹³ἐν τῇ ἡμέρᾳ ταύτῃ εἰσῆλθεν Νωε . . . εἰς τὴν κιβωτόν.

Gen 7:6–7, 10–13 LXX

⁶Now Noah was six hundred years old when the flood of water came over the earth. ⁷Noah entered . . . into the ark because of the water of the flood . . . ¹⁰And after seven days the water of the flood came over the earth. ¹¹In the six hundreth year of Noah's life, the second month, the 27th day of the month, on this day all the fountains of the abyss let loose and the cataracts of heaven opened, ¹²and rain fell upon the earth for forty days and nights. ¹³On this day Noah . . . entered the ark.

Gen 19:23–26 LXX

²³ὁ ἥλιος ἐξῆλθεν ἐπὶ τὴν γῆν, καὶ Λωτ εἰσῆλθεν εἰς Σηγωρ, ²⁴καὶ κύριος ἔβρεξεν ἐπὶ Σοδομα καὶ Γομορρα θεῖον καὶ πῦρ παρὰ κυρίου ἐκ τοῦ οὐρανοῦ. ²⁵καὶ κατέστρεψεν τὰς πόλεις ταύτας καὶ πᾶσαν τὴν περίοικον καὶ πάντας τοὺς κατοικοῦντας ἐν ταῖς πόλεσιν καὶ πάντα τὰ ἀνατέλλοντα ἐκ τῆς γῆς. ²⁶καὶ ἐπέβλεψεν ἡ γυνὴ αὐτοῦ εἰς τὰ ὀπίσω καὶ ἐγένετο στήλη ἁλός.

Gen 19:23–26 LXX

²³The sun had rise on the earth and Lot entered Segor. ²⁴And the Lord rained down upon Sodom and Gomorrah brimstone and fire from the Lord out of heaven; ²⁵and he overthrew these cities and all the surrounding area and all those who dwelt in the cities and everything that grew on the ground. ²⁶And his wife looked back and became a stele or salt.

$[^{31}$ἐν ἐκείνῃ τῇ ἡμέρᾳ ὃς ἔσται ἐπὶ τοῦ δώματος καὶ τὰ σκεύη αὐτοῦ ἐν τῇ οἰκίᾳ, μὴ καταβάτω ἆραι αὐτά, καὶ ὁ ἐν ἀγρῷ ὁμοίως μὴ ἐπιστρεψάτω εἰς τὰ ὀπίσω.]

$[^{32}$μνημονεύετε τῆς γυναικὸς Λώτ.]

^{33}ὃς ἐὰν ζητήσῃ τὴν ψυχὴν αὐτοῦ περιποιήσασθαι ἀπολέσει αὐτήν, ὃς δ᾽ ἂν ἀπολέσῃ, ζῳογονήσει αὐτήν.

^{34}λέγω ὑμῖν, ταύτῃ τῇ νυκτὶ **ἔσονται δύο** ἐπὶ κλίνης μιᾶς, ὁ **εἷς παραλημφθήσεται καὶ** ὁ ἕτερος ἀφεθήσεται·

^{35}ἔσονται **δύο ἀλήθουσαι** ἐπὶ τὸ αὐτό, ἡ μία **παραλημφθήσεται ἡ δὲ ἑτέρα ἀφεθήσεται.**

⇨ Q 14:26–27; 17:33 [S56]

40 τότε **δύο ἔσονται** ἐν τῷ ἀγρῷ, **εἷς παραλαμβάνεται καὶ εἷς ἀφίεται·**

^{41}**δύο ἀλήθουσαι** ἐν τῷ μύλῳ, **μία παραλαμβάνεται καὶ μία ἀφίεται·**

$[^{42}$γρηγορεῖτε οὖν, ὅτι οὐκ οἴδατε ποίᾳ ἡμέρᾳ ὁ κύριος ὑμῶν ἔρχεται].

$[^{37}$καὶ ἀποκριθέντες λέγουσιν αὐτῷ· ποῦ κύριε; ὁ δὲ εἶπεν αὐτοῖς·]

ὅπου τὸ σῶμα, ἐκεῖ καὶ οἱ ἀετοὶ ἐπισυναχθήσονται.

^{28}**ὅπου** ἐὰν ᾖ **τὸ πτῶμα, ἐκεῖ συναχθήσονται οἱ ἀετοί.**

Matt 24:40: εσονται δυο (Luke): ℵ* B 892 *pc* aur h-l r¹ [NA²⁵] / δυο εσονται: ℵ² D L W Koine Θ 067 λ φ lat [NA²⁶; HG].

Luke 17:33: και ος² (ε)αν: A (D) R W Koine Θ 063 λ sa [NA²⁵; HG] / ος δ᾽ αν (Mark 8:35): 𝔭⁷⁵ ℵ B L Ψ 579 892

pc bo [NA²⁶] / και ος δ᾽ αν: φ // απολεσει²: A L N R Γ Δ 063 1010 *al* [NA²⁵] / απολεση: B D W Koine Θ Ψ λ φ [NA²⁶; HG].

Luke 17:36: δυο εσονται εν τω αγρω· εις παραλημφθησεται και ο ετερος αφεθησεται (Matt): (D) φ 700 *al* lat sy / omit: *rell*; [NA²⁵·²⁶; HG].

Notes

Q 17:23–24, 26–27, 30, 34–35, 37b

In Q: Most authors. Hawkins (1911: 111) and Lührmann (72) assert that the Markan parallel makes a non-Markan source for 17:23 doubtful. Harnack (106–107) excludes 17:30.

[Luke 17:22]

In Q: Crossan 1983: 178, 203, 345. Easton Lk 264; Hunter 145; Kümmel 1957: 29; Marshall Lk 659 (hesitantly); Polag 76–77, 90–91; Schnackenburg 1971: 228–29; Schürmann 1968: 222 (but see idem, 1975: 139 n. 82).

Easton suggests that Matthew omitted v. 22 because it did not fit his context in chap. 24. Both Polag and Schnackenburg concede that the verse is redactional, but posit a Q text lying behind v. 22. Polag conjectures εἶπεν δὲ τοῖς μαθηταῖς αὐτοῦ· as the original introduction. Schnackenburg argues that the phrase ἐλεύσονται ἡμέραι, which is an Old Testament locution (Amos 4:2; 8:11; 9:13; Jer 7:32; 9:24; 16:14, etc.), derives from a transitional phrase in Q which connected 17:20b–21 (⇨ [S65]) and Q 17:23.

Not in Q (Lukan): Bultmann 1963: 130; Creed Lk 220;

Fitzmyer Lk 1164; Grundmann Lk 342; Hoffmann; Kloppenborg 1987: 154–55; Klostermann Lk 175; Laufen 1980: 362; Lührmann 72; Müller 1908: 55; Schenk; Schulz 278; Schürmann 1975: 139 n. 82; Zmijewski 1972: 398–403, 417–19.

[Luke 17:25]

In Q: Bussmann 92–93: Matthew omitted the saying in the course of his rearrangement of Q and his insertion of Markan material into Matt 24. Hunter 145; Manson 142–43; Schmid 335 n. 2 (with hesitations); Weiss 1907: 86.

Not in Q (Lukan): Most authors, although Marshall (Lk 661–62) expresses hesitations on excluding the verse: the view of Manson, Weiss and Bussmann deserves "more consideration than it usually receives."

(Q 17:28–29)

In Q: Crossan 1983: 176–79, 203, 345; Easton Lk 265; Grundmann Lk 342; Hunter 145; Kloppenborg 1987: 157; Klostermann Lk 175–76; Manson 143; Marshall Lk 662; Polag 78; Rigaux 1970: 422; Schenk 122; Schmid 338; Schmithals Lk 175, 177 (hesitantly); Schnackenburg

Mark 13:15–16 ⇨ Luke 17:31–32
¹⁵ὁ [δὲ] ἐπὶ τοῦ δώματος μὴ καταβάτω μηδὲ εἰσελθάτω
ἆραί τι ἐκ τῆς οἰκίας αὐτοῦ, ¹⁶ καὶ ὁ εἰς τὸν ἀγρὸν μὴ
ἐπιστρεψάτω εἰς τὰ ὀπίσω ἆραι τὸ ἱμάτιον αὐτοῦ.

Matt 24:17–18
¹⁷ὁ ἐπὶ τοῦ δώματος μὴ καταβάτω ἆραι τὰ ἐκ τῆς οἰκίας
αὐτοῦ, ¹⁸καὶ ὁ ἐν τῷ ἀγρῷ μὴ ἐπιστρεψάτω ὀπίσω ἆραι
τὸ ἱμάτιον αὐτοῦ.

GThom 61a
ⲡⲉϫⲉ ⲓ̅ⲥ̅ ⲟⲩⲛ̄ ⲥⲛⲁⲩ ⲛⲁⲙⲧⲟⲛ ⲙ̄ⲙⲁⲩ ϩⲓ ⲟⲩϭⲗⲟϭ
ⲡⲟⲩⲁ ⲛⲁⲙⲟⲩ ⲡⲟⲩⲁ ⲛⲁⲱⲛϩ.

Job 39:27–30 LXX ⇨ Q 17:37b
²⁷ἐπὶ δὲ σῷ προστάγματι ὑψοῦται ἀετός, γὺψ δὲ ἐπὶ
νοσσιᾶς αὐτοῦ καθεσθεὶς αὐλίζεται ²⁸ἐπ' ἐξοχῇ πέτρας
καὶ ἀποκρύφῳ; ²⁹ἐκεῖσε ὢν ζητεῖ τὰ σῖτα, πόρρωθεν οἱ
ὀφθαλμοὶ αὐτοῦ σκοπεύουσιν· ³⁰ νεοσσοὶ δὲ αὐτοῦ
φύρονται ἐν αἵματι, οὗ δ' ἂν ὦσι τεθνεῶτες, παραχρῆμα
εὑρίσκονται.

Mark 13:15–16
¹⁵Let anyone on the housetop not go down, nor enter to
remove anything from his house; ¹⁶and whoever is in the
field should not go back to get his cloak.

Matt 24:17–18
¹⁷Let anyone on the housetop not go down to remove
possessions from his house; ¹⁸and whoever is in the field
should not go back to get his cloak.

GThom 61a
Jesus said, "Two will rest on a couch: one will die, one
will live."

Job 39:27–30 LXX
²⁷Is it at your command that the eagle mounts up, and
sitting upon its nest the vulture spends its time, ²⁸on high
and hidden crags? ²⁹From there he seeks his food, at a
great distance his eyes observe; ³⁰its young are stained
with blood, and wherever there are dead, they are
immediately found.

1971: 231; Schneider Lk 356; Schürmann 1975: 139; Weiss 1907: 86; Zeller 89 (undecided).

The main arguments for the inclusion of these verses are: (1) It is not typical of Lukan redaction to create such expansions and easier to explain Matthew's omission than Luke's addition (Weiss; Easton; Rigaux). (2) Q elsewhere employs double illustrations (Easton; Schnackenburg). (3) Luke preserves the "poetic form" of the passage (Manson). (4) Luke's redactional interest lies not in vv. 28–29 but in vv. 31–32. A reference to Gen 19 in his source occasioned his insertion of vv. 31–32 (Kloppenborg). (5) Matthew's omission may be explained as a result of his change of focus from the unexpectedness of the end to humanity's ignorance of it (Weiss; Schmid) or as a result of his rearrangement of chap. 24 (Schnackenburg; Schneider), or as a result of his concern for brevity (Manson).

The lack of evidence of a Lukan creation, coupled with resistance to the idea that Matthew would have omitted the saying had he seen it in Q has led some to posit a Q^{Lk} version: Bultmann 1963: 117; Geiger 1973: 92–94; Lührmann 72–74, 82–83; Sato 1984:66; Schulz 278, 280 (possibly); Steinhauser 1981: 209–10; Tödt 1965: 49, 51.

Not in Q: Creed Lk 221; Fitzmyer Lk 1165: vv. 28–32 derive from L. Harnack; Hawkins 1911: 115; Hoffmann; Meyer 51; Müller 1908: 8, 19, 55; Schulz 278, 280 (possibly); Zeller 89 (undecided); Zmijewski 1972: 452–57 (with hesitations).

[Luke 17:31–32]
In Q: Crossan 1983: 92, 178 (v. 31 is possibly in Q); Grundmann Lk 342; Hunter 145; Lambrecht 1966: 342–46; idem 1967: 157–59; Manson 144; Marshall Lk 664; Polag 78.

Manson and Marshall note the artificiality of the verses and argue that Luke would not have added such inappropriate material. Lambrecht notes some minor agreements against Mark: the use of a plural object of $\dot{\alpha}\rho\alpha\iota$ and the common omission of $\mu\eta\delta\grave{\epsilon}$ $\epsilon\dot{\iota}\sigma\epsilon\lambda\theta\acute{\alpha}\tau\omega$ (Mark 13:15).

Not in Q: Bultmann 1963: 117; Easton Lk 265; Fitzmyer Lk 1165 (from L, not Mark); Harnack; Kloppenborg 1987: 158; Klosterman Lk 176; Lührmann 72; Meyer 51; Müller 1908: 55; Schenk; Schmid Lk 277; Schmithals Lk 177; Schnackenburg 1971: 231–32; Schulz 278; Weiss 1907: 86–87; Zeller 90; Zmijewski 1972: 473–78.

Those who exclude vv. 31–32 normally argue that they are based on Mark 13:15–16. The insertion was created for homiletic purposes and owes its place to vv. 28–29, not *vice versa* (Easton) or to the catchwords "in the day[s]" (Fitzmyer).

Q 17:33
Placement: ⇨ [S56]

[Luke 17:36] ⇨ Textual notes
Manson (146) argues that the omission of v. 36 was due to a scribe who thought the verse inappropriate to the context. Most authors exclude the verse from Luke (and hence from Q) on textual grounds.

[Q 17:37a]
In Q: Hunter 146; Manson 147; Polag 90 (uncertain); Schmid 336. Since both Manson and Schmid hold that the Lukan placement of 17:37b is original, they argue that Matthew dropped the introduction when he relocated it.

Not in Q: Bultmann 1963: 335–36; Bussmann 94; Easton Lk 266; Fitzmyer Lk 1165; Grundmann Lk 342; Lührmann 72; Kloppenborg 1987: 156; Marshall Lk 669; Meyer 51; Müller 1908: 14; Schenk 120; Schmithals Lk 178; Schulz 280 and n. 122; Steinhauser 1981: 302.

Q 17:37b
The main difficulty associated with this verse is its placement. In favor of Matthean order: Easton Lk 265; Fitzmyer Lk 1165, 1173; Geiger 1973: 73; Harnack 105, 270; Hoffmann 1969: 136; Laufen 1980: 370; Lührmann 72; Marshall Lk 668–69; Meyer 51; Polag 76; Schenk 120; Schmithals Lk 178; Schulz 280; Tödt 1965: 48; Zeller 89; Zmijewski 1972: 506–10. The arguments advanced in support of Matthew include: (1) Both Q 17:24 and 17:37b concern visible heavenly phenomena and thus belong together as a double-saying (Geiger; Lührmann; Schulz) (2). Luke displaced the verse when he inserted Luke 17:25 (Easton; Tödt) or transferred it so that it would serve as a climax (Easton; Fitzmyer) or moved it to eliminate the infelicitous association of the Son of Man and the eagle saying (Schulz; Tödt).

Others favor the Lukan location: Bussmann 94; Manson 147; Sato 1984: 50; Schmid 336; Schnackenburg 1971: 233–34; Schürmann 1975: 139; Steinhauser 1981: 302; Taylor 1972: 113 (with hesitations); Weiss 1907: 88. Bussmann's conclusion is predicated on his ascription of 17:25 to Q. Schmid argues that Matthew's placement is the more difficult and hence secondary but Taylor thinks that Matthew's order is smoother, and secondary to the "roughness of Luke's enigmatic form." Steinhauser points out that although Luke frequently animates his account with introductory questions (e.g., 17:37a), he does so without disturbing the relative order of his sources.

Matt 24:23–28, 37–42

[²³ Then if any one says to you, 'Lo, here is the Christ!' or 'There he is!' do not believe it. ²⁴ For false Christs and false prophets will arise and perform great signs and wonders, so as to lead astray, if possible, even the elect. ²⁵ Behold, I have told you beforehand.]
²⁶ So, if they say to you, 'Behold, he is in the wilderness,' do not go out there; if they say, 'Behold, he is in the secret chambers, do not believe it. ²⁷ For as the lightning comes from the east and flashes to the west, so will be the coming of the Son of man.

²⁸ Wherever the corpse is, there the eagles will be gathered.

³⁷ For as were the days of Noah, so will be the coming of the Son of man. ³⁸ For just as in those days before the flood they were eating and drinking, marrying and being married, up to the day when Noah entered the ark, ³⁹ and they did not know until the flood came and took them all,

so also will be the coming of the Son of man.

⁴⁰ Then two men will be in the field; one is taken and one is left. ⁴¹ Two women will be grinding at the mill; one is taken and one is left.

[⁴² Watch therefore, for you do not know on what day your Lord is coming.]
²⁸ Wherever the corpse is, there the eagles will be gathered.

Luke 17:22–37

[²² And he said to the disciples, "The days are coming when you will long to see one of the days of the Son of man, and you will not see it.]

²³ And they will say to you, 'Lo, there!' or 'Lo, here!' Do not go, do not follow them. ²⁴ For as lightning flashes and lights up the sky from one side to the other, so will the Son of man be in his day.

[²⁵ But first he must suffer many things and be rejected by this generation.]
[³⁷ And they said to him, "Where, Lord?" He said to them,]
"Where the body is, there the eagles will be gathered together."
²⁶ And as it was in the days of Noah, so will it be in the days of the Son of man. ²⁷ They ate, they drank, they married, they were being married, up to the day when Noah entered the ark, and the flood came and destroyed them all.
(²⁸ Likewise as it was in the days of Lot—they ate, they drank, they bought, they sold, they planted, they built, ²⁹ but on the day when Lot left Sodom fire and sulphur rained from heaven and destroyed them all—)
³⁰ so will it be on the day when the Son of man is revealed.
[³¹ On that day, let whoever is on the housetop, with his goods in the house, not come down to remove them; and whoever is in the field should not go back.]
[³² Remember Lot's wife.]
³³ Whoever seeks to gain his life will lose it, but whoever loses his life will keep it.
³⁴ I tell you, in that night there will be two in one bed; the one will be taken and the other left. ³⁵ There will be two women grinding together; the one will be taken and the other left."
[³⁷ And they said to him, "Where, Lord?" He said to them,]
"Where the body is, there the eagles will be gathered together."

Matt 25:14–30

¹⁴Ὥσπερ γὰρ **ἄνθρωπος** ἀποδημῶν ἐκάλεσεν τοὺς ἰδίους **δούλους** καὶ παρέδωκεν αὐτοῖς τὰ ὑπάρχοντα αὐτοῦ, ¹⁵καὶ ᾧ μὲν **ἔδωκεν** πέντε τάλαντα, ᾧ δὲ δύο, ᾧ δὲ ἕν, ἑκάστῳ κατὰ τὴν ἰδίαν δύναμιν, καὶ ἀπεδήμησεν.

εὐθέως ¹⁶πορευθεὶς ὁ τὰ πέντε τάλαντα λαβὼν ἠργάσατο ἐν αὐτοῖς καὶ ἐκέρδησεν ἄλλα πέντε· ¹⁷ ὡσαύτως ὁ τὰ δύο ἐκέρδησεν ἄλλα δύο. ¹⁸ὁ δὲ τὸ ἓν λαβὼν ἀπελθὼν ὤρυξεν γῆν καὶ ἔκρυψεν τὸ ἀργύριον τοῦ κυρίου αὐτοῦ.
¹⁹μετὰ δὲ πολὺν χρόνον ἔρχεται ὁ κύριος τῶν δούλων ἐκείνων καὶ συναίρει λόγον μετ' αὐτῶν.
²⁰καὶ προσελθὼν ὁ τὰ πέντε τάλαντα λαβὼν προσήνεγκεν ἄλλα πέντε τάλαντα **λέγων· κύριε**, πέντε τάλαντά μοι παρέδωκας· ἴδε ἄλλα πέντε τάλαντα ἐκέρδησα. ²¹ἔφη **αὐτῷ** ὁ κύριος αὐτοῦ· εὖ, **δοῦλε ἀγαθὲ** καὶ πιστέ, ἐπὶ ὀλίγα ἦς **πιστός**, ἐπὶ πολλῶν σε καταστήσω· εἴσελθε εἰς τὴν χαρὰν τοῦ κυρίου σου.
²²προσελθὼν [δὲ] **καὶ** ὁ τὰ δύο τάλαντα εἶπεν· **κύριε**, δύο τάλαντά μοι παρέδωκας· ἴδε ἄλλα δύο τάλαντα ἐκέρδησα. ²³ἔφη αὐτῷ ὁ κύριος αὐτοῦ· εὖ, δοῦλε ἀγαθὲ καὶ πιστέ, ἐπὶ ὀλίγα ἦς πιστός, ἐπὶ πολλῶν σε καταστήσω· εἴσελθε εἰς τὴν χαρὰν τοῦ κυρίου σου.
²⁴προσελθὼν δὲ **καὶ** ὁ τὸ ἓν τάλαντον εἰληφὼς εἶπεν· **κύριε, ἔγνων σε ὅτι σκληρὸς εἶ ἄνθρωπος**, θερίζων ὅπου **οὐκ ἔσπειρας καὶ** συνάγων ὅθεν **οὐ** διεσκόρπισας, ²⁵καὶ **φοβηθεὶς** ἀπελθὼν ἔκρυψα τὸ τάλαντόν σου ἐν τῇ γῇ· ἴδε ἔχεις τὸ σόν.
²⁶ἀποκριθεὶς δὲ ὁ κύριος αὐτοῦ εἶπεν **αὐτῷ· πονηρέ δοῦλε** καὶ ὀκνηρέ,
ᾔδεις ὅτι θερίζω ὅπου **οὐκ ἔσπειρα καὶ** συνάγω ὅθεν οὐ διεσκόρπισα; ²⁷ἔδει σε οὖν βαλεῖν τὰ ἀργύριά μου τοῖς τραπεζίταις, καὶ **ἐλθὼν ἐγὼ** ἐκομισάμην **ἂν** τὸ ἐμὸν **σὺν τόκῳ.**

Luke 19:11–27

[¹¹Ἀκουόντων δὲ αὐτῶν ταῦτα προσθεὶς εἶπεν παραβολὴν διὰ τὸ ἐγγὺς εἶναι Ἰερουσαλὴμ αὐτὸν καὶ δοκεῖν αὐτοὺς ὅτι παραχρῆμα μέλλει ἡ βασιλεία τοῦ θεοῦ ἀναφαίνεσθαι].
¹²εἶπεν οὖν· **ἄνθρωπός** τις εὐγενὴς ἐπορεύθη εἰς χώραν μακρὰν λαβεῖν ἑαυτῷ βασιλείαν καὶ ὑποστρέψαι.
¹³καλέσας δὲ δέκα **δούλους** ἑαυτοῦ **ἔδωκεν** αὐτοῖς δέκα μνᾶς καὶ εἶπεν πρὸς αὐτούς· πραγματεύσασθε ἐν ᾧ ἔρχομαι.

[¹⁴οἱ δὲ πολῖται αὐτοῦ ἐμίσουν αὐτὸν καὶ ἀπέστειλαν πρεσβείαν ὀπίσω αὐτοῦ λέγοντες· οὐ θέλομεν τοῦτον βασιλεῦσαι ἐφ' ἡμᾶς. ¹⁵καὶ ἐγένετο ἐν τῷ ἐπανελθεῖν αὐτὸν λαβόντα τὴν βασιλείαν]

καὶ εἶπεν φωνηθῆναι αὐτῷ τοὺς δούλους τούτους οἷς δεδώκει τὸ ἀργύριον, ἵνα γνοῖ τί διεπραγματεύσαντο.
¹⁶παρεγένετο δὲ ὁ πρῶτος **λέγων· κύριε**, ἡ μνᾶ σου δέκα προσηργάσατο μνᾶς.

¹⁷ καὶ εἶπεν **αὐτῷ· εὖγε, ἀγαθὲ δοῦλε**, ὅτι ἐν ἐλαχίστῳ **πιστὸς** ἐγένου, ἴσθι ἐξουσίαν ἔχων ἐπάνω δέκα πόλεων.
¹⁸**καὶ** ἦλθεν ὁ δεύτερος λέγων· ἡ μνᾶ σου, **κύριε**, ἐποίησεν πέντε μνᾶς.
¹⁹εἶπεν δὲ καὶ τούτῳ· καὶ σὺ ἐπάνω γίνου πέντε πόλεων.

²⁰**καὶ** ὁ ἕτερος ἦλθεν λέγων· **κύριε**, ἰδοὺ ἡ μνᾶ σου ἣν εἶχον ἀποκειμένην ἐν σουδαρίῳ· ²¹ἐφοβούμην γάρ σε, ὅτι **ἄνθρωπος** αὐστηρὸς **εἶ**, αἴρεις ὃ **οὐκ ἔθηκας, καὶ θερίζεις ὃ οὐκ ἔσπειρας.**

²²λέγει **αὐτῷ·**
ἐκ τοῦ στόματός σου κρινῶ σε, **πονηρὲ δοῦλε**.
ᾔδεις ὅτι ἐγὼ ἄνθρωπος αὐστηρός εἰμι, αἴρων ὃ **οὐκ ἔθηκα, καὶ θερίζων ὃ οὐκ ἔσπειρα.**
²³καὶ διὰ τί **οὐκ ἔδωκάς μου** τὸ ἀργύριον ἐπὶ τράπεζαν; **κἀγὼ ἐλθὼν** **σὺν τόκῳ ἂν** αὐτὸ ἔπραξα.

Mark 13:34

³⁴῾Ως ἄνθρωπος ἀπόδημος ἀφεὶς τὴν οἰκίαν αὐτοῦ καὶ δοὺς τοῖς δούλοις αὐτοῦ τὴν ἐξουσίαν ἑκάστῳ τὸ ἔργον αὐτοῦ καὶ τῷ θυρωρῷ ἐνετείλατο ἵνα γρηγορῇ.

Matt 24:45–47 ⇨ Q 12:42–46 [S45]

⁴⁵Τίς ἄρα ἐστὶν ὁ πιστὸς δοῦλος καὶ φρόνιμος ὃν κατέστησεν ὁ κύριος ἐπὶ τῆς οἰκετείας αὐτοῦ τοῦ δοῦναι αὐτοῖς τὴν τροφὴν ἐν καιρῷ; ⁴⁶μακάριος ὁ δοῦλος ἐκεῖνος ὃν ἐλθὼν ὁ κύριος αὐτοῦ εὑρήσει οὕτως ποιοῦντα· ⁴⁷ἀμὴν λέγω ὑμῖν ὅτι ἐπὶ πᾶσιν τοῖς ὑπάρχουσιν αὐτοῦ καταστήσει αὐτόν.

Luke 12:42b–44 ⇨ Q 12:42–46 [S45]

⁴². . . τίς ἄρα ἐστὶν ὁ πιστὸς οἰκονόμος ὁ φρόνιμος, ὃν καταστήσει ὁ κύριος ἐπὶ τῆς θεραπείας αὐτοῦ τοῦ διδόναι ἐν καιρῷ [τὸ] σιτομέτριον; ⁴³μακάριος ὁ δοῦλος ἐκεῖνος, ὃν ἐλθὼν ὁ κύριος αὐτοῦ εὑρήσει ποιοῦντα οὕτως· ⁴⁴ἀληθῶς λέγω ὑμῖν ὅτι ἐπὶ πᾶσιν τοῖς ὑπάρχουσιν αὐτοῦ καταστήσει αὐτόν.

GNaz 18

᾽Επεὶ δὲ τὸ εἰς ἡμᾶς ἧκον ῾Εβραϊκοῖς χαρακτῆρσιν εὐαγγέλιον τὴν ἀπειλὴν οὐ κατὰ τοῦ ἀποκρύψαντος ἐπῆγεν, ἀλλὰ κατὰ τοῦ ἀσώτως ἐζηκότος· τρεῖς γὰρ δούλους περιεῖχε, τὸν μὲν καταφαγόντα τὴν ὕπαρξιν τοῦ δεσπότου μετὰ πορνῶν καὶ αὐλητρίδων, τὸν δὲ πολλαπλασιάσαντα τὴν ἐργασίαν, τὸν δὲ κατακρύψαντα τὸ τάλαντον· εἶτα τὸν μὲν ἀποδεχθῆναι, τὸν δὲ μεμφθῆναι μόνον, τὸν δὲ συγκλεισθῆναι δεσμωτηρίῳ ἐφίστημι, μήποτε κατὰ τὸν Ματθαῖον μετὰ τὴν συμπλήρωσιν τοῦ λόγου τοῦ κατὰ τοῦ μηδὲν ἐργασαμένου ἢ ἑξῆς ἐπιλεγομένη ἀπειλὴ οὐ περὶ αὐτοῦ, ἀλλὰ περὶ τοῦ προτέρου κατ᾽ ἐπανάληψιν λέλεκται, τοῦ ἐσθίοντος καὶ πίνοντος μετὰ τῶν μεθυόντων.

2 Clem 8:5

⁵λέγει γὰρ ὁ κύριος ἐν τῷ εὐαγγελίῳ· εἰ τὸ μικρὸν οὐκ ἐτηρήσατε, τὸ μέγα τίς ὑμῖν δώσει; λέγω γὰρ ὑμῖν, ὅτι ὁ πιστὸς ἐν ἐλαχίστῳ καὶ ἐν πολλῷ πιστός ἐστιν.

Mark 13:34

³⁴It is like a man going on a journey, when he leaves home and places his servants in charge, each with his own work, and orders the doorkeeper to be on watch.

Matt 24:45–47

⁴⁵Who then is the faithful and wise servant, whom his master has put in charge of his household, to give them their meals on time? ⁴⁶Blessed is that servant whom his master when he comes will find so doing. ⁴⁷Amen, I tell you, he will put him in charge of all his possessions.

Luke 12:42b–44

⁴². . . Who then is the faithful and wise steward, whom his master will put in charge of his household staff, to give them their food allowance on time? ⁴³Blessed is that servant whom his master when he comes will find so doing. ⁴⁴Truly, I tell you, he will put him in charge of all his possessions.

GNaz 18

But since the Gospel [written] in Hebrew characters which has come into our hands enters the threat not against the man who had hid [the talent], but against him who had lived dissolutely — for he [the master] had three servants: one who squandered his master's substance with harlots and flute-girls, one who multiplied the gain, and one who hid the talent; and accordingly one was accepted [with joy], another merely rebuked, and another cast into prison — I wonder whether in Matthew the threat which is uttered after the word against the man who did nothing may refer not to him, but by epanalepsis to the first who had feasted and drunk with the drunken.

2 Clem 8:5

⁵For the Lord says in the gospel, "If ye did not guard that which is small, who shall give you that which is great? For I tell you that he who is faithful in that which is least, is faithful also in that which is much."

²⁸ἄρατε οὖν ἀπ᾽ αὐτοῦ τὸ τάλαντον
καὶ δότε τῷ ἔχοντι τὰ δέκα τάλαντα·

²⁹τῷ γὰρ ἔχοντι παντὶ δοθήσεται καὶ
περισσευθήσεται, τοῦ δὲ μὴ ἔχοντος καὶ ὃ
ἔχει ἀρθήσεται ἀπ᾽ αὐτοῦ.

[³⁰καὶ τὸν ἀρχεῖον δοῦλον ἐκβάλετε εἰς τὸ σκότος τὸ
ἐξώτερον· ἐκεῖ ἔσται ὁ κλαυθμὸς καὶ ὁ βρυγμὸς τῶν
ὀδόντων].

[²⁴καὶ τοῖς παρεστῶσιν εἶπεν·]
ἄρατε   ἀπ᾽ αὐτοῦ τὴν μνᾶν
καὶ δότε τῷ τὰς δέκα μνᾶς ἔχοντι
— ²⁵καὶ εἶπαν αὐτῷ· κύριε, ἔχει δέκα μνᾶς
— ²⁶λέγω ὑμῖν ὅτι
παντὶ τῷ ἔχοντι δοθήσεται,
                    ἀπὸ δὲ τοῦ μὴ ἔχοντος καὶ ὃ
ἔχει ἀρθήσεται.
[²⁷πλὴν τοὺς ἐχθρούς μου τούτους τοὺς μὴ
θελήσαντάς με βασιλεῦσαι ἐπ᾽ αὐτοὺς ἀγάγετε ὧδε
καὶ κατασφάξατε αὐτοὺς ἔμπροσθέν μου].

τράπεζα ⇨ Luke 19:23 [S68]

Matt 25:22: προσελθων: 𝔭³⁵ ℵ* B *pc* sa [NA²⁵] /
προσελθων δε: ℵ² A C D L W Koine Θ 074 0133 λ φ 1 vg
sy^h mae bo [NA²⁶; HG].

Luke 19:15: τις τι διεπραγματευσατο: A (R W) Koine Θ
047 063 0272 λ φ lat sy^p.h [NA²⁵; HG] / τι
διεπραγματευσαντο: ℵ B D L Ψ 579 e sy^s.c sa bo [NA²⁶] //
26: append απ αυτου (Matt): ℵ² A D R W Koine Θ Ψ 063
λ φ [HG] / txt: ℵ* B K L 1241 *pc* sa bo; Mcion [NA²⁵.²⁶].

GThom 41

ⲡⲉϫⲉ ⲓ̅ⲥ̅ ϫⲉ ⲡⲉⲧⲉⲩⲛ̅ⲧⲁϥ ϩⲛ̅ ⲧⲉϥϭⲓϫ ⲥⲉⲛⲁϯ ⲛⲁϥ ⲁⲩⲱ ⲡⲉⲧⲉ ⲙⲛ̅ⲧⲁϥ ⲡⲕⲉϣⲏⲙ ⲉⲧⲟⲩⲛ̅ⲧⲁϥ ⲥⲉⲛⲁϥⲓⲧϥ̅ ⲛ̅ⲧⲟⲟⲧϥ.

Mark 4:25

²⁵ὃς γὰρ ἔχει, δοθήσεται αὐτῷ·
          καὶ ὃς οὐκ ἔχει, καὶ ὃ ἔχει
ἀρθήσεται ἀπ' αὐτοῦ.

Matt 13:12

¹²ὅστις γὰρ ἔχει, δοθήσεται αὐτῷ καὶ
περισσευθήσεται· ὅστις δὲ οὐκ ἔχει, καὶ ὃ ἔχει
ἀρθήσεται ἀπ' αὐτοῦ.

Luke 8:18b

¹⁸. . . ὃς ἂν γὰρ ἔχῃ, δοθήσεται αὐτῷ·
          καὶ ὃς ἂν μὴ ἔχῃ, καὶ ὃ δοκεῖ ἔχειν
ἀρθήσεται ἀπ' αὐτοῦ.

GThom 41

Jesus said, "Whoever has something in hand will be given more, and whoever has nothing will be deprived of even the little that person has."

Mark 4:25

²⁵ For the one who has will be given more; and from the one who has not, even what he has will be taken away.

Matt 13:12

¹² For the one who has will be given more, and he will have abundance; but from the one who has not, even what he has will be taken away.

Luke 8:18b

¹⁸ . . . for whoever has will be given more, and from the one who has not, even what he thinks that he has will be taken away.

Q 19:12–13, 15b–25

The substantial disagreements between Matthew and Luke, as well as the somewhat different narrative lines, account for serious source critical disputes. If the parable derived from Q, then either Matthew or Luke (or both) redacted it rather substantially. It is usual to argue that Luke 19:12, 14–15a, 24a, 27 betray a secondary development due either to Lukan allegorizing or to the insertion of a second parable having to do with a throne claimant, and perhaps echoing Josephus' account of Archelaus (*Bell.* 2.80–100; *Ant.* 17.299–320). As Schmid (342–43) points out, it is unlikely that Matthew would have omitted this material had he known it. This additional material may derive from pre–Lukan tradition (Easton Lk 282; Harnack 126; Marshall Lk 701–702) or it might derive from Luke's hand (Bultmann 1963: 176; Creed Lk 232; Fitzmyer Lk 1231; Klostermann Lk 186; Lührmann 70–71; Manson 313 [with hesitations]; Schenk 126–27; Schmithals Lk 187; Schulz 288).

In Q: Bussmann 98–100, 111; Crossan 1983: 197–202, 203, 345; Easton Lk 282–84; Edwards 1976: 142–44; Fitzmyer Lk 79, 1230–31; Hawkins 1911: 117 (with considerable probability); Hoffmann 5, 42, 48–49; Kilpatrick 1946: 32; Klostermann Lk 186 (probably); Lührmann 70–71. Marshall (Lk 701–702) argues that Matthew and Luke depend upon two different recensions of Q. Meyer 58–61; Müller 1908: 9, 56 (hesitantly); Polag 80 (conjectural); Schenk 125–26; Schmithals Lk 186–87; Schulz 288–98; Schürmann 1982: 125, 131. Streeter 1911b: 188; idem, 1924: 282–83: Matthew's account is a conflation of Q and M (a version similar to that of *GNaz* 18), while Luke reproduces Q. Weiss 1907: 269–70: Luke's version is from L and Matthew takes his from Q. Wernle 1899: 91; Zeller 83.

Not in Q: The relatively slight degree of verbal agreement is most often cited as the reason for excluding the pericope from Q. Thus Grundmann Lk 14; Harnack 122–26; Hunter 164, 183. Klostermann Mt 201 (but see above); Knox 1957: 45, 110; Manson 245, 313; Schmid 342–43; Vassiliadis 1978: 69; Weiser 1971: 226–58. Harnack also mentions the possibility of the influence of Mark 13:34, while Weiser rejects attempts to explain the divergences solely in terms of Matthean and Lukan redaction; hence separate traditions must be posited.

Q 19:26

In Q: Crossan 1983: 197–202, 203, 345; Easton Lk 283–84; Fitzmyer Lk 1232; Harnack 34 (with hesitations); Hawkins 1911: 111; Hoffmann; Kilpatrick 1946: 87; Marshall Lk 708; Meyer 58; Müller 1908: 9, 56; Polag 82; Schenk 126; Schulz 292; Weiss 1907: 271; Zeller 84 and most authors, apart from those who exclude all of Q 19:12–25.

Not in Q: Vassiliadis 1978: 68: Proverbial sayings may be due to the influence of the oral tradition.

[Luke 19:27; Matt 25:30]

Not in Q: Bultmann 1963: 176; Easton Lk 284; Kilpatrick 1946: 75; Meyer 58; Müller 1908: 56; Polag 83; Schenk 126; Schulz 292–93 and most authors.

Matt 25:14–30

¹⁴"For it is like the case of a man going on a journey. He called his servants and entrusted to them his property; ¹⁵to one he gave five talents, to another two, to another one, each according to his ability. Then he went away.

¹⁶Immediately the one who had received the five talents went and traded with them; and he made another five talents. ¹⁷So also, he who had the two talents made another two talents. ¹⁸But the one who had received the one talent went and dug in the ground and hid his master's money. ¹⁹Now after a long time the master of those servants came and settled accounts with them. ²⁰And he who had received the five talents came forward, bringing the other five talents, saying, 'Master, you delivered to me five talents; here I have made another five talents.' ²¹His master said to him, 'Well done, good and faithful servant; you have been trustworthy in a small matter, I will put you in charge of much; enter into the joy of your master.' ²²Then the one who had the two talents also came forward, saying, 'Master, you delivered to me two talents; here I have made another two talents.' ²³His master said to him, 'Well done, good and faithful servant; you have been trustworthy in a small matter, I will put you in charge of much; enter into the joy of your master.' ²⁴He who had received the one talent also came forward, saying, 'Master, I knew you to be a hard man, reaping where you did not sow, and gathering where you did not scatter; ²⁵and being afraid, I went and hid your talent in the ground. Here you have what is yours.' ²⁶But his master answered him, 'You wicked and slothful servant! You knew that I reap where I have not sowed, and gather where I have not scattered? ²⁷Then you ought to have invested my money with the bankers, and when I came I might have received what was my own with interest. ²⁸So take the talent from him, and give it to him who has the ten talents. ²⁹For the one who has will be given more, and he will have in abundance; but from the one who has not, even what he has will be taken away.

[³⁰And cast the worthless servant into the outer darkness; out there will be weeping and gnashing of teeth.]'"

Luke 19:11–27

[¹¹As they heard these things, he proceeded to tell a parable, because he was near to Jerusalem, and because they supposed that the reign of God was to appear immediately.]
¹²He said therefore, "A nobleman went into a far country to receive a kingdom and then to return. ¹³Calling ten of his servants, he gave them ten minas, and said to them, 'Do business with these till I come.'

[¹⁴But his citizens hated him and sent an embassy after him, saying, 'We do not want this man to reign over us.' ¹⁵When he returned, having received the kingdom,]

he said to summon these servants to whom he had given the money, that he might know what they had made in business. ¹⁶The first came, saying, 'Master, your mina has made ten additional minas.' ¹⁷And he said to him, 'Well done, good servant! Because you have been trustworthy in a very little, you shall have authority over ten cities.' ¹⁸And the second came, saying, 'Master, your mina has made five minas.' ¹⁹And he said to him, 'And you are to be over five cities.' ²⁰And the other came, saying, 'Master, here is your mina, which I kept stored in a napkin; ²¹for I was afraid of you, because you are a severe man; you withdraw what you did not deposit, and reap what you did not sow.' ²²He said to him, 'From your own mouth I will condemn you, you wicked servant! You knew that I was a severe man, withdrawing what I did not deposit and reaping what I did not sow? ²³Why indeed then did you not put my money into the bank, and when I came I might have collected it with interest?'

[²⁴And he said to those who stood by,]
'Take the mina from him, and give it to him who has the ten.' ²⁵And they said to him, 'Lord, he has ten minas!' ²⁶'I tell you, that every one who has will be given more; but from the one has not, even what he has will be taken away.

[²⁷But as for these enemies of mine, who did not want me to reign over them, bring them here and slay them before me.]'"

Matt 19:27–29

[²⁷τότε ἀποκριθεὶς ὁ Πέτρος εἶπεν αὐτῷ· ἰδοὺ ἡμεῖς ἀφήκαμεν πάντα καὶ ἠκολουθήσαμέν σοι· τί ἄρα ἔσται ἡμῖν; ²⁸ὁ δὲ Ἰησοῦς εἶπεν αὐτοῖς· ἀμὴν λέγω ὑμῖν ὅτι]

υ̲μ̲ε̲ῖ̲ς̲ ο̲ἱ̲ ἀκολουθήσαντές μοι

ἐν τῇ παλιγγενεσίᾳ ὅταν καθίσῃ ὁ υἱὸς τοῦ ἀνθρώπου ἐπὶ θρόνου δόξης αὐτοῦ, **καθήσεσθε** καὶ ὑμεῖς **ἐπὶ δώδεκα θρόνους κρίνοντες τὰς δώδεκα φυλὰς τοῦ** Ἰσραήλ.

[²⁹καὶ πᾶς ὅστις ἀφῆκεν οἰκίας ἢ ἀδελφοὺς ἢ ἀδελφὰς ἢ πατέρα ἢ μητέρα ἢ τέκνα ἢ ἀγροὺς ἕνεκεν τοῦ ὀνόματός μου, ἑκατονταπλασίονα λήμψεται καὶ ζωὴν αἰώνιον κληρονομήσει].

Matt 19:28: και αυτοι: ℵ D L Z λ 1 124 892 *pc*; Or [NA²⁵; HG] / και υμεις²: B C W Koine Δ Θ φ lat [NA²⁶]

Luke 22:24–30

[²⁴Ἐγένετο δὲ καὶ φιλονεικία ἐν αὐτοῖς, τὸ τίς αὐτῶν δοκεῖ εἶναι μείζων. ²⁵ὁ δὲ εἶπεν αὐτοῖς· οἱ βασιλεῖς τῶν ἐθνῶν κυριεύουσιν αὐτῶν καὶ οἱ ἐξουσιάζοντες αὐτῶν εὐεργέται καλοῦνται. ²⁶ὑμεῖς δὲ οὐχ οὕτως, ἀλλ᾽ ὁ μείζων ἐν ὑμῖν γινέσθω ὡς ὁ νεώτερος καὶ ὁ ἡγούμενος ὡς ὁ διακονῶν. ²⁷τίς γὰρ μείζων, ὁ ἀνακείμενος ἢ ὁ διακονῶν; οὐχὶ ὁ ἀνακείμενος; ἐγὼ δὲ ἐν μέσῳ ὑμῶν εἰμι ὡς ὁ διακονῶν].

²⁸υ̲μ̲ε̲ῖ̲ς̲ δέ ἐστε ο̲ἱ̲ διαμεμενηκότες μετ᾽ ἐμοῦ ἐν τοῖς πειρασμοῖς μου· ²⁹κἀγὼ διατίθεμαι ὑμῖν καθὼς διέθετό μοι ὁ πατήρ μου βασιλείαν, ³⁰ἵνα ἔσθητε καὶ πίνητε ἐπὶ τῆς τραπέζης μου ἐν τῇ βασιλείᾳ μου, καὶ **καθήσεσθε** **ἐπὶ θρόνων** **τὰς δώδεκα φυλὰς κρίνοντες τοῦ** Ἰσραήλ.

Notes

Q 22:28–30

In Q: Bammel 1970: 39–50; Crossan 1983: 202–203; Edwards 1976: 144–45; Fitzmyer Lk 1413; Harnack 95; Hawkins 1911: 117 (with considerable probability); Hoffmann 5, 42, 150; Kloppenborg 1987: 164–65; Lührmann 75; Marshall Lk 815; Meyer 61–63; Polag 78 (conjectural); Schenk 129–30; Schmid 310; Schmithals Lk 211; Schulz 330–36; Schürmann 1982: 136; Streeter 1911b: 202 (but see below); Weiss 1907: 122; Zeller 88.

Some authors also include Matthew's (ἀμὴν) λέγω ὑμῖν ὅτι: Fitzmyer Lk 1413 ("certainly" in Q); Marshall Lk 815; Schenk 129; Schulz 331. Others, however, consider

it to be redactional or borrowed from Mark 10:29: Dupont 1964: 712 n.2; Harnack 95; Meyer 61; Polag 79; Schmithals Lk 211.

Not in Q: Bussmann 104: The wording is too divergent to posit a Q text here. Easton Lk 326: The verbal disagreements make it very uncertain that this came from Q. Hunter 160, 186; Manson 339; Müller 1908: 6, 55, 58; Streeter 1924: 288 (but see above): This is an example of two divergent versions of a saying, one from M and the other from L. Tödt 1965: 64–65: Matt 19:28 is not from Q, but originated, like Q, in early Palestinian Christianity. Vassiliadis 1978: 70; Wernle 1899: 92.

Matt 19:27–29
[27 Then Peter answered him, "Behold, we have left everything and followed you. What then shall we have?" 28 Jesus said to them, "Amen, I tell you,]

at the Renewal, when the Son of man sits on his glorious throne, you who have followed me will also sit on twelve thrones, judging the twelve tribes of Israel.

[29 And every one who has left households or brothers or sisters or father or mother or children or lands, for my name's sake, will receive a hundredfold, and inherit eternal life.]"

Luke 22:24–30
[24 A dispute also arose among them, which of them was to be regarded as the greatest. 25 But he said to them, "The kings of the Gentiles exercise lordship over them; and those in authority over them are called benefactors. 26 But not so with you; rather let the greatest among you become as the youngest, and the leader as one who serves. 27 For which is the greater, one who reclines at table, or one who serves? Is it not the one who relines at table? But I am among you as one who serves.]
28 "You are those who have persevered with me in my trials; 29 and I assign to you, as my Father assigned to me, a kingdom, 30 that you may eat and drink at my table in my kingdom, and sit on thrones judging the twelve tribes of Israel."

Parallels

Mark 10:28–30 ⇨ Matt 19:27–28a, 29
28 Ἤρξατο λέγειν ὁ Πέτρος αὐτῷ· ἰδοὺ ἡμεῖς ἀφήκαμεν πάντα καὶ ἠκολουθήκαμέν σοι· 29 ἔφη ὁ Ἰησοῦς· ἀμὴν λέγω ὑμῖν, οὐδείς ἐστιν ὃς ἀφῆκεν οἰκίαν ἢ ἀδελφοὺς ἢ ἀδελφὰς ἢ μητέρα ἢ πατέρα ἢ τέκνα ἢ ἀγροὺς ἕνεκεν ἐμοῦ καὶ ἕνεκεν τοῦ εὐαγγελίου, 30 ἐὰν μὴ λάβῃ ἑκατονταπλασίονα νῦν ἐν τῷ καιρῷ τούτῳ οἰκίας καὶ ἀδελφοὺς καὶ ἀδελφὰς καὶ μητέρας καὶ τέκνα καὶ ἀγροὺς μετὰ διωγμῶν, καὶ ἐν τῷ αἰῶνι τῷ ἐρχομένῳ ζωὴν αἰώνιον.

Mark 10:28–30
28 Peter began to say to him, "Behold, we have left everything and followed you." 29 Jesus said, "Amen, I tell you, there is no one who has left household or brothers or sisters or mother or father or children or lands, for my sake and for the gospel, 30 who will not receive a hundredfold now in this time, houses and brothers and sisters and mothers and children and lands, with persecutions, and in the age to come eternal life."

Wis 3:8 LXX
8 κρινοῦσιν ἔθνη καὶ κρατήσουσιν λαῶν, καὶ βασιλεύσει αὐτῶν κύριος εἰς τοὺς αἰῶνας.

Wis 3:8 LXX
8 They [the righteous] will govern nations and rule over peoples, and the Lord will reign over them forever.

Sir 4:15 LXX
15 ὁ ὑπακούων αὐτῆς κρινεῖ ἔθνη, καὶ ὁ προσέχων αὐτῇ κατασκηνώσει πεποιθώς.

Sir 4:15 LXX
15 He who obeys her [Wisdom] will judge the nations, and whoever gives heed to her will dwell secure.

Christian Hermann Weisse   *(1801–1866)*

Born August 10, 1801 in Leipzig. From 1828 Weisse lectured in philosophy and theology at the University of Leipzig as a *Privatdozent* (Lecturer) and later professor. In his *Die evangelische Geschichte kritisch und philosophisch bearbeitet* [The Gospel History examined critically and philosophically] (Leipzig, 1838), Weisse adapted earlier work by Freidrich Schleiermacher and Karl Lachmann and became the first to propose that Matthew and Luke used as sources both Mark and a source of sayings. He was later (in 1856) to lament that no one had yet followed him in treading "the path that has been blazed by the investigations of Schleiermacher and Lachmann."

Heinrich Julius Holtzmann   *(1832–1910)*

Born May 17, 1832 in Karlsruhe. Holtzmann taught successively at Heidelberg and Strassburg. When he wrote his *Die synoptischen Evangelien: Ihr Ursprung und geschichtlicher Charakter* [The Synoptic Gospels: Their Origin and Historical Character] (Leipzig, 1863) there was practically no consensus regarding gospel origins. After summarizing the previous work on the Synoptic gospels, Holtzmann put forth a modified version of Weisse's hypothesis (involving an *Urmarkus* [primitive version of Mark] which he later discarded). His treatment was in large measure responsible for the emergence of a German consensus favoring the Two Document Hypothesis, as it was later to be called.

Bernhard Weiss   *(1827–1918)*

Born June 20, 1827 in Königsberg. Weiss taught New Testament in Königsberg (1852–63), Kiel (1863–77) and Berlin (1877–1908). Known as a conservative, Weiss contributed several volumes to the newly founded Meyer commentary series, as well as *Lehrbuch der Einleitung in das Neue Testament* (Berlin, 1886, 1893[3]) [ET: *A Manual of Introduction to the New Testament* (2 vols.; New York, 1887–89)] and *Die Quellen des Lukasevangeliums* [The Sources of the Gospel of Luke] (Stuttgart and Berlin, 1907). He took an "expanded" view of Q, and included in it many narrative passages found in Mark.

Adolf (von) Harnack   (1851–1930)

Born May 7, 1851 in Dorpat. Reputed as one of the most influential German theologians and church historians, Harnack studied church history in Dorpat and Leipzig and held positions at Leipzig, Giessen, Marburg and, from 1888 to 1921, at Berlin. Harnack was a prolific writer, contributing to all areas of church history and New Testament, and is perhaps best known for his history of dogma and *Das Wesen des Christentums* (Leipzig, 1900) [ET: *What is Christianity?* (New York, 1957)]. Harnack founded the Kirchenväterkommission, *Texte und Untersuchungen zur Geschichte der altchristlichen Literatur,* and *Theologische Literatur-Zeitung*, and was a member of the Prussian Academy of Sciences, founder of the Evangelical-social Congress, director of the Prussian State Library, and president of the Kaiser Wilhelm-Gesellschaft zur Förderung der Wissenschaft (now the Max Planck Gesellschaft). In 1914 Kaiser Wilhelm raised him to the status of hereditary noble.

Among Harnack's lasting contributions was his *Sprüche und Reden Jesu* (Leipzig, 1907) [ET: *The Sayings of Jesus* (London and New York, 1908)] which was the first detailed reconstruction and commentary on Q.

Photograph reproduced with permission from *Aus der Werkstaat des Vollendeten*, Alfred Töpelmann, Berlin, 1930.

Burnet Hillman Streeter   (1874–1937)

Born November 17, 1874 in Croydon. Dean of Pembroke College from 1899, he became in 1905 a Fellow of Queen's College, Oxford. There Streeter joined the "Seminar" which met in the home of the Lady Margaret Professor of Divinity, William Sanday and, along with Sanday, Sir John C. Hawkins, W. C. Allen and others, produced *Oxford Studies in the Synoptic Problem* (Oxford, 1911). His *The Four Gospels* (London, 1924) became the classic British statement of the "fundamental solution" to the Synoptic problem. Streeter proposed a "four document hypothesis" (Mark, Q, M and L) which also involved a "Proto-Luke" (Q + L) as an intermediary step to Luke.

Painting reproduced with permission from The Queen's College, Oxford.

Thomas Walter Manson   (1893–1958)

Born July 22, 1893 in Tynemouth. Manson studied at Glasgow and Cambridge, and taught at Westminster College, Cambridge, and Mansfield College, Oxford. He succeeded C. H. Dodd both at Oxford and in the Rylands Professorship at Manchester. Manson helped found the Studiorum Novi Testamenti Societas, was made a Fellow of the British Academy, honorary member of the Society of Biblical Literature and corresponding fellow of the Akademie der Wissenschaften zu Göttingen. His major contribution to Q studies was his *The Sayings of Jesus* (London, 1937, 1949) which represented the first full-length commentary and reconstruction of Q in English.

Photograph reproduced with permission from *New Testament Essays: Studies in Memory of Thomas Walter Manson, 1893–1958*, Manchester University Press, 1959.

*C*oncordance: Introduction

This concordance contains all of the vocabulary appearing in the Matthean and Lukan texts deemed most likely to have derived from Q. This includes all of the unbracketed texts in the parallel Matthew and Luke columns and those texts enclosed in parentheses, i.e., those *Sondergut* texts for which relatively strong arguments may be cited in support of their origin in Q. It also includes Matt 9:32–34 [S29] and Matt 16:1–2a, 4 [S32] which are treated as parallel to Matt 12:22–24 // Luke 11:14–15 and Matt 12:38–39 // Luke 11:16, 29 respectively.

The vocabulary of those pericopae or portions of pericopae which appear in square brackets [redactional material or *Sondergut* not in Q] or in angle brackets ⟨in Q but unrecoverable⟩ is excluded from the concordance. More particularly, the following materials are *excluded:*

1. texts which are cited merely to provide an indication of the redactional setting into which Matthew and Luke have placed Q texts (e.g., Matt 9:36 [S22]; Luke 14:15 [S55]);
2. redactional introductions, insertions and conclusions (e.g., Matt 5:43 [S9]; Luke 6:39a [S11]);
3. entire pericopae (e.g., Matt 3:13–17 // Luke 3:21–22 [S5]) or portions of pericopae (e.g., Luke 11:53–54 [S34]) which have a low probability of deriving from Q and
4. those transitional and introductory passages which, although an origin in Q is highly likely, have been so thoroughly rewritten by Matthew and Luke that the *Vorlage* is no longer visible (e.g., Matt 5:1–2 // Luke 6:12, 17, 20a [S7]; Matt 7:28 // Luke 7:10a [S15]).

Sigla

Obviously, the policy of concording all of the Matthean and Lukan vocabulary occurring in pericopae which derive from Q means that along with Q vocabulary this concordance unavoidably contains words that derive from the redactional work of the evangelists or, conceivably, from two different versions of Q. The following sigla are used to distinguish the types of concordance entries:

*   The asterisk marks occurrences of vocabulary that appears in both Matthew and Luke at the same relative location. Notwithstanding the possibility of coincidental redactional agreements, the asterisked occurrences represent the *minimal Q vocabulary*.

An agreement is defined as the use of a word by both evangelists so that it either has the same or analogous syntactical position in a sentence or clause, or has the same or analogous semantic function within the sentence. This does not necessarily imply agreement in inflection or in word order. For example, for Matt 5:3: ἡ βασιλεία τῶν οὐρανῶν // Luke 6:20b: ἡ βασιλεία τοῦ θεοῦ, the occurrences of ἡ and βασιλεία are marked with an asterisk, as are those of the differently inflected definite articles, τῶν (Matt) and τοῦ (Luke). Likewise, agreements in vocabulary but disagreements in word order and registered as agreements. For example, in Matt 12:45: ἑπτὰ ἕτερα πνεύματα πονηρότερα ἑαυτοῦ // Luke 11:24: ἕτερα πνεύματα πονηρότερα ἑαυτοῦ ἑπτά, all of the entries are marked with * indicating agreement.

(*) Sixteen pairs of agreements appear as (*). This siglum designates agreement in the use of the same verbal stem but differences in prefix. For example, at Q 17:37 Luke uses ἐπισυνάγω where Matthew has συνάγω. Under the occurrences of συνάγω, Matt 24:28 is marked with (*) to signal the partial agreement with the ἐπισυνάγω of Luke 17:37. In each such agreement, the cognate verb or verbs are listed after the main entry:

συνάγω ⇨ ἐπισυνάγω.

(φ) The concordance also notes synonyms or other substitutes in the parallel gospel. Thus, for example, at Luke 11:43 where Luke has ἀγαπάω, the Matthean parallel has φιλέω. Synonyms and other substitutes are listed in parentheses following the main entry (and after any cognate verbs [see above]). Where the parallel gospel contains a synonym or substitute, an abbreviated form of the word (normally, the first letter or letters) appears in parentheses immediately following the entry for the main verb. For example,

ἀγαπάω (⇨ φιλέω)
Luke [4/9] . . . 11:43 (φ)

(S) The designation "S" is used to mark vocabulary which appears in *Sondergut* passages which are deemed likely to have derived from Q. These include Matt 5:41; 7:2a; 11:23b–24 and Luke 6:24–26, 34–35b, 37c, 38ab; 7:3–5, 20; 9:61–62; 11:21–22 (cf. Matt 12:29 // Mark 3:27); 11:27–28, 36; 12:13–14, 16–21, 49; 13:25 (cf. Matt 25:10–12); 15:8–10; and 17:28–29. Although Matt 25:10–12 is presented as a secondary parallel to Luke 13:25 and hence its vocabulary does not appear in the concordance, there are several items of agreement with Luke 13:25. These agreements are noted with the Lukan entries in the concordance, e.g., θύρα . . . 13:25 (S; cf. Matt 25:10).

–   Entries with no marking indicate that the other synoptist either lacks a specific parallel for the vocabulary, or employs quite different vocabulary.

[1/2] The first digit indicates the number of Matthew–Luke agreements in the use of the word, and the second digit gives the total number of occurrences concorded. The figure in parentheses includes agreements in the main and cognate forms of a verb.

Statistics

The following statistics are based on the concorded vocabulary.

	Matthean Q Pericopae	*Lukan Q Pericopae*
Total Words:	4464	4652
Total Vocabulary:	812	857
Agreements:	2414 (2430)*	2400 (2416)
Percent Agreement:	54.08 (54.43)	51.59 (51.93)

* The figures in parentheses include the sixteen agreements in cognate verbs.

Needless to say, the statistics for the Matthew–Luke agreements would be significantly higher if the considerable number of close synonyms such as ἀμφιάζω (Luke 12:28) and ἀμφιέννυμι (Matt 6:30) or μεθύσκω (Luke 12:45) and μεθύω (Matt 24:49) had been counted as agreements.

It will be seen that the figures for Matthean agreements are fourteen (14) greater than those for Luke. This is due to a few instances of double-agreement, i.e., where two Matthean texts are parallel to a single Lukan one (or *vice versa*). The following pericopae show double agreements:

Matthew
Matt 9:32–34 // 12:22–24 // Luke 11:14–15 (adding 15 agreements to Matthew).
Matt 12:38–39 // 16:1–2a, 4 // Luke 11:16, 29 (adding 15 agreements to Matthew).
Matt 25:27 καί, ἐγώ // Luke 19:13: κἀγώ (adding 2 agreement to Matthew).

Luke
Luke 7:19 // 7:20 // Matt 11:3 (adding 6 agreements to Luke).
Luke 10:9 // 10:11 // Matt 10:7 (adding 4 agreements to Luke).
Luke 11:29 // 12:54a // Matt 16:2 (adding 1 agreement to Luke).
Luke 14:11 // 18:14 // Matt 23:12 (adding 6 agreements to Luke).
Luke 19:13: κἀγώ // Matt 25:27 καί, ἐγώ (adding 1 agreement to Luke).

The Matthean concordance has 32 double agreements, the Lukan has 18, for a net surplus or 14 in Matthew's favor. The additional (32) Matthean words are:

ἄρχων, γενεά, δίδωμι, δέ (2), δαιμόνιον (2), εἰ, ἐν, ἐκβάλλω, Ἰωνᾶ, καί (3), κωφός (2), λαλέω, μή, οὐ, ὄχλος, πονηρός, σημεῖον (4), αὐτή, ἐγώ, τό, τόν, οἱ, τῶν, τά.

The additional (18) Lukan words are:

βασιλεία, δέ, εἰμί, ἑαυτός (2), ἔρχομαι, ἐγγίζω, ἤ, κἀγώ, προσδοκάω, ταπεινόω (2), ὑψόω (2), σύ, τοῦ, ὁ, ἡ.

Organization

The vocabulary is arranged by dictionary form rather than by inflected form. The only exceptions to this rule are the cases of the pronouns αὐτός, ἐγώ, σύ, ἡμεῖς and ὑμεῖς and all occurrences of the definite article. These are arranged by inflection and listed at the end of the concordance. In organizing the concordance the taxomony of the Bauer, Arndt, Gingrich and Danker lexicon has been followed. Thus εἶπον and λέγω are concorded separately.

Matthean and Lukan references are given in canonical order. Since the organization of the synopsis in general follows Lukan order, the full parallel display of the occurrence of any Lukan word may be located easily. In order to assist the user in locating the sections of the synopsis in which Matthean verses are displayed, a table of Matthean verses and their corresponding Lukan parallels is provided.

Matthean Q Texts in the Concordance

Matthew	Luke	Section No.	Matthew	Luke	Section No.
3:7–10	3:7–9	S3	11:2–6	7:18–23	S16
3:11–12	3:16–17	S4	11:7–11	7:24–28	S17
4:1–11	4:1–13	S6	11:11–12	16:16	S18, S61
5:3–4, 6	6:23–23	S8	11:16–19	7:31–35	S20
5:11–12	6:20b–21	S8	11:20–24	10:13–15	S23
5:13	14:34–35	S57	11:25–27	10:21–22	S25
5:15	11:33	S33	12:22–30	11:14–23	S29
5:18	16:17	S61	12:32	12:10	S38
5:25–26	12:57–59	S48	12:33b, 34b	6:43–44	S13
5:32	16:18	S61	12:35	6:45	S13
5:39b–42	6:27–35	S9	12:38–42	11:16, 29–32	S32
5:44–47	6:27–35	S9	12:43–45	11:24–26	S30
5:48	6:36	S10	13:16–17	10:23–24	S26
6:9–13	11:2–4	S27	13:31–32	13:18–19	S49
6:19–21	12:33–34	S42	13:33	13:20–21	S49
6:22–23	11:34–36	S33	15:14	6:40	S11
6:24	16:13	S60	16:1–2a	11:16	S32
6:25–33	12:22–31	S41	16:2–3	12:54–56	S47
7:1–2	6:37–38	S10	16:4	11:29	S32
7:3–5	6:41–42	S12	17:20b	17:6b	S64
7:7–11	11:9–13	S28	18:6–7	17:1b–2	S62
7:12	6:31	S9	18:12–13	15:4–7	S58
7:13–14	13:24	S50	18:15	17:3b	S63
7:16b, 18	6:43–45	S13	18:21b–22	17:4	S63
7:21	6:46	S14	19:28b	22:28–30	S68
7:22–23	13:26–27	S14, S50	20:16	13:30	S51
7:24–27	6:47–49	S14	22:1–10	14:16–24	S55
8:5–13	7:1b–10	S15	23:4, 6	11:46, 43	S34
8:11–12	13:28–29	S15, S51	23:12	14:11/18:14b	S54
8:18–22	9:57–60	S21	23:13	11:52	S34
9:32–34	11:14–15	S29	23:23	11:42	S34
9:37–38	10:2	S22	23:25–28	11:39–41, 44	S34
10:7–16a	10:2–12	S22	23:29–32	11:47–48	S34
10:19	12:11–12	S39	23:34–36	11:49–51	S34
10:24–25	6:39	S11	23:37–39	13:34–35	S34, S52
10:26–27	12:2–3	S35	24:26–28	17:23–24, 37b	S66
10:28–31	12:4–7	S36	24:37–41	17:26–30, 34–35	S66
10:32–33	12:8–9	S37	24:43–44	12:39–40	S44
10:34–36	12:51–53	S46	24:45–51	12:42b–46	S45
10:37–39	14:26–27; 17:33	S56	25:10–12	13:25	S50
10:40	10:16	S24	25:14–29	19:12–13, 15b–26	S67

Concordance

῞Αβελ
Matt [1/1] 23:35*
Luke [1/1] 11:51*

᾿Αβραάμ
Matt [3/3] 3:9* 3:9* 8:11*
Luke [3/3] 3:8* 3:8* 13:28*

ἀγαθοποιέω (▷ ἀσπάζομαι)
Luke [0/3] 6:33 (α) 6:33 6:35 (S)

ἀγαθός (▷ καλός)
Matt [5/10] 5:45 7:11* 7:11 7:18 (κ) 12:35*
12:35* 12:35* 22:10 25:21* 25:23
Luke [5/7] 6:45* 6:45* 6:45* 11:13* 12:18 (S)
12:19 (S) 19:17*

ἀγαλλιάω (▷ σκιρτάω)
Matt [0/1] 5:12 (σ)
Luke [0/1] 10:21

ἀγαπάω (▷ φιλέω)
Matt [4/4] 5:44* 5:46* 5:46* 6:24*
Luke [4/9] 6:27* 6:32* 6:32* 6:32 6:32 6:35
(S) 7:5 (S) 11:43 (φ) 16:13*

ἀγάπη (▷ ἔλεος)
Luke [0/1] 11:42 (ε)

ἀγγαρεύω
Matt [0/1] 5:41 (S)

ἄγγελος
Matt [2/3] 4:6* 4:11 11:10*
Luke [2/6] 4:10* 7:24 7:27* 12:8 12:9 15:10
(S)

ἁγιάζω
Matt [1/1] 6:9*
Luke [1/1] 11:2*

ἅγιος
Matt [2/3] 3:11* 4:5 12:32*
Luke [2/6] 3:16* 4:1 10:21 11:13 12:10* 12:12

ἀγορά
Matt [2/2] 11:16* 23:7*
Luke [2/2] 7:32* 11:43*

ἀγοράζω
Luke [0/3] 14:18 14:19 17:28 (S)

ἀγρός (▷ κῆπος, κλίνη)
Matt [2/5] 6:28 6:30* 13:31 (κη) 22:5* 24:40
(κλ)
Luke [2/2] 12:28* 14:18*

ἄγω ▷ ἀνάγω (▷ παραλαμβάνω)
Luke [0(1)/2] 4:1(*) 4:9 (π)

ἀγωνίζομαι
Luke [0/1] 13:24

ἀδελφή
Luke [0/1] 14:26

ἀδελφός
Matt [4/7] 5:47 7:3* 7:4* 7:5* 18:15* 18:15
18:21
Luke [4/7] 6:41* 6:42* 6:42 6:42* 12:13 (S)
14:26 17:3*

ἄδηλος
Luke [0/1] 11:44

ᾅδης
Matt [1/1] 11:23*
Luke [1/1] 10:15*

ἀδικία (▷ ἀνομία)
Luke [0/1] 13:27 (α)

ἄδικος (▷ ἀχάριστος)
Matt [0/1] 5:45 (α)

ἀδυνατέω
Matt [0/1] 17:20

ἀετός
Matt [1/1] 24:28*
Luke [1/1] 17:37*

ἀθετέω
Luke [0/4] 10:16 10:16 10:16 10:16

αἷμα
Matt [3/4] 23:30 23:35* 23:35* 23:35*
Luke [3/3] 11:50* 11:51* 11:51*

αἴρω (▷ ἀπόλλυμι, δανείζω, κλείω, λαμβάνω,
συνάγω)
Matt [3/4] 4:6* 24:39 (α) 25:28* 25:29*
Luke [3/9] 4:11* 6:29 (λ) 6:30 (δ) 11:22 (S)
11:52 (κ) 19:21 (σ) 19:22 (σ) 19:24* 19:26*

αἰτέω
Matt [6/6] 5:42* 7:7* 7:8* 7:9* 7:10* 7:11*
Luke [6/6] 6:30* 11:9* 11:10* 11:11* 11:12*
11:13*

αἰών
Matt [0/1] 12:32

ἀκαθαρσία
Matt [0/1] 23:27

ἀκάθαρτος
Matt [1/1] 12:43*
Luke [1/1] 11:24*

ἄκανθα
Matt [1/1] 7:16*
Luke [1/1] 6:44*

ἀκολουθέω (▷ διαμένω, ἔρχομαι)
Matt [3/5] 8:10* 8:19* 8:22* 10:38 (ε) 19:28
(δ)
Luke [3/4] 7:9* 9:57* 9:59* 9:61 (S)

ἀκούω (▷ δέχομαι, μετανοέω)
Matt [10/15] 7:24* 7:26* 8:10* 10:14 10:27*
11:2 11:4* 11:5* 12:24 12:42* 13:16 13:17*
13:17* 13:17* 18:15 (μ)
Luke [10/17] 6:27 6:47* 6:49* 7:3 (S) 7:9*
7:22* 7:22* 10:16 (δ) 10:16 (δ) 10:24* 10:24*
10:24* 11:28 (S) 11:31* 12:3* 14:35 14:35

ἀκρασία (▷ πονηρία)
Matt [0/1] 23:25 (π)

ἅλας
Matt [2/2] 5:13* 5:13*
Luke [2/2] 14:34* 14:34*

ἄλευρον
Matt [1/1] 13:33*
Luke [1/1] 13:21*

ἀλήθω
Matt [1/1] 24:41*
Luke [1/1] 17:35*

ἀληθῶς (▷ ἀμήν)
Luke [0/1] 12:44 (α)

ἁλίζω (▷ ἀρτύω)
Matt [0/1] 5:13 (α)

ἀλλά (▷ δέ)
Matt [5/9] 4:4 5:15* 6:13 7:21 8:8* 10:34*
11:8* 11:9* 18:22
Luke [5/8] 6:27 (δ) 7:7* 7:25* 7:26* 11:33*
11:42 12:7 (δ) 12:51*

ἀλλήλων (▷ ἕτερος)
Luke [0/1] 7:32 (ε)

ἄλλος (▷ ἕτερος)
Matt [2/10] 5:39* 8:9* 13:31 13:33 22:4 25:16
25:17 25:20 25:20 25:22
Luke [2/4] 6:29* 7:8* 7:19 (ε) 7:20 (ε)

ἄλων
Matt [1/1] 3:12*
Luke [1/1] 3:17*

ἀλώπηξ
Matt [1/1] 8:20*
Luke [1/1] 9:58*

ἁμαρτάνω
Matt [2/2] 18:15* 18:21*
Luke [2/2] 17:3* 17:4*
ἁμαρτία (⇨ ὀφείλημα)
Luke [0/1] 11:4 (ο)
ἁμαρτωλός (⇨ ἐθνικός, τελώνης)
Matt [1/1] 11:19*
Luke [1/7] 6:32 (τ) 6:33 (ε) 6:34 (S) 6:34 (S)
7:34* 15:7 15:10 (S)
ἀμελέω
Matt [0/1] 22:5
ἀμήν (⇨ ἀληθῶς, ναί)
Matt [0/10] 5:18 5:26 8:10 10:15 11:11 13:17
17:20 18:13 23:36 (ν) 24:47 (α)
ἄμμος
Matt [0/1] 7:26
ἀμφιάζω (⇨ ἀμφιέννυμι)
Luke [0/1] 12:28 (α)
ἀμφιέννυμι (⇨ ἀμφιάζω)
Matt [1/2] 6:30 (α) 11:8*
Luke [1/1] 7:25*
ἀμφότεροι
Matt [1/1] 15:14*
Luke [1/1] 6:39*
ἄν
Matt [5/16] 5:18 5:18 5:26 10:11* 10:11
10:14* 10:33 11:21* 11:23 (S) 12:32 18:6
23:30 23:39 24:43 24:43* 25:27*
Luke [5/11] 10:5 10:8* 10:10* 10:13* 12:8
12:39* 13:25 (S) 17:6 17:6 17:33 19:23*
ἀναβλέπω
Matt [1/1] 11:5*
Luke [1/1] 7:22*
ἀναγκάζω
Luke [0/1] 14:23
ἀνάγκη
Matt [0/1] 18:7
Luke [0/1] 14:18
ἀνάγω ⇨ ἄγω (⇨ παραλαμβάνω)
Matt [0(1)/1] 4:1(*)
Luke [0/1] 4:5 (π)
ἀνακάμπτω (⇨ ἐπιστρέφω)
Luke [0/1] 10:6 (ε)
ἀνάκειμαι
Matt [0/1] 22:10
ἀνακλίνω
Matt [1/1] 8:11*
Luke [1/1] 13:29*
ἀνάπαυσις
Matt [1/1] 12:43*
Luke [1/1] 11:24*
ἀναπαύω
Luke [0/1] 12:19 (S)
ἀνάπειρος
Luke [0/1] 14:21
ἀνάπτω
Luke [0/1] 12:49 (S)

ἀνατέλλω
Matt [0/1] 5:45
Luke [0/1] 12:54
ἀνατολή
Matt [1/2] 8:11* 24:27
Luke [1/1] 13:29*
ἀνέκλειπτος
Luke [0/1] 12:33
ἀνεκτός
Matt [2/3] 10:15* 11:22* 11:24 (S)
Luke [2/2] 10:12* 10:14*
ἄνεμος
Matt [1/3] 7:25 7:27 11:7*
Luke [1/1] 7:24*
ἀνένδεκτος
Luke [0/1] 17:1
ἄνευ
Matt [0/1] 10:29
ἄνηθον (⇨ πήγανον)
Matt [0/1] 23:23 (π)
ἀνήρ (⇨ ἄνθρωπος)
Matt [1/3] 7:24 (α) 7:26 (α) 12:41*
Luke [1/5] 7:20 (S) 11:31 11:32* 14:24 16:18
ἄνθρωπος (⇨ ἀνήρ, πατήρ, υἱός)
Matt [24/35] 4:4* 5:13 7:9 (π) 7:12* 8:9* 8:20*
9:32 10:32* 10:33* 10:35 (ν) 10:36 11:8*
11:19* 11:19* 12:32* 12:35* 12:40*
12:43* 12:45* 13:31* 18:7 18:12* 19:28 22:2*
23:4* 23:7 23:13 23:28 24:27* 24:37* 24:39*
24:44* 25:14* 25:24*
Luke [24/35] 4:4* 6:22 6:22 6:26 (S) 6:31*
6:45* 6:48 (α) 6:49 (α) 7:8* 7:25* 7:31 7:34*
7:34* 9:58* 11:24* 11:26* 11:30* 11:44
11:46* 12:8* 12:8 12:9* 12:10* 12:14 (S)
12:16 (S) 12:40* 13:19* 14:16* 15:4* 17:24*
17:26* 17:30* 19:12* 19:21* 19:22
ἀνίστημι
Matt [1/1] 12:41*
Luke [1/1] 11:32*
ἀνοίγω
Matt [2/2] 7:7* 7:8*
Luke [2/3] 11:9* 11:10* 13:25 (S; cf. Matt
25:11)
ἀνομία (⇨ ἀδικία)
Matt [0/2] 7:23 (α) 23:28
ἀντέχω
Matt [1/1] 6:24*
Luke [1/1] 16:13*
ἀντί
Luke [0/2] 11:11 12:3
ἀντίδικος
Matt [1/2] 5:25* 5:25
Luke [1/1] 12:58*
ἀντιμετρέω ⇨ μετρέω
Luke [0(1)/1] 6:38(*)
ἄνυδρος
Matt [1/1] 12:43*
Luke [1/1] 11:24*

ἀξίνη
Matt [1/1] 3:10*
Luke [1/1] 3:9*
ἄξιος (⇨ μαθητής)
Matt [2/9] 3:8* 10:10* 10:11 10:13 10:13
10:37 (μ) 10:37 10:38 (μ) 22:8
Luke [2/3] 3:8* 7:4 (S) 10:7*
ἀξιόω
Luke [0/1] 7:7
ἀπαγγέλλω
Matt [1/1] 11:4*
Luke [1/3] 7:18 7:22* 14:21
ἀπάγω
Matt [0/2] 7:13 7:14
ἀπαιτέω (⇨ ἀποστρέφω)
Luke [0/2] 6:30 (α) 12:20 (S)
ἀπαλλάσσω
Luke [0/1] 12:58
ἀπαρνέομαι ⇨ ἀρνέομαι
Luke [0(1)/1] 12:9(*)
ἅπας (⇨ πᾶς)
Matt [0/2] 6:32 24:39 (π)
Luke [0/1] 4:6 (π)
ἀπελπίζω
Luke [0/1] 6:35 (S)
ἀπέρχομαι ⇨ ἐξέρχομαι (⇨ πορεύομαι)
Matt [2/5] 8:19* 8:21* 22:5 25:18 25:25
Luke [2(3)/5] 7:24 (π) 9:57* 9:59* 9:60
17:23(*)
ἀπέχω
Matt [0/2] 6:24 (S) 7:6
ἄπιστος (⇨ ὑποκριτής)
Luke [0/1] 12:46 (ν)
ἁπλοῦς
Matt [1/1] 6:22*
Luke [1/1] 11:34*
ἀπό (⇨ ἐκ, ἐπί, παρά)
Matt [12/21] 3:7* 5:18 5:42* 6:13 7:16 (εκ)
7:16 (εκ) 7:23* 8:11* 10:28* 11:12* 11:19*
11:25* 12:38 (π) 12:43* 18:7 23:34 23:35*
23:39 24:27 (εκ) 25:28* 25:29*
Luke [12/29] 3:7* 4:1 4:13 6:29 6:30* 7:6
7:35* 10:21* 11:24* 11:50 11:50 11:51* 11:51
(επ) 12:4* 12:20 (S) 12:52 12:57 12:58 13:25
(S) 13:27* 13:29* 13:29 14:18 16:16* 16:18
17:29 (S) 17:29 (S) 19:24* 19:26*
ἀποδεκατόω
Matt [1/1] 23:23*
Luke [1/1] 11:42*
ἀποδημέω
Matt [0/2] 25:14 25:15
ἀποδίδωμι
Matt [1/1] 5:26*
Luke [1/1] 12:59*
ἀποθήκη
Matt [2/2] 3:12* 6:26*
Luke [2/3] 3:17* 12:18 (S) 12:24*

ἀποκαλύπτω
  Matt [3/3] 10:26* 11:25* 11:27*
  Luke [3/4] 10:21* 10:22* 12:2* 17:30
ἀπόκειμαι
  Luke [0/1] 19:20
ἀποκλείω
  Luke [0/1] 13:25 (S; cf. Matt 25:10 [κλείω])
ἀποκρίνομαι
  Matt [2/9] 4:4* 8:8 11:4* 11:25 12:38 12:39
  16:2 22:1 25:26
  Luke [2/5] 4:4* 4:8 4:12 7:22* 13:25 (S; cf.
  Matt 25:12)
ἀποκρύπτω ▷ κρύπτω
  Luke [0(1)/1] 10:21(*)
ἀποκτείνω (▷ φονεύω)
  Matt [3/5] 10:28* 10:28 22:6 23:34* 23:37*
  Luke [3/6] 11:47 11:48 (φ) 11:49* 12:4* 12:5
  13:34*
ἀπολαμβάνω
  Luke [0/1] 6:34 (S)
ἀπόλλυμι (▷ αἴρω, ἐμβάλλω, πλανάω, φονεύω)
  Matt [2/4] 10:28 (ε) 10:39* 10:39* 22:7
  Luke [2/10] 11:51 (φ) 15:4 (π) 15:4 (π) 15:6
  15:8 (S) 15:9 (S) 17:27 (a) 17:29 (S) 17:33*
  17:33*
ἀπολογέομαι (▷ λαλέω)
  Luke [0/1] 12:11 (λ)
ἀπολύω
  Matt [2/2] 5:32* 5:32*
  Luke [2/4] 6:37 (S) 6:37 (S) 16:18* 16:18*
ἀπομάσσω (▷ ἐκτινάσσω)
  Luke [0/1] 10:11 (ε)
ἀποστέλλω
  Matt [6/7] 10:16* 11:10* 10:40* 22:3* 22:4
  23:34* 23:37*
  Luke [6/8] 7:3 (S) 7:20 (S) 7:27* 10:3* 10:16*
  11:49* 13:34* 14:17*
ἀπόστολος (▷ γραμματεύς, σοφός)
  Luke [0/1] 11:49 (σ, γ)
ἀποστρέφω (▷ ἀπαιτέω)
  Matt [0/1] 5:42 (a)
ἀποτάσσω
  Luke [0/1] 9:61 (S)
ἀποχωρέω (▷ ἀφίστημι)
  Matt [0/1] 7:23 (a)
ἅπτω (▷ καίω)
  Luke [0/2] 11:33 (κ) 15:8 (S)
ἀπώλεια
  Matt [0/1] 7:13
ἄρα (▷ ὥστε)
  Matt [2/2] 12:28* 24:45*
  Luke [2/3] 11:20* 11:48 (ω) 12:42*
ἀργύριον
  Matt [1/2] 25:18 25:27*
  Luke [1/2] 19:15 19:23*
ἄργυρος
  Matt [0/1] 10:9

ἀρήν (▷ προβάτον)
  Luke [0/1] 10:3 (π)
ἀριθμέω
  Matt [1/1] 10:30*
  Luke [1/1] 12:7*
ἄριστον
  Matt [0/1] 22:4
ἀρκετός
  Matt [0/1] 10:25
ἀρνέομαι ▷ ἀπαρνέομαι
  Matt [1(2)/2] 10:33* 10:33(*)
  Luke [1/1] 12:9*
ἄροτρον
  Luke [0/1] 9:62 (S)
ἁρπαγή
  Matt [1/1] 23:25*
  Luke [1/1] 11:39*
ἁρπάζω
  Matt [0/2] 11:12 12:29
ἄρτι
  Matt [0/2] 11:12 23:39
ἄρτος (▷ ᾠόν)
  Matt [3/4] 4:3* 4:4* 6:11* 7:9 (ω)
  Luke [3/4] 4:3* 4:4* 7:33 11:3*
ἀρτύω (▷ ἁλίζω)
  Luke [0/1] 14:34 (a)
ἀρχή
  Luke [0/1] 12:11
ἄρχομαι (▷ δοκέω)
  Matt [2/2] 11:7* 24:49*
  Luke [2/7] 3:8 (δ) 7:24* 11:29 12:45* 13:25 (S)
  13:26 14:18
ἄρχων
  Matt [2/2] 9:34* 12:24*
  Luke [1/2] 11:15* 12:58
ἄσβεστος
  Matt [1/1] 3:12*
  Luke [1/1] 3:17*
ἀσθενέω (▷ ἀσθενής)
  Matt [0/1] 10:8 (a)
ἀσθενής (▷ ἀσθενέω)
  Luke [0/1] 10:9 (a)
ἀσπάζομαι (▷ ἀγαθοποιέω, λέγω)
  Matt [0/2] 5:47 (a) 10:12 (λ)
  Luke [0/1] 10:4
ἀσπασμός
  Matt [1/1] 23:7*
  Luke [1/1] 11:43*
ἀσσάριον
  Matt [1/1] 10:29*
  Luke [1/1] 12:6*
ἀστραπή
  Matt [1/1] 24:27*
  Luke [1/2] 11:36 (S) 17:24*
ἀστράπτω (▷ ἐξέρχομαι)
  Luke [0/1] 17:24 (ε)

αὐλέω
  Matt [1/1] 11:17*
  Luke [1/1] 7:32*
αὐλή
  Luke [0/1] 11:21 (S)
αὐξάνω
  Matt [2/2] 6:28* 13:32*
  Luke [2/2] 12:27* 13:19*
αὔριον
  Matt [1/1] 6:30*
  Luke [1/1] 12:28*
αὐστηρός (▷ σκληρός)
  Luke [0/2] 19:21 (σ) 19:22
ἀφανίζω (▷ διαφθείρω)
  Matt [0/2] 6:19 6:20 (δ)
ἀφίημι (▷ ἀφίστημι, ἐάω, καταλείπω, κερδαίνω,
  κωλύω, παρέρχομαι, παρίημι)
  Matt [10/17] 4:11 (αφ) 5:40 (κω) 6:12* 6:12*
  7:4* 8:22* 12:32* 12:32* 15:14 18:12 (κα)
  18:21* 23:13 (κω) 23:23 (παρερχ) 23:23 (παριη)
  23:38* 24:40* 24:41*
  Luke [10/12] 6:42* 9:60* 11:4* 11:4* 12:10*
  12:10* 12:39 (ε) 13:35* 17:3 (κερ) 17:4* 17:34*
  17:35*
ἀφίστημι (▷ ἀποχωρέω, ἀφίημι)
  Luke [0/2] 4:13 (αφ) 13:27 (απ)
ἀφορίζω
  Luke [0/1] 6:22
ἄφρων (▷ τυφλός)
  Luke [0/2] 11:40 (τ) 12:20 (S)
ἀχάριστος (▷ ἄδικος)
  Luke [0/1] 6:35 (a)
ἄχρι
  Matt [1/1] 24:38*
  Luke [1/2] 4:13 17:27*
ἄχυρον
  Matt [1/1] 3:12*
  Luke [1/1] 3:17*

βαθύνω
  Luke [0/1] 6:48
βαλλάντιον (▷ θησαυρός, χρυσός)
  Luke [0/2] 10:4 (χ) 12:33 (θ)
βάλλω (▷ δίδωμι, σπείρω)
  Matt [5/9] 3:10* 4:6* 5:13* 5:25* 6:30* 8:6
  10:34 (δ) 10:34 25:27 (δ)
  Luke [5/7] 3:9* 4:9* 12:28* 12:49 (S) 12:58*
  13:19 (σ) 14:35*
βαπτίζω (▷ βάπτισμα)
  Matt [2/2] 3:11* 3:11*
  Luke [2/3] 3:7 (β) 3:16* 3:16*
βάπτισμα (▷ βαπτίζω)
  Matt [0/1] 3:7 (β)
Βαπτιστής
  Matt [1/1] 11:11 11:12
  Luke [0/2] 7:20 (S) 7:33
Βαραχίας
  Matt [0/1] 23:35

βαρύς
  Matt [0/2] 23:4 23:23
βασανίζω
  Matt [0/1] 8:6
βασιλεία (▷ γνῶσις)
  Matt [14/17] 4:8* 5:3* 6:10* 6:33* 7:21 8:11*
  8:12* 10:7* 11:11* 11:12* 12:25* 12:26*
  12:28* 13:31* 13:33* 22:2 23:13 (γ)
  Luke [15/20] 4:5* 6:20* 7:28* 9:60 9:62 (S)
  10:9* 10:11* 11:2* 11:17* 11:18* 11:20*
  12:31* 13:18* 13:20* 13:28* 13:29* 16:16*
  19:12 22:29 22:30
βασίλειος (▷ βασιλεύς)
  Luke [0/1] 7:25 (β)
βασιλεύς (▷ βασίλειος, δίκαιος, οἰκοδεσπότης)
  Matt [0/3] 11:8 (β) 22:2 22:7 (o)
  Luke [0/1] 10:24 (δ)
βασίλισσα
  Matt [1/1] 12:42*
  Luke [1/1] 11:31*
βαστάζω (▷ κτάομαι, λαμβάνω, λύω)
  Matt [0/1] 3:11 (λυω)
  Luke [0/3] 10:4 (κ) 11:27 (S) 14:27 (λαμ)
βάτος (▷ τρίβολος)
  Luke [0/1] 6:44 (τ)
Βεελζεβούλ
  Matt [2/2] 12:24* 12:27*
  Luke [2/2] 11:15* 11:19*
Βηθσαϊδά(ν)
  Matt [1/1] 11:21*
  Luke [1/1] 10:13*
βιάζω
  Matt [1/1] 11:12*
  Luke [1/1] 16:16*
βιαστής
  Matt [0/1] 11:12
βλασφημέω (▷ εἶπον)
  Luke [0/1] 12:10 (ε)
βλέπω (▷ ὁράω)
  Matt [3/5] 7:3* 11:4 (o) 12:22 13:16* 13:17*
  Luke [3/7] 6:41* 6:42 9:62 (S) 10:23* 10:23
  10:24* 11:33
βόθυνος
  Matt [1/1] 15:14*
  Luke [1/1] 6:39*
βορρᾶς
  Luke [0/1] 13:29
βούλομαι
  Matt [1/1] 11:27*
  Luke [1/1] 10:22*
βοῦς
  Luke [0/1] 14:19
βρέχω
  Matt [0/1] 5:45
  Luke [0/1] 17:29 (S)
βροχή (▷ πλήμμυρα)
  Matt [0/2] 7:25 (π) 7:27

βρυγμός
  Matt [1/2] 8:12* 24:51
  Luke [1/1] 13:28*
βρῶσις
  Matt [0/2] 6:19 6:20

γαμέω
  Matt [2/2] 5:32* 24:38*
  Luke [2/4] 14:20 16:18 16:18* 17:27*
γαμίζω
  Matt [1/1] 24:38*
  Luke [1/1] 17:27*
γάμος (▷ δεῖπνον, οἶκος)
  Matt [0/6] 22:2 (δ) 22:3 22:4 22:8 22:9 22:10
  (o)
γάρ (▷ δέ, διά, καί, μήτι, ὅτι, οὐχί, ὡς)
  Matt [17/36] 3:9* 4:6* 4:10 5:12* 5:18 (δε)
  5:46 (κ) 6:21* 6:24* 6:32* 6:32 (δε) 7:2 (S) 7:8*
  7:12 7:25 (δια) 8:9* 10:10* 10:19* 10:26 (δε)
  10:35* 11:13 11:18* 12:33* 12:34* 12:40*
  13:17* 16:2 16:3 17:20 18:7 23:13 23:39 (δε)
  24:27* 24:37 (κ) 24:38 25:14 25:29
  Luke [17/31] 3:8* 4:10* 6:23 (οτι) 6:23* 6:26
  (S) 6:32 6:33 6:38 (κ) 6:43 6:44* 6:44 (μ) 6:45*
  7:5 (S) 7:6 7:8* 7:33* 10:7* 10:24* 11:4 (ω)
  11:10* 11:30* 12:12* 12:23 (ουχι) 12:30*
  12:34* 12:52* 12:58 14:24 16:13* 17:24*
  19:21
γε
  Luke [0/1] 10:6
γέεννα
  Matt [1/1] 10:28*
  Luke [1/1] 12:5*
γείτων
  Luke [0/2] 15:6 15:9 (S)
γελάω (▷ παρακαλέω)
  Luke [0/2] 6:21 (π) 6:25 (S)
γεμίζω (▷ πίμπλημι)
  Luke [0/1] 14:23 (π)
γέμω
  Matt [1/1] 23:25* 23:27
  Luke [1/1] 11:39*
γενεά
  Matt [6/6] 11:16* 12:39* 12:41* 12:42* 16:4*
  23:36*
  Luke [5/8] 7:31* 11:29 11:29* 11:30 11:31*
  11:32* 11:50 11:51*
γέννημα
  Matt [1/1] 3:7*
  Luke [1/1] 3:7*
γεννητός
  Matt [1/1] 11:11*
  Luke [1/1] 7:28*
γεύομαι
  Luke [0/1] 14:24
γῆ
  Matt [4/14] 5:13 5:18* 6:10 6:19 10:15 10:29

10:34* 11:24 (S) 11:25* 12:40 12:42* 23:35
25:18 25:25
  Luke [4/8] 6:49 10:21* 11:31* 12:49 (S)
12:51* 12:56 14:35 16:17*
γίνομαι (▷ εἰμί, ἔχω, καταβαίνω)
  Matt [7/18] 4:3* 5:18 5:45 6:10 8:13 10:25
(ει) 11:21* 11:21* 11:23 (S) 11:23 (S) 11:26*
12:45* 13:32* 16:2 18:12 (εχ) 18:13 23:26 (ει)
24:44*
  Luke [7/21] 4:3* 6:36 (ει) 6:48 (κ) 6:49 (ει)
10:13* 10:13* 10:21* 11:14 11:26* 11:27 (S)
11:30 (ει) 12:40* 12:54 12:55 13:19* 14:22
15:10 (S) 17:26 17:28 (S) 19:17 (ει) 19:19
γινώσκω (▷ ἐπιγινώσκω (▷ οἶδα)
  Matt [4/8] 7:23 (o) 10:26* 12:33* 16:3 (o)
24:39 24:43* 24:50* 25:24
  Luke [4(5)/7] 6:44* 10:11 10:22(*) 12:2*
12:39* 12:46* 19:15
γνῶσις (▷ βασιλεία)
  Luke [0/1] 11:52 (β)
Γόμορρα
  Matt [0/1] 10:15
γραμματεύς (▷ ἀπόστολος, νομικός)
  Matt [0/8] 8:19 12:38 23:13 (ν) 23:23 23:25
23:27 23:29 23:34 (a)
γράφω (▷ εἶπον)
  Matt [4/5] 4:4* 4:6* 4:7 (ε) 4:10* 11:10*
  Luke [4/4] 4:4* 4:8* 4:10* 7:27*
γρηγορέω
  Matt [0/1] 24:43
γυνή
  Matt [3/3] 5:32* 11:11* 13:33*
  Luke [3/7] 7:28* 11:27 (S) 13:21* 14:20 14:26
15:8 (S) 16:18*

δαιμονίζομαι (▷ δαιμόνιον)
  Matt [0/2] 9:32 (δ) 12:22 (δ)
δαιμόνιον
  Matt [8/10] 7:22 9:33* 9:34* 9:34* 10:8
11:18* 12:24* 12:24* 12:27* 12:28*
  Luke [6/7] 7:33* 11:14 (δ) 11:14* 11:15*
11:15* 11:19* 11:20*
δάκτυλος (▷ πνεῦμα)
  Matt [1/1] 23:4*
  Luke [1/2] 11:20 (π) 11:46*
δανείζω (▷ αἴρω)
  Matt [0/1] 5:42 (a)
  Luke [0/3] 6:34 (S) 6:34 (S) 6:35 (S)
Δαυίδ
  Matt [0/1] 12:23
δέ (▷ ἀλλά, γάρ, ἤ, καί, ὅτι, οὖν, πλήν, τε, τότε)
  Matt [34/78] 3:7 (ουν) 3:10* 3:11* 3:12* 4:4
(κ) 5:13* 5:32 5:44 (a) 6:20 6:23* 6:27* 6:29*
6:30* 6:33 (π) 7:3* 7:3* 8:5 8:10* 8:11 8:12
8:20* 8:21* 8:22* 9:37* 9:32 (κ) 9:34* 10:7 (κ)
10:11 (κ) 10:12* 10:13* 10:19* 10:28 (κ) 10:28
10:30 (a) 10:33* 11:2 (κ) 11:7* 11:11* 11:12
11:16 (ουν) 12:24* 12:25* 12:28* 12:32*

12:39* 12:43 13:16 13:32 (κ) 15:14 16:2*
16:3* 18:6 18:15 22:5 22:5 22:6 22:7 22:8 23:4
(οτι) 23:4 (κ) 23:6 23:12 (οτι) 23:13 23:23*
23:25* 23:27 23:28 24:43* 24:48* 24:49 (τε)
25:15 25:15 25:18 25:19 (κ) 25:22 25:24 25:26
25:29*
Luke [33/91] 3:9* 3:16* 3:17* 4:1 (τοτε) 4:3 (κ)
4:9 (τοτε) 6:40 6:41* 6:41* 6:46 6:48 (κ) 6:49
(κ) 7:2 7:3 (S) 7:4 (S) 7:6 (κ) 7:6 7:9* 7:20 (S)
7:24* 7:28* 9:58* 9:59 9:59* 9:60* 9:60 9:61
(S) 9:61 (S) 9:62 (S) 10:2 (τοτε) 10:2* 10:5*
10:6* 10:7 10:10 (κ) 10:16 11:2 11:11 (η) 11:14
(κ) 11:15* 11:16 (κ, τοτε) 11:17* 11:18 11:19
(κ) 11:20* 11:22 (S) 11:27 (S) 11:28 (S) 11:29*
11:34* 11:39* 11:42* 11:46 11:47 11:48 (κ)
12:2 (γ) 12:4 12:5 12:8 12:9* 12:10* 12:11*
12:13 (S) 12:14 (S) 12:16 (S) 12:20 (S) 12:20
(S) 12:22 12:25* 12:27* 12:28* 12:30 (γ)
12:39* 12:45* 12:54*12:56* 12:57 13:28
13:35 (γ) 14:16 (κ) 14:34* 16:17 (γ) 17:29 (S)
17:33 (κ) 17:35 (κ) 18:14 (κ) 19:13 (κ) 19:16 (κ)
19:19 19:26* 22:28

δεῖ
Matt [1/2] 23:23* 25:27
Luke [1/2] 11:42* 12:12

δείκνυμι
Matt [1/1] 4:8*
Luke [1/1] 4:5*

δεινῶς
Matt [0/1] 8:6

δεῖπνον (⇨ γάμος)
Matt [0/1] 23:6
Luke [0/3] 14:16 (γ) 14:17 14:24

δέκα
Matt [1/1] 25:28*
Luke [1/7] 15:8 (S) 19:13 19:13 19:16 19:17
19:24* 19:25

δένδρον
Matt [6/6] 3:10* 3:10* 7:18* 7:18* 12:33*
13:32*
Luke [6/6] 3:9* 3:9* 6:43* 6:43* 6:44* 13:19*

δεξιός
Matt [0/1] 5:39

δέομαι
Matt [1/1] 9:38*
Luke [1/1] 10:2*

δεσμεύω (⇨ φορτίζω)
Matt [0/1] 23:4 (φ)

δεσμωτήριον
Matt [0/1] 11:2

δεῦτε
Matt [0/1] 22:4

δεύτερος
Luke [0/1] 19:18

δέχομαι (⇨ ἀκούω)
Matt [1/5] 10:14* 10:40 (α) 10:40 (α) 10:40
10:40
Luke [1/2] 10:8 10:10*

δέω
Matt [0/1] 12:29

διά (⇨ γάρ)
Matt [6/10] 4:4 6:25* 7:13* 7:13 11:2 12:27*
12:43* 18:7* 23:34* 24:44
Luke [6/9] 6:48 (γ) 11:19* 11:24* 11:49*
12:22* 13:24* 14:20 17:1* 19:23

διαβλέπω
Matt [1/1] 7:5*
Luke [1/1] 6:42*

διάβολος (⇨ πειράζω)
Matt [2/4] 4:1* 4:5 4:8 4:11*
Luke [2/4] 4:2* 4:3 (π) 4:6 4:13*

διαγγέλλω
Luke [0/1] 9:60

διαδίδωμι
Luke [0/1] 11:22 (S)

διακαθαίρω (⇨ διακαθαρίζω)
Luke [0/1] 3:17 (δ)

διακαθαρίζω (⇨ διακαθαίρω)
Matt [0/1] 3:12 (δ)

διακονέω
Matt [0/1] 4:11

διακρίνω (⇨ δοκιμάζω)
Matt [0/1] 16:3 (δ)

διαλογίζομαι
Luke [0/1] 12:16 (S)

διαμένω (⇨ ἀκολουθέω)
Luke [0/1] 22:28 (α)

διαμερίζω ⇨ μερίζω (⇨ διχάζω)
Luke [0(2)/4] 11:17(*) 11:18(*) 12:52 12:53 (δ)

διαμερισμός (⇨ μάχαιρα)
Luke [0/1] 12:51 (μ)

διανόημα (⇨ ἐνθύμησις)
Luke [0/1] 11:17 (ε)

διαπραγματεύομαι
Luke [0/1] 19:15

διαρπάζω
Matt [0/1] 12:29

διασκορπίζω (⇨ τίθημι)
Matt [0/2] 25:24 (τ) 25:26 (τ)

διασῴζω (⇨ θεραπεύω)
Luke [0/1] 7:3 (θ)

διατίθημαι
Luke [0/2] 22:29 22:29

διαφέρω
Matt [2/2] 6:26* 10:31*
Luke [2/2] 12:7* 12:24*

διαφθείρω (⇨ ἀφανίζω)
Luke [0/1] 12:33 (α)

διαφυλάσσω
Luke [0/1] 4:10

διδάσκαλος
Matt [2/4] 8:19 10:24* 10:25* 12:38
Luke [2/3] 6:40* 6:40* 12:13 (S)

διδάσκω (⇨ δίδωμι)
Luke [0/2] 12:12 (δ) 13:26

δίδωμι (⇨ βάλλω, διδάσκω)
Matt [12/14] 4:9* 5:42* 6:11* 7:7* 7:11*
7:11* 10:8 10:19 (δ) 12:39* 16:4* 24:45*
25:15* 25:28* 25:29*
Luke [11/21] 4:6* 4:6 6:30* 6:38 (S) 6:38 (S)
6:38 (S) 11:3* 11:9* 11:13* 11:13* 11:29*
11:41 12:33 12:42* 12:51 (β) 12:58 19:13*
19:15 19:23 (β) 19:24* 19:26*

διέξοδος
Matt [0/1] 22:9

διέρχομαι
Matt [1/1] 12:43*
Luke [1/1] 11:24*

δίκαιος (⇨ βασιλεύς)
Matt [0/6] 5:45 13:17 (β) 23:28 23:29 23:35
23:35
Luke [0/2] 12:57 15:7

δικαιοσύνη
Matt [0/2] 5:6 6:33

δικαιόω
Matt [1/1] 11:19*
Luke [1/1] 7:35*

διό
Luke [0/1] 7:7

διορύσσω (⇨ ἐγγίζω)
Matt [1/3] 6:19 6:20 (ε) 24:43*
Luke [1/1] 12:39*

διχάζω (⇨ διαμερίζω)
Matt [0/1] 10:35 (δ)

διχοτομέω
Matt [1/1] 24:51*
Luke [1/1] 12:46*

διψάω
Matt [0/1] 5:6

διώκω (⇨ ἐπηρεάζω, πιστεύω, ποιέω)
Matt [1/4] 5:11 5:12 (πο) 5:44 (ε) 23:34*
Luke [1/2] 11:49* 17:23 (πι)

δοκέω (⇨ ἄρχομαι, νομίζω)
Matt [1/3] 3:9 (α) 18:12 24:44*
Luke [1/2] 12:40* 12:51 (ν)

δοκιμάζω (⇨ διακρίνω)
Luke [0/3] 12:56 (δ) 12:56 14:19

δοκός
Matt [3/3] 7:3* 7:4* 7:5*
Luke [3/3] 6:41* 6:42* 6:42*

δόμα
Matt [1/1] 7:11*
Luke [1/1] 11:13*

δόξα
Matt [2/3] 4:8* 6:29* 19:28
Luke [2/2] 4:6* 12:27*

δουλεύω
Matt [2/2] 6:24* 6:24*
Luke [2/2] 16:13* 16:13*

δοῦλος (⇨ οἰκονόμος, παῖς)
Matt [10/17] 8:9* 10:24 10:25 22:3* 22:4 22:6
22:8* 22:10 24:45 (ο) 24:46* 24:48* 24:50*
25:14* 25:19* 25:21* 25:23 25:26*

Luke [10/16] 7:2 (π) 7:3 (S) 7:8* 7:10 (π)
12:43* 12:45* 12:46* 14:17* 14:21 14:21*
14:22 14:23 19:13* 19:15* 19:17* 19:22*

δραχμή
Luke [0/3] 15:8 (S) 15:8 (S) 15:9 (S)

δύναμαι (⇨ εἰμί, ἔχω, οἶδα)
Matt [4/9] 3:9* 6:24* 6:24* 6:27* 7:18 (ει)
10:28 (εχ) 10:28 (εχ) 12:29 16:3 (ο)
Luke [4/10] 3:8* 6:39 6:42 12:25* 12:26 14:20
14:26 14:27 16:13* 16:13*

δύναμις
Matt [1/4] 7:22 11:21* 11:23 (S) 25:15
Luke [1/1] 10:13*

δύο
Matt [3/12] 5:41 (S) 6:24* 10:10 10:29 24:40*
24:41* 25:15 25:17 25:17 25:22 25:22 25:22
Luke [3/7] 7:18 12:6 12:52 12:52 16:13*
17:34* 17:35*

δυσβάστακτος
Matt [1/1] 23:4*
Luke [1/1] 11:46*

δυσμή
Matt [1/2] 8:11* 24:27
Luke [1/2] 12:54 13:29*

δώδεκα
Matt [1/2] 19:28 19:28*
Luke [1/1] 22:30*

δῶμα
Matt [1/1] 10:27*
Luke [1/1] 12:3*

δωρεάν
Matt [0/2] 10:8 10:8

ἐάν (⇨ εἰ, ὅταν, ἐπάν)
Matt [10/25] 4:9* 5:13* 5:32 5:46 (ει) 5:47*
6:22 (ο) 6:23 (επ) 7:12 8:19* 10:13* 10:13 (ει)
11:6* 11:27* 12:29 (επ) 12:32 15:14 17:20 (ει)
18:12 18:13 18:15* 18:15* 22:9 24:26 24:28
24:48*
Luke [10/15] 4:6 4:7* 6:33* 6:34 (S) 7:23*
9:57* 10:6* 10:22* 12:45* 14:34* 15:8 (S)
17:3* 17:3* 17:4 17:33

ἑαυτός, -ή, -όν (⇨ αὐτοῦ, αὐτῆς, ἴδιος, ὑμῖν)
Matt [7/10] 3:9* 8:22* 12:25* 12:25 12:26*
12:45 12:45* 23:12* 23:12* 23:31
Luke [9/21] 3:8* 9:60* 11:17* 11:18* 11:21
(S) 11:26* 12:17 (S) 12:21 (S) 12:33 (υ) 12:57
13:19 (αυτου) 13:34 (αυτης) 14:11* 14:11*
14:26 14:26 14:27 (αυτου) 18:14* 18:14*
19:12 19:13 (ι)

ἐάω (⇨ ἀφίημι)
Matt [0/1] 24:43 (α)

ἑβδομηκοντάκις
Matt [0/1] 18:22

ἐγγίζω (⇨ διορύσσω)
Matt [1/1] 10:7*
Luke [2/3] 10:9* 10:11* 12:33 (δ)

ἐγείρω (⇨ εἰμί)
Matt [3/5] 3:9* 10:8 11:5* 11:11 (ε) 12:42*
Luke [3/4] 3:8* 7:22* 11:31* 13:25 (S)

ἐγκρύπτω
Matt [1/1] 13:33*
Luke [1/1] 13:21*

ἐθνικός (⇨ ἁμαρτωλός)
Matt [0/1] 5:47 (α)

ἔθνος
Matt [1/1] 6:32*
Luke [1/2] 7:5 (S) 12:30*

εἰ (⇨ ἐάν, ἵνα)
Matt [14/18] 4:3* 4:6* 5:13 6:30* 6:23* 7:11*
11:21* 11:23 (S) 11:27* 11:27* 12:24 12:26*
12:27* 12:28* 12:39* 16:4* 23:30 24:43*
Luke [13/20] 4:3* 4:9* 6:32 (ε) 10:6 (ε) 10:13*
10:22* 10:22* 11:13* 11:18* 11:19* 11:20*
11:29* 11:36* 12:26 12:28* 12:39* 12:49 (S)
14:26 17:2 (ι) 17:6 (ε)

εἰμί (⇨ γίνομαι, δύναμαι, ἐγείρω, ἔχω, παρομοιάζω,
ὑπάρχω)
Matt [45/78] 3:11 3:11* 4:3* 4:6* 5:3* 5:11*
5:13 5:25 5:25 5:48 (γ) 5:48* 6:21* 6:21*
6:22* 6:22* 6:22* 6:23* 6:23 6:23* 6:25*
6:30* 7:9 7:11 (υ) 7:12 7:13 7:14 7:27 (γ) 8:8*
8:9* 8:12* 10:11 10:13* 10:13 10:15* 10:24*
10:26* 10:30 10:37* 10:37 10:38* 11:3* 11:6*
11:8* 11:10* 11:11* 11:16* 11:22* 11:24 (S)
12:23 12:27* 12:30* 12:30* 12:40 (γ) 12:40*
13:31* 13:32 13:32 13:33* 15:14 20:16* 22:8
22:8 23:28 23:30 23:30 23:31* 24:26 24:27*
24:28 24:37* 24:38 24:39* 24:40* 24:45*
24:51 25:21 (γ) 25:23 25:24*
Luke [46/93] 3:16* 4:3* 4:7 4:9* 6:20* 6:22*
6:32 (εχ) 6:33 (π) 6:34 (S) 6:35 (S) 6:35 (γ)
6:35 6:36* 6:40 (γ) 6:40* 6:43 (δ) 6:47 6:48
6:49 7:2 7:4 (S) 7:6* 7:8* 7:19* 7:20* 7:23*
7:25* 7:27* 7:28 (εγ) 7:28* 7:31 7:32* 9:62 (S)
10:6* 10:12* 10:14* 10:22 10:22 11:14 11:14
11:19* 11:21 (S) 11:23* 11:23* 11:29 11:30*
11:34* 11:34* 11:34* 11:34* 11:35* 11:36 (S)
11:41 (γ) 11:44 (π) 11:48* 12:2* 12:6 12:20 (S)
12:23* 12:24 12:28* 12:34* 12:34* 12:42*
12:52 12:55 13:18* 13:19 13:21* 13:25 (S)
13:27 13:28* 13:30 13:30* 13:30 13:30 14:17
14:22 14:26* 14:27* 14:35 15:7 16:17 17:1
17:24* 17:26* 17:30* 17:34* 17:35 19:17
19:21* 19:22 22:28

εἶπον (⇨ βλασφημέω, γράφω, λαλέω, λέγω,
ὁμολογέω, φήμι)
Matt [18/32] 3:7 (λε) 4:3* 4:3* 4:4 4:9* 5:11
7:4 (λε) 7:22 (λε) 8:8* 8:10* 8:13 8:19* 8:21*
10:27* 11:3 (λε) 11:4* 11:25* 12:24* 12:25*
12:32* 12:32 (β) 12:39 (λε) 16:2 (λε) 17:20 (λε)
22:1* 22:4* 23:39* 24:26* 24:48* 25:22 (λε)
25:24 (λε) 25:26 (λε)
Luke [18/60] 4:3* 4:3* 4:6* 4:8 (λε) 4:9 (λε)
4:12 (φ) 4:12 (γ) 6:26 (S) 7:7* 7:9* 7:20 (S)

7:22* 9:57* 9:58 (λε) 9:59 9:59* 9:60 (λε) 9:61
(S) 9:62 (S) 10:10 10:21* 11:2 11:15* 11:17*
11:27 (S) 11:28 (S) 11:46 11:49 12:3* 12:10*
12:11 (λα) 12:12 (λα) 12:13 (S) 12:13 (S) 12:14
(S) 12:16 (S) 12:18 (S) 12:19 (S) 12:20 (S)
12:22 12:45* 13:20 (λα) 13:25 (S; cf. Matt
25:12) 13:27 (ο) 13:35* 14:16* 14:17* 14:18
14:19 14:20 14:21 (λε) 14:22 14:23 17:23*
19:12 19:13 19:15 19:17 (φ) 19:19 (φ) 19:25

εἰρήνη
Matt [2/4] 10:13* 10:13 10:34* 10:34
Luke [2/5] 10:5 10:6 10:6* 11:21 (S) 12:51*

εἰς (⇨ ἐν, ἐπί, ἕως, κατά, πρός)
Matt [19/42] 3:11 3:10* 3:12* 4:1 (εν) 4:5* 4:8
5:13* 5:25* 5:39 (επι) 6:13* 6:26 6:26 6:30*
7:13 7:14 7:21 8:5* 8:12 9:38* 10:9 10:10
10:11* 10:12* 10:27 11:7* 12:29 (π) 12:41*
12:44* 13:33* 15:14* 18:6 18:15 18:21* 22:3
22:4 22:5 22:9 22:10* 23:34 24:38* 25:21
25:23
Luke [19/43] 3:9* 3:17* 4:9* 6:38 (S) 6:39*
7:1* 7:10 7:24* 9:61 (S) 9:62 (S) 10:2* 10:5*
10:7 10:8* 10:10 10:10 10:11 11:4* 11:24*
11:32* 11:33 11:49 (π) 12:5 (εν) 12:10 (κ)
12:10 (κ) 12:19 (S) 12:21 (S) 12:28* 12:58*
13:19 (εν) 13:19 13:21* 14:21 14:23* 14:35*
14:35 15:6 16:16 17:2 (εν) 17:4* 17:24 (εως)
17:27* 19:12

εἷς (⇨ ἕτερος, τις)
Matt [9/18] 5:18 5:18* 5:41 (S) 6:24* 6:24*
6:27 6:29* 8:19 (τ) 10:29* 18:6* 18:12* 24:40*
24:40 (ε) 24:41* 24:41 (ε) 25:15 25:18 25:24
Luke [9/16] 11:46 12:6* 12:27* 12:52 14:18
15:4* 15:7 15:8 (S) 15:10 (S) 16:13* 16:13*
16:17* 17:2* 17:34 17:34* 17:35*

εἰσάγω
Luke [0/1] 14:21

εἰσέρχομαι
Matt [10/15] 7:13* 7:13* 7:21 8:5* 8:8*
10:11* 10:12* 12:29 12:45* 23:13* 23:13*
23:13 24:38* 25:21 25:23
Luke [10/12] 7:1* 7:6* 10:5* 10:8* 10:10
11:26* 11:52* 11:52* 13:24* 13:24* 14:23
17:27*

εἰσπορεύομαι
Luke [0/1] 11:33

εἰσφέρω (⇨ παραδίδωμι)
Matt [1/1] 6:13*
Luke [1/2] 11:4* 12:11 (π)

ἐκ (⇨ ἀπό, ἐν, ἔξω)
Matt [13/17] 3:9* 6:27* 7:4 (εν) 7:5* 7:5 (εν)
7:9* 10:29* 12:33* 12:34* 12:35* 12:35*
12:42* 16:1* 18:12* 23:25 23:34* 23:34
Luke [13/24] 3:8* 6:42* 6:44* 6:44 (α) 6:44 (α)
6:45* 6:45* 6:45* 10:7 10:11 (εξω) 11:11*
11:13 (εν) 11:15 11:16* 11:27 (S) 11:31*
11:49* 12:6* 12:13 (S) 12:25* 15:4 15:4*
17:24 (α) 19:22

ἕκαστος
  Matt [0/1] 25:15
  Luke [0/1] 6:44
ἑκατόν
  Matt [1/1] 18:12*
  Luke [1/1] 15:4*
ἑκατοντάρχης
  Matt [2/3] 8:5* 8:8* 8:13
  Luke [2/2] 7:2* 7:6*
ἐκβάλλω (▷ θεραπεύω, προφέρω)
  Matt [11/16] 7:4* 7:5* 7:5* 7:22 8:12* 9:33*
  9:34* 9:38* 10:8 12:24* 12:26 12:27* 12:27*
  12:28* 12:35 (π) 12:35 (π)
  Luke [10/11] 6:22 6:42* 6:42* 6:42* 10:2*
  11:14* 11:15* 11:19* 11:19* 11:20* 13:28*
ἐκεῖ
  Matt [4/6] 6:21* 8:12* 12:45* 17:20 24:28*
  24:51
  Luke [4/7] 10:6 11:26* 12:18 (S) 12:34*
  13:28* 17:23 17:37*
ἐκεῖθεν
  Matt [1/1] 5:26*
  Luke [1/1] 12:59*
ἐκεῖνος (▷ κἀκεῖνος (▷ αὐτή, οὗτος)
  Matt [7/17] 7:22 7:25* 7:27* 8:13 10:14
  10:15* 10:19 (α) 11:25 (α) 12:45* 22:7 22:10
  24:38 24:43 (ο) 24:46* 24:48* 24:50* 25:19
  Luke [7/11] 4:2 6:23 6:48* 6:49* 10:12 10:12*
  11:26* 12:43* 12:45* 12:46* 14:24
ἐκζητέω (▷ ἔρχομαι, ἥκω)
  Luke [0/2] 11:50 (ε) 11:51 (η)
ἐκκόπτω
  Matt [1/1] 3:10*
  Luke [1/1] 3:9*
ἐκπειράζω
  Matt [1/1] 4:7*
  Luke [1/1] 4:12*
ἐκπορεύομαι (▷ ἔρχομαι)
  Matt [0/1] 4:4
  Luke [0/1] 3:7 (ε)
ἐκριζόω (▷ μεταβαίνω)
  Luke [0/1] 17:6 (μ)
ἐκτινάσσω (▷ ἀπομάσσω)
  Matt [0/1] 10:14 (α)
ἐκτός
  Matt [0/1] 23:26
ἐκχέω
  Matt [1/1] 23:35*
  Luke [1/1] 11:50*
ἐλάχιστος (▷ ὀλίγος)
  Luke [0/2] 12:26 19:17 (ο)
ἐλέγχω (▷ ἐπιτιμάω)
  Matt [0/1] 18:15 (ε)
ἐλεημοσύνη
  Luke [0/2] 11:41 12:33
ἔλεος (▷ ἀγάπη)
  Matt [0/1] 23:23 (α)

ἐλπίζω
  Luke [0/1] 6:34 (S)
ἐμαυτοῦ
  Matt [1/1] 8:9*
  Luke [1/2] 7:7 7:8*
ἐμβάλλω (▷ ἀπόλλυμι)
  Luke [0/1] 12:5 (α)
ἐμβλέπω (▷ κατανοέω)
  Matt [0/1] 6:26 (κ)
ἐμός (▷ αὐτό)
  Matt [0/1] 25:27 (α)
ἐμπί(μ)πλημι
  Luke [0/1] 6:25 (S)
ἐμπίπρημι
  Matt [0/1] 22:7
ἐμπίπτω ▷ πίπτω
  Luke [0(1)/1] 6:39(*)
ἐμπορία
  Matt [0/1] 22:5
ἔμπροσθεν (▷ ἐνώπιον)
  Matt [4/7] 10:32* 10:32* 10:33 (ε) 10:33 (ε)
  11:10* 11:26* 23:13
  Luke [4/4] 7:27* 10:21* 12:8* 12:8*
ἐν (▷ εἰς, ἐκ, ἐπί)
  Matt [47/87] 3:9* 3:11 3:11* 3:12* 5:12*
  5:13* 5:15 5:25* 5:45 6:9 6:10 6:20* 6:23*
  6:29* 7:2 (S) 7:2 7:3* 7:3* 7:4* 7:11 (εκ) 7:21
  7:22 8:6 8:10* 8:11* 8:13 9:33 9:34* 10:11
  10:15* 10:16* 10:19 10:27* 10:27* 10:28
  (εις) 10:32* 10:32* 10:32 10:33 11:2 11:6*
  11:8* 11:8* 11:11* 11:11* 11:16* 11:21*
  11:21* 11:21* 11:22* 11:23 (S) 11:23 (S)
  11:24 (S) 11:25* 12:24* 12:27* 12:27* 12:28*
  12:32 12:32 12:40 12:40 12:41* 12:42* 13:31
  (εις) 13:32* 18:6 (εις) 19:28 22:1 23:6 23:6*
  23:7* 23:30 23:30 23:34 23:39* 24:26 24:26
  24:38 24:40 (επι) 24:41 (επι) 24:45* 24:48*
  24:50* 24:50* 25:16 25:25
  Luke [46/79] 3:8* 3:16* 3:17* 4:1 4:1 (εις) 4:2
  4:5 6:23 6:23* 6:41* 6:41* 6:42 (εκ) 6:42* 6:42
  (εκ) 7:9* 7:23* 7:25* 7:25 7:25* 7:28* 7:28*
  7:32* 9:57 10:3* 10:7 10:9 10:12* 10:13*
  10:13* 10:13* 10:14* 10:21* 10:21 11:15*
  11:19* 11:19* 11:20* 11:21 (S) 11:27 (S)
  11:31* 11:32* 11:35* 11:43* 11:43* 12:3*
  12:3* 12:3 12:8* 12:8* 12:12* 12:17 (S)
  12:27* 12:28 12:33* 12:42* 12:45* 12:46*
  12:46* 12:51 (επι) 12:52 12:58* 13:19* 13:26
  13:28 13:29* 13:35* 14:34* 15:4 (επι) 15:7
  17:6 17:24 17:26 17:26 17:28 (S) 19:13 19:17
  (επι) 19:20 22:28 22:30
ἔνδοξος (▷ μαλακός)
  Luke [0/1] 7:25 (μ)
ἔνδυμα
  Matt [1/1] 6:25* 6:28
  Luke [1/1] 12:23*

ἐνδύω
  Matt [1/1] 6:25*
  Luke [1/1] 12:22*
ἔνειμι (▷ ἐντός)
  Luke [0/1] 11:41 (ε)
ἕνεκα -εν
  Matt [1/2] 5:11* 10:39
  Luke [1/1] 6:22*
ἐνενήκοντα
  Matt [2/2] 18:12* 18:13*
  Luke [2/2] 15:4* 15:7*
ἔνθεν
  Matt [0/1] 17:20
ἐνθύμησις (▷ διανόημα)
  Matt [0/1] 12:25 (δ)
ἐννέα
  Matt [2/2] 18:12* 18:13*
  Luke [2/2] 15:4* 15:7*
ἐντέλλω
  Matt [1/1] 4:6*
  Luke [1/1] 4:10*
ἐντός (▷ ἔνειμι)
  Matt [0/1] 23:26 (ε)
ἐντεῦθεν
  Luke [0/1] 4:9
ἔντιμος
  Luke [0/1] 7:2
ἐνώπιον (▷ ἔμπροσθεν)
  Luke [0/6] 4:7 12:6 12:9 (ε) 12:9 (ε) 13:26
  15:10 (S)
ἐξέρχομαι (▷ ἀπέρχομαι (▷ ἀστράπτω)
  Matt [8(9)/12] 5:26* 9:32 10:11 10:14* 11:7*
  11:8* 11:9* 12:43* 12:44* 22:10* 24:26(*)
  24:27 (ασ)
  Luke [8/12] 7:24* 7:25* 7:26* 10:10* 11:14
  11:24* 11:24* 12:59* 14:18 14:21 14:23*
  17:29 (S)
ἐξετάζω
  Matt [0/1] 10:11
ἐξίστημι (▷ θαυμάζω)
  Matt [0/1] 12:23 (θ)
ἐξομολογέω
  Matt [1/1] 11:25*
  Luke [1/1] 10:21*
ἐξουσία
  Matt [1/1] 8:9*
  Luke [1/5] 4:6 7:8* 12:5 12:11 19:17
ἔξω (▷ ἐκ, ἐξώτερος)
  Matt [1/2] 5:13* 10:14 (εκ)
  Luke [1/3] 13:25 (S) 13:28 (εξ) 14:35*
ἔξωθεν
  Matt [1/3] 23:25* 23:27 23:28
  Luke [1/2] 11:39* 11:40
ἐξώτερος (▷ ἔξω)
  Matt [0/1] 8:12 (ε)
ἐπαθροίζω
  Luke [0/1] 11:29

ἐπαίρω
Luke [0/1] 11:27 (S)
ἐπάν (▷ ἐάν)
Luke [0/2] 11:22 (ε) 11:34 (ε)
ἐπαναπαύομαι (▷ ἔρχομαι)
Luke [0/1] 10:6 (ε)
ἐπάνω (▷ ἐπί)
Luke [0/3] 11:44 19:17 (ε) 19:19 (ε)
ἐπέρχομαι
Luke [0/1] 11:22 (S)
ἐπερωτάω (▷ ζητέω)
Matt [0/1] 16:1 (ζ)
ἐπηρεάζω (▷ διώκω)
Luke [0/1] 6:28 (δ)
ἐπί (▷ ἀπό, εἰς, ἐν, ἐπάνω, κατά, πρός)
Matt [17/37] 3:7 4:4* 4:4 4:5* 4:6* 5:15*
5:45* 5:45 6:10 6:19 6:27* 7:24* 7:25 7:26*
10:13* 10:27* 10:29 10:34 (εν) 12:26* 12:28*
18:12 (εν) 18:13* 18:13* 19:28 19:28* 22:5
22:9 23:4 23:35 23:35 23:36 (α) 24:45* 24:47*
25:21 (εν) 25:21 (επ) 25:23 25:23 (επ)
Luke [17/44] 4:4* 4:9* 4:11* 6:29 (εἰς) 6:35*
6:48* 6:49* 9:62 (S) 10:6* 10:6 (π) 10:9 11:17
(κ) 11:17 (κ) 11:18* 11:20* 11:22 (S) 11:33*
12:3* 12:11 12:14 (S) 12:25* 12:42* 12:44*
12:49 (S) 12:52 12:52 12:53 12:53 (κ) 12:53
12:53 (κ) 12:53 12:53 (κ) 12:54 12:58 15:4 15:5
15:7* 15:7* 15:10 (S) 17:34 (εν) 17:35 (εν)
19:23 22:30 22:30*
ἐπιβάλλω
Luke [0/1] 9:62 (S)
ἐπιγινώσκω ▷ γινώσκω
Matt [0(1)/2] 11:27(*) 11:27
ἐπιδείκνυμι
Matt [0/1] 16:1
ἐπιδίδωμι
Matt [2/2] 7:9* 7:10*
Luke [2/2] 11:11* 11:12*
ἐπιζητέω ▷ ζητέω
Matt [1(3)/3] 6:32* 12:39(*) 16:4(*)
Luke [1/1] 12:30*
ἐπιθυμέω (▷ θέλω)
Matt [0/1] 13:17 (θ)
ἐπιλανθάνομαι (▷ πίπτω)
Luke [0/1] 12:6 (π)
ἐπιμελῶς
Luke [0/1] 15:8 (S)
ἐπιούσιος
Matt [1/1] 6:11*
Luke [1/1] 11:3*
ἐπιστρέφω ▷ ὑποστρέφω (▷ ἀνακάμπτω)
Matt [0(1)/2] 10:13 (α) 12:44(*)
Luke [0/1] 17:4
ἐπισυνάγω ▷ συνάγω
Matt [1/2] 23:37* 23:37
Luke [1(2)/2] 13:34* 17:37(*)
ἐπιτάσσω
Luke [0/1] 14:22

ἐπιτίθημι
Matt [0/1] 23:4
Luke [0/1] 15:5
ἐπιτιμάω (▷ ἐλέγχω)
Luke [0/1] 17:3 (ε)
ἐπιτρέπω
Matt [1/1] 8:21*
Luke [1/2] 9:59* 9:61 (S)
ἑπτά
Matt [1/2] 12:45* 18:22
Luke [1/1] 11:26*
ἑπτάκις
Matt [2/2] 18:21* 18:22*
Luke [2/2] 17:4* 17:4*
ἐργάζομαι (▷ ἐργάτης)
Matt [0/2] 7:23 (ε) 25:16
ἐργασία
Luke [0/1] 12:58
ἐργάτης (▷ ἐργάζομαι)
Matt [3/3] 9:37* 9:38* 10:10*
Luke [3/4] 10:2* 10:2* 10:7* 13:27 (ε)
ἔργον (▷ τέκνον)
Matt [0/2] 11:2 11:19 (τ)
Luke [0/1] 11:48
ἔρημος (▷ ὄρος)
Matt [2/4] 4:1* 11:7* 23:38 24:26
Luke [2/3] 4:1* 7:24* 15:4 (o)
ἐρημόω
Matt [1/1] 12:25*
Luke [1/1] 11:17*
ἔρχομαι ▷ προσέρχομαι (▷ ἀκολουθέω, ἐκζητέω,
ἐκπορεύομαι, ἐπαναπαύομαι, παραγίνομαι)
Matt [18/29] 3:7 (εκπ) 3:11* 6:10* 7:25 7:27
8:7* 8:9* 8:9* 10:13 (επ) 10:34 (πα) 10:34
10:35 11:3* 11:18* 11:19* 12:42* 12:44*
13:32 18:7* 18:7* 22:3 23:35 (εκζ) 23:39*
24:39* 24:43* 24:44* 24:46* 25:19 25:27*
Luke [19(21)/32] 3:16* 6:47 7:3* 7:7 7:8* 7:8*
7:19* 7:20* 7:33* 7:34* 11:2* 11:25* 11:31*
12:45 13:35* 12:39* 12:40* 12:43* 12:49 (S)
12:54 14:17 14:20 14:26 14:27 (α) 15:6 17:1*
17:1* 17:27* 19:13 19:18(*) 19:20(*) 19:23*
ἐρωτάω
Luke [0/3] 7:3 (S) 14:18 14:19
ἐσθίω (▷ νηστεύω, τρώγω)
Matt [5/5] 6:25* 6:31* 11:18* 11:19* 24:49*
Luke [5/13] 4:2 (ν) 7:33* 7:34* 10:7 10:8
12:19 (S) 12:22* 12:29* 12:45* 13:26 17:27 (τ)
17:28 (S) 22:30
ἔσχατος
Matt [4/4] 5:26* 12:45* 20:16* 20:16*
Luke [4/4] 11:26* 12:59* 13:30* 13:30*
ἔσωθεν
Matt [1/3] 23:25* 23:27 23:28
Luke [1/2] 11:39* 11:40
ἕτερος (▷ ἀλλήλων, ἄλλος, εἷς)
Matt [4/6] 6:24* 6:24* 8:21* 11:3 (αλλος)
11:16 (αλληλων) 12:45*

ἐπιτίθημι
Luke [4/12] 9:59* 9:61 (S) 11:16 11:26* 14:19
14:20 16:13* 16:13* 16:18 17:34 (ε) 17:35 (ε)
19:20
ἔτι
Matt [0/1] 5:13
Luke [0/2] 14:22 14:26
ἑτοιμάζω
Matt [0/1] 22:4
Luke [0/1] 12:20 (S)
ἕτοιμος
Matt [2/3] 22:4* 22:8 24:44*
Luke [2/2] 12:40* 14:17*
ἔτος
Luke [0/1] 12:19 (S)
εὖ (▷ εὖγε)
Matt [0/2] 25:21 (ε) 25:23
εὐαγγελίζω
Matt [1/1] 11:5*
Luke [1/1] 7:22* 16:16
εὖγε (▷ εὖ)
Luke [0/1] 19:17 (ε)
εὐγενής
Luke [0/1] 19:12
εὐδία
Matt [0/1] 16:2
εὐδοκία
Matt [1/1] 11:26*
Luke [1/1] 10:21*
εὔθετος (▷ ἰσχύω)
Luke [0/2] 9:62 (S) 14:35 (ι)
εὐθέως
Matt [0/1] 25:15
εὐθύς
Luke [0/2] 6:49 12:54
εὔκοπος
Luke [0/1] 16:17
εὐλογέω
Matt [1/1] 23:39*
Luke [1/2] 6:28 13:35*
εὐνοέω
Matt [0/1] 5:25
εὑρίσκω (▷ ζητέω, ζῳογονέω)
Matt [7/12] 7:7* 7:8* 7:14 8:10* 10:39 (ζη)
10:39 (ζω) 12:43* 12:44* 18:13* 22:9 22:10
24:46*
Luke [7/13] 7:9* 7:10 11:9* 11:10* 11:24*
11:25* 12:43* 15:4 15:5* 15:6 15:8 (S) 15:9 (S)
15:9 (S)
εὐρύχωρος
Matt [0/1] 7:13
εὐφορέω
Luke [0/1] 12:16 (S)
εὐφραίνω
Luke [0/1] 12:19 (S)
ἐχθρός
Matt [1/2] 5:44* 10:36
Luke [1/2] 6:27* 6:35 (S)

ἔχιδνα
Matt [1/1] 3:7*
Luke [1/1] 3:7*

ἔχω (▷ γίνομαι, δύναμαι, εἰμί)
Matt [10/12] 3:9* 5:46 (ε) 8:9* 8:20* 8:20*
11:18* 17:20* 25:25 25:28* 25:29* 25:29*
25:29*
Luke [10/26] 3:8* 7:2 7:8* 7:33* 9:58* 9:58*
11:36 (S) 12:4 (δ) 12:5 (δ) 12:17 (S) 12:19 (S)
14:18 14:18 14:19 14:35 15:4 (γ) 15:7 15:8 (S)
17:6* 19:17 19:20 19:24* 19:25 19:26* 19:26*
19:26*

ἕως (▷ εἰς, μέχρι, ὡς)
Matt [6/17] 5:18 5:18 5:25 (ω) 5:26* 10:11
11:12 11:13 (μ) 11:23* 11:23* 13:33* 18:21
18:22 18:22 23:35* 23:39* 24:27 (ε) 24:39
Luke [6/8] 10:15* 10:15* 11:51* 12:59*
13:21* 13:35 15:4 15:8 (S)

Ζαχαρίας
Matt [1/1] 23:35*
Luke [1/1] 11:51*

ζάω
Matt [1/1] 4:4*
Luke [1/1] 4:4*

ζεύγη
Luke [0/1] 14:19

ζητέω ▷ ἐπιζητέω (▷ ἐπερωτάω, εὑρίσκω,
μεριμνάω)
Matt [4/5] 6:33* 7:7* 7:8* 12:43* 18:12
Luke [4(5)/10] 11:9* 11:10* 11:16 (επερ)
11:24* 11:29(*) 12:29 (μ) 12:31* 13:24 15:8
(S) 17:33 (ευ)

ζύμη
Matt [1/1] 13:33*
Luke [1/1] 13:21*

ζυμόω
Matt [1/1] 13:33*
Luke [1/1] 13:21*

ζωή
Matt [0/1] 7:14

ζῳογονέω (▷ εὑρίσκω)
Luke [0/1] 17:33 (ζ)

ζώνη
Matt [0/1] 10:9

ἤ (▷ καί, δέ, οὐδέ)
Matt [9/22] 5:18* 6:24* 6:24* 6:25 6:31 (κ)
6:31 (κ) 7:4 7:9 (δ) 7:10* 7:16 (ο) 10:11 10:14
10:15* 10:19* 10:37 (κ) 10:37 11:3* 11:22*
11:24 (S) 12:25 12:29 18:13*
Luke [10/16] 7:19* 7:20* 10:12* 10:14*
11:12* 12:11* 12:11 12:14 (S) 12:51 15:7*
15:8 (S) 16:13* 16:13* 16:17* 17:2 17:23

ἤδη
Matt [1/1] 3:10*
Luke [1/4] 3:9* 7:6 12:49 (S) 14:17

ἡδύοσμον
Matt [1/1] 23:23*
Luke [1/1] 11:42*

ἥκω (▷ ἐκζητέω)
Matt [2/3] 8:11* 23:36 (ε) 24:50*
Luke [2/3] 12:46* 13:29* 13:35

ἡλικία
Matt [1/1] 6:27*
Luke [1/1] 12:25*

ἥλιος
Matt [0/1] 5:45

ἡμέρα (▷ παρουσία, σήμερον)
Matt [5/13] 4:2* 7:22 10:15* 11:12 11:22
11:24 (S) 12:40 12:40 23:30 24:37* 24:38
24:38* 24:50*
Luke [5/14] 4:2* 4:2 6:23 10:12* 11:3 (σ)
12:46* 17:4 17:24 (π) 17:26* 17:26 (π) 17:27*
17:28 (S) 17:29 (S) 17:30 (π)

θάλασσα
Matt [1/1] 18:6*
Luke [1/2] 17:2* 17:6

θάπτω
Matt [2/2] 8:21* 8:22*
Luke [2/2] 9:59* 9:60*

θαυμάζω (▷ ἐξίστημι)
Matt [2/2] 8:10* 9:33*
Luke [2/2] 7:9* 11:14* (ε)

θεάομαι
Matt [1/1] 11:7*
Luke [1/1] 7:24*

θεῖον
Luke [0/1] 17:29 (S)

θέλημα
Matt [0/2] 6:10 7:21

θέλω (▷ ἐπιθυμέω)
Matt [3/8] 5:40 5:42 7:12* 12:38 22:3 23:4
23:37* 23:37*
Luke [3/6] 4:6 6:31* 10:24 (ε) 12:49 (S) 13:34*
13:34*

θεμέλιος
Luke [0/2] 6:48 6:49

θεμελιόω (▷ οἰκοδομέω)
Matt [0/1] 7:25 (ο)

θεός (▷ οὐρανός, πατήρ)
Matt [9/11] 3:9* 4:3* 4:4 4:6* 4:7* 4:10* 6:24*
6:30* 6:33 12:28* 12:28*
Luke [9/30] 3:8* 4:3* 4:8* 4:9* 4:12* 6:20 (ο)
7:28 (ο) 9:60 9:62 (S) 10:9 (ο) 10:11 (ο) 11:20*
11:20* 11:28 (S) 11:42 11:49 12:6 (π) 12:8 (π)
12:9 (π) 12:20 (S) 12:21 (S) 12:24 (π) 12:28*
13:18 (ο) 13:20 (ο) 13:28 13:29 (ο) 15:10 (S)
16:13* 16:16 (ο)

θεραπεία (▷ οἰκετεία)
Luke [0/1] 12:42 (ο)

θεραπεύω (▷ διασῴζω, ἐκβάλλω)
Matt [1/3] 8:7 (δ) 10:8* 12:22 (ε)
Luke [1/1] 10:9*

θερίζω
Matt [3/3] 6:26* 25:24* 25:26*
Luke [3/3] 12:24* 19:21* 19:22*

θερισμός
Matt [3/3] 9:37* 9:38* 9:38*
Luke [3/3] 10:2* 10:2* 10:2*

θηλάζω
Luke [0/1] 11:27 (S)

θησαυρίζω (▷ ποιέω, πωλέω)
Matt [0/2] 6:19 (πω) 6:20 (πο)
Luke [0/1] 12:21 (S)

θησαυρός (▷ βαλλάντιον)
Matt [3/5] 6:19 (β) 6:20* 6:21* 12:35* 12:35
Luke [3/3] 6:45* 12:33* 12:34*

θλίβω
Matt [0/1] 7:14

θρηνέω
Matt [1/1] 11:17*
Luke [1/1] 7:32*

θρίξ
Matt [1/1] 10:30*
Luke [1/1] 12:7*

θρόνος
Matt [1/2] 19:28 19:28*
Luke [1/1] 22:30*

θυγάτηρ (▷ τέκνον)
Matt [1/2] 10:35* 10:37 (τ)
Luke [1/2] 12:53 12:53*

θύρα (▷ πύλη)
Luke [0/3] 13:24 (π) 13:25 (S; cf. Matt 25:10)
13:25 (S)

θυσιαστήριον
Matt [1/1] 23:35*
Luke [1/1] 11:51*

θύω
Matt [0/1] 22:4

Ἰακώβ
Matt [1/1] 8:11*
Luke [1/1] 13:28*

ἰάομαι (▷ ὑγιαίνω)
Matt [1/2] 8:8* 8:13 (υ)
Luke [1/1] 7:7*

ἴδε (▷ ἰδού)
Matt [0/3] 25:20 25:22 25:25 (ι)

ἴδιος (▷ ἑαυτός, σός)
Matt [0/3] 22:5 25:14 (ε) 25:15
Luke [0/2] 6:41 (σ) 6:44

ἰδού (▷ ἴδε)
Matt [9/14] 4:11 7:4 9:32 10:16* 11:8* 11:10*
11:19* 12:41* 12:42* 22:4 23:34 23:38*
24:26* 24:26*
Luke [9/13] 6:23 7:25* 7:27* 7:34* 10:3*
11:31* 11:32* 11:41 13:30 13:35* 17:23*
17:23* 19:20 (ι)

ἱερόν
Matt [1/1] 4:5*
Luke [1/1] 4:9*

'Ιερουσαλήμ
  Matt [2/2] 23:37* 23:37*
  Luke [2/3] 4:9 13:34* 13:34*
'Ιησοῦς
  Matt [5/12] 4:1* 4:7* 4:10* 8:10* 8:13 8:20*
    8:22 11:4 11:7 11:25 18:22 22:1
  Luke [5/10] 4:1* 4:4 4:8* 4:12* 7:3 (S) 7:4 (S)
    7:6 7:9* 9:58* 9:62 (S)
ἱκανός
  Matt [2/2] 3:11* 8:8*
  Luke [2/2] 3:16* 7:6*
ἱμάς
  Luke [0/1] 3:16
ἱμάτιον
  Matt [1/1] 5:40*
  Luke [1/2] 6:29* 7:25
ἱματισμός
  Luke [0/1] 7:25
ἵνα (⇨ εἰ, καί, ὅπως)
  Matt [3/7] 4:3* 7:1 7:12* 8:8* 10:25 18:6 (ε)
    23:26
  Luke [3/10] 4:3* 6:31* 6:34 (S) 7:6* 11:33 (κ)
    11:50 (ο) 14:23 17:2 19:15 22:30
'Ιορδάνης
  Luke [0/1] 4:1
'Ιουδαῖος
  Luke [0/1] 7:3 (S)
'Ισαάκ
  Matt [1/1] 8:11*
  Luke [1/1] 13:28*
ἴσος
  Luke [0/1] 6:34 (S)
'Ισραήλ
  Matt [2/3] 8:10* 9:33 19:28*
  Luke [2/2] 7:9* 22:30*
ἵστημι (⇨ πίπτω)
  Matt [2/3] 4:5* 12:25 (π) 12:26*
  Luke [2/3] 4:9* 11:18* 13:25 (S)
ἰσχυρός
  Matt [2/3] 3:11* 12:29* 12:29
  Luke [2/3] 3:16* 11:21* 11:22 (S)
ἰσχύω (⇨ εὔθετος)
  Matt [0/1] 5:13 (ε)
  Luke [0/2] 6:48 13:24
ἰχθύς
  Matt [1/1] 7:10*
  Luke [1/2] 11:11* 11:11
'Ιωάννης
  Matt [6/7] 11:2* 11:4* 11:7* 11:11* 11:12
    11:13* 11:18*
  Luke [6/9] 7:18 7:18* 7:20 (S) 7:22* 7:24
    7:24* 7:28* 7:33* 16:16*
'Ιωνᾶς
  Matt [5/5] 12:39* 12:40* 12:41* 12:41* 16:4*
  Luke [4/4] 11:29* 11:30* 11:32* 11:32*
ἰῶτα
  Matt [0/1] 5:18

κἀγώ (⇨ ἐγώ)
  Matt [0/2] 10:32 10:33
  Luke [1/3] 11:9 19:23* (ε) 22:29
καθαιρέω
  Luke [0/1] 12:18 (S)
καθαρίζω
  Matt [2/4] 10:8 11:5* 23:25* 23:26
  Luke [2/2] 7:22* 11:39*
καθαρός
  Matt [1/1] 23:26*
  Luke [1/1] 11:41*
κάθημαι
  Matt [2/3] 11:16* 19:28*
  Luke [2/3] 7:32* 10:13 22:30*
καθίζω
  Matt [0/1] 19:28
καθίστημι
  Matt [2/4] 24:45* 24:47* 25:21 25:23
  Luke [2/3] 12:14 (S) 12:42* 12:44*
καθοπλίζω
  Luke [0/1] 11:21 (S)
καθώς (⇨ ὡς, ὥσπερ)
  Luke [0/6] 6:31 6:36 (ως) 11:30 (ωσπ) 17:26
    (ωσπ) 17:28 (S) 22:29
καί (⇨ δέ, γάρ, ἤ, ἵνα, οὐδέ, οὖν, οὕτως, ὅπως, τότε,
    ὥστε)
  Matt [165/294] 3:7 3:9* 3:10* 3:11* 3:12
    3:12* 4:2* 4:2 4:3 (δ) 4:5* 4:6* 4:6* 4:8 4:8*
    4:9* 4:10* 4:11 4:11 5:6 5:11* 5:11 5:12* 5:15
    5:15 (ι) 5:18* 5:25* 5:25* 5:32* 5:39* 5:40*
    5:40* 5:40 5:41 (S) 5:42* 5:44 5:45* 5:45 5:45
    5:46* 5:47* 5:47* 6:10 6:12* 6:12* 6:13* 6:19
    6:19 6:19 6:20 6:21* 6:24* 6:24* 6:24* 6:25*
    6:26* 6:28 6:30* 6:33 6:33* 7:2 (γ) 7:4 7:5*
    7:7* 7:7* 7:7* 7:8* 7:8* 7:10* 7:12 7:12 7:13
    7:13 7:14 7:14 7:22* 7:22* 7:23* 7:24* 7:25
    7:25 7:25 (δ) 7:25 7:25* 7:26 (δ) 7:26* 7:27
    7:27 7:27 7:27 7:27* 7:27* 7:27* 8:6 8:7 (δ) 8:8 8:8*
    8:9* 8:9* 8:9* 8:9* 8:9* 8:9* 8:9* 8:10* 8:11*
    8:11* 8:11* 8:11* 8:12* 8:13 8:13* 8:19*
    8:20* 8:20* 8:21 8:22 9:33 (δ) 9:33* 10:13*
    10:14 (δ) 10:15 10:25 10:26* 10:27* 10:28
    10:28 10:28 10:29* 10:30* 10:35* 10:35*
    10:36 10:37 10:38 10:38* 10:39 (δ) 10:40*
    11:4* 11:4* 11:5 11:5* 11:5 11:5 11:6* 11:9*
    11:12* 11:13* 11:17* 11:17* 11:18* 11:19*
    11:19* 11:19* 11:19* 11:19* 11:21* 11:21*
    11:22* 11:23* 11:25* 11:25* 11:25* 11:27*
    11:27* 12:22 12:22 (δ) 12:22 12:23* 12:23
    12:25* 12:26* 12:27 (δ) 12:29 12:29* 12:30*
    12:32* 13:32* 13:32 12:35* 12:38 12:39
    12:39* 12:40 12:40 12:41* 12:41* 12:42*
    12:42* 12:43* 12:44* 12:45 12:45* 12:45*
    12:45* 13:16 13:17* 13:17* 13:17* 13:17*
    16:1 (δ) 16:1 16:3* 16:4 16:4* 17:20* 17:20
    18:6* 18:12* 18:12* 18:13* 18:15 18:21 19:28
    20:16* 22:1 (δ) 22:3* 22:3 22:4 22:4 22:6 22:7
  22:7 22:9* 22:10 22:10 22:10 23:4 23:4 23:6
    23:7* 23:7 23:12* 23:13 23:23 23:23* 23:23*
    23:23* 23:23* 23:23 23:25 23:25* 23:25*
    23:26 23:27 23:27 23:28 23:28 23:29 23:29
    23:30 23:32 (δ) 23:34* 23:34 23:34 23:34
    23:34* 23:35* 23:37* 23:37* 24:27 24:38
    24:38 24:39* 24:39* 24:39 24:40* 24:41 (δ)
    24:43 24:44* 24:45 24:49* 24:49* 24:50*
    24:51* 24:51* 24:51 25:14 25:15 (δ) 25:15
    25:16 25:18 25:19 25:20 (δ) 25:21 25:22*
    25:23 25:24* 25:24* 25:25 25:26 25:26*
    25:27* 25:28* 25:29 25:29*
  Luke [162/320] 3:8* 3:9 3:9* 3:16* 3:17* 4:1
    4:2* 4:2 4:4 (δ) 4:5 4:6* 4:6* 4:6 4:8 (τ) 4:8*
    4:9* 4:9* 4:11* 4:12 4:13 (τ) 6:22 6:22 6:22*
    6:23* 6:25 (S) 6:29* 6:29* 6:29* 6:30* 6:31
    (ουν) 6:32 (γ) 6:32* 6:33* 6:33* 6:34 (S) 6:34
    (S) 6:35 (S) 6:35 (S) 6:35 (S) 6:35 (οπως) 6:35*
    6:36 6:37 6:37 (ι) 6:37 6:37 6:37 (S) 6:38 6:42*
    6:45 6:46 6:47 6:47* 6:48 6:48 6:48* 6:49*
    6:49* 6:49* 7:5 (S) 7:7* 7:8* 7:8* 7:8* 7:8*
    7:8* 7:8* 7:8* 7:9* 7:10* 7:18 (δ) 7:18 7:22*
    7:22* 7:22* 7:23* 7:25 7:26* 7:31 7:32 7:32*
    7:32* 7:33* 7:34* 7:34* 7:34* 7:34* 7:35*
    9:57* 9:58* 9:58* 9:61 (S) 9:62 (S) 10:4 10:6*
    10:7 10:8 (δ) 10:8 10:9 (δ) 10:9 10:10 10:11
    10:13* 10:13* 10:14* 10:15* 10:16* 10:21
    10:21* 10:21* 10:21* 10:22* 10:22 (ουδε)
    10:22* 10:24* 10:24* 10:24* 10:24* 11:4*
    11:4* 11:4* 11:9* 11:9* 11:9* 11:10* 11:10*
    11:11 11:12* 11:14 (δ τ) 11:14 11:14* 11:17*
    11:18* 11:22* 11:23* 11:24* 11:25* 11:25*
    11:26* 11:26* 11:26* 11:27 (S) 11:28 (S)
    11:29* 11:30 11:31* 11:31* 11:32* 11:32*
    11:34 11:34 11:39* 11:39* 11:40 11:41 11:42*
    11:42* 11:42* 11:42* 11:43* 11:44 11:46
    11:46 (δ) 11:48 11:49 11:49* 11:49 11:49*
    11:51* 11:52 (ουδε) 12:2* 12:3* 12:4 (δ) 12:6*
    12:7* 12:8 12:10* 12:11 12:11 12:17 (S) 12:18
    (S) 12:18 12:18 (S) 12:18 (S) 12:19 (S)
    12:21 (S) 12:23* 12:24* 12:28* 12:29 (ουν)
    12:29 (η) 12:29 (η) 12:31* 12:33 12:34*
    12:40* 12:45* 12:45 12:45* 12:45 12:46*
    12:46* 12:46* 12:49 (S) 12:52 12:53 12:53*
    12:53* 12:54 12:54 12:55* 12:55 12:56 12:57
    12:58* 12:58* 12:59 13:18 13:19 (S 13:19*
    13:19 (ωστε) 13:20 13:24 13:25 (S; cf. Matt
    25:10) 13:25 (S) 13:25 (S) 13:25 (S) 13:26*
    13:26* 13:27* 13:28* 13:28* 13:28* 13:28
    13:29 13:29* 13:29 13:29 13:29* 13:30
    (ουτως) 13:30* 13:34* 13:34* 14:11* 14:16
    14:17* 14:18 14:18 14:19 14:19 14:20 14:20
    14:21 14:21 14:21* 14:21 14:21 14:21 14:22
    14:22 14:23 14:23 14:26 (η) 14:26 14:26
    14:26 14:26 14:26 14:26 14:27* 14:34 15:4*
    15:4* 15:5* 15:6 15:6 15:8 (S) 15:8* 15:9 (S)
    15:9* 16:13* 16:13* 16:13* 16:16* 16:16*

16:17* 16:18 16:18* 17:2* 17:3 17:4 17:4
17:6* 17:6 17:23 (ουν) 17:26 (γ) 17:26 17:27*
17:27* 17:29 (S) 17:29 (S) 17:34* 17:37 19:12
19:13 19:15 (δ) 19:17 19:18* 19:19 19:19
19:20* 19:21* 19:22* 19:23 19:24* 19:25
19:26* 22:30 22:30

καιρός (⇨ ὥρα)
  Matt [2/3] 11:25 (ω) 16:3* 24:45*
  Luke [2/3] 4:13 12:42* 12:56*

καίω (⇨ ἅπτω)
  Matt [0/1] 5:15 (a)

κἀκεῖ
  Matt [0/1] 10:11

κἀκεῖνος
  Matt [1/1] 23:23*
  Luke [1/1] 11:42*

κακός
  Matt [0/1] 24:48

κακῶς
  Luke [0/1] 7:2

κάλαμος
  Matt [1/1] 11:7*
  Luke [1/1] 7:24*

καλέω (⇨ λέγω)
  Matt [3/7] 22:3* 22:4* 22:3 22:8 22:9 23:7
  25:14*
  Luke [3/5] 6:46 (λ) 14:16* 14:17* 14:24
  19:13*

καλός (⇨ ἀγαθός)
  Matt [2/2] 3:10* 7:18*
  Luke [2/5] 3:9* 6:38 (S) 6:43 (a) 6:43* 14:34

καλύπτω ⇨ συγκαλύπτω
  Matt [0(1)/1] 10:26(*)

καλῶς
  Luke [0/3] 6:26 (S) 6:27 6:48

καρδία
  Matt [3/4] 6:21* 12:34* 12:40 24:48*
  Luke [3/4] 6:45 6:45* 12:34* 12:45*

καρπός
  Matt [5/5] 3:8* 3:10* 7:18* 7:18* 12:33*
  Luke [5/6] 3:8* 3:9* 6:43* 6:43* 6:44* 12:17
  (S)

κάρφος
  Matt [3/3] 7:3* 7:4* 7:5*
  Luke [3/3] 6:41* 6:42* 6:42*

κατά (⇨ εἰς, ἐπί)
  Matt [1/10] 5:11 10:35 (επ) 10:35 (επ) 10:35
  (επ) 12:25 (επ) 12:25 (επ) 12:30* 12:32 (εις)
  12:32 (εις) 25:15
  Luke [1/6] 6:23 6:26 (S) 10:4 11:3 11:23*
  17:30

καταβαίνω (⇨ γίνομαι)
  Matt [1/3] 7:25 (γ) 7:27 11:23*
  Luke [1/1] 10:15*

καταβολή
  Luke [0/1] 11:50

καταδικάζω
  Luke [0/2] 6:37 6:37

κατακαίω
  Matt [1/1] 3:12*
  Luke [1/1] 3:17*

κατακλυσμός
  Matt [1/2] 24:38 24:39*
  Luke [1/1] 17:27*

κατακρίνω
  Matt [2/2] 12:41* 12:42*
  Luke [2/2] 11:31* 11:32*

καταλείπω (⇨ ἀφίημι)
  Luke [0/1] 15:4 (a)

καταμανθάνω (⇨ κατανοέω)
  Matt [0/1] 6:28 (κ)

κατανοέω (⇨ ἐμβλέπω, καταμανθάνω)
  Matt [1/1] 7:3*
  Luke [1/3] 6:41* 12:24 (ε) 12:27 (κ)

καταπατέω
  Matt [0/1] 5:13

καταποντίζω (⇨ ῥίπτω)
  Matt [0/1] 18:6 (ρ)

καταράομαι
  Luke [0/1] 6:28

καταρτίζω
  Luke [0/1] 6:40

κατασκευάζω
  Matt [1/1] 11:10*
  Luke [1/1] 7:27*

κατασκηνόω
  Matt [1/1] 13:32*
  Luke [1/1] 13:19*

κατασκήνωσις
  Matt [1/1] 8:20*
  Luke [1/1] 9:58*

κατασύρω
  Luke [0/1] 12:58

καταφρονέω
  Matt [1/1] 6:24*
  Luke [1/1] 16:13*

κατοικέω
  Matt [1/1] 12:45*
  Luke [1/1] 11:26*

κάτω
  Matt [1/1] 4:6*
  Luke [1/1] 4:9*

καύσων
  Luke [0/1] 12:55

Καφαρναούμ
  Matt [2/2] 8:5* 11:23*
  Luke [2/2] 7:1* 10:15*

κεῖμαι
  Matt [1/1] 3:10*
  Luke [1/2] 3:9* 12:19 (S)

κεραία
  Matt [1/1] 5:18*
  Luke [1/1] 16:17*

κερδαίνω (⇨ ἀφίημι)
  Matt [0/5] 18:15 (a) 25:16 25:17 25:20 25:22

κεφαλή
  Matt [2/2] 8:20* 10:30*
  Luke [2/2] 9:58* 12:7*

κῆπος (⇨ ἀγρός)
  Luke [0/1] 13:19 (a)

κήρυγμα
  Matt [1/1] 12:41*
  Luke [1/1] 11:32*

κηρύσσω
  Matt [1/2] 10:7 10:27*
  Luke [1/1] 12:3*

κῆτος
  Matt [0/1] 12:40

κιβωτός
  Matt [1/1] 24:38*
  Luke [1/1] 17:27*

κινέω (⇨ προσψαύω)
  Matt [0/1] 23:4 (π)

κλάδος
  Matt [1/1] 13:32*
  Luke [1/1] 13:19*

κλαίω (⇨ πενθέω, κόπτω)
  Luke [0/3] 6:21 (π) 6:25 (S) 7:32 (κ)

κλαυθμός
  Matt [1/2] 8:12* 24:51
  Luke [1/1] 13:28*

κλείς (⇨ κλείω)
  Luke [0/1] 11:52 (κ)

κλείω (⇨ αἴρω, κλείς)
  Matt [0/1] 23:13 (a κ)

κλέπτης
  Matt [2/3] 6:19 6:20* 24:43*
  Luke [2/2] 12:33* 12:39*

κλέπτω
  Matt [0/2] 6:19 6:20

κληρονομία
  Luke [0/1] 12:13 (S)

κλίβανος
  Matt [1/1] 6:30*
  Luke [1/1] 12:28*

κλίνη (⇨ ἀγρός)
  Luke [0/1] 17:34 (a)

κλίνω
  Matt [1/1] 8:20*
  Luke [1/1] 9:58*

κοδράντης (⇨ λεπτός)
  Matt [1/1] 5:26 (λ)

κοιλία
  Matt [0/1] 12:40
  Luke [0/1] 11:27 (S)

κοινωνός
  Matt [0/1] 23:30

κόκκος
  Matt [2/2] 13:31* 17:20*
  Luke [2/2] 13:19* 17:6*

κολλάω
  Luke [0/1] 10:11

κόλπος
    Luke [0/1] 6:38 (S)
κομίζω (⇨ πράσσω)
    Matt [0/1] 25:27 (π)
κονιάω
    Matt [0/1] 23:27
κονιορτός
    Matt [1/1] 10:14*
    Luke [1/1] 10:11*
κοπιάω
    Matt [1/1] 6:28*
    Luke [1/1] 12:27*
κοπρία
    Luke [0/1] 14:35
κόπτω (⇨ κλαίω)
    Matt [0/1] 11:17 (κ)
κόραξ (⇨ πετεινόν)
    Luke [0/1] 12:24 (π)
κοσμέω
    Matt [1/2] 12:44* 23:29
    Luke [1/1] 11:25*
κόσμος (⇨ οἰκουμένη)
    Matt [0/2] 4:8 (ο) 18:7
    Luke [0/2] 11:50 12:30
κρατέω
    Matt [0/1] 22:6
κρεμάννυμι (⇨ περίκειμαι)
    Matt [0/1] 18:6 (π)
κρίμα
    Matt [0/1] 7:2 (S)
κρίνον
    Matt [1/1] 6:28*
    Luke [1/1] 12:27*
κρίνω
    Matt [3/6] 5:40 7:1* 7:1* 7:2 (S) 7:2 (S) 19:28*
    Luke [3/5] 6:37* 6:37* 12:57 19:22 22:30*
κρίσις
    Matt [4/6] 10:15 11:22* 11:24 (S) 12:41*
    12:42* 23:23*
    Luke [4/4] 10:14* 11:31* 11:32* 11:42*
κριτής
    Matt [3/3] 5:25* 5:25* 12:27*
    Luke [3/4] 11:19* 12:14 (S) 12:58* 12:58*
κρούω
    Matt [2/2] 7:7* 7:8*
    Luke [2/3] 11:9* 11:10* 13:25 (S)
κρύπτη
    Luke [0/1] 11:33
κρυπτός
    Matt [1/1] 10:26*
    Luke [1/1] 12:2*
κρύπτω (⇨ ἀποκρύπτω)
    Matt [0(1)/3] 11:25(*) 25:18 25:25
κτάομαι (⇨ βαστάζω)
    Matt [0/1] 10:9 (β)
κύμινον (⇨ λάχανον)
    Matt [0/1] 23:23 (λ)

κύριος
    Matt [17/30] 4:7* 4:10* 6:24* 7:21* 7:21*
    7:22 7:22 8:6 8:8* 8:21* 9:38* 10:24 10:25
    11:25* 18:21 23:39* 24:45* 24:46* 24:48*
    24:50* 25:18 25:19 25:20* 25:21 25:21 25:22*
    25:23 25:23 25:24* 25:26
    Luke [17/24] 4:8* 4:12* 6:46* 6:46* 7:6* 7:19
    9:59* 9:61 (S) 10:2* 10:21* 12:42* 12:43*
    12:45* 12:46* 13:25 (S; cf. Matt 25:11) 13:35*
    14:21 14:22 14:23 16:13* 19:16* 19:18*
    19:20* 19:25
κωλύω (⇨ ἀφίημι)
    Luke [0/2] 6:29 (α) 11:52 (α)
κώμη
    Matt [0/1] 10:11
κωφός
    Matt [5/5] 9:32* 9:33* 11:5* 12:22* 12:22*
    Luke [3/3] 7:22* 11:14* 11:14*

λαλέω (⇨ ἀπολογέομαι, εἶπον)
    Matt [3/6] 9:33* 10:19 (α, ε) 10:19 (ε) 12:22*
    12:34* 13:33 (ε)
    Luke [2/3] 6:45* 11:14* 12:3
λαμβάνω (⇨ αἴρω, βαστάζω)
    Matt [3/10] 5:40 (α) 7:8* 10:8 10:38 (β) 13:31*
    13:33* 25:16 25:18 25:20 25:24
    Luke [3/5] 6:34 (S) 11:10* 13:19* 13:21*
    19:12
λάμπω (⇨ φαίνω)
    Matt [0/1] 5:15
    Luke [0/1] 17:24 (φ)
λατρεύω
    Matt [1/1] 4:10*
    Luke [1/1] 4:8*
λάχανον (⇨ κύμινον)
    Matt [0/1] 13:32
    Luke [1/1] 11:42 (κ)
λέγω (⇨ ἀσπάζομαι, εἶπον, καλέω, ὁμολογέω, φημί)
    Matt [26/51] 3:9* 3:9* 4:6 (ε) 4:10 (ε) 5:18
    5:26* 5:32 5:44* 6:25* 6:29* 6:31 7:21 (κ) 8:6
    8:7 8:9* 8:10* 8:11 8:20 (ε) 8:22 (ε) 9:33 9:34
    (ε) 9:37* 10:7* 10:15* 10:27 11:7* 11:9*
    11:11* 11:17* 11:18* 11:19* 11:22 11:24 (S)
    12:23 12:38 12:44* 13:17* 13:31* 16:2* 17:20
    18:13* 18:22 18:22 22:1 22:4 22:8 (ε) 23:30
    23:36* 23:39* 24:47* 25:20*
    Luke [26/61] 3:7 (ε) 3:8* 3:8* 6:27* 6:42 (ε)
    6:46 7:4 (S) 7:6 (φ) 7:8* 7:9* 7:19 (ε) 7:20 (S)
    7:24* 7:26* 7:28* 7:32* 7:33* 7:34* 10:2*
    10:5 (α) 10:9* 10:12* 10:24* 11:2 11:9 11:24*
    11:27 (S) 11:29 (ε) 11:51* 12:4 12:5 12:8 12:16
    (S) 12:17 (S) 12:22* 12:27* 12:44* 12:51
    12:54 12:54* 12:55 12:59* 13:18* 13:24
    13:25 (S; cf. Matt 25:11) 13:26 (ε) 13:27 (ο)
    13:35* 14:24 15:6 15:7* 15:9 (S) 15:10 (S)
    17:4 17:6 (ε) 17:34 19:16* 19:18 (ε) 19:20 (ε)
    19:22 (ε) 19:26

λεπρός
    Matt [1/2] 10:8 11:5*
    Luke [1/1] 7:22*
λεπτός (⇨ κοδράντης)
    Luke [0/1] 12:59 (κ)
λίαν
    Matt [0/1] 4:8
λιθοβολέω
    Matt [1/1] 23:37*
    Luke [1/1] 13:34*
λίθος (⇨ μύλος, σκορπίος)
    Matt [3/4] 3:9* 4:3* 4:6* 7:9 (σ)
    Luke [3/4] 3:8* 4:3* 4:11* 17:2 (μ)
λόγος
    Matt [3/7] 5:32 7:24* 7:26* 8:8* 10:14 12:32*
    25:19
    Luke [3/4] 6:47* 7:7* 11:28 (S) 12:10*
λοιπός
    Matt [0/1] 22:6
    Luke [0/1] 12:26
λύκος
    Matt [1/1] 10:16*
    Luke [1/1] 10:3*
λυσιτελέω (⇨ συμφέρω)
    Luke [0/1] 17:2 (σ)
λυχνία
    Matt [1/1] 5:15*
    Luke [1/1] 11:33*
λύχνος
    Matt [2/2] 5:15* 6:22*
    Luke [2/4] 11:33* 11:34* 11:36 (S) 15:8 (S)
λύω (⇨ βαστάζω)
    Luke [0/1] 3:16 (β)
Λώτ
    Luke [0/2] 17:28 (S) 17:29 (S)

μαθητής (⇨ ἄξιος)
    Matt [2/5] 8:21 9:37 10:24* 10:25 11:2*
    Luke [2/6] 6:40* 7:18 7:18* 12:22 14:26 (α)
    14:27 (α)
μακάριος
    Matt [7/7] 5:3* 5:4* 5:6* 5:11* 11:6* 13:16*
    24:46*
    Luke [7/9] 6:20* 6:21* 6:21* 6:22* 7:23*
    10:23* 11:27 (S) 11:28 (S) 12:43*
μακράν
    Luke [0/1] 7:6
μακρός
    Luke [0/1] 19:12
μαλακός (⇨ ἔνδοξος)
    Matt [1/2] 11:8* 11:8 (ε)
    Luke [1/1] 7:25*
μᾶλλον
    Matt [3/5] 6:26* 6:30* 7:11* 10:28 18:13
    Luke [3/3] 11:13* 12:24* 12:28*
μαμωνᾶς
    Matt [1/1] 6:24*
    Luke [1/1] 16:13*

μαρτυρέω (▷ μάρτυς)
    Matt [0/1] 23:31 (μ)
μάρτυς (▷ μαρτυρέω)
    Luke [0/1] 11:48 (μ)
μαστιγόω
    Matt [0/1] 23:34
μαστός
    Luke [0/1] 11:27 (S)
μάχαιρα (▷ διαμερισμός)
    Matt [0/1] 10:34 (δ)
μέγας
    Matt [3/4] 7:27* 11:11* 11:11* 13:32
    Luke [3/5] 6:49* 7:28* 7:28* 12:18 (S) 14:16
μεθύσκω (▷ μεθύω)
    Luke [0/1] 12:45 (μ)
μεθύω (▷ μεθύσκω)
    Matt [0/1] 24:49 (μ)
μέλλω
    Matt [1/2] 3:7* 12:32
    Luke [1/2] 3:7* 7:2
μέν
    Matt [2/10] 3:11* 9:37* 10:13 13:32 16:3 22:5
    22:8 23:27 23:28 25:15
    Luke [2/3] 3:16* 10:2* 11:48
μενοῦν
    Luke [0/1] 11:28 (S)
μένω
    Matt [1/2] 10:11* 11:23 (S)
    Luke [1/1] 10:7*
μερίζω ▷ διαμερίζω
    Matt [0(2)/3] 12:25(*) 12:25 12:26(*)
    Luke [0/1] 12:13 (S)
μεριμνάω (▷ ζητέω)
    Matt [4/5] 6:25* 6:27* 6:28* 6:31 (ζ) 10:19*
    Luke [4/4] 12:11* 12:22* 12:25* 12:26*
μεριστής
    Luke [0/1] 12:14 (S)
μέρος
    Matt [1/1] 24:51*
    Luke [1/2] 11:36 (S) 12:46*
μέσος
    Matt [1/1] 10:16*
    Luke [1/1] 10:3*
μεστός
    Matt [0/1] 23:28
μετά
    Matt [6/12] 5:25* 5:41 (S) 8:11 12:30* 12:30*
    12:41* 12:42* 12:45 24:49 24:51* 25:19 25:19
    Luke [6/10] 11:23* 11:23* 11:31* 11:32* 12:4
    12:5 12:13 (S) 12:46* 12:58* 22:28
μεταβαίνω (▷ ἐκριζόω, φυτεύω)
    Matt [0/2] 17:20 (ε) 17:20 (φ)
    Luke [0/1] 10:7
μετανοέω (▷ ἀκούω)
    Matt [2/2] 11:21* 12:41*
    Luke [2/6] 10:13* 11:32* 15:7 15:10 (S) 17:3
    (α) 17:4

μετάνοια
    Matt [1/2] 3:8* 3:11
    Luke [1/2] 3:8* 15:7
μεταξύ
    Matt [1/2] 18:15 23:35*
    Luke [1/1] 11:51*
μετεωρίζομαι (▷ περιβάλλω)
    Luke [0/1] 12:29 (π)
μετρέω ▷ ἀντιμετρέω
    Matt [1(2)/2] 7:2* 7:2(*)
    Luke [1/1] 6:38*
μέτρον
    Matt [1/2] 7:2* 23:32
    Luke [1/2] 6:38 (S) 6:38*
μέχρι (▷ ἕως)
    Matt [0/1] 11:23 (S)
    Luke [0/1] 16:16 (ε)
μή (▷ μηδέ, μήτε, οὐ)
    Matt [30/41] 3:9* 3:10* 5:13 5:18 5:26* 5:42*
    6:13* 6:19 6:25* 6:31* 7:1* 7:1* 7:9 7:10
    7:26* 10:9* 10:10* 10:13* 10:14* 10:19*
    10:26 10:28* 10:28* 10:31* 10:34 11:6*
    11:23* 11:27* 11:27* 12:24 12:29 12:30*
    12:30* 12:39* 16:4* 18:13 (ο) 23:23* 23:39*
    24:26* 24:26 (μηδε) 25:29*
    Luke [29/43] 3:8* 3:9* 6:29 6:30* 6:37* 6:37*
    6:37 6:37 6:49* 7:6 7:33 7:33 (μητε) 10:4*
    10:4* 10:4 (μηδε) 10:6* 10:7 10:10* 10:15*
    10:22* 10:22* 11:4* 11:23* 11:23* 11:24 (ο)
    11:29* 11:35 11:36 (S) 11:42* 12:4* 12:4*
    12:7* 12:11* 12:21 (S) 12:22* 12:29* 12:29
    12:33 12:59* 13:35* 17:1 17:23* 19:26*
μηδέ (▷ μή)
    Matt [1/7] 6:25* 10:9 10:9 10:10 10:10 10:10
    (μ) 10:14
    Luke [1/2] 12:22* 17:23 (μ)
μηδείς
    Luke [0/2] 6:35 (S) 10:4
μήποτε
    Matt [2/2] 5:25* 4:6*
    Luke [2/2] 4:11* 12:58*
μήτε (▷ μή)
    Matt [1/2] 11:18 (μ) 11:18*
    Luke [1/1] 7:33*
μήτηρ
    Matt [2/2] 10:35* 10:37*
    Luke [2/3] 12:53 12:53* 14:26*
μήτι (▷ οὐ)
    Matt [0/2] 7:16 (ο) 12:23
    Luke [0/1] 6:39
μικρός
    Matt [2/3] 11:11* 13:32 18:6*
    Luke [2/2] 7:28* 17:2*
μίλιον
    Matt [0/1] 5:41 (S)
μισέω (▷ φιλέω)
    Matt [1/1] 6:24*
    Luke [1/4] 6:22 6:27 14:26 (φ) 16:13*

μισθός (▷ τροφή, χάρις)
    Matt [1/2] 5:12* 5:46 (χ)
    Luke [1/3] 6:23* 6:35 (S) 10:7 (τ)
μνᾶ (▷ τάλαντον)
    Luke [0/9] 19:13 (τ) 19:16 (τ) 19:16 (τ) 19:18
    (τ) 19:18 (τ) 19:20 (τ) 19:24 (τ) 19:24 (τ) 19:25
μνημεῖον (▷ τάφος)
    Matt [1/1] 23:29*
    Luke [1/2] 11:44 (τ) 11:47*
μόδιος
    Matt [1/1] 5:15*
    Luke [1/1] 11:33*
μοιχαλίς
    Matt [0/2] 12:39 16:4
μοιχάω (▷ μοιχεύω)
    Matt [0/1] 5:32 (μ)
μοιχεύω (▷ μοιχάω)
    Matt [1/1] 5:32*
    Luke [1/2] 16:18* 16:18 (μ)
μόνος
    Matt [2/5] 4:4* 4:10* 5:47 8:8 18:15
    Luke [2/2] 4:4* 4:8*
μυλικός (▷ μύλος)
    Luke [0/1] 17:2 (μ)
μύλος (▷ λίθος μυλικός)
    Matt [0/2] 18:6 (λ μ) 24:41
μωραίνω
    Matt [1/1] 5:13*
    Luke [1/1] 14:34*
μωρός
    Matt [0/1] 7:26
ναί (▷ ἀμήν)
    Matt [2/2] 11:9* 11:26*
    Luke [2/4] 7:26* 10:21* 11:51 (α) 12:5
ναός (▷ οἶκος)
    Matt [0/1] 23:35 (ο)
νεκρός
    Matt [3/5] 8:22* 8:22* 10:8 11:5* 23:27
    Luke [3/3] 7:22* 9:60* 9:60*
νεφέλη
    Luke [0/1] 12:54
νήθω
    Matt [1/1] 6:28*
    Luke [1/1] 12:27*
νήπιος
    Matt [1/1] 11:25*
    Luke [1/1] 10:21*
νηστεύω (▷ ἐσθίω)
    Matt [0/1] 4:2 (ε)
νικάω
    Luke [0/1] 11:22 (S)
Νινευίτης
    Matt [1/1] 12:41*
    Luke [1/2] 11:30 11:32*
νομίζω (▷ δοκέω)
    Matt [0/1] 10:34 (δ)

νομικός (⊳ γραμματεύς, Φαρισαῖος)
  Luke [0/2] 11:46 11:52 (γ, Φ)
νόμος
  Matt [2/4] 5:18* 7:12 11:13* 23:23
  Luke [2/2] 16:16* 16:17*
νοσσιά (⊳ νοσσίον)
  Luke [0/1] 13:34 (ν)
νοσσίον (⊳ νοσσιά)
  Matt [0/1] 23:37 (ν)
νότος
  Matt [1/1] 12:42*
  Luke [1/3] 11:31* 12:55 13:29
νύμφη
  Matt [1/1] 10:35*
  Luke [1/2] 12:53 12:53*
νῦν
  Luke [0/6] 6:21 6:21 6:25 (S) 6:25 (S) 11:39
  12:52
νύξ (⊳ τότε)
  Matt [0/3] 4:2 12:40 12:40
  Luke [0/2] 12:20 (S) 17:34 (τ)
Νῶε
  Matt [2/2] 24:37* 24:38*
  Luke [2/2] 17:26* 17:27*

ὁδηγέω
  Matt [1/1] 15:14*
  Luke [1/1] 6:39*
ὁδηγός
  Matt [0/1] 15:14
ὁδός
  Matt [3/7] 5:25* 7:13 7:14 10:10 11:10* 22:9
  22:10*
  Luke [3/5] 7:27* 9:57 10:4 12:58* 14:23*
ὀδούς
  Matt [1/2] 8:12* 24:51
  Luke [1/1] 13:28*
ὅθεν (⊳ ὅς)
  Matt [1/3] 12:44* 25:24 (ο) 25:26 (ο)
  Luke [1/1] 11:24*
οἶδα (⊳ γινώσκω, δύναμαι)
  Matt [5/5] 6:32* 7:11* 12:25* 24:43* 25:26*
  Luke [5/10] 11:13* 11:17* 11:44 12:30*
  12:39* 12:56 (γ) 12:56 (δ) 13:25 (S; cf. Matt
  25:12) 13:27 (ο) 19:22*
οἰκετεία (⊳ θεραπεία)
  Matt [0/1] 24:45 (θ)
οἰκέτης
  Luke [0/1] 16:13
οἰκία (⊳ οἶκος)
  Matt [5/13] 5:15 7:24* 7:25* 7:26* 7:27* 8:6
  10:12* 10:13 10:14 12:25 (ο) 12:29 12:29
  24:43 (ο)
  Luke [5/10] 6:48* 6:48* 6:49* 6:49* 7:6 10:5*
  10:7 10:7 10:7 15:8 (S)
οἰκιακός
  Matt [0/1] 10:36

οἰκοδεσπότης (⊳ βασιλεύς)
  Matt [1/1] 24:43*
  Luke [1/3] 12:39* 13:25 (S) 14:21 (β)
οἰκοδομέω (⊳ θεμελιόω)
  Matt [3/3] 7:24* 7:26* 23:29*
  Luke [3/8] 6:48* 6:48 (θ) 6:49* 7:5 (S) 11:47*
  11:48 12:18 (S) 17:28 (S)
οἰκονόμος (⊳ δοῦλος)
  Luke [0/1] 12:42 (δ)
οἶκος (⊳ βασίλειος, γάμος, ναός, οἰκία)
  Matt [2/3] 11:8 (β) 12:44* 23:38*
  Luke [2/12] 7:10 9:61 (S) 10:5 11:17 (ο) 11:17
  11:24* 11:51 (ν) 12:39 (ο) 12:52 13:35* 14:23
  (γ) 15:6
οἰκουμένη (⊳ κόσμος)
  Luke [0/1] 4:5 (κ)
οἰκτρίμων (⊳ τέλειος)
  Luke [0/2] 6:36 (τ) 6:36 (τ)
οἶνος
  Luke [0/1] 7:33
οἰνοπότης
  Matt [1/1] 11:19*
  Luke [1/1] 7:34*
ὀκνηρός
  Matt [0/1] 25:26
ὀλιγόπιστος
  Matt [1/1] 6:30*
  Luke [1/1] 12:28*
ὀλίγος (⊳ ἐλάχιστος)
  Matt [1/4] 7:14 (cf. Luke 13:23) 9:37* 25:21
  (ε) 25:23
  Luke [1/1] 10:2*
ὅλος
  Matt [2/3] 6:22* 6:23 13:33*
  Luke [2/4] 11:34* 11:36 (S) 11:36 (S) 13:21*
ὄμβρος
  Luke [0/1] 12:54
ὅμοιος (⊳ ὁμοιόω)
  Matt [3/3] 11:16* 13:31* 13:33*
  Luke [3/8] 6:47 6:48 (ο) 6:49 (ο) 7:31 7:32*
  13:18* 13:19 13:21*
ὁμοιόω (⊳ ὅμοιος)
  Matt [1/4] 7:24 (ο) 7:26 (ο) 11:16* 22:2
  Luke [1/3] 7:31* 13:18 13:20
ὁμοίως (⊳ οὕτως)
  Luke [0/2] 6:31 (ο) 17:28 (S)
ὁμολογέω (⊳ λέγω)
  Matt [2/3] 7:23 (λ) 10:32* 10:32*
  Luke [2/2] 12:8* 12:8*
ὀνειδίζω
  Matt [1/1] 5:11*
  Luke [1/1] 6:22*
ὀνικός
  Matt [0/1] 18:6
ὄνομα
  Matt [2/5] 6:9* 7:22 7:22 7:22 23:39*
  Luke [2/3] 6:22 11:2* 13:35*

ὀπίσω
  Matt [1/2] 3:11 10:38*
  Luke [1/2] 9:62 (S) 14:27*
ὅπου (⊳ ὅς)
  Matt [4/9] 6:19 6:19 6:20* 6:20 6:21* 8:19*
  24:28* 25:24 (ο) 25:26 (ο)
  Luke [4/4] 9:57* 12:33* 12:34* 17:37*
ὅπως (⊳ ἵνα, καί)
  Matt [1/3] 5:45 (κ) 9:38* 23:35 (ι)
  Luke [1/2] 7:3 (S) 10:2*
ὁράω (⊳ βλέπω)
  Matt [5/7] 3:7 11:8* 11:9* 12:38 13:17*
  13:17* 23:39*
  Luke [5/9] 7:22 (β) 7:25* 7:26* 10:24* 10:24*
  12:54 13:28 13:35* 14:18
ὀργή
  Matt [1/1] 3:7*
  Luke [1/1] 3:7*
ὀργίζω
  Matt [1/1] 22:7*
  Luke [1/1] 14:21*
ὄρνις
  Matt [1/1] 23:37*
  Luke [1/1] 13:34*
ὄρος (⊳ ἔρημος, συκάμινος)
  Matt [0/3] 4:8 17:20 (σ) 18:12 (ε)
ὀρύσσω
  Matt [0/1] 25:18
ὀρχέομαι
  Matt [1/1] 11:17*
  Luke [1/1] 7:32*
ὅς, ἥ, ὅ (⊳ ὁ, ὅθεν, ὅπου, ὅσος, ὅστις, τοῦ, τῷ)
  Matt [28/44] 3:11* 3:12* 5:32 (ο) 7:2 (S) 7:2*
  7:9 10:11* 10:14* 10:26* 10:26* 10:27 (οσος)
  10:27* 10:38 (οστις) 11:4* 11:6* 11:10*
  11:10* 11:16 11:27* 12:32* 12:32 (τω) 13:17*
  13:17* 13:31* 13:32 13:33* 13:33* 18:6 18:7*
  22:5 22:5 22:10 23:35 (τον) 23:37* 24:38*
  24:44* 24:45* 24:46* 24:50* 24:50* 25:15
  25:15 25:15 25:29*
  Luke [28/62] 3:16* 3:17* 4:6 6:34 (S) 6:38*
  6:46 6:48 (οστις) 6:49 7:2 7:4 (S) 7:22* 7:23*
  7:27* 7:27* 7:32 10:5 10:8* 10:10* 10:22*
  10:23 10:24* 10:24* 11:22 (S) 11:27 (S) 12:2*
  12:2* 12:3 12:3* 12:8 (οστις) 12:10* 12:12
  12:20 (S) 12:24 12:40* 12:42* 12:43* 12:46*
  12:46* 13:19* 13:21* 13:21* 13:25 (S) 13:30
  13:30 13:34* 14:22 15:8 (S) 15:9 (S) 17:1*
  17:27* 17:29 (S) 17:30 17:33 (ο) 17:33 (ο)
  19:13 19:15 19:20 19:21 (οπου) 19:21 (οθεν)
  19:22 (οπου) 19:22 (οθεν) 19:26*
ὅσος (⊳ ὅς)
  Matt [0/2] 7:12 22:9
  Luke [0/1] 12:3 (ος)
ὀστέον
  Matt [0/1] 23:27
ὅστις (⊳ ὅς, ὁ, τῷ)
  Matt [0/12] 5:25 5:39 (τω) 5:41 (S) 7:24 (ο)

7:24 (ος) 7:26 10:32 (ος) 10:33 (ο) 22:2 23:12
23:12 23:27
Luke [0/2] 14:27 (ος) 15:7

ὅταν (⇨ ἐάν)
Matt [3/5] 5:11* 10:19* 12:43* 13:32 19:28
Luke [3/12] 6:22* 6:22 6:26 (S) 11:2 11:21 (S)
11:24* 11:34 (ε) 11:36 (S) 12:11* 12:54 12:55
13:28

ὅτε
Luke [0/1] 13:35

ὅτι (⇨ γάρ)
Matt [26/38] 3:9* 4:6* 5:3* 5:4* 5:6* 5:12 (γ)
5:32 5:45* 6:26* 6:29 6:32* 7:13* 7:23 8:11
10:7 10:34* 11:21* 11:23 (S) 11:24 (S) 11:25*
11:26* 12:41* 12:42* 13:16 13:16 13:17*
18:13* 23:13* 23:23* 23:25 23:27* 23:29*
23:31 24:43* 24:44* 24:47* 25:24* 25:26*
Luke [26/50] 3:8* 4:4 4:6 4:10* 4:11 4:12
6:20* 6:21* 6:21* 6:24 (S) 6:25 6:25 (S)
6:35* 7:4 (S) 10:11 10:12 10:13* 10:21*
10:21* 10:24* 11:31* 11:32* 11:42* 11:43
11:44* 11:46 11:47* 11:48 11:52* 12:17 (S)
12:24* 12:30* 12:39* 12:40* 12:44* 12:51*
12:54 12:55 13:24* 14:11 14:17 14:24 15:6
15:7* 15:9 (S) 18:14 19:17 19:21* 19:22*
19:26

οὐ, οὐκ, οὐχ (⇨ μή, μήτι, οὐδείς, οὐδέποτε, οὐχί,
πόσος)
Matt [38/56] 3:11* 4:4* 4:7* 5:18 5:26* 6:20
6:24* 6:26* 6:26 (π) 6:28* 6:30 (π) 7:3* 7:18*
7:21 7:22 7:25* 8:8* 8:20* 10:24* 10:26*
10:26* 10:29* 10:34 (ουχι) 10:37* 10:37
10:38* 10:38* 11:11 (ουδεις) 11:17* 11:17*
12:24 12:25 12:32* 12:39* 12:43 (μη) 13:17*
13:17* 16:3* 16:4* 18:22 22:3 22:8 23:4*
23:13* 23:30 23:37* 23:39* 24:39 24:43*
24:44* 24:50* 24:50* 25:24* 25:24* 25:26
25:26*
Luke [37/59] 3:16* 4:2 4:4* 4:12* 6:37 6:37
6:40* 6:41* 6:42 6:43* 6:44 (μητι) 6:46 6:48*
7:6 7:6* 7:32* 7:32* 9:58* 10:24* 10:24*
11:29* 11:40 11:44 11:46* 11:52* 12:2* 12:2*
12:6* 12:10* 12:17 (S) 12:24* 12:24 12:27*
12:33 12:39* 12:40* 12:46* 12:46* 12:56*
12:57 12:59* 13:24 13:25 (S; cf. Matt 25:12)
13:27 (ουδεποτε) 13:34* 13:35* 14:20 14:26
14:26* 14:27* 14:27* 15:4 (ουχι) 15:7* (μη)
16:13* 19:21* 19:21* 19:22 19:22* 19:23

οὐαί
Matt [7/9] 11:21* 11:21* 18:7 18:7* 23:13*
23:23* 23:25 23:27* 23:29*
Luke [7/13] 6:24 (S) 6:25 (S) 6:25 (S) 6:26 (S)
10:13* 10:13* 11:42* 11:43 11:44* 11:46
11:47* 11:52* 17:1*

οὐδέ (⇨ ἤ, καί, οὐδείς)
Matt [5/10] 5:15 (ο) 6:20 6:26* 6:26* 6:28*
6:29* 7:18* 10:24 11:27 (κ) 23:13 (κ)

Luke [5/11] 6:43* 6:44 (η) 7:7 7:9 (ο) 11:33
12:24* 12:24* 12:26 12:27* 12:27* 12:33

οὐδείς (⇨ οὐ, οὐδέ, οὔτε)
Matt [3/6] 5:13 (οντε) 6:24* 8:10 (ουδε) 10:26*
11:27* 17:20
Luke [3/8] 4:2 7:28 (ον) 9:62 (S) 10:22* 11:33
(ουδε) 12:2* 14:24 16:13*

οὐδέποτε (⇨ οὐ)
Matt [0/2] 7:23 (ο) 9:33

οὖν (⇨ δέ, καί)
Matt [5/19] 3:8* 3:10* 5:48 6:9 6:22 6:23*
6:31 (κ) 7:11* 7:12 (κ) 7:24 9:38* 10:26 10:31
10:32 (δ) 12:26 22:9 24:26 (κ) 25:27 25:28
Luke [5/13] 3:7 (δ) 3:8* 3:9* 4:7 7:31 (δ) 10:2*
11:13* 11:35 11:36* 12:26 (κ) 13:18 14:34
19:12

οὐράνιος
Matt [0/3] 5:48 6:26 6:32

οὐρανός (⇨ θεός)
Matt [10/29] 5:3 (θ) 5:12* 5:18* 5:45 6:9 6:10
6:20* 6:26 7:11* 7:21 7:21 8:11 (θ) 8:20* 10:7
(θ) 10:32 10:33 11:11 (θ) 11:12 (θ) 11:23*
11:25* 13:31 (θ) 13:32* 13:33 (θ) 16:1* 16:2
16:3 16:3* 22:2 23:13
Luke [10/14] 6:23* 9:58* 10:15* 10:21*
11:13* 11:16* 12:33* 12:56* 13:19* 15:7
16:17* 17:24 17:24 17:29 (S)

οὖς
Matt [1/2] 10:27* 13:16
Luke [1/2] 12:3* 14:35

οὔτε (⇨ οὐδείς)
Matt [0/4] 6:20 6:20 12:32 12:32
Luke [0/2] 14:35 (ο) 14:35

οὗτος (⇨ ἐκεῖνος)
Matt [20/30] 3:9* 4:9 4:3* 6:25* 6:29* 6:32*
6:32* 6:33* 7:12 7:24 7:26 8:9* 8:9* 11:7
11:10* 11:16* 11:25* 12:23 12:24 12:27*
12:32 12:41* 12:42* 17:20* 18:6* 23:23*
23:34* 23:36 23:36* 24:44
Luke [20/41] 3:8* 4:3* 4:6 7:4 (S) 7:8* 7:8* 7:9
7:18 7:27* 7:31* 10:5 10:11 10:21* 11:19*
11:27 (S) 11:29 11:30 11:31* 11:32* 11:42*
11:49* 11:50 11:51* 12:4 12:5 12:18 (S) 12:20
(S) 12:22* 12:27* 12:30* 12:30* 12:31* 12:39
(ε) 12:56 14:20 14:21 17:2* 17:6* 17:34 19:15
19:19

οὕτως (⇨ ὁμοίως)
Matt [6/13] 5:12 6:9 6:30* 7:12 (ο) 9:33 11:26*
12:40* 20:16 23:28 24:27* 24:37* 24:39
24:46*
Luke [6/10] 10:21* 11:30* 12:21 (S) 12:28*
12:43* 12:54 15:7 15:10 (S) 17:24* 17:26*

οὐχί (⇨ γάρ, οὐ)
Matt [1/5] 5:46 5:47 6:25 (γ) 10:29* 18:12 (ο)
Luke [1/4] 6:39 12:6* 12:51 (ο) 15:8 (S)

ὀφειλέτης (⇨ ὀφείλω)
Matt [0/1] 6:12 (ο)

ὀφείλημα (⇨ ἁμαρτία)
Matt [0/1] 6:12 (α)

ὀφείλω (⇨ ὀφειλέτης)
Luke [0/1] 11:4 (ο)

ὀφθαλμός
Matt [9/10] 6:22* 6:22* 6:23 7:3* 7:3* 7:4*
7:4* 7:5* 7:5* 13:16*
Luke [9/9] 6:41* 6:41* 6:42* 6:42* 6:42*
6:42* 10:23* 11:34* 11:34*

ὄφις
Matt [1/1] 7:10*
Luke [1/1] 11:11*

ὄχλος (⇨ Σαδδουκαῖος, Φαρισαῖος)
Matt [3/3] 9:33* 11:7* 12:23*
Luke [2/8] 3:7 (Φ Σ) 7:9 7:24* 11:14* 11:27 (S)
11:29 12:13 (S) 12:54

ὄψιος
Matt [0/1] 16:2

παιδίον
Matt [1/1] 11:16*
Luke [1/1] 7:32*

παιδίσκη (⇨ σύνδουλος)
Luke [0/1] 12:45 (σ)

παῖς (⇨ δοῦλος, σύνδουλος)
Matt [1/3] 8:6 (δ) 8:8* 8:13 (δ)
Luke [1/2] 7:7* 12:45 (σ)

πάλαι
Matt [1/1] 11:21*
Luke [1/1] 10:13*

παλαιόω
Luke [0/1] 12:33

παλιγγενεσία
Matt [0/1] 19:28

πάλιν
Matt [0/4] 4:7 4:8 22:1 22:4
Luke [0/2] 6:43 13:20

πανοπλία
Luke [0/1] 11:22 (S)

παρά (⇨ ἀπό)
Matt [0/1] 8:10
Luke [0/3] 6:34 (S) 10:7 11:16 (α)

παραβολή
Matt [0/3] 13:31 13:33 22:1
Luke [0/1] 12:16 (S)

παραγίνομαι (⇨ ἔρχομαι, προσέρχομαι)
Luke [0/5] 7:4 (S) 7:20 (S) 12:51 (ε) 14:21
19:16 (π)

παραδίδωμι (⇨ δίδωμι, εἰσφέρω)
Matt [2/6] 5:25* 10:19 (ε) 11:27* 25:14 (δ)
25:20 25:22
Luke [2/3] 4:6 10:22* 12:58*

παραιτέομαι
Luke [0/3] 14:18 14:18 14:19

παρακαλέω (⇨ γελάω)
Matt [1/2] 5:4 (γ) 8:5*
Luke [1/1] 7:4*

παράκλησις
Luke [0/1] 6:24 (S)
παραλαμβάνω (⇨ ἄγω, ἀνάγω)
Matt [3/5] 4:5 (αγ) 4:8 (αν) 12:45* 24:40*
24:41*
Luke [3/3] 11:26* 17:34* 17:35*
παραλυτικός
Matt [0/1] 8:6
παρατίθημι
Matt [0/1] 13:31
Luke [0/1] 10:8
παρεκτός
Matt [0/1] 5:32
παρέρχομαι (⇨ ἀφίημι, πίπτω)
Matt [1/2] 5:18* 5:18 (π)
Luke [1/2] 11:42 (α) 16:17*
παρέχω (⇨ στρέφω)
Luke [0/2] 6:29 (σ) 7:4 (S)
παρίημι (⇨ ἀφίημι)
Luke [0/1] 11:42 (α)
παρομοιάζω (⇨ εἰμί)
Matt [0/1] 23:27 (ε)
παρουσία (⇨ ἡμέρα)
Matt [0/3] 24:27 (η) 24:37 (η) 24:39 (η)
παροψίς (⇨ πίναξ)
Matt [0/1] 23:25 (π)
πᾶς (⇨ ἅπας, πόλυς)
Matt [13/31] 3:10* 4:4 4:8* 4:9 (α) 5:11 5:15
5:18 5:32* 6:29* 6:32* 6:33 7:8* 7:12 7:21
7:24* 7:26 10:30* 10:32* 11:13 11:27* 12:23
12:25* 12:25 13:32 22:4 22:10 23:27 23:35
23:36 24:47* 25:29*
Luke [13/34] 3:9* 4:5* 4:7 4:13 6:26 (S) 6:30
6:40 6:47* 7:18 7:35 10:22* 11:4 11:10*
11:17* 11:41 11:42 11:50 12:7* 12:8* 12:10
12:18 (S) 12:27* 12:30* 12:44* 13:27 13:28
(π) 14:11 14:18 16:16 16:18* 17:27 (α) 17:29
(S) 18:14 19:26*
πατήρ (⇨ ἄνθρωπος, θεός, ὕψιστος)
Matt [14/21] 3:9* 5:45 (υ) 5:48* 6:9* 6:26 (θ)
6:32* 7:11* 7:21 8:21* 10:29 (θ) 10:32 (θ)
10:33 (θ) 10:35* 10:37* 11:25* 11:26* 11:27*
11:27* 11:27* 23:30* 23:32
Luke [14/20] 3:8* 6:23 6:26 (S) 6:36* 9:59*
10:21* 10:21* 10:22* 10:22* 10:22* 11:2*
11:11 (α) 11:13* 11:47* 11:48 12:30* 12:53
12:53* 14:26* 22:29
πείζω
Luke [0/1] 6:38 (S)
πείθω
Luke [0/1] 11:22 (S)
πεινάω
Matt [2/2] 4:2* 5:6*
Luke [2/3] 4:2* 6:21* 6:25 (S)
πειράζω (⇨ διάβολος)
Matt [2/3] 4:1* 4:3 (δ) 16:1*
Luke [2/2] 4:2* 11:16*

πειρασμός
Matt [1/1] 6:13*
Luke [1/3] 4:13 11:4* 22:28
πέλαγος
Matt [0/1] 18:6
πέμπω
Matt [1/2] 11:2* 22:7
Luke [1/3] 7:6 7:10 7:19*
πενθερά
Matt [1/1] 10:35*
Luke [1/2] 12:53 12:53*
πενθέω (⇨ κλαίω)
Matt [0/1] 5:4 (κ)
Luke [0/1] 6:25 (S)
πέντε
Matt [0/7] 25:15 25:16 25:16 25:20 25:20
25:20 25:20
Luke [0/5] 12:6 12:52 14:19 19:18 19:19
πέρας
Matt [1/1] 12:42*
Luke [1/1] 11:31*
περί (⇨ ὑπέρ)
Matt [5/5] 4:6* 6:28* 11:7* 11:10* 18:6*
Luke [5/8] 4:10* 6:28 (υ) 7:3 (S) 7:18 7:24*
7:27* 12:26* 17:2*
περιβάλλω (⇨ μετεωρίζομαι)
Matt [1/2] 6:29* 6:31 (μ)
Luke [1/1] 12:27*
περίκειμαι (⇨ κρεμάννυμι)
Luke [0/1] 17:2 (κ)
περιπατέω
Matt [1/1] 11:5*
Luke [1/2] 7:22* 11:44
περιποιέω
Luke [0/1] 17:33
περίσσευμα
Matt [1/1] 12:34*
Luke [1/1] 6:45*
περισσεύω
Matt [0/1] 25:29
περισσός (⇨ χάρις)
Matt [0/1] 5:47 (χ)
περισσότερος
Matt [1/1] 11:9*
Luke [1/2] 7:26* 12:4
πετεινόν (⇨ κόραξ)
Matt [2/3] 6:26 (κ) 8:20* 13:32*
Luke [2/3] 9:58* 12:24 13:19*
πέτρα
Matt [1/2] 7:24* 7:25
Luke [1/1] 6:48*
πήγανον (⇨ ἄνηθον)
Luke [0/1] 11:42 (α)
πήρα
Matt [1/1] 10:10*
Luke [1/1] 10:4*

πῆχυς
Matt [1/1] 6:27*
Luke [1/1] 12:25*
πίμπλημι (⇨ γεμίζω)
Matt [0/1] 22:10 (γ)
πίναξ (⇨ παροψίς)
Luke [0/1] 11:39 (π)
πίνω
Matt [5/6] 6:25 6:31* 11:18* 11:19* 24:38*
24:49*
Luke [5/10] 7:33* 7:34* 10:7 12:19 (S) 12:29*
12:45* 13:26 17:27* 17:28 (S) 22:30
πίπτω ⇨ ἐμπίπτω, συμπίπτω (⇨ ἐπιλανθάνω,
ἵστημι, παρέρχομαι)
Matt [0(2)/5] 4:9 7:25 7:27(*) 10:29 (ε)
15:14(*)
Luke [0/2] 11:17 (ι) 16:17 (π)
πιστεύω (⇨ διώκω)
Matt [0/3] 8:13 18:6 24:26 (δ)
πίστις
Matt [2/3] 8:10* 17:20* 23:23
Luke [2/2] 7:9* 17:6*
πιστός
Matt [2/5] 24:45* 25:21 25:21* 25:23 25:23
Luke [2/2] 12:42* 19:17*
πλανάω (⇨ πλανάω)
Matt [0/3] 18:12 (π) 18:12 (π) 18:13
πλατεῖα
Matt [0/1] 7:13
Luke [0/3] 10:10 13:26 14:21
πλήμμυρα (⇨ βροχή)
Luke [0/1] 6:48 (β)
πλήν (⇨ δέ)
Matt [2/3] 11:22* 11:24 (S) 18:7*
Luke [2/7] 6:24 (S) 6:35 (S) 10:11 10:14*
11:41 12:31 (δ) 17:1*
πλήρης
Luke [0/1] 4:1
πληρόω
Matt [0/1] 23:32
πλούσιος
uke [0/2] 6:24 (S) 12:16 (S)
πλουτέω
Luke [0/1] 12:21 (S)
πνεῦμα (⇨ δάκτυλος)
Matt [5/7] 3:11* 4:1* 5:3 12:28 (δ) 12:32*
12:43* 12:45*
Luke [5/9] 3:16* 4:1* 4:1 10:21 11:13 11:24*
11:26* 12:10* 12:12
πνέω
Matt [0/2] 7:25 7:27
Luke [0/1] 12:55
πόθεν
Luke [0/2] 13:25 (S) 13:27
ποιέω (⇨ διώκω, εἰμί, θησαυρίζω)
Matt [15/19] 3:8* 3:10* 5:32 5:46 5:47 (ε)
5:47* 7:12* 7:12* 7:18* 7:18* 7:21* 7:22
7:24* 7:26* 8:9* 8:9* 22:2* 23:23* 24:46*

Luke [15/25] 3:8* 3:9* 6:23 (δ) 6:26 (S) 6:27
6:31* 6:31* 6:33* 6:43* 6:43* 6:46* 6:49*
6:47* 7:8* 7:8* 11:40 11:40 11:42* 12:4 12:17
(S) 12:18 (S) 12:33 (θ) 12:43* 14:16* 19:18

ποῖος (⊳ τίς)
  Matt [1/1] 24:43*
  Luke [1/4] 6:32 (τ) 6:33 (τ) 6:34 (S) 12:39*

πόλις
  Matt [3/8] 4:5 10:11* 10:14* 10:15* 12:25
  22:7 23:34 23:34
  Luke [3/7] 10:8* 10:10 10:11* 10:12* 14:21
  19:17 19:19

πολύς (⊳ πᾶς, πόσος)
  Matt [8/16] 3:7 5:12* 6:25* 6:30 (πο) 7:13*
  7:22 7:22 8:11 (πα) 9:37* 10:31* 12:41*
  12:42* 13:17* 25:19 25:21 25:23
  Luke [8/12] 6:23* 6:35 (S) 10:2* 10:24*
  11:31* 11:32* 12:7* 12:19 (S) 12:19 (S) 12:23*
  13:24* 14:16

πονηρία (⊳ ἀκρασία)
  Luke [0/1] 11:39 (α)

πονηρός (⊳ σαπρός)
  Matt [11/14] 5:11* 5:45* 6:13 6:23* 7:11*
  7:18 (σ) 12:35* 12:35* 12:35* 12:39* 12:45*
  16:4* 22:10 25:26*
  Luke [10/10] 6:22* 6:35* 6:45* 6:45* 6:45*
  11:13* 11:26* 11:29* 11:34* 19:22*

πορεύομαι (⊳ ἀπέρχομαι)
  Matt [5/9] 8:9* 8:9* 10:7 11:4* 11:7 (π) 12:45*
  18:12* 22:9 25:16
  Luke [5/9] 7:6 7:8* 7:8* 7:22* 9:57 11:26*
  14:19 15:4* 19:12

πορνεία
  Matt [0/1] 5:32

ποσάκις (⊳ ἑπτάκις)
  Matt [1/2] 18:21 (π) 23:37*
  Luke [1/1] 13:34*

πόσος (⊳ οὐ, πολύς)
  Matt [1/2] 6:23 7:11*
  Luke [1/3] 11:13* 12:24 (ο) 12:28 (ο, π)

ποταμός
  Matt [2/2] 7:25* 7:27*
  Luke [2/2] 6:48* 6:49*

ποτήριον
  Matt [1/2] 23:25* 23:26
  Luke [1/1] 11:39*

ποῦ
  Matt [1/1] 8:20*
  Luke [1/2] 9:58* 12:17 (S)

πούς
  Matt [2/2] 4:6* 10:14*
  Luke [2/2] 4:11* 10:11*

πραγματεύομαι
  Luke [0/1] 19:13

πράκτωρ (⊳ ὑπηρέτης)
  Luke [0/2] 12:58 (υ) 12:58

πράσσω (⊳ κομίζω)
  Luke [0/1] 19:23 (κ)

πρεσβύτερος
  Luke [0/1] 7:3 (S)

πρό
  Matt [1/3] 5:12 11:10* 24:38
  Luke [1/1] 7:27*

πρόβατον (⊳ ἀρήν)
  Matt [1/2] 10:16 (α) 18:12*
  Luke [1/2] 15:4* 15:6

πρός (⊳ εἰς, ἐπί)
  Matt [3/5] 3:10* 4:6* 10:13 (επι) 23:34 (εις)
  23:37*
  Luke [3/24] 3:9* 4:4 4:11* 6:47 7:3 (S) 7:4 (S)
  7:7 7:19 7:20 (S) 7:20 (S) 7:24 9:57 9:59 9:62
  (S) 10:2 12:3 (εις) 12:16 (S) 12:22 12:58 13:34*
  14:23 14:26 17:4 19:13

προσδοκάω
  Matt [2/2] 11:3* 24:50*
  Luke [3/3] 7:19* 7:20* 12:46*

προσεργάζομαι
  Luke [0/1] 19:16

προσέρχομαι ⊳ ἔρχομαι (⊳ παραγίνομαι)
  Matt [0(2)/8] 4:3 4:11 8:5 8:19 16:1 25:20 (π)
  25:22(*) 25:24(*)

προσεύχομαι
  Matt [2/2] 5:44* 6:9*
  Luke [2/2] 6:28* 11:2*

προσκαλέω
  Luke [0/1] 7:18

προσκόπτω (⊳ προσρήσσω)
  Matt [1/2] 4:6* 7:27 (π)
  Luke [1/1] 4:11*

προσκυνέω
  Matt [2/2] 4:9* 4:10*
  Luke [2/2] 4:7* 4:8*

προσπίπτω (⊳ προσρήσσω)
  Matt [0/1] 7:25 (π)

προσρήσσω (⊳ προσκόπτω, προσπίπτω)
  Luke [0/2] 6:48 (προσπ) 6:49 (προσκ)

προστίθημι
  Matt [2/2] 6:27* 6:33*
  Luke [2/2] 12:25* 12:31*

προσφέρω
  Matt [0/3] 9:32 12:22 25:20

προσφωνέω
  Matt [1/1] 11:16*
  Luke [1/1] 7:32*

προσψαύω (⊳ κινέω)
  Luke [0/1] 11:46 (κ)

πρόσωπον
  Matt [2/2] 11:10* 16:3*
  Luke [2/2] 7:27* 12:56*

προφέρω (⊳ ἐκβάλλω)
  Luke [0/2] 6:45 (ε) 6:45 (ε)

προφητεύω
  Matt [0/2] 7:22 11:13

προφήτης (⊳ δίκαιος)
  Matt [8/12] 5:12* 7:12 11:9* 11:9* 11:13*

12:39 13:17* 23:29* 23:30 23:31 23:34*
23:37*
  Luke [8/10] 6:23* 7:26* 7:26* 10:24* 11:49*
  11:47* 11:50 (δ) 13:28 13:34* 16:16*

πρωΐ
  Matt [0/1] 16:3

πρωτοκαθεδρία
  Matt [1/1] 23:6*
  Luke [1/1] 11:43*

πρωτοκλισία
  Matt [0/1] 23:6

πρῶτος
  Matt [5/8] 6:33 7:5* 8:21* 12:29 12:45*
  20:16* 20:16* 23:26
  Luke [5/9] 6:42* 9:59* 9:61 (S) 10:5 11:26*
  13:30* 13:30 14:18 19:16

πτερύγιον
  Matt [1/1] 4:5*
  Luke [1/1] 4:9*

πτέρυξ
  Matt [1/1] 23:37*
  Luke [1/1] 13:34*

πτύον
  Matt [1/1] 3:12*
  Luke [1/1] 3:17*

πτῶμα (⊳ σῶμα)
  Matt [0/1] 24:28 (σ)

πτῶσις (⊳ ῥήγμα)
  Luke [0/1] 7:27 (ρ)

πτωχός
  Matt [2/2] 5:3* 11:5*
  Luke [2/3] 6:20* 7:22* 14:21

πύλη (⊳ θύρα)
  Matt [0/3] 7:13 (θ) 7:13 7:14

πῦρ
  Matt [3/3] 3:10* 3:11* 3:12*
  Luke [3/5] 3:9* 3:16* 3:17* 12:49 (S) 17:29 (S)

πυρράζω
  Matt [0/2] 16:2 16:3

πωλέω (⊳ θησαυρίζω)
  Matt [1/1] 10:29*
  Luke [1/3] 12:6* 12:33 (θ) 17:28 (S)

πῶς
  Matt [4/5] 6:28* 7:4* 10:19* 12:26* 12:29
  Luke [4/5] 6:42* 11:18* 12:11* 12:27* 12:56

ῥαββί
  Matt [0/1] 23:7

ῥάβδος
  Matt [0/1] 10:10

ῥαπίζω (⊳ τύπτω)
  Matt [0/1] 5:39 (τ)

ῥῆγμα (⊳ πτῶσις)
  Luke [0/1] 6:49 (π)

ῥῆμα
  Matt [0/1] 4:4

ῥίζα
Matt [1/1] 3:10*
Luke [1/1] 3:9*
ῥίπτω (⇨ καταποντίζω)
Luke [0/1] 17:2 (κ)
ῥύμη
Luke [0/1] 14:21
ῥύομαι
Matt [0/1] 6:13

Σαδδουκαῖος (⇨ ὄχλος)
Matt [0/2] 3:7 (ο) 16:1
σάκκος
Matt [1/1] 11:21*
Luke [1/1] 10:13*
σαλεύω
Matt [1/1] 11:7*
Luke [1/3] 6:38 (S) 6:48 7:24*
σαπρός (⇨ πονηρός)
Matt [1/1] 7:18*
Luke [1/2] 6:43 (π) 6:43*
σαρόω
Matt [1/1] 12:44*
Luke [1/2] 11:25* 15:8 (S)
σατανᾶς
Matt [1/3] 4:10 12:26* 12:26
Luke [1/1] 11:18*
σάτον
Matt [1/1] 13:33*
Luke [1/1] 13:21*
σεαυτοῦ
Matt [1/1] 4:6*
Luke [1/1] 4:9*
σημεῖον
Matt [8/9] 12:38* 12:39* 12:39* 12:39* 16:1*
16:3 16:4* 16:4* 16:4*
Luke [4/5] 11:16* 11:29* 11:29* 11:29* 11:30
σήμερον (⇨ ἡμέρα)
Matt [1/4] 6:11 (η) 6:30* 11:23 (S) 16:3
Luke [1/1] 12:28*
σής
Matt [1/2] 6:19 6:20*
Luke [1/1] 12:33*
σιαγών
Matt [1/1] 5:39*
Luke [1/1] 6:29*
Σιδών
Matt [2/2] 11:21* 11:22*
Luke [2/2] 10:13* 10:14*
σίναπι
Matt [2/2] 13:31* 17:20*
Luke [2/2] 13:19* 17:6*
σιτομέτριον (⇨ τροφή)
Luke [0/1] 12:42 (τ)
σιτιστός
Matt [0/1] 22:4

σῖτος
Matt [1/1] 3:12*
Luke [1/2] 3:17* 12:18 (S)
σκανδαλίζω
Matt [2/2] 11:6* 18:6*
Luke [2/2] 7:23* 17:2*
σκάνδαλον
Matt [1/3] 18:7 18:7* 18:7
Luke [1/1] 17:1*
σκάπτω
Luke [0/1] 6:48
σκεῦος
Matt [0/1] 12:29
σκιρτάω (⇨ ἀγαλλιάω)
Luke [0/1] 6:23 (α)
σκληρός (⇨ αὐστηρός)
Matt [0/1] 25:24 (α)
σκοπέω
Luke [0/1] 11:35
σκορπίζω
Matt [1/1] 12:30*
Luke [1/1] 11:23*
σκορπίος (⇨ λίθος)
Luke [0/1] 11:12 (λ)
σκοτεινός
Matt [1/2] 6:23*
Luke [1/2] 11:34* 11:36 (S)
σκοτία
Matt [1/1] 10:27*
Luke [1/1] 12:3*
σκότος
Matt [1/3] 6:23* 6:23 8:12
Luke [1/1] 11:35*
σκύλλω
Luke [0/1] 7:6
σκῦλον
Luke [0/1] 11:22 (S)
Σόδομα
Matt [1/3] 10:15* 11:23 (S) 11:24 (S)
Luke [1/2] 10:12* 17:29 (S)
Σολομών
Matt [3/3] 6:29* 12:42* 12:42*
Luke [3/3] 11:31* 11:31* 12:27*
σός (⇨ ἴδιος, σοῦ)
Matt [0/5] 7:3 (ι) 7:22 7:22 7:22 25:25
Luke [0/1] 6:30 (σ)
σουδάριον
Luke [0/1] 19:20
σοφία
Matt [2/2] 11:19* 12:42*
Luke [2/3] 7:35* 11:31* 11:49
σοφός (⇨ ἀπόστολος, γραμματεύς)
Matt [1/2] 11:25* 23:34 (α, γ)
Luke [1/1] 10:21*
σπείρω (⇨ βάλλω)
Matt [3/4] 6:26* 13:31 (β) 25:24* 25:26*
Luke [3/3] 12:24* 19:21* 19:22*

σπέρμα
Matt [0/1] 13:32
σποδός
Matt [1/1] 11:21*
Luke [1/1] 10:13*
σπουδαίως
Luke [0/1] 7:4 (S)
σταυρός
Matt [1/1] 10:38*
Luke [1/1] 14:27*
σταυρόω
Matt [0/1] 23:34
σταφυλή
Matt [1/1] 7:16*
Luke [1/1] 6:44*
στέγη
Matt [1/1] 8:8*
Luke [1/1] 7:6*
στενός
Matt [1/2] 7:13* 7:14
Luke [1/1] 13:24*
στιγμή
Luke [0/1] 4:5
στόμα
Matt [1/2] 4:4 12:34*
Luke [1/2] 6:45* 19:22
στράτευμα
Matt [0/1] 22:7
στρατιώτης
Matt [1/1] 8:9*
Luke [1/1] 7:8*
στρέφω (⇨ παρέχω)
Matt [0/1] 5:39 (π)
Luke [0/1] 7:9
στρουθίον
Matt [2/2] 10:29* 10:31*
Luke [2/2] 12:6* 12:7*
στυγνάζω
Matt [0/1] 16:3
συγκαλέω
Luke [0/2] 15:6 15:9 (S)
συγκαλύπτω ⇨ καλύπτω
Luke [0(1)/1] 12:2(*)
συγχαίρω
Luke [0/2] 15:6 15:9 (S)
συκάμινος (⇨ ὄρος)
Luke [0/1] 17:6 (ο)
σῦκον
Matt [1/1] 7:16*
Luke [1/1] 6:44*
συλλέγω
Matt [1/1] 7:16*
Luke [1/1] 6:44*
συμπίπτω ⇨ πίπτω
Luke [0(1)/1] 6:49(*)
συμφέρω (⇨ λυσιτελέω)
Matt [0/1] 18:6 (λ)

σύν
Matt [1/1] 25:27*
Luke [1/2] 7:6 19:23*

συνάγω ▷ ἐπισυνάγω (▷ αἴρω)
Matt [2(3)/7] 3:12* 6:26 12:30* 22:10 24:28(*)
25:24 (α) 25:26 (α)
Luke [2/4] 3:17* 11:23* 12:17 (S) 12:18 (S)

συναγωγή
Matt [1/2] 23:6* 23:34
Luke [1/3] 7:5 (S) 11:43* 12:11

συναίρω
Matt [0/1] 25:19

σύνδουλος (▷ παιδίσκη, παῖς)
Matt [0/1] 24:49 (π π)

συνετός
Matt [1/1] 11:25*
Luke [1/1] 10:21*

συνευδοκέω
Luke [0/1] 11:48

συντελέω
Luke [0/2] 4:2 4:13

σχολάζω
Matt [0/1] 12:44

σῶμα (▷ πτῶμα)
Matt [6/7] 6:22* 6:22* 6:23* 6:25* 6:25*
10:28* 10:28
Luke [6/8] 11:34* 11:34* 11:34* 11:36 (S)
12:4* 12:22* 12:23* 17:37 (π)

τάλαντον (▷ μνᾶ)
Matt [0/13] 25:15 (μ) 25:16 25:20 25:20 25:20
(μ) 25:20 (μ) 25:22 25:22 (μ) 25:22 (μ) 25:24
25:25 (μ) 25:28 (μ) 25:28 (μ)

ταμεῖον
Matt [0/1] 24:26
Luke [0/2] 12:3 12:24

ταπεινόω
Matt [2/2] 23:12* 23:12*
Luke [4/4] 14:11* 14:11* 18:14* 18:14*

τάσσω
Luke [0/1] 7:8

ταῦρος
Matt [0/1] 22:4

τάφος (▷ μνημεῖον)
Matt [0/2] 23:27 (τ) 23:29 (τ)

ταχέως
Luke [0/1] 14:21

ταχύς
Matt [0/1] 5:25

τε (▷ δέ)
Matt [0/1] 22:10
Luke [0/2] 12:45 (δ) 14:26

τέκνον (▷ ἔργον, θυγάτηρ)
Matt [3/3] 3:9* 7:11* 23:37*
Luke [3/5] 3:8* 7:35 (ε) 11:13* 13:34* 14:26
(θ)

τέλειος (▷ οἰκτρίμων)
Matt [0/2] 5:48 (ο) 5:48 (ο)

τελευτάω
Luke [0/1] 7:2

τελώνης (▷ ἁμαρτωλός)
Matt [1/2] 5:46 (α) 11:19*
Luke [1/1] 7:34*

τεσσεράκοντα
Matt [1/2] 4:2* 4:2
Luke [1/1] 4:2*

τίθημι (▷ διασκορπίζω)
Matt [2/2] 5:15* 24:51*
Luke [2/5] 6:48 11:33* 12:46* 19:21 (δ) 19:22
(δ)

τις, τι (▷ εἷς, Φαρισαῖος)
Matt [0/4] 11:27 12:29 12:38 18:12
Luke [0/12] 7:2 7:18 9:57 (ε) 11:15 (φ) 11:27
(S) 11:36 (S) 12:4 12:13 (S) 12:16 (S) 14:16
14:26 19:12

τίς, τί (▷ μή, ποῖος)
Matt [18/25] 3:7* 5:13* 5:46 (π) 5:47 (π) 6:25*
6:25 6:25* 6:27* 6:28* 6:31* 6:31* 6:31 (μ)
7:3* 7:9* 7:14 10:11 10:19* 10:19 11:7* 11:8*
11:9* 11:16* 12:27* 18:12* 24:45*
Luke [18/36] 3:7* 6:41* 6:46 6:47 7:24* 7:25*
7:26* 7:31* 7:31 10:22 10:22 11:11* 11:19*
12:5 12:11* 12:11 12:14 (S) 12:17 (S) 12:20 (S)
12:22* 12:22* 12:25* 12:26* 12:29* 12:29*
12:42* 12:49 (S) 12:57 13:18 13:18 13:20
14:34* 15:4* 15:8 (S) 19:15 19:23

τόκος
Matt [1/1] 25:27*
Luke [1/1] 19:23*

τόπος
Matt [1/1] 12:43*
Luke [1/2] 11:24* 14:22

τοσοῦτος,-αύτη,-οῦτον
Matt [1/1] 8:10*
Luke [1/1] 7:9*

τότε (▷ δέ, καί)
Matt [4/14] 4:1 (δ) 4:5 (δ) 4:10 (κ) 4:11 (κ) 7:5*
7:23 9:37 (δ) 12:22 (κ) 12:29 12:38 (δ) 12:44*
12:45* 22:8* 24:40
Luke [4/6] 6:42* 11:24* 11:26* 13:26 14:21*
16:16

τράπεζα (▷ τραπεζίτης)
Luke [0/2] 19:23 (τ) 22:30

τραπεζίτης (▷ τράπεζα)
Matt [0/1] 25:27 (τ)

τράχηλος
Matt [1/1] 18:6*
Luke [1/1] 17:2*

τρεῖς
Matt [1/5] 12:40 12:40 12:40 12:40 13:33*
Luke [1/3] 12:52 12:52 13:21*

τρέφω
Matt [1/1] 6:26*
Luke [1/1] 12:24*

τρίβολος (▷ βάτος)
Matt [0/1] 7:16 (β)

τρόπος
Matt [1/1] 23:37*
Luke [1/1] 13:34*

τροφή (▷ μισθός, σιτομέτριον)
Matt [1/3] 6:25* 10:10 (μ) 24:45 (σ)
Luke [1/1] 12:23*

τρυγάω
Luke [0/1] 6:44

τρυφή
Luke [0/1] 7:25

τρώγω (▷ ἐσθίω)
Matt [0/1] 24:38 (ε)

τύπτω (▷ ῥαπίζω)
Matt [1/1] 24:49*
Luke [1/2] 6:29 (ρ) 12:45*

Τύρος
Matt [2/2] 11:21* 11:22*
Luke [2/2] 10:13* 10:14*

τυφλός (▷ ἄφρων)
Matt [3/7] 11:5* 12:22 15:14 15:14 15:14*
15:14* 23:26 (α)
Luke [3/4] 6:39* 6:39* 7:22* 14:21

ὑβρίζω
Matt [0/1] 22:6

ὑγιαίνω (▷ ἰάομαι)
Luke [0/1] 7:10 (ι)

ὕδωρ
Matt [1/1] 3:11*
Luke [1/1] 3:16*

υἱός (▷ ἄνθρωπος, τέκνον)
Matt [16/23] 4:3* 4:6* 5:45* 7:9* 8:12 8:20*
10:37 (τ) 11:19* 11:27* 11:27* 11:27* 12:23
12:27* 12:32* 12:40* 19:28 22:2 23:31 23:35
24:27* 24:37* 24:39* 24:44*
Luke [16/21] 4:3* 4:9* 6:22 6:35* 7:34* 9:58*
10:6 10:22* 10:22* 10:22* 11:11* 11:19*
11:30* 12:8 12:10* 12:40* 12:53 (α) 12:53
17:24* 17:26* 17:30*

ὑμέτερος (▷ αὐτῶν)
Luke [0/1] 6:20 (α)

ὑπάγω
Matt [0/4] 4:10 5:41 (S) 8:13 18:15
Luke [0/2] 10:3 12:58

ὑπακούω
Luke [0/1] 17:6

ὑπάρχω (▷ εἰμί, θησαυρός, φορέω)
Matt [1/2] 24:47* 25:14
Luke [1/5] 7:25 (φ) 11:13 (ε) 11:21 (S) 12:33
(θ) 12:44*

ὑπέρ (▷ περί)
Matt [1/5] 5:44 (π) 10:24* 10:24 10:37 10:37
Luke [1/1] 6:40*

ὑπερεκχύννω
Luke [0/1] 6:38 (S)

ὑπηρέτης (▷ πράκτωρ)
Matt [0/1] 5:25 (π)

ὑπό
Matt [8/11] 4:1 4:1* 5:13 5:15* 8:8* 8:9* 8:9*
11:7* 11:27* 23:7 23:37*
Luke [8/11] 3:7 4:2* 7:6* 7:8* 7:8* 7:24*
10:22* 11:33* 13:34* 17:24 17:24

ὑποδείκνυμι
Matt [1/1] 3:7*
Luke [1/3] 3:7* 6:47 12:5

ὑπόδημα
Matt [2/2] 3:11* 10:10*
Luke [2/2] 3:16* 10:4*

ὑπόκρισις
Matt [0/1] 23:28

ὑποκριτής (⇨ ἄπιστος)
Matt [1/7] 7:5* 23:13 23:23 23:25 23:27 23:29
24:51 (α)
Luke [1/2] 6:42* 12:56

ὑποστρέφω ⇨ ἐπιστρέφω
Luke [0(1)/4] 4:1 7:10 11:24(*) 19:12

ὕστερος
Matt [0/1] 4:2

ὑψηλός
Matt [0/1] 4:8

ὕψιστος (⇨ πατήρ)
Luke [0/1] 6:35 (π)

ὑψόω
Matt [3/3] 11:23* 23:12* 23:12*
Luke [5/5] 10:15* 14:11* 14:11* 18:14*
18:14*

φάγος
Matt [1/1] 11:19*
Luke [1/1] 7:34*

φαίνω (⇨ λάμπω)
Matt [0/4] 9:33 23:27 23:28 24:27 (λ)

Φαρισαῖος (⇨ νομικός, ὄχλος, τις)
Matt [2/11] 3:7 (ο) 9:34 (τ) 12:24 (τ) 12:38
16:1 23:13 (ν) 23:23* 23:25* 23:26 23:27
23:29
Luke [2/3] 11:39* 11:42* 11:43

φεύγω
Matt [1/1] 3:7*
Luke [1/1] 3:7*

φημί (⇨ εἶπεν, λέγω)
Matt [0/4] 4:7 (ε) 8:8 (λ) 25:21(ε) 25:23 (ε)

φθάνω
Matt [1/1] 12:28*
Luke [1/1] 11:20*

φιλέω (⇨ ἀγαπάω, μισέω)
Matt [0/3] 10:37 (μ) 10:37 23:6 (α)

φίλος
Matt [1/1] 11:19*
Luke [1/5] 7:6 7:34* 12:4 15:6 15:9 (S)

φοβέω
Matt [4/5] 10:26 10:28* 10:28* 10:31* 25:25*
Luke [4/6] 12:4* 12:5 12:5* 12:5 12:7* 19:21*

φονεύς
Matt [0/1] 22:7

φονεύω (⇨ ἀποκτείνω, ἀπόλλυμι)
Matt [0/2] 23:31 (αποκτ) 23:35 (απολ)

φορέω (⇨ ὑπάρχω)
Matt [0/1] 11:8 (υ)

φορτίζω (⇨ δεσμεύω)
Luke [0/1] 11:46 (δ)

φορτίον
Matt [1/1] 23:4*
Luke [1/2] 11:46* 11:46

φραγμός
Luke [0/1] 14:23

φρόνιμος
Matt [1/2] 7:24 24:45*
Luke [1/1] 12:42*

φυλακή (⇨ ὥρα)
Matt [1/2] 5:25* 24:43 (ω)
Luke [1/1] 12:58*

φυλάσσω
Luke [0/2] 11:21 (S) 11:28 (S)

φυλή
Matt [1/1] 19:28*
Luke [1/1] 22:30*

φυτεύω (⇨ μεταβαίνω)
Luke [0/2] 17:6 (μ) 17:28 (S)

φωλεός
Matt [1/1] 8:20*
Luke [1/1] 9:58*

φωνέω
Luke [0/1] 19:15

φωνή
Luke [0/1] 11:27 (S)

φῶς
Matt [2/2] 6:23* 10:27*
Luke [2/3] 11:33 11:35* 12:3*

φωτεινός
Matt [1/1] 6:22*
Luke [1/3] 11:34* 11:36 (S) 11:36 (S)

φωτίζω
Luke [0/1] 11:36 (S)

χαίρω
Matt [2/2] 5:12* 18:13*
Luke [2/2] 6:23* 15:5*

χαλκός
Matt [0/1] 10:9

χαρά
Matt [0/2] 25:21 25:23
Luke [0/2] 15:7 15:10 (S)

χάρις (⇨ μισθός, περισσός)
Luke [0/3] 6:32 (μ) 6:33 (π) 6:34 (S)

χειμών
Matt [0/1] 16:3

χείρ
Matt [2/2] 3:12* 4:6*
Luke [2/3] 3:17* 4:11* 9:62 (S)

χείρων
Matt [1/1] 12:45*
Luke [1/1] 11:26*

χιτών
Matt [1/2] 5:40* 10:10
Luke [1/1] 6:29*

Χοραζίν
Matt [1/1] 11:21*
Luke [1/1] 10:13*

χορτάζω
Matt [1/1] 5:6*
Luke [1/1] 6:21*

χόρτος
Matt [1/1] 6:30*
Luke [1/1] 12:28*

χρεία
Luke [0/1] 15:7

χρῄζω
Matt [1/1] 6:32*
Luke [1/1] 12:30*

χρηστός
Luke [0/1] 6:35

Χριστός
Matt [0/1] 11:2

χρονίζω
Matt [1/1] 24:48*
Luke [1/1] 12:45*

χρόνος
Matt [0/1] 25:19
Luke [0/1] 4:5

χρυσός (⇨ βαλλάντιον)
Matt [0/1] 10:9 (β)

χωλός
Matt [1/1] 11:5*
Luke [1/2] 7:22* 14:21

χώρα
Luke [0/2] 12:16 (S) 19:12

χωρίς
Luke [0/1] 6:49

ψεύδομαι
Matt [0/1] 5:11

ψευδοπροφήτης
Luke [0/1] 6:26 (S)

ψυχή
Matt [3/6] 6:25* 6:25* 10:28 10:28 10:39*
10:39
Luke [3/7] 12:19 (S) 12:19 (S) 12:20 (S) 12:22*
12:23* 14:26 17:33*

ὧδε
Matt [2/2] 12:41* 12:42*
Luke [2/4] 11:31* 11:32* 14:21 17:23

ὦμος
Matt [0/1] 23:4
Luke [0/1] 15:5

ᾠόν (⇨ ἄρτος)
Luke [0/1] 11:12 (α)

ὥρα (⇨ καιρός, φυλακή)
Matt [3/4] 8:13 10:19* 24:44* 24:50*

Luke [3/6] 10:21 (κ) 12:12* 12:39 (φ) 12:40* 12:46* 14:17

ὡραῖος
  Matt [0/1] 23:27

ὡς (▷ γάρ, καθώς)
  Matt [4/10] 5:48 (κ) 6:10 6:12 (γ) 6:29* 8:13 10:16* 10:25* 10:25 17:20* 24:38
  Luke [4/8] 6:22 6:40* 10:3* 11:36 (S) 11:44 12:27* 12:58 17:6*

ὡσαύτως
  Matt [0/1] 25:17

ὥσπερ (▷ καθώς)
  Matt [1/4] 12:40 (κ) 24:27* 24:37 (κ) 25:14
  Luke [1/1] 17:24*

ὥστε (▷ ἄρα, καί)
  Matt [0/3] 12:22 13:32 (κ) 23:31 (a)

Pronouns and Articles (concorded by inflection)

αὐτός
  Matt [1/1] 3:11*
  Luke [1/6] 3:16* 6:35 6:42 7:5 (S) 11:17 11:28 (S)

αὐτό (▷ ἐμός)
  Matt [2/3] 5:46 5:47* 18:13*
  Luke [2/6] 6:33* 11:14 14:35 15:4* 17:35 19:23 (ε)

αὐτοῦ (▷ ἑαυτός)
  Matt [27/59] 3:12* 3:12* 3:12* 4:6* 5:25 5:32* 5:41 (S) 5:45 6:27* 6:29* 6:33* 7:9 7:24 7:26 8:5 8:13 8:21 9:37 9:38* 10:10* 10:24 10:25* 10:25 10:35 10:36 10:38 (ε) 10:39* 10:39 11:2* 11:11* 12:26* 12:29 12:29* 13:31 (ε) 13:32* 18:6* 18:15 19:28 22:2 22:3* 22:5 22:6 22:7 22:8* 23:26 24:43 24:45* 24:46* 24:47* 24:48* 24:49 24:51* 25:14 25:18 25:21 25:23 25:26 25:28* 25:29
  Luke [27/43] 3:7 3:16 3:17* 3:17* 3:17* 4:10* 4:13 6:40* 6:45 7:3 (S) 7:6 7:18 7:18* 7:28* 10:2* 10:7* 11:16 11:18* 11:21 (S) 11:22 (S) 11:22 (S) 11:22* 12:22 12:25* 12:27* 12:31* 12:39* 12:42* 12:43* 12:44* 12:45* 12:46* 12:58 13:19* 14:17* 14:21 14:21* 15:5 16:18* 17:2* 17:24 17:33* 19:24*

αὐτῆς (▷ ἑαυτός)
  Matt [2/6] 7:13 7:27 10:35 10:35* 11:19* 23:37 (ε)
  Luke [2/3] 7:35* 10:10 12:53*

αὐτῷ
  Matt [18/32] 4:3* 4:6* 4:7* 4:8* 4:9* 4:10* 4:10* 4:11 5:39 5:40 7:9* 7:10* 8:5 8:7 8:19* 8:20* 8:21 8:22* 9:32 10:32* 11:3 12:22 12:32* 12:32 12:38 18:6* 18:13 18:21* 18:22 25:21* 25:23 25:26*
  Luke [19/30] 4:3* 4:5* 4:6* 4:8* 4:8* 4:9* 4:12* 7:2 7:6 7:9 9:58* 9:60* 11:11* 11:12* 11:27 (S) 12:8* 12:10* 12:13 (S) 12:14 (S) 12:20 (S) 14:16* 14:18 17:2* 17:3* 17:3 17:4* 19:15 19:17* 19:22* 19:25

αὐτῇ (▷ ἐκεῖνος)
  Matt [2/3] 10:11 12:39* 16:4*
  Luke [1/5] 10:7 10:9 10:21 11:29* 12:12 (ε)

αὐτόν
  Matt [7/14] 4:5* 4:5 4:8* 4:11 5:15 7:11* 8:5* 8:7 10:33 12:22 16:1 18:15* 24:47* 24:51*
  Luke [8/17] 4:4 4:5* 4:9* 7:3 (S) 7:3 (S) 7:4* 7:9 7:20 (S) 9:57* 9:62 (S) 10:6* 11:13* 11:22 (S) 11:27 (S) 12:44* 12:46* 14:18

αὐτήν
  Matt [7/10] 5:32 7:14 10:12 10:13* 10:39* 10:39* 11:12* 12:41* 12:42* 23:37*
  Luke [5/9] 4:6 6:48 6:48 11:32* 13:18 13:34* 16:16* 17:33* 17:33*

αὐτοί (▷ ἡμεῖς, ὑμεῖς)
  Matt [2/4] 5:4 5:6 12:27* 23:4*
  Luke [2/5] 11:4 (η) 11:19* 11:46* 11:48 11:52 (v)

αὐτά
  Matt [2/3] 6:26* 11:25* 23:4
  Luke [1/5] 6:23 6:26 (S) 10:21* 14:19 17:30

αὐτῶν (▷ ὑμέτερος, ὑμῶν)
  Matt [5/13] 4:8* 5:3 (υμετ) 6:26 10:29* 9:32 12:25* 18:12* 22:7 23:4 (υμων) 23:30 23:34* 23:34 25:19
  Luke [5/11] 4:2 4:6* 6:23 6:26 (S) 9:57 10:7 11:15 11:17* 11:49* 12:6* 15:4*

αὐτοῖς (▷ ὑμῖν)
  Matt [4/15] 3:7 3:7 7:12* 7:23 (v) 11:4* 12:25* 12:39 13:31 13:33 16:1 16:2 22:1* 24:45 25:14 25:16
  Luke [3/8] 6:31* 7:6 7:22* 10:9 11:2 11:17* 15:6 19:13

αὐτούς (▷ ὑμᾶς)
  Matt [1/4] 7:24* 7:26 10:26 15:14
  Luke [3/10] 6:32 6:47* 10:2 11:31* 11:47 11:48 11:49 (v) 12:16 (S) 12:24* 19:13

ἐγώ (▷ κἀγώ)
  Matt [5/11] 3:11* 5:32 5:44 8:7 8:9* 10:16 11:10 12:27* 12:28* 23:34 25:27* (κ)
  Luke [4/5] 3:16* 7:9* 11:19* 11:20* 19:22

ἐμοῦ, μου
  Matt [18/30] 3:11 3:11* 5:11 7:21 7:23* 7:24* 7:26 8:6 8:8* 8:8* 8:9* 8:21* 10:32 10:33 10:37* 10:37 10:38* 10:38* 10:39 11:10 11:27* 12:30* 12:30* 12:30* 12:44* 18:21 22:4 22:4 24:48* 25:27*
  Luke [20/36] 3:16* 4:7 6:47* 7:6* 7:7* 7:8* 7:27* 9:59* 9:61 (S) 10:16* 10:22* 11:23* 11:23* 11:23* 11:24* 12:4 12:13 (S) 12:13 (S) 12:17 (S) 12:18 12:18 (S) 12:19 12:45* 13:27* 14:23 14:24 14:26* 14:27* 14:27* 15:6 19:23* 22:28* 22:28 22:29 22:30 22:30

ἐμοί, μοι
  Matt [7/11] 4:9 7:21* 7:22 8:21* 8:22* 10:32* 11:6* 11:27* 19:28* 25:20 25:22
  Luke [5/10] 4:6 7:23* 9:59* 9:59* 9:61 (S) 10:22* 12:8* 15:6 15:9 (S) 22:29

ἐμέ, με (▷ σε)
  Matt [5/9] 10:33* 10:37 10:37 10:40* 10:40* 10:40* 18:6 18:21 (σ) 23:39*
  Luke [5/11] 6:46* 6:47 10:16 10:16* 10:16* 12:9* 12:14 (S) 13:35* 14:18 14:19 14:26

σύ
  Matt [2/2] 11:3* 11:23*
  Luke [3/6] 4:7 7:19* 7:20* 9:60 10:15* 19:19

σου (▷ σός, ὑμῶν)
  Matt [23/36] 4:6* 4:6* 4:7* 4:10* 5:25* 5:39 5:40* 5:42 (σ) 6:9* 6:10 6:10* 6:21 (v) 6:21 (v) 6:22* 6:22* 6:23 6:23* 7:3* 7:4* 7:4* 7:4* 7:5* 7:5* 11:10* 11:10* 11:10* 11:26* 12:38 18:15* 18:15 18:15 18:15 23:37* 25:21 25:23 25:25
  Luke [23/33] 4:7 4:8* 4:10* 4:11* 4:12* 6:29* 6:41* 6:42* 6:42* 6:42* 6:42* 7:27* 7:27* 7:27* 10:21* 11:2* 11:2* 11:34 11:34* 11:34* 11:34* 11:36 (S) 12:20 (S) 12:20 (S) 12:58* 13:26 13:34* 17:3* 19:16 19:18 19:20 19:22

σοι
  Matt [7/12] 4:9* 5:26* 5:40 6:23* 8:13 8:19* 11:21* 11:21* 11:23 (S) 11:24 (S) 11:25* 18:22
  Luke [7/8] 4:6* 9:57* 9:61 (S) 10:13* 10:13* 10:21* 11:35* 12:59*

σε (▷ ἐμέ, με)
  Matt [5/10] 4:6* 5:25* 5:39* 5:41 (S) 5:42* 18:15 25:21 25:23 25:24* 25:27
  Luke [5/17] 4:10 4:11* 6:29* 6:30* 7:7 7:20 (S) 11:27 (S) 11:36 (S) 12:58* 12:58 12:58 14:18 14:19 17:4 (μ) 17:4 19:21* 19:22

ἡμεῖς (▷ αὐτοί)
  Matt [0/1] 6:12 (a)

ἡμῶν (▷ ὑμῶν)
  Matt [3/5] 6:9 6:11* 6:12* 6:12* 23:30 (v)
  Luke [2/4] 7:5 (S) 11:3* 11:4* 13:26

ἡμῖν
  Matt [2/2] 6:11* 6:12*
  Luke [3/5] 7:5 11:3* 11:4* 11:4* 13:25 (S; cf. Matt 25:11)

ἡμᾶς
  Matt [1/2] 6:13* 6:13
  Luke [1/2] 7:20 (S) 11:4*

ὑμεῖς (▷ αὐτοί)
  Matt [5/13] 5:13 5:48 6:9 6:26* 7:11* 7:12 10:31 19:28* 19:28 23:13 (a) 23:28 23:32* 24:44*
  Luke [6/8] 10:24 11:13* 11:39* 11:48* 12:24* 12:29 12:40* 22:28*

ὑμῶν (▷ αὐτῶν, ἡμῶν, σου)
  Matt [12/29] 5:11 5:12* 5:12 5:44 5:45 5:47 5:48* 6:25 6:25 6:26 6:27* 6:32* 7:9* 7:11* 7:11 10:9 10:13* 10:13 10:14 10:14 10:29 10:30* 12:27* 12:27 13:16 13:16 23:32 23:34 23:38*

Luke [13/27] 6:22 6:23* 6:24 (S) 6:27* 6:35 (S)
6:35 (S) 6:36* 6:38 (S) 10:6* 10:11 10:16*
11:11* 11:13* 11:19* 11:19* 11:39 11:46 (a)
11:47 (η) 11:48 12:7* 12:25* 12:30* 12:33
12:34 (σ) 12:34 (σ) 13:35* 15:4

ὑμῖν (▷ αὐτοῖς, ἑαυτός)

Matt [31/41] 3:7* 3:9* 5:18 5:32 5:44* 6:19
6:20 (ε) 6:25* 6:29* 6:33* 7:2* 7:7* 7:7* 7:12*
8:10* 8:11 10:15* 10:19* 10:27 11:9* 11:11*
11:17* 11:21* 11:22 11:22* 11:24 (S) 13:17*
17:20 17:20* 18:12 18:13* 23:13* 23:23*
23:25* 23:27* 23:29* 23:36* 23:38* 23:39*
24:26* 24:47*

Luke [29/56] 3:7* 3:8* 6:24 (S) 6:25 (S) 6:27*
6:31* 6:32 6:33 6:34 (S) 6:38 (S) 6:38* 6:47
7:9* 7:26* 7:28* 7:32* 10:8 10:11 10:11
10:12* 10:13* 10:14* 10:24* 11:9 11:9* 11:9*
11:41 11:42* 11:43 11:44* 11:46 11:47*
11:51* 11:52* 12:4 12:5 12:5 12:8 12:22*
12:27* 12:31* 12:44* 12:51 13:24 13:25 (S; cf.
Matt 25:12) 13:27 (a) 13:35* 13:35* 14:24
15:7* 15:10 (S) 17:6* 17:23* 17:34 19:26
22:29

ὑμᾶς (▷ αὐτούς)

Matt [13/15] 3:11* 3:11* 5:11* 5:44* 5:46*
6:30* 7:23* 10:13* 10:14* 10:16* 10:19*
10:40* 12:28* 23:34 (a) 23:35

Luke [13/24] 3:16* 3:16* 6:22* 6:22 6:26 (S)
6:27 6:28 6:28* 6:32* 6:33 10:3* 10:6* 10:8
10:9 10:10* 10:16 11:20* 12:11* 12:12* 12:14
(S) 12:28* 13:25 (S; cf. Matt 25:12) 13:27*
13:28

Articles

Matt [377/653]
Luke [374/638]

ὁ (▷ ὅς, ὅστις)

Matt [71/117] 3:9* 3:11* 4:1 4:3* 4:4 4:4* 4:5
4:7* 4:8 4:10* 4:11* 5:12* 5:18* 5:25 5:25*
5:32* 5:48* 5:48 6:9 6:21* 6:22* 6:22* 6:22*
6:23 6:26* 6:26 6:30* 6:32* 6:32 7:8* 7:8*
7:9* 7:11* 7:11* 7:12 7:21 7:21 7:26* 8:6 8:8*
8:8* 8:10* 8:12* 8:12* 8:13 8:13 8:20* 8:20*
8:22 9:33* 9:37* 10:10* 10:25* 10:25 10:25
10:37 10:37 10:39 (os) 10:39 (os) 10:40*
10:40* 11:2* 11:3* 11:4 11:7 11:11* 11:13*
11:19* 11:25 11:26* 11:27* 11:27* 11:27*
12:23 12:26* 12:30* 12:30* 12:35* 12:35*
12:39 12:40* 16:2 16:2 16:3 18:15* 18:21
18:22 19:28 22:1 22:7* 22:8 22:10 23:38*
23:39* 24:39* 24:43* 24:43 24:44* 24:45*
24:45 24:46* 24:46 24:48* 24:48 24:50*
24:51 24:51 25:16 25:17 25:18 25:19 25:20*
25:21 25:22* 25:23 25:24* 25:26

Luke [78/114] 3:8* 3:16* 4:3* 4:4 4:4* 4:6
4:8* 4:12* 4:13* 6:23* 6:35 (S) 6:36* 6:40*
6:45* 6:45* 6:47 (οστις) 6:48* 6:49* 6:49* 7:6
7:6* 7:7* 7:9* 7:18* 7:19* 7:20 (S) 7:20* 7:28*

7:33 7:34* 9:58* 9:58* 9:59 9:62 (S) 10:2*
10:7* 10:16* 10:16* 10:16 10:21* 10:22*
10:22* 10:22* 10:22* 10:22* 11:10* 11:10*
11:11* 11:13* 11:13* 11:14* 11:18* 11:21*
11:23* 11:23* 11:30* 11:34* 11:34* 11:34*
11:36 (S) 11:40 11:46 12:8 12:9 (οστις) 12:14
(S) 12:20 (S) 12:21 (S) 12:24* 12:28* 12:30*
12:34* 12:39* 12:39* 12:40* 12:42* 12:42
12:42* 12:43* 12:43* 12:45* 12:45* 12:46*
12:58* 12:58 13:25 13:28* 13:28* 13:35*
13:35* 14:11 14:11 14:16 14:18 14:21 14:21*
14:22 14:23 14:23 14:35 16:16* 16:18* 16:18
(os) 17:3* 17:24* 17:27* 17:30* 17:34 17:34
18:14 18:14 19:16* 19:18* 19:20* 22:29

ἠ

Matt [18/32] 3:10* 5:3* 5:18* 6:10* 6:21*
6:25* 7:4* 7:13 7:13 7:13 7:14 7:14 7:14 7:25
7:27 7:27* 10:7* 10:13 10:13* 10:13 11:12*
11:19* 12:26* 12:28* 13:31* 13:33* 22:2
23:37* 24:27* 24:27 24:37 24:39

Luke [15/25] 3:9* 6:20* 7:35* 10:6* 10:9*
10:11* 11:2* 11:18* 11:20* 11:27 (S) 11:27 (S)
11:29 11:49 12:16 (S) 12:23* 12:34* 13:18*
13:34* 16:16* 17:24* 17:35 17:35 19:16 19:18
19:20

τό

Matt [32/53] 3:7 3:12* 3:12* 4:5 5:13* 5:13*
5:40* 5:46 5:47* 6:9* 6:10 6:22* 6:23* 6:23*
6:23* 6:23 6:25* 7:3* 7:3* 7:4* 7:5* 7:21 8:12
8:12 10:27* 10:28* 12:33 12:34* 12:39*
12:41* 12:43* 16:3* 16:4* 18:7 18:12 22:4
23:23* 23:23* 23:23 23:23* 23:25* 23:26
23:26 23:32 24:28* 24:51* 25:18 25:18 25:24
25:25 25:25 25:27 25:28*

Luke [33/57] 3:17* 3:17* 4:9* 6:22 6:29*
6:33* 6:41* 6:41* 6:42* 6:42* 6:42 6:42 6:45
6:45 6:45* 6:48 6:49* 7:5 (S) 11:2* 11:3
11:24* 11:29* 11:32* 11:33 11:34* 11:34*
11:35* 11:35* 11:36 (S) 11:39* 11:39 11:40
11:40 11:42* 11:42* 11:50 11:50 12:3* 12:4*
12:5 12:10* 12:12 12:23* 12:42 12:46* 12:56*
12:57 12:59* 14:34* 14:34* 15:4 15:6 15:6
17:35 17:37* 19:15 19:23*

τοῦ (▷ ὅς)

Matt [51/86] 4:1 4:1* 4:3* 4:5* 4:6* 4:8* 5:18*
5:45 5:45 6:13 6:22* 6:22* 6:24* 6:25* 6:26
6:28 6:30 6:33 7:3* 7:4* 7:5* 7:5* 7:5* 7:21
7:21 8:20* 8:20* 9:33* 9:38* 9:38* 10:29*
10:32* 10:32 10:33 10:33 10:35 10:36 11:2
11:11 11:12 11:19* 11:25* 11:27* 12:28*
12:29* 12:32* 12:32* 12:32* 12:32 12:33*
12:34 12:35* 12:35* 12:39 12:40 12:40*
12:43* 12:45* 13:32* 16:1 16:3* 19:28 19:28*
23:23 23:25* 23:26 23:35 23:35 23:35 23:35
23:35* 24:27* 24:27* 24:37 24:37* 24:37*
24:38 24:39* 24:39* 24:44 24:45* 24:50*
25:18 25:21 25:23 25:29*

Luke [53/80] 4:1 4:2* 4:3* 4:9* 4:9* 4:10
6:20* 6:22 6:22 6:29 6:30 6:41* 6:42* 6:42*
6:44* 6:45* 6:45* 7:3 (S) 7:28* 7:34* 9:58*
9:58* 9:60 9:62 (S) 10:2* 10:2* 10:7* 10:9*
10:11* 10:15 10:21* 10:22* 11:14* 11:20*
11:24* 11:26* 11:27 (S) 11:28 (S) 11:30*
11:34* 11:39* 11:39* 11:42 11:49 11:51 (os)
11:51* 11:51 12:6* 12:8 12:8* 12:9 12:10*
12:13 12:23* 12:30 12:40* 12:42* 12:46*
12:52 12:56 12:58* 13:18* 13:19* 13:20*
13:28 13:29* 14:17 14:24 15:10 (S) 16:13*
16:16* 16:17* 17:1 17:24* 17:26* 17:26*
17:30* 19:22 19:26* 22:30*

τῆς

Matt [17/24] 3:7* 3:8* 5:13 6:19 6:25* 7:13*
8:12* 10:10* 10:14 10:14* 10:30* 10:35*
10:35* 11:23 (S) 11:25* 12:34 12:40 12:41*
12:42* 12:42* 18:6* 23:25* 23:35 24:45*

Luke [15/24] 3:7* 3:8* 4:5* 6:45 6:49* 7:6
7:31* 10:11* 10:21* 11:31* 11:31* 11:32*
11:50 11:51* 11:52 12:7* 12:23* 12:42* 12:56
13:24* 14:21 17:4 17:24 22:30

τῷ (▷ ὅς, ὅστις)

Matt [18/40] 3:9* 5:3 5:25* 5:25* 5:25* 5:40
5:42 6:25* 7:3* 7:3* 7:4* 7:4* 7:8* 7:22 7:22
7:22 8:9* 8:10* 8:13 9:33 9:34* 10:25 10:27*
11:2 11:25 12:24 12:32 12:32 13:31 17:20*
18:6 18:7 18:7 22:2 23:4* 23:30 24:40 24:41
25:28* 25:29*

Luke [20/30] 3:8* 4:1 4:3* 6:23* 6:29 (οστις)
6:41* 6:41* 6:42* 6:42* 6:42* 6:42* 7:8* 7:9*
7:9* 10:5 10:21 10:21 11:10* 11:15* 11:27 (S)
12:3* 12:10 (os) 12:13 (S) 12:22* 12:58* 14:21
14:21* 15:7 19:24* 19:26*

τῇ

Matt [14/23] 3:12* 5:15 5:25* 6:25* 6:29*
7:22 7:25* 7:27* 8:6 8:11* 8:13 10:15* 10:19*
10:27* 11:11* 12:40 12:40 12:41* 12:42*
19:28 24:26 24:48* 25:25

Luke [17/34] 3:17* 4:1* 6:23 6:48* 7:28* 9:57
9:62 (S) 10:7 10:12 10:12* 10:14 10:21 11:30
11:31* 11:32* 11:36 (S) 12:3* 12:12* 12:19 (S)
12:20 (S) 12:22* 12:27* 12:45* 12:51 12:58*
13:28* 13:29* 14:17 15:4 17:6* 17:6 17:24
17:34 22:30

τόν

Matt [26/33] 3:9* 3:12* 4:6* 4:7* 4:10* 5:15*
5:26* 5:40* 5:42 5:45 6:11* 6:11* 6:24* 6:24*
6:30* 8:21* 9:38* 10:14* 10:24* 10:24 10:28*
10:38* 10:40* 11:10* 11:27* 11:27* 12:22*
12:26 12:29 12:44* 18:6* 18:15 22:5

Luke [28/43] 3:8* 3:16 3:17* 4:8* 4:11* 4:12*
6:29* 6:38 (S) 6:40* 7:3 (S) 7:4 (S) 7:10 7:10
7:19 7:27* 9:59* 9:61 (S) 10:2* 10:11* 10:11
10:16* 11:3* 11:3* 11:11 11:24* 11:28 (S)
11:33* 12:5* 12:10* 12:18 (S) 12:28* 12:39*
12:56* 12:58* 14:17* 14:23 14:26 14:27* 15:6
16:13* 16:13* 16:17* 17:2*

τήν

Matt [28/52] 3:10* 3:12* 3:12* 4:1* 4:5 4:8*
5:6 5:15* 5:32* 5:39* 5:39* 6:27* 6:33* 6:33
7:3* 7:5* 7:13 7:14 7:21 7:23 7:24 7:24* 7:25
7:26 7:26* 8:8* 8:20* 10:12 10:28 10:29
10:34* 10:39* 10:39 11:7* 11:10* 11:16*
12:29 12:29* 12:42* 22:5 22:7 23:6 23:13
23:23* 23:23 23:36* 24:38* 24:43* 24:45
25:15 25:21 25:23
Luke [32/57] 3:9* 3:17* 3:17* 4:6 4:6* 6:24 (S)
6:29* 6:29* 6:41* 6:41 6:42* 6:42* 6:48*
6:49* 7:5 (S) 7:6* 7:24* 7:27* 9:58* 9:60 9:62
(S) 10:4 11:21 (S) 11:22 (S) 11:31* 11:33*
11:42* 11:42* 11:43* 11:52 12:5 12:13 (S)
12:20 (S) 12:25* 12:31* 12:49 (S) 12:53
12:53* 12:53 12:53* 12:54 13:20* 13:25 (S)
13:25 (S; cf. Matt 25:10) 13:34* 14:26 14:26
14:26 15:8 (S) 15:9 (S) 16:17* 16:18* 17:2*
17:24 17:27* 17:33* 19:24*

οἱ

Matt [18/36] 4:3* 5:3* 5:4* 5:6* 5:46* 5:47*
7:12* 7:12 7:13 7:14 7:23 7:25* 7:25 7:27*
7:27 8:12 9:33* 9:34 9:37* 10:36 11:8* 11:13*
12:23* 12:24 12:27* 13:16* 16:1 19:28* 20:16
20:16 22:4 22:5 22:6 22:8 22:10 24:28*
Luke [15/31] 6:20* 6:21* 6:21* 6:22 6:23 6:25
(S) 6:25 (S) 6:26 (S) 6:26 (S) 6:31* 6:32* 6:33*
7:4 (S) 7:10 7:18 7:20 7:25* 10:2* 10:23*
10:23 11:14* 11:19* 11:28 (S) 11:33 11:39
11:44 11:44 11:47* 16:16* 17:37* 22:28*

αἱ

Matt [5/7] 8:20* 10:30* 11:21* 11:21* 11:23
(S) 11:23 (S) 24:37*
Luke [4/4] 9:58* 10:13* 10:13* 12:7*

τά

Matt [18/33] 3:11* 6:12* 6:26 6:28* 6:32*
8:20* 9:34* 11:2 11:8 12:24* 12:27* 12:28*
12:29 12:45* 13:16 13:32* 16:3 18:7* 18:12*
18:12 22:4 22:7 23:23 23:29* 23:37* 23:37*
25:14 25:16 25:17 25:20 25:22 25:27* 25:28*
Luke [14/29] 6:23 6:26 (S) 6:30 6:34 (S) 9:58*
9:62 (S) 10:7 10:8 11:15* 11:17* 11:19*
11:20* 11:21 (S) 11:22* 11:26* 11:41 11:44
11:44 11:47* 12:18 (S) 12:27* 12:30* 12:33
13:19* 13:34* 14:26 15:4* 17:1* 17:30

τῶν

Matt [29/51] 3:7 3:9* 3:10* 5:3* 5:13 5:44*
7:21 8:11* 8:12* 8:21 9:34* 10:7* 10:14*
10:27* 10:28* 10:32* 10:33* 11:2* 11:8
11:11* 11:12 11:12* 11:19* 12:24* 12:38
12:42* 12:45* 13:31* 13:32 13:32 13:33*
16:3* 18:6* 18:6 18:7 22:2 22:9 23:4* 23:7
23:13 23:13 23:29* 23:29 23:30* 23:30 23:31
23:32 24:49 24:51* 24:51 25:19*
Luke [19/32] 3:8* 3:9* 3:16* 6:28* 6:47* 7:3
(S) 7:18* 7:24 7:35* 11:15* 11:26* 11:29
11:31 11:31* 11:46* 11:47* 11:48 11:50 12:3*
12:4* 12:8* 12:8 12:9* 12:9 12:24 12:26
12:48* 13:28* 14:24 14:24 15:10 (S) 17:2*

τοῖς

Matt [11/26] 4:6* 5:12* 5:15 6:9 6:12 7:11*
7:11 7:11* 7:21 8:10* 9:37 10:32 10:33 11:7*
11:8* 11:16 13:32* 18:13 18:13 22:4* 22:8*
23:6 23:28 24:26 24:47* 25:27
Luke [8/27] 3:7 4:10* 6:23* 6:24 (S) 6:26 (S)
6:27 6:27 7:25* 7:32 9:61 (S) 11:13* 11:13*
11:30 11:42 11:43 11:46 11:46 11:48 11:52
12:3 12:4 12:33 12:44* 12:54 13:19* 14:17*
22:28

ταῖς

Matt [2/7] 11:16 23:6* 23:7* 23:30 23:34
24:38 24:38
Luke [3/7] 4:2 11:43* 11:43* 13:26 17:26*
17:26 17:28 (S)

τούς

Matt [13/26] 5:12* 5:12 5:44* 5:46* 5:47*
7:24* 7:26 8:22* 8:22* 10:14 22:3* 22:3 22:3
22:4 22:6 22:7 22:9 23:4 23:7* 23:13* 23:29
23:31 23:37* 23:37* 24:49* 25:14
Luke [14/29] 6:27* 6:28 6:32* 6:32 6:33* 6:35
(S) 6:35 7:24* 7:31 9:60* 9:60* 10:9 10:11*
11:43* 11:46* 11:52* 12:17 (S) 12:22 12:24
12:45* 13:28 13:34* 13:34* 14:21 14:26 15:5
15:6 15:6 19:15*

τάς

Matt [6/8] 4:8* 10:9 12:25* 19:28* 22:9
22:10* 23:6* 23:37*
Luke [6/15] 4:5* 10:10 11:4* 12:11 12:11
12:11 12:18 (S) 12:45 13:34* 14:21 14:23*
14:26 15:9 (S) 19:24* 22:30*

Formulae

The λέγω ὑμῖν (σοί) formula.

1. Q 3:8
   Matt 3:9: λέγω γὰρ ὑμῖν ὅτι
   Luke 3:8: λέγω γὰρ ὑμῖν ὅτι
2. Q 6:27
   Matt 5:44: ἐγὼ δὲ λέγω ὑμῖν
   Luke 6:27: Ἀλλὰ ὑμῖν λέγω τοῖς ἀκούουσιν
3. [Q 6:29]
   Matt 5:39: [ἐγὼ δὲ λέγω ὑμῖν]
   Luke 6:29: No introductory formula
4. Q 7:9
   Matt 8:10: ἀμὴν λέγω ὑμῖν
   Luke 7:9: λέγω ὑμῖν
5. Q 7:26
   Matt 11:9: ναί, λέγω ὑμῖν
   Luke 7:26: ναί, λέγω ὑμῖν
6. Q 7:28
   Matt 11:11: ἀμὴν λέγω ὑμῖν
   Luke 7:28: λέγω ὑμῖν
7. Q 10:12
   Matt 10:15: ἀμὴν λέγω ὑμῖν
   Luke 10:12: λέγω ὑμῖν ὅτι
8. Q 10:14
   Matt 11:22: πλὴν λέγω ὑμῖν
   Luke 10:14: πλὴν
9. (Q/Matt 11:24)
   Matt 11:24: (πλὴν λέγω ὑμῖν ὅτι)
   Luke 10:15: No parallel
10. Q 10:24
    Matt 13:17: ἀμὴν γὰρ λέγω ὑμῖν ὅτι
    Luke 10:24: λέγω γὰρ ὑμῖν ὅτι
11. Q 11:9
    Matt 7:7: No introductory formula
    Luke 11:9: Κἀγὼ ὑμῖν λέγω
12. Q 11:51
    Matt 23:36: ἀμὴν λέγω ὑμῖν
    Luke 11:51: ναὶ λέγω ὑμῖν

13. Q 12:3
    Matt 10:27: ὃ λέγω ὑμῖν ἐν τῇ σκοτίᾳ εἴπατε ἐν τῷ φωτί
    Luke 12:3: ἀνθ' ὧν ὅσα ἐν τῇ σκοτίᾳ εἴπατε ἐν τῷ φωτὶ ἀκουσθήσεται
14. Q 12:4
    Matt 10:28: No introductory formula
    Luke 12:4: Λέγω δὲ ὑμῖν τοῖς φίλοις μου
15. Q 12:5
    Matt 10:28: No parallel
    Luke 12:5: ναὶ λέγω ὑμῖν
16. Q 12:8
    Matt 10:32: No introductory formula
    Luke 12:8: Λέγω δὲ ὑμῖν
17. [Q/Matt 12:31]
    Matt 12:31: [διὰ τοῦτο λέγω ὑμῖν] (cf. Mark 3:28)
    Luke: No parallel
18. [Q/Matt 10:23]
    Matt 10:23: [ἀμὴν γὰρ λέγω ὑμῖν]
    Luke: No parallel
19. Q 12:22
    Matt 6:25: Διὰ τοῦτο λέγω ὑμῖν
    Luke 12:22: διὰ τοῦτο λέγω ὑμῖν
20. Q 12:27
    Matt 6:29: λέγω δὲ ὑμῖν ὅτι
    Luke 12:27: λέγω δὲ ὑμῖν
21. Q 12:44
    Matt 24:47: ἀμὴν λέγω ὑμῖν ὅτι
    Luke 12:44: ἀληθῶς λέγω ὑμῖν ὅτι
22. Q 12:51
    Matt 10:34: οὐκ . . . ἀλλά
    Luke 12:51: οὐχί, λέγω ὑμῖν, ἀλλά
23. Q 12:59
    Matt 5:26: ἀμὴν λέγω σοι
    Luke 12:59: λέγω σοι
24. Q 13:24
    Matt 7:13: πολλοί εἰσιν οἱ εἰσερχόμενοι
    Luke 13:24: πολλοί, λέγω ὑμῖν, ζητήσουσιν εἰσελθεῖν

25. Q 13:29
    Matt 8:11: λέγω δὲ ὑμῖν ὅτι
    Luke 13:29: No introductory formula
26. Q 13:35
    Matt 23:39: λέγω γὰρ ὑμῖν
    Luke 13:35: λέγω δὲ ὑμῖν
27. Q 14:24
    Matt 22:10: No parallel
    Luke 14:24: λέγω γὰρ ὑμῖν ὅτι
28. Q 15:7
    Matt 18:13: ἀμὴν λέγω ὑμῖν ὅτι
    Luke 15:7: λέγω ὑμῖν ὅτι
29. (Q 15:10)
    Matt: No parallel
    Luke 15:10: οὕτως, λέγω ὑμῖν, γίνεται χαρὰ
30. Q 16:17
    Matt 5:18: Ἀμὴν γὰρ λέγω ὑμῖν
    Luke 16:17: No introductory formula
31. Q 16:18
    Matt 5:32: ἐγὼ δὲ λέγω ὑμῖν ὅτι
    Luke 16:18: No introductory formula
32. Q 17:4
    Matt 18:22: οὐ λέγω σοι . . . ἀλλά
    Luke 17:4: No introductory formula
33. Q 17:6
    Matt 17:20: ἀμὴν γὰρ λέγω ὑμῖν
    Luke 17:6: No introductory formula
34. Q 17:34
    Matt 24:40: No introductory formula
    Luke 17:34: λέγω ὑμῖν
35. Q 19:26
    Matt 25:28: No introductory formula
    Luke 19:26: λέγω ὑμῖν ὅτι
36. Q 22:28
    Matt 19:28 [ἀμὴν λέγω ὑμῖν] (cf. Mark 10:29)
    Luke 22:28: No introductory formula

Compound Christological titles

[For simple titles (Christ, Lord, teacher, etc.) consult the Concordance.]

A. The Coming One

37. Q 3:16
Matt 3:11: ὁ δὲ ὀπίσω μου ἐρχόμενος ἰσχυρότερός μού ἐστιν.
Luke 3:16: ἔρχεται δὲ ὁ ἰσχυρότερός μου.

38. Q 7:19–20
Matt 11:3: σὺ εἶ ὁ ἐρχόμενος ἢ ἕτερον προσδοκῶμεν;
Luke 7:19: σὺ εἶ ὁ ἐρχόμενος ἢ ἄλλον προσδοκῶμεν;
Luke 7:20: σὺ εἶ ὁ ἐρχόμενος ἢ ἄλλον προσδοκῶμεν;

39. Q 13:35
Matt 23:39: εὐλογημένος ὁ ἐρχόμενος ἐν ὀνόματι κυρίου.
Luke 13:35: εὐλογημένος ὁ ἐρχόμενος ἐν ὀνόματι κυρίου.

B. Son of God

40. Q 4:3
Matt 4:3: εἰ υἱὸς εἶ τοῦ θεοῦ. . .
Luke 4:3: εἰ υἱὸς εἶ τοῦ θεοῦ. . .

41. Q 4:9
Matt 4:6: εἰ υἱὸς εἶ τοῦ θεοῦ. . .
Luke 4:9: εἰ υἱὸς εἶ τοῦ θεοῦ. . .

C. Son of Man

42. Q 6:22
Matt 5:11: μακάριοί ἐστε ὅταν ὀνειδίσωσιν ὑμᾶς καὶ διώξωσιν καὶ εἴπωσιν πᾶν πονηρὸν καθ’ ὑμῶν ψευδόμενοι ἕνεκεν ἐμοῦ.
Luke 6:22: μακάριοί ἐστε ὅταν μισήσωσιν ὑμᾶς οἱ ἄνθρωποι, καὶ ὅταν ἀφορίσωσιν ὑμᾶς καὶ ὀνειδίσωσιν καὶ ἐκβάλωσιν τὸ ὄνομα ὑμῶν ὡς πονηρὸν ἕνεκα τοῦ υἱοῦ τοῦ ἀνθρώπου·

43. Q 7:34
Matt 11:19: ἦλθεν ὁ υἱὸς τοῦ ἀνθρώπου ἐσθίων καὶ πίνων, καὶ λέγουσιν· ἰδοὺ ἄνθρωπος φάγος καὶ οἰνοπότης, τελωνῶν φίλος καὶ ἁμαρτωλῶν.
Luke 7:34: ἐλήλυθεν ὁ υἱὸς τοῦ ἀνθρώπου ἐσθίων καὶ πίνων, καὶ λέγετε· ἰδοὺ ἄνθρωπος φάγος καὶ οἰνοπότης, φίλος τελωνῶν καὶ ἁμαρτωλῶν.

44. Q 9:58
Matt 8:20: αἱ ἀλώπεκες φωλεοὺς ἔχουσιν καὶ τὰ πετεινὰ τοῦ οὐρανοῦ κατασκηνώσεις, ὁ δὲ υἱὸς τοῦ ἀνθρώπου οὐκ ἔχει ποῦ τὴν κεφαλὴν κλίνῃ.
Luke 9:58: αἱ ἀλώπεκες φωλεοὺς ἔχουσιν καὶ τὰ πετεινὰ τοῦ οὐρανοῦ κατασκηνώσεις, ὁ δὲ υἱὸς τοῦ ἀνθρώπου οὐκ ἔχει ποῦ τὴν κεφαλὴν κλίνῃ.

45. Q 11:30
Matt 12:40: ὥσπερ γὰρ ἦν Ἰωνᾶς ἐν τῇ κοιλίᾳ τοῦ κήτους τρεῖς ἡμέρας καὶ τρεῖς νύκτας, οὕτως ἔσται ὁ υἱὸς τοῦ ἀνθρώπου ἐν τῇ καρδίᾳ τῆς γῆς τρεῖς ἡμέρας καὶ τρεῖς νύκτας.
Luke 11:30: καθὼς γὰρ ἐγένετο Ἰωνᾶς τοῖς Νινευίταις σημεῖον, οὕτως ἔσται καὶ ὁ υἱὸς τοῦ ἀνθρώπου τῇ γενεᾷ ταύτῃ.

46. Q 12:8
Matt 10:32: Πᾶς οὖν ὅστις ὁμολογήσει ἐν ἐμοὶ ἔμπροσθεν τῶν ἀνθρώπων, ὁμολογήσω κἀγὼ ἐν αὐτῷ ἔμπροσθεν τοῦ πατρός μου τοῦ ἐν τοῖς οὐρανοῖς·
Luke 12:8: πᾶς ὃς ἂν ὁμολογήσῃ ἐν ἐμοὶ ἔμπροσθεν τῶν ἀνθρώπων, καὶ ὁ υἱὸς τοῦ ἀνθρώπου ὁμολογήσει ἐν αὐτῷ ἔμπροσθεν τῶν ἀγγέλων τοῦ θεοῦ·

47. Q 12:10
Matt 12:32: καὶ ὃς ἐὰν εἴπῃ λόγον κατὰ τοῦ υἱοῦ τοῦ ἀνθρώπου, ἀφεθήσεται αὐτῷ· ὃς δ’ ἂν εἴπῃ κατὰ τοῦ πνεύματος τοῦ ἁγίου, οὐκ ἀφεθήσεται αὐτῷ οὔτε ἐν τούτῳ τῷ αἰῶνι οὔτε ἐν τῷ μέλλοντι.
Luke 12:10: Καὶ πᾶς ὃς ἐρεῖ λόγον εἰς τὸν υἱὸν τοῦ ἀνθρώπου, ἀφεθήσεται αὐτῷ· τῷ δὲ εἰς τὸ ἅγιον πνεῦμα βλασφημήσαντι οὐκ ἀφεθήσεται.

48. [Q/Matt 10:23]
Matt 10:23: [ὅταν δὲ διώκωσιν ὑμᾶς ἐν τῇ πόλει ταύτῃ, φεύγετε εἰς τὴν ἑτέραν· ἀμὴν γὰρ λέγω ὑμῖν, οὐ μὴ τελέσητε τὰς πόλεις τοῦ Ἰσραηλ ἕως ἂν ἔλθῃ ὁ υἱὸς τοῦ ἀνθρώπου.]
Luke: No parallel

49. Q 12:40
Matt 24:44: διὰ τοῦτο καὶ ὑμεῖς γίνεσθε ἕτοιμοι, ὅτι ᾗ οὐ δοκεῖτε ὥρᾳ ὁ υἱὸς τοῦ ἀνθρώπου ἔρχεται.

Luke 12:40: καὶ ὑμεῖς γίνεσθε ἕτοιμοι, ὅτι ᾗ ὥρᾳ οὐ δοκεῖτε ὁ υἱὸς τοῦ ἀνθρώπου ἔρχεται.

50. Q 17:24
Matt 24:27: ὥσπερ γὰρ ἡ ἀστραπὴ ἐξέρχεται ἀπὸ ἀνατολῶν καὶ φαίνεται ἕως δυσμῶν, οὕτως ἔσται ἡ παρουσία τοῦ υἱοῦ τοῦ ἀνθρώπου·
Luke 17:24: ὥσπερ γὰρ ἡ ἀστραπὴ ἀστράπτουσα ἐκ τῆς ὑπὸ τὸν οὐρανὸν εἰς τὴν ὑπ’ οὐρανὸν λάμπει, οὕτως ἔσται ὁ υἱὸς τοῦ ἀνθρώπου ἐν τῇ ἡμέρᾳ αὐτοῦ·

51. Q 17:26
Matt 24:37: ὥσπερ γὰρ αἱ ἡμέραι τοῦ Νῶε, οὕτως ἔσται ἡ παρουσία τοῦ υἱοῦ τοῦ ἀνθρώπου·
Luke 17:26: καὶ καθὼς ἐγένετο ἐν ταῖς ἡμέραις Νῶε, οὕτως ἔσται καὶ ἐν ταῖς ἡμέραις τοῦ υἱοῦ τοῦ ἀνθρώπου.

52. Q 17:30
Matt 24:39: οὕτως ἔσται καὶ ἡ παρουσία τοῦ υἱοῦ τοῦ ἀνθρώπου·
Luke 17:30: κατὰ τὰ αὐτὰ ἔσται ᾗ ἡμέρᾳ ὁ υἱὸς τοῦ ἀνθρώπου ἀποκαλύπτεται.

53. Q 22:28
Matt 19:28: ὑμεῖς οἱ ἀκολουθήσαντές μοι ἐν τῇ παλιγγενεσίᾳ ὅταν καθίσῃ ὁ υἱὸς τοῦ ἀνθρώπου ἐπὶ θρόνου δόξης αὐτοῦ, καθήσεσθε καὶ ὑμεῖς ἐπὶ δώδεκα θρόνους κρίνοντες τὰς δώδεκα φυλὰς τοῦ Ἰσραήλ.
Luke 22:28–30: ὑμεῖς δέ ἐστε οἱ διαμεμενηκότες μετ’ ἐμοῦ ἐν τοῖς πειρασμοῖς μου· κἀγὼ διατίθεμαι ὑμῖν καθὼς διέθετό μοι ὁ πατήρ μου βασιλείαν, ἵνα ἔσθητε καὶ πίνητε ἐπὶ τῆς τραπέζης μου ἐν τῇ βασιλείᾳ μου, καὶ καθήσεσθε ἐπὶ θρόνων τὰς δώδεκα φυλὰς κρίνοντες τοῦ Ἰσραήλ.

*B*ibliography

1. Primary Sources

Apocrypha

2 Esdras 1—2 (5 Ezra)
Robert L. Bensly, ed. *The Fourth Book of Ezra: The Latin Version edited from the MSS*. Intro. by M. R. James. Texts and Studies 3/2. Cambridge: Cambridge Univ. Press, 1895; repr. Nendeln/Liechtenstein: Kraus, 1967.
Bruce M. Metzger, trans. "The Fourth Book of Ezra," *The Old Testament Pseudepigrapha*. ed. James H. Charlesworth. 2 vols. Garden City, N.Y.: Doubleday & Co., 1983, 1985. 1:517–59.

Apocryphon of James
Francis E. Williams, ed. and trans. "NHC I,2: The Apocryphon of James," *Nag Hammadi Codex I (The Jung Codex). Introduction, Texts, Translations, Indices*. ed Harold W. Attridge. NHS 22. Leiden: E. J. Brill, 1985. 13–53.
Francis E. Williams and Dieter Mueller, trans. "The Apocryphon of James (I, 2)," *The Nag Hammadi Library in English*. ed. James M. Robinson. San Francisco: Harper & Row, 1977. 29–36.

Dialogue of the Savior
Stephen Emmel, ed. and trans. *Nag Hammadi Codex III, 5: The Dialogue of the Savior*. NHS 26. Leiden: E. J. Brill, 1984.

Gospel of the Ebionites
2   Epiphanius, *Haer.* 30.13.4–5 (ed. Holl, 350). Trans.: Philipp Vielhauer, *NTApoc* 2:157.
3   Epiphanius, *Haer.* 30.13.6 (ed. Holl, 350). Trans.: Philipp Vielhauer, *NTApoc* 2:157.

Gospel of the Egyptians (*apud* Ps-Titum)
fr. 3   Donatien de Bruyne, "Epistulam Titi, Discipuli Pauli, De Dispositione Sanctimonii," *Révue Bénédictine* 37 (1925) 60, lines 492–93. Trans. by author.

Gospel of the Hebrews
2   Jerome, *Comm. in Isaiam* 4 on Isa 11:2 (Migne, *PL* 24:148). Trans.: Philipp Vielhauer, *NTApoc* 2:163–64 (modified slightly).
3   Origen, *Comm. in Johannem* 2.12 (ed. Preuschen, 67); *Hom. in Jeremiam* 15.4 (ed. Nautin, 2:122). Trans.: Philipp Vielhauer, *NTApoc* 2:164.

4a, 4b   Clement Alex., *Strom.* 2.9.45.5 (ed. Stählin, 137); Clement Alex., *Strom.* 5.14.96.3 (ed. Stählin, 389). Trans.: Philipp Vielhauer, *NTApoc* 2:164.

Gospel of Mary
George MacRae and R. McL. Wilson, ed. and trans. "The Gospel According to Mary BG, *1*:7,1–19,5," *Nag Hammadi Codices V,2–5 and VI with Papyrus Berolinensis 8502, 1 and 4*. ed. Douglas M. Parrott. NHS 11. Leiden: E. J. Brill, 1979. 453–71.
George MacRae and R. McL. Wilson, trans. "The Gospel of Mary (BG 8502, *1*)," *The Nag Hammadi Library in English*. ed. James M. Robinson. San Francisco: Harper & Row, 1977. 471–74.

Gospel of the Nazarenes
2   Jerome, *Dial. contra Pelag.* 3.2 (Migne, *PL* 23:597–98). Trans.: Philipp Vielhauer, *NTApoc* 2:146–47 (modified slightly).
5   Jerome, *Comm. in Mattheum* 6:11 (ed. Bonnard, 132). Trans.: Philipp Vielhauer, *NTApoc* 2:147.
6   NT Cod. 1424 ad Matt 7:5 Trans.: Philipp Vielhauer, *NTApoc* 2:147.
15   Jerome, *Dial. contra Pelag.* 3.2 (Migne, *PL* 23:598). Trans.: Philipp Vielhauer, *NTApoc* 2:148.
18   Eusebius, *Theophania* 22 (ed. Klostermann, 6). Trans.: Philipp Vielhauer, *NTApoc* 2:149.

Gospel of Thomas
A. Guillaumont, Henri-Charles Puech, Gilles Quispel, Walter Till and Yassah Abd al Masîh, ed. *The Gospel According to Thomas*. Leiden: E. J. Brill; New York and Evanston: Harper & Row, 1959.
Thomas O. Lambdin, trans. "The Gospel of Thomas (II, *2*)," *The Nag Hammadi Library in English*. ed. James M. Robinson. San Francisco: Harper & Row, 1977. 117–130.

Gospel of Truth
Harold W. Attridge and George W. MacRae, ed. and trans. "NHC I,3: The Gospel of Truth," *Nag Hammadi Codex I (The Jung Codex). Introduction, Texts, Translations, Indices*. ed. Harold W. Attridge. NHS 22. Leiden: E. J. Brill, 1985, 55–122.
George W. MacRae, trans. "The Gospel of Truth (I, *3* and XII, *2*)," *The Nag Hammadi Library in English*. ed. James M. Robinson. San Francisco: Harper & Row, 1977. 37–49.

Papyrus Egerton 2

H. Idris Bell and T. C. Skeat, ed. and trans. *Fragments of an Unknown Gospel and other Early Christian Papyri*. London: British Museum, 1935.

Papyrus Oxyrhynchus 1, 654, 655

Harold W. Attridge, ed. and trans. "Appendix: The Greek Fragments," *Nag Hammadi Codex II, 2–7, together with XIII, 2*, Brit. Lib. Or. 4926(1) and P. Oxy. 1, 654, 655*. ed. Bentley Layton. NHS 20–21. Leiden: E. J. Brill, 1988.

Papyrus Oxyrhynchus 840

B. P. Grenfell and A. S. Hunt, ed. and trans. *The Oxyrhynchus Papyri. Part V*. Egypt Exploration Fund. Graeco-Roman Memoirs 8. London: Egypt Exploration Society, 1908.

Papyrus Oxyrhynchus 1224

B. P. Grenfell and A. S. Hunt, ed. and trans. *The Oxyrhynchus Papyri. Part X*. Egypt Exploration Fund. Graeco-Roman Memoirs 13. London: Egypt Exploration Society, 1914.

Teachings of Silvanus

Yvonne Janssens, ed. *Les Leçons de Silvanos (NH VII,4)*. Bibliothèque copte de Nag Hammadi, Section "Textes" 13. Québec: Les Presses de l'Université Laval, 1983.

Malcolm Peel and Jan Zandee, trans. "The Teachings of Silvanus (VII, *4*)," *The Nag Hammadi Library in English*. ed. James M. Robinson. San Francisco: Harper & Row, 1977. 346–61.

Testament of Abraham

Michael E. Stone, ed. and trans. *The Testament of Abraham*. SBLTT 2; Pseudepigrapha Series 2. Missoula, Mont.: Scholars Press, 1972.

Thomas the Contender

John D. Turner, ed. *The Book of Thomas the Contender*. SBLDS 23. Missoula, Mont.: Scholars Press, 1975.

John D. Turner, trans. "The Book of Thomas the Contender (II, *7*)," *The Nag Hammadi Library in English*. ed. James M. Robinson. San Francisco: Harper & Row, 1977. 188–94.

Early Christian Literature

Clement of Alexandria

Strom. Otto Stählin, ed. *Clemens Alexandrinus*. 2. Band, *Stromata Buch I–VI*. GCS 15. Leipzig: J. C. Hinrichs, 1906.

1 Clement

1 Clem. Kirsopp Lake, ed. and trans. "The First Epistle of Clement to the Corinthians," *Apostolic Fathers*. LCL. 2 vols. Cambridge, Mass.: Harvard Univ. Press; London: Heinemann, 1912. 1:3–121.

2 Clement

2 Clem. Kirsopp Lake, ed. and trans. "The Second Epistle of Clement to the Corinthians," *Apostolic Fathers*. LCL. 2 vols.

Cambridge, Mass.: Harvard Univ. Press; London: Heinemann, 1912. 1:125–63.

Didache

Did Kirsopp Lake, ed. and trans. "The Didache, or Teaching of the Twelve Apostles," *Apostolic Fathers*. LCL. 2 vols. Cambridge, Mass.: Harvard Univ. Press; London: Heinemann, 1912. 1:305–33.

Epiphanius

Haer. Karl Holl, ed. *Epiphanius: Ancoratus und Panarion*. 1. Band, *Ancoratus und Panarion Haer 1—33*. GCS. Leipzig: J. C. Hinrichs, 1915.

Eusebius

Hist. eccl. Kirsopp Lake and J. E. L. Oulton, ed. and trans. *Eusebius: Ecclesiastical History*. LCL. 2 vols. Cambridge, Mass.: Harvard Univ. Press; London: Heinemann, 1926, 1932.

Theophania Erich Klostermann, ed. *Apocrypha II: Gospels*. Materials for the use of Theological Lectures and Students 8. Cambridge: Deighton, Bell & Co., 1904. 6 (text of *Theophania* 22).

Jerome

Comm. in Isaiam *Commentaria in Isaiam prophetam*, Migne, *PL* 24 (= *Hieronymi Opera Omnia* 4).

Comm. in Mattheum Emile Bonnard, ed. and trans. *Saint Jérôme: Commentaire sur S. Matthieu. Tome I (Livres I–II)*. SC 242. Paris: Les editions du Cerf, 1977.

Dial. contra. Pelag. *Dialogus contra Pelagianos*, Migne, *PL* 23: 495–590 (= *Hieronymi Opera Omnia* 2–3).

Mani *Epistula Fundamenti*

Cited in Augustine *Contra Epistulam Manichaei quam vocant Fundamenti*. Migne, *PL* 42: 181.

Origen

Comm. in Johannem Erwin Preuschen, ed. *Origenes Werke*. 4. Band, *Der Johanneskommentar*. GCS. Leipzig: J. C. Hinrichs, 1903.

Hom. in Jeremiam Pierre Nautin, ed. and trans. *Homélies sur Jérémie.*. SC 232, 238. 2 vols. Paris: Les editions du Cerf, 1976–1977.

De oratione Paul Koetschau, ed. *Origenes Werke*. 2. Band, *Die Schrift vom Gebet*. GCS. Leipzig: J. C. Hinrichs, 1899.

Polycarp of Smyrna

Phil. Kirsopp Lake, ed. and trans. "The Epistle of Polycarp to the Philippians," *Apostolic Fathers*. LCL. 2 vols. Cambridge, Mass.: Harvard Univ. Press; London: Heinemann, 1912. 1:280–301.

Pseudo-Clementine Homilies

Ps. Clem. Hom B. Rehm, ed. *Die Pseudoclementinen*. 1, *Homilien*. GCS 42. Berlin: Akademie Verlag; Leipzig: J. C. Hinrichs, 1953.

2. Secondary Sources

Aland, Kurt, ed.
1978   *Synopsis Quattuor Evangeliorum. Locis parallelis evangeliorum apocryphorum et patrum adhibitis.* 10. ed. Stuttgart: Deutsche Bibelstiftung (13. revidierte Auflage, 1985).

Arens, Eduardo
1976   *The* HΛΘΟΝ – *Sayings in the Synoptic Tradition.* Orbis biblicus et orientalis 10. Göttingen: Vandenhoeck & Ruprecht; Freiburg, Sw.: Universitätsverlag.

Argyle, A. W.
1952–53   "The Accounts of the Temptation of Jesus in Relation to the Q-Hypothesis," *ExpT* 64: 382.

Bammel, Ernst
1970   "Das Ende von Q." Pp. 39–50 in *Verborum Veritas: Festschrift für Gustav Stählin zum 70. Geburtstag.* ed. O. Böcher und K. Haacker. Wuppertal: Rolf Brockhaus.

Bartsch, H. W.
1960   "Feldrede und Bergpredigt. Redaktionsarbeit in Luk 6," *TZ* 16: 5–18.

Barth, Gerhard
1963   "Matthew's Understanding of the Law." Pp. 58–164 in G. Bornkamm, G. Barth and H. J. Held, *Tradition and Interpretation in Matthew.* trans. P. Scott. Philadelphia: Westminster Press.

Beare, F. W.
1962   *The Earliest Records of Jesus.* New York and Nashville: Abingdon Press.
1970   "The Mission of the Disciples and the Mission Charge: Matthew 10 and Parallels," *JBL* 89: 1–13.

Broer, Ingo.
1975   "Die Antithesen und der Evangelist Matthäus. Vesuch, eine alte These zu revidieren," *BZ* NF 19: 50–63.

Bultmann, Rudolf K.
1963   *History of the Synoptic Tradition.* trans. John Marsh. Oxford: Basil Blackwell [trans. from 2d ed., 1931].

Busse, Ulrich
1979   *Die Wunder des Propheten Jesus: Die Rezeption, Komposition und Interpretation der Wundertradition im Evangelium des Lukas.* FzB 24. 2d ed. Würzburg: Echter.

Bussmann, Wilhelm
—   *Synoptische Studien. 2. Heft. Zur Redenquelle.* Halle [Saale]: Buchhandlung des Waisenhauses, 1929.

Carlston, Charles E.
1982   "Wisdom and Eschatology in Q," in Delobel 1982: 101–19.

Catchpole, David
1983a   "Q and the 'Friend at Midnight' (Luke xi.5–8/9)," *JTS* NS 34: 407–24.

1983b   "Reproof and Reconciliation in the Q community: A study of the tradition-history of Mt 18,15–17.21/Lk 17,3–4," *SNTU* 8: 79–90.
1986   "Jesus and the Community of Israel — The Inaugural Discourse in Q," *BJRL* 68: 296–316.

Chilton, Bruce
1979   *God in Strength: Jesus' Announcement of the Kingdom.* SNTU B/1. Freistadt: F. Plöchl.

Coppens, Joseph
1981   *Le fils de l'homme néotestamentaire.* La Relève apocalyptique du messianisme royal 3. BETL 55. Leuven: Uitgeverij Peeters and Leuven Univ. Press.

Creed, J. M.
Lk   *The Gospel According to St. Luke.* London: Macmillan & Co., 1950.

Crossan, John Dominic
1983   *In Fragments: The Aphorisms of Jesus.* San Francisco: Harper & Row.
1985   "Divine Immediacy and Human Immediacy." Paper presented at Oct 1985 meeting of the Jesus Seminar, St. Meinrads, Indiana.

Davies, W. D.
1966   *The Setting of the Sermon on the Mount.* Cambridge: At the Univ. Press.

Delobel, Joel, ed.
1982   *Logia: Les Paroles de Jésus — The Sayings of Jesus.* BETL 59. Leuven: Uitgeverij Peeters and Leuven Univ. Press.

Dibelius, Martin
1911   *Die urchristliche Überlieferung von Johannes dem Täufer.* FRLANT 15. Göttingen: Vandenhoeck & Ruprecht.
1935   *From Tradition to Gospel.* New York: Charles Scribner's Sons [trans. from 2d. ed., 1933].

Dupont, Jacques
1964   "Le Logion de douze trônes (Mt 19,28; Lc 22,28–30)," *Bib* 45:355–92; repr. as pp. 706–43 in *Etudes sur les évangiles synoptiques.* ed. Frans Neirynck. BETL 70:1–2. Leuven: Uitgeverij Peeters and Leuven Univ. Press, 1985.
1967   "Beaucoup viendront du levant et du couchant . . .," *SciEccl* 19: 153–67.
1969   *Les Béatitudes.* Vol. 1, *Le problème littéraire.* EBib. 2d ed. Paris: J. Gabalda et Cie.
1973   *Les Béatitudes.* Vol. 3, *Les Evangélistes.* EBib. Paris: Gabalda et Cie.

Easton, Burton
Lk   *The Gospel According to St. Luke.* New York: Charles Scribner's Sons; Edinburgh: T. & T. Clark, 1926.
1913   "The Beezebul Sections," *JBL* 32: 57–73.

Edwards, Richard A.
1971   *The Sign of Jonah in the Theology of the Evangelists and Q.* SBT 2/18. London: SCM Press.

1975 *A Concordance to Q.* SBLSBS 7. Missoula, Mont.: Scholars Press.

1976 *A Theology of Q.* Philadelphia: Fortress Press.

1982 "Matthew's Use of Q in Chapter Eleven," in Delobel 1982: 256–75.

Ernst, J.

Lk *Das Evangelium nach Lukas.* RNT 3. Regensburg: Pustet, 1977.

Fitzmyer, Joseph A.

Lk *The Gospel According to Luke.* AB 28–28a. New York: Doubleday & Co., 1981, 1985.

Frankemölle, Hubert

1971 "Die Makarismen (Mt 5,1–12; Lk 6,20–23). Motive und Umfang der redaktionellen Komposition," *BZ* NF 15: 52–75.

Fuchs, A.

1979 *Die Entwicklung der Beelzebulkontroverse bei den Synoptikern.* SNTU Serie B/5. Linz: SNTU.

Garland, David E.

1979 *The Intention of Matthew 23.* NovTSup 52. Leiden: E. J. Brill.

Geiger, Ruthild

1973 *Die lukanischen Endzeitgreden: Studien zur Eschatologie des Lukas-Evangeliums.* Europäische Hochschulschriften 23/16. Bern and Frankfurt: Herbert und Peter Lang.

Grundmann, Walter

Lk *Das Evangelium nach Lukas.* THKNT 3. 10th ed. Berlin: Evangelische Verlagsanstalt, 1984 [1st ed. 1961].

Mt *Das Evangelium nach Matthäus.* THKNT 1. 5th ed. Berlin: Evangelische Verlagsanstalt. 1981 [1st. ed. 1968].

Guelich, Robert A.

1976a "The Antitheses of Matthew v. 21–48: Traditional or Redactional?" *NTS* 22: 444–56.

1976b "The Matthean Beatitudes: 'Entrance Requirements' or Eschatological Blessings," *JBL* 95: 415–34.

Haenchen, Ernst

1951 "Matthäus 23," *ZTK* 48: 38–63.

Hahn, Ferdinand

1965 *Mission in the New Testament.* trans. F. Clarke. SBT 1/47. London: SCM Press [trans. from 1963 ed.].

1969 *The Titles of Jesus in Christology.* trans. H. Knight and G. Ogg. London: Lutterworth [trans. from 1963 ed.].

1970 "Das Gleichnis von der Einladung zum Festmahl." Pp. 51–82 in *Verborum Veritas. Festschrift für Gustav Stählin zum 70. Geburtstag.* ed. O. Böcher und K. Haacker. Wuppertal: Rolf Brockhaus.

Harnack, Adolf von

— *The Sayings of Jesus: The Second Source of St. Matthew and St. Luke.* New Testament Studies 3. trans. J. R. Wilkinson. London: Williams & Norgate; New York: G. P. Putnam's Sons, 1908 [trans. from 1907 ed.].

Haupt, Walther

1913 *Worte Jesu und Gemeindeüberlieferung: Eine Untersuchung zur Quellengeschichte des Synopse.* Untersuchungen zum Neuen Testament 3. Leipzig: J. C. Hinrichs.

Havener, Ivan

1987 *Q: The Sayings of Jesus.* Good News Studies 19. Wilmington: Michael Glazier.

Hawkins, John C.

1909 *Horae Synopticae.* 2d ed. Oxford: At the Clarendon Press; repr. 1968.

1911 "Probabilities as to the so-called Double Tradition of St. Matthew and St. Luke." Pp. 95–140 in *Oxford Studies in the Synoptic Problem.* ed. W. Sanday. Oxford: At the Clarendon Press.

Hengel, Martin

1981 *The Charismatic Leader and his Followers.* New York: Crossroad [trans. from 1968 ed.].

Hoffmann, Paul

— *Studien zur Theologie der Logienquelle.* NTAbh NF 8. 2d ed. Münster: Aschendorff, 1975.

1967 "Πάντες ἐργάται ἀδικίας. Redaktion und Tradition in Lk 13,22–30," *ZNW* 58: 188–214.

1969 "Die Anfänge der Theologie in der Logienquelle." Pp. 134–52 in *Gestalt und Anspruch.* ed. J. Schreiner. Würzburg: Echter.

1971 "Lk 10,5–11 in der Instruktionsreden der Logienquelle." Pp. 37–53 in *EKKNT Vorarbeiten 3.* Zurich: Benzinger; Neukirchen: Neukirchener Verlag.

1984 "Tradition und Situation: Zur 'Verbindlichkeit' des Gebots der Feindesliebe in der synoptischen Überlieferung und in der gegenwärtigen Friedensdiskussion." Pp. 50–118 in *Ethik im Neuen Testament.* ed. Karl Kertelge. Quaestiones disputatae 102. Freiburg, Basel and Vienna: Herder & Herder.

Hübner, Hans

1973 *Das Gesetz in der synoptischen Tradition.* Witten: Luther Verlag.

Huck, Albert and Heinrich Greeven

1981 *Synopse der drei ersten Evangelien mit Beigabe der johanneischen Parallelstellen.* 13th ed. rev. by Heinrich Greeven. Tübingen: J. C. B. Mohr (Paul Siebeck).

Huck, Albert and Hans Lietzmann

1936 *Synopse der drei ersten Evangelien.* 9th ed. rev. by Hans Lietzmann. Tübingen: J. C. B. Mohr (Paul Siebeck); 12th ed. 1975.

Hunter, A. M.

— *The Work and Words of Jesus.* London: SCM Press, 1950.

Jacobson, Arland Dean
— "Wisdom Christology in Q." Ph.D. diss., Claremont Graduate School, 1978
1982a "The Literary Unity of Q," *JBL* 101: 365–89.
1982b "The Literary Unity of Q: Lc 10,2–16 and Parallels as a Test Case," in Delobel 1982: 419–23.
Jeremias, Joachim
1980 *Die Sprache des Lukasevangeliums.* MeyerK Sonderband. Göttingen: Vandenhoeck & Ruprecht.
Käsemann, Ernst
1964 "Lukas 11:14–28." Vol. 2, pp. 242–48 in *Exegetische Versuche und Besinnungen.* Göttingen: Vandenhoeck & Ruprecht.
Kilpatrick, G. D.
1946 *The Origins of the Gospel According to St. Matthew.* Oxford: At the Clarendon Press.
Klein, G.
1964 "Die Prüfung der Zeit (Lukas 12,54–56)," *ZTK* 61: 373–90.
Kloppenborg, John S.
1978 "Wisdom Christology in Q," *Laval théologique et philosophique* 34: 129–47.
1985 "Q 11:14–26: Work Sheets for Reconstruction," *SBLASP* 24: 133–51.
1987 *The Formation of Q: Trajectories in Ancient Wisdom Collections.* Studies in Antiquity and Christianity. Philadelphia: Fortress Press.
Klostermann, Erich
Lk *Das Lukasevanglium.* HNT 5. 3d. ed. Tübingen: J. C. B. Mohr (Paul Siebeck), 1975.
Mt *Das Matthäusevangelium.* HNT 4. 4th ed. Tübingen: J. C. B. Mohr (Paul Siebeck), 1971.
Knox, Wilfred L.
1957 *The Sources of the Synoptic Gospels.* ed. H. Chadwick. 2. vols. Cambridge: At the Univ. Press.
Kümmel, W. G.
1957 *Promise and Fulfilment: The Eschatological Message of Jesus.* SBT 1/23. London: SCM; repr. 1974 [trans. from 3d. ed., 1956].
Lambrecht, J.
1966 "Die Logia-Quellen von Markus 13," *Bib* 47: 321–60.
1967 *Die Redaktion der Markus-Apokalypse: Literarische Analyse und Strukturuntersuchung.* AnBib 28. Rome: Pontifical Biblical Institute.
1982 "Q—Influence on Mark 8,34—9,1," in Delobel 1982: 277–304.
1985 *The Sermon on the Mount.* Good News Studies 14. Wilmington: Michael Glazier.
Laufen, Rudolf
1980 *Die Doppelüberlieferung der Logienquelle und des Markusevangeliums.* BBB 54. Bonn: Hanstein.
Légasse, S.
1962 "L'Homme fort de Luc xi.21–22," *NovT* 5: 5–9.

Linton, Olof
1972 "The Q Problem Reconsidered." Pp. 43–59 in *Studies in New Testament and Early Christian Literature. Essays in Honor of Allen P. Wikgren.* ed. D. E. Aune. NovTSup 33. Leiden: E. J. Brill.
Lührmann, Dieter
— *Die Redaktion der Logienquelle.* WMANT 33. Neukirchen-Vluyn: Neukirchener Verlag, 1969.
1972 "Liebet eure Feinde (Lk 6,27–36/Mt 5,39–48)," *ZTK* 69: 412–38.
1985 *Synopse der Q-Überlieferungen.* Privately circulated ms (1985).
Luz, Ulrich
Mt *Das Evangelium nach Matthäus (Mt 1—7).* EKKNT 1/1. Neukirchen-Vluyn: Neukirchener Verlag; Zurich: Beinzinger, 1985.
1983 "Sermon on the Mount/Plain: Reconstruction of QMt and QLk," *SBLASP* 22: 473–79.
1985 "Q 10:2–16; 11:14–23," *SBLASP* 24: 101–102.
Manson, T. W.
— *The Sayings of Jesus.* London: SCM Press, 1937; repr. 1949.
Marshall, I. Howard
Lk *Commentary on Luke.* Exeter: Paternoster; Grand Rapids: Wm. B. Eerdmans, 1978.
März, Claus-Peter
1985 "'Feuer auf die Erde zu werfen, bin ich gekommen . . .' Zum Verständnis und zur Entstehung von Lk 12,49." Pp. 479–511 in *A Cause de l'Evangile: Mélanges offerts à Dom Jacques Dupont.* Lectio divine 123. Paris: Les éditions du Cerf.
1986 "Lk 12,54b–56 par Mt 16,2b.3 und die Akoluthie der Redequelle," *SNTU* 11: 83–96.
Meyer, P. D.
— "The Community of Q." Diss. University of Iowa, 1967.
1970 "The Gentile Mission in Q," *JBL* 89: 405–17.
Michaelis, Christine
1968 "Die Π–Alliteration der Subjektsworte der ersten 4 Seligpreisungen in MT. v 3–6 und ihre Bedeutung für den Aufbau der Seligpreisungen bei MT., LK. und in Q," *NovT* 10: 148–61.
Minear, Paul
1970 "False Prophecy and Hypocrisy in the Gospel of Matthew." Pp. 76–93 in *Neues Testament und Kirche. Festschrift R. Schnackenburg.* ed. J. Gnilka. Freiburg: Herder & Herder.
Moffatt, James
1918 *An Introduction to the Literature of the New Testament.* 3d ed. Edinburgh: T. & T. Clark.
Morgenthaler, Robert
1971 *Statistische Synopse.* Zurich and Stuttgart: Gotthelf Verlag.

Müller, G. H.
1908   *Zur Synopse. Untersuchung über die Arbeitsweise des Lk und Mt und ihre Quellen.* FRLANT 11. Göttingen: Vandenhoeck & Ruprecht.

Mussner, Franz
1967   "Das 'Gleichnis' vom gestrengen Mahlherrn (Lk 13,22–30)." Pp. 113–24 in *Praesentia Salutis.* Düsseldorf: Patmos.

Neirynck, Frans
1982   "Recent Developments in the Study of Q," in Delobel 1982: 29–75.

Neirynck, Frans and Frans Van Segbroek
1982   "Q Bibliography," in Delobel 1982: 561–86.
1984   *New Testament Vocabulary: A Companion Volume to the Concordance.* BETL 65. Leuven: Leuven Univ. Press and Uitgeverij Peeters.
1986   "Q Bibliography: Additional List 1981–1985." *ETL* 62: 157–65.

Percy, Ernst
1953   *Die Botschaft Jesu: Eine traditionskritische und exegetische Untersuchung.* Lund: C. W. K. Gleerup.

Piper, John
1979   *Love Your Enemies: Jesus' Love Command in the Synoptic Gospels.* SNTSMS 38. Cambridge: At the Univ. Press.

Plummer, Alfred
Lk   *The Gospel According to S. Luke.* ICC. 4th ed. Edinburgh: T. & T. Clark, 1901.

Polag, Athanasius
—   *Fragmenta Q: Textheft zur Logienquelle.* Neukirchen-Vluyn: Neukirchener Verlag, 1979
1977   *Die Christologie der Logienquelle.* WMANT 45. Neukirchen-Vluyn: Neukirchener Verlag.

Rengstorf, K.
Lk   *Das Evangelium nach Lukas.* NTD 3. 10th ed. Göttingen: Vandenhoeck und Ruprecht, 1965.

Rigaux, B.
1970   "La petite apocalypse de Luc (xvii, 22–37)." Pp. 407–38 in *Ecclesia a Spiritu Sancto edocta.* BETL 27. Gembloux: Duculot.

Sato, Migaku
1984   "Q und Prophetie: Studien zur Gattungs- und Traditionsgeschichte der Quelle Q." Inauguraldissertation, Universität Bern.

Schelkle, K. H.
1983   "Israel und Kirche im Anfang," *TQ* 163: 86–95.

Schenk, Wolfgang
—   *Synopse zur Redenquelle der Evangelien: Q Synopse und Rekonstruktion in deutscher Übersetzung mit kurzen Erläuterungen.* Düsseldorf: Patmos, 1981.

Schlosser, Jacques
1980   *Le Règne de Dieu dans les dits de Jésus.* EBib. Paris: Gabalda et Cie.

Schmid, Josef
—   *Matthäus und Lukas: Eine Untersuchung des Verhältnisses ihrer Evangelien.* BibS(F) 23/2–4. Freiburg: Herder & Herder, 1930.
Lk   *Das Evangelium nach Lukas.* RNT 3. 4th ed. Regensburg: Pustet, 1960.

Schmithals, Walter
Lk   *Das Evangelium nach Lukas.* Zuricher Bibelkommentare 3,1. Zurich: Theologischer Verlag, 1980.
1985   *Einleitung in die drei ersten Evangelien.* De Gruyter Lehrbuch. Berlin: Walter de Gruyter.

Schnackenburg, Rudolf
1963   *God's Rule and Kingdom.* trans. John Murray. New York: Herder & Herder [trans. from 1963 ed.].
1971   "Der eschatologische Abschnitt Lk 17,20–37." *Mélanges bibliques en hommage au R. P. Beda Rigaux.* Gembloux: Duculot, 1970. 213–23; repr. as pp. 220–43 in *Schriften zum Neuen Testament.* Munich: Kösel.

Schneider, Gerhard
Lk   *Das Evangelium nach Lukas.* Ökumenischer Taschenbuchkommentar zum NT 3/1–2. 2d ed. Gütersloh: Gerd Mohn; Würzburg: Echter, 1984.

Scholer, David M.
1986   "Q Bibliography: 1981—1986." *SBLASP* 25: 27–36.

Schönle, V.
1982   *Johannes, Jesus und die Juden: Die theologische Position des Matthäus und des Verfassers der Redenquelle im Lichte von Mt. 11.* BBET 17. Franfurt a/Main and Bern: Peter Lang.

Schulz, Siegfried
—   *Q. Die Spruchquelle der Evangelisten.* Zurich: Theologischer Verlag, 1972.

Schürmann, Heinz
Lk   *Das Lukasevangelium.* HTKNT 3/1. Freiburg, Basel and Vienna: Herder & Herder, 1969.
1968   *Traditionsgeschichtliche Untersuchungen.* Düsseldorf: Patmos.
1975   "Beobachtungen zum Menschensohn-Titel in der Redequelle." Pp. 124–47 in *Jesus und der Menschensohn. Für Anton Vögtle.* ed. R. Pesch and R. Schnackenburg. Freiburg: Herder & Herder.
1982   "Das Zeugnis der Redequelle für die Basileia-Verkündigung Jesu," in Delobel 1982: 121–200.
1986   "Die Redekomposition wider 'dieses Geschlecht' und seine Führung in der Redenquelle (vgl. Mt 23,1–39 par Lk 1,37–54): Bestand—Akoluthie—Kompositionsformen," *SNTU* 11:33–81.

Schweizer, Eduard
Mt   *Das Evangelium nach Matthäus.* NTD 2. Göttingen: Vandenhoeck & Ruprecht, 1973; 3d. ed., 1981.
1974   *Matthäus und seine Gemeinde.* SBS 71. Stuttgart: KBW.

Soiron, Thaddeus
1916   *Die Logia Jesu: Eine literarkritische und literar-geschichtliche Untersuchung zum synoptischen Problem.* NTAbh 6,4. Münster: Aschendorff.

Steck, Odil Hannes
1967   *Israel und das gewaltsame Geschick der Propheten.* WMANT 23. Neukirchen-Vluyn: Neukirchener Verlag.

Steinhauser, Michael G.
1981   *Doppelbildworte in den synoptischen Evangelien. Eine form- und traditionskritische Studie.* FzB 44. Würzburg: Echter.

Strecker, Georg
1971a   *Der Weg der Gerechtigkeit.* FRLANT 82. 5. Aufl. Göttingen: Vandenhoeck & Ruprecht.
1971b   "Die Makarismen der Bergpredigt," *NTS* 17: 255–70.
1978   "Die Antithesen der Bergpredigt (Mt 5 21–48 par)," *ZNW* 69: 36–72.
1985   *Die Bergpredigt: Ein exegetischer Kommentar.* 2d ed. Göttingen: Vandenhoeck & Ruprecht.

Streeter. B. H.
1911a   "On the Original Order of Q." Pp. 141–64 in *Oxford Studies in the Synoptic Problem.* Oxford: At the Clarendon Press.
1911b   "The Original Extent of Q." Pp. 185–208 in *Oxford Studies in the Synoptic Problem.* Oxford: At the Clarendon Press.
1924   *The Four Gospels.* London: Macmillan & Co.

Suggs, M. Jack
1975   "The Antitheses as Redactional Products." Pp. 433–444 in *Jesus Christus in Historie und Theologie.* ed. G. Strecker. Tübingen: J. C. B. Mohr (Paul Siebeck); repr. as pp. 93–107 in *Essays on the Love Command.* Philadelphia: Fortress Press, 1978.

Taylor, Vincent
1972   "The Original Order of Q." Pp. 246–69 in *New Testament Essays: Studies in Memory of T. W. Manson.* Manchester: Manchester University, 1959; repr. as pp. 95–118 in *New Testament Essays.* London: Epworth 1970; Grand Rapids: Wm. B. Eerdmans, 1972.

Tödt, H. E.
1965   *The Son of Man in the Synoptic Tradition.* trans. D. M. Barton. London: SCM Press [trans. from 2d. ed., 1963].

Trilling, Wolfgang
1959   "Die Täufertradition bei Matthäus," *BZ* NF 3: 271–89.
1964   *Das Wahre Israel: Studien zur Theologie des Matthäus- Evangeliums.* SANT 10. 3d ed. Munich: Kösel.

Tuckett, Christopher
1983   "The Beatitudes: A Source-Critical Study," *NovT* 25: 193–216.

Vassiliadis, P.
1978   "The Nature and Extent of the Q Document," *NovT* 20: 49– 73.
1982   "The Original Order of Q: Some Residual Cases," in Delobel 1982: 379–87.

Vögtle, Anton
1971a   "Der Spruch vom Jonaszeichen." Pp. 103–36 in *Das Evangelium und die Evangelien.* Düsseldorf: Patmos.
1971b   "Wunder und Wort in urchristlicher Glaubenswerbung." Pp. 219–42 in *Das Evangelium und die Evangelien.* Düsseldorf: Patmos.

Walter, N.
1968   "Die Bearbeitung der Seligpreisungen durch Matthäus," *SE* 4 [= TU 102]: 246–58.

Wanke, Joachim
1980   "Kommentarworte: Älteste Kommentierungen von Herrenworte," *BZ* NF 24: 208–33.

Wegner, Uwe
1985   *Das Hauptmann von Kafarnaum.* WUNT 2/14. Tübingen: J. C. B. Mohr (Paul Siebeck).

Weiser, A.
1971   *Die Knechtsgleichnisse der synoptischen Evangelien.* SANT 29. Munich: Kösel.

Weiss, B.
1901   *Die Evangelien des Markus und Lukas.* MeyerK 1/2. 9th ed. Göttingen: Vandenhoeck & Ruprecht.
1907   *Die Quellen des Lukasevangeliums.* Stuttgart and Berlin: J. G. Cotta.

Weiss, Johannes
1900   *Die Predigt Jesu von Reiche Gottes.* 2d. ed. Göttingen: Vandenhoeck & Ruprecht.

Wellhausen, Julius
1911   *Einleitung in die drei ersten Evangelien.* 2d ed. Berlin: Reimer [1st ed. 1905].

Wernle, Paul
1899   *Die synoptische Frage.* Leipzig, Freiburg and Tübingen: J. C. B. Mohr (Paul Siebeck).

Wilson, S. G.
1973   *The Gentiles and the Gentile Mission in Luke–Acts.* SNTSMS 23. Cambridge: At the University Press.

Wink, Walter
1968   *John the Baptist in the Gospel Tradition.* SNTSMS 7. Cambridge: At the Univ. Press.

Worden, Ronald D.
—   "A Philological Analysis of Luke 6:20b–49 and Parallels." Ph.D. Diss. Princeton Theological Seminary, 1973.

Zeller, Dieter
—   *Kommentar zur Logienquelle.* Stuttgarter kleiner Kommentar, Neues Testament 21. Stuttgart: KBW, 1984.
1971–72   "Das Logion Mt 8,11f/Lk 13,28f und das Motiv der Völkerwallfahrt," *BZ* NF 15: 222–37; 16: 84–93.

1977   *Die weisheitlichen Mahnsprüche bei den Synoptikern.*
        FzB 17. Würzburg: Echter.

1982   "Redaktionsprozesse und weckselnder 'Sitz im
        Leben' beim Q- Material," in Delobel 1982: 395–409.

Zmijewski, J.

1972   *Die Eschatologiereden des Lukas-evangeliums: Eine*
        traditions- und redaktionsgeschichtliche Unter-
        suchungen zu Lk 21,5–36 und Lk 17,20–37. BBB 40.
        Bonn: Peter Hanstein.

*I*ndex Locorum

*C*olophon

Designed & composed by Polebridge Press, Inc., Sonoma, California.

Printed & bound by Edwards Brothers, Inc., Ann Arbor, Michigan.

Display lines are set in Galliard Italic.

Text lines are set in Times Roman, Ibycus Greek, Ibycus Coptic, & Ibycus Hebrew.

10132